P9-CMF-726

To my friend Tom.

Toshi   1957 march.

THE YOMEI GATE, SHRINES OF NIKKÔ.

UNBEATEN TRACKS IN JAPAN

AN ACCOUNT OF

TRAVELS ON HORSEBACK IN THE INTERIOR

INCLUDING

VISITS TO THE ABORIGINES OF YEZO AND THE SHRINES
OF NIKKÔ AND ISÉ

By ISABELLA L. BIRD

AUTHOR OF 'A LADY'S LIFE IN THE ROCKY MOUNTAINS' 'SIX
MONTHS IN THE SANDWICH ISLANDS'
ETC. ETC.

IN TWO VOLUMES. — VOL. I.

WITH MAP AND ILLUSTRATIONS

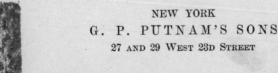

NEW YORK
G. P. PUTNAM'S SONS
27 AND 29 WEST 23D STREET

To the Memory

OF

LADY PARKES,

WHOSE KINDNESS AND FRIENDSHIP ARE AMONG MY
MOST TREASURED REMEMBRANCES
OF JAPAN,

These Volumes

ARE GRATEFULLY AND REVERENTLY
DEDICATED.

PREFACE.

HAVING been recommended to leave home, in April 1878, in order to recruit my health by means which had proved serviceable before, I decided to visit Japan, attracted less by the reputed excellence of its climate, than by the certainty that it possessed in an especial degree those sources of novel and sustained interest, which conduce so essentially to the enjoyment and restoration of a solitary health-seeker. The climate disappointed me, but though I found the country a study rather than a rapture, its interest exceeded my largest expectations.

This is not a "Book on Japan," but a narrative of travels in Japan, and an attempt to contribute something to the sum of knowledge of the present condition of the country, and it was not till I had travelled for some months in the interior of the main island and in Yezo, that I decided that my materials were novel enough to render the contribution worth making. From Nikkô northwards my route was altogether off the beaten track, and had never been traversed in its entirety by any European. I lived among the Japanese, and saw their mode of living, in regions unaffected by European contact. As a lady travelling alone, and the first European lady who had been seen in several districts through which my route lay, my experiences differed more or less widely from those of preceding travellers; and I am able to offer a fuller account of the aborigines of Yezo, obtained by actual acquaintance with them, than has hitherto been given. These are my chief reasons for offering these volumes to the public.

It was with some reluctance that I decided that they should consist mainly of letters written on the spot for my sister and a circle of personal friends; for this form of publication involves the sacrifice of artistic arrangement and literary treatment, and necessitates a certain amount of egotism; but, on the other hand, it places the reader in the position of the traveller, and makes him share the vicissitudes of travel, discomfort, difficulty, and tedium, as well as novelty and enjoyment. The "beaten tracks," with the exception of Nikkô, have been dismissed in a few sentences, but where their features have undergone marked changes within a few years, as in the case of Tôkiyô (Yedo), they have been sketched more or less slightly. Many important subjects are necessarily passed over, and others are briefly summarised in the "Chapter on Japanese Public Affairs."

In Northern Japan, in the absence of all other sources of information, I had to learn everything from the people themselves, through an interpreter, and every fact had to be disinterred by careful labour from amidst a mass of rubbish. The Ainos supplied the information which is given concerning their customs, habits, and religion; but I had an opportunity of comparing my notes with some taken about the same time by Mr. Heinrich Von Siebold of the Austrian Legation, and of finding a most satisfactory agreement on all points.

Some of the Letters give a less pleasing picture of the condition of the peasantry than the one popularly presented, and it is possible that some readers may wish that it had been less realistically painted; but as the scenes are strictly representative, and I neither made them nor went in search of them, I offer them in the interests of truth, for they illustrate the nature of a large portion of the material with which the Japanese Government has to work in building up the New Civilisation.

Accuracy has been my first aim, but the sources of error are many, and it is from those who have studied Japan the most carefully, and are the best acquainted with its difficulties, that I shall receive the most kindly allowance, if, in spite of carefulness, I have fallen into mistakes.

The Transactions of the English and German Asiatic Societies of Japan, and papers on special Japanese subjects, including "A Budget of Japanese Notes," in the *Japan Mail* and *Tôkiyô Times*, gave me valuable help, and I gratefully acknowledge the assistance afforded me in many ways by Sir Harry S. Parkes, K.C.B., and Mr. Satow of H.B.M.'s Legation, Principal Dyer, Mr. Chamberlain of the Imperial Naval College, Mr. F. V. Dickins, and others, whose kindly interest in my work often encouraged me when I was disheartened by my lack of skill; but, in justice to these and other kind friends, I am anxious to claim and accept the fullest measure of personal responsibility for the opinions expressed, which, whether right or wrong, are wholly my own.

The concluding chapter, which treats briefly of Public Affairs, is based upon facts courteously supplied by the Japanese Government, and on official documents, and may be useful in directing attention to the sources from which it is taken. The illustrations, with the exception of three, which are by a Japanese artist, have been engraved from sketches of my own, or Japanese photographs.

I am painfully conscious of the defects of these volumes, but I venture to present them to the public in the hope that, in spite of their demerits, they may be accepted as an honest attempt to describe things as I saw them in Japan, on land journeys of more than 1,400 miles.

Since the letters passed through the press, the beloved and only sister to whom, in the first instance, they were written, to whose able and careful criticism they owe much, and whose loving interest was the inspiration alike of my travels and of my narratives of them, has passed away, and the concluding chapter has been revised and completed under the shadow of this great grief. I have, therefore, to request my readers to pardon its faults of style and somewhat abrupt termination.

ISABELLA L. BIRD.

September 1880.

CONTENTS OF VOL. I.

CHINESE AND SERVANTS.

THEATRICAL.

WORSHIP.

THE JOURNEY BEGUN.

FROM KASUKABÉ TO NIKKÔ.

KANAYA'S HOUSE.

NIKKÔ.

A WATERING-PLACE.

DOMESTIC LIFE.

EVENING EMPLOYMENTS.

SHOPPING.

SCANT COSTUMES.

DIRT AND DISEASE.

HIGH FARMING.

A MALARIOUS DISTRICT.

EXTREME FILTHINESS.

A RIVER JOURNEY.

MISSIONS.

BUDDHISM.

NIIGATA.

THE SHOPS.

ADULTERATIONS.

FOOD.

DISCOMFORTS.

A PROSPEROUS DISTRICT.

A JAPANESE DOCTOR.

A FEARFUL DISEASE.

FUNERAL CEREMONIES.

POLICEMEN.

A HOSPITAL VISIT.

THE POLICE FORCE.

ITO'S VIRTUES AND FAULTS.

A WEDDING CEREMONY.

A HOLIDAY.

A NARROW ESCAPE.

SHIRASAWA.

LIST OF ILLUSTRATIONS.

GLOSSARY OF JAPANESE WORDS

FOR WHICH ACTUAL ENGLISH EQUIVALENTS DO NOT EXIST

SIMPLE RULES FOR THE PRONUNCIATION OF JAPANESE WORDS.

The vowels are pronounced as in Italian, with the exception of *u*, which takes the sound given to the same letter in English in "put," "full," etc.

Consonants are sounded as in English; but *g*, except at the beginning of a word, is pronounced like *ng* in singing. The *h* is distinctly aspirated. *Hi* is almost like *sh*.

Amado. Outside shutters sliding in grooves; lit. "rain-doors."

Andon. A square or circular paper lantern in a lacquer or wooden frame, 3 feet high.

Bentô bako. Occasional meal or luncheon box of varnished wood or lacquer, with several compartments.

Butsu-dana. Buddhist altar shelf.

Chaya. A house where tea and other refreshments are sold, to be eaten or drunk on the premises; lit. "tea-house."

Daïmiyô. Territorial nobles under the old *régime*, with annual revenues estimated at 10,000 *koku* of rice, and upwards; lit. "great name."

Daidokoro. An open kitchen.

Doma. A small yard within the entrance of houses; lit. "earth-space."

Eta. Men who had to do with dead animals, hides, etc. A pariah class estimated at 3,000,000, whose disabilities are now removed.

Fusuma. Sliding screens covered with wall paper.

Geisha. A professional woman, possessed of the accomplishments of playing, singing, and dancing.

Hakama. Full petticoat trousers, formerly worn only by the *Samurai.*

Haori. A short, sleeved mantle worn by both sexes.

Heimin. The commonalty. All classes below the nobility and gentry.

Hibachi. A charcoal brazier.

Itama. An unmatted floor. Applied to the polished ledge on which people sit to wash their feet at the entrance of a house; lit. "board-space."

Irori. A square depression in the middle of a floor, used as a fire-place.

Jishindo. A small door in the *amado;* lit. "earthquake-door."

Jôrôya. A house of ill-fame.

Kago. A covered basket, in which a traveller is carried by two men.

Kakemono. A hanging picture.

Kak'ké. A disease similar to the *beri-beri* of Ceylon; lit. "leg-humour."

Kaimiyô. The name given to persons after death.

Kaitakushi. Department for the colonisation of Yezo.

Kamado. A kitchen fire.

Kami-dana. A Shintô shrine-shelf.

Kashitsukeya. A non-respectable *yadoya.*

Kimono. A long, sleeved robe, open in front and folding over, worn by both sexes with a girdle.

Kugé. Nobles of the Mikado's court under the old *régime.*

Kura. A "godown." A fireproof storehouse.

Kuruma. A *jinrikisha* or man-power carriage; lit. a "wheel" or "vehicle."

Kuwazoku. The new name for the nobility in general.

Makimono. A picture roll, or illuminated scroll.

Mago. A pack-horse leader.

Maro (Polynesian). A loin cloth six inches broad.

Matsuri. A religious festival.

Mekaké. Concubine.

Saké. Rice beer containing from 11 to 17 per cent of alcohol.

Sakura. A species of wild cherry. [*Prunus cerasus.*]

Samurai. The retainers of the *daimiyô* under the old *régime* "two-sworded" men.

Shizoku. The gentry. Equivalent to *Samurai.*

Shôgun (Tycoon). The Mikado's chief vassal; erroneously styled by foreigners "The Temporal Emperor." Abolished. Full title, Sei-i-Tai Shôgun, "Barbarian-quelling generalissimo," bestowed by the Mikado upon his son, Yamato-daké-no-mikoto, conqueror of the aborigines of the north and west of the main island, B.C. 86. The first hereditary Shôgun was Minomoto Yoritomo, A.D. 1190, the greatest, Iyéyasu, the founder of the Tokugawa dynasty two centuries ago, the last, Keiki, now living in retirement at Shidzuoka.

Shôji. Sliding screens with translucent paper.

Shômiyô. A territorial noble with an annual revenue of less than 10,000 *koku* of rice; lit. "small name."

Tabako-bon. A wooden tray with fire-pot and ash-pot.

Tatami. House-mats, 5 feet 9 inches by 3 feet, stuffed to a thickness of 2½ inches, and covered with a finely-woven surface.

Teishiu (pronounced *teishi*). Used for the house-master, or host of a *yadoya;* also for husband by wife.

Tokonoma. An alcove with a polished floor; lit. "bed-place."

Torii. A sacred gateway. A portal over entrance of avenue leading to temples and shrines; lit. "bird's rest."

Yadoya. A Japanese inn.

Zen. A small lacquered stand 6 inches high, supplied as a dining-table to each person at a meal.

WORDS USED IN COMBINATION.

Bashi. A bridge, as Setabashi.

Kawa or *gawa.* A river, as Kanagawa.

Machi. A street, as Teramachi.

Sawa. A swamp or defile, as Shirasawa.

Togé. A pass, as Sannotogé.

Yama. A mountain, as Asamayama.

Zan or *san.* A syllable affixed to mountains whose names are supposed to be of Chinese origin, as Nikkôzan.

INTRODUCTORY CHAPTER.

To those of my readers who are familiar with Japan I offer an apology for a chapter of elementary facts, and ask them to omit it. The few who have never previously read a book on Japan, and the many who have forgotten what they read, or whose far eastern geography is rusty, or in whose memories the curious inventions of some early voyagers stick, or who still believe in *hara kiri* and the existence of a shadowy Mikado at Kiyôto, and a solid Shôgun at Tôkiyô, are requested to read it.

If an eminent writer found that "educated Britons" required more than one re-statement of the fact that the coco palm and the cacao bush are not one and the same thing, it is not surprising that such facts as that the "Spiritual" and "Temporal" Emperors are fictions of the past, and that the most northern part of Japan with its Siberian winter is south of the most southern point of England, are not always fresh in the memory. Were it so, such questions and remarks as the following could not be uttered by highly educated, and, in some respects, well-informed people. By a general officer's wife, " Is Sir Harry Parkes Governor of Japan?" By a borough M.P., " Is there any hope of the abolition of slavery in Japan?" By a county M.P., " Is the

Viceroy of Japan appointed for life?" By one gentleman holding an official appointment in India to another,
both having been crammed for Civil Service examinations within the last two years, "Japan belongs to Russia now, doesn't it?" "Yes, I think China ceded it in
return for something or other a few years ago," and in
the same connection, an officer holding a high military
appointment contended not only that Japan belongs to
Russia, but that it is on the Asiatic mainland, and was
only convinced of his error by being confronted with
the map; the mistake in both the latter cases probably
arising out of a hazy recollection that Japan surren-
dered Saghalien to Russia a few years ago in exchange
for some small islands.

The suppositions that Sir Harry Parkes is Governor
of Japan, that Japan is tributary to China, that the
Japanese are Roman Catholics, that Christianity is prohibited, that the people of the interior are savages, and
that the climate is tropical, have been repeated over and
over again in my hearing by educated people, and mistakes equally grotesque frequently find their way into
the newspapers; so true is it that, unless we are going
to travel in a country, to fight it, or to colonise it, our
information is seldom either abundant or accurate, and
highly imaginative accounts by early travellers, the long
period of mysterious seclusion, and the changes which
have succeeded each other with breathless rapidity during the last eleven years, create a special confusion in
our ideas of Japan.

So rapid, indeed, have these changes been, that on
turning to Chambers's admirable *Encyclopædia*, I find
that the edition of 1863 states that there are two Emperors, Spiritual and Secular, that Japan is ruled by an
aristocracy of hereditary *daimiyô*, that the weapons used
by the army are matchlocks and even bows and arrows,

that the navy is composed of war junks, that the iron cash is the only circulating medium, that the most remarkable of existing customs is *hara kiri*, that only men of rank can enter a city on horseback, and that the area of the Empire is estimated at 265,000 square miles, — many of which statements were substantially correct sixteen years ago.

The few facts which follow are merely given for the purpose of making the succeeding Letters intelligible. Sixteen days' sail from America, forty-two from England, and four from Hong Kong, Japan lies only 20 miles from Kamtchatka, and a day's sail in a junk from the Asian mainland of Corea. The Japanese Empire, which is said to be composed of 3800 islands, extends from Lat. 24° to 50° 40′ N., and from Long. 124° to 156° 38′ E., that is to say, that its northern extremity is a little south of the Land's End, and its southern a little north of Nubia. Straggling over 26° of latitude, and extending southwards to within thirty miles of the Tropic of Cancer, a man may enjoy a nearly perpetual summer in Yakunoshima, or shiver in the rigours of a Siberian winter in Northern Yezo. The traveller's opinion of the climate depends very much upon whether he goes to Japan from the east or west. If from Singapore or China, he pronounces it bracing, healthful, delicious; if from California, damp, misty, and enervating. Then there are good and bad seasons, cold or mild winters, cool or hot summers, dry or wet years, and other variations, besides a greater variety of actual climates than the mere extent of latitude warrants.

Thus the eastern coasts are warmed by the Kuro Shiwo, the gulf-stream of the North Pacific, and the western are chilled during many months of the year by a cold north-west wind from the Asiatic mainland, which gathers moisture from the Sea of Japan, while the climate of Northern Yezo is Siberianised by the cold current from the Sea of Okotsk. Climate is further modified by the influence of the monsoons, but, on the whole, it may be said that the summer is hot, damp, and cloudy, and the winter cold, bright, and relatively dry; that the spring and autumn are briefer and more vivid than in England; that the skies are brighter, and the sun hotter and more lavish of his presence; that there is no sickly season; that there are no diseases of locality; and that Europeans and their children thrive well in all parts of the Empire.

There are, however, certain drawbacks, such as the throbbing and jerking of frequent earthquakes, the liability to typhoons in July, August, and September, the uncertainty as to the intentions of certain dormant but not extinct volcanoes, and mild malaria.

The area of this much-disintegrated Empire is 147,582 square miles, *i.e.* it is considerably larger than Great Britain and Ireland, Prussia, or Italy, considerably smaller than France, and not so large as any one of the eighteen provinces into which China is divided. Among its 3800 islands Honshiu [Nipon], Kiushiu, Shikoku, and Yezo, are the most important. These islands are among the most mountainous in the world; there are several active volcanoes, and the extinct ones, of which the well-known Fujisan, 13,080 feet high, is the loftiest, are almost innumerable. The area of forest is four times as great as that of the cultivated land; the lakes are few, and, with the exception of Lake Biwa, small; the streams are countless, but the rivers are mostly short and badly suited for navigation. There are few harbours on the east coast, and almost none on the west, but such as there are, are deep and capacious. The soil is mainly disintegrated basalt, and is not naturally very prolific. The scenery is often grand, and nearly always pretty, and if there be monotony, it is, as Baron Hubner says, "the poetry of monotony." The luxuriance of the vegetation and the greenness in spring and throughout the summer are so wonderful that the islands of the Japanese Archipelago might well be called the Emerald Isles. Even winter fails to bring brownness and bareness. Evergreens of 150 varieties compensate for the leaflessness of the deciduous trees, every landscape is bright with the verdure of springing crops, and camellias with their crimson blossoms light up leafage covered with snow. The mountains of Japan are covered with forest, and the valleys and plains are exquisitely tilled gardens.

The Empire is very rich in flowers, and especially in flowering shrubs. Azaleas, camellias, hydrangeas, and magnolias all delight the eye in their seasons with a breadth and blaze of colour which cannot be described, and irises, peonies, cherries, and plums, have their special festivals. The classic lotus with its great pink or white cups, the *Paulownia Imperialis*, a tree which bears erect foxglove blossoms, deutzias with their graceful flowers, rhododendrons, wistaria, and many greenhouse friends, are as common as hawthorns and hedgeroses with us. Savatier enumerates 1699 species of dicotyledonous plants in Japan, and the monocotyledonous are proportionately numerous. Among the former are eight species of magnolia, seven of hydrangea, twenty of rhododendron, fourteen of ilex, twenty-two of maple, twenty-two of oak, four of pine, and nine of fir. Among the novelties in flowering shrubs and gorgeous lilies, the English ivy, sundew, mistletoe, buttercup, marsh marigold, purple and white clover, honeysuckle, coltsfoot, sow thistle, veronica, and many others, rejoice the traveller's eye by their familiar homeliness. Among the trees which claim homage either from their beauty or majesty, the *Cryptomeria japonica*, the *Camellia japonica*, the *Zelkawa keaki* (a species of elm), the *Salisburia adiantifolia*, the *Magnolia hyperleuca*, and the *Persimmon*, are in the first rank, and the eye rests with special delight on the great bamboo, whose feathery, bright green foliage massed against groves of coniferæ seems to combine the tropics with the temperate zone. The 26° of latitude through which the Empire extends give it an infinite variety of vegetation, from the rigid pine and scrub oak of Yezo to the palms, bananas, and sugar-cane of Kiushiu. Ferns are abundant and very varied, but indigenous fruits are few, small, sour, and tasteless.

The fauna is meagre, consisting chiefly of deer, bears, wolves, wild boars, badgers, foxes, monkeys, snakes, and small ground animals; eagles, hawks, herons, quails, pheasants, and storks, are numerous, and crows are innumerable, but birds of sweet voice and brilliant plumage are mournfully rare, and silence is a characteristic of nature in Japan; nor do imported animals make up for the lack of indigenous ones. They have no place in Japanese landscape. There are no grass fields or velvety pasture lands, or farmyards knee-deep in straw, and flocks and herds form no part of the wealth of the Japanese farmer. Oxen are used for draught alone, and not by any means generally. Horses are used as beasts of burden and for riding, but the Japanese horse is a mean, sorry brute, a grudging, ungenerous animal, trying to human patience and temper, with three *movements* (not by any means to be confounded with paces) — a drag, a roll, and a scramble. The ass, mule, and pig, are only to be seen on experimental farms. Cowardly yellow dogs, much given to nocturnal howling, miserable misrepresentations of the Scotch collie, abound, and are probably indigenous, besides which there are imported lap-dogs dwarfish and objectionable, and domestic cats, mostly with only rudimentary tails. Ducks and the ubiquitous barn-door fowl are everywhere. Mosquitoes are nearly universal between April and October, and insects which stab and sting abound.

Railroads have been introduced between Yokohama and Tôkiyô, and Kobe, Kiyôto, and Otsu, seventy-six miles in all. The main roads vary in width from thirty feet to that of mere rude bridle tracks, and the bye-roads are narrow tracks only passable for pack-horses. Nearly all travelling must be done on foot or on pack-horses, or in covered bamboo baskets, called *kago*, carried by men, or on the level in *kurumas*, two-wheeled vehicles drawn by men. There are *yadoyas* or inns on most of the routes, and post stations where horses and coolies can be procured at fixed rates.

The population of 34,358,404 souls, or about 230 to the square mile, is larger by a million than that of the United Kingdom, exceeds that of Prussia by nine millions, and that of Italy by seven millions, but is less than that of France by a million and a half. With the exception of 12,000 Ainos, and about 5000 Europeans, Americans, and Chinese, this population is absolutely homogeneous, and yellow skins, dark, elongated eyes, and dark, straight hair, are the rule. The same language, with certain immaterial provincialisms, is spoken by all the Japanese of the Empire, and similar uniformity prevails in temples, dwelling-houses, and costume.

Japan is beyond the limits of "Oriental magnificence." Colour and gilding are only found in the temples; palaces and cottages are alike of grey wood; architecture scarcely exists; wealth, if there be any, makes no display; dull blues, browns, and greys, are the usual colours of costume; jewellery is not worn; everything

is poor and pale, and a monotony of meanness characterises the towns.

The Japanese of the treaty ports are contaminated
and vulgarised by intercourse with foreigners; those of
the interior, so far from being "savages," are kindly,
gentle, and courteous, so much so, that a lady with no
other attendant than a native servant can travel, as I
have done, for 1200 miles through little-visited regions,
and not meet with a single instance of incivility or
extortion.

Foreigners in Japan are still under restrictions, *i.e.*
they are only allowed to settle and trade in Yokohama,
Nagasaki, Tôkiyô, Kobe, Osaka, Hakodaté, and Niigata.
Nor can they travel beyond a radius of 25 miles from
the "treaty ports," without a "passport," or formal permission from the Government, obtainable only for a
given time and route. Foreigners are not under Japanese jurisdiction, but are tried for offences in their own
consular Courts, and their privilege of "extra-territori-
ality" is regarded as a great grievance by the Japanese,
and is a constant bone of contention between the
Japanese and Foreign Governments.

The mystery of a "Spiritual Emperor," secluded in
Kiyôto, and a "Temporal Emperor" reigning in Yedo
no longer exists; the Shogunate is abolished, Yedo has
become Tôkiyô; the *daimiyô*, shorn of their power and
titles, have retired into private life; the "two-sworded"
men are extinct, and the Mikado, a modern-looking man
in European dress, reigns by divine right in Tôkiyô,
with European appliances of "ironclads," "Armstrongs,"
and "needle guns," and the *prestige* of being the one
hundred and twenty-third in direct descent from the
Sun Goddess, the chief deity in the Pantheon of the
national religion. His government is a modified despotism, with tendencies at times in a constitutional

direction. Slavery is unknown, and class disabilities
no longer exist.

Shintô, a rude form of nature and myth worship,
probably indigenous, containing no moral code, and few
if any elements of religion, is the "state," and "state
endowed" church, but Buddhism, imported from Corea
in the sixth century, and disestablished since the restoration of the Mikado, has a firmer hold on the masses,
the higher classes contenting themselves with a system
of secular philosophy while giving a nominal adhesion
to Shintô for political purposes. Christianity is quietly
tolerated, and Protestants, Roman Catholics, and Greeks,
claim among them about 27,000 converts.

Politically, old Japan is no more. The grandeur of
its rulers, its antique chivalry, its stately etiquette, its
ceremonial costume, its punctilious suicides, and its
codes of honour, only exist on the stage. Its traditional customs, its rigid social order, its formal politeness, its measured courtesies, its ignorant patriotism,
its innumerable and enslaving superstitions, linger still
in the interior, specially in the regions where a debased
and corrupt form of Buddhism holds sway. Over great
districts of country on the unbeaten track which I
traversed from Nikkô to Aomori, the rumble of the
wheels of progress is scarcely yet heard, and the Japanese peasant lives and thinks as his fathers lived and
thought before him.

Since my return, I have frequently been asked
whether the rage for western civilisation is likely to be
more than a passing fancy, and whether the civilisation
itself is more than a temporary veneering? It is only
seven years since the mission of Iwakura and his colleagues visited Europe and America with the view of
investigating western civilisation and transplanting its
best results to Japanese soil, and only nine since the

magnificent and complicated system of Japanese feudalism was swept away. Of the men who rule Japan, only
two are "aristocrats." With the impetus of the new
movement, springing mainly from the people, and from
within, not from without, we have undoubtedly two of
the elements of permanence.

Many Europeans ridicule Japanese progress as "imitation," Chinese and Coreans contemplate it with ill-
concealed anger, not unmixed with jealousy, yet Japan
holds on her course, and, without venturing to predict
her future, I see no reason to distrust the permanence
of a movement which has isolated her from other Orien
tal nations, and which, in spite of very many extravagances and absurdities, is growing and broadening daily.
The religion, letters, and civilisation which she received
from China through Corea ("veenering," it may have
been said), have lasted for twelve centuries. The civilisation which comes from the far West in the nineteenth
century is not a more sweeping wave than that which
came from Corea in the sixth, and is likely to produce
equally enduring results, specially and certainly if
Christianity overthrows Buddhism, the most powerful
influence from without which has hitherto affected
Japan.

The transformations which are being accomplished are
under the direction of foreigners in Government service,
and of Japanese selected for their capacities, who have
studied for some years in Europe and America; and the
Government has spared neither trouble nor expense in
securing the most competent assistance in all departments, and it is only in comparatively few instances that
it has been badly advised by interested aliens for the
furtherance of personal or other ends. About 500 foreigners have been at one time or other in its service, and
though they may have met with annoyances and exasper-

ations, the terms of their contracts have been faithfully adhered to. Some of these gentlemen are decorated with high-sounding titles during their brief engagements; but it must be remembered that they are there as helpers only, without actual authority, as servants and not masters, and that, with a notable exception, the greater their energy, ability, and capacity for training, the sooner are their services dispensed with, and one department after another passes from foreign into native management. The retention of foreign *employés* forms no part of the programme of progress. " Japan for the Japanese " is the motto of Japanese patriotism; the " Barbarians " are to be used, and dispensed with as soon as possible.

Of the present foreign staff the great majority are teachers ; considerably more than half are English, and Anglo-Saxon influences in science, culture, and political ideas and economy, are paramount in the transformation of the Empire.

With these few introductory remarks, I ask my readers to land with me on the shores of the " Empire of the Rising Sun," and to accompany me with patient kindliness on my long wanderings.

FIRST IMPRESSIONS.

First View of Japan — A Vision of Fujisan — A Hybrid City — Japanese *Sampans* — "Pullman Cars" — Undignified Locomotion —
Paper Money — The Drawbacks of Japanese Travelling.

ORIENTAL HOTEL, YOKOHAMA, *May* 21.

EIGHTEEN days of unintermitted rolling over "desolate rainy seas" brought the "City of Tokio" early
yesterday morning to Cape King, and by noon we were
steaming up the Gulf of Yedo, quite near the shore.
The day was soft and grey with a little faint blue sky,
and though the coast of Japan is much more prepossessing than most coasts, there were no startling surprises either of colour or form.   Broken wooded ridges,
deeply cleft, rise from the water's edge, grey, deep-
roofed villages cluster about the mouths of the ravines,
and terraces of rice cultivation, bright with the greenness of English lawns, run up to a great height among
dark masses of upland forest.   The populousness of
the coast is very impressive, and the gulf every where
was equally peopled with fishing-boats, of which we
passed not only hundreds but thousands in five hours.
The coasts and sea were pale, and the boats were pale
too, their hulls being unpainted wood, and their sails
pure white duck.   Now and then a high-sterned junk
drifted by like a phantom galley, then we slackened
speed to avoid exterminating a fleet of triangular-look-
ing fishing-boats with white square sails, and so on
through the greyness and dumbness hour after hour.

For long I looked in vain for Fujisan, and failed to see it, though I heard ecstasies all over the deck, till accidentally looking heavenwards instead of earthwards, I saw far above any possibility of height, as one would

FUJISAN.

have thought, a huge, truncated cone of pure snow, 13,080 feet above the sea, from which it sweeps upwards in a glorious curve, very wan, against a very pale blue sky, with its base and the intervening country veiled in a pale grey mist.[1] It was a wonderful vision, and shortly, as a vision, vanished. Except the cone of Tristan d'Acunha — also a cone of snow — I never saw a mountain rise in such lonely majesty, with nothing

[1] This is an altogether exceptional aspect of Fujisan, under exceptional atmospheric conditions. The mountain usually looks broader and lower, and is often compared to an inverted fan.

near or far to detract from its height and grandeur. No wonder that it is a sacred mountain, and so dear to the Japanese that their art is never weary of representing it. It was nearly fifty miles off when we first saw it.

The air and water were alike motionless, the mist was still and pale, grey clouds lay restfully on a bluish sky, the reflections of the white sails of the fishing boats scarcely quivered; it was all so pale, wan, and ghastly, that the turbulence of crumpled foam which we left behind us, and our noisy, throbbing progress, seemed a boisterous intrusion upon sleeping Asia.

The gulf narrowed, the forest-crested hills, the terraced ravines, the picturesque grey villages, the quiet beach life, and the pale blue masses of the mountains of the interior, became more visible. Fuji retired into the mist in which he enfolds his grandeur for most of the summer; we passed Reception Bay, Perry Island, Webster Island, Cape Saratoga, and Mississippi Bay — American nomenclature which perpetuates the successes of American diplomacy, and not far from Treaty Point came upon a red light-ship with the words "Treaty Point" in large letters upon her. Outside of this no foreign vessel may anchor.

The ports open to the trade, and under certain restrictions to the residence of foreigners, are Yokohama, (Kanagawa), Kobe, Nagasaki, Niigata, and Hakodaté in Yezo.

Close within the light-ship is the pretty bay which forms Yokohama Harbour, but the pale blue waters of the Gulf of Yedo, speckled with the white sails of countless fishing-boats, run up for twenty miles to the northwards to the city of Yedo or Tôkiyô. The Bluff, a range of low hills running abruptly into the sea on the left, and losing itself inland on the right, covered with bungalows, large and small, and buildings with flagstaffs, which are the English, German, and American Naval Hospitals, and the Bund, an irregular terrace of great length carried along the shore on a stone-faced embankment, are the first things which attract attention. Below the Bluff is the settlement, mostly foreign, and then a Japanese town of low grey houses and monotonous grey roofs spreads itself over an extensive plain.

Yokohama is not imposing in any way — these hybrid cities never are; its Bluff represents the suburbs of Boston; its Bund, the suburbs of Birkenhead, with a semi-tropical hallucination; and the Japanese town, mean and ineffective, represents I know not what, unless industrious poverty. Along the Bund are the Grand and International Hotels, the club-house, and several of the "hongs," or houses of business, that of the old firm of Jardine, Matheson, and Co., being No. 1. All these stand in gardens and shrubberies, and have a broad carriage drive between them and the sea. Then there are the British Consulate, imposingly ugly, the Union Church, partly built with money contributed in the Hawaiian Islands, unimposingly so, a few other buildings scarcely less offensive, the Japanese Post Office, Custom House, and Saibanchô or Court House, new, and built substantially in foreign style by foreign architects, and a huddle of mean erections which look like warehouses.

There are two *hatobas* or jetties, English and French — dreary projections resembling breakwaters, with sloping faces of undressed stone, but there are neither docks nor wharves, and a fleet of large ships, mostly steamers, were receiving or discharging cargo at their moorings. Iron-clads and wooden war-ships bearing the flags of England, France, America, Italy, and Russia, lay in apparent amity, and among them a handsome Japanese steam corvette, lately built in England, flying the Japan-

ese flag — a red ball on a white ground. Among the
merchantmen were two fine mail steamers from Hakodaté and Shanghai belonging to the Mitsu Bishi Co., a
Japanese line which is gradually acquiring a monopoly
of the Japanese coasting and China trade.

The bustle among my fellow-passengers, many of
whom were returning home, and all of whom expected
to be met by friends, left me at leisure as I looked at
unattractive, unfamiliar Yokohama, and the pale grey
land stretched out before me, to speculate somewhat
sadly on my destiny on these strange shores, on which
I have not even an acquaintance. On mooring, we
were at once surrounded by crowds of native boats
called by foreigners *sampans*, and Dr. Gulick, a near
relation of my Hilo friends, came on board to meet his
daughter, welcomed me cordially, and relieved me of
all the trouble of disembarkation. These *sampans* are
very clumsy-looking, but are managed with great dexterity by the boatmen, who gave and received any number of bumps with much good nature, and without any
of the shouting and swearing in which competitive boatmen usually indulge.

The partially triangular shape of these boats approaches that of a salmon-fisher's punt used on certain
British rivers. Being floored gives them the appearance
of being absolutely flat-bottomed; but though they tilt
readily, they are very safe, being heavily built, and fitted together with singular precision with wooden bolts
and a few copper cleets. They are *sculled*, not what
we should call rowed, by two or four men with very
heavy oars made of two pieces of wood working on pins
placed on outrigger bars. The men scull standing, and
use the thigh as a rest for the oar. They all wear a
single, wide-sleeved, scanty, blue cotton garment, not
fastened or girdled at the waist, straw sandals, kept on

by a thong passing between the great toe and the others, and if they wear any head-gear, it is only a wisp of blue cotton tied round the forehead. The one garment is only an apology for clothing, and displays lean concave chests and lean muscular limbs. The skin is very yellow, and often much tattooed with mythical beasts. The charge for *sampans* is fixed by tariff, so the traveller

TRAVELLING RESTAURANT.

lands without having his temper ruffled by extortionate demands.

The first thing that impressed me on landing was that there were no loafers, and that all the small, ugly, kindly-looking, shrivelled, bandy-legged, round-shouldered, concave-chested, poor-looking beings in the streets had some affairs of their own to mind. At the top of the landing-steps there was a portable restaurant, a neat and most compact thing, with charcoal stove, cooking and eating utensils complete; but it looked as if it were made by and for dolls, and the mannikin who kept it was not five feet high. At the custom-house we were attended to by minute officials in blue uniforms of European pattern, and leather boots; very civil creatures, who opened and examined our trunks carefully, and strapped them up again, contrasting pleasingly with the insolent and rapacious officials who perform the same duties at New York.

Outside were about fifty of the now well-known *jin-ri-ki-shas*, and the air was full of a buzz produced by the rapid reiteration of this uncouth word by fifty tongues. This conveyance, as you know, is a feature of Japan, growing in importance every day. It was only invented seven years ago, and already there are nearly 23,000 in one city, and men can make so much more by drawing them than by almost any kind of skilled labour, that thousands of fine young men desert agricultural pursuits and flock into the towns to make draught-animals of themselves, though it is said that the average duration of a man's life after he takes to running is only five years, and that the runners fall victims in large numbers to aggravated forms of heart and lung disease Over tolerably level ground a good runner can trot forty miles a day, at a rate of about four miles an hour. They are registered and taxed at 8s. a year for one carrying two persons, and 4s. for one which carries one only, and there is a regular tariff for time and distance.

The *kuruma* or jin-ri-ki-sha [1] consists of a light perambulator body, an adjustible hood of oiled paper, a velvet or cloth lining and cushion, a well for parcels

[1] I continue hereafter to use the Japanese word *kuruma* instead of the Chinese word *Jin-ri-ki-sha*. *Kuruma*, literally a wheel or vehicle, is the word commonly used by the *Jin-ri-ki-sha* men and other Japanese for the "man-power-carriage," and is certainly more euphonious. From *kuruma* naturally comes *kurumaya* for the *kuruma* runner.

under the seat, two high slim wheels, and a pair of shafts connected by a bar at the ends. The body is usually lacquered and decorated according to its owner's taste. Some show little except polished brass, others are alto-gether inlaid with shells known as Venus's ear, and others are gaudily painted with contorted dragons, or groups of peonies, hydrangeas, chrysanthemums, and mythical personages. They cost from £2 upwards. The shafts rest on the ground at a steep incline as you get in — it must require much practice to enable one to mount with ease or dignity — the runner lifts them up, gets into them, gives the body a good tilt back-wards, and goes off at a smart trot. They are drawn by one, two, or three men, according to the speed de-sired by the occupants. When rain comes on, the man puts up the hood, and ties you and it closely up in a covering of oiled paper, in which you are invisible. At night, whether running or standing still, they carry prettily painted circular paper lanterns 18 inches long. It is most comical to see stout, florid, solid-looking merchants, missionaries, male and female, fashionably dressed ladies, armed with card cases, Chinese compra-dores, and Japanese peasant men and women flying along Main Street, which is like the decent respectable High Street of a dozen forgotten country towns in England, in happy unconsciousness of the ludicrousness of their appearance; racing, chasing, crossing each other, their lean, polite, pleasant runners in their great hats shaped like inverted bowls, their incomprehensible blue tights, and their short blue overshirts with badges or charac-ters in white upon them, tearing along, their yellow faces streaming with perspiration, laughing, shouting, and avoiding collisions by a mere shave.

After a visit to the Consulate I entered a *kuruma* and, with two ladies in two more, was bowled along at a furious pace by a laughing little mannikin down Main Street, a narrow, solid, well-paved street with well-made side walks, kerb stones, and gutters, with iron lamp-posts, gas lamps, and foreign shops all along its length, to this quiet hotel recommended by Sir Wyville Thomson, which offers a refuge from the nasal twang of my fellow voyagers who have all gone to the caravanserais on the Bund. The host is a Frenchman, but he relies on a Chinaman; the servants are Japanese "boys" in Japanese clothes; and there is a Japanese "groom of the chambers" in faultless English costume, who perfectly appals me by the elaborate politeness of his manner.

Almost as soon as I arrived I was obliged to go in search of Mr. Fraser's office in the settlement, I say *search*, for there are no names on the streets, where there are numbers they have no sequence, and I met no Europeans on foot to help me in my difficulty. Yokohama does not improve on further acquaintance. It has a dead-alive look. It has irregularity without picturesqueness, and the grey sky, grey sea, grey houses, and grey roofs, look harmoniously dull. No foreign money except the Mexican dollar passes in Japan, and Mr. Fraser's compradore soon metamorphosed my English gold into Japanese *satsu* or paper money, a bundle of *yen* nearly at par just now with the dollar, packets of 50, 20, and 10 *sen* notes, and some rouleaux of very neat copper coins. The initiated recognise the different denominations of paper money at a glance by their differing colours and sizes, but at present they are a distracting mystery to me. The notes are pieces of stiff paper with Chinese characters at the corners, near which, with exceptionally good eyes or a magnifying glass, one can discern an English word denoting the value. They are very neatly executed, and are ornamented with the chrysanthemum crest of the Mikado and the interlaced dragons of the Empire.

I long to get away into real Japan. Mr. Wilkinson, H.B.M.'s acting consul, called yesterday, and was extremely kind. He thinks that my plan for travelling in the interior is rather too ambitious, but that it is perfectly safe for a lady to travel alone, and agrees with every body else in thinking that legions of fleas and the miserable horses are the great drawbacks of Japanese travelling. I. L. B.

THE OLD AND THE NEW.

Sir Harry Parkes — An "Ambassador's Carriage" — Blurs and Hieroglyphs — Cart Coolies — A supposed Concession to Foreign Opinion — Regulations.

YOKOHAMA, *May* 22.

TO-DAY has been spent in making new acquaintances, instituting a search for a servant and a pony, receiving many offers of help, asking questions and receiving from different people answers which directly contradict each other. Hours are early. Thirteen people called on me before noon. Ladies drive themselves about the town in small pony carriages attended by running grooms called *bettos*. The foreign merchants keep *kurumas* constantly standing at their doors, finding a willing, intelligent coolie much more serviceable than a lazy, fractious, capricious Japanese pony, and even the dignity of an "Ambassador Extraordinary and Minister Plenipotentiary" is not above such a lowly conveyance, as I have seen to-day. My last visitors were Sir Harry and Lady Parkes, who brought sunshine and kindliness into the room, and left it behind them. Sir Harry is a young-looking man scarcely in middle life, slight, active, fair, blue-eyed, a thorough Saxon, with sunny hair and a sunny smile, a sunshiny geniality in his manner, and bearing no trace in his appearance of his thirty years of service in the East, his sufferings in the prison at Peking, and the various attempts upon his life in Japan. He and Lady Parkes were most truly kind, and encourage me so heartily in my largest projects for travelling in the interior, that I shall start as soon as I have secured a servant. When they went away they jumped into *kurumas*, and it was most amusing to see the representative of England hurried down the street in a perambulator with a tandem of coolies.

I write of Sir Harry Parkes, as he is a public character, but I can only allude to the kindness shown to me by others here, and to the way in which several people are taking a great deal of trouble to facilitate my arrangements for seeing Japan. Though the day is sunshiny, I don't admire Yokohama any more than at first. It is dull and has no salient points, and it looks as if it had seen busier if not better days; but already the loneliness of a solitary arrival and the feeling of being a complete stranger have vanished, and I am suffering mainly from complete mental confusion, owing to the rapidity with which new sights and ideas are crowding upon me. My reading of books on Japan, and the persistent pumping of my Japanese fellow-voyagers for the last three weeks, might nearly as well have been omitted, for the country presents itself to me as a complete blur, or a page covered with hieroglyphs to which I have no key. Well, I have months to spend here, and I must begin at the alphabet, see everything, hear everything, read everything, and delay forming opinions as long as possible.

As I look out of the window, I see heavy, two-wheeled man-carts drawn and pushed by four men each, on which nearly all goods, stones for building, and all else, are carried. The two men who pull press with hands and thighs against a cross-bar at the end of a heavy pole, and the two who push apply their shoulders to beams which project behind, using their thick, smoothly shaven skulls as the motive power when they push their heavy loads uphill. Their cry is impressive and melancholy. They draw incredible loads, but as if the toil which often makes every breath a groan or a gasp were not enough, they shout incessantly with a coarse, guttural grunt, something like *Ha huida, Ho huida, wa ho, Ha huida*, etc. The inference from the

JAPANESE MAN-CART.

sight is that human labour is cheap and abundant. Government has made nudity a punishable offence in this and other cities, and these poor cart coolies toil in the same precarious and inconvenient garment that the boatmen wear. My inference is, that the compulsory wearing of clothing is a concession to foreign opinion. I may be wrong in both cases. It is not unwise perhaps to start with Professor Griffis's dictum that "the Government is Asiatic, despotic, and idolatrous." My first impression is that the country is much governed. One comes in contact with "regulations" on landing in the fixed tariff for *sampans* and *kurumas*, the notifications on boards, the neat policemen, the lanterns on conveyances, the rejection of foreign coin, the postal regulations, and many others; and — must I say it? — in the absence of extortionate demands! **I. L. B.**

YEDO.

Yedo and Tôkiyô — The Yokohama Railroad — The Effect of Misfits — The Plain of Yedo — Personal Peculiarities — First Impressions of Tôkiyô — H.B.M.'s Legation — An English Home.

H.B.M.'s LEGATION, YEDO, *May* 24.

I HAVE dated my letter Yedo, according to the usage of the British Legation, but popularly the new name of Tôkiyô, or Eastern Capital, is used, Kiyôto, the Mikado's former residence having received the name of Saikiô, or Western Capital, though it has now no claim to be regarded as a capital at all. Yedo belongs to the old *régime* and the Shôgunate, Tôkiyô to the new *régime* and the Restoration, with their history of ten years. It would seem an incongruity to travel to *Yedo* by railway, but quite proper when the destination is Tôkiyô.

The journey between the two cities is performed in an hour by an admirable, well-metalled, double track railroad, 18 miles long, with iron bridges, neat stations, and substantial roomy termini, built by English engineers at a cost known only to Government, and opened by the Mikado in 1872. The Yokohama station is a handsome and suitable stone building, with a spacious approach, ticket offices on our plan, roomy waiting-rooms for different classes — uncarpeted, however, in consideration of Japanese clogs — and supplied with the daily papers. There is a department for the weighing and labelling of luggage, and on the broad covered stone platform at both termini, a barrier with turnstiles, through which, except by special favour, no ticketless person can pass. Except the ticket clerks, who are Chinese, and the guards and engine-drivers, who are English, the officials are Japanese in European dress. Outside the stations, instead of cabs, there are *kurumas*, which carry luggage as well as people. Only luggage in the hand is allowed to go free, the rest is weighed, numbered, and charged for, a corresponding number being given to its owner to present at his destination. The fares are, 3d class, an *ichibu*, or about 1s.; 2d class, 60 *sen*, or about 2s. 4d.; and 1st class, a *yen*, or about 3s. 8d. The tickets are collected as the passengers pass through the barrier at the end of the journey. The English-built cars differ from ours in having seats along the sides, and doors opening on platforms at both ends. On the whole the arrangements are Continental rather than British. The first-class cars are expensively fitted up with deeply cushioned, red morocco seats, but carry very few passengers, and the comfortable seats, covered with fine matting, of the 2d class are very scantily occupied, but the 3d class vans are crowded with Japanese, who have taken to railroads as readily as to *kurumas*. This line earns about $8,000,-000 a year.

The Japanese look most diminutive in European dress. Each garment is a misfit, and exaggerates the miserable *physique*, and the national defects of concave chests and bow legs. The lack of "complexion" and of hair upon the face makes it nearly impossible to judge of the ages of men. I supposed that all the railroad officials were striplings of 17 or 18, but they are men from 25 to 40 years old.

It was a beautiful day, like an English June day, but hotter, and though the *Sakura* (wild cherry) and its kin, which are the glory of the Japanese spring, are over, everything is a young, fresh green yet, and in all the beauty of growth and luxuriance. The immediate neighbourhood of Yokohama is beautiful, with abrupt wooded hills, and small picturesque valleys, but after passing Kanagawa the railroad enters upon the immense plain of Yedo, said to be 90 miles from north to south, on whose northern and western boundaries faint blue mountains of great height hovered dreamily in the blue haze, and on whose eastern shore for many miles the clear blue wavelets of the Gulf of Yedo ripple, always as then, brightened by the white sails of innumerable fishing-boats. On this fertile and fruitful plain stand not only the capital with its million of inhabitants, but a number of populous cities, and several hundred thriving agricultural villages. Every foot of land which can be seen from the railroad is cultivated by the most careful spade husbandry, and much of it is irrigated for rice. Streams abound, and villages of grey wooden houses with grey thatch, and grey temples with strangely curved roofs, are scattered thickly over the landscape. It is all homelike, liveable, and pretty, the country of an industrious people, for not a weed is to be seen, but no very striking features or peculiarities arrest one at first sight unless it be the crowds everywhere.

You don't take your ticket for Tôkiyô, but for Shinagawa or Shinbashi, two of the many villages which have grown together into the capital. Yedo is hardly seen before Shinagawa is reached, for it has no smoke and no long chimneys; its temples and public buildings are seldom lofty; the former are often concealed among thick trees, and its ordinary houses seldom reach a height of 20 feet. On the right a blue sea with fortified islands upon it, wooded gardens with massive retaining walls, hundreds of fishing-boats lying in creeks or drawn

up on the beach; on the left a broad road on which
kurumas are hurrying both ways, rows of low, grey
houses, mostly tea-houses and shops, and as I was asking " Where is Yedo?" the train came to rest in the
terminus — the Shinbashi railroad station, and disgorged
its 200 Japanese passengers with a combined clatter of
400 clogs — a new sound to me. These clogs add three
inches to their height, but even with them few of the
men attained 5 feet 7 inches, and few of the women 5
feet 2 inches; but they look far broader in the national
costume, which also conceals the defects of their figures.
So lean, so yellow, so ugly, yet so pleasant-looking, so
wanting in colour and effectiveness; the women so very
small and tottering in their walk; the children so
formal-looking and such dignified burlesques on the
adults, I feel as if I had seen them all before, so like
are they to their pictures on trays, fans, and tea-pots.
The hair of the women is all drawn away from their
faces, and is worn in chignons, and the men, when they
don't shave the front of their heads and gather their
back hair into a quaint queue drawn forward over the
shaven patch, wear their coarse hair about three inches
long in a refractory undivided mop.

Davis, an orderly from the Legation, met me, one of
the escort cut down and severely wounded when Sir H.
Parkes was attacked in the street of Kiyôtô in March
1868 on his way to his first audience of the Mikado.
Hundreds of *kurumas*, and covered carts with four
wheels drawn by one miserable horse, which are the
omnibuses of certain districts of Tôkiyô, were waiting
outside the station, and an English brougham for me
with a running *betto*. The Legation stands in Kôjimachi on very elevated ground above the inner moat of
the historic " Castle of Yedo," but I cannot tell you
anything of what I saw on my way thither, except that

there were miles of dark, silent, barrack-like buildings, with highly ornamental gateways, and long rows of projecting windows with screens made of reeds — the feudal mansions of Yedo — and miles of moats with lofty grass embankments or walls of massive masonry 50 feet high, with kiosk-like towers at the corners, and curious, roofed gateways, and many bridges, and acres of lotus leaves. Turning along the inner moat, up a steep slope, there are, on the right, its deep green waters, the great grass embankment surmounted by a dismal wall overhung by the branches of coniferous trees which surrounded the palace of the Shôgun, and on the left sundry *yashikis*, as the mansions of the *daimiyô* were called, now in this quarter mostly turned into hospitals, barracks, and Government offices. On a height, the most conspicuous of them all, is the great red gateway of the *yashiki*, now occupied by the French Military Mission, formerly the residence of Ii Kamon no Kami, one of the great actors in recent historic events, who was assassinated not far off, outside the Sakaruda gate of the castle. Besides these, barracks, parade grounds, policemen, *kurumas*, carts pulled and pushed by coolies, pack-horses in straw sandals, and dwarfish, slatternly-looking soldiers in European dress made up the Tôkiyô that I saw between Shinbashi and the Legation.

H.B.M.'s Legation has a good situation near the Foreign Office, several of the Government departments, and the residences of the ministers, which are chiefly of brick in the English suburban villa style. Within the compound, with a brick archway with the Royal Arms upon it for an entrance, are the Minister's residence, the Chancery, two houses for the two English Secretaries of Legation, and quarters for the escort.

It is an English house and an English home, though,

with the exception of a venerable nurse, there are no English servants. The butler and footman are tall Chinamen, with long pig-tails, black satin caps, and long blue robes; the cook is a Chinaman, and the other servants are all Japanese, including one female servant, a sweet, gentle, kindly girl about 4 feet 5 in height, the wife of the head "housemaid.", None of the servants speak anything but the most aggravating "pidgun" English, but their deficient speech is more than made up for by the intelligence and service of the orderly in waiting, who is rarely absent from the neighbourhood of the hall door, and attends to the visitors' book and to all messages and notes. There are two real English children of six and seven, with great capacities for such innocent enjoyments as can be found within the limits of the nursery and garden. The other inmate of the house is a beautiful and attractive terrier called "Rags," a Skye dog, who unbends "in the bosom of his family," but ordinarily is as imposing in his demeanour as if he, and not his master, represented the dignity of the British Empire.

The Japanese Secretary of Legation is Mr. Ernest Satow, whose reputation for scholarship, specially in the department of history, is said by the Japanese themselves to be the highest in Japan [1] — an honourable distinction for an Englishman, and won by the persevering industry of fifteen years. The scholarship connected with the British Civil Service is not, however, monopolised by Mr. Satow, for several gentlemen in the consular service, who are passing through the various grades of student interpreters, are distinguishing themselves not alone by their facility in colloquial

[1] Often in the later months of my residence in Japan, when I asked educated Japanese questions concerning their history, religions, or ancient customs, I was put off with the answer, "You should ask Mr. Satow, he could tell you."

Japanese, but by their researches in various departments of Japanese history, mythology, archæology, and literature. Indeed it is to their labours, and to those of a few other Englishmen and Germans, that the Japanese of the rising generation will be indebted for keeping alive not only the knowledge of their archaic literature, but even of the manners and customs of the first half of this century.   I. L. B.

CUSTOMS AND DRESS.

Lifeless Heat — Street Sights in Tôkiyô — The Foreign Concession — The Missionary Quarter — Architectural Vulgarities — The Imperial Gardens — Costume and Behaviour — Female Inelegance

H.B.M.'s LEGATION, YEDO, *May* 27.

So far I am not much pleased with the climate. There is no elasticity in the air. It has been warm and damp ever since I came, with a sky either covered with masses of clouds or suffused with a grey mist. Friday was admitted by everybody to be a wretched day, with lifeless heat and a continuous drizzle.

In the afternoon I drove to the Foreign Concession to pay some visits. We passed miles of *yashikis* and enclosed vacant spaces, where *yashikis* once were; crossed rivers, moats, and canals; saw hundreds of boats with thatched roofs lying on water or mud, smelt villanous smells from crowded canals and open black drains; saw coolies in umbrella hats and straw rain cloaks, and all the world carrying paper umbrellas; saw a street, a hive of busy, crowded industries, the lower front of each house a shop, whose novel and ingenious wares amazed me; saw women with bright complexions, shining hair, shaven eyebrows and blackened teeth, clattering and tottering on high clogs; saw *kurumas* with their passengers completely hidden by envelopes of yellow oiled paper; — but saw never a horse or horse-carriage !

Tsukiji (" filled-up land ") is the Concession in which

alone foreigners may live who are not in Japanese
employment. The land is raised upon a fine embankment facing the gulf near the entrance of the Sumida
River, and is elsewhere moated in by canals crossed by
several bridges. As a place for foreign trade Tôkiyô
has proved a complete failure. There are very few
foreign merchants, and the foreign hotels are insignificant and little patronised. The U.S. Legation still
clings to Tsukiji, though the ministers of the other
great powers all live inside the moats in the neighbourhood of the Government offices. The roads are broad
and neatly kept, but the aspect of the Concession is
dull and desolate, and people live near enough to
each other to be hourly fretted by the sight of each
other's dreary doings.

There is a complete nest of Missionary Church edifices, a wonderful testimony to the shattered unity of
the Christian Church, and the number of houses occupied by missionaries is very large. It must be painful
to them to be compelled to huddle together in this
narrow locality. Besides their houses and churches
they have several boarding-schools for girls, and a
Union Theological College, supported jointly by the
American Presbyterian, Reformed Presbyterian, and
Scotch United Presbyterian bodies. This last body
has five missionaries here, one of whom, Dr. Faulds, a
medical missionary, has opened a small hospital. The
S.P.G. Society has four missionaries here, the C.M.S.
only one, and the Canadian Methodists one. Most
of them meet monthly in a united conference. The
Young Men's Christian Association has lately opened
rooms in Tsukiji, with more than the usual attractions.

At the C.M.S. house I met Mr. Fyson from Niigata
on the Sea of Japan, and Mr. Dening from Hakodaté

in Yezo, with their respective wives, who were very kind, and asked me to visit them. We talked over the *pros* and *cons* of my proposed journey, some thinking it impracticable, others encouraging it. The special points discussed were "the Food Question," which is yet unsolved, and whether it is best to buy a pony or trust to pack-horses.

Everything looked as dull and dismal as wide, deserted streets, a dead level, and a warm drizzle could make it. I am much astonished by the aggressions made here by western architectural ideas. *Yedo* is chiefly represented by the grandeur of the castle walls, banks, and moats, the *yashikis*, many of which are showing signs of unarrested decay, and the crowded streets of warehouses and wholesale produce merchants in the neighbourhood of the Nihon Bashi, the bridge from which all the distances in Japan are said to be measured. *Tôkiyô* and the new *régime* are architecturally represented by the ministerial villas of stone-faced brick, with red brick garden walls, the Engineering College, really solid and handsome, and a number of barracks, departments, police stations, colleges, and schools, in a debased Europeanised or Americanised style, built of wood, painted white, with a superabundance of oblong glass windows, and usually without verandahs, looking like inferior warehouses, or taverns in the outskirts of San Francisco, as vulgar and dismally ugly as they can be, and more like confectionery than building. It is certainly not under the advice of Mr. Chastel de Boinville, the architect of the Engineering College, that the Government has thus vulgarised the new capital, making parts of it, except for the clean, smooth roads, to look more like the outskirts of Chicago or Melbourne than an Oriental city.

Sir H. and Lady Parkes enter into my travelling

plans with much zest and kindness, offering the practical advice and help which their extensive travelling
experience suggests, and not interposing any obstacles.
Indeed, Sir H. not only approves of my plan of travelling northwards through the interior, but suggests
some additions. I only hope the actual journey may
be as pleasant as planning it on the map has been.
Sir Harry advises me not to buy a pony, as it would
fall sick for want of proper food, lose its shoes, and
involve an additional plague in the shape of a *betto*.

May 29. — The weather is once more fine, with the
mercury a little over 70°, and taking advantage of it,
we walked in the Fukiagé Gardens, private pleasure-
grounds of the Mikado, which in these new days are
open by ticket to the public every Saturday. They are
a noble specimen of the perfection to which the Japanese have brought the art of landscape-gardening. The
park, for such it is, is so beautifully laid out, and the
inequalities of the ground are so artistically taken advantage of, that in one or two places the effect of mountain scenery is almost produced. The trees are most
tastefully grouped and contrasted, the feathery, light
green bamboo being always massed against a dark background of coniferæ, while huge deciduous trees with
heavy, pendant foliage, and shrubs and ferns at their
feet, have been chosen to shade and droop over the
winding walks. The broad lawns are smooth shaven,
and the gravel walks are as absolutely faultless as those
at Kew. Below a very pretty cascade there is a small
lake surrounded by trees of great size and beauty, and
on its bank a carpeted glass pavilion, in which, after
much diplomacy, the Mikado consented to receive the
Duke of Edinburgh, and for the first time to recognise
a fellow mortal as of royal rank. This park is in the
heart of the Castle enclosure, and its associations are all

with the Shôgunate. Here former rulers, unseen of
their people, took their dreary exercise, and minute representations of the Empire which they had never seen
were created — a toy-farm, for instance, toy padi fields,
and other toy industries.

What a contrast! Instead of the mysterious state of
the Shôgun and the glitter of the *daimiyôs* trains, there
were thousands of gentle courteous people of the lower
orders enjoying the bright afternoon in their national
costume, which, except in the case of children and very
young girls, rarely emancipates itself from the bonds of
dull blues, greys, and browns, harmonious but ineffective. The basis of this costume for both sexes consists
of the *kimono*, a very scanty dressing-gown, made of
several straight widths of cotton or silk, 15 inches wide,
without gores or shoulder seams, but hollowed out at
the neck, which it exposes freely. The " armholes " are
merely long openings in the seams, and the sleeve —
a most important part of the dress, which plays a very
leading part in the classical dances and in romantic
poetry — is simply a width of the same stuff from 3
feet to 10 feet long, doubled, joined, and attached to a
portion of the armhole. The sleeve often hangs down
nearly to the ground, and women at their work put on
an arrangement of braces called *tasuki* for binding these
long bags under their armpits. I call them bags, for
the sides are sewn up from the lower end to a short distance below the arms, and are used for stowing away all
sorts of things. Certain charms and " pocket " idols are
carried in the sleeve, and food, and the paper squares
used for pocket handkerchiefs, which when new are carried in the girdles, after being used once, are dropped
into the sleeve, until an opportunity occurs for throwing
them away out of doors. The sleeve is used invariably
for wiping away tears, and is mentioned frequently in

very ancient poetry, as in an ode translated by Mr. F
V. Dickens, which is not less than 600 years old.

> " When last each other we embraced,
>   A solemn vow of faith we swore,
> And sealed it with the tears that chased
>   Adown our cheeks, our *drenched sleeves* o'er."

But it is possible to grow prosy over sleeves, so I will
only add that it is only women and children who have
a prescriptive right to folly, who wear them so long as
nearly to touch the ground.

The *kimono* has no "fit," and slouches over the shoulders. It is folded over in front by the men from left to
right, and by the women from right to left, and is confined at the waist by a girdle or *obi.* In the case of men
this is the width of a hand, and in that of women it is
a foot wide and ten feet long. It is passed twice round
the waist, and tied behind in an enormous bow, sometimes with two ends, sometimes with one ; but the fashion here is to stiffen it and make the bow lengthwise and
fasten it up between the shoulders, when it looks like a
pillow-slip. It is the most important article of a woman's
dress. No woman, or girl child is ever seen out of
doors without it, and the art of tying it is one of the
most important parts of a girl's education. It frequently costs more than the whole of the dress. Women carry handkerchiefs, charms, and many other things
in its broad folds, and men attach their purses, smoking
apparatus, fan, and portable pen and ink to it. The
great size of the bow at the back, and the tightness
with which the scanty *kimono* is drawn *forwards*, makes
every woman look as if she stooped. A *haori* or short
upper garment, of exactly the same make, but loose,
and only clasped over the chest by a cord, is often worn
by both sexes over the *kimono*. The front of the *kimo*

no is wide and loose, and is used as a receptacle for many things. Men sometimes carry their children tucked within the fronts of their dresses, and I have seen as many as seven books and a map taken out of the same capacious reservoir. Many of the younger men now wear *hakama*, or full petticoat trousers (formerly only worn by the Samurai), drawn over the *kimono* with the *haori* outside, but so far as the usual dress of the lower classes is concerned, it is only by the *obi* and the hair that you can tell a man from a woman. Foot mittens of white cloth, with a separate place for the great toe, are worn, and make the naturally small feet look big and awkward. It is very aristocratic for women to walk with an infirm gait, turning the feet inwards. The foot-gear out of doors consists of very high clogs made of the light wood of the *Paulownia Imperialis*, kept on by a leather thong which passes between the great toe and the others. These encumbrances increase the natural awkwardness of the Japanese gait, as the foot cannot be raised in walking. Hats are not worn by either sex, but the female hair is most elaborately dressed in chignons and bows, and is carefully drawn back from the face. A great many of the men wear their badge or crest, stamped in white, upon their *haoris*. No jewellery is worn, one or two pins in the hair being the only ornaments.

There were hundreds of children, dressed exactly like their parents, except that for them, as for young girls, touches of scarlet are admissible. Boys begin to wear the *obi* at three years old, girls, in their cradles, I should think. Little, solemn, old-fashioned bundles they looked, the boys with their heads shaven, except for tufts of hair over the brow and each ear, creatures to whom one would never venture to talk child's talk or seduce into a romp.

The female dress is surely not graceful, tumbling off at the shoulders, as tightly dragged round the hips as the most inconvenient of English dresses, though to the *front* not the back, so narrow as to impede locomotion, and too long for muddy weather. Tottering with turned-in feet on high wooden clogs, with limbs so tightly swathed that only the shortest steps are possible, a heavy chignon on the head, and the monstrous bow of the *obi* giving the top-heavy wearer the appearance of tumbling forward, the diminutive Japanese women look truly helpless. We have given Japan railroads, telegraphs, ironclads, and many other things; have we borrowed from her the "Grecian bend," the tied-back, sheath-like dresses, the restricting skirts, and the tottering walk?

The women never walked with the men, but in groups by themselves, with their children, and often carried their babies "pick-a-back." The men also walked with and carried children, but there were no family groups. Though the women wear nothing on their heads, there is a gentle modesty and womanliness about their faces which is pleasing. All looked happy, but there was nothing like frolic, and the quiet, courteous behaviour contrasted remarkably with that of a Saturday afternoon crowd at home. There must be a reliable habit of good behaviour among the masses, for there was not a policeman in the Gardens; and there must be enough of them and to spare, for nearly 6000 are stationed in Tôkiyô.

Though foreigners are so common here, we were regarded as interesting or diverting objects, and while Sir Harry with great animation was recalling some diplomatic experiences, a crowd grouped itself about us, staring vacantly with great black eyes, and with open mouths showing blackened teeth, but so courteously that one could not feel being stared at. In going out we met the Chinese ministers, big, fat, over-clothed, and ungainly, in violet brocade robes over primrose brocade skirts, with two much conventionalised boys. When I was presented they bowed nearly to the earth, and then, by a strange incongruity, shook hands. I. L. B.

TEMPLES.

Narrow Grooves — Topics of Talk — A Pair of Ponies — The Shrine₁
of Shiba — "Afternoon Tea" —The English Church.

H.B.M.'s LEGATION, YEDO.

FOREIGN life in Tôkiyô is much like life at home,
except that it has fewer objects and less variety, and
except in a small *clique* of scholars and *savans* talk runs
in somewhat narrow grooves.   Except the members of
the legations, and the missionaries, most of the foreigners here are in the employment of the Japanese Government, and their engagements are for terms of years.
It is no part of the plan of the able men who lead the
new Japanese movement to keep up a permanent foreign
staff.   To get all they can out of foreigners, and then
to dispense with their services is their idea.   The telegraph department has passed out of foreign leading-
strings this week, and other departments will follow as
soon as possible.

The Naval College has English instructors, the Medical College is under the charge of Germans, the Imperial University has English-speaking teachers, the Engineering College has a British Principal, assisted by a
large British staff, and a French Military Commission
teaches European drill and tactics to the army.   The
changes in the teaching staff are frequent, and people
talk not only of actual but possible changes, whose
engagement expires next month or next year, the proba-
bilities of its renewal, the reduced salary on which Mr

——— is remaining, the certainty that Mr. ———'s engagement will not be renewed, and guess what he will do
with himself and what sum he has saved; whether Mr.
———'s salary is paid in *satsu* or coin, and the present
discount on *satsu*. One happiness of being at the Legation is that gossip is utterly discouraged, and that one
is not subjected to wearisome and profitless talk. If I
cannot enter into the discussions on the actual fate of
Yoshitsuné, or the mysterious meaning of the *tomoyé*,
there is a satisfaction in hearing the learned *sough* about
my ears.

"Afternoon teas" have reached Tôkiyô, and Lady
Parkes took me to one at the house of Mr. Hawes, one
of the teachers at the Naval College. Lady P. drove a
pair of chestnut ponies of perfect beauty, fiery creatures,
much given to belligerent and other erratic proceedings,
and apparently only kept from running away by skilful
restraint. The inspector of the escort rode in front, but
only to show us the way, for Yedo, which lately swarmed
with foreigner-hating, two-sworded bravos, the retainers
of the *daimiyô*, is now so safe that a foreign lady can
drive through its loneliest or most crowded parts without any other attendant than a *betto*. There are no
side walks, and the people are so unused to such flying
vehicles as Lady Parkes's phaeton, that only the alarming yells of the *betto* who ran in front secured a narrow
lane for our progress.

Passing through the mean, bewildering streets of
Tôkiyô, we drove through a gateway into a region where
forest trees make a solemn shade, and the hum of the
city is unheard, a region of countless temples and
temple-courts, and stately tombs where six of the Shôguns "lie in glory, every one in his own house."
Grandly roofed red portals, arabesques in gold and
colour, coloured cloisters in which no footfall is ever

heard, groves and avenues of magnificent cryptomeria, cool in summer and green in winter, falling water, blossoming shrubs, marvels of Japanese art in lacquer and bronze, and a hush as of death, make Shiba the most solemn and fascinating resort to which one can betake one's self. Formerly hundreds of priests lived within the enclosure, and their houses and the guest-chambers for visitors and pilgrims constituted almost a town by themselves, but the "old order" has changed, the bare Shintô faith has displaced the highly decorated ceremonial of Buddhism, the priests are dispersed; an English Episcopal Service is held in one of the small temples, and the Government has allotted priest and pilgrim houses, temples and colleges, as residences to the foreigners in its service.

Thus only our "afternoon tea" deserves mention, for our host lives in the house of the priest of a small Fox temple; there is a small shrine in his garden, and the priest brings offerings of food every morning to two foxes or badgers which live underneath it. The house, an irregular wooden one, with deep eaves forming the verandah, looks like a doll's house, not fit to bear the tread of heavy men. By means of grooves in the floor with sliding partitions of lacquer and paper, it can be transformed in two minutes from a house with one or two large rooms, into a house with five or six small ones. The floor is laid with what, if they were upright, we should call *panels* of matting, very white and fine. All foreigners' houses here are turned to some extent into museums of Japanese objects of "bigotry and virtue," which furnish both the rooms and topics for talk. The forms and colours, and even the materials, differ so widely from those used in the West that it must require a prolonged education of the eye for the appreciation of many of them. Some which are treasured I think decidedly ugly, others take me by storm at once; but I rebel against being coerced into admiration of a work of art because it is old, or because it is Japanese, and I shall not buy anything till I have been in Japan six months, and certainly shall not take home a thousand teapots, as an English lady curio-hunter is doing!

Lieut. Hawes gave us some strawberries, which have lately been introduced, and they had a good flavour, but people think they will soon lose it, as other exotic fruits have done before them. A day or two ago we had some fully ripe strawberries of a pale pea-green colour, with a strong odour and flavour, not of strawberries, but of the Catawba grape!

"And the next day was the Sabbath." This is a word which of course has no meaning here, so it was through streets of unresting industries that we drove to the quiet groves of Shiba, to the small temple in which liturgical worship is held, where a simple communion-table has taken the place of the altar and the shrine of Buddha, and a few seats on the matted floor accommodate the scanty congregation. The temple is open on one side to a wooded creek in which the blue iris and lotus are growing abundantly. Birds, if they did not sing, chirped in the trees, and hundreds of iridescent flies, blue and scarlet dragon-flies, and butterflies with black and gold wings, rejoiced over the water in the bright May sunshine. It is not wonderful that the lotus flower and leaf should have been taken as sacred emblems, they seem so naturally to belong to religious use. At this time the castle moats and the temple ponds are covered with their grand, peltate, blue-green leaves, gemmed with spheres of dew.

> "The lotus blooms round every azure creek,"

but nobody knows anything about "the yellow lotus dust!"   I. L. B.

CHINESE AND SERVANTS.

Dr. Hepburn — The Yokohama Bluff — "John Chinaman" — Chinese *Compradores* — Engaging a Servant — First Impressions of Ito — A Solemn Contract — The Food Question.

H.B.M.'s Legation, Yedo, June 7.

I WENT to Yokohama for a week to visit Dr. and Mrs. Hepburn on the Bluff. Bishop and Mrs. Burdon of Hong Kong were also guests, and it was very pleasant. Dr. Hepburn is about the oldest foreign resident, having been here nineteen years. He came in the strange days of the old *régime* as a medical missionary, and, before the Japanese opened hospitals and dispensaries with qualified medical attendance, he received as many as 7000 patients in a year, and they came from great distances to get his advice. He does not consider that the practice of healing is now needed in Japan to secure a hearing for Christianity, and, being in failing health, has retired from medical work. He is a man of extensive acquaintance with many Japanese matters, and the standard Japanese English Dictionary is the fruit of his nearly unaided philological labours during a period of thirteen years. He is now one of three scholars who are translating the New Testament into Japanese, and, although a layman, takes charge of a native congregation in Yokohama. His extensive information, scientific attainments, calm judgment, and freedom from bias, make him a very interesting man. He is by no means enthusiastic about the Japanese, or sanguine re-

garding their future in any respect, and evidently thinks
them deficient in solidity.

The Bluff is very pretty with a New England pretti-
ness, and everything is neat and trim. It is well laid
out with steep roads with pretty bungalows on both
sides, half hidden by thick shrubberies and hedges, and
azaleas, roses, and other flowering shrubs just now
brighten the daintily kept grounds. Owing to the extreme steepness of the hill, both the seaward and inland
views are very fine, and the morning and evening
glimpses of Fujisan are magnificent. The native town
lies below with its innumerable novelties, but I cannot
at present attempt to describe what I see, for I have
not yet succeeded in grasping even the barest outlines.
Japan is a great empire with a most ancient and elaborate civilisation, and offers as much novelty perhaps as
an excursion to another planet!

One cannot be a day in Yokohama without seeing
quite a different class of orientals from the small,
thinly dressed, and usually poor-looking Japanese. Of
the 2500 Chinamen who reside in Japan, over 1100
are in Yokohama, and if they were suddenly removed,
business would come to an abrupt halt. Here, as
everywhere, the Chinese immigrant is making himself
indispensable. He walks through the streets with his
swinging gait and air of complete self-complacency, as
though he belonged to the ruling race. He is tall and
big, and his many garments with a handsome brocaded
robe over all, his satin pantaloons, of which not much
is seen, tight at the ankles, and his high shoes, whose
black satin tops are slightly turned up at the toes, make
him look even taller and bigger than he is. His head
is mostly shaven, but the hair at the back is plaited
with a quantity of black purse twist into a queue which
reaches to his knees, above which, set well back, he

wears a stiff, black satin skull-cap, without which he is
never seen. His face is very yellow, his long dark eyes
and eyebrows slope upwards towards his temples, he
has not the vestige of a beard, and his skin is shiny.
He looks thoroughly "well-to-do." He is not unpleas-
ing-looking, but you feel that as a Celestial he looks
down upon you. If you ask a question in a merchant's
office, or change your gold into *satsu*, or take your railroad or steamer ticket, or get change in a shop, the inevitable Chinaman appears. In the street he swings
past you with a purpose in his face; as he flies past you
in a *kuruma* he is bent on business; he is sober and
reliable, and is content to "squeeze" his employer
rather than to rob him — his one aim in life is money.
For this he is industrious, faithful, self-denying; and he
has his reward.

Within an hour of arriving one hears the new word
"compradore," and it is as compradores that the Chinese have the confidence, and in business matters something of the control, of this foreign community. Each
firm has its Chinese compradore, a factotum, middle-
man, and occasionally a tyrant. The Japanese producers, and in many cases even the brokers, never see
the foreign merchant, but deal with him through this
Chinaman, who, having added "pidgun" Japanese to
"pidgun" English, is further aided by his acquaintance
with his own written character, which is largely used
here. With a certain amount of deference to his employer's wishes, he arranges the purchase and sale of
goods, the hiring and payment of coolies, the changing
of money, and much else. Trusted as he is by the foreign merchants, who scarcely grudge him what he
regards as legitimate "squeezes," he is abhorred by the
Japanese dealers, from whom he exacts "squeezes" on
everything, and who have no check upon his rapacity.

The Chinamen who are not compradores are money-changers, brokers, and clerks, and it is in their power any d⸱⸱ to lock the wheels of Yokohama finance. You cannot know what your money is worth, or the rate of exchange, or any of the mysteries of finance, without appealing to the sleek well-dressed, imperturbable, " defiantly comfortable," Chinaman. Japanese politeness is almost servile in its attitude and expression, the Chinaman is independent, almost supercilious. In life, as in death, he owes nothing to any one. He has his benevolent association, guilds, and temple, and if he is so unfortunate as not to return alive to spend his fortune in his own country, he ensures that his remains shall be taken there for their final rest. A more industrious and thriving nationality does not exist in Japan.

Several of my kind new acquaintances interested themselves about the (to me) vital matter of a servant interpreter, and many Japanese came to "see after the place." The speaking of intelligible English is a *sine quâ non*, and it was wonderful to find the few words badly pronounced and worse put together, which were regarded by the candidates as a sufficient qualification. Can you speak English? "Yes." What wages do you ask? "Twelve dollars a month." This was always said glibly, and in each case sounded hopeful. Who have you lived with? A foreign name distorted out of all recognition as was natural, was then given. Where have you travelled? This question usually had to be translated into Japanese, and the usual answer was, "The Tokaido, the Nakasendo, to Kiyôto, to Nikkô," naming the beaten tracks of countless tourists. Do you know anything of Northern Japan and the Hokkaido?

"No," with a blank, wondering look. At this stage in every case Dr. Hepburn compassionately stepped in

as interpreter, for their stock of English was exhausted.
Three were regarded as promising.   One was a sprightly
youth who came in a well-made European suit of light-
coloured tweed, a laid-down collar, a tie with a diamond.
(?) pin, and a white shirt, so stiffly starched, that he
could hardly bend low enough for a bow even of European profundity.   He wore a gilt watch-chain with a
locket, the corner of a very white cambric pocket handkerchief dangled from his breast pocket, and he held a
cane and a felt hat in his hand.   He was a Japanese
dandy of the first water.   I looked at him ruefully.
To me starched collars are to be an unknown luxury
for the next three months.   His fine foreign clothes
would enhance prices everywhere in the interior, and
besides that, I should feel a perpetual difficulty in asking menial services from an exquisite.   I was therefore
quite relieved when his English broke down at the second question.

The second was a most respectable-looking man of
thirty-five in a good Japanese dress.   He was highly
recommended, and his first English words were promising, but he had been cook in the service of a wealthy
English official who travelled with a large retinue, and
sent servants on ahead to prepare the way.   He knew
really only a few words of English, and his horror at
finding that there was "no master," and that there
would be no woman servant, was so great, that I hardly
know whether he rejected me, or I him.

The third, sent by Mr. Wilkinson, wore a plain Japanese dress, and had a frank, intelligent face.   Though
Dr. Hepburn spoke with him in Japanese, he thought
that he knew more English than the others, and that
what he knew would come out when he was less agitated.   He evidently understood what I said, and
though I had a suspicion that he would turn out to

be the "master," I thought him so prepossessing that I nearly engaged him on the spot. None of the others merit any remark.

However, when I had nearly made up my mind in his favour, a creature appeared without any recommendation at all, except that one of Dr. Hepburn's servants was acquainted with him. He is only eighteen, but this is equivalent to twenty-three or twenty-four with us, and only 4 feet 10 inches in height, but though bandy-legged is well proportioned, and strong-looking. He has a round and singularly plain face, good teeth, much elongated eyes, and the heavy droop of his eyelids almost caricatures the usual Japanese peculiarity. He is the most stupid-looking Japanese that I have seen, but, from a rapid, furtive glance in his eyes now and then, I think that the stolidity is partly assumed. He said that he had lived at the American Legation, that he had been a clerk on the Osaka railroad, that he had travelled through northern Japan by the eastern route and in Yezo, with Mr. Maries, a botanical collector, that he understood drying plants, that he could cook a little, that he could write English, that he could walk twenty-five miles a day, and that he thoroughly understood getting through the interior! This would-be paragon had no recommendations, and accounted for this by saying that they had been burned in a recent fire in his father house. Mr. Maries was not forthcoming, and more than this, I suspected and disliked the boy. However, he understood my English and I his, and being very anxious to begin my travels, I engaged him for twelve dollars a month, and soon afterwards he came back with a contract, in which he declares by all that he holds most sacred, that he will serve me faithfully for the wages agreed upon, and to this document he affixed his seal and I my name. The next day he asked me for a

month's wages in advance, which I gave him, but Dr.
H. consolingly suggested that I should never see him
again!

Ever since the solemn night when the contract was
signed, I have felt under an incubus, and since he appeared here yesterday punctual to the appointed hour,
I have felt as if I had a veritable "old man of the sea"
upon my shoulders. He flies up stairs and along the
corridors as noiselessly as a cat, and already knows
where I keep all my things. Nothing surprises or
abashes him, he bows profoundly to Sir Harry and
Lady Parkes when he encounters them, but is obviously
"quite at home" in a Legation, and only allowed one
of the orderlies to show him how to put on a Mexican
saddle and English bridle out of condescension to my
wishes. He seems as sharp or "smart" as can be, and
has already arranged for the first three days of my journey. His name is Ito, and you will doubtless hear
much more of him, as he will be my good or evil genius
for the next three months.

As no English lady has yet travelled alone through
the interior, my project excites a very friendly interest
among my friends, and I receive much warning and
dissuasion, and a little encouragement. The strongest
because the most intelligent dissuasion comes from Dr.
Hepburn, who thinks that I ought not to undertake the
journey, and that I shall never get through to the Tsugaru Strait. If I accepted much of the advice given to
me, as to taking tinned meats and soups, claret, and a
Japanese maid, I should need a train of at least six
pack-horses! As to fleas, there is a lamentable consen-
sus of opinion that they are the curse of Japanese
travelling during the summer, and some people recom-
mend me to sleep in a bag drawn tightly round the
throat, others to sprinkle my bedding freely with insect

powder, others to smear the skin all over with carbolic oil, and some to make a plentiful use of dried and powdered flea-bane. All admit, however, that these are but feeble palliatives. Hammocks unfortunately cannot be used in Japanese houses.

The "Food Question" is said to be the most important one for all travellers, and it is discussed continually with startling earnestness, not alone as regards my tour. However apathetic people are on other subjects, the mere mention of this one rouses them into interest. All have suffered or may suffer, and everyone wishes to impart his own experience, or to learn from that of others. Foreign ministers, professors, missionaries, merchants, all discuss it with becoming gravity as a question of life and death, which by many it is supposed to be. The fact is that except at a few hotels in popular resorts which are got up for foreigners, bread, butter, milk, meat, poultry, coffee, wine, and beer, are unattainable, that fresh fish is rare, and that unless one can live on rice, tea, and eggs, with the addition now and then of some tasteless fresh vegetables, food must be taken, as the fishy and vegetable abominations known as "Japanese food" can only be swallowed and digested by a few, and that after long practice.[1]

Another, but far inferior difficulty on which much stress is laid, is the practice common among native servants of getting a "squeeze" out of every money transaction on the road, so that the cost of travelling is often doubled, and sometimes trebled, according to the skill and capacity of the servant. Three gentlemen who have travelled extensively, have given me lists of

[1] After several months of travelling in some of the roughest parts of the interior, I should advise a person in average health — and none other should travel in Japan — not to encumber himself with tinned meats, soups, claret, or any eatables or drinkables except Liebig's extract of meat.

the prices which I ought to pay, varying in different districts, and largely increased on the beaten track of tourists, and Mr. Wilkinson has read these to Ito, who offered an occasional remonstrance. Mr. W. remarked after the conversation, which was in Japanese, that he thought I should have to " look sharp after money matters " — a painful prospect, as I have never been able to manage anybody in my life, and shall surely have no control over this clever, cunning, Japanese youth, who on most points will be able to deceive me as he pleases.

On returning here I found that Lady Parkes had made most of the necessary preparations for me, and that they include two light baskets with covers of oiled paper, a travelling bed or stretcher, a folding chair, and an india-rubber bath, all which she considers as necessaries for a person in feeble health on a journey of such long duration. This week has been spent in making acquaintances in Tôkiyô, seeing some characteristic sights, and in trying to get light on my tour, but little seems known by foreigners of northern Japan, and a Government department, on being applied to, returned an itinerary, leaving out 140 miles of the route that I dream of taking, on the ground of "insufficient information," on which Sir Harry cheerily remarked, " You will have to get your information as you go along, and that will be all the more interesting." Ah! but how ?

I. L. B.

THEATRICAL.

H.B.M.'s LEGATION, YEDO, *June* 7.

ON Friday we went by formal invitation to the opening of the new Shintomi Theatre, which is to introduce
a new era in the Japanese drama. Hitherto, though a
passion for the play is general in Japan, theatre-going
has been an enjoyment confined by custom to the middle and lower classes, and the idea of the Mikado, Iwakura, Terashima, or any others of the Ministry honour-
ing public theatricals with their presence would be
regarded as simply monstrous; but there are private
theatres at the palace, where the Emperor and Court
witness the *Nô*, the mediæval lyric drama of Japan,
"the very aristocracy of the histrionic art." But as
Japan is following western example in so many ways, it
has occurred to Morita, the enterprising proprietor of
this new theatre, that a regenerated drama with an
improved stage, and a light and well-ventilated audito-
rium, "would, as in Europe, be a means of recreation
worthy of the highest in the land," and produce the
result indicated in a Japanese proverb quoted by a
native paper, the *Meiroku Zasshi*, on this very subject,
"There is nothing that unites the highest and lowest so
much as community of entertainment."

Theatres are called *shibaiya*, "turf places," because the first performances were held on grass plots. The origin of the drama in Japan, as in most other countries, was religious, its primary object being to propitiate the gods. At first it consisted of dancing to an orchestral accompaniment by masked and quaintly costumed male dancers. Two such dances, one of Japanese origin, founded on some of the oldest Shintô traditions, and introduced from China in the sixth century A.D., still exist; but the earliest approach to a play was a dance by an actor dressed up as an old man early in the ninth century, and three centuries later a woman named Iso no Zuiji, who is regarded by some as the mother of the Japanese drama, danced and postured in the costume of the Court nobles. It was only in 1624 that a man by the Shôgun's order opened the first theatre in Yedo. The play-houses are mostly in one street, called after him Saruwaka Street.[1]

In the last three centuries the drama has come down from legend to history, and from history to the common doings of ordinary men and women, and the adoption of elaborate scenery, the multiplication of performers, and the disintegration of the dramatic unity of the piece, have gradually brought about new conditions, out of which has been developed the modern drama or melodrama. The best of the Japanese classical plays are still partially historical. One of the most popular

[1] In the *Cornhill Magazine*, Oct. 1876, Mr. B. H. Chamberlain gives a very interesting and popular account of the *Nô*, the ancient lyric drama, accompanied by a translation of *The Deathstone*, a play with two *dramatis personæ*, a priest and a maiden, and a chorus. The drama opens with a speech by the Priest. "I am a priest, and Gen-o is my name. With a heart ever fixed upon the path of wisdom, I had long groaned over the imperfection of my spiritual insight. But now I see clear, and with the sacerdotal besom I shall sweep the cobwebs from the eyes of men." The *Deathstone* is well worth reading as a specimen of the performances which are among the greatest pleasures of the most highly cultivated Japanese.

of these is " The forty-seven Ronins," founded on the
tale so simply told in Mr. Mitford's *Tales of Old Japan*.
Of the worst, many of which are the most popular, I
believe that the less that is said the better. Several of
the native papers accuse the theatre of being the great
corrupter of the youth of Japan, and the *Meiroku
Zasshi* advocates theatrical reform on the ground that
theatrical performances generally are "immoral, false,
nonsensical, and tedious." In the " Code of morals for
women," it is enjoined that no woman under forty
should go to the theatre, but this wise prohibition is
very generally violated among the lower classes. It
is only from the best historical plays, however, that the
rising generation can learn anything of the costumes,
customs, manners, and etiquette of the old *régime*, and
it is easy to understand the fascination which the theatre wields over people to whom it offers the only reproduction of that stately national life of which all men of
thirty have an adult remembrance.

The profession of an actor is hereditary, and MS.
instructions are carefully handed down in his family.
Actors have been looked upon as a degraded class, but
their disabilities along with those of the *etá*, a pariah
caste, are now removed. One family of actors, that to
which Ichikawa Danijirô, the most famous of living
Japanese actors, belongs, was an exception to the general rule of degradation. Under the Shôguns women
were prohibited from acting with men, but there are
female theatrical companies, said, however, to be neither
popular nor numerous. The beardlessness of the ordinary Japanese renders the " get up " of a man as a
woman an easy thing, but the imitated voice is most
unpleasing, and there is a stiffness and lack of grace
about female parts so filled. Women are now being
introduced into theatrical companies. The story of a

play is said to be forcibly told, but the action of the body and face is, according to western notions, forced and exaggerated, while doleful music and the plaintive wailing of the chorus unduly intensify the expression of grief and despair. Many foreigners interested in Japanese archaic matters, and tolerably acquainted with the language, are much fascinated by the classical drama, but if the representation at the Shintomi Theatre was at all typical, I should describe it as slow and tedious.

An ordinary Japanese play begins at 6 or 10 A.M., lasts the whole day, and possibly two or three successive days, and at Tôkiyô extends into the night. There are intervals between the acts in which many playgoers adjourn for refreshments to the neighbouring tea-houses, but it is quite correct for refreshments to be served to parties in the theatre itself, and even on this opening day tea-house servants continuously carried lacquer trays with tea, rice, and sandwiches to the occupants of the compartments or boxes. Of course smoking is allowed, as it is in temples and everywhere else. When the performances are carried on after dark, a row of candles is placed in front of the stage, and attendants, with additional candles fixed on long sticks, hold them so as to throw light upon the faces of those actors who are speaking or grimacing. Boys in loose black caps, who are supposed to be invisible, crouch behind the performers in order to remove articles no longer required, or to slip an unseen support under an actor who has to sustain the same position for any length of time. The stage used for the *Nô* dramas is a plain, square, wooden room, supported by pillars and open on all sides but one, and that, according to immemorial usage, is painted with a pine tree, three small pine trees being planted or placed in the court which separates the stage from the spectators. There is no ornament at all. But the ordinary stage is provided with scenery which is nearly brought to perfection, and the costumes are gorgeous in the extreme, many of them being of great antiquity and absolutely price-'ess, owing to the beauty of the antique needlework.

Morita's invitation was extended to the diplomatic body, the foreigners in Government employment, and to a large number of the higher Japanese officials. The whole neighbourhood was *en fête*. The great tea-houses, which sell theatre tickets which ensure both seats and refreshments, were gay with flags and col-oured paper lanterns, and the theatre doors were only kept clear for visitors by rows of policemen, who quietly kept back the crowd which blocked the street. A steward in European evening dress handed us to our seats in the front row of the gallery facing the stage, one half of which was reserved for foreigners, and the other half for Japanese officialdom, and the seats both in it and the side galleries were covered with very ugly carpets for the occasion. In the long delay before the opening, tea and ices were handed to the invited guests.

The building is very plain and bare. The stage for that day was destitute of scenery and ornament, and was arranged for the *Nô* performance. Were it not so, it would have been equipped with a turn-table, a trap or ascent, and topsy-turvy scenes. The whole is of pure white wood. The floor or pit is occupied with compartments, which were crowded with men, women, and children, talking, smoking, and eating. Two raised wooden walks called "flower paths," by which the actors enter and retire on some occasions, pass through the pit. There is a very neat ceiling, which, like the whole of the carpenters' work, is highly finished in

fine white wood. The greatest innovation is that two
gasaliers have been introduced, and gas footlights have
replaced the dismal row of tallow candles and the
black "supers" who used to follow the actors about
with lighted tapers on the end of rods. The theatre
is seated for 2000 people, but you must not understand
by that that it has seats, for the boxes are only finely
matted pens in which the playgoers sit on the floor in
the usual position of squatting on the heels. The only
decorations were a profusion of white flags with the
badges of the actors in red upon them, interspersed
with flags and paper lanterns of red and white, the
national colours. The effect of this almost monotonous simplicity was a harmonious prettiness which
pleased and rested the eyes. The stage was partially
concealed, not by a "drop scene," but by a pure white
curtain with the badge of the theatre in red upon it,
red and white being the only colours used.

Before the performance, attendants presented each
invited guest with a pretty, white fan, ornamented in
red with the Chinese characters which form Morita's
name. The people are so far fortunate whose written
characters lend themselves so readily to the purposes
of simple and tasteful ornament. When delay had
become nearly insupportable, and the noisy music of
marine and military bands, which performed alternately, had rasped sensitive nerves to the extreme limit
of endurance, a curtain at the side of the stage was
drawn aside, and Morita, accompanied by forty actors
in European evening dress, advanced to the front and
right of the stage, those who perform as females group-
ing themselves on the left, dressed in *kimono* and
hakama. The actors in European dress arranged them
selves in a dismal line, an awkward squad. Alas for
them! Where was Ichikawa Danijirô, the idol of play-

goers, with whose stately figure in brocaded robes I had become familiar from countless photographs, and where the host of grand, two-sworded lesser luminaries in the rich draperies of the old *régime?* Fanny Parkes, aged six, said, "Papa, how *very* funny all those ugly men look!" and if she had been aged sixty she could not have made a more apt remark. The yellow, featureless faces, all alike, the bullet-shaped craniums, the coarse cropped hair bristling up from the head, the flat chests, round shoulders, and lean, ill-shaped legs, were exhibited in all their ugliness in western dress, for the first, and I hope for the last time. The clothes looked as if they had all been made for one man, and that man not one of the forty who were present. It is true that they had got into them, but that is very different from wearing them. They stood in one deplorable attitude, with lean arms hanging limp by their sides, hands crammed into badly-fitting white kid gloves, and looking like miscreants awaiting castigation.

Morita read the following address in Japanese : —

SPOKEN at the Shintomi Theatre, Yedo, on the day of the opening of the new house.

"Some persons with a taste for histrionic performances, filled with regret at the inutility of these performances consequent on their general corruption, acquainted Morita, proprietor of the Shimabara Theatre, and the chief actors, with their desire of effecting alterations both in the arrangements of the house and the character of the dramas exhibited, of avoiding all indecency, and making propriety the end and aim of bringing on the boards such living historical pictures as might persuade to virtue and deter from vice, and of thus obtaining, on the one hand, the result of helping towards the improvement of manners and morals, and on the other that of constituting this house the chief place of relaxation for nobles and distinguished men, as also for the Ministers of foreign countries — in a word, for the *élite* of society — results which might, to some degree, prove of service to the cause of orderly government, and form one feature in the advance of society along the path of civilisation. Morita and the actors have, in consequence, spared no effort; and not only the arrangement of the house and the tendency of the dramas, but even the behaviour and the manners of the performers have been subjected to reform, so as to lead them to hope for the patronage of the *élite* of society. Now has arrived the day when the theatre stands completed. They solemnly inaugurate it with a ceremonial based on that observed at the inauguration of banks and similiar useful institutions; they have invited the military band to discourse music; they have requested the honour of the presence of all the *élite* of society, of the Governor, of the greater, middle, and lesser Inspectors of Police, of the higher officials, of the nobility, of the chief merchants, and of the Ministers of foreign countries, and what they expect from the auspices of so brilliant an inauguration is the commencement of the era of theatrical reform."

After this the favourite actor followed with another in the same strain, on behalf of himself and his brethren. Although one's sense of the ludicrous must be excited by the aping of European costume, yet Morita's address has a special interest and importance as an additional evidence of the desire for *reform from within,* and as being altogether in sympathy with the great Japanese movement in the direction of western civilisation. His attempt to purify the stage is in harmony with the action of the Government in prohibiting the sale of pictures and figures of an immoral tendency, in suppressing many immoral exhibitions, in enforcing the wearing of clothing out of doors in the cities, in prohibiting promiscuous bathing in the public bath-houses, and in many other ways providing for the improvement, at least in externals, of the public morals.

After an interval, during which tea and champagne were provided in the galleries, and much feasting went on in the pit, the curtain rose upon the *Nô* stage and its performers. Mr. Chamberlain, the scholarly author of the paper on this performance, in the *Cornhill Magazine* for October 1876, tried to rouse me to some enthusiasm about this ancient lyric drama; but in spite of his explanations, the splendour of the dresses, and the antique dignity of the actors, I found it most tedious, and the strumming, squalling, mewing, and stamping by which the traditional posturings are accompanied, are to a stranger absolutely exasperating. This was followed by a short play, the scene of which was laid in the Old Palace in Kiyôto, and concluded with a comic pastoral, in which troops of actors and "actresses" danced and frolicked down the "flower paths," waving branches of blossoming cherry. The costumes in the *Nô* were gorgeous, some of them probably several centuries old, and the dresses in the pastoral were exquisitely beautiful. The latter was indeed a lovely spectacle.   I. L. B.

WORSHIP.

Kwan-non Temple — Uniformity of Temple Architecture — A *Kurama* Expedition — A Perpetual Festival — The *Ni-ô* — The Limbo of Vanity — Heathen Prayers — Binzuru — The Fox-God — A Group of Devils — Floral Monstrosities — Japanese Womankind — New Japan — An *Eléqante*.

H.B.M.'s LEGATION, YEDO, *June* 9.

ONCE for all I will describe a Buddhist temple, and it shall be the popular temple of Asakusa, which keeps fair and festival the whole year round, and is dedicated to the "thousand-armed" Kwan-non, the goddess of mercy.[1] Writing generally, it may be said that in design, roof, and general aspect, Japanese Buddhist temples are all alike. The sacred architectural idea expresses itself in nearly the same form always. There is the single or double roofed gateway, with highly coloured figures in niches on either side; the paved temple-court, with more or fewer stone or bronze lanterns; *amainu*, or heavenly dogs, in stone on stone pedestals; stone

---

[1] Kuhan-on, pronounced Kwan-non, the goddess of mercy, the most popular Divinity of the Japanese Pantheon, is imported from China, where she is known as Kwanyin. The following note and legend of her origin have been given to me by Mr. F. V. Dickens. "Probably Kwanyin was found as a principal goddess among the Chinese by the Buddhist missionaries on their arrival from India, and by them was made out to be their own deity Avalòkitêswara, who is male, and head of the church. Her name means the onlooker, the hearer of prayers, or rather, of the sound of prayers. The Chinese say she was a daughter of Chong Wang (B.C. 696), and was put into a convent and ordered to be executed because she refused to marry in accordance with her father's wishes The executioner's sword broke, and in consequence

sarcophagi, roofed over or not, for holy water; a flight of steps; a portico, continued as a verandah all round the temple; a roof of tremendously disproportionate size and weight, with a peculiar curve; a square or oblong hall divided by a railing from a " chancel " with a high and low altar, and a shrine containing Buddha, or the divinity to whom the chapel is dedicated; an incense-burner, and a few ecclesiastical ornaments. The symbols, idols, and adornments, depend upon the sect to which the temple belongs, or the wealth of its votaries, or the fancy of the priests. Some temples are packed full of gods, shrines, banners, bronzes, brasses, tablets, and ornaments, and others, like those of the Monto sect, are so severely simple, that with scarcely an alteration they might be used for Christian worship to-morrow.

The foundations consist of square stones on which the uprights rest. These are of elm, and are united at intervals by longitudinal pieces. The great size and enormous weight of the roofs arises from the trusses being formed of one heavy frame being built upon another in diminishing squares till the top is reached, the main beams being formed of very large timbers put on in their natural state. They are either very heavily and ornamentally tiled, or covered with sheet copper ornamented with gold, or thatched to a depth of from one

she was stifled. She went to hell, but hell immediately turned into paradise ; and Yama, its king, disgusted with the change, sent her back to life on a lotus flower. Then her father fell sick, and she cured him by cutting off the flesh of her arms, and feeding him with it. A statue was ordered to be erected to her with eyes and arms complete, but by a misunderstanding of the word ch'uën (complete) for Ts'ien, a thousand, it was provided with a thousand arms and eyes." The "thousand-armed Kwan-non" came to Japan with the Buddhist propagandists, and her *cultus* is one of the most popular in the Empire. The temple of Sanjiusangendo at Kiyôto contains (it is said) 33,000 representations of this divinity, a thousand of which are larger than life. It is one of the most impressive sights in Japan.

to three feet, with fine shingles or bark. The casing of
the walls on the outside is usually thick elm planking
either lacquered or unpainted, and that of the inside is
of thin, finely planed and bevelled planking of the beautiful wood of the *Retinospora obtusa*. The lining of the
roof is in flat panels, and where it is supported by pillars, they are invariably circular, and formed of the
straight, finely grained stem of the *Retinospora obtusa*.
The projecting ends of the roof beams under the eaves
are either elaborately carved, lacquered in dull red, or
covered with copper, as are the joints of the beams.
Very few nails are used, the timbers being very beautifully joined by mortices and dovetails, other methods
of junction being unknown.

Mr. Chamberlain and I went in a *kuruma* hurried
along by three liveried coolies, through the three miles
of crowded streets which lie between the Legation and
Asakusa, once a village, but now incorporated with this
monster city, to the broad street leading to the Adzuma
Bridge over the Sumida river, one of the few stone
bridges in Tôkiyô, which connects east Tôkiyô, an uninteresting region, containing many canals, storehouses,
timber-yards, and inferior *yashikis*, with the rest of the
city. This street, marvellously thronged with pedestrians and *kurumas*, is the terminus of a number of city
"stage lines," and twenty wretched-looking covered
waggons, with still more wretched ponies, were drawn
up in the middle, waiting for passengers. Just there
plenty of real Tôkiyô life is to be seen, for near a shrine
of popular pilgrimage there are always numerous places
of amusement, innocent and vicious, and the vicinity of this temple is full of restaurants, tea-houses,
minor theatres, and the resorts of dancing and singing
girls.

A broad paved avenue, only open to foot-passengers,

leads from this street to the grand entrance, a colossal
two-storied double-roofed *mon* or gate, painted a rich
dull red. On either side of this avenue are lines of
booths, which make a brilliant and lavish display of
their contents, toy-shops, shops for smoking apparatus,
and shops for the sale of ornamental hair-pins predom-
inating. Nearer the gate are booths for the sale of
rosaries for prayer, sleeve and bosom idols of brass and
wood in small shrines, amulet bags, representations of
the jolly-looking Daikoku, the god of wealth, the most
popular of the household gods of Japan, shrines, memorial tablets, cheap *ex votos*, sacred bells, candlesticks,
and incense-burners, and all the endless and various
articles connected with Buddhist devotion, public and
private. Every day is a festival-day at Asakusa; the
temple is dedicated to the most popular of the great
divinities; it is the most popular of religious resorts;
and whether he be Buddhist, Shintôist, or Christian, no
stranger comes to the capital without making a visit to
its crowded courts, or a purchase at its tempting booths.
Not to be an exception, I invested in bouquets of fire-
work flowers, 50 flowers for 2 *sen*, or 1d., each of which,
as it slowly consumes, throws off fiery coruscations,
shaped like the most beautiful of snow crystals. I was
also tempted by small boxes at 2 *sen* each, containing
what look like little slips of withered pith, but which,
on being dropped into water, expand into trees and
flowers.

Down a paved passage on the right there is an artificial river, not over clean, with a bridge formed of one
curved stone, from which a flight of steps leads up to a
small temple with a magnificent bronze bell. At the
entrance several women were praying. In the same
direction are two fine bronze Buddhas, seated figures,
one with clasped hands, the other holding a lotus, both

with "The light of the world" upon their brows. The grand red gateway into the actual temple courts has an extremely imposing effect, and besides it is the portal to the first great heathen temple that I have seen, and it made me think of another temple whose courts were equally crowded with buyers and sellers, and of a "whip of small cords" in the hand of One who claimed both the temple and its courts as His "Father's House." Not with less righteous wrath would the gentle founder of Buddhism purify the unsanctified courts of Asakusa. Hundreds of men, women, and children passed to and fro through the gateway in incessant streams, and so they are passing through every daylight hour of every day in the year, thousands becoming tens of thousands on the great *matsuri* days, when the *mikoshi* or sacred car, containing certain symbols of the god, is exhibited, and after sacred mimes and dances have been performed, is carried in a magnificent, antique procession to the shore and back again. Under the gateway on either side are the *Ni-ô* or two kings, gigantic figures in flowing robes, one red and with an open mouth, representing the *Yo*, or male principle of Chinese philosophy, the other green, and with the mouth firmly closed, representing the *In*, or female principle. They are hideous creatures, with protruding eyes, and faces and figures distorted and corrupted into a high degree of exaggerated and convulsive action. These figures guard the gates of most of the larger temples, and small prints of them are pasted over the doors of houses to protect them against burglars. Attached to the grating in front were a number of straw sandals, hung up by people who pray that their limbs may be as muscular as those of the *Ni-ô*.

Passing through this gate we were in the temple court proper, and in front of the temple itself, a building of imposing height and size, of a dull red colour, with a grand roof of heavy iron grey tiles, with a sweeping curve which gives grace as well as grandeur. The timbers and supports are solid, and of great size, but in common with all Japanese temples, whether Buddhist or Shintô, the edifice is entirely of wood. A broad flight of narrow, steep, brass-bound steps lead up to the porch, which is formed by a number of circular pillars supporting a very lofty roof, from which paper lanterns ten feet long are hanging. A gallery runs from this round the temple, under cover of the eaves. There is an outer temple, un-matted, and an inner one behind a grating, into which those who choose to pay for the privilege of praying in comparative privacy, or of having prayers said for them by the priests, can pass.

In the outer temple, the noise, confusion, and perpetual motion, are bewildering. Crowds on clattering clogs pass in and out, pigeons, of which hundreds live in the porch, fly over your head, and the whirring of their wings mingles with the tinkling of bells, the beating of drums and gongs, the high-pitched drone of the priests, the low murmur of prayers, the rippling laughter of girls, the harsh voices of men, and the general buzz of a multitude. There is very much that is highly grotesque at first sight. Men squat on the floor selling amulets, rosaries, printed prayers, incense sticks, and other wares. *Ex votos* of all kinds hang on the wall and on the great round pillars. Many of these are rude Japanese pictures. The subject of one is the blowing-up of a steamer in the Sumidagawa with the loss of 100 lives, when the donor was saved by the grace of Kwannon.[1] Numbers of memorials are from people who

[1] In a native Guide to Yedo, the date of this Temple of Sensoji is attributed to the thirteenth century, and its origin to a noble who fell into disgrace at Court, and having become a *Ronin*, or masterless man, fell into such straits that he became a fisherman. One day he went to

offered up prayers here, and have been restored to health or wealth. Others are from junk men whose lives have been in peril. There are scores of men's queues and a few dusty braids of women's hair offered on account of vows or prayers, usually for sick relatives, and among them all, on the left hand, are a large mirror in a gaudily gilt frame, and a framed picture of the P. M. S. *China!* Above this incongruous collection are splendid wood carvings, and frescoes of angels, among which the pigeons find a home free from molestation.

Near the entrance there is a superb incense burner in the most massive style of the older bronzes, with a mythical beast rampant upon it, and in high relief round it the Japanese signs of the zodiac, the rat, ox, tiger, rabbit, dragon, serpent, horse, goat, monkey, cock, dog, and hog. Clouds of incense rise continually from the perforations round the edge, and a black-toothed woman who keeps it burning is perpetually receiving small coins from the worshippers, who then pass on to the front of the altar to pray. The high altar, and indeed all that I should regard as properly the temple are pro-tected by a screen of coarsely netted iron wire. This holy of holies is full of shrines and gods, gigantic candlesticks, colossal lotuses of gilded silver, offerings, lamps, lacquer, litany books, gongs, drums, bells, and all the mysterious symbols of a faith which is a system of morals and metaphysics to the educated and initiated, and an idolatrous superstition to the masses. In this interior the light was dim, the lamps burned low, the atmosphere was heavy with incense, and amidst its fumes shaven priests in chasubles and stoles moved noiselessly

the Sumida to fish, but at every cast of the net brought up only a small figure of the goddess Kwan-non. To whatever spot he sculled, the same luck pursued him, so carrying home the image he enshrined it, and the endowments of subsequent devotees raised its buildings to the dignity of being the first temple in Yeddo.

over the soft matting round the high altar on which Kwan-non is enshrined, lighting candles, striking bells, and murmuring prayers. In front of the screen is the treasury, a wooden chest 14 feet by 10, with a deep slit, into which all the worshippers cast copper coins with a ceaseless clinking sound.

There too they pray, if that can be called prayer which frequently consists only in the repetition of an uncomprehended phrase in a foreign tongue, bowing the head, raising the hands and rubbing them, murmuring a few words, telling beads, clapping the hands, bowing again, and then passing out, or on to another shrine to repeat the same form. Merchants in silk clothing, soldiers in shabby French uniforms, farmers, coolies in "vile raiment," mothers, maidens, swells in European clothes, even the *samurai* policemen, bow before the goddess of mercy. Most of the prayers were offered rapidly, a mere momentary interlude in the gurgle of careless talk, and without a pretence of reverence; but some of the petitioners obviously brought real woes in simple "faith." I specially noticed two men in stylish European clothes, who prostrated themselves over and over again, and remained before the altar several minutes, offering low-voiced prayers, with closed eyes, and every sign of genuine earnestness, and several women in obvious distress, probably about sick persons, who offered their prayers with a pleading agony, no less real than that which ascends to our Father in heaven from anguished hearts in England.

In one shrine there is a large idol, spotted all over with pellets of paper, and hundreds of these are sticking to the wire netting which protects him. A worshipper writes his petition on paper, or better still, has it written for him by the priest, chews it to a pulp, and spits it at the divinity. If, having been well aimed, it passes through the wire and sticks, it is a good omen, if it lodges in the netting the prayer has probably been unheard. The Ni-ô, and some of the gods outside the temple are similarly disfigured. On the left there is a shrine with a screen, to the bars of which innumerable prayers have been tied. On the right, accessible to all, sits Binzuru, one of Buddha's original sixteen disciples. His face and appearance have been calm and amiable, with something of the quiet dignity of an elderly country gentleman of the reign of George III., but he is now worn and defaced, and has not much more of eyes, nose, and mouth, than the Sphinx, and the polished, red lacquer has disappeared from his hands and feet, for Binzuru is a great medicine god, and centuries of sick people have rubbed his face and limbs, and then have rubbed their own. A young woman went up to him, rubbed the back of his neck, and then rubbed her own. Then a modest-looking girl, leading an ancient woman with badly inflamed eyelids and paralysed arms, rubbed his eyelids, and then gently stroked the closed eyelids of the crone. Then a coolie, with a swelled knee, applied himself vigorously to Binzuru's knee, and more gently to his own. Remember, this is the great temple of the populace, and "not many rich, not many noble, not many mighty," enter its dim, dirty, crowded halls.[1]

But the great temple to Kwan-non is not the only sight of Asakusa. Outside it are countless shrines and temples, huge stone *Amainu*, or heavenly dogs, on rude blocks of stone, large cisterns of stone and bronze with and without canopies, containing water for the ablutions of the worshippers, cast iron *Amainu* on hewn

---

[1] I visited this temple alone many times afterwards, and each visit deepened the interest of my first impressions. There is always enough of change and novelty to prevent the interest from flagging, and the mild but profoundly superstitious form of heathenism which prevails in Japan is nowhere better represented.

stone pedestals — a recent gift — bronze and stone
lanterns, a stone prayer-wheel in a stone post, figures of
Buddha with the serene countenance of one who rests
from his labours, stone idols, on which devotees have
pasted slips of paper inscribed with prayers, with sticks

STONE LANTERNS.

of incense rising out of the ashes of hundreds of former
sticks smouldering before them, blocks of hewn stone
with Chinese and Sanskrit inscriptions, an eight-sided
temple in which are figures of the "Five Hundred Disciples" of Buddha, a temple with the roof and upper
part of the walls richly coloured, the circular Shintô
mirror in an inner shrine, a bronze treasury outside with
a bell which is rung to attract the god's attention, a
striking five-storied pagoda, with much red lacquer, and
the ends of the roof-beams very boldly carved, its heavy
eaves fringed with wind bells, and its uppermost roof

terminating in a graceful copper spiral of great height, with the "sacred pearl" surrounded by flames for its finial. Near it, as near most temples, is an upright frame of plain wood with tablets, on which are inscribed the names of donors to the temple, and the amount of their gifts.

Among the many shrines is an Inari or Fox temple, fox-worship being one of the most universal superstitions in Japan. The foxes, however, are only the servants of a mythical personage named Uga, to whom is ascribed the honour of the discovery and cultivation of the rice plant. Popularly, however, the honours due to Inari Sama (the name under which Uga was deified) are paid to his servants. Before two gilded foxes in this shrine there was a tray on which small bowls of rice and foxes moulded in sugar were placed as offerings. Shintô *gohei*, strips of paper cut and folded in a special fashion, and usually attached to a white wand, and supposed to represent the Shintô *kami*, or gods, who are simply deified heroes, were in the same temple, and there were Shintô *torii* in wood and stone near the entrance.

There is a handsome stone-floored temple to the south east of the main building, to which we were the sole visitors. It is lofty and very richly decorated. In the centre is an octagonal revolving room, or rather shrine of rich red lacquer most gorgeously ornamented. It rests on a frame of carved black lacquer, and has a lacquer gallery running round it, on which several richly decorated doors open. On the application of several shoulders to this gallery the shrine rotates. It is in fact a revolving library of the Buddhist Scriptures, and a single turn is equivalent to a single pious perusal of them. It is an exceedingly beautiful specimen of ancient decorative lacquer work. At the back part of the temple is a draped brass figure of Buddha, with one hand raised — a dignified piece of casting. All the Buddhas have Hindoo features, and the graceful drapery and Oriental repose which have been imported from India contrast singularly with the grotesque extravagances of the indigenous Japanese conceptions. In the same temple are four monstrously extravagant figures carved in wood, life size, with clawed toes on their feet, and two great fangs in addition to the teeth in each mouth. The heads of all are surrounded with flames, and are backed by golden circlets. They are extravagantly clothed, in garments which look as if they were agitated by a violent wind; they wear helmets and partial suits of armour, and hold in their right hands something between a monarch's sceptre and a priest's staff. They have goggle eyes and open mouths, and their faces are in distorted and exaggerated action. One, painted bright red, tramples on a writhing devil painted bright pink, another, painted emerald green, tramples on a sea-green devil, an indigo blue monster tramples on a sky-blue fiend, and a bright pink monster treads under his clawed feet a flesh-coloured demon. I cannot give you any idea of the hideousness of their aspect, and was much inclined to sympathise with the more innocent-looking fiends whom they were maltreating. They occur very frequently in Buddhist temples, and are said by some to be assistant torturers to Yemma, the lord of hell, and are called by others "The gods of the Four Quarters."

The temple grounds are a most extraordinary sight. No English fair in the palmiest days of fairs ever presented such an array of attractions. Behind the temple are archery galleries in numbers, where girls, hardly so modest-looking as usual, smile and smirk, and bring straw-coloured tea in dainty cups, and tasteless sweetmeats on lacquer trays, and smoke their tiny pipes, and offer you bows of slender bamboo strips, two feet long, with rests for the arrows, and tiny cherry-wood arrows, bone-tipped, and feathered red, blue, and white, and smilingly, but quite unobtrusively, ask you to try your skill or luck at a target hanging in front of a square drum, flanked by red cushions. A click, a boom, or a hardly audible " thud " indicate the result. Nearly all the archers were grown-up men, and many of them spend hours at a time in this childish sport.

All over the grounds booths with the usual charcoal fire, copper boiler, iron kettle of curious workmanship, tiny cups, fragrant aroma of tea, and winsome, graceful girls, invite you to drink and rest, and more solid but less inviting refreshments are also to be had. Rows of pretty paper lanterns decorate all the stalls. Then there are photograph galleries, mimic tea-gardens, tableaux in which a large number of groups of life-size figures with appropriate scenery are put into motion by a creaking wheel of great size, matted lounges for rest, stands with saucers of rice, beans and peas for offerings to the gods, the pigeons, and the two sacred horses, Albino ponies, with pink eyes and noses, revoltingly greedy creatures, eating all day long and still craving for more. There are booths for singing and dancing, and under one a professional story-teller was reciting to a densely packed crowd one of the old, popular stories of crime. There are booths where for a few *rin* you may have the pleasure of feeding some very ugly and greedy apes, or of watching mangy monkeys which have been taught to prostrate themselves Japanese fashion. One of the greatest sights is a collection of tableaux, life-size figures, the work of one artist who, after visiting the thirty-three great temples of the goddess of mercy, was so impressed by her power and goodness that he

created thirty-five groups, in order to show his countrymen the benefits of her *cultus*. These figures are wonderfully true to life, and wear real garments. In most
of the tableaux the goddess is represented as a lovely
and gentle woman — a Madonna, but with divine power.
Mr. Griffis, in *The Mikado's Empire*, gives an interesting
account of each. The two most curious, as representing
two articles of the Buddhist faith — future punishment
and metempsychosis — are tableaux of a hungry robber
appropriating the temple offerings, with a painting near
him showing his coming destiny, in which there are
devils and a red-hot cart with axles of fire, and one of a
man suffering from violent headache, who is directed
by Kwan-non to the spot where the buried skull which
belonged to him in a former state of existence is being
split open by the root of a tree which is growing through
the eye-socket. On removing the root the pain ceases!
The catalogue of sights is only half exhausted. Besides
the regular sights, there are gardens to the left of the
temple, in which dwarf azaleas are still blooming, and
which display to thousands of admirers the great floral
sights of Japan in their turn, camellias in January,
plum-blossoms in early March, cherry-blossoms in April,
the sacred lotus in July, and chrysanthemums in November. The Japanese are passionately fond of certain
flowers, and the "cherry viewing," the "iris and peony
viewing," the "lotus viewing," and the "maple viewing," are excursions which are part of the annual routine of Japanese life. The badges of many of the most
celebrated families are floral. The Imperial or public
badge of the Mikado is an open chrysanthemum with
sixteen petals; his palace, or private badge represents
blossoms and leaves of *Paulownia Imperialis*, and the
celebrated badge of the Shôguns of the Tokugawa dynasty is three leaves of a species of mallow, united at

their tips. But in the Asakusa gardens at this season it is less the natural than the artificial beauties which attract. Much of the "highest art" in Japanese gardening consists in distorting, deforming, dwarfing, exaggerating, and thwarting nature. The borders are clipped tea-plants, shrubs and trees are carefully trained and clipped into the likeness of umbrellas, boats, houses, men with foreign hats, tortoises, storks, and cats, and the beloved form of Fuji is represented several times. It is curious that the gardeners choose the most rigid and intractable of pines, the *Pinus massoniana* or *Pinus parviflora* for their most difficult experiments, and that the same pines are subject to operations for the production of dwarfishness and deformity in almost every garden in Japan. There are guilds of florists, the occupation is hereditary, and different families possess hereditary skill in the different deformities which are produced. Carefully dwarfed trees of various kinds, strange variegation of leaves and flowers, painstaking exaggerations of calyx, corolla, or pistil, and careful development and perpetuation of sundry strange freaks of nature, make these gardens no less than the grand forest trees left to their own ways, both in them and the temple courts, very interesting to a new comer.

But here, as everywhere, people interested me more than things. Their devout but more frequently irreverent worship, their gross and puerile superstitions, the total absence of beggars and disorderly characters, the childish amusements of men and women, the formal dress and gravity of children, the singular mixture of religion and amusement, the extreme but not disrespectful curiosity with which foreigners are still regarded, the absence of groups in which father, mother, and children, enjoy themselves together, yet the perfect freedom with which women move among men, the attention paid to children by parents of both sexes, the diminutive size of the people, the exposed but modest faces of the women, the clean and well-dressed appearance of all, their extreme quietness, the courtesy and good order preserved by the thousands who thronged the temple and its grounds during the afternoon, and the fact that not a single policeman was present, made a deep impression upon me.

Though the women, especially the girls, are modest, gentle, and pleasing-looking, I saw nothing like even passable good looks. The noses are flat, the lips thick, and the eyes of the sloping Mongolian type; and the common custom of shaving off the eyebrows and blackening the teeth (though less common in Tôkiyô than formerly), together with an obvious lack of soul, give nearly all faces an inane, vacant expression. The narrow, scanty dresses enable one to judge of the *physique*, and physically they look below par, as if the race were wearing out. Their shoulders are round and very falling, their chests and hips narrow, their hands and feet very small, their stature from four feet eight inches to five feet one inch. They look as if a girl passed from girlhood to middle age almost at once when weighted with the cares of maternity. The children look too big and heavy to be carried pick-a-back by their little mothers, and they too look deficient in robust vitality, and dwindle as they grow up. The men don't look much better. They are usually from five feet to five feet five inches, and their *physique* is wretched, leanness without muscle being the general rule. They impress me as the ugliest and the most pleasing people I have ever seen, as well as the neatest and most ingenious.

This letter is far too long, but to pass over Asakusa and its novelties when the impression of them is fresh

would be to omit one of the most interesting sights in
Japan. On the way back we passed red mail-carts like
those in London, a squadron of cavalry in European
uniforms and with European saddles, and the carriage
of the Minister of Marine, an English brougham with a
pair of horses in English harness, and an escort of six
troopers — a painful precaution adopted since the political assassination of Okubo, the Home Minister, three
weeks ago. So the old and the new in this great city
contrast with and jostle each other. The Mikado and
his ministers, naval and military officers and men, the
whole of the civil officials and the police, wear European
clothes, as well as a number of dissipated-looking young
men who aspire to represent "young Japan." Carriages, and houses in English style, with carpets, chairs.
and tables, are becoming increasingly numerous, and
the bad taste which regulates the purchase of foreign
furnishings is as marked as the good taste which everywhere presides over the adornment of the houses in
purely Japanese style. Happily these expensive and
unbecoming innovations have scarcely affected female
dress, and some ladies who adopted our fashions have
given them up because of their discomfort and manifold
difficulties and complications.

The Empress on State occasions appears in scarlet
satin *hakama*, and flowing robes, and she and the Court
ladies invariably wear the national costume. I have
only seen two ladies in European dress; and this was
at a dinner party here, and they were the wives of Mr.
Mori the go-ahead Vice-Minister for Foreign affairs, and
of the Japanese Consul at Hong Kong; and both by
long residence abroad have learned to wear it with ease.
The wife of Saigo the Minister of Education called one
day in an exquisite Japanese dress of dove-coloured silk
crêpe, with a pale pink underdress of the same material,

which showed a little at the neck and sleeves. Her
girdle was of rich dove-coloured silk, with a ghost of a
pale pink blossom hovering upon it here and there. She
had no frills or fripperies of any description, or ornaments except a single pin in her chignon, and with a
sweet and charming face she looked as graceful and
dignified in her Japanese costume as she would have
looked exactly the reverse in ours. Their costume has
one striking advantage over ours. A woman is perfectly *clothed* if she has one garment and a girdle on, and
perfectly *dressed* if she has two. There is a difference
in features and expression, much exaggerated, however,
by Japanese artists, between the faces of high-born
women and those of the middle and lower classes. I
decline to admire fat faces, pug noses, thick lips, long
eyes, turned up at the outer corners, and complexions
which owe much to powder and paint. The habit of
painting the lips with a reddish-yellow pigment, and of
heavily powdering the face and throat with pearl powder, is a repulsive one. But it is hard to pronounce
any unfavourable criticism on women who have so
much kindly grace of manner.   I. L. B.

THE JOURNEY BEGUN.

Fears — Travelling Equipments — Passports — Coolie Costume — A
Yedo Diorama — Rice Culture — Tea Houses — A Traveller's Reception — The Inn at Kasukabé — Lack of Privacy — A Concourse
of Noises — A Nocturnal Alarm — A Vision of Policemen — A
Budget from Yedo.

KASUKABÉ, *June* 10.

FROM the date you will see that I have started on my
long journey, though not upon the "unbeaten tracks"
which I hope to take after leaving Nikkô, and my first
evening alone in the midst of this crowded Asian life is
strange, almost fearful. I have suffered from nervous-
ness all day — the fear of being frightened, of being
rudely mobbed as threatened by Mr. Campbell of Islay,
of giving offence by transgressing the rules of Japanese
politeness — of, I know not what! Ito is my sole reliance, and he may prove a "broken reed." I often
wished to give up my project, but was ashamed of my
cowardice when, on the best authority, I received assur-
ances of its safety.[1]

The preparations were finished yesterday, and my
outfit weighed 110 lbs., which, with Ito's weight of 90
lbs., is as much as can be carried by an average Japanese horse. My two painted wicker-boxes lined with
paper and with waterproof covers are convenient for
the two sides of a pack-horse. I have a folding-chair —

[1] The list of my equipments is given as a help to future travellers,
especially ladies, who desire to travel long distances in the interior of
Japan. One wicker basket is enough, as I afterwards found.

for in a Japanese house there is nothing but the floor to sit upon, and not even a solid wall to lean against — an air-pillow for *kuruma* travelling, an india-rubber bath, sheets, a blanket, and last, and more important than all else, a canvas stretcher on light poles, which can be put together in two minutes; and being 2½ feet high is supposed to be secure from fleas. The "Food Question" has been solved by a modified rejection of all advice! I have only brought a small supply of Liebig's extract of meat, 4 lbs. of raisins, some chocolate, both for eating and drinking, and some brandy in case of need. I have my own Mexican saddle and bridle, a reasonable quantity of clothes, including a loose wrapper for wearing in the evening, some candles, Mr. Brunton's large map of Japan, volumes of the Transactions of the English Asiatic Society, and Mr. Satow's Anglo-Japanese Dictionary. My travelling dress is a short costume of dust-coloured striped tweed, with strong laced boots of unblacked leather, and a Japanese hat, shaped like a large inverted bowl, of light bamboo plait, with a white cotton cover, and a very light frame inside, which fits round the brow and leaves a space of 1½ inch between the hat and the head for the free circulation of air. It only weighs 2½ ounces, and is infinitely to be preferred to a heavy pith helmet, and, light as it is, it protects the head so thoroughly, that though the sun has been unclouded all day and the mercury at 86°, no other protection has been necessary. My money is in bundles of 50 *yen*, and 50, 20, and 10 *sen* notes, besides which I have some rouleaux of copper coins. I have a bag for my passport, which hangs to my waist. All my luggage, with the exception of my saddle, which I use for a footstool, goes into one *kuruma*, and Ito, who is limited to 12 lbs., takes his along with him.

I have three *kurumas*, which are to go to Nikkô,

ninety miles, in three days, without change of runners, for about eleven shillings each.

Passports usually define the route over which the foreigner is to travel, but in this case Sir H. Parkes has obtained one which is practically unrestricted, for it permits me to travel through all Japan north of Tôkiyô and in Yezo without specifying any route. This precious document, without which I should be liable to be arrested and forwarded to my consul, is of course in Japanese, but the cover gives in English the regulations under which it is issued. A passport must be applied for, for reasons of "health, botanical research, or scientific investigation." Its bearer must not light fires in woods, attend fires on horseback, trespass on fields, enclosures, or game-preserves, scribble on temples, shrines, or walls, drive fast on a narrow road, or disregard notices of "No thoroughfare." He must "conduct himself in an orderly and conciliating manner towards the Japanese authorities and people;" he "must produce his passport to any officials who may demand it," under pain of arrest; and while in the interior "is forbidden to shoot, trade, to conclude mercantile contracts with Japanese, or to rent houses or rooms for a longer period than his journey requires."

Nikkô, *June* 13. — This is one of the paradises of Japan! It is a proverbial saying, "He who has not seen Nikkô must not use the word kek'ko" (splendid, delicious, beautiful); but of this more hereafter. My attempt to write to you from Kasukabé failed, owing to the onslaught of an army of fleas, which compelled me to retreat to my stretcher, and the last two nights, for this and other reasons, writing has been out of the question.

I left the Legation at 11 A.M. on Monday and reached Kasukabé at 5 P.M., the runners keeping up an easy

trot the whole journey of twenty-three miles; but the
halts for smoking and eating were frequent.

These *kuruma*-runners wore short blue cotton drawers, girdles with tobacco pouch and pipe attached, short
blue cotton shirts with wide sleeves, and open in front,
reaching to their waists, and blue cotton handkerchiefs
knotted round their heads, except when the sun was

A KURUMA.

very hot, when they took the flat, flag discs two feet in
diameter, which always hang behind *kurumas*, and are
used either in sun or rain, and tied them on their heads.
They wore straw sandals, which had to be replaced
twice on the way. Blue and white towels hung from
the shafts to wipe away the sweat, which ran profusely
down the lean, brown bodies. The upper garment
always flew behind them, displaying chests and backs

elaborately tattooed with dragons and fishes. Tattooing has recently been prohibited; but it was not only a favourite adornment, but a substitute for perishable clothing.

Most of the men of the lower classes wear their hair in a very ugly fashion, — the front and top of the head being shaved, the long hair from the back and sides being drawn up and tied, then waxed, tied again, and cut short off, the stiff queue being brought forward and laid, pointing forwards, along the back part of the top of the head. This top-knot is shaped much like a short clay pipe. The shaving and dressing the hair thus require the skill of a professional barber. Formerly the hair was worn in this way by the *samurai*, in order that the helmet might fit comfortably, but it is now the style of the lower classes mostly and by no means invariably.

Blithely, at a merry trot, the coolies hurried us away from the kindly group in the Legation porch, across the inner moat and along the inner drive of the castle, past gateways and retaining walls of Cyclopean masonry, across the second moat, along miles of streets of sheds and shops, all grey, thronged with foot-passengers and *kurumas*, with packhorses loaded two or three feet above their backs, the arches of their saddles red and gilded lacquer, their frontlets of red leather, their "shoes" straw sandals, their heads tied tightly to the saddle-girth on either side, great white cloths figured with mythical beasts in blue hanging down loosely under their bodies; with coolies dragging heavy loads to the guttural cry of *Hai! huida!* with children whose heads were shaved in hideous patterns; and now and then, as if to point a moral lesson in the midst of the whirling diorama, a funeral passed through the throng, with a priest in rich robes, mumbling prayers, a covered barrel containing the corpse, and a train of mourners in blue dresses with white wings. Then we came to the fringe of Yedo, where the houses cease to be continuous, but all that day there was little interval between them. All had open fronts, so that the occupations of the inmates, the "domestic life" in fact, were perfectly visible. Many of these houses were road-side *chayas*, or tea-houses, and nearly all sold sweetmeats, dried fish, pickles, *mochi*, or uncooked cakes of rice dough, dried persimmons, rain hats, or straw shoes for man or beast. The road, though wide enough for two carriages (of which we saw none), was not good, and the ditches on both sides were frequently neither clean nor sweet. Must I write it? The houses were mean, poor, shabby, often even squalid, the smells were bad, and the people looked ugly, shabby, and poor, though all were working at something or other.

The country is a dead level, and mainly an artificial mud flat or swamp, in whose fertile ooze various aquatic birds were wading, and in which hundreds of men and women were wading too, above their knees in slush; for this plain of Yedo is mainly a great rice-field, and this is the busy season of rice-planting; for here, in the sense in which we understand it, they do not "cast their bread upon the waters." There are eight or nine leading varieties of rice grown in Japan, all of which, except an upland species, require mud, water, and much puddling and nasty work. Rice is the staple food and the wealth of Japan. Its revenues were estimated in rice. Rice is grown almost wherever irrigation is possible.

The grain, after being soaked till it is on the verge of sprouting, is sown thickly in small patches, which are flooded every night to a depth of two or three inches, and dried off during the day. When the seedlings are well up, fish manure or refuse oil is put over

them to force them on, and in about fifty days, when
the patch is covered with plants about three inches
high, whose brilliant green gladdens the eye just now
all about Yokohama, the people take them up in bundles of three or four, and plant them in tufts, in lines,
leaving a foot between each tuft as well as between
each line. The planting, however, is by no means
general yet, and I saw a great deal of a preliminary
operation, in which a horse with a straw saddle, to
which an instrument composed of several deep teeth is
attached, travels up and down in the slush, followed by
a man who guides him, not by reins, but by a long
bamboo attached to the side of his nose. This process
tears up the old rice roots, disintegrates the soil, and
mixes up the manure with it; for the rice-fields are
very heavily manured — as are all Japanese crops —
with everything which is supposed to possess fertilising
qualities. Where this ploughing was over, a thick
bubbly scum lay on the black water, giving off the
smell of a "pestilent fen" under the hot sun.

Rice is commonly planted in fields formed by terra-
cing sloping ground, in which case irrigation is easily
obtained; but on this level plain, water is laboriously
raised from the main canals into narrow ditches at a
higher level, by means of a portable and very ingenious
"treadmill" pump, which is made to revolve in a sci-
entifically constructed trough, by a man who perpetually ascends its floats. It somewhat resembles a paddle wheel of eight feet in diameter. When irrigation
is wanted at any particular spot, this contrivance is
carried to the intersection of the higher with the lower
ditch, and fixed there with bamboo uprights on each
side, with a rail across to give support to the man who
works it with his feet, just as the tread-wheel is worked
in prison. When the pump is needed elsewhere it is

only necessary to remove it, and bank up the cutting in the dyke. As far as I could see across the slush, there were wheels at work, up which copper-skinned men, naked, except for the *maro* or loin-cloth, were industriously climbing.

The rice-fields are usually very small and of all shapes. A quarter of an acre is a good-sized field. The rice-crop planted in June is not reaped till November, but in the meantime it needs to be " puddled " three times, *i.e.* for all the people to turn into the slush, and grub out all the weeds and tangled aquatic plants, which weave themselves from tuft to tuft, and puddle up the mud afresh round the roots. It grows in water till it is ripe, when the fields are dried off. An acre of the best land produces annually about fifty-four bushels of rice, and of the worst about thirty.

On the plain of Yedo, besides the nearly continuous villages along the causewayed road, there are islands, as they may be called, of villages surrounded by trees, and hundreds of pleasant oases on which wheat ready for the sickle, onions, millet, beans, and peas, were flourishing. There were lotus ponds too in which the glorious lily, *Nelumbo nucifera*, is being grown for the sacrilegious purpose of being eaten! Its splendid classical leaves are already a foot above the water. A species of *Sagittaria* is also grown in water for food, but both it and the lotus are luxuries. There are neither hedges nor fences anywhere, but the peasant proprietors are well acquainted with their boundaries, and no land-gluttons have arisen yet to add "field to field." Except that in some cases horses and oxen are used for ploughing the rice-fields, the whole cultivation is by hand, and not a weed is to be seen. Rows of the *Paulownia Imperialis*, grown for the sake of the lightness of its wood, which is used for making clogs, do not improve the somewhat monotonous landscape.

After running cheerily for several miles, my men bowled me into a tea-house, where they ate and smoked while I sat in the garden, which consisted of baked mud, smooth stepping stones, a little pond with some goldfish, a deformed pine, and a stone lantern. Observe that foreigners are wrong in calling the Japanese houses of entertainment indiscriminately " tea-houses." A tea-house or *chaya* is a house at which you can obtain tea and other refreshments, rooms to eat them in, and attendance. That which to some extent answers to an hotel is a *yadoya*, which provides sleeping accommodation and food as required. The licenses are different. Tea-houses are of all grades, from the three-storied erections, gay with flags and lanterns, in the great cities and at places of popular resort, down to the road-side tea-house, as represented in the engraving, with three or four lounges of dark-coloured wood under its eaves, usually occupied by naked coolies in all attitudes of easiness and repose. The floor is raised about eighteen inches above the ground, and in these tea-houses is frequently a matted platform with a recess called the *doma*, literally " earth-space," in the middle, round which runs a ledge of polished wood called the *itama*, or " board space," on which travellers sit while they bathe their soiled feet with the water which is immediately brought to them; for neither with soiled feet nor in foreign shoes must one advance one step on the matted floor. On one side of the *doma* is the kitchen with its one or two charcoal fires, where the coolies lounge on the mats and take their food and smoke, and on the other the family pursue their avocations. In almost the smallest tea-house there are one or two rooms at the back, but all the life and interest are in the open front. In the small tea-houses there is only an *irori*, a square hole in the floor, full of sand or white ash, on which the live charcoal for cooking purposes is placed, and small racks for food and eating utensils; but in the large ones there is a row of charcoal stoves, and the walls are garnished up to the roof with shelves, and the lacquer tables and lacquer and china ware used by the guests. The large tea-houses contain the possibilities for a number of rooms which

ROAD-SIDE TEA-HOUSE.

can be extemporised at once by sliding paper panels, called *fusuma*, along grooves in the floor and in the ceiling or cross-beams.

When we stopped at wayside tea-houses the runners bathed their feet, rinsed their mouths, and ate rice, pickles, salt fish, and "broth of abominable things," after which they smoked their tiny pipes, which give them three whiffs for each filling. As soon as I got out at any of these, one smiling girl brought me the *tabako-bon*, a square wood or lacquer tray, with a china or bamboo charcoal-holder and ash-pot upon it, and another presented me with a *zen*, a small lacquer table about six inches high, with a tiny teapot with a hollow handle at right angles with the spout, holding about an English tea-cupful, and two cups without handles or saucers, with a capacity of from ten to twenty thimblefuls each. The hot water is merely allowed to rest a minute on the tea-leaves, and the infusion is a clear straw-coloured liquid with a delicious aroma and flavour, grateful and refreshing at all times. If Japanese tea " stands," it acquires a coarse bitterness and an unwholesome astringency. Milk and sugar are not used. A clean-looking wooden or lacquer pail with a lid is kept in all tea-houses, and though hot rice, except to order, is only ready three times daily, the pail always contains cold rice, and the coolies heat it by pouring hot tea over it. As you eat, a tea-house girl, with this pail beside her, squats on the floor in front of you, and fills your rice bowl till you say, " Hold, enough ! " On this road it is expected that you leave three or four *sen* on the tea-tray for a rest of an hour or two and tea.

All day we travelled through rice-swamps, along a much-frequented road, as far as Kasukabé, a good-sized but miserable-looking town, with its main street like one of the poorest streets in Tôkiyô, and halted for the night at a large *yadoya*, with downstairs and upstairs rooms, crowds of travellers, and many evil smells. On entering, the house-master or landlord, the *teishi*, folded his hands and prostrated himself, touching the floor with his forehead three times. It is a large, rambling old house, and fully thirty servants were bustling about in the *daidokoro*, or great open kitchen. I took a room upstairs [*i.e.* up a steep step-ladder of dark, polished

wood], with a balcony under the deep eaves. The front
of the house upstairs was one long room with only sides
and a front, but it was immediately divided into four
by drawing sliding screens or panels, covered with
opaque wall papers, into their proper grooves. A back
was also improvised, but this was formed of frames with
panes of translucent paper, like our tissue paper, with
sundry holes and rents. This being done, I found myself the possessor of a room about sixteen feet square,
without hook, shelf, rail, or anything on which to put
anything, nothing in short but a matted floor. Do not
be misled by the use of this word matting. Japanese
house-mats, *tatami*, are as neat, refined, and soft a covering for the floor as the finest Axminster carpet. They
are 5 feet 9 inches long, 3 feet broad, and 2½ inches
thick. The frame is solidly made of coarse straw, and
this is covered with very fine woven matting, as nearly
white as possible, and each mat is usually bound with
dark blue cloth. Temples and rooms are measured by
the number of mats they contain, and rooms must be
built for the mats, as they are never cut to the rooms.
They are always level with the polished grooves or
ledges which surround the floor. They are soft and
elastic, and the finer qualities are very beautiful. They
are as expensive as the best Brussels carpet, and the
Japanese take great pride in them, and are much ag-
grieved by the way in which some thoughtless foreigners stamp over them with dirty boots. Unfortunately
they harbour myriads of fleas.

Outside my room an open balcony with many similar
rooms ran round a forlorn aggregate of dilapidated
shingle roofs and water-butts. These rooms were all
full. Ito asked me for instructions once for all, put up
my stretcher under a large mosquito net of coarse green
canvas with a fusty smell, filled my bath, brought me

some tea, rice, and eggs, took my passport to be copied by the house-master, and departed, I know not whither. I tried to write to you, but fleas and mosquitoes prevented it, and besides, the *fusuma* were frequently noiselessly drawn apart, and several pairs of dark, elongated eyes surveyed me through the cracks; for there were two Japanese families in the room to the right, and five men in that to the left. I closed the sliding windows, with translucent paper for window panes, called *shôji*, and went to bed; but the lack of privacy was fearful, and I have not yet sufficient trust in my fellow-creatures to be comfortable without locks, walls, or doors! Eyes were constantly applied to the sides of the room, a girl twice drew aside the *shôji* between it and the corridor, a man, who I afterwards found was a blind man, offering his services as a shampooer, came in and said some (of course) unintelligible words, and the new noises were perfectly bewildering. On one side a man recited Buddhist prayers in a high key; on the other a girl was twanging a *samisen*, a species of guitar; the house was full of talking and splashing, drums and tomtoms were beaten outside; there were street cries innumerable, and the whistling of the blind shampooers, and the resonant clap of the fire watchman who perambulates all Japanese villages, and beats two pieces of wood together in token of his vigilance, were intolerable. It was a life of which I knew nothing, and the mystery was more alarming than attractive; my money was lying about, and nothing seemed easier than to slide a hand through the *fusuma* and appropriate it. Ito told me that the well was badly contaminated, the odours were fearful; illness was to be feared as well as robbery! So unreasonably I reasoned![1]

[1] My fears, though quite natural for a lady alone, had really no justification. I have since travelled 1200 miles in the interior, and in Yezo,

My bed is merely a piece of canvas nailed to two wooden bars. When I lay down the canvas burst away from the lower row of nails with a series of cracks, and sank gradually till I found myself lying on a sharp-edged pole which connects the two pair of trestles, and the helpless victim of fleas and mosquitoes. I lay for three hours, not daring to stir lest I should bring the canvas altogether down, becoming more and more nervous every moment, and then Ito called outside the

SIR HARRY'S MESSENGER.

shôji, "It would be best, Miss Bird, that I should see you." What horror can this be? I thought, and was not reassured when he added, "Here's a messenger from the Legation, and two policemen want to speak to you." On arriving I had done the correct thing in giving the house-master my passport, which, according to law, he had copied into his book, and had sent a dupli-

with perfect safety and freedom from alarm, and I believe that there is no country in the world in which a lady can travel with such absolute security from danger and rudeness as in Japan.

cate copy to the police-station, and this intrusion near midnight was as unaccountable as it was unwarrantable. Nevertheless the appearance of the two manikins in European uniforms, with the familiar batons and bull's-eye lanterns, and with manners which were respectful without being deferential, gave me immediate relief. I should have welcomed twenty of their species, for their presence assured me of the fact that I am known and registered, and that a Government which, for special reasons, is anxious to impress foreigners with its power and omniscience, is responsible for my safety.

While they spelt through my passport by their dim lantern, I opened the Yedo parcel, and found that it contained a tin of lemon sugar, a most kind note from Sir Harry Parkes, and a packet of letters from you. While I was attempting to open the letters, Ito, the policemen, and the lantern glided out of my room, and I lay uneasily till daylight, with the letters and telegram for which I had been yearning for six weeks, on my bed unopened!

Already I can laugh at my fears and misfortunes, as I hope you will. A traveller must buy his own experience, and success or failure depends mainly on personal idiosyncrasies. Many matters will be remedied by experience as I go on, and I shall acquire the habit of feeling secure; but lack of privacy, bad smells, and the torments of fleas and mosquitoes are, I fear, irremediable evils. **I. L. B.**

FROM KASUKABÉ TO NIKKÔ.

A Coolie falls ill — Peasant Costume — Varieties in Threshing — The Tochigi *yadoya* — Farming Villages — A Beautiful Region — An *In Memoriam* Avenue — A Doll's Street — Nikkô — The Journey's End — Coolie Kindliness.

BY seven the next morning the rice was eaten, the room as bare as if it had never been occupied, the bill of 80 *sen* paid, the house-master and servants with many *sayo naras*, or farewells, had prostrated themselves, and we were away in the *kurumas* at a rapid trot. At the first halt my runner, a kindly, good-natured creature, but absolutely hideous, was seized with pain and vomiting, owing, he said, to drinking the bad water at Kasukabé, and was left behind. He pleased me much by the honest independent way in which he provided a substitute, strictly adhering to his bargain, and never asking for a gratuity on account of his illness. He had been so kind and helpful that I felt quite sad at leaving him there ill, — only a coolie to be sure, only an atom among the 34,000,000 of the Empire, but not less precious to our Father in heaven than any other. It was a brilliant day, with the mercury 86° in the shade, but the heat was not oppressive. At noon we reached the Toré, and I rode on a coolie's tattooed shoulders through the shallow part, and then, with the *kurumas*, some ill-disposed pack-horses, and a number of travellers, crossed in a flat-bottomed boat. The boatmen, travellers, and cultivators, were nearly or altogether without clothes.

but the richer farmers worked in the fields in curved bamboo hats as large as umbrellas, *kimonos* with large sleeves not girt up, and large fans attached to their girdles. Many of the travellers whom we met were without hats, but shielded the front of the head by holding a fan between it and the sun. Probably the inconvenience of the national costume for working men partly accounts for the general practice of getting rid of it. It is such a hindrance even in walking, that most pedestrians have "their loins girded up" by taking the middle of the hem at the bottom of the *kimono* and tucking it under the girdle. This, in the case of many, shows woven, tight-fitting, elastic, white cotton pantaloons, reaching to the ankles. After ferrying another river at a village from which a steamer plies to Tôkiyô, the country became much more pleasing, the rice-fields fewer, the trees, houses, and barns larger, and, in the distance, high hills loomed faintly through the haze. Much of the wheat, of which they don't make bread but vermicelli, is already being carried. You see wheat stacks ten feet high moving slowly, and while you are wondering, you become aware of four feet moving below them; for all the crop is carried on horses' if not on human backs. I went to see several threshing-floors, clean, open spaces outside barns, where the grain is laid on mats and threshed by two or four men with heavy revolving flails. Another method is for women to beat out the grain on racks of split bamboo laid lengthwise; and I saw yet a third practised both in the fields and barn-yards, in which women pass handfuls of stalks backwards through a sort of carding instrument with sharp iron teeth placed in a slanting position, which cuts off the ears, leaving the stalk unbruised. This is probably "the sharp threshing instrument, having teeth" mentioned by Isaiah. The ears are then rubbed be-

tween the hands. In this region the wheat was win-
nowed altogether by hand, and after the wind had
driven the chaff away, the grain was laid out on mats
to dry. Sickles are not used, but the reaper takes a
handful of stalks and cuts them off close to the ground
with a short, straight knife, fixed at a right angle with
the handle. The wheat is sown in rows with wide spaces
between them, which are utilised for beans and other
crops, and no sooner is it removed than *daikon* (*Raphanus sativus*), cucumbers, or some other vegetable, takes
its place, as the land under careful tillage and copious
manuring bears two, and even three crops in the year.
The soil is trenched for wheat as for all crops except
rice, not a weed is to be seen, and the whole country
looks like a well-kept garden. The barns in this district are very handsome, and many of their grand roofs
have that concave sweep with which we are familiar in
the pagoda. The eaves are often eight feet deep, and
the thatch three feet thick. Several of the farm-yards
have handsome gateways like the ancient "lychgates"
of some of our English churchyards much magnified.
As animals are not used for milk, draught, or food, and
there are no pasture lands, both the country and the
farm-yards have a singular silence and an inanimate
look; a mean-looking dog and a few fowls being the
only representatives of domestic animal life. I long
for the lowing of cattle and the bleating of sheep

At 6 we reached Tochigi, a large town, formerly the
castle town of a *daimiyô*. Its special manufacture is
rope of many kinds, a great deal of hemp being grown
in the neighbourhood. Many of the roofs are tiled, and
the town has a more solid and handsome appearance
than those that we had previously passed through. But
from Kasukabé to Tochigi was from bad to worse. I
nearly abandoned Japanese travelling altogether, and,

if last night had not been a great improvement, I think
I should have gone ignominiously back to Tôkiyô. The
yadoya was a very large one, and as sixty guests had
arrived before me, there was no choice of accommodation, and I had to be contented with a room enclosed
on all sides not by *fusuma* but *shôji*, and with barely
room for my bed, bath, and chair, under a fusty green
mosquito net, which was a perfect nest of fleas. One
side of the room was against a much-frequented passage,
and another opened on a small yard upon which three
opposite rooms also opened, crowded with some not very
sober or decorous travellers. The *shôji* were full of
holes, and often at each hole I saw a human eye. Privacy was a luxury not even to be recalled. Besides the
constant application of eyes to the *shôji*, the servants,
who were very noisy and rough, looked into my room
constantly without any pretext; the host, a bright,
pleasant-looking man, did the same; jugglers, musicians,
blind shampooers, and singing girls, all pushed the
screens aside; and I began to think that Mr. Campbell
was right, and that a lady should not travel alone in
Japan. Ito, who had the room next to mine, suggested
that robbery was quite likely, and asked to be allowed
to take charge of my money; but did not decamp with
it during the night! I lay down on my precarious
stretcher before eight, but as the night advanced, the
din of the house increased till it became truly diabolical, and never ceased till after one. Drums, tom-toms,
and cymbals were beaten; *kotos* and *samisens* screeched
and twanged; *geishas* (professional women with the accomplishments of dancing, singing, and playing) danced,
accompanied by songs whose jerking discords were most
laughable; story-tellers recited tales in a high key, and
the running about and splashing close to my room
never ceased. Late at night my precarious *shôji* were

accidentally thrown down, revealing a scene of great hilarity, in which a number of people were bathing and throwing water over each other.

The noise of departures began at daylight, and I was glad to leave at seven. Before you go the *fusuma* are slidden back, and what was your room becomes part of a great, open, matted space — an arrangement which effectually prevents fustiness. Though the road was up a slight incline, and the men were too tired to trot, we made thirty miles in nine hours. The kindliness and courtesy of the coolies to me and to each other was a constant source of pleasure to me. It is most amusing to see the elaborate politeness of the greetings of men clothed only in hats and *maros*. The hat is invariably removed when they speak to each other, and three profound bows are never omitted.

Soon after leaving the *yadoya* we passed through a wide street with the largest and handsomest houses I have yet seen on both sides. They were all open in front; their highly-polished floors and passages looked like still water; the *kakemonos*, or wall-pictures on their side-walls, were extremely beautiful; and their mats were very fine and white. There were large gardens at the back, with fountains and flowers, and streams crossed by light stone bridges sometimes flowed through the houses. From the signs I supposed them to be *yadoyas*, but on asking Ito why we had not put up at one of them, he replied that they were all *kashitsukeya*, or tea-houses of disreputable character — a very sad fact.[1]

As we journeyed, the country became prettier and

---

[1] In my northern journey I was very frequently obliged to put up with rough and dirty accommodation, because the better sort of houses were of this class. If there are few sights which shock the traveller, there is much even on the surface to indicate vices which degrade and enslave the manhood of Japan.

prettier, rolling up to abrupt wooded hills with moun·
tains in the clouds behind. The farming villages are
comfortable and embowered in wood, and the richer
farmers seclude their dwellings by closely-clipped hedges
or rather screens, two feet wide, and often twenty feet
high. Tea grew near every house, and its leaves were
being gathered and dried on mats. Signs of silk culture began to appear in shrubberies of mulberry trees,
and white and sulphur yellow cocoons were lying in the
sun along the road in flat trays. Numbers of women
sat in the fronts of the houses weaving cotton cloth fifteen inches wide, and cotton yarn, mostly imported from
England, was being dyed in all the villages, the dye
used being a native indigo, the *Polygonum tinctorium.*
Old women were spinning, and young and old usually pursued their avocations with wise-looking babies
tucked into the backs of their dresses, and peering cun-
ningly over their shoulders. Even little girls of seven
and eight were playing at children's games with babies
on their backs, and those who were too small to carry
real ones had big dolls strapped on in similar fashion.
Innumerable villages, crowded houses, and babies in all,
give one the impression of a very populous country.

As the day wore on in its brightness and glory the
pictures became more varied and beautiful. Great
snow-slashed mountains looked over the foothills, on
whose steep sides the dark blue green of pine and
cryptomeria was lighted up by the spring tints of
deciduous trees. There were groves of cryptomeria on
small hills crowned by Shintô shrines, approached by
grand flights of stone stairs. The red gold of the harvest fields contrasted with the fresh green and exquisite
leafage of the hemp; rose and white azaleas lighted
up the copse-woods; and when the broad road passed
into the colossal avenue of cryptomeria which over

shadows the way to the sacred shrines of Nikkô, and tremulous sunbeams and shadows flecked the grass, I felt that Japan was beautiful, and that the mud flats of Yedo were only an ugly dream!

Two roads lead to Nikkô. I avoided the one usually taken by Utsunomiya, and by doing so lost the most magnificent of the two avenues, which extends for nearly fifty miles along the great highway called the Oshiu-kaido. Along the Reiheishi-kaido, the road by which I came, it extends for thirty miles, and the two, broken frequently by villages, converge upon the village of Imaichi, eight miles from Nikkô, where they unite, and only terminate at the entrance of the town. They are said to have been planted as an offering to the buried Shôguns by a man who was too poor to place a bronze lantern at their shrines. A grander monument could not have been devised, and they are probably the grandest things of their kind in the world. The avenue of the Reiheishi-kaido is a good carriage road with sloping banks eight feet high, covered with grass and ferns. At the top of these are the cryptomeria, then two grassy walks, and between these and the cultivation a screen of saplings and brushwood. A great many of the trees become two at four feet from the ground. Many of the stems are twenty-seven feet in girth; they do not diminish or branch till they have reached a height of from 50 to 60 feet, and the appearance of altitude is aided by the longitudinal splitting of the reddish coloured bark into strips about two inches wide. The trees are pyramidal, and at a little distance resemble cedars. There is a deep solemnity about this glorious avenue with its broad shade and dancing lights, and the rare glimpses of high mountains. Instinct alone would tell one that it leads to something which must be grand and beautiful like itself. It is broken occasionally by small villages with big bells suspended between double poles; by wayside shrines with offerings of rags and flowers; by stone effigies of Buddha and his disciples, mostly defaced or overthrown, all wearing the same expression of beatified rest and indifference to mundane affairs; and by temples of lacquered wood falling to decay, whose bells sent their surpassingly sweet tones far on the evening air.

Imaichi, where the two stately aisles unite, is a long up-hill street, with a clear mountain stream enclosed in a stone channel, and crossed by hewn stone slabs running down the middle. In a room built over the stream, and commanding a view up and down the street, two policemen sat writing. It looks a dull place without much traffic, as if oppressed by the stateliness of the avenues below it and the shrines above it, but it has a quiet *yadoya* where I had a good night's rest, although my canvas bed was nearly on the ground. We left early this morning in drizzling rain, and went straight up-hill under the cryptomeria for eight miles. The vegetation is as profuse as one would expect in so damp and hot a summer climate, and from the prodigious rainfall of the mountains; every stone is covered with moss, and the road-sides are green with the *Protococcus viridis* and several species of *Marchantia*. We were among the foothills of the Nantaizan mountains at a height of 1000 feet, abrupt in their forms, wooded to their summits, and noisy with the dash and tumble of a thousand streams. The long street of Hachiishi, with its steep-roofed, deep-eaved houses, its warm colouring, and its steep roadway with steps at intervals, has a sort of Swiss picturesqueness as you enter it, as you must, on foot, while your *kurumas* are hauled and lifted up the steps; nor is the resemblance given by steep roofs, pines, and mountains

patched with coniferæ, altogether lost as you ascend
the steep street, and see wood carvings and quaint baskets of wood and grass offered everywhere for sale. It
is a truly dull, quaint street, and the people come out
to stare at a foreigner as if foreigners had not become
common events since 1870, when Sir H. and Lady
Parkes, the first Europeans who were permitted to visit
Nikkô, took up their abode in the Imperial Hombô. It
is a doll's street with small low houses, so finely matted,
so exquisitely clean, so finically neat, so light and delicate, that even when I entered them without my boots
I felt like a "bull in a china shop," as if my mere
weight must smash through and destroy. The street
is so painfully clean that I should no more think of
walking over it in muddy boots than over a drawing-
room carpet. It has a silent mountain look, and most
of its shops sell specialties, lacquer work, boxes of
sweetmeats made of black beans and sugar, all sorts
of boxes, trays, cups, and stands, made of plain, polished
wood, and more grotesque articles made from the roots
of trees.

It was not part of my plan to stay at the beautiful
yadoya which receives foreigners in Hachiishi, and I
sent Ito half a mile farther with a note in Japanese to
the owner of the house where I now am, while I sat on
a rocky eminence at the top of the street, unmolested
by anybody, looking over to the solemn groves upon
the mountains, where the two greatest of the Shôguns
"sleep in glory." Below, the rushing Daiyagawa,
swollen by the night's rain, thundered through a narrow gorge. Beyond, colossal flights of stone stairs
stretch mysteriously away among cryptomeria groves,
above which tower the Nikkôsan mountains. Just
where the torrent finds its impetuosity checked by two
stone walls, it is spanned by a bridge, 84 feet long by

18 wide, of dull red lacquer, resting on two stone piers on either side, connected by two transverse stone beams. A welcome bit of colour it is amidst the masses of dark greens and soft greys, though there is nothing imposing in its structure, and its interest consists in being the Mihashi, or Sacred Bridge, built in 1636, formerly open only to the Shôguns, the envoy of the Mikado, and to pilgrims twice a year. Both its gates are locked. Grand and lonely Nikkô looks, the home of rain and mist. *Kuruma* roads end here, and if you wish to go any farther you must either walk, ride, or be carried.

Ito was long away, and the coolies kept addressing me in Japanese, which made me feel helpless and solitary, and eventually they shouldered my baggage, and descending a flight of steps, we crossed the river by the secular bridge, and shortly met my host, Kanaya, a very bright, pleasant-looking man, who bowed nearly to the earth. Terraced roads in every direction lead through cryptomerias to the shrines; and this one passes many a stately enclosure, but leads away from the temples, and though it is the highway to Chiuzenjii, a place of popular pilgrimage, Yumoto, a place of popular resort, and several other villages, it is very rugged, and having flights of stone steps at intervals, is only practicable for horses and pedestrians.

At the house, with the appearance of which I was at once delighted, I regretfully parted with my coolies, who had served me kindly and faithfully. They had paid me many little attentions, such as always beating the dust out of my dress, inflating my air-pillow, and bringing me flowers, and were always grateful when I walked up hills; and just now, after going for a frolic to the mountains, they called to wish me good-bye, bringing branches of azaleas.   I. L. B.

KANAYA'S HOUSE.

A Japanese Idyll — Musical Stillness — My Rooms — Floral Lecorations — Kanaya and his Household — Table Equipments.

KANAYA'S, NIKKÔ, *June* 15.

I DON'T know what to write about my house. It is a Japanese idyll; there is nothing within or without which does not please the eye, and after the din of *yadoyas*, its silence, musical with the dash of waters and the twitter of birds, is truly refreshing. It is a simple but irregular two-storied pavilion, standing on a stone-faced terrace approached by a flight of stone steps. The garden is well laid out, and, as peonies, irises, and azaleas are now in blossom, it is very bright. The mountain, with its lower part covered with red azaleas, rises just behind, and a stream which tumbles down it supplies the house with water, both cold and pure, and another, after forming a miniature cascade, passes under the house and through a fishpond with rocky islets into the river below. The grey village of Irimichi lies on the other side of the road shut in with the rushing Daiya, and beyond it are high, broken hills, richly wooded, and slashed with ravines and waterfalls.

Kanaya's sister, a very sweet, refined-looking woman, met me at the door and divested me of my boots. The two verandahs are highly polished, so are the entrance and the stairs which lead to my room, and the mats are so fine and white that I almost fear to walk over them even in my stockings. The polished stairs lead to a highly polished, broad verandah with a beautiful view, from which you enter one large room, which, being too large, was at once made into two. Four highly polished steps lead from this into an exquisite room at the back, which Ito occupies, and another polished staircase into the bath-house and garden. The whole front of my room is composed of *shôji*, which slide back during the day. The ceiling is of light wood crossed by bars of

KANAYA'S HOUSE.

dark wood, and the posts which support it are of dark polished wood. The panels are of wrinkled sky blue paper splashed with gold. At one end are two alcoves with floors of polished wood, called *tokonoma*. In one hangs a *kakemono*, or wall-picture, a painting of a blossoming branch of the cherry on white silk —— a perfect piece of art, which in itself fills the room with freshness and beauty. The artist who painted it painted nothing but cherry blossoms, and fell in the rebellion. On a shelf in the other alcove is a very valuable cabinet with sliding doors, on which peonies are painted on a gold ground. A single spray of rose azalea in a pure white vase hanging on one of the polished posts, and a single iris in another, are the only decorations. The mats are very fine and white, but the only furniture is a folding screen with some suggestions of landscape in Indian ink. I almost wish that the rooms were a little less exquisite, for I am in constant dread of spilling the ink, indenting the mats, or tearing the paper windows. Downstairs there is a room equally beautiful, and a large space where all the domestic avocations are carried on. There is a *kura*, or fireproof storehouse, with a tiled roof on the right of the house.

Kanaya leads the discords at the Shintô shrines; but his duties are few, and he is chiefly occupied in perpetually embellishing his house and garden. His mother, a venerable old lady, and his sister, the sweetest and most graceful Japanese woman but one that I have seen, live with him. She moves about the house like a floating fairy, and her voice has music in its tones. A half-witted servant man and the sister's boy and girl complete the family. Kanaya is the chief man in the village, and is very intelligent and apparently well educated. He has divorced his wife, and his sister has practically divorced her husband. Of late, to help his income, he has let these charming rooms to foreigners who have brought letters to him, and he is very anxious to meet their views, while his good taste leads him to avoid Europeanising his beautiful home.

Supper came up on a *zen*, or small table six inches high, of old gold lacquer, with the rice in a gold lacquer bowl, and the teapot and cup were fine Kaga porcelain. For my two rooms with rice and tea I pay

2s. a day. Ito forages for me, and can occasionally get chickens at 10d. each and a dish of trout for 6d., and eggs are always to be had for 1d. each. It is extremely interesting to live in a private house and to see the externalities at least of domestic life in a Japanese middle-class home. I. L. B.

NIKKÔ.

The Beauties of Nikkô — The Burial of Iyéyasu — The Approach to the great Shrines — The Yomei Gate — Gorgeous Decorations — Simplicity of the Mausoleum — The Shrine of Iyémitsu — Religious Art of Japan and India — An Earthquake — Beauties of Wood-carving.

KANAYA'S, NIKKÔ, *June* 21.

I HAVE been at Nikkô for nine days, and am therefore entitled to use the word " *Kek'ko!* "

Nikkô has a distinct individuality. This consists not so much in its great beauty and variety, as in its solemn grandeur, its profound melancholy, its slow and sure decay, and the historical and religious atmosphere from which one can never altogether escape. It is a place of graves too, of constant rain and strange stillness, and its glories lie in the past. I have paid almost daily visits to the famous shrines; but their decorations are so profuse, and their mythological allusions so complicated, that instead of attempting any detailed description, I must content myself with giving the slightest possible sketch of what I suppose may fairly be ranked among the most beautiful scenes in the world.

Nikkô means "sunny splendour," and its beauties are celebrated in poetry and art all over Japan. Mountains for a great part of the year clothed or patched with snow, piled in great ranges round Nantaisan their monarch, worshipped as a god; forests of magnificent timber; ravines and passes scarcely explored; dark green lakes sleeping in endless serenity; the deep abyss of Kêgon, into which the waters of Chiuzenjii plunge from a height of 250 feet; the bright beauty of the falls of Kiri Furi, the loveliness of the gardens of Dainichi-do; the sombre grandeur of the passes through which the Daiyagawa forces its way from the upper regions; a gorgeousness of azaleas and magnolias; and a luxuri-ousness of vegetation perhaps unequalled in Japan, are only a few of the attractions which surround the shrines of the two greatest Shôguns.

To a glorious resting-place on the hill-slope of Hotoké Iwa, sacred since 767, when a Buddhist saint, called Shôdô Shônin, visited it, and declared the old Shintô deity of the mountain to be only a manifestation of Buddha, Hidetada, the second Shôgun of the Tokugawa dynasty, conveyed the corpse of his father Iyéyasu in 1617. It was a splendid burial. An Imperial envoy, a priest of the Mikado's family, court nobles from Kiyôto, and hundreds of *daimiyôs*, captains, and nobles of inferior rank, took part in the ceremony. An army of priests in rich robes during three days intoned a sacred classic 10,000 times, and Iyéyasu was deified by a decree of the Mikado under a name signifying "light of the east, great incarnation of Buddha." An envoy of high rank was subsequently sent by the Emperor to the shrine once a year, to offer not the ordinary *gohei*, or shreds of paper attached to a long wand which are to be seen in every Shintô shrine, but *gohei* solidly gilt. The other Shôgun who is buried here is Iyémitsu, the able grandson of Iyéyasu. He finished the Nikkô temples and those of Toyeisan at Uyeno in Yedo. The less important Shôguns of the line of Tokugawa are buried in Uyeno and Shiba, in Yedo. Since the restora-tion, and what may be called the disestablishment of Buddhism, the shrine of Iyéyasu has been shorn of all

its glories of ritual, and its magnificent Buddhist paraphernalia; the 200 priests who gave it splendour are
scattered, and six Shintô priests alternately attend upon
it as much for the purpose of selling tickets of admission
as for any priestly duties.

All roads, bridges, and avenues here lead to these
shrines, but the grand approach is by the Red Bridge,
and up a broad road with steps at intervals and stone-
faced enbankments at each side, on the top of which
are belts of cryptomeria. At the summit of this ascent
is a fine granite *torii*, 27 feet 6 inches high, with columns
3 feet 6 inches in diameter, offered by the *daimiyô* of
Chikuzen in 1618 from his own quarries. After this
come 118 magnificent bronze lanterns on massive stone
pedestals, each of which is inscribed with the posthumous title of Iyéyasu, the name of the giver, and a
legend of the offering — all the gifts of *daimiyô* — a
holy water cistern made of a solid block of granite, and
covered by a roof resting on twenty square granite pillars, and a bronze bell, lantern, and candelabra of
marvellous workmanship, offered by the kings of Corea
and Liukiu. On the left is a five-storied pagoda, 104
feet high, richly carved in wood and as richly gilded
and painted. The signs of the zodiac run round the
lower story.

The grand entrance gate is at the top of a handsome
flight of steps forty yards from the *torii*. A looped
white curtain with the Mikado's crest in black hangs
partially over the gateway, in which, beautiful as it is,
one does not care to linger, to examine the gilded
amainu in niches, or the spirited carvings of tigers
under the eaves, for the view of the first court over-
whelms one by its magnificence and beauty. The whole
style of the buildings, the arrangements, the art of
every kind, the thought which inspires the whole, are

exclusively Japanese, and the glimpse from the *Ni-ô* gate is a revelation of a previously undreamed-of beauty both in form and colour.

Round the neatly-pebbled court, which is enclosed by a bright red timber wall, are three gorgeous buildings which contain the treasures of the temple, a sumptuous stable for the three sacred Albino horses which are kept for the use of the god, a magnificent granite cistern of holy water, fed from the Sômendaki cascade, and a highly decorated building, in which a complete collection of Buddhist Scriptures is deposited. From this a flight of steps leads into a smaller court containing a bell-tower "of marvellous workmanship and ornamentation," a drum tower, hardly less beautiful, a shrine, the candelabra, bell, and lantern mentioned before, and some very grand bronze lanterns.

From this court another flight of steps ascends to the Yomei gate, whose splendour I contemplated day after day with increasing astonishment. The white columns which support it have capitals formed of great red-throated heads of the mythical *kirin*. Above the architrave is a projecting balcony which runs all round the gateway with a railing carried by dragons' heads. In the centre two white dragons fight eternally. Underneath, in high relief, there are groups of children playing, then a network of richly painted beams, and seven groups of Chinese sages. The high roof is supported by gilded dragons' heads with crimson throats. In the interior of the gateway there are side-niches painted white, which are lined with gracefully designed arabesques founded on the *botan* or peony. A piazza, whose outer walls of twenty-one compartments are enriched with magnificent carvings of birds, flowers, and trees, runs right and left, and encloses on three of its sides another court, the fourth side of which is a ter-

minal stone wall built against the side of the hill. On
the right are two decorated buildings, one of which
contains a stage for the performance of the sacred
dances, and the other an altar for the burning of cedar
wood incense. On the left is a building for the reception of the three sacred cars which were used during
festivals. To pass from court to court is to pass from
splendour to splendour; one is almost glad to feel that
this is the last, and that the strain on one's capacity for
admiration is nearly over.

In the middle is the sacred enclosure, formed of gilded
trellis-work with painted borders above and below,
forming a square of which each side measures 150 feet,
and which contains the *haiden* or chapel. Underneath
the trellis-work are groups of birds with backgrounds
of grass, very boldly carved in wood and richly gilded
and painted. From the imposing entrance through a
double avenue of cryptomeria, among courts, gates, temples, shrines, pagodas, colossal bells of bronze, and lanterns inlaid with gold, you pass through this final court
bewildered by magnificence, through golden gates, into
the dimness of a golden temple, and there is — simply
a black lacquer table with a circular metal mirror upon
it!

Within is a hall finely matted, 42 feet wide, by 27
from front to back, with lofty apartments on each side,
one for the Shôgun and the other "for his Holiness the
Abbot." Both of course are empty. The roof of the
hall is panelled and richly frescoed. The Shôgun's
room contains some very fine *fusuma* on which *kirin*
(fabulous monsters) are depicted on a dead gold ground,
and four oak panels, 8 feet by 6, finely carved, with the
phœnix in low relief variously treated. In the Abbot's
room there are similar panels adorned with hawks spirit-
edly executed. The only ecclesiastical ornament among

the dim splendours of the chapel is the plain gold *gohei*. Steps at the back lead into a chapel paved with stone, with a fine panelled ceiling representing dragons on a dark blue ground. Beyond this some gilded doors lead into the principal chapel, containing four rooms which are not accessible; but if they correspond with the outside, which is of highly polished black lacquer relieved by gold, they must be severely magnificent.

But not in any one of these gorgeous shrines did Iyéyasu decree that his dust should rest. Re-entering the last court, it is necessary to leave the enclosures altogether by passing through a covered gateway in the eastern piazza into a stone gallery, green with mosses and hepaticæ. Within, wealth and art have created a fairyland of gold and colour; without, Nature, at her stateliest, has surrounded the great Shôgun's tomb with a pomp of mournful splendour. A staircase of 240 stone steps leads to the top of the hill, where, above and behind all the stateliness of the shrines raised in his honour, the dust of Iyéyasu sleeps in an unadorned but Cyclopean tomb of stone and bronze, surmounted by a bronze urn. In front is a stone table decorated with a bronze incense burner, a vase with lotus blossoms and leaves in brass, and a bronze stork bearing a bronze candlestick in its mouth. A lofty stone wall surmounted by a balustrade, surrounds the simple but stately enclosure, and cryptomeria of large size growing up the back of the hill create perpetual twilight round it. Slant rays of sunshine alone pass through them, no flower blooms or bird sings, only silence and mournfulness surround the grave of the ablest and greatest man that Japan has produced.

Impressed as I had been with the glorious workmanship in wood, bronze, and lacquer, I scarcely admired less the masonry of the vast retaining walls, the stone

gallery, the staircase and its balustrade, all put together
without mortar or cement, and so accurately fitted that
the joints are scarcely affected by the rain, damp, and
aggressive vegetation of 260 years. The steps of the
staircase are fine monoliths, and the coping at the side,
the massive balustrade, and the heavy rail at the top,
are cut out of solid blocks of stone from 10 to 18
feet in length. Nor is the workmanship of the great
granite cistern for holy water less remarkable. It is so
carefully adjusted on its bed, that the water brought
from a neighbouring cascade rises and pours over each
edge in such carefully equalised columns that, as Mr.
Satow says, "it seems to be a solid block of water
rather than a piece of stone."

The temples of Iyémitsu are close to those of Iyéyasu,
and though somewhat less magnificent, are even more
bewildering, as they are still in Buddhist hands, and
are crowded with the gods of the Buddhist Pantheon
and the splendid paraphernalia of Buddhist worship, in
striking contrast to the simplicity of the lonely Shintô
mirror in the midst of the blaze of gold and colour. In
the grand entrance gate are gigantic *Ni-ô*, the Buddhist
Gog and Magog, vermilion coloured, and with draperies painted in imitation of flowered silk. A second pair,
painted red and green, removed from Iyémitsu's temple,
are in niches within the gate. A flight of steps leads
to another gate, in whose gorgeous niches stand hideous
monsters, in human form, representing the gods of wind
and thunder. Wind has crystal eyes, and a half-jolly,
half-demoniacal expression. He is painted green, and
carries a wind-bag on his back, a long sack tied at each
end, with the ends brought over his shoulders and held
in his hands. The god of thunder is painted red, with
purple hair on end, and stands on clouds holding thun-
derbolts in his hand. More steps, and another gate

containing the Tennô, or gods of the four quarters, boldly carved and in strong action, with long eye-teeth, and at last the principal temple is reached. An old priest who took me over it on my first visit, on passing the gods of wind and thunder said, " We used to believe in these things, but we don't now," and his manner in speaking of the other deities was rather contemptuous. He requested me, however, to take off my hat as well as my shoes at the door of the temple. Within there was a gorgeous shrine, and when an acolyte drew aside the curtain of cloth of gold the interior was equally imposing, containing Buddha and two other figures of gilded brass, seated cross-legged on lotus flowers, with rows of petals several times repeated, and with that look of eternal repose on their faces which is reproduced in the commonest roadside images. In front of the shrine several candles were burning, the offerings of some people who were having prayers said for them, and the whole was lighted by two lamps burning low. On a step of the altar a much-contorted devil was crouching uneasily, for he was subjugated, and by a grim irony, made to carry a massive incense-burner on his shoulders. In this temple there were more than a hundred idols standing in rows, many of them life-size, some of them trampling devils under their feet, but all hideous, partly from the bright greens, vermilions, and blues with which they are painted. Remarkable muscular development characterises all, and the figures or faces are all in vigorous action of some kind, generally grossly exaggerated.

For the second time I noticed the singular contrast between the horrible or grotesque creations of Japanese religious fancy, with their contorted figures and gaudy, fly-away tags of dress, and the Oriental calm of face, figure, and drapery of the imported Buddha, the crea-

tion of the religious art of India. The teeth of all the
Japanese gods in this temple were most unpleasantly
conspicuous. Some idols (such as the farmers' and sailors' gods) were in shrines, and there were many small
offerings of rice and sweetmeats before them. The
priests sell pieces of paper inscribed with the names of
these divinities as charms against shipwreck and failure
of the rice crops, and Ito bought a number of the latter,
having been commissioned to do so by several rice farmers at Yokohama. It is not the pilgrim season, but several pilgrims were there, offering candles, incense, and
rice.

While we were crossing the court there were two
shocks of earthquake; all the golden wind-bells which
fringe the roofs rang softly, and a number of priests ran
into the temple and beat various kinds of drums for the
space of half an hour. Iyémitsu's tomb is reached by
flights of steps on the right of the chapel. It is in the
same style as Iyéyasu's, but the gates in front are of
bronze, and are inscribed with large Sanskrit characters
in bright brass. One of the most beautiful of the many
views is from the uppermost gate of the temple. The
sun shone on my second visit and brightened the spring
tints of the trees on Hotoké Iwa, which was vignetted
by a frame of dark cryptomeria.

Thus far, with Mr. Satow's help, I have gone over the
principal objects of interest, omitting very many, but I
should add that a large temple is being constructed on
the right of the entrance avenue for the reception of
the Buddhist insignia, which have been ejected from
Iyéyasu's shrine. Tickets of admission to each shrine
are sold for 7d. each, but it is not clear that the money
so raised is for repairs, and as wood, paint, and gilding
cannot last for ever, and the Japanese Government is
more intent upon material progress than upon preserv-

ing its antiquities, it is a question whether these shrines are not destined to decay with the decaying faiths of the people   I have reduced my description to the baldness of a hand-book in absolute despair.

Some of the buildings are roofed with sheet-copper, but most of them are tiled. Tiling, however, has been raised almost to the dignity of a fine art in Japan. The tiles themselves are a coppery grey, with a suggestion of metallic lustre about it. They are slightly concave, and the joints are covered by others quite convex, which come down like massive tubes from the ridge pole, and terminate at the eaves with discs on which the Tokugawa badge is emblazoned in gold, as it is everywhere on these shrines where it would not be quite out of keeping. The roofs are so massive that they require all the strength of the heavy carved timbers below, and like all else, they gleam with gold, or that which simulates it.

The shrines are the most wonderful work of their kind in Japan. In their stately setting of cryptomeria, few of which are less than 20 feet in girth at 3 feet from the ground, they take one prisoner by their beauty, in defiance of all rules of western art, and compel one to acknowledge the beauty of forms and combinations of colour hitherto unknown, and that lacquered wood is capable of lending itself to the expression of a very high idea in art. Gold has been used in profusion, and black, dull red, and white, with a breadth and lavishness quite unique. The bronze fret-work alone is a study, and the wood-carving needs weeks of earnest work for the mastery of its ideas and details. One screen or railing only has 60 panels, each 4 feet long, carved with marvellous boldness and depth in open work, representing peacocks, pheasants, storks, lotuses, peonies, bamboos, and foliage. The fidelity to form and colour in the birds, and the reproduction of the glory of motion, could not be excelled.

Yet the flowers please me even better. Truly the artist has revelled in his work, and has carved and painted with joy. The lotus leaf retains its dewy bloom, the peony its shades of creamy white, the bamboo leaf still trembles on its graceful stem, in contrast to the rigid needles of the pine, and countless corollas, in all the perfect colouring of passionate life, unfold themselves amidst the leafage of the gorgeous tracery. These carvings are from 10 to 15 inches deep, and single feathers in the tails of the pheasants stand out fully 6 inches in front of peonies nearly as deep.

The details fade from my memory daily as I leave the shrines, and in their place are picturesque masses of black and red lacquer and gold, gilded doors opening without noise, halls laid with matting so soft that not a footfall sounds, across whose twilight the sunbeams fall aslant on richly arabesqued walls and panels carved with birds and flowers, and on ceilings panelled and wrought with elaborate art, of inner shrines of gold, and golden lilies six feet high, and curtains of gold brocade, and incense fumes, and colossal bells and golden ridge poles; of the mythical fauna, *kirin*, dragon, and *howo*, of elephants, apes, and tigers, strangely mingled with flowers and trees, and golden tracery, and diaper work on a gold ground, and lacquer screens, and pagodas, and groves of bronze lanterns, and shaven priests in gold brocade, and Shintô attendants in black lacquer caps, and gleams of sunlit gold here and there, and simple monumental urns, and a mountain-side covered with a cryptomeria-forest, with rose azaleas lighting up its solemn shade.[1]   I. L. B.

[1] The Japanese Government has recently undertaken the charge of the repairs of the shrines of Nikkô and Shiba ; so that the fear of these exquisite creations of art falling into decay is now at an end.   **January 1880.**

A WATERING-PLACE.

A Japanese Pack-horse and Pack-saddle — The Mountain-road to
Chiuzenjii — A Deserted Village — The Pilgrim Season — Rose
Azaleas — *Yadoya* and Attendant — A native Watering-place —
The Sulphur Baths — A "Squeeze" — A welcome Arrival.

YASHIMAYA, YUMOTO, NIKKÔZAN MOUNTAINS, *June 22.*

TO-DAY I have made an experimental journey on
horseback, have done fifteen miles in eight hours of continuous travelling, and have encountered for the first
time the Japanese pack-horse, an animal of which many
unpleasing stories are told, and which has hitherto been
as mythical to me as the *kirin* or dragon. I have neither
been kicked, bitten, nor pitched off, however, for mares
are used exclusively in this district, gentle creatures
about fourteen hands high, with weak hind-quarters,
and heads nearly concealed by shaggy manes and forelocks.   They are led by a rope round the nose, and go
barefoot, except on stony ground, when the *mago*, or
man who leads them, ties straw sandals on their feet.
The pack-saddle is composed of two packs of straw
eight inches thick, faced with red, and connected before and behind by strong oak arches gaily painted or
lacquered.   There is for a girth a rope loosely tied
under the body, and the security of the load depends
on a crupper, usually a piece of bamboo attached to the
saddle by ropes strung with wooden counters, and another rope round the neck, into which you put your
foot as you scramble over the high front upon the top

of the erection. The load must be carefully balanced,
or it comes to grief, and the *mago* handles it all over
first, and if an accurate division of weight is impossible,
adds a stone to one side or the other. Here, women
who wear enormous rain hats and gird their *kimonos*
over tight blue trousers, both load the horses and lead
them. I dropped upon my loaded horse from the top
of a wall, the ridges, bars, tags, and knotted rigging of

JAPANESE PACK-HORSE.

the saddle being smoothed over by a folded *futon*, or
wadded cotton quilt, and I was then fourteen inches
above the animal's back, with my feet hanging over his
neck. You must balance yourself carefully, or you
bring the whole erection over, but balancing soon becomes a matter of habit. If the horse does not stumble, the pack-saddle is tolerable on level ground, but
most severe on the spine in going up-hill, and so intol-

erable in going down that I was relieved when I found
that I had slid over the horse's head into a mud-hole;
and you are quite helpless, as he does not understand a
bridle, if you have one, and blindly follows his leader,
who trudges on six feet in front of him.

The first part of the road is tolerable, though there are
several flights of steps, and lies through a glen among
waterfalls, temples, scattered farms, and poor hamlets, in
which most of the people were making wooden trays
which are lacquered in Hachiishi. When we reached
the hamlet of Magaeshi (horse turn back) Ito and the
female *mago* stopped to smoke at a wayside tea-house
with a lovely garden, and I walked on for two miles
along the rude zigzag track through what in freshets is
the broad bed of a rampageous torrent, and is now a
wreck of lava boulders threaded by the impetuous
Daiyagawa. The glen becomes a gorge with lofty
walls of basalt, the rushing stream is crossed frequently
on bridges made of poles loosely covered with soil and
twigs, Nantaisan apparently blocks all progress several
times, but still the river and the track circumvent him,
till, after ascending 2000 feet through a gorge of ever-
increasing grandeur, we came to a precipice and a
broad chasm banked across, from which there is a magnificent view of snow-slashed mountains, cleft by two
converging ravines of great depth, terminating in
ledges over which two fine waterfalls precipitate themselves. It is said that there are 740 steps in the seven
miles between Nikkô and Chiuzenjii, most of which are
on the final two miles. A bridle track zigzags up the
steep sides of mountains, and, to facilitate the ascent,
there are long staircases of logs, which the horses don't
like, and they have made tracks on each edge consisting of mud-holes over a foot deep, with corrugations
between them.

Views through the trees became more and more magnificent, and at the top of the ascent, by which we had attained a height of 3000 feet, we came upon the lovely lake of Chiuzenjii lying asleep at the feet of Nantaisan, a mirror of peace, reflecting in its unrippled waters the deep green of the steep, wooded hills on its farther shore. Nantaisan is worshipped, and on its rugged summit 3500 feet above the lake, there is a small Shintô shrine with a rock beside it on which about a hundred rusty sword-blades lie — offerings made by remorseful men whose deeds of violence haunted them till they went there on pilgrimage and deposited the instruments of their crimes before the shrine of the mountain god. A singularly mournful-looking, deserted village of rows of long, grey, barrack-like houses, skirts the lake for some distance, and the two or three tea-houses which exist hardly give it the appearance of being inhabited. Even these are closed in October for the winter, and twelve men take turns of five days each to look after the property. But in July the quiet village is crowded with pilgrims, and the long, grey barracks are thronged, for on a steep acclivity there is a large red temple with a black *torii*, a very sacred place indeed, for it is the original shrine of the Gongen of Nikkô. There is nothing solemn or devout in ordinary Japanese pilgrimage. Except under special circumstances, it is merely a holiday "outing," a grandly sociable frolic.

I followed a priest with a shaven skull on a horse led by a girl, through several miles of dense wood of oak, horse and Spanish chestnuts, pines, elm, and several species of maples, with a lavish undergrowth of azalea, privet, syringa, hydrangea, grape vines, bamboo grass, and several beautiful flowering shrubs that I do not know, the path following the curve of the lake so closely that one hears its tiny wavelets lapping on the shingle the whole time. The thing that pleased me most was a blaze of rose-crimson azaleas fully fifteen feet high, such a mass of blossom, that their leaves, if they had any, were concealed. The path for some distance was lighted by them. I saw two thick snakes about four feet long, one green, the other red and brown, coiled up on the flat branches of trees, apparently in a torpid state.

On leaving the lake the track makes a steep ascent, the boom of tumbling water is heard, and a sudden turn shows a dilapidated log bridge, and a vigorous mountain torrent cascading its way between rocky walls green with every species of damp greenery, with great cedars and chestnuts bending over it, and maples with finely incised leaves in every rift. Cedars had long since fallen across it, and were green with moss and ferns; even maples had found roothold in their gigantic stems, and the whole arcade, as far as I could see, was lighted with rose azaleas, touched here and there by the slant rays of the afternoon sun. It was so exquisitely lovely that, resting on a prostrate Buddha, I was glad to wait an hour for my attendants, whom I had left drinking (tea) and smoking at Chiuzenjii.

Passing over a swampish level, another ascent brought us to the Yumoto lake, a lovely sheet of deep green water, deeply shadowed by high, heavily timbered mountains, and into a forest of extreme beauty, where the ground looks as if a mountain of rock had been blown into pieces, some huge, some small, but all with sharp angles. Not an exposed fragment was to be seen. They were all smothered in the greenery which riots in damp, exquisite mosses, liverworts, *Hymenophyllums*, and the filmy and feathery *Trichomanes radicans*. The trees were all magnificent cedars, and there was a fragrant twilight in their deep shade, only lighted by flame-coloured azaleas.

The pace of the pack-horse was so aggravating that I was glad to emerge from the chilly wood upon the lake, from which the last sunlight was fading, for it is walled in by high mountains, one of which, Shiraneyama, just above Yumoto, is 8500 feet high, and its deep ravines are still full of snow lying among the trees. The road ends here, though good pedestrians, well guided, can cross the mountains in two directions. The entrance to Yumoto is disfigured by an open bathhouse, in which numbers of nude people were lying in fumes of sulphuretted hydrogen; for this *cul de sac* is a famous watering-place, much resorted to in cases of rheumatism and obstinate skin diseases; and several sulphur springs, after being utilised in baths, fall into the lake at this point with a strong sulphurous smell rising from blue water with a yellow scum upon it.

The hard day's journey ended in an exquisite *yadoya*, beautiful within and without, and more fit for fairies than for travel-soiled mortals. The *fusuma* are light planed wood with a sweet scent, the matting nearly white, the balconies polished pine. On entering, a smiling girl brought me some plum-flower tea with a delicate almond flavour, a sweatmeat made of beans and sugar, and a lacquer bowl of frozen snow. After making a difficult meal from a fowl of much experience, I spent the evening out of doors, as a Japanese watering-place is an interesting novelty.

There is scarcely room between the lake and the mountains for the picturesque village with its trim neat houses one above another, built of reddish cedar newly planed. The snow lies ten feet deep here in winter, and on October 10 the people wrap their beautiful dwellings up in coarse matting, not even leaving the roofs uncovered, and go to the low country till May 10, leaving one man in charge, who is relieved once a week. Were the houses mine I should be tempted to wrap them up on every rainy day! I did quite the wrong

ATTENDANT AT TEA-HOUSE.

thing in riding here. It is proper to be carried up in a *kago* or covered basket.

The village consists of two short streets, 8 feet wide, composed entirely of *yadoyas* of various grades, with a picturesquely varied frontage of deep eaves, graceful balconies, rows of Chinese lanterns, and open lower

fronts. The place is full of people, and the four bathing-sheds were crowded. Some energetic invalids bathe
twelve times a day! Everyone who was walking about
carried a blue towel over his arm, and the rails of the
balconies were covered with blue towels hanging to dry.
There can be very little amusement. The mountains
rise at once from the village, and are so covered with
jungle that one can only walk in the short streets or
along the track by which I came. There is one covered
boat for excursions on the lake, and a few *geishas* were
playing the *samisen;* but as gaming is illegal, and there
is no place of public resort except the bathing-sheds,
people must spend nearly all their time in bathing,
sleeping, smoking, and eating. The great spring is beyond the village, in a square tank in a mound. It bubbles up with much strength, giving off fetid fumes.
There are broad boards laid at intervals across it, and
people crippled with rheumatism go and lie for hours
upon them, for the advantage of the sulphurous steam.
The temperature of the spring is 130° F.; but after the
water has travelled to the village along an open wooden
pipe, it is only 84°. Yumoto is over 4000 feet high, and
very cold.

Irimichi. — Before leaving Yumoto I saw the *modus
operandi* of a "squeeze." I asked for the bill, when,
instead of giving it to me, the host ran upstairs and
asked Ito how much it should be, the two dividing the
overcharge. Your servant gets a "squeeze" on everything you buy, and on your hotel expenses, and, as it is
managed very adroitly, and you cannot prevent it, it is
best not to worry about it so long as it keeps within
reasonable limits.

In returning I visited the Yû-no-taki Falls, formed by
the overflow of the Yumoto Lake, in which a large body
of water, in rushing over finely corrugated black rock

at an angle of 40°, is divided into thousands of separate cascades with the appearance of shred silk. Another fall, Kégon-no-taki, where the Daiya leaps from the Chiuzenjii Lake into a deep cauldron with a foreground of rose azaleas then lighted by a sunbeam, and a background of abrupt but very lofty mountains covered with coniferæ, was a magnificent sight, and scarcely less so the vanishing of the Daiya into a stupendous cleft. A zigzag path on the face of the precipice tends to a view-point 200 feet below, with the amusing notice that no old people, young children, or people who have had too much *saké*, are to go down. Wherever a view is specially beautiful there are sure to be covered seats and possibilities for eating, and this was not an exception.

Torrents of rain came on, the rivers and streams swelled rapidly; the reverberation of the 200 waterfalls which Nikkô is said to possess filled the air; the horse slid rather than stepped down the muddy hill-sides. Near Irimichi the road became a rapid, which cascaded over the stone steps with some violence, and I arrived with clothing and baggage soaked, to find a foreign gentleman and lady drying their clothes on the front of my balcony, and my lovely rooms occupied. I was so rejoiced, however, to see people of my own race and speech, that I gladly took the back room, and as soon as we were all equipped in dry clothes, I made their acquaintance, and found that they were Mr. and Mrs. Chauncey Goodrich from Peking on their honeymoon journey.[1]   I. L. B.

---

[1] We fraternised very cordially, and I heard afterwards with deep regret that Mrs. Goodrich, who was then suffering from the effect of the bad water at Kasukabé, only lived for a few weeks.

DOMESTIC LIFE.

Peaceful Monotony — A Japanese School — A dismal Ditty — Punishment — A Children's Party — A juvenile Belle — Female Names — A juvenile Drama — Needlework — Calligraphy — Kanaya — Daily Routine — An Evening's Entertainment — Planning Routes — The God-shelf.

IRIMICHI, NIKKÔ, *June* 23.

MY peacefully monotonous life here is nearly at an end. The people are so quiet and kindly, though almost too still, and I have learned to know something of the externals of village life, and have become quite fond of the place. But the climate is a disappointment. When it does not rain the air is like a vapour bath, and when it rains, which it generally does, it pours in even torrents. The temperature is from 72° to 86°, and in the steaminess needles rust, books and boots become covered with mildew, and the roads and walls grow greener every day with the *Protococcus viridis*. The air is very relaxing, and does not dispose one for long walks, though I have made a point of seeing everything, usually accompanied by Kanaya and Ito. After the temples, the waterfalls, and the grand views of the horseshoe range of snowy mountains which surrounds Nikkô, with its five principal peaks of Nantai, Akanagi, Niôho, and the great and little Manago, and after surveying from a hill, called Tozama, the plain I crossed from Yedo, stretching away beyond the billowy undulations of the foothills, as far as the Tsukuba peaks, the village life around has been my chief, or rather I should say my first, interest.

The village of Irimichi, which epitomises for me at present the village life of Japan, consists of about three hundred houses built along three roads, across which steps in fours and threes are placed at intervals. Down the middle of each a rapid stream runs in a stone channel, and this gives endless amusement to the children, specially to the boys, who devise many ingenious models and mechanical toys, which are put in motion by water wheels. But at 7 A.M. a drum beats to summon the children to a school whose buildings would not discredit any school-board at home. Too much Europeanised I thought it, and the children looked very uncomfortable sitting on high benches in front of desks, instead of squatting, native fashion. The school apparatus is very good, and there are fine maps on the walls. The teacher, a man about twenty-five, made very free use of the black-board, and questioned his pupils with much rapidity. The best answer moved its giver to the head of the class, as with us. Obedience is the foundation of the Japanese social order, and with children accustomed to unquestioning obedience at home the teacher has no trouble in securing quietness, attention, and docility. There was almost a painful earnestness in the old-fashioned faces which pored over the school books; even such a rare event as the entrance of a foreigner failed to distract these childish students. The younger pupils were taught chiefly by object lessons, and the older were exercised in reading geographical and historical books aloud, a very high key being adopted, and a most disagreeable tone, both with the Chinese and Japanese pronunciation. Arithmetic and the elements of some of the branches of natural philosophy are also taught. The children recited a verse of poetry which I understood contained the whole of the simple syllabary. It has been translated thus : —

" Colour and perfume vanish away.
  What can be lasting in this world ?
  To-day disappears in the abyss of nothingness ;
  It is but the passing image of a dream, and causes only a slight
    trouble."

It is the echo of the wearied sensualist's cry " Vanity
of vanities, all is vanity," and indicates the singular
Oriental distaste for life, but is a dismal ditty for young
children to learn. The Chinese classics, formerly the
basis of Japanese education, are now mainly taught as
a vehicle for conveying a knowledge of the Chinese
character, in acquiring even a moderate acquaintance
with which the children undergo a great deal of useless
toil.

The penalties for bad conduct used to be a few blows
with a switch on the front of the leg, or a slight burn
with the *moxa* on the forefinger — still a common punishment in households ; but I understood the teacher to
say that detention in the schoolhouse is the only punishment now resorted to, and he expressed great disappro-
bation of our plan of imposing an added task. When
twelve o'clock came the children marched in orderly
fashion out of the school grounds, the boys in one division and the girls in another, after which they quietly
dispersed.

The Government has already done a great deal in
putting education within the reach of all classes, but
there are as yet no effective compulsory arrangements,
and out of an estimated school population of 5,000,000,
only something over 2,000,000 are actually at school.
Teaching is likely to add considerably to the occupations
open to women; 800 are already so employed. The
Nikkô teacher is appointed by the local Government,
but his pay depends on school fees and on voluntary
contributions. The fees are from a halfpenny to three

half-pence monthly, according to the means of the parents; but this does not include ink, paper, slates, or books. He told me that there are thirteen grades of teachers. He is in the eighth, and receives £1 per month.

On going home, the children dine, and in the evening, in nearly every house, you hear the monotonous hum of the preparation of lessons. After dinner they are liberated for play, but the girls often hang about the house with babies on their backs the whole afternoon nursing dolls. One evening I met a procession of sixty boys and girls, all carrying white flags with black balls, except the leader, who carried a white flag with a gilded ball, and they sang or rather howled as they walked; but the other amusements have been of a most sedentary kind. The mechanical toys, worked by water-wheels in the stream, are most fascinating.

Formal children's parties have been given in this house, for which formal invitations, in the name of the house-child, a girl of twelve, are sent out. About 3 P.M. the guests arrive, frequently attended by servants; and this child, Haru, receives them at the top of the stone steps, and conducts each into the reception room, where they are arranged according to some well-understood rules of precedence. Haru's hair is drawn back, raised in front, and gathered into a double loop, in which some scarlet *crêpe* is twisted. Her face and throat are much whitened, the paint terminating in three points at the back of the neck, from which all the short hair has been carefully extracted with pincers. Her lips are slightly touched with red paint, and her face looks like that of a cheap doll. She wears a blue, flowered silk *kimono*, with sleeves touching the ground, a blue girdle lined with scarlet, and a fold of scarlet *crêpe* lies between her painted neck and her *kimono.*

On her little feet she wears white *tabi*, socks of cotton cloth, with a separate place for the great toe, so as to allow the scarlet-covered thongs of the finely lacquered clogs, which she puts on when she stands on the stone steps to receive her guests, to pass between it and the smaller toes. All the other little ladies were dressed in the same style, and all looked like ill-executed dolls. She met them with very formal but graceful bows.

When they were all assembled, she and her very graceful mother, squatting before each, presented tea and sweetmeats on lacquer trays, and then they played at very quiet and polite games till dusk. They addressed each other by their names with the honorific prefix *O*, only used in the case of women, and the respectful affix *San;* thus Haru becomes O-Haru-San, which is equivalent to "Miss." A mistress of a house is addressed as *O-Kami-San*, and *O-Kusuma* — something like "my lady" — is used to married ladies. Women have no surnames; thus you do not speak of Mrs. Saguchi, but of the wife of Saguchi *San;* and you would address her as *O-Kusuma*. Among the children's names were *Haru*, Spring; *Yuki*, Snow; *Hana*, Blossom; *Kiku*, Chrysanthemum; *Gin*, Silver.

One of their games was most amusing, and was played with some spirit and much dignity. It consisted in one child feigning sickness, and another playing the doctor, and the pompousness and gravity of the latter, and the distress and weakness of the former, were most successfully imitated. Unfortunately the doctor killed his patient, who counterfeited the death sleep very effectively with her whitened face; and then followed the funeral and the mourning. They dramatise thus weddings, dinner-parties, and many other of the events of life. The dignity and self-possession of these chil-dren are wonderful. The fact is that their initiation into all that is required by the rules of Japanese etiquette begins as soon as they can speak, so that by the time they are ten years old they know exactly what to do and avoid under all possible circumstances. Before they went away, tea and sweetmeats were again handed round, and as it is neither etiquette to refuse them, nor to leave anything behind that you have once taken, several of the small ladies slipped the residue into their capacious sleeves. On departing, the same formal courtesies were used as on arriving.

Yuki, Haru's mother, speaks, acts, and moves with a charming gracefulness. Except at night, and when friends drop in to afternoon tea, as they often do, she is always either at domestic avocations, such as cleaning, sewing, or cooking, or planting vegetables, or weeding them. All Japanese girls learn to sew and to make their own clothes, but there are none of the mysteries and difficulties which make the sewing lesson a thing of dread with us. The *kimono, haori,* and girdle, and even the long hanging sleeves, have only parallel seams, and these are only tacked or basted, as the garments, when washed, are taken to pieces, and each piece, after being very slightly stiffened, is stretched upon a board to dry. There is no underclothing, with its bands, frills, gussets, and buttonholes; the poorer women wear none, and those above them wear, like Yuki, an underdress of a frothy-looking silk *crêpe*, as simply made as the upper one. There are circulating libraries here, as in most villages, and, in the evening, both Yuki and Haru read love stories, or accounts of ancient heroes and heroines, dressed up to suit the popular taste, written in the easiest possible style. Ito has about ten volumes of novels in his room, and spends half the night in reading them.

Both Yuki and Haru write easily, but female writing

is different from that of men, being, as is usual with us, more of a running hand, and the style is non-classical, and, besides containing many abbreviations and expressions not in use among men, a syntax varying from that of the ordinary spoken language is used, and the *hiragana*, or simple syllabary, and a special size and quality of paper, and a feminine gracefulness in curving the characters, are also matters of etiquette.

Yuki's son, a lad of thirteen, often comes to my room to display his skill in writing the Chinese character. He is a very bright boy, and shows considerable talent for drawing. Indeed, it is only a short step from writing to drawing. Giotto's o hardly involved more breadth and vigour of touch than some of these characters. They are written with a camel's hair brush dipped in Indian ink, instead of a pen, and this boy, with two or three vigorous touches, produces characters a foot long, such as are mounted and hung as tablets outside the different shops. Yuki plays the *samisen*, which may be regarded as the national female instrument, and Haru goes to a teacher daily for lessons on the same.

The art of arranging flowers is taught in manuals, the study of which forms part of a girl's education, and there is scarcely a day in which my room is not newly decorated. It is an education to me; I am beginning to appreciate the extreme beauty of solitude in decoration. In the alcove hangs a *kakemono* of exquisite beauty, a single blossoming branch of the cherry. On one panel of a folding screen there is a single iris. The vases which hang so gracefully on the polished posts contain each a single peony, a single iris, a single azalea, stalk, leaves, and corolla, all displayed in their full beauty. Can anything be more grotesque and barbarous than our "florists' bouquets," a series of concentric rings of flowers of divers colours, bordered by maidenhair and a piece of stiff lace paper, in which stems, leaves, and even petals are brutally crushed, and the grace and individuality of each flower systematically destroyed?

Kanaya is the chief man in this village, besides being the leader of the dissonant squeaks and discords which represent music at the Shintô festivals, and in some mysterious back region he compounds and sells drugs. Since I have been here the beautification of his garden has been his chief object, and he has made a very respectable waterfall, a rushing stream, a small lake, a rustic bamboo bridge, and several grass banks, and has transplanted several large trees. He kindly goes out with me a good deal, and as he is very intelligent, and Ito is proving an excellent, and, I think, a faithful interpreter, I find it very pleasant to be here.

They rise at daylight, fold up the wadded quilts or *futons* on and under which they have slept, and put them and the wooden pillows, much like stereoscopes in shape, with little rolls of paper or wadding on the top, into a press with a sliding door, sweep the mats carefully, dust all the woodwork and the verandahs, open the *amado* — wooden shutters which, by sliding in a groove along the edge of the verandah, box in the whole house at night, and retire into an ornamental projection in the day — and throw the paper windows back. Breakfast follows, then domestic avocations, dinner at one, and sewing, gardening, and visiting till six, when they take the evening meal.

Visitors usually arrive soon afterwards and stay till eleven or twelve. Japanese chess, story-telling, and the *samisen* fill up the early part of the evening, but later, an agonising performance, which they call singing, begins, which sounds like the very essence of heathenishness, and consists mainly in a prolonged vibrating "No."

As soon as I hear it I feel as if I were among savages. *Saké* or rice-beer is always passed round before the visitors leave, in little cups with the gods of luck at the bottom of them. *Saké*, when heated, mounts readily to the head, and a single, small cup excites the half-witted man-servant to some very foolish musical performances. I am sorry to write it, but his master and mistress take great pleasure in seeing him make a fool of himself, and Ito, who is from policy a total abstainer, goes into convulsions of laughter.

One evening I was invited to join the family, and they entertained me by showing me picture and guide books. Most Japanese provinces have their guide-books, illustrated by woodcuts of the most striking objects, and giving itineraries, names of *yadoyas*, and other local information. One volume of pictures very finely executed on silk was more than a century old. Old gold lacquer and china, and some pieces of antique embroidered silk, were also produced for my benefit, and some musical instruments of great beauty, said to be more than two centuries old. None of these treasures are kept in the house, but in the *kura* or fireproof storehouse close by. The rooms are not encumbered by ornaments; a single *kakemono*, or fine piece of lacquer or china appears for a few days and then makes way for something else; so they have variety as well as simplicity, and each object is enjoyed in its turn without distraction.

Kanaya and his sister often pay me an evening visit, and, with Brunton's map on the floor, we project astonishing routes to Niigata, which are usually abruptly abandoned on finding a mountain chain in the way with never a road over it. The life of these people seems to pass easily enough, but Kanaya deplores the want of money; he would like to be rich, and intends to build a hotel for foreigners.

The only vestige of religion in his house is the *kami-dana* or god-shelf, on which stands a wooden shrine like a Shintô temple, which contains the memorial tablets to deceased relations. Each morning a sprig of evergreen and a little rice and *saké* are placed before it, and every evening a lighted lamp.

EVENING EMPLOYMENTS.

Darkness visible — Nikkô Shops — Girls and Matrons — Night and Sleep — Parental Love — Childish Docility — Hair-dressing — Skin Diseases — The Moxa — Acupuncture.

I DON'T wonder that the Japanese rise early, for their evenings are cheerless, owing to the dismal illumination. In this and other houses the lamp consists of a square or circular lacquer stand, with four uprights 2½ feet high, and panes of white paper. A flatted iron dish is suspended in this full of oil, with the pith of a rush with a weight in the centre laid across it, and one of the projecting ends is lighted. This wretched apparatus is called an *andon*, and round its wretched " darkness visible " the family huddles, the children to play games and learn lessons, and the women to sew; for the Japanese daylight is short and the houses are dark. Almost more deplorable is a candlestick of the same height as the *andon*, with a spike at the top which fits into a hole at the bottom of a " farthing candle " of vegetable wax, with a thick wick made of rolled paper, which requires constant snuffing, and, after giving for a short time a dim and jerky light, expires with a bad smell. Lamps, burning mineral oils, native and imported, are being manufactured on a large scale, but apart from the peril connected with them, the carriage of oil into country districts is very expensive. No Japanese would think of sleeping without having an *andon* burning all night in his room.

These villages are full of shops. There is scarcely a house which does not sell something. Where the buyers come from, and how a profit can be made, is a mystery. Many of the things are eatables, such as dried fishes, 1½ inch long, impaled on sticks; cakes, sweetmeats composed of rice, flour, and very little sugar; circular lumps of rice dough, called *mochi;* roots boiled in brine; a white jelly made from beans; and ropes, straw shoes for men and horses, straw cloaks, paper umbrellas, paper waterproofs, hair pins, tooth picks, tobacco pipes, paper *mouchoirs,* and numbers of other trifles made of bamboo, straw, grass, and wood. These goods are on stands, and in the room behind, open to the street, all the domestic avocations are going on, and the housewife is usually to be seen boiling water or sewing with a baby tucked into the back of her dress. A lucifer factory has recently been put up, and in many house fronts men are cutting up wood into lengths for matches. In others they are husking rice, a very laborious process, in which the grain is pounded in a mortar sunk in the floor by a flat-ended wooden pestle attached to a long horizontal lever, which is worked by the feet of a man, invariably naked, who stands at the other extremity.

In some women are weaving, in others spinning cotton. Usually there are three or four together, the mother, the eldest son's wife, and one or two unmarried girls. The girls marry at sixteen, and shortly these comely, rosy, wholesome-looking creatures pass into haggard, middle-aged women with vacant faces, owing to the blackening of the teeth and removal of the eyebrows, which, if they do not follow betrothal, are resorted to on the birth of the first child. In other houses women are at their toilet, blackening their teeth before circular metal mirrors placed in folding stands on the mats, or performing ablutions, unclothed to the waist.

The village is very silent early, while the children are at school; their return enlivens it a little, but they are quiet even at play; at sunset the men return, and things are a little livelier; you hear a good deal of splashing in baths, and after that they carry about and play with their younger children, while the older ones prepare lessons for the following day by reciting them in a high, monotonous twang. At dark, the paper windows are drawn, the *amado*, or external wooden shutters are closed, the lamp is lighted before the family shrine, supper is eaten, the children play at quiet games round the *andon;* and about ten the quilts and wooden pillows are produced from the press, the *amado* are bolted, and the family lies down to sleep in one room. Small trays of food and the *tabako-bon* are always within reach of adult sleepers, and one grows quite accustomed to hear the sound of ashes being knocked out of the pipe at intervals during the night. The children sit up as late as their parents, and are included in all their conversation.

I never saw people take so much delight in their offspring, carrying them about, or holding their hands in walking, watching and entering into their games, supplying them constantly with new toys, taking them to picnics and festivals, never being content to be without them, and treating other people's children also with a suitable measure of affection and attention. Both fathers and mothers take a pride in their children. It is most amusing about six every morning to see twelve or fourteen men sitting on a low wall, each with a child under two in his arms, fondling and playing with it, and showing off its *physique* and intelligence. To judge from appearances, the children form the chief topic at this morning gathering. At night, after the houses are shut up, looking through the long fringe of rope or rattan which conceals the sliding door, you see the father, who wears nothing but a *maro* in "the bosom of his family," bending his ugly, kindly face over a gentle-looking baby, and the mother, who more often than not has dropped the *kimono* from her shoulders, enfolding two children destitute of clothing, in her arms. For some reasons they prefer boys, but certainly girls are equally petted and loved. The children, though for our ideas too gentle and formal, are very prepossessing in looks and behaviour. They are so perfectly docile and obedient, so ready to help their parents, so good to the little ones, and, in the many hours which I have spent in watching them at play, I have never heard an angry word, or seen a sour look or act. But they are little men and women rather than children, and their old-fashioned appearance is greatly aided by their dress, which, as I have remarked before, is the same as that of adults.

There are, however, various styles of dressing the hair of girls, by which you can form a pretty accurate estimate of any girl's age up to her marriage, when the *coiffure* undergoes a definite change. The boys all look top heavy and their heads of an abnormal size, partly from a hideous practice of shaving the head altogether for the first three years. After this the hair is allowed to grow in three tufts, one over each ear, and the other at the back of the neck: as often, however, a tuft is grown at the top of the back of the head. At ten, the crown alone is shaved and a forelock is worn, and at fifteen, when the boy assumes the responsibilities of manhood, his hair is allowed to grow like that of a man. The grave dignity of these boys, with the grotesque patterns on their big heads, is most amusing.

Would that these much exposed skulls were always smooth and clean! It is painful to see the prevalence of such repulsive maladies as *scabies*, scald-head, ringworm, sore eyes, and unwholesome-looking eruptions, and fully 30 per cent of the village people are badly seamed with smallpox.

The absence of clothing enables one to study the human frame, and I have been puzzled by the constant appearance of eight round marks like burns, four on each side of the spine, and often as many on the legs, the chest and sides frequently coming in for their share. These marks are produced by *mogusa* (moxa), small cones of the dried wool of the *Artemisia vulgaris*, which are lighted and laid on the skin. It is really the exception where the back is not scarred by its use. Here, these little mugwort cones are to be found in most houses, and people are burned in the spring, just as in England blood-letting was formerly customary at the same season. I saw the operation performed by a mother on her son, who bore it with great equanimity, but the suppurating sore which follows is sometimes very painful. It is not only the old national remedy for many forms of disease, but it is believed that its use six times is a specific against an attack of *kak'ké*, (the *beri-beri* of Ceylon and India) which the Japanese justly dread. Another national remedy is acupuncture, and even non-professional people frequently employ it. One evening Yuki suffered from neuralgia or toothache, and Kanaya produced a very fine gilt steel needle, and stretching the skin of her cheek very tightly, thrust it in perpendicularly, rolling it gently between his fingers till it attained the desired depth. There is a drug, or compound of "a hundred drugs," on which they place such great reliance, that the men carry a small box of it with them in their girdles to the fields, to take in case of any pain or uncomfortable feeling. Ito is never without it, and is constantly offering it to me. It is a dark brown powder, with an aromatic taste, and a pinch of it diffuses a genial glow through the whole frame!

SHOPPING.

Shops and Shopping — Calculations — The Barber's Shop — A Paper
  Waterproof — Ito's Vanity — The Worship of Daikoku —Prepa-
  rations for the Journey — Transport and Prices — Money and
  Measurements.

I HAVE had to do a little shopping in Hachiishi for
my journey. The shop-fronts, you must understand,
are all open, and at the height of the floor, about two
feet from the ground, there is a broad ledge of polished
wood on which you sit down. A woman everlastingly
boiling water on a bronze *hibachi* or brazier, shifting the
embers about deftly with brass tongs like chopsticks,
and with a baby looking calmly over her shoulders, is
the shopwoman ; but she remains indifferent till she
imagines that you have a definite purpose of buying,
when she comes forward bowing to the ground, and I
politely rise and bow too. Then I or Ito ask the price
of a thing, and she names it, very likely asking 4s. for
what ought to sell at 6d. You say 3s., she laughs and
says 3s. 6d., you say 2s., she laughs again and says 3s.,
offering you the *tabako-bon*. Eventually the matter is
compromised by your giving her 1s., at which she
appears quite delighted. With a profusion of bows
and "*sayo naras*" on each side, you go away with the
pleasant feeling of having given an industrious woman
twice as much as the thing was worth to her, and less
than what it is worth to you !

Between your offers the saleswoman makes great use

of the *soroban*, a frame enclosing some rows of balls moving on thick wires, which is used in all business transactions in Japan, and its use is such a habit, that a Japanese cannot add two and two together without it. She is so intent upon the balls that you imagine at first that she is making an elaborate calculation as to whether it would be possible for her to make even a fractional profit out of the sum offered. Ito says that they ask a Japanese the sum they mean to take, and that foreigners, by "bullying" and beating them down, get things for less than natives, who are too polite to follow the same course. In some shops, when I went away feeling that the price asked, say fifty *sen*, was quite unreasonable, the saleswoman shuffled after me offering me the same thing for twenty. At each shop, as soon as I sat down, a crowd, mainly composed of women and children, collected in front, nearly all with babies on their backs, contemplating me with a quiet, grave, inane stare, somewhat embarrassing.

There are several barbers' shops, and the evening seems a very busy time with them. This operation partakes of the general want of privacy of the life of the village, and is performed in the raised open front of the shop. Soap is not used, and the process is a painful one. The victims let their garments fall to their waists, and each holds in his left hand a lacquered tray to receive the croppings. The ugly Japanese face at this time wears a most grotesque expression of stolid resignation as it is held and pulled about by the operator, who turns it in all directions, that he may judge of the effect that he is producing. The shaving the face till it is smooth and shiny, and the cutting, waxing, and tying of the queue with twine made of paper, are among the evening sights of Nikkô.

Lacquer and things curiously carved in wood are the

great attractions of the shops, but they interest me far less than the objects of utility in Japanese daily life, with their ingenuity of contrivance and perfection of adaptation and workmanship. A seed shop, where seeds are truly idealised, attracts me daily. Thirty varieties are offered for sale, as various in form as they are in colour, and arranged most artistically on stands, while some are put up in packages decorated with what one may call a facsimile of the root, leaves, and flower, in water colours. A lad usually lies on the mat behind executing these very creditable pictures — for such they are — with a few bold and apparently careless strokes with his brush. He gladly sold me a peony as a scrap for a screen for three *sen.* My purchases, with this exception, were necessaries only — a paper waterproof cloak, " a circular," black outside and yellow inside, made of square sheets of oiled paper cemented together, and some large sheets of the same for covering my baggage; and I succeeded in getting Ito out of his obnoxious black wide-awake into a basin-shaped hat like mine, for ugly as I think him, he has a large share of personal vanity, whitens his teeth, and powders his face carefully before a mirror, and is in great dread of sunburn. He powders his hands too, and polishes his nails, and never goes out without gloves.

I am surprised at the poverty of these villages. There is no upper class, and a middle class is represented by Kanaya and another man on the other side of the river. The people "rise early, and eat the bread of carefulness," are all in debt, and in Irimichi, which has lately suffered from a great fire, only keep themselves afloat. I am very sorry for them, not only because they are poor, but because, though superstitious, they are materialists, and worship Daikoku, the god of wealth, with their bodies and spirits. I wish they were all

Christians, *i.e.* that they were pure, truthful, self-denying followers of our Lord Christ, and realised the pithy
description of the godly man given in the Prayer-book
translation of Psalm cxii., "He is merciful, loving, and
righteous."

To-morrow I leave luxury behind, and plunge into
the interior, hoping to emerge somehow upon the Sea
of Japan. No information can be got here except
about the route to Niigata which I have decided not to
take, so, after much study of Brunton's map, I have
fixed upon one place, and have said positively, "I go to
Tajima." If I reach it I can get farther, but all I can
learn is, "It's a very bad road, it's all among the mountains." Ito, who has a great regard for his own comforts, tries to dissuade me from going, by saying that I
shall lose mine, but as these kind people have ingen-
iously repaired my bed by doubling the canvas and
lacing it into holes in the side poles,[1] and as I have
lived for the last three days on rice, eggs, and coarse vermicelli about the thickness and colour of earthworms,
this prospect does not appal me! In Japan there is a
Land Transport Company, called *Riku-un-kaisha*, with
a head-office in Tôkiyô, and branches in various towns
and villages. It arranges for the transport of travellers
and merchandise by pack-horses and coolies at certain
fixed rates, and gives receipts in due form. It hires the
horses from the farmers, and makes a moderate profit
on each transaction, but saves the traveller from difficulties, delays, and extortions. The prices vary considerably in different districts, and are regulated by the
price of forage, the state of the roads, and the number
of hireable horses. For a *ri*, nearly 2½ miles, they

---

[1] I advise every traveller in the ruder regions of Japan to take a
similar stretcher and a good mosquito net. With these he may defy all
ordinary discomforts.

charge from 6 to 10 *sen* for a horse and the man who leads it, for a *kuruma* with one man from 4 to 9 *sen*, for the same distance, and for baggage coolies, about the same. [This Transport Company is admirably organised. I employed it in journeys of over 1200 miles, and always found it efficient and reliable.] I intend to make use of it always, much against Ito's wishes, who reckoned on many a prospective "squeeze" in dealings with the farmers.

My journey will now be entirely over "unbeaten tracks," and will lead through what may be called "Old Japan," and as it will be natural to use Japanese words for money and distances for which there are no English terms, I give them here. A *yen* is a note representing a dollar, or about 3s. 7d. of our money; a *sen* is something less than a halfpenny; a *rin* is a thin round coin of iron or bronze, with a square hole in the middle, of which 10 make a *sen*, and 1000 a *yen;* and a *tempo* is a handsome oval bronze coin with a hole in the centre, of which 5 make 4 *sen*. Distances are measured by *ri, chô,* and *ken*. Six feet make one *ken*, sixty *ken*, one *chô*, and thirty-six *chô* one *ri*, or nearly 2½ English miles. When I write of a road I mean a bridle-path from four to eight feet wide, *kuruma* roads being specified as such. **I. L. B.**

SCANT COSTUMES.

Comfort disappears — Fine Scenery — An Alarm — A Farm-house —
An unusual Costume — Bridling a Horse — Female Dress and
Ugliness — Babies — My *Mago* — Beauties of the Kinugawa — A
Buddhist Cemetery — Fujihara — My Servant — Horse-shoes — An
absurd Mistake.

FUJIHARA, *June* 24.

ITO's informants were right. Comfort was left behind at Nikkô!

A little woman brought two depressed-looking mares
at 6 this morning; my saddle and bridle were put on
one, and Ito and the baggage on the other; my hosts
and I exchanged cordial good wishes and obeisances,
and with the woman dragging my sorry mare by a rope
round her nose, we left the glorious shrines and solemn
cryptomeria groves of Nikkô behind, passed down its
long, clean street, and where the *In Memoriam* avenue
is densest and darkest turned off to the left by a path
like the bed of a brook, which afterwards, as a most
atrocious trail, wound about among the rough boulders
of the Daiya, which it crosses often on temporary
bridges of timbers covered with branches and soil.
After crossing one of the low spurs of the Nikkôsan
mountains, we wound among ravines whose steep sides
are clothed with maple, oak, magnolia, elm, pine, and
cryptomeria, linked together by festoons of the redundant *Wistaria chinensis*, and brightened by azalea and
syringa clusters. Every vista was blocked by some
grand mountain, waterfalls thundered, bright streams

glanced through the trees, and in the glorious sunshine of June the country looked most beautiful.

We travelled less than a *ri* an hour, as it was a mere flounder either among rocks or in deep mud, the woman in her girt-up dress and straw sandals trudging bravely along, till she suddenly flung away the rope, cried out, and ran backwards, perfectly scared by a big grey snake, with red spots, much embarrassed by a large frog which he would not let go, though, like most of his kind, he was alarmed by human approach, and made desperate efforts to swallow his victim and wriggle into the bushes. After crawling for three hours, we dismounted at the mountain farm of Kohiaku, on the edge of a rice valley, and the woman counted her packages to see that they were all right, and without waiting for a gratuity turned homewards with her horses. I pitched my chair in the verandah of a house near a few poor dwellings inhabited by peasants with large families, the house being in the barn-yard of a rich *saké* maker. I waited an hour, grew famished, got some weak tea and boiled barley, waited another hour and yet another, for all the horses were eating leaves on the mountains. There was a little stir. Men carried sheaves of barley home on their backs, and stacked them under the eaves. Children, with barely the rudiments of clothing, stood and watched me hour after hour, and adults were not ashamed to join the group, for they had never seen a foreign woman, a fork, or a spoon. Do you remember a sentence in Dr. Macgregor's last sermon? "What strange sights some of you will see!" Could there be a stranger one than a decent-looking middle-aged man, lying on his chest in the verandah, raised on his elbows, and intently reading a book, clothed only in a pair of spectacles? Besides that curious piece of still life, women frequently drew water from a well by the primitive contrivance of a beam suspended across an upright, with the bucket at one end, and a stone at the other.

When the horses arrived, the men said they could not put on the bridle, but after much talk it was managed by two of them violently forcing open the jaws of

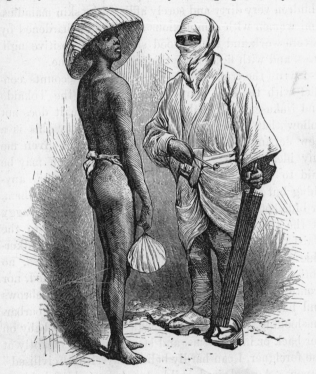

SUMMER AND WINTER COSTUME.

the animal, while a third seized a propitious moment for slipping the bit into her mouth. At the next change a bridle was a thing unheard of, and when I suggested that the creature would open her mouth voluntarily if the bit were pressed close to her teeth, the standers-by mockingly said, "No horse ever opens his

mouth except to eat or to bite," and were only convinced after I had put on the bridle myself. The new
horses had a rocking gait like camels, and I was glad
to dispense with them at Kisagoi, a small upland hamlet, a very poor place, with poverty-stricken houses,
children very dirty and sorely afflicted by skin maladies,
and women with complexions and features hardened by
severe work and much wood smoke into positive ugliness, and with figures anything but statuesque.

I write the truth as I see it, and if my accounts conflict with those of tourists who write of the Tokaido
and Nakasendo, of Lake Biwa and Hakone, it does not
follow that either is inaccurate. But truly this is a
new Japan to me, of which no books have given me
any idea, and it is not fairyland. The men may be
said to wear nothing. Few of the women wear anything but a short petticoat wound tightly round them,
or blue cotton trousers very tight in the legs and baggy
at the top, with a blue cotton garment open to the
waist tucked into the band, and a blue cotton handkerchief knotted round the head. From the dress, no
notion of the sex of the wearer could be gained, nor
from the faces, if it were not for the shaven eyebrows
and black teeth. The short petticoat is truly barbar-
ous-looking, and when a woman has a nude baby on
her back or in her arms, and stands staring vacantly at
the foreigner, I can hardly believe myself in "civilised"
Japan. A good-sized child, strong enough to hold up
his head, sees the world right cheerfully looking over
his mother's shoulders, but it is a constant distress to
me to see small children of six and seven years old
lugging on their backs gristly babies, whose shorn
heads are frizzling in the sun and "wobbling" about as
though they must drop off, their eyes, as nurses say,
"looking over their heads." A number of silkworms

are kept in this region, and in the open barns groups of men in nature's costume, and women unclothed to their waists, were busy stripping mulberry branches. The houses were all poor, and the people dirty both in their clothing and persons. Some of the younger women might possibly have been comely, if soap and water had been plentifully applied to their faces, but soap is not used, and such washing as the garments get is only the rubbing them a little with sand in a running stream. I will give you an amusing instance of the way in which one may make absurd mistakes. I heard many stories of the viciousness and aggressiveness of pack-horses, and was told that they were muzzled to prevent them from pasturing upon the haunches of their companions and making vicious snatches at men. Now I find that the muzzle is only to prevent them from eating as they travel. Mares are used exclusively in this region, and they are the gentlest of their race. If you have the weight of baggage reckoned at one horse-load, though it should turn out that the weight is too great for a weakly animal, and the Transport Agent distributes it among two or even three horses, you only pay for one; and though our *cortége* on leaving Kisagoi consisted of four small, shock-headed mares who could hardly see through their bushy forelocks, with three active foals, and one woman and three girls to lead them, I only paid for two horses at 7 *sen* a *ri*.

My *mago*, with her toil-hardened thoroughly good-natured face rendered hideous by black teeth, wore straw sandals, blue cotton trousers with a vest tucked into them, as poor and worn as they could be, and a blue cotton towel knotted round her head. As the sky looked threatening she carried a straw rain-cloak, a thatch of two connected capes, one fastening at the neck, the other at the waist, and a flat hat of flags 2½ feet in diameter hung at her back like a shield. Up and down, over rocks and through deep mud, she trudged with a steady stride, turning her kind, ugly face at intervals to see if the girls were following. I like the firm hardy gait which this unbecoming costume permits, better than the painful shuffle imposed upon the more civilised women by their tight skirts and high clogs.

From Kohiaku the road passed through an irregular grassy valley between densely-wooded hills, the valley itself timbered with park-like clumps of pine and Spanish chestnuts, but on leaving Kisagoi the scenery changed. A steep rocky track brought us to the Kinugawa, a clear rushing river, which has cut its way deeply through coloured rock, and is crossed at a considerable height by a bridge with an alarmingly steep curve, from which there is a fine view of high mountains, and among them Futarayama, to which some of the most ancient Shintô legends are attached. We rode for some time within hearing of the Kinugawa, catching magnificent glimpses of it frequently — turbulent and locked in by walls of porphyry, or widening and calming and spreading its aquamarine waters over great slabs of pink and green rock — lighted fitfully by the sun, or spanned by rainbows, or pausing to rest in deep shady pools, but always beautiful. The mountains through which it forces its way on the other side are precipitous and wooded to their summits with coniferæ while the less abrupt side, along which the track is carried, curves into green knolls in its lower slopes, sprinkled with grand Spanish chestnuts scarcely yet in blossom, with maples which have not yet lost the scarlet which they wear in spring as well as autumn, and with many flowering trees and shrubs which are new to me, and with an undergrowth of red azaleas, syringa, blue hydrangea — the very blue of heaven — yellow raspberries, ferns, clematis, white and yellow lilies, blue irises, and fifty other trees and shrubs entangled and festooned by the wistaria, whose beautiful foliage is as common as is that of the bramble with us. The redundancy of the vegetation was truly tropical, and the brilliancy and variety of its living greens, dripping with recent rain, were enhanced by the slant rays of the afternoon sun.

We passed several crowded burial-grounds; indeed, along that valley, the dead seemed more numerous than the living. They are very neatly kept, the gravestones, which even the poorest manage to procure, being placed closely together in rows which are three feet apart. On many of these Buddha, or *a* Buddha, sat with folded hands in endless inanity. Three feet, with our ideas of sepulture, is a small allowance for a grave, but the Buddhists are not buried in a recumbent position, and the poorer classes are interred in closed pine tubs bound with bamboo hoops, into which the body is forcibly compressed in a squatting attitude, with the head bowed. The funeral rites, however, in all cases are respectful, and carefully carried out.

The few hamlets we passed are of farm-houses only, the deep-eaved roofs covering in one sweep, dwelling-house, barn, and stable. In every barn unclothed people were pursuing various industries. We met strings of pack-mares, tied head and tail, loaded with rice and *saké*, and men and women carrying large creels full of mulberry leaves. The ravine grew more and more beautiful, and an ascent through a dark wood of arrowy cryptomeria brought us to this village exquisitely situated, where a number of miniature ravines, industriously terraced for rice, come down upon the great chasm of the Kinugawa. Eleven hours of travelling have brought me eighteen miles!

Ikari, June 25. — Fujihara has forty-six farm-houses and a *yadoya*, all dark, damp, dirty, and draughty, a combination of dwelling-house, barn, and stable. The *yadoya* consisted of a *daidokoro*, or open kitchen, and stable below, and a small loft above, capable of division, and I found on returning from a walk, six Japanese in extreme *déshabille*, occupying the part through which I had to pass. On this being remedied, I sat down to write, but was soon driven upon the balcony, under the eaves, by myriads of fleas, which hopped out of the mats as sandhoppers do out of the sea sand, and even in the balcony hopped over my letter. There were two outer walls of hairy mud with living creatures crawling in the cracks; cobwebs hung from the uncovered rafters. The mats were brown with age and dirt, the rice was musty, and only partially cleaned, the eggs had seen better days, and the tea was musty.

I saw everything out of doors with Ito, the patient industry, the exquisitely situated village, the evening avocations, the quiet dulness, and then contemplated it all from my balcony and read the sentence (from a paper in the Transactions of the Asiatic Society) which had led me to devise this journey, "There is a most exquisitely picturesque but difficult route up the course of the Kinugawa, which seems almost as unknown to Japanese as to foreigners." There was a pure lemon-coloured sky above, and slush a foot deep below. A road, at this time a quagmire, intersected by a rapid stream, crossed in many places by planks, runs through the village. This stream is at once "lavatory" and "drinking fountain." People come back from their work, sit on the planks, take off their muddy clothes and wring them out, and bathe their feet in the current. On either side are the dwellings, in front of which are much-decayed manure heaps, and the women were engaged in breaking them up and treading them into a pulp with their bare feet. All wear the vest and trousers at their work, but only the short petticoats in their houses, and I saw several respectable mothers of families cross the road and pay visits in this garment only, without any sense of impropriety. The younger children wear nothing but a string and an amulet. The persons, clothing, and houses are alive with vermin, and if the word squalor can be applied to independent and industrious people, they were squalid. Beetles, spiders, and wood-lice held a carnival in my room after dark, and the presence of horses in the same house brought a number of horse-flies. I sprinkled my stretcher with insect powder, but my blanket had been on the floor for one minute, and fleas rendered sleep impossible. The night was very long. The *andon* went out, leaving a strong smell of rancid oil. The primitive Japanese dog, a cream-coloured wolfish-looking animal, the size of a collie, very noisy and aggressive, but as cowardly as bullies usually are, was in great force in Fujihara, and the barking, growling, and quarrelling of these useless curs continued at intervals until daylight; and when they were not quarrelling they were howling. Torrents of rain fell, obliging me to move my bed from place to place to get out of the drip. At 5 Ito came and entreated me to leave, whimpering, " I've had no sleep, there are thousands and thousands of fleas ! " He has travelled by another route to the Tsugaru Strait through the interior, and says that he would not have believed that there was such a place in Japan, and that people in Yokohama will not believe it when he tells them of it and of the costume of the women. He is " ashamed for a foreigner to see such a place," he says. His cleverness in travelling and his singular intelligence surprise me daily. He is very anxious to speak *good*

English, as distinguished from "common" English, and to get new words with their correct pronunciation and spelling. Each day he puts down in his note-book all the words that I use that he does not quite understand, and in the evening brings them to me and puts down their meaning and spelling with their Japanese equivalents. He speaks English already far better than many professional interpreters, but would be more pleasing if he had not picked up some American vulgarisms and free-and-easy ways. It is so important to me to have a good interpreter, or I should not have engaged so young and inexperienced a servant; but he is so clever that he is now able to be cook, laundryman, and general attendant as well as courier and interpreter, and I think it is far easier for me than if he were an older man. I am trying to manage him, because I saw that he meant to manage me, specially in the matter of "squeezes." He is intensely Japanese, his patriotism has all the weakness and strength of personal vanity, and he thinks everything inferior that is foreign. Our manners, eyes, and modes of eating, appear simply odious to him. He delights in retailing stories of the bad manners of Englishmen, describes them as "roaring out *ohio* to every one on the road," frightening the tea-house nymphs, kicking or slapping their coolies, stamping over white mats in muddy boots, acting generally like ill-bred Satyrs, exciting an ill-concealed hatred in simple country districts, and bringing themselves and their country into contempt and ridicule.[1] He is very anxious about my good behaviour, and as I am equally anxious to be courteous everywhere in Japanese fashion, and not to violate the general rules of Japanese etiquette, I take his suggestions as to what I ought to do

[1] This can only be true of the behaviour of the lowest excursionists from the Treaty Ports.

and avoid in very good part, and my bows are growing more profound every day! The people are so kind and courteous, that it is truly brutal in foreigners not to be kind and courteous to them. You will observe that I am entirely dependent on Ito, not only for travelling arrangements, but for making inquiries, gaining information, and even for companionship, such as it is; and our being mutually embarked on a hard and adventurous journey will, I hope, make us mutually kind and considerate. Nominally, he is a Shintôist, which means nothing. At Nikkô I read to him the earlier chapters of St. Luke, and when I came to the story of the Prodigal Son I was interrupted by a somewhat scornful laugh and the remark, "Why, all this is our Buddha over again!"

To-day's journey, though very rough, has been rather pleasant. The rain moderated at noon, and I left Fujihara on foot, wearing my American "mountain dress" and Wellington boots, — the only costume in which ladies can enjoy pedestrian or pack-horse travelling in this country, — with a light straw mat — the waterproof of the region — hanging over my shoulders, and so we plodded on with two baggage horses through the ankle-deep mud, till the rain cleared off, the mountains looked through the mist, the augmented Kinugawa thundered below, and enjoyment became possible, even in my half-fed condition. Eventually I mounted a pack-saddle, and we crossed a spur of Takadayama at a height of 2100 feet on a well-devised series of zigzags, eight of which in one place could be seen one below another. The forest there is not so dense as usual, and the lower mountain slopes are sprinkled with noble Spanish chestnuts. The descent was steep and slippery, the horse had tender feet, and after stumbling badly, eventually came down, and I went over his head to the great distress of the kindly female *mago*. The straw shoes tied with wisps round the pasterns are a great nuisance. The "shoe-strings" are always coming untied, and the shoes only wear about two *ri* on soft ground, and less than one on hard. They keep the feet so soft and spongy that the horses can't walk without them at all, and as soon as they get thin, your horse begins to stumble, the *mago* gets uneasy, and presently you stop; four shoes, which are hanging from the saddle, are soaked in water and are tied on with much coaxing, raising the animal fully an inch above the ground. Anything more temporary and clumsy could not be devised. The bridle paths are strewn with them, and the children collect them in heaps to decay for manure. They cost 3 or 4 *sen* the set, and in every village men spend their leisure time in making them.

Along this route an automatic rice-cleaner appears frequently, and is mysteriously fascinating. You see a wooden shed completely closed, with something of the look of a miniature water-mill about it, and always prettily situated on the verge of a mountain stream. A dull thump at regular intervals proceeds from the interior; no one is ever to be seen near it, but at one end you are attracted by a stream led into the hollowed end of a log, or into a scoop attached to a beam. As the scoop fills it sinks, and raises a lever with a heavy wooden hammer at its other end, and when full it tilts, the water runs out, and the hammer falls into a mortar filled with rice, and is lifted again *ad infinitum*, as the scoop is refilled, the rate of the thumps depending upon the amount of water in the stream.

At the next stage, called Takahara, we got one horse for the baggage, crossed the river and the ravine, and by a steep climb reached a solitary *yadoya* with the usual open front and *irori*, round which a number of people, old and young, were sitting. When I arrived, a whole bevy of nice-looking girls took to flight, but were soon recalled by a word from Ito to their elders. Lady Parkes, on a side-saddle and in a riding-habit, has been taken for a man till the people saw her hair, and a young friend of mine who is very pretty and has a beautiful complexion, when travelling lately with her husband, was supposed to be a man who had shaven off his beard. I wear a hat, which is a thing only worn by women in the fields as a protection from sun and rain, my eyebrows are unshaven, and my teeth are unblackened, so these girls supposed me to be a foreign man. Ito in explanation said, " They haven't seen any, but everybody brings them tales how rude foreigners are to girls, and they are awful scared." There was nothing eatable but rice and eggs, and I ate them under the concentrated stare of eighteen pairs of dark eyes. The hot springs, to which many people afflicted with sores resort, are by the river, at the bottom of a rude flight of steps, in an open shed, but I could not ascertain their temperature, as a number of men and women were sitting in the water. They bathe four times a day, and remain for an hour at a time.

We left for the five mile's walk to Ikari in a torrent of rain by a newly made path completely shut in with the cascading Kinugawa, and carried along sometimes low, sometimes high, on props projecting over it from the face of the rock. I do not expect to see anything lovelier in Japan.

The river, always crystal-blue or crystal-green, largely increased in volume by the rains, forces itself through gates of brightly-coloured rock, by which its progress is repeatedly arrested, and rarely lingers for rest in all its sparkling, rushing course. It is walled in by high mountains gloriously wooded and cleft by dark ravines down which torrents were tumbling in great drifts of foam crashing and booming, boom and crash multiplied by many an echo, and every ravine afforded glimpses far back of more mountains, clefts, and waterfalls, and such over-abundant vegetation that I welcomed the sight of a grey cliff or bare face of rock. Along the path there were fascinating details composed of the manifold greenery which revels in damp heat, ferns, mosses, *confervæ*, fungi, trailers, shading tiny rills which dropped down into grottoes feathery with the exquisite *Trichomanes radicans*, or drooped over the rustic path and hung into the river, and overhead the finely incised and almost feathery foliage of several varieties of maple admitted the light only as a green mist. The spring tints have not yet darkened into the monotone of summer, rose azaleas still light the hillsides, and masses of cryptomeria give depth and shadow. Still, beautiful as it all is, one sighs for something which shall satisfy one's craving for startling individuality and grace of form, as in the coco-palm and banana of the tropics. The featheriness of the maple, and the arrowy straightness and pyramidal form of the cryptomeria, please me better than all else; but why criticise? Ten minutes of sunshine would transform the whole into fairyland.

There were no houses and no people. Leaving this beautiful river we crossed a spur of a hill, where all the trees were matted together by a very fragrant white honeysuckle, and came down upon an open valley where a quiet stream joins the loud-tongued Kinugawa, and another mile brought us to this beautifully-situated hamlet of twenty-five houses, surrounded by mountains, and close to a mountain stream called the Okawa. The names of Japanese rivers gives one very little geographical information from their want of continuity. A river changes its name several times in a course of thirty or

forty miles, according to the districts through which it
passes. This is my old friend the Kinugawa, up which
I have been travelling for two days. Want of space is
a great aid to the picturesque. Ikari is crowded together on a hill slope, and its short, primitive-looking
street, with its warm browns and greys, is quite attractive in "the clear shining after rain." My halting-
place is at the express office at the top of the hill, a
place like a big barn, with horses at one end and a liv-
ing-room at the other, and in the centre much produce
awaiting transport, and a group of people stripping
mulberry branches. The nearest *daimiyô* used to halt
here on his way to Tôkiyô, so there are two rooms for
travellers, called *daimiyôs'* rooms, fifteen feet high, handsomely ceiled in dark wood, the *shôji* of such fine work
as to merit the name of fret-work, the *fusuma* artistically decorated, the mats clean and fine, and in the alcove
a sword-rack of old gold lacquer. Mine is the inner
room, and Ito and four travellers occupy the outer one.
Though very dark it is luxury after last night. The
rest of the house is given up to the rearing of silkworms. The house-masters here and at Fujihara are
not used to passports, and Ito, who is posing as a town-
bred youth, has explained and copied mine, all the village men assembling to hear it read aloud. He does
not know the word used for "scientific investigation,"
but in the idea of increasing his own importance by
exaggerating mine, I hear him telling the people that
I am *gakusha, i.e.* learned! There is no police station
here, but every month policemen pay domiciliary visits
to these outlying *yadoyas* and examine the register of
visitors.

This is a much neater place than the last, but the
people look stupid and apathetic, and I wonder what
they think of the men who have abolished the *daimiyô*

and the feudal *régime*, have raised the *eta* to citizenship, and are hurrying the empire forward on the tracks of western civilisation!

Since shingle has given place to thatch there is much to admire in the villages, with their steep roofs, deep eaves and balconies, the warm russet of roofs and walls, the quaint confusion of the farm-houses, the hedges of camellia and pomegranate, the bamboo clumps and persimmon orchards, and (in spite of dirt and bad smells) the generally satisfied look of the peasant proprietors.

No food can be got here except rice and eggs, and I am haunted by memories of the fowls and fish of Nikkô, to say nothing of the "flesh pots" of the Legation, and

> "——A sorrow's crown of sorrow
> Is remembering happier things!"

The mercury falls to 70° at night, and I generally awake from cold at 3 A.M., for my blankets are only summer ones, and I dare not supplement them with a quilt, either for sleeping on or under, because of the fleas which it contains. I usually retire about 7.30, for there is almost no twilight, and very little inducement for sitting up by the dimness of candle or *andon*, and I have found these days of riding on slow, rolling, stumbling horses very severe, and if I were anything of a walker, should certainly prefer pedestrianism.

I. L. B.

DIRT AND DISEASE.

A Fantastic Jumble — The "Quiver" of Poverty — The Watershed — From Bad to Worse — The Rice Planter's Holiday — A Diseased Crowd — Amateur Doctoring — The Hot Bath — Want of Cleanliness — Insanitary Houses — Rapid Eating — Premature Old Age.

KURUMATOGÉ, *June* 30.

AFTER the hard travelling of six days the rest of Sunday in a quiet place at a high elevation is truly delightful! Mountains and passes, valleys and rice-swamps, forests and rice-swamps, villages and rice-swamps; poverty, industry, dirt, ruinous temples, prostrate Buddhas, strings of straw-shod pack-horses; long, grey, featureless streets, and quiet, staring crowds, are all jumbled up fantastically in my memory. Fine weather accompanied me through beautiful scenery from Ikari to Yokokawa, where I ate my lunch in the street to avoid the innumerable fleas of the tea-house, with a circle round me of nearly all the inhabitants. At first the children, both old and young, were so frightened that they ran away, but by degrees they timidly came back, clinging to the skirts of their parents (skirts in this case being a metaphorical expression), running away again as often as I looked at them. The crowd was filthy and squalid beyond description. Why should the "quiver" of poverty be so very full? one asks as one looks at the swarms of gentle, naked, old-fashioned children, born to a heritage of hard toil, to be, like their parents, devoured by vermin, and pressed hard for taxes. A horse kicked off my saddle before it was girthed, the crowd scattered right and left, and work, which had been suspended for two hours to stare at the foreigner, began again.

A long ascent took us to the top of a pass 2500 feet in height, a projecting spur not 30 feet wide, with a grand view of mountains and ravines, and a maze of involved streams, which unite in a vigorous torrent, whose course we followed for some hours, till it expanded into a quiet river, lounging lazily through a rice-swamp of considerable extent. The map is blank in this region, but I judged, as I afterwards found rightly, that at that pass we had crossed the watershed, and that the streams thenceforward no longer fall into the Pacific, but into the Sea of Japan. At Itosawa the horses produced stumbled so intolerably that I walked the last stage, and reached Kayashima, a miserable village of fifty-seven houses, so exhausted, that I could not go farther, and was obliged to put up with worse accommodation even than at Fujihara, with less strength for its hardships.

The *yadoya* was simply awful. The *daidokoro* had a large wood fire burning in a trench, filling the whole place with stinging smoke, from which my room, which was merely screened off by some dilapidated *shôji*, was not exempt. The rafters were black and shiny with soot and moisture. The house-master, who knelt persistently on the floor of my room till he was dislodged by Ito, apologised for the dirt of his house, as well he might. Stifling, dark, and smoky, as my room was, I had to close the paper windows, owing to the crowd which assembled in the street. There was neither rice nor soy, and Ito, who values his own comfort, began to speak to the house-master and servants loudly and roughly, and to throw my things about, a style of acting which I promptly terminated, for nothing could be more hurtful to a foreigner, or more unkind to the people, than for a servant to be rude and bullying; and the man was most polite, and never approached me but on bended knees. When I gave him my passport, as the custom is, he touched his forehead with it, and then touched the earth with his forehead.

I found nothing that I could eat except black beans and boiled cucumbers. The room was dark, dirty, vile, noisy, and poisoned by sewage odours, as rooms unfortunately are very apt to be. At the end of the rice-planting there is a holiday for two days, when many offerings are made to Inari, the god of rice-farmers; and the holiday-makers kept up their revel all night, and drums, stationary and peripatetic, were constantly beaten in such a way as to prevent sleep.

A little boy, the house-master's son, was suffering from a very bad cough, and a few drops of chlorodyne, which I gave him, allayed it so completely, that the cure was noised abroad in the earliest hours of the next morning, and by five o'clock nearly the whole population was assembled outside my room, with much whispering and shuffling of shoeless feet, and applications of eyes to the many holes in the paper windows. When I drew aside the *shôji*, I was disconcerted by the painful sight which presented itself, for the people were pressing one upon another, fathers and mothers holding naked children covered with skin-disease or with scald-head, or ringworm, daughters leading mothers nearly blind, men exhibiting painful sores, children blinking with eyes infested by flies, and nearly closed with ophthalmia, and all, sick and well, in truly "vile raiment," lamentably dirty and swarming with vermin, the sick asking for medicine, and the well either bringing the sick or gratifying an apathetic curiosity. Sadly I told them that I did not understand their manifold "diseases and torments," and that if I did, I had no stock of medicines, and that in my own country the constant washing of clothes, and the constant application of water to the skin, accompanied by friction with clean cloths, would be much relied upon by doctors for the cure and prevention of similar cutaneous diseases. To pacify them, I made some ointment of animal fat and flowers of sulphur, extracted with difficulty from some man's hoard, and told them how to apply it to some of the worst cases. The horse, being unused to a girth, became fidgety as it was being saddled, creating a *stampede* among the crowd, and the *mago* would not touch it again. They are as much afraid of their gentle mares as if they were panthers. All the children followed me for a considerable distance, and a good many of the adults made an excuse for going in the same direction.

I was entirely unprepared for the *apparent* poverty and *real* dirt and discomfort that I have seen since leaving Nikkô. With us poverty of the squalid kind is usually associated with laziness and drunkenness, but here the first is unknown, and the last is rare among the peasant proprietors. Their industry is ceaseless, they have no Sabbaths, and only take a holiday when they have nothing to do. Their spade husbandry turns the country into one beautifully kept garden, in which one might look vainly for a weed. They are economical and thrifty, and turn everything to useful account. They manure the ground heavily, understand the rotation of crops, and have little if anything to learn in the way of improved agricultural processes. I am too new a comer to venture an opinion on the subject. The appearance of poverty may be produced by apathy regarding comforts to which they have not been accustomed. The dirt is preventible, and the causes of the prevalence of cutaneous diseases among children are not far to seek. There can be no doubt of the want of cleanliness in nearly the whole district that I have passed through, and this surprises me.

The people tell me that they take a bath once a week. This sounds well, but when looked into, its merit diminishes. This bath in private houses consists of a tub four feet high, and sufficiently large to allow of an average-sized human being crouching in it in the ordinary squatting position. It is heated by charcoal in such a way that the fumes have occasionally proved fatal. The temperature ranges from 110° to 125°, and fatal syncope among old people is known to occur during immersion. The water in private bath tubs is used without any change by all the inmates of a house, and in the public baths by a large number of customers. The bathing is not for purification, but for the enjoyment of a sensuous luxury. Soap is not used, and friction is apologised for by a general dabbing with a soft and dirty towel. The intermediate washing consists in putting the feet into hot water when they are covered with mud, washing the hands and face, or giving them a slap with a damp towel.

These people wear no linen, and their clothes, which are seldom washed, are constantly worn, night and day, as long as they will hold together. They seal up their houses as hermetically as they can at night, and herd together in numbers in one sleeping-room, with its atmosphere vitiated to begin with by charcoal and tobacco fumes, huddled up in their dirty garments in wadded quilts, which are kept during the day in close cupboards, and are seldom washed from one year's end to another. The *tatami*, beneath a tolerably fair exterior, swarm with insect life, and are receptacles of dust, organic matters, etc. The hair, which is loaded with oil and bandoline, is dressed once a week, or less often in these districts, and it is unnecessary to enter into any details regarding the distressing results, and much besides may be left to the imagination. The persons of the people, especially of the children, are infested with vermin, and one fruitful source of skin sores is the irritation arising from this cause. The floors of houses, being concealed by mats, are laid down carelessly with gaps between the boards, and as the damp earth is only eighteen inches or two feet below, emanations of all kinds enter the mats and pass into the rooms. Where the drinking water is taken from wells situated in the midst of crowded houses, contamination may be regarded as certain, either from the direct effect of insanitary arrangements within the houses, or from percolations into the soil from gutters outside, choked with decomposing organic matter. In the farming villages, as a general rule, the sewage is kept in large tubs sunk into the earth at the house door, from whence it is removed in open buckets to the fields.

The houses in this region (and I believe everywhere) are hermetically sealed at night, both in summer and winter, the *amado*, which are made without ventilators, literally boxing them in, so that unless they are falling to pieces, which is rarely the case, none of the air vitiated by the breathing of many persons, by the emanations from their bodies and clothing, by the miasmata produced by defective domestic arrangements, and by the fumes from charcoal *hibachi*, can ever be renewed. Exercise is seldom taken from choice, and unless the women work in the fields, they hang over charcoal fumes the whole day for five months of the year, engaged in interminable processes of cooking, or in the attempt to get warm. Much of the food of the peasantry is raw or half-raw salt fish, and vegetables rendered indigestible by being coarsely pickled, all bolted with the most marvellous rapidity, as if the one object of life were to rush through a meal in the shortest possible time. The married women look as if they had never known youth, and their skin is apt to be like tanned leather. At Kayashima I asked the house-master's wife, who looked about fifty, how old she was (a polite question in Japan), and she replied twenty-two — one of many similar surprises. Her boy was five years old, and was still unweaned.

This digression disposes of one aspect of the population.[1]

---

[1] Many unpleasant details have necessarily been omitted. If the reader requires any apology for those which are given here and elsewhere, it must be found in my desire to give such a faithful picture of peasant life, as I saw it in Northern Japan, as may be a contribution to the general sum of knowledge of the country, and, at the same time, serve to illustrate some of the difficulties which the Government has to encounter in its endeavour to raise masses of people as deficient as these are in some of the first requirements of civilisation.   I. L. B.

HIGH FARMING.

A Japanese Ferry — The *Wistaria Chinensis* — The Crops — A Chinese Drug — Etiquette in Cultivation — A Corrugated Road — The Pass of Sanno — Various Vegetation — An Ungainly Undergrowth — Preponderance of Men — The Shrines of Nature-worship — Apparent Decay of Religion.

WE changed horses at Tajima, formerly a *daimiyô's* residence, and, for a Japanese town, rather picturesque. It makes and exports clogs, coarse pottery, coarse lacquer, and coarse baskets.

After travelling through rice-fields varying from thirty yards square to a quarter of an acre, with the tops of the dykes utilised by planting dwarf beans along them, we came to a large river, the Arakai, along whose affluents we had been tramping for two days, and, after passing through several filthy villages, thronged with filthy and industrious inhabitants, crossed it in a scow. High forks planted securely in the bank on either side sustained a rope formed of several strands of the wistaria knotted together. One man hauled on this hand over hand, another poled at the stern, and the rapid current did the rest. In this fashion we have crossed many rivers subsequently. Tariffs of charges are posted at all ferries, as well as at all bridges where charges are made, and a man sits in an office to receive the money.

The wistaria, which is largely used where a strength and durability exceeding that of ordinary cables is required, seems universal. As a dwarf it covers the hills and road-sides, and as an aggressive *liana* it climbs the tallest trees and occasionally kills them, cramping and compressing them mercilessly, and finally riots in its magnificent luxuriance over their dead branches. Several times I have thought that I had come upon a new species of tree of great beauty, and have found it to be an elm or cryptomeria killed and metamorphosed by this rampageous creeper. Some of its twisted stems are as thick as a man's body. In pleasure-grounds it is trellised and trained so as to form bowers of large size, a single tree often allowing 100 people to rest comfortably under its shadow.

Villages with their ceaseless industries succeeded each other rapidly, and the crops were more varied than ever; wheat, barley, millet, rice, hemp, beans (which in their many varieties rank next to rice as the staple food), pease, water melons, cucumbers trained on sticks like peas, sweet potato, egg plants, tiger lilies, a purple colea the leaves of which are eaten like spinach, lettuces, and indigo. Patches of a small yellow chrysanthemum occurred frequently. The petals are partially boiled, and are eaten with vinegar as a dainty. The most valuable crop of this region is *ninjin*, the Chinese *ginseng*, the botanical *Panax repens*. In the Chinese pharmacopeia it occupies a leading place (even apart from superstitions which are connected with it), and is used for fevers as we use quinine. It has at times been sold in the east for its weight in gold, and, though the price has fallen to 40s. per lb., the profit on its cultivation is considerable. The ginseng exported annually from Japan is worth, on arrival in China, £200,000, and in another two years more than double the present crop will be placed in the market. The exquisite neatness of Japanese cultivation culminates in *ninjin.*

It is sown on beds 27 feet long, 2½ broad, 1 high,
and 2 apart. In each bed there are 438 seed-holes, and
in each hole three seeds. I mention this as an instance
of the minute etiquette which regulates all processes in
this curiously formal country. As a protection from
the sun, neatly-made straw roofs cover the beds both
in winter and summer. Only the strong plants are
allowed to survive the first year. In the fifth year the
roots are taken up, scalded, and roasted in trays at a
gentle heat from four to eight days, according to their
size. The stalks and leaves are boiled down to make a
black, coarse jelly, much like liquorice, but very bitter,
which is used in cases of debility. *Sesamum Orientale*,
from which an oil is made, which is used both for the
hair and for frying fish, began to be cultivated. The
use of this in frying is answerable for one of the most
horrific smells in Japan. It is almost worse than
daikon.

The country was really very beautiful. The views
were wider and finer than on the previous days, taking
in great sweeps of peaked mountains, wooded to their
summits, and from the top of the Pass of Sanno the
clustered peaks were glorified into unearthly beauty in
a golden mist of evening sunshine. I slept at a house
combining silk farm, post office, express office, and
daimiyô's rooms, at the hamlet of Ouchi, prettily situated in a valley with mountainous surroundings, and
leaving early on the following morning, had a very
grand ride, passing in a crateriform cavity the pretty
little lake of Oyakê, and then ascending the magnificent pass of Ichikawa. We turned off what, by ironi-
cal courtesy, is called the main road, upon a villanous
track, consisting of a series of lateral corrugations,
about a foot broad, with depressions between them
more than a foot deep, formed by the invariable tread-

ing of the pack-horses in each other's footsteps. Each
hole was a quagmire of tenacious mud, the ascent of
2400 feet was very steep, and the *mago* adjured the
animals the whole time with *Hai! Hai! Hai!* which is
supposed to suggest to them that extreme caution is
requisite. Their shoes were always coming untied, and
they wore out two sets in four miles. The top of the
pass, like that of a great many others, is a narrow
ridge, on the farther side of which the track dips
abruptly into a tremendous ravine, along whose side
we descended for a mile or so in company with a river
whose reverberating thunder drowned all attempts at
speech. A glorious view it was, looking down between
the wooded precipices to a rolling wooded plain, lying
in depths of indigo shadow, bounded by ranges of
wooded mountains, and overtopped by heights heavily
splotched with snow! The vegetation was significant
of a milder climate. The magnolia and bamboo re-
appeared, and tropical ferns mingled with the beautiful blue hydrangea, the yellow Japan lily, and the
great blue campanula. There was an ocean of trees
entangled with a beautiful trailer (*Actinidia polygama*)
with a profusion of white leaves, which, at a distance,
look like great clusters of white blossoms. But the
rank undergrowth of the forests of this region is not
attractive. Many of its component parts deserve the
name of weeds, being gawky, ragged umbels, coarse
docks, rank nettles, and many other things which I
don't know, and never wish to see again. Near the
end of this descent my mare took the bit between her
teeth and carried me at an ungainly gallop into the
beautifully situated, precipitous village of Ichikawa,
which is absolutely saturated with moisture by the
spray of a fine waterfall which tumbles through the
middle of it, and its trees and roadside are green with

the *Protococcus viridis*. The Transport Agent there was a woman. Women keep *yadoyas* and shops, and cultivate farms as freely as men. Boards giving the number of inhabitants, male and female, and the number of horses and bullocks, are put up in each village, and I noticed in Ichikawa, as everywhere hitherto, that men preponderate.[1]

Everywhere there are conical hills densely wooded with cryptomeria, and scarcely one is without a steep flight of handsome stone stairs with a stone or wooden *torii* at its base. From below, the top is involved in mystery, but, on ascending into what is truly a "solemn shade," one usually finds a small, wooden shrine, and some tokens of worship, such as a few flowers, a little rice, or a sprig of evergreen. These "groves" and "high places" are the shrines of the old nature and hero worship which has its symbols "on every high hill, and under every green tree." In some places there is merely a red *torii* with some wisps of straw dangling from it at the entrance of a grove; in others, a single venerable tree or group of trees is surrounded with a straw rope with straw tassels dangling from it — the sign of sacredness; in others, again, a paved path under a row of decaying grey *torii* leads to nothing. The grand flights of stone stairs up to the shrines in the groves are the great religious feature of this part of the country, and seem to point to a much more pious age than the present. The Buddhist temples have lately been few, and though they are much more pretentious than the Shintô shrines, and usually have stone lanterns and monuments of various kinds in their grounds, they are shabby and decaying, the paint is wearing off the wood, and they have an unmistakable

[1] The excess of males over females in the capital is 36,000, and in the whole Empire nearly half a million.

look of "disestablishment," not supplemented by a vigorous "voluntaryism." One of the most marked features of this part of the country is the decayed look of the religious edifices and symbols. Buddhas erect but without noses, moss and lichen covered, here and there, with strips of pink cloth tied round their necks, and Buddhas prostrate among grass and weeds, are every where. One passes hundreds of them in a single day's journey.

In contrast to the neglect of religious symbols is the fact that the burial-grounds, even the lonely ones on the wild hill-sides, are always well kept, the head-stones are always erect, and on most graves there are offerings of fresh flowers. Near several of the villages there are cemeteries less carefully kept, with monuments of quite a different shape, where the pack-horses of the region are interred. This evening is so very fine that I will break off my letter here. It is more than long enough already. **I. L. B.**

A MALARIOUS DISTRICT.

The Plain of Wakamatsu — A Noble Tree — Light Costume — The Takata Crowd — Japanese Paper — A Congress of Schoolmasters — Timidity of a Crowd — Bad Roads — Vicious Horses — Mountain Scenery — A Picturesque Inn — Swallowing a Fish-bone — Poverty and Suicide — An Inn-kitchen — England Unknown! — My Breakfast Disappears.

KURUMATOGÉ, *June* 30.

A SHORT ride took us from Ichikawa to a plain about eleven miles broad by eighteen long. The large town of Wakamatsu stands near its southern end, and it is sprinkled with towns and villages. The great lake of Iniwashiro is not far off. The plain is rich and fertile. In the distance the steep roofs of its villages with their groves look very picturesque. As usual not a fence or gate is to be seen, or any other hedge than the tall one used as a screen for the dwellings of the richer farmers. I must confess that it is a lovely plain, well wooded and watered, its thriving villages half hidden by persimmon and walnut-trees, and its fertile acres so magnificently tilled that even at this prolific season not a weed is to be seen. The lacquer-tree (*Rhus vernicifera*) abounds, and one of the finest of the native trees, *keaki,* the Japanese elm (*Zelkowa keaki*), grows to an immense size. I measured the girth of one of these which was surrounded by the Shintô straw rope, and found it 36 feet 10 inches, at four feet from the ground, and the spread of its thick drooping foliage was noble in proportion. Tea grows in every garden, and mulberry-trees everywhere show that sericulture is one of the leading industries of the district, and the paper mulberry (*Broussonettia papyrifera*) is also abundant.

Bad roads and bad horses detracted from my enjoyment. One hour of a good horse would have carried me across the plain; as it was, seven weary hours were expended upon it. The day degenerated, and closed in still, hot rain, the air was stifling and electric, the saddle slipped constantly from being too big, the shoes were more than usually troublesome, the horseflies tormented, and the men and horses crawled. The rice-fields were undergoing a second process of puddling, and many of the men engaged in it wore only a hat, and a fan attached to the girdle.

An avenue of cryptomeria and two handsome and somewhat gilded Buddhist temples denoted the approach to a place of some importance, and such Takata is, as being a large town with a considerable trade in silk, rope, and *ninjin*, and the residence of one of the higher officials of the *ken* or prefecture. The street is a mile long, and every house is a shop. The general aspect is mean and forlorn. In these little-travelled districts, as soon as one reaches the margin of a town, the first man one meets turns and flies down the street, calling out the Japanese equivalent of "Here's a foreigner!" and soon blind and seeing, old and young, clothed and naked, gather together. At the *yadoya* the crowd assembled in such force that the house-master removed me to some pretty rooms in a garden; but then the adults climbed on the house-roofs which overlooked it, and the children on a palisade at the end, which broke down under their weight, and admitted the whole inundation; so that I had to close the *shôji*, with the fatiguing consciousness during the whole time of nominal rest of a multitude surging outside. Then five policemen in black alpaca frock-coats and white trousers invaded my precarious privacy, desiring to see my passport — a demand never made before except where I halted for the night. In their European clothes they cannot bow with Japanese punctiliousness but they were very polite, and expressed great annoy· ance at the crowd, and dispersed it; but they had hard- ly disappeared when it gathered again. When I went out I found fully 1000 people helping me to realize how the crowded cities of Judea sent forth people clothed much as these are when the Miracle-Worker from Gali- lee arrived, but not what the fatigue of the crowding and buzzing must have been to One who had been preaching and working during the long day. These Japanese crowds, however, are quiet and gentle, and never press rudely upon one. I could not find it in my heart to complain of them except to you. Four of the policemen returned, and escorted me to the out- skirts of the town. The noise made by 1000 people shuffling along in clogs is like the clatter of a hail- storm.

Paper plays such an important part in Japan that I was very glad to learn a little about it at a farm near Takata, to which I took an introduction, and found the farmer very polite. The *Broussonettia papyrifera* is the plant from which the Polynesians make their *tapa* or paper cloth. In Japan its culture is a most impor- tant industry. Plants of the Buddlea and Hibiscus species are also used, but only in small quantities, for mixing with the bark of the paper mulberry. Over sixty kinds of paper are manufactured, and etiquette prescribes the use which is made of each. To say noth- ing of walls, windows, cups, pocket-handkerchiefs, lan- terns, string, wrappers, cloaks, hats, baggage-covers, it is used domestically and professionally for all purposes for which we use lint, bandages, and cloths, and the consumption of it is enormous. It is so tenacious as to be nearly untearable, and even the finest kind, an exquisite and almost diaphanous fabric, soft like the most delicate silk *crêpe*, in which fine gold lacquer is usually wrapped, can only be torn with difficulty.

At this farm paper was being made in a small quantity for home use. The farmer, Tanaka, said that the paper mulberry shoots, after being allowed to grow to a length of five feet, are cut annually, and soaked in water for several days, after which the bark is taken off and boiled in ley; the inner and whiter bark which is used for making the better qualities of paper, being separated from the outer. He was only using the coarsest. The bark is beaten, as in Hawaii, into a pulp, and a small quantity is taken up on a frame and allowed to dry in the sun. Tanaka was making a coarse grey kind, used for covering the pads which soften the wooden pillows of the poorest classes. The sheets, 14 inches by 10 inches, are sold at three for a farthing.

After this there was a dismal tramp of five hours through rice-fields. The moist climate and the fatigue of this manner of travelling are deteriorating my health, and the pain in my spine, which has been daily increasing, was so severe that I could neither ride nor walk for more than twenty minutes at a time; and the pace was so slow that it was six when we reached Bangé, a commercial town of 5000 people, literally in the rice-swamp, mean, filthy, damp, and decaying, and full of an overpowering stench from black, slimy ditches. The mercury was 84°, and hot rain fell fast through the motionless air. We dismounted in a shed full of bales of dried fish, which gave off an overpowering odour, and wet and dirty people crowded in to stare at the foreigner till the air seemed unbreathable.

But there were signs of progress. A three days' congress of schoolmasters was being held; candidates for vacant situations were being examined; there were lengthy educational discussions going on, specially on the subject of the value of the Chinese classics as a part of education; and every inn was crowded.

Bangé was malarious: there was so much malarious fever that the Government had sent additional medical assistance; the hills were only a *ri* off, and it seemed essential to go on. But not a horse could be got till 10 P M; the road was worse than the one I had travelled; the pain became more acute, and I more exhausted, and I was obliged to remain. Then followed a weary hour, in which the Express Agent's five emissaries were searching for a room, and considerably after dark I found myself in a rambling old overcrowded *yadoya*, where my room was mainly built on piles above stagnant water, and the mosquitoes were in such swarms as to make the air dense, and after a feverish and miserable night I was glad to get up early and depart.

Fully 2000 people had assembled. After I was mounted I was on the point of removing my Dollond from the case, which hung on the saddle horn, when a regular stampede occurred, old and young running as fast as they possibly could, children being knocked down in the haste of their elders. Ito said that they thought I was taking out a pistol to frighten them, and I made him explain what the object really was, for they are a gentle, harmless people, whom one would not annoy without sincere regret. In many European countries, and certainly in some parts of our own, a solitary lady-traveller in a foreign dress would be exposed to rudeness, insult, and extortion, if not to actual danger; but I have not met with a single instance of incivility or real overcharge, and there is no rudeness even about the crowding. The *mago* are anxious that I should not get wet or be frightened, and very scrupulous in seeing that all straps and loose things are safe at the end of the journey, and instead of hanging about asking for gratuities, or stopping to drink and gossip, they quickly unload the horses, get a paper from the Transport Agent, and go home. Only yesterday a strap was missing, and though it was after dark, the man went back a *ri* for it, and refused to take some *sen* which I wished to give him, saying he was responsible for delivering everything right at the journey's end. They are so kind and courteous to each other, which is very pleasing. Ito is not pleasing or polite in his manner to me, but when he speaks to his own people he cannot free himself from the shackles of etiquette, and bows as profoundly and uses as many polite phrases as anybody else.

In an hour the malarious plain was crossed, and we have been among piles of mountains ever since. The infamous road was so slippery that my horse fell several times, and the baggage horse, with Ito upon him, rolled head over heels, sending his miscellaneous pack in all directions. Good roads are really the most pressing need of Japan. It would be far better if the Government were to enrich the country by such a remunerative outlay as making passable roads for the transport of goods through the interior, than to impoverish it by buying iron-clads in England, and indulging in expensive western vanities.

That so horrible a road should have so good a bridge as that by which we crossed the broad river Agano is surprising. It consists of twelve large scows, each one secured to a strong cable of plaited wistaria, which crosses the river at a great height, so as to allow of the scows and the plank bridge which they carry rising and falling with the twelve feet variation of the water.

Ito's disaster kept him back for an hour, and I sat meanwhile on a rice-sack in the hamlet of Katakado, a collection of steep-roofed houses huddled together on a height above the Agano. It was one mob of pack-horses, over 200 of them, biting, squealing, and kicking. Before I could dismount, one vicious creature struck at me violently, but only hit the great wooden stirrup. I could hardly find any place out of the range of hoofs or teeth. My baggage horse showed great fury after he was unloaded. He attacked people right and left with his teeth, struck out savagely with his fore feet, lashed out with his hind ones, and tried to pin his master up against a wall.

Leaving this fractious scene, we struck again through the mountains. Their ranges were interminable, and every view from every fresh ridge grander than the last, for we were now near the lofty range of the Aidzu Mountains, and the double-peaked Bandaisan, the abrupt precipices of Itoyasan, and the grand mass of Miyojintaké in the south-west, with their vast snow-fields and snow-filled ravines, were all visible at once. These summits of naked rock or dazzling snow, rising above the smothering greenery of the lower ranges into a heaven of delicious blue, gave exactly that individuality and emphasis which to my thinking Japanese scenery usually lacks. Riding on first, I arrived alone at the little town of Nozawa to encounter the curiosity of a crowd, and, after a rest, we had a very pleasant walk of three miles along the side of a ridge above a rapid river with fine gray cliffs on its farther side, with a grand view of the Aidzu giants violet coloured in a golden sunset.

The sound of the bronze bells of temples floated with a sweet mournfulness on the still air, making one forget that the lowing of kine and bleating of sheep, which would have been more appropriate to such a pastoral-looking region, were absent.

At dusk we came upon the picturesque village of Nojiri, on the margin of a rice-valley, but I shrank from spending Sunday in a hole, and having spied a solitary house on the very brow of a hill 1500 feet higher, I dragged out the information that it was a tea-house, and came up to it. It took three quarters of an hour to climb the series of precipitous zigzags by which this remarkable pass is surmounted; darkness came on, accompanied by thunder and lightning, and just as we arrived a tremendous zigzag of blue flame lit up the house and its interior, showing a large group sitting round a wood fire, and then all was thick darkness again. It was a most startling effect. This house is magnificently situated, almost hanging over the edge of the knife-like ridge of the pass of Kuruma, on which it is situated. It is the only *yadoya* I have been at from which there has been any view. The villages are nearly always in the valleys, and the best rooms are at the back, and have their prospects limited by the paling of the conventional garden. If it were not for the fleas, which are here in legions, I should stay longer, for the view of the Aidzu snow is delicious, and, as there are only two other houses, one can ramble without being mobbed.

In one, a child two and a half years old swallowed a fish-bone last night, and has been suffering and crying all day, and the grief of the mother so won Ito's sympathy that he took me to see her. She had walked up and down with it for eighteen hours, but never thought of looking into its throat, and was very unwilling that I should do so. The bone was visible, and easily removed with a crochet needle. An hour later the mother sent a tray with a quantity of cakes and coarse confectionery upon it as a present, with the piece of dried seaweed which always accompanies a gift. Before night seven people with sore legs applied for "advice." The sores were all superficial and all alike, and their owners said that they had been produced by the incessant rubbing of the bites of ants.

On this summer day the country looks as prosperous as it is beautiful, and one would not think that acute poverty could exist in the steep-roofed village of Nojiri which nestles at the foot of the hill; but two hempen ropes dangling from a cryptomeria just below tell the sad tale of an elderly man who hanged himself two days ago, because he was too poor to provide for a large family; and the house-mistress and Ito tell me that when a man who has a young family gets too old or feeble for work, he often destroys himself.

Suicide appears very common. When a young man and woman wish to marry, and the consent of the parents is refused, they often bind themselves together and drown themselves. [This is such a frequent offence that the new Code imposes penal servitude for ten years on people arrested in the commission of it.] Women never hang themselves, but, as may be expected, suicide is more common among them than among men, and an acute sense of shame, lovers' quarrels, cruelties practised upon *geishas* and others by those who are their taskmasters for a term of years, the loss of personal charms through age or illness, and even the dread of such loss, are the most usual causes. In these cases they usually go out at night, and after filling their capacious hanging sleeves with stones, jump into a river or well. I have passed two wells which are at present disused in consequence of recent suicides.

My hostess is a widow with a family, a good-natured, bustling woman, with a great love of talk. All day her house is open all round, having literally no walls. The roof and solitary upper room are supported on posts, and my ladder almost touches the kitchen fire. During the day-time the large matted area under the roof has no divisions, and groups of travellers and *magos* lie about; for every one who has toiled up either side of Kurumatogé takes a cup of "tea with eating," and the house-mistress is busy the whole day. A big well is near the fire. Of course there is no furniture; but a shelf runs under the roof on which there is a Buddhist god-house, with two black idols in it, one of them being that much-worshipped divinity, Daikoku, the god of wealth. Besides a rack for kitchen utensils, there is only a stand on which are six large brown dishes with food for sale — salt shell-fish, in a black liquid, dried trout impaled on sticks, sea slugs in soy, a paste made of pounded roots, and green cakes made of the slimy river *confervæ*, pressed and dried — all ill-favoured and unsavoury viands. This afternoon a man without clothes was treading flour paste on a mat, a traveller in a blue silk robe was lying on the floor smoking, and five women in loose attire, with elaborate chignons and blackened teeth, were squatting round the fire. At the house-mistress's request I wrote a eulogistic description of the view from her house, and read it in English, Ito translating it, to the very great satisfaction of the assemblage. Then I was asked to write on four fans. The woman has never heard of England. It is not "a name to conjure with" in these wilds. Neither has she heard of America. She knows of Russia as a great power, and of course of China, but there her knowledge ends, though she has been at Tôkiyô and Kiyôto.

July 1.— I was just falling asleep last night, in spite of mosquitoes and fleas, when I was roused by much talking and loud outcries of poultry; and Ito carrying a screaming, refractory hen, and a man and woman whom he had with difficulty bribed to part with it, appeared by my bed. I feebly said I would have it boiled for breakfast, but when Ito called me this morning he told me with a most rueful face that just as he was going to kill it it had escaped to the woods! In order to understand my feelings you must have experienced what it is not to have tasted fish, flesh, or fowl, for ten days! The alternative was eggs and some of the paste which the man was treading yesterday on the mat cut into strips and boiled! It was coarse flour and buckwheat, so you see I have learned not to be particular!   I. L. B.

EXTREME FILTHINESS.

An Infamous Road — Monotonous Greenery — Abysmal Dirt — Low Lives — The Lacquer Tree — Lacquer Poisoning — The Wax Tree and Wax Candles — The Tsugawa *Yadoya* — Politeness — A Shipping Port — A "Foreign Devil."

TSUGAWA, *July* 2.

YESTERDAY'S journey was one of the most severe I have yet had, for in ten hours of hard travelling I only accomplished fifteen miles. The road from Kurumatogé westwards is so infamous that the stages are sometimes little more than a mile. Yet it is by it, so far at least as the Tsugawa river, that the produce and manufactures of the rich plain of Aidzu with its numerous towns, and of a very large interior district, must find an outlet at Niigata. In defiance of all modern ideas it goes straight up and straight down hill, at a gradient that I should be afraid to hazard a guess at, and at present it is a perfect quagmire, into which great stones have been thrown, some of which have subsided edgewise, and others have disappeared altogether. It is the very worst road I ever rode over, and that is saying a good deal! Kurumatogé was the last of seventeen mountain passes, over 2000 feet high, which I have crossed since leaving Nikkô. Between it and Tsugawa the scenery, though on a smaller scale, is of much the same character as hitherto — hills wooded to their tops, cleft by ravines which open out occasionally to divulge more distant ranges, all smothered in greenery, which, when I am ill-pleased, I am inclined to call "rank vegetation." Oh that an abrupt scaur, or a strip of flaming desert, or something salient and brilliant, would break in, however discordantly, upon this monotony of green!

The villages of that district must, I think, have reached the lowest abyss of filthiness in Hozawa and Saikaiyama. Fowls, dogs, horses, and people herded together in sheds black with wood smoke, and manure heaps drained into the wells. No young boy wore any clothing. Few of the men wore anything but the *maro*, the women were unclothed to their waists, and such clothing as they had was very dirty, and held together by mere force of habit. The adults were covered with inflamed bites of insects, and the children with skin-disease. Their houses were dirty, and as they squatted on their heels, or lay face downwards, they looked little better than savages. Their appearance and the want of delicacy of their habits are simply abominable, and in the latter respect they contrast to great disadvantage with several savage peoples that I have been among. If I had kept to Nikkô, Hakone, Miyanoshita, and similar places visited by foreigners with less time, I should have formed a very different impression. Is their spiritual condition, I often wonder, much higher than their physical one? They are courteous, kindly, industrious, and free from gross crimes; but, from the conversations that I have had with Japanese, and from much that I see, I judge that their standard of foundational morality is very low, and that life is neither truthful nor pure.

All that remains to them of religion is a few superstitions, and futurity, whether as regards hope or fear, is a blank about which they hardly trouble themselves. Truly they are in sore need of ameliorating influences, and of being lifted up to that type of highest manliness and womanliness which constitutes the Christian ideal. If they were less courteous and kindly one

would be less painfully exercised about their condition,
which, however, under its best aspects, is devoid of the
highest elements of noble living. The day's tramp
through mire ended in a broad valley surrounded by
abrupt conical hills, and varied by conical knolls
covered with the dark cryptomeria. The lacquer tree
(*Rhus v.*) grows abundantly throughout the region. It
does not attain a larger size than our ordinary ash,
which it much resembles in general aspect. It is grown
for the sake of that celebrated varnish which gives its
name to the most beautiful of Japanese manufactures.
The trees are all scarred with numerous longitudinal
incisions from which the substance exudes in the early
spring. As taken from the tree it is of the colour and
consistence of thick cream, but becomes dark on exposure to the air. Lacquer is used for all kinds of purposes, from the golden shrines of Shiba and Nikkô,
down to the rice bowl in which the humblest coolie
takes his meal. I can no more fancy Japan without
lacquer than without paper, and combinations of the
two are universal. The finely lacquered articles which
are sold in the shops are enriched with five coats of the
varnish, and good old lacquer bears the contact of live
embers without blistering. The seed of the lacquer
tree produces a good deal of oil. The smell or touch,
or both combined, of new lacquer produces in a great
many people, both natives and foreigners, a very uncomfortable malady known as "lacquer poisoning,"
which in mild cases affects the skin only, but in severe
ones the system generally. Ito will on no account
touch a lacquer tree, or take shelter under one from
the rain.

Its kinsman, the *Rhus succedanea*, from which vegetable wax is made, is grown to a small extent in this
district. I associate it with many a dismal evening in

which I have attempted to write to you by the curiously fitful light of a greenish candle with a thick paper wick which burns smokily, giving off a tallowy smell. The wax as exported to England for use in the manufacture of wax-candles is carefully bleached, but for home use the bean-shaped, dark yellow kernel, after being deprived of its husk by a process analogous to rice-husking, is only steamed to soften it, then pressed, and the oil which is the result is received into earthen vessels, in which it hardens into a bluish green mass, ready to be made into candles.

I put up here at a crowded *yadoya*, where they have given me two cheerful rooms in the garden away from the crowd. Ito's great desire on arriving at any place is to shut me up in my room, and keep me a close prisoner till the start the next morning; but here I emancipated myself, and enjoyed myself very much sitting in the *daidokoro*. The house-master is of the *samurai* or two-sworded class, now, as such, extinct. His face is longer, his lips thinner, and his nose straighter and more prominent than those of the lower class, and there is a difference in his manner and bearing. I have had a great deal of interesting conversation with him.

In the same open space his clerk was writing at a lacquer desk of the stereotyped form, a low bench with the ends rolled over, a woman was tailoring, coolies were washing their feet on the *itama*, and several more were squatting round the *irori* smoking and drinking tea. A coolie servant washed some rice for my dinner, but before doing so took off his clothes, and the woman who cooked it let her *kimono* fall to her waist before she began to work, as is customary among respectable women. The house-master's wife and Ito talked about me unguardedly I asked what they were saying. "She says," said he, " that you are very polite — for a foreigner," he added. I asked what she meant, and found that it was because I took off my boots before I stepped on the matting, and bowed when they handed me the *tabako-bon*.

We walked through the town to find something eatable for to-morrow's river journey, but only succeeded in getting wafers made of white of egg and sugar, balls made of sugar and barley flour, and beans coated with sugar. Thatch, with its picturesqueness, has disappeared, and the Tsugawa roofs are of strips of bark weighted with large stones ; but as the houses turn their gable ends to the street, and there is a promenade the whole way under the eaves, and the street turns twice at right angles and terminates in temple grounds on a bank above the river, it is less monotonous than most Japanese towns. It is a place of 3000 people, and a good deal of produce is shipped from hence to Niigata by the river. To-day it is thronged with pack-horses. I was much mobbed, and one child formed the solitary exception to the general rule of politeness by calling me a name equivalent to the Chinese *Fan Kwai*, "Foreign Devil;" but he was severely chidden, and a policeman has just called with an apology. A slice of fresh salmon has been produced, and I think I never tasted anything so delicious. I have finished the first part of my land journey, and leave for Niigata by boat to-morrow morning.   I. L. B.

A RIVER JOURNEY.

A Hurry — The Tsugawa Packet-boat — Running the Rapids — Fantastic Scenery — The River-life — Vineyards — Dıying Barley —
Summer Silence — The Outskirts of Niigata — The Church Mission House.

NIIGATA, *July* 4.

THE boat for Niigata was to leave at 8, but at 5 Ito
roused me by saying they were going at once, as it was
full, and we left in haste, the house-master running to
the river with one of my large baskets on his back
to "speed the parting guest." Two rivers unite to form
a stream over whose beauty I would gladly have lingered, and the morning, singularly rich and tender in its
colouring, ripened into a glorious day of light without
glare, and heat without oppressiveness. The "packet"
was a stoutly built boat, 45 feet long by 6 broad, pro-
pelled by one man sculling at the stern, and another
pulling a short broad-bladed oar, which worked in a
wistaria loop at the bow. It had a croquet mallet nan-
dle about 18 inches long, to which the man gave a
wriggling turn at each stroke. Both rower and sculler
stood the whole time, clad in umbrella hats. The fore
part and centre carried bags of rice and crates of pottery, and the hinder part had a thatched roof, which,
when we started, sheltered twenty-five Japanese, but
we dropped them at hamlets on the river, and reached
Niigata with only three. I had my chair on the top of
the cargo, and found the voyage a delightful change
from the fatiguing crawl through quagmires at the rate

of from 15 to 18 miles a day. This trip is called "running the rapids of the Tsugawa," because for about twelve miles the river, hemmed in by lofty cliffs, studded with visible and sunken rocks, making several abrupt turns and shallowing in many places, hurries a boat swiftly downwards; and it is said that it requires long practice, skill, and coolness on the part of the boatmen to prevent grave and frequent accidents. But if they are rapids, they are on a small scale, and look anything but formidable. With the river at its present height the boats run down forty-five miles in eight hours, charging only 30 *sen* or 1s. 3d., but it takes from five to seven days to get up, and much hard work in poling and towing.

The boat had a thoroughly "native" look, with its bronzed crew, thatched roof, and the umbrella hats of all its passengers hanging on the mast. I enjoyed every hour of the day. It was luxury to drop quietly down the stream, the air was delicious, and having heard nothing of it, the beauty of the Tsugawa came upon me as a pleasant surprise, besides that every mile brought me nearer the hoped-for home letters. Almost as soon as we left Tsugawa the downward passage was apparently barred by fantastic mountains, which just opened their rocky gates wide enough to let us through, and then closed again. Pinnacles and needles of bare, flushed rock rose out of luxuriant vegetation — Quiraing without its bareness, the Rhine without its ruins, and more beautiful than both. There were mountains connected by ridges no broader than a horse's back, others with great grey buttresses, deep chasms cleft by streams, temples with pagoda roofs on heights, sunny villages with deep thatched roofs hidden away among blossoming trees, and through rifts in the nearer ranges glimpses of snowy mountains.

After a rapid run of twelve miles through this enchanting scenery, the remaining course of the Tsugawa
is that of a broad, full stream winding marvellously
through a wooded and tolerably level country, partially
surrounded by snowy mountains. The river life was
very pretty. Canoes abounded, some loaded with vegetables, some with wheat, others with boys and girls
returning from school. *Sampans* with their white puck-
ered sails in flotillas of a dozen at a time crawled up
the deep water, or were towed through the shallows by
crews frolicking and shouting. Then the scene changed
to a broad and deep river with a peculiar alluvial smell
from the quantity of vegetable matter held in suspension, flowing calmly between densely wooded, bamboo
fringed banks, just high enough to conceal the surrounding country. No houses, or nearly none, are to be
seen, but signs of a continuity of population abound.
Every hundred yards almost there is a narrow path to
the river through the jungle, with a canoe moored at
its foot. Erections like gallows, with a swinging bamboo, with a bucket at one end and a stone at the other,
occurring continually, show the vicinity of households
dependent upon the river for their water supply. Wherever the banks admitted of it horses were being washed
by having water poured over their backs with a dipper,
naked children were rolling in the mud, and cackling
of poultry, human voices, and sounds of industry were
ever floating towards us from the dense greenery of the
shores, making one feel without seeing that the margin
was very populous. Except the boatmen and myself,
no one was awake during the hot, silent afternoon — it
was dreamy and delicious. Occasionally, as we floated
down, vineyards were visible with the vines trained on
horizontal trellises, or bamboo rails often forty feet long,
nailed horizontally on cryptomeria to a height of twenty

feet, on which small sheaves of barley were placed astride to dry till the frame was full.

More forest, more dreams, then the forest and the abundant vegetation altogether disappeared, the river opened out among low lands and banks of shingle and sand, and by 3 we were on the outskirts of Niigata, whose low houses, with rows of stones upon their roofs, spread over a stretch of sand, beyond which is a sandy roll with some clumps of firs. Tea-houses with many balconies studded the river-side, and pleasure parties were enjoying themselves with *geishas* and *saké*, but on the whole, the water-side streets are shabby and tumble down, and the landward side of the great city of western Japan is certainly disappointing; and it was difficult to believe it a Treaty Port, for the sea was not in sight, and there were no consular flags flying. We poled along one of the numerous canals, which are the carriage ways for produce and goods, among hundreds of loaded boats, landed in the heart of the city, and, as the result of repeated inquiries, eventually reached the Church Mission House, an unshaded wooden building without verandahs, close to the Government Buildings, where I was most kindly welcomed by Mr. and Mrs. Fyson.

The house is plain, simple, and inconveniently small, but doors and walls are great luxuries, and you cannot imagine how pleasing the ways of a refined European household are after the eternal babblement and indecorum of the Japanese. **I. L. B.**

ITINERARY OF ROUTE FROM NIKKÔ TO NIIGATA

(KINUGAWA ROUTE.)

From Tôkiyô to

	No. of houses.	Ri.	Chô.
Nikkô		36	
Kohiaku	6	2	18
Kisagoi	19	1	18
Fujihara	46	2	19
Takahara	15	2	10
Ikari	25	2	
Nakamiyo	10	1	24
Yokokawa	20	2	21
Itosawa	38	2	34
Kayashima	57	1	4
Tajima	250	1	21
Toyonari	120	2	12
Atomi	34	1	
Ouchi	27	2	12
Ichikawa	7	2	22
Takata	420	2	11
Bangé	910	3	4
Katakado	50	1	20
Nosawa	306	3	24
Nojiri	110	1	27
Kurumatogé	3		9
Hozawa	20	1	14
Torige	21	1	
Sakaiyama	28		24
Tsugawa	615	2	18
Niigata	50,000 souls	18	
		Ri. 101	6

About 247 miles.

MISSIONS.

Christian Missions — Niigata as a Mission Station — The Two Missionaries — The Result of three Years of Work — Daily Preaching — The Medical Mission — The Hospital — Difficulties of Missionaries in Japan.

OUR Lord's command, "Go ye into all the world, and preach the gospel to every creature," was never better defined than by the Duke of Wellington in the famous phrase in which he called it "The marching orders" of the Church. Widely as we may differ in theory regarding the ultimate destiny of the heathen, "all who profess and call themselves Christians" agree that it is the Church's duty to fulfil Christ's injunction with unquestioning obedience, leaving the issue to Him.

It is one thing, however, to take a conventional interest in Foreign Missions at home, and another to consider them in presence of 34,000,000 of heathen. In the latter case, one is haunted by a perpetual sense of shame, first, for one's own selfishness and apathy, and then for the selfishness and apathy thousands of times multiplied, which are content to enjoy the temporal blessings by which Christianity has been accompanied, and the hope of "life and immortality," unembittered by the thought of the hundreds of millions who are living and dying without these blessings and this hope. In travelling among the Japanese, I have often felt the shadowiness and conventionality of much of what is called belief, for if righteous and humane men and women were truly convinced that these people, without Christianity, are doomed to perish everlastingly, it would be more than a few prayers, pounds, and shillings, which would be spent upon their conversion ; and numbers would come forward at their own cost to save their brethren and sisters from a doom, which, in an individual instance, no one can contemplate without unspeakable horror.

Niigata is an important city of 50,000 people, the capital of the large and populous province of Echigo. It is the only Treaty Port on the west side of Japan, and as such, is the only town between Hakodaté and Nagasaki (a distance of 1100 miles, with a population of many millions, mostly uncontaminated by intercourse with foreigners), in which a missionary is allowed to live, and Protestant Christianity has taken possession of this outpost, with a force of TWO MEN — Mr. Fyson and Dr. Palm — who have no necessary connection with each other, and who, if they were not the good and sensible men that they are, might consequently present the unseemly spectacle of disunion, and rival, or even antagonistic effort.

Dr. Palm, as a medical man sent out by the Edinburgh Medical Missionary Society, is naturally without a colleague, and is assisted by the cordial co-operation of the Japanese doctors ; but it is an obscure policy in the Church Missionary Society to leave a solitary missionary in this isolated region for three years, to battle unaided with the difficulties of the language and the infinite discouragement arising from the indifference and fickleness of the Japanese.

I have the highest respect for both the Niigata missionaries. They are true, honest, conscientious men, not sanguine or enthusiastic, but given up to the work of making Christianity known in the way which seems best to each of them, because they believe it to be the work indicated by the Master. They are alike incapable of dressing up "cases for reports," of magnifying trifling encouragements, of suppressing serious discouragements, or of responding in any unrighteous way to the pressure brought to bear upon missionaries by persons at home, who are naturally anxious for results. Dr. Palm, for some time a childless widower, has had it in his power to itinerate regularly and extensively among the populous towns and villages contained within the treaty limits of twenty-five miles. Mr. and Mrs. Fyson offer what is very important in this land of loose morals, the example of a virtuous Christian home, in which servants are treated with consideration and justice, and in which a singularly sensitive conscientiousness penetrates even the smallest details. The missionaries are accused of speaking atrocious Japanese, and of treating the most sacred themes in the lowest coolie vernacular; but Mr. Fyson aims at scholarship, and Ito, who is well educated, but abhors missionaries, says, that though he is not fluent, "the Japanese that he has is really good." Mrs. Fyson speaks colloquial Japanese readily, and besides having a Bible class, is on very friendly terms with many of her female neighbours, who talk to her confidentially, and in whom she feels a great interest. Her real regard for the Japanese women, and the sympathetic, womanly way in which she enters not only into their difficulties, but into their different notions of morals, please me much.

Mr. Fyson itinerates at certain seasons of the year. He finds strong prejudices against Christianity in the country, and extreme indifference in the city. On his first tours great crowds came to hear of the new "way," but that kind of interest has diminished. Among the lower classes it is believed that the missionaries are in the pay of the English Government with a view to ulterior political designs; that the eyes of converts are taken out immediately after death, if not before, to be used in the preparation of an ointment; that the missionaries have the power to spirit away money which has been carefully concealed, and the like!

The local authorities of Echigo make no actual opposition to the promulgation of Christianity, and until lately the rural priests were indifferent to it. On one occasion a Shintô priest gave Mr. Fyson leave to preach in a place belonging to him, with the remark that the country was "sunk in Buddhism," and on another a Buddhist priest allowed him to preach from the steps of a temple. In Niigata the Buddhist priests think it desirable to assail the new "way," and the local newspaper has opened its columns for their attacks, and for replies by Christian converts. There are many persons who have learned enough about Christianity to admit its reasonableness and its superiority to other religions in point of morality, but who are so indifferent to all religion that they go no farther. Of those who come to the open preaching every Sunday afternoon in a building attached to the mission-house, some go so far as to make inquiries concerning Christianity; but it often turns out that they have been actuated by some mercenary motive. As "the outward and visible sign" of three years of earnest work Mr. Fyson has baptized seven persons, with five of whom I received the communion according to the English form. He has a very energetic and intelligent native catechist who itinerates and collects considerable audiences. Difficulties are often raised regarding the hire of rooms for Christian preaching. It is not "correct" for a missionary to preach in the open air. It places him on a level with "monkey-players," jugglers, and other vagabond characters!

Of late the Buddhists have established daily preachings in one or two of the Niigata temples, and the preachers, who are chosen for their oratorical gifts, attract large audiences, composed chiefly of women, and exclusively of persons of the lower classes. Practically the difficulty in the way of Christianity is the general indifference to *all* religion. The "religious faculty" appears to be lost out of the Japanese nature. It is a complete mistake to suppose that because the old faiths are decaying Japan is ripe for the introduction of a new one. The Empire has embarked on a career of material progress. Everything which tends in that direction is eagerly appropriated and assimilated, that which does not is rejected as of no account. I asked a highly-educated and thoughtful young Japanese, who had just returned from a course of some years of scientific study in America, if he had ever studied religion, and his answer embodies at least the view of the educated classes, "*No, I had no time for anything that had no practical bearing.*"

The main object of my journey to Niigata was to learn something of the Medical Mission work done by Dr. Palm. This work seeks the worker, throngs him, crowds upon him. It goes through endless useful ramifications, spreads scientific truth in the treatment of diseases, removes prejudice against the practice of surgery and foreign drugs, dethrones superstitious quackery, introduces common sense and an improved hygiene, invites intelligent co-operation in its temporal part, and last, but not least, smooths the way for the gospel of the Good Physician by which it is always accompanied. These are the unanswerable pleas for Medical Missions in Japan.

In Dr. Palm Medical Missions have a very valuable agent. He is a well-equipped medical man, a lover and student of his profession, as well as a missionary. He is judicious, solid, and conscientious in all his work; there is no "scamping" in his dispensary or hospital, and when he has trained his assistants to do anything as well as he can do it himself, he trusts it to them under his supervision. He has gained the cordial good will of a large body of Japanese doctors, who co-operate with him in the towns and villages, and are introducing the most approved methods of European treatment under his auspices. He is an earnest and patient student of the language, both in its colloquial and literary forms. He has studied the Japanese character closely. He is not enthusiastic, and gives at least their full weight to the difficulties which lie in the way of Christianity, avoiding all hopeful forecasts of its future, content to do the work which demands his whole time and ability. He is an upright, honourable man, and as such, has gained general respect. He has baptized thirty-one converts after periods of severe probation, and the general conduct of the members of this infant church is without reproach. Mr. Oshikawa, his missionary assistant, is a man of much talent and energy, and a very able preacher. His whole heart is in Christian work, and he itinerates very extensively. The dispensary assistant is well trained and careful.

Recently the doctor of Suibara, one of the earliest village stations, has been baptized. He is a man of scholarship, a competent medical practitioner, and for a year and a half has co-operated with Dr. Palm at Suibara, undertaking all the expenses of the preaching place, and heartily furthering both the medical and evangelistic work. Still more recently another doctor from the island of Sado was baptized. There cannot be better evidence of the esteem in which Dr. Palm is held, than the circumstance that this man was in Niigata by an arrangement lately made with Dr. Palm by the Government, for teaching the treatment of eye diseases to the native practitioners in different parts of the province. He was previously disposed towards Christianity by some remarks in a medical book in Chinese, written by Dr. Dudgeon, and the daily addresses at the dispensary made him decide to embrace Christianity.

The native doctors have such a high value for "The English Doctor" that if it were not for passport restrictions, he would constantly be called into consultation by them beyond treaty limits. Amusing things frequently occur in the work. Lately, at the earnest request of the relatives of a patient, who were fully aware of the risk, Dr. Palm performed a very serious operation, under very unfavourable and difficult circumstances, and the patient died. The Japanese doctor, who was of the old Chinese School of Medicine (a school of consummate quackery and superstition), was so impressed with the wonders of English surgery that, though the operation was unsuccessful, he abandoned his system and sent away his three medical pupils, telling them that he had decided to learn European medicine, and that they must do the same!

In many cases the requests for Dr. Palm's regular services come from Japanese doctors, who, under these circumstances, arrange to secure a preaching place. At the town of Nakajo six young doctors have established a dispensary, which, at their request, is visited by Dr. Palm once a month. At the large town of Nagaoka, beyond treaty limits, there is a Government hospital, with three native doctors and a number of pupils, and so anxious were these for English skill that they procured a passport and gave Dr. Palm $10 for his expenses on each visit. There, and in every place, preaching accompanies healing.

In Buddhist places dislike of the foreigner, his religion, and his medicine, are often equally strong; while in Shintô places the two first are matters of indifference, and the last is eagerly sought. Just at the time of my visit the local Government feebly attempted to put a stop to evangelism in country places, and the police gave notice that in future no rooms were to be let for the purposes of preaching, stating that a similar notice had been served on Dr. Palm. This was never done, however, and .the matter dropped. The police also interfered with Mr. Fyson's native evangelist by asking him to produce his license to preach, but there is no ordinance on this subject, and as he, like Dr. Palm, showed the inclination to maintain his right, the thing was thereafter let alone.

Dr. Palm lives in a small Japanese house in the centre of the city, near the dispensary and the recently opened hospital, both of which I visited. At the dispensary between sixty and seventy patients are treated daily. They were clean and very well dressed. On the day of my visit fully half of them were suffering from diseases of the eyes. On arriving at the rooms before 9 A.M., each receives a ticket giving the order in which his case is to be attended to. An address on Christianity is always given, but some who have received tickets go away, only returning when they think that their turn has arrived, and Dr. Palm does not think it wise to bring undue pressure to bear upon them with regard to hearing the gospel. The people seem very independent, and insist on paying for their medicines, except in the case of a few who are quite destitute. The medicines are made up by Japanese assistants.

Six weeks before my visit Dr. Palm rented a house for a hospital for surgical cases. There was one severe case of cancer, and the rest were cases of spinal abscesses and hip-joint diseases. He has provided beds for the patients, to render nursing and dressing easier, but there is at first a great objection to using them. The people are frightened, and think that they shall fall off on the floor. The nursing, as is to be expected in Japan, is the weak point. It is undertaken by a respectable man and his wife, but a lady surgical nurse would be invaluable. The rooms are tolerably ventilated, and as the antiseptic treatment is used, Dr. Palm does not dread gangrene, but they are dark and unsuitable for operations — so dark, indeed, that Dr. Palm was obliged to bring one severe case of cancer to a room opening from his own sitting-room. The hospital patients pay 10 *sen* a day, *i.e.* nearly 3s. per week. The dispensary patients pay so liberally that, including native contributions, the hospital and dispensary are nearly self-supporting. The hospital accommodates twelve patients, and its expenses during last year were £319, and the receipts from patients £316!

The rapid increase of Medical Missionary work is most surprising. The work began four years ago, and had to contend not only with prejudices against the Christianity with which it is nobly associated, but against "foreign drugs," and specially against surgical operations. In the first year the number of patients was under 500. Last year it exceeded 5000, and 1500 of these were treated in thirteen country stations, in co-operation with native doctors, who supply the medicines under Dr. Palm's instructions, and obtain clinical teaching from him. Last year the confidence of the people had been so far won, that 174 submitted to surgical operations, and some of these of a serious kind were undertaken in the country, and left in charge of Japanese doctors, who treated them antiseptically. Dr. Palm regards the younger doctors as intelligent and fairly educated, and anxious to improve in their profession. Last year a number of them formed a Society for Mutual Improvement and the discussion of medical topics, and invited Dr. Palm to become its president and give them a lecture once a month. He is now doing so, and as some of them are acquainted with English, he furnishes them with the *British Medical Journal*, from which suitable translations are made.

In connection with the work of healing, invaluable *per se*, the gospel has permeated the very populous district within treaty limits. Indifference, contempt, and hatred prevail, yet we may hope that for seed so widely sown the two missionaries at Niigata may yet bring home the sheaves with rejoicing from these unpromising harvest fields.

Much of the sympathy given to missionaries at home is altogether misplaced. In Japan they are provided with comfortable houses and sufficient incomes, and even the isolation of Niigata, as Mr. and Mrs. Fyson would testify, is not felt by people who have work to do. The phrase " taking their lives in their hands " has no significance, and they incur no perils either from people or climate. On other grounds, missionaries placed in this and similar isolated positions deserve a sympathy which they rarely receive. A medical missionary has at least the exercise of his profession, which if he be a man of the right sort is an absorbing interest, and his work seeks him out sometimes even before he is ready for it. A simply evangelistic missionary, on the contrary, has to seek and make his work, and to deal with an indifferent and inert mass.

Both have to acquire by severe study something of a

most difficult and uncertain language before entering upon teaching, and even when they have made some progress they must long remain in doubt as to whether the words they use convey their meaning. For the solitary evangelistic missionary fresh difficulties arise when inquirers and candidates for baptism begin to gather around him. On his unaided responsibility he has to try to discern character, motives, and general fitness for admission into a church whose purity it is essential to conserve. He must find out a man's personal circumstances, his history, past and present, and do this discreetly and often by wading through the mire of prevarication and misrepresentation. Questions arise whether a man is to be admitted who is unable to relinquish his work on the Lord's Day, or who gets his living by means which we deem questionable, and perhaps, when everything appears satisfactory, it leaks out that he has more wives than one, or something equally unsuitable. Each case stands by itself and is involved in various complications, and must be judged on its merits and without assistance in a country in which the attainment of truth on any subject is a matter of special difficulty. I. L. B.

NOTE. — Since the above notes were written the cholera has visited Niigata, and Mission work for the time has suffered considerably, as the ignorant people were readily made to believe that the Christians had poisoned the wells. Peasants armed with spears were on the watch for Christian missionaries, and Dr. Palm's preaching-place in Nakajo was demolished in a riot. A very strong spirit of dislike, both to foreigners and their religion, manifested itself throughout the Province of Echigo, but things are gradually resuming their wonted course.

I. L. B

BUDDHISM.

Temple Street — Interior of a Temple — Resemblances between Buddhist and Roman Ritual — A Popular Preacher — Nirvana — Gentleness of Buddhism — Japanese distaste to "Eternal Life" — A new Obstacle in the way of Christianity.

NIIGATA, *July* 6.

THERE is a street here called Teramachi, or Temple Street. On one side, for nearly its whole length, there are Buddhist temples, temple grounds, and priests' houses, the other side is mainly composed of *jôrôyas*. These temples are mostly handsome and spacious. The panelled ceilings and the rows of pillars which support them are of the finely grained and richly coloured wood of the *Retinospora obtusa*. In all nearly one half of the area is railed off from the "laity." In each the high altar is magnificent, and altogether free from frippery and meretricious ornament. The altar-pieces proper consist of an incense burner with a perforated cover in the centre, flower vases on either side, and candelabra placed to the right and left of the flower vases, all of bronze, and often designed after ancient Chinese patterns, the originals of which are said to have travelled from India with the early Buddhist propagandists. On the whole, the Niigata temples are ecclesiastical and devotional-looking, and if a few of the Buddhist insignia were removed, they might be used for Christian worship without alteration. Their brass vessels are very beautiful, and their chalices,

flagons, lamps, and candlesticks are classical in form
and severely simple.

On the altars are draped, standing figures of Buddha
with glories round their heads, in gorgeous shrines,
looking like Madonnas, and below them the altar-
pieces previously mentioned, fresh flowers in the vases,

BUDDHIST PRIESTS.

and the curling smoke of incense diffusing a dreamy fragrance. Antique lamps, burning low and never extin-
guished, hang in front of the shrine. The fumes of
incense, the tinkling of small bells, lighted candles on
the high altar, the shaven crowns and flowing vestments
of the priests, the prostrations and processions, the

chanting of litanies in an unknown tongue, the " chancel rail," the dim light, and many other resemblances,
both slight and important, recall the gorgeousness of the
Roman ritual. From whence came the patterns of all
these shrines, lamps, candlesticks, and brazen vessels,
which Buddhist, Ritualist, Greek, and Romanist alike
use, the tongues of flame in the temples, the holy
water, the garments of the officiating priests, the candles and flowers on the altar, the white robes of the
pilgrims, and all the other coincident affinities which
daily startle one? Even the shops of the shrine-makers
look like " ecclesiastical decoration " shops in Oxford
Street.

Nor was the likeness lessened by the vast throng of
worshippers telling their beads on their brown rosaries
as they murmured their prayers, squatting on the matted floor of the great temple into which we went to
hear the afternoon preaching. It was a very striking
sight. The priestly orator sat on a square erection
covered with violet silk, just within the rail. He wore
a cassock of brocaded amber satin, a violet stole and
hood, and a chasuble of white silk gauze, and held a
rosary in his hand. A portion of the Buddhist Scriptures lay on his lap, and from a text in this he preached
with indescribable vehemence and much gesticulation,
in a most singular, high-pitched key, painful to listen
to. His subject was future punishment, *i.c.* the tortures
of the Buddhist hells. When he came to the conclu-
sion of the first part, in which he worked himself into
the semblance of a maniac, he paused abruptly and repeated the words, " Namû amida Butsû," and all the
congregation, slightly raising the hands on which the
rosaries were wound, answered with the roar of a
mighty response, " Eternal Buddha, save." Then he
retired behind the altar, and the adult worshippers,

relaxing their fixed attitudes, lighted their pipes and talked, and the children crawled about in the crowd. Then the priest, bowing as he passed the altar, took his place again on the rostrum, but before he began part two of his discourse, the prayer "Eternal Buddha, save" murmured low through the temple like the sound of many waters, and so for two hours the service was continued. Outside, under a canopy, the holy water stands, and on the steps leading to the entrance are ranged in rows the clogs and umbrellas of the worshippers. In the temple, the minister of a faith which is losing its hold upon the people, as at home was exhorting a congregation to follow the moral precepts of its founder, and emphasising his exhortations by portraying the punishments which await the guilty, — tortures and horrors which the pen cannot describe, — and the transmigration of the impure soul through the bodies of hateful beasts. Is there a household or a heart purer or better to-night, I wonder, for the tremendously energetic sermon of the popular preacher?

In the grounds of that temple there is a very fine bronze figure of Buddha seated in the usual attitude upon a lotus blossom. The Buddhist who, by purity and righteousness, escapes the tortures of hell, reaches the state of Nirvana in which he is represented. He is not sleeping, he is not waking, he is not acting, he is not thinking, his consciousness is doubtful — he exists — that is all — his work is done — a hazy beatitude, a negation remain. This is the best future to which the devout Buddhist can aspire. The greatest evil is life. The greatest good is Nirvana, or death in life.

I never visit a Buddhist temple without giving Buddhism full credit for having taught the lessons of mercy, gentleness, and reverence for life, to an Asiatic people. No victims have ever smoked upon its altars, its shady groves have never been scenes of cruelty and horror, and it has no Moloch to which children have ever passed through the fire. Such has been the reverence for life in all its forms which Buddhism has inculcated, that the theological, and even the Scriptural phraseology used concerning the atonement of Christ, are undoubtedly in the first instance abhorrent to the Japanese mind, and the whole Levitical system of sacrifice, and such statements as "Without shedding of blood there is no remission," are doubtless calculated to repel inquirers into the Christian faith. The Japanese have no notion of sin, and much time must elapse before Christian teaching can revolutionise their ideas on that and other subjects.

Again, the notion of "eternal life," which thrilled the Hawaiians with a new joy, is more likely to suggest a curse than a "gift of God." Shintôism has no teachings concerning a future, Buddhism promises to the pure total nonentity, or the annihilation of consciousness, or a measure of conscious personality in absorption into the holy Sâkya. Distaste for prolonged existence is essentially Oriental; weariness of life, even in the midst of its enjoyments, oppresses the Asiatic, and to the ignorant peasantry of Japan eternal life presents itself under the popular form of the Buddhist doctrine of metempsychosis, as almost endless birth and death, with new sufferings under each new form, sinking into lower and lower hells, or painfully rising to higher and higher heavens, to the blessed doom of impersonality. "Eternal life" then represents an almost endless chain whose links are successive existences. The common Japanese proverb, "If you hate a man let him live," epitomises the Japanese idea of the unsatisfactoriness of life.

Another obstacle in the way of Christianity (and all

these are apart from the deeply rooted and genuine dislike to the purity of its morality) is that the Japanese
students who are educated by their Government in
England or America return and tell their countrymen
that no one of any intelligence or position now believes
in Christianity, and that it is an exploded system, only
propped up by the clergy and the uneducated masses.
Yet, for all this and much more, and in spite of the very
slow progress which Christianity has made, any one who
attempts to forecast the future of Japan without any
reference to it, is making a very serious mistake.

I. L. B.

NIIGATA.

Abominable Weather — Insect Pests — Absence of Foreign Trade —
A refractory River — Progress — The Japanese City — Water
Highways — Niigata Gardens — Ruth Fyson — The Winter Climate
— A Population in Wadding.

NIIGATA, *July* 9

I HAVE spent over a week in Niigata, and leave it
regretfully to-morrow, rather for the sake of the friends
I have made than for its own interests. I never experienced a week of more abominable weather. The sun
has been seen just once, the mountains, which are thirty miles off, not at all. The clouds are a brownish
grey, the air moist and motionless, and the mercury has
varied from 82° in the day to 80° at night. The household is afflicted with lassitude and loss of appetite.
Evening does not bring coolness, but myriads of flying,
creeping, jumping, running creatures, all with power
to hurt, which replace the day mosquitoes, villains
with spotted legs, which bite and poison one without
the warning hum. The night mosquitoes are legion.
There are no walks except in the streets and the public
gardens, for Niigata is built on a sand spit, hot and
bare. Neither can you get a view of it without climbing to the top of a wooden look-out.

Niigata is a Treaty Port without foreign trade, and
almost without foreign residents. Not a foreign ship
visited the port either last year or this. There are
only two foreign firms, and these are German, and only
eighteen foreigners, of which number except the mis-

sionaries, nearly all are in Government employment. Its river, the Shinano, is the largest in Japan, and it and its affluents bring down a prodigious volume of water. But Japanese rivers are much choked with sand and shingle washed down from the mountains. In all that I have seen, except those which are physically limited by walls of hard rock, a river bed is a waste of sand, boulders, and shingle, through the middle of which, among sand-banks and shallows, the river proper takes its devious course. In the freshets which occur to a greater or less extent every year, enormous volumes of water pour over these wastes, carrying sand and detritus down to the mouths, which are all obstructed by bars. Of these rivers the Shinano, being the biggest, is the most refractory, and has piled up a bar at its entrance through which there is only a passage seven feet deep, which is perpetually shallowing. The minds of engineers are much exercised upon the Shinano, and the Government is most anxious to deepen the channel and give Western Japan what it has not — a harbour; but the expense of the necessary operation is enormous, and in the meantime a limited ocean traffic is carried on by junks and by a few small Japanese steamers which call outside.[1] There is a British Vice Consulate, but except as a step few would accept such a dreary post or outpost.

But Niigata is a handsome, prosperous city of 50,000 inhabitants, the capital of the wealthy province of Echigo, with a population of one and a half millions,

[1] By one of these, not fitted up for passengers, I have sent one of my baskets to Hakodaté, and by doing so have come upon one of the vexatious restrictions by which foreigners are harassed. It would seem natural to allow a foreigner to send his personal luggage from one Treaty Port to another without going through a number of formalities which render it nearly impossible, but it was only managed by Ito sending mine in his own name to a Japanese at Hakodaté, with whom he is slightly acquainted.

and is the seat of the *Kenrei*, or provincial governor, of the chief law courts, of fine schools, a hospital, and barracks. It is curious to find in such an excluded town a school deserving the designation of a college, as it includes intermediate, primary, and normal schools, an English school with 150 pupils, organised by English and American teachers, an engineering school, a geological museum, splendidly equipped laboratories, and the newest and most approved scientific and educational apparatus. The Government Buildings, which are grouped near Mr. Fyson's, are of painted white wood, and are imposing from their size and their innumerable glass windows. There is a large hospital[1] arranged by a European doctor, with a medical school attached, and it, the *Kenchô*, the *Saibanchô*, or Court House, the schools, the barracks, and a large bank, which is rivalling them all, have a go-ahead, Europeanised look, bold, staring, and tasteless. There are large public gardens, very well laid out, and with finely gravelled walks. There are 300 street lamps which burn the mineral oil of the district.

Yet, because the riotous Shinano persistently bars it out from the sea, its natural highway, the capital of one of the richest provinces of Japan is "left out in the cold," and the province itself, which yields not only rice, silk, tea, hemp, *ninjin*, and indigo, in large quantities, but gold, copper, coal, and petroleum, has to send most of its produce to Yedo across ranges of mountains, on the backs of pack-horses, by roads scarcely less infamous than the one by which I came.

---

[1] This hospital is large and well ventilated, but has not as yet succeeded in attracting many in-patients; out-patients, specially sufferers from ophthalmia, are very numerous. The Japanese chief physician regards the great prevalence of the malady in this neighbourhood as the result of damp, the reflection of the sun's rays from sand and snow, inadequate ventilation, and charcoal fumes.

The Niigata of the Government, with its signs of progress in a western direction, is quite unattractive-looking as compared with the genuine Japanese Niigata, which is the neatest, cleanest, and most comfortable-looking town I have yet seen, and altogether free from the jostlement of a foreign settlement. It is renowned for the beautiful tea-houses which attract visitors from distant places, and for the excellence of the theatres, and is the centre of the recreation and pleasure of a large district. It is so beautifully clean that, as at Nikkô, I should feel reluctant to walk upon its well-swept streets in muddy boots. It would afford a good lesson to the Edinburgh authorities, for every vagrant bit of straw, stick, or paper, is at once pounced upon and removed, and no rubbish may stand for an instant in its streets except in a covered box or bucket. It is correctly laid out in square divisions, formed by five streets over a mile long, crossed by very numerous short ones, and is intersected by canals, which are its real roadways. I have not seen a pack-horse in the streets; everything comes in by boat, and there are few houses in the city which cannot have their goods delivered by canal very near to their doors. These water-ways are busy all day, but in the early morning, when the boats come in loaded with the vegetables without which the people could not exist for a day, the bustle is indescribable. The cucumber boats just now are the great sight. The canals are usually in the middle of the streets, and have fairly broad roadways on both sides. They are much below the street level, and their nearly perpendicular banks are neatly faced with wood, broken at intervals by flights of stairs. They are bordered by trees, among which are many weeping willows; and as the river water runs through them, keeping them quite sweet, and they are crossed at short intervals by light bridges, they form a very attractive feature of Niigata.

The houses have very steep roofs of shingle, weighted with stones, and as they are of very irregular heights, and all turn the steep gables of the upper stories streetwards, the town has a picturesqueness very unusual in Japan. The deep verandahs are connected all along

STREET AND CANAL.

the streets, so as to form a sheltered promenade when the snow lies deep in winter. With its canals with their avenues of trees, its fine public gardens and clean, picturesque streets, it is a really attractive town; but its improvements are recent, and were only lately completed by Mr. Masakata Kusumoto, now Governor of Tôkiyô. There is no appearance of poverty in any part of the town, but if there be wealth, it is carefully concealed. One marked feature of the city is the number of streets of dwelling-houses with projecting windows of wooden *slats*, through which the people can see without being seen, though at night, when the *andons* are lit, we saw, as we walked from Dr. Palm's, that in most cases families were sitting round the *hibachi* in a *déshabille* of the scantiest kind.

The fronts are very narrow, and the houses extend backwards to an amazing length, with gardens in which flowers, shrubs, and mosquitoes are grown, and bridges are several times repeated, so as to give the effect of fairyland as you look through from the street. The principal apartments in all Japanese houses are at the back, looking out on these miniature landscapes, for a landscape is skilfully dwarfed into a space often not more than 30 feet square. A lake, a rockwork, a bridge, a stone lantern, and a deformed pine, are indispensable, but whenever circumstances and means admit of it, quaintnesses of all kinds are introduced. Small pavilions, retreats for tea-making, reading, sleeping in quiet and coolness, fishing under cover, and drinking *saké;* bronze pagodas, cascades falling from the mouths of bronze dragons; rock caves, with gold and silver fish darting in and out; lakes with rocky islands, streams crossed by green bridges, just high enough to allow a rat or frog to pass under; lawns, and slabs of stone for crossing them in wet weather, grottoes, hills, valleys, groves of miniature palms, cycas, and bamboo; and dwarfed trees of many kinds, of purplish and dull green hues, are cut into startling likenesses of beasts and creeping things, or stretch distorted arms over tiny lakes.

I have walked about a great deal in Niigata, and when with Mrs. Fyson, who is the only European lady here at present, and her little Ruth, a pretty Saxon child of three years old, we have been followed by an immense crowd, as the sight of this fair creature, with golden curls falling over her shoulders, is most fascinating. Both men and women have gentle, winning ways with infants, and Ruth, instead of being afraid of the crowds, smiles upon them, bows in Japanese fashion, speaks to them in Japanese, and seems a little disposed to leave her own people altogether. It is most difficult to make her keep with us, and two or three times, on missing her, and looking back, we have seen her seated, native fashion, in a ring in a crowd of several hundred people, receiving a homage and admiration from which she was most unwillingly torn. The Japanese have a perfect passion for children, but it is not good for European children to be much with them, as they corrupt their morals, and teach them to tell lies.

The climate of Niigata and of most of this great province contrasts unpleasantly with the region on the other side of the mountains, warmed by the gulf-stream of the North Pacific, in which the autumn and winter, with their still atmosphere, bracing temperature, and blue and sunny skies, are the most delightful seasons of the year. Thirty-two days of snow-fall occur on an average. The canals and rivers freeze, and even the rapid Shinano sometimes bears a horse. In January and February the snow lies three or four feet deep, a veil of clouds obscures the sky, people inhabit their upper rooms to get any daylight, pack-horse traffic is suspended, pedestrians go about with difficulty in rough snow-shoes, and for nearly six months the coast is unsuitable for navigation, owing to the prevalence of strong, cold, north-west winds. In this city people in wadded clothes, with only their eyes exposed, creep about under the verandahs. The population huddles round *hibachis* and shivers, for the mercury which rises to 92° in summer, falls to 15° in winter. And all this is in Latitude 37° 55′ — three degrees south of Naples!

I. L. B.

THE SHOPS.

Mean Streets — Curio Shops — Idealised Tubs — Hair-Pins — Coarse
Lacquer — Graven Images — Ecclesiastical Paraphernalia — Shoddy — Booksellers' Shops — Literature for Women — Careful Domestic Training — Literary Copyright — Book-Binding — Paper
Lanterns — Blue China — Quack Medicines — Criticisms.

NIIGATA, *July* 9.

THE "gorgeous east" is not a phrase which applies
to anything in Japan except to a few of the temples.
The cities, with their low, grey, wooden houses, are singularly mean, and the shops, as far as outward appearance goes, are as mean as all else; for the best textile
goods cannot be exposed for fear of injury from damp,
dust, and rain, and though there are a number of
"curio," or, as we should call them, second-hand shops,
they only expose common things in the street. The
china, confectionery, toy, and shrine shops, make the
best show. If one has time and patience, by diving
into a small back shop, or climbing by a steep ladder
into a loft, one may chance to see priceless things in
old lacquer; but each article is hidden away in its own
well-made deal box and its many wrappings of soft silk,
or *crêpe*-like paper. The coopers' and basket-makers'
shops contain articles of exquisite neatness of workmanship and singular adaptability. I never pass a
cooper's without longing to become a purchaser. A
common tub, by careful choice of woods and attention
to taste and neatness of detail, is turned into an *objet*

d'art. The basket-work, coarse and fine, is simply wonderful, from the great bamboo cages which are used to
hold stones in their place for breakwaters, down to the
grasshoppers, spiders, and beetles of such deceptively
imitative art that you feel inclined to brush them off the
fine plaited fans to which they are artificially attached.
Shops of the same kind herd together; thus, in one
long street, one sees little except toy-shops with stuffed
and china animals on wheels, windmills and water
wheels, toy idols and idol cars, battledores and shuttle
cocks, sugar toys of all kinds, and dolls of all sizes. A
short street contains few but barbers' shops, another is
devoted to the sale of wigs, chignons, toupées, and the
switches of coarse black hair which the women inter-
weave dexterously with their own. An adjacent street
is full of shops where all sorts of pins for the hair are
sold, from the plain brass or silver pin costing a trifle,
to the elaborate tortoise-shell pin with a group of birds
or bamboos finely carved, costing 8 or 12 *yen* at least.
I counted 117 different kinds of ornamental hair-pins!
In the same street are sold the stiff pads over which the
universal chignon is rolled. Not far off there is a street
chiefly taken up with clogs, of which thousands of pairs
are annually made in Niigata; then another with paper
umbrellas, sun and rain hats, paper waterproof cloaks
and baggage-wrappers, straw shoes for men and horses,
straw rain-cloaks, and straw rain-mats; then rows of
shops for pack-saddles, with gay fronts of red lacquer.
In the principal streets, though it is quite usual to see
eight or ten shops of one kind together, there is a tolerable mixture. Niigata is famous for coarse lacquer
such as is sold in London shops and at bazaars, trays
with a black or red ground, with birds, bamboos, or
peonies sprawling across it in gold paint. Similar trays
with legs, *zen*, or tables, are sold in sets of ten for fam-

ily use, as well as rice-bowls, rice pails and ladles, pillows, and numberless other articles of household utility. A sort of seaweed lacquer is also manufactured.

In the same street with these lacquer shops are the ecclesiastical furniture shops. At the back of these one can see the whole process, as described by Isaiah, of graving a god, from the rude block to the last delicate touches. There are all the household gods, among which Daikoku, the grinning god of wealth, never fails to attract one's attention, and gods of all sizes, from those eight feet high down to those an inch long in gold-embroidered bags, worn as charms by children, and others of delicate workmanship, which are carried in the sleeves of adults. I have one of the latter, representing the goddess of mercy. The case is a lotus bud, well executed in dark wood, which, on being removed, leaves a pedestal on which a draped female figure stands, with a glory touched with gold round her head, a golden sceptre by her side, and one pair of arms quietly folded across her breast, while about ten more come out from behind her, but are so dexterously managed as not to suggest any idea of monstrosity. The expression of both face and figure is one of majestic serenity. The whole is about four inches high, and is the most exquisite piece of wood-carving that I have ever seen. There are gorgeous shrines for temples, in which Buddha stands in endless calm, and shrines for his disciples, and family shrines of all sizes and prices, from bronze and gold at 200 *yen* down to unpainted wood at a dollar, tablets for the *kaimiyô* or dead name, in black or gold, candlesticks and incense-burners in bronze and brass, brass lotuses six feet high, altar-cloths richly worked in gold, drums, gongs, bells, and the numerous musical instruments used in temple worship, and hundreds of different articles more or less elabo rate used in the perplexing symbolism of the worship of some of the Buddhist sects. Shops for incense, which is consumed in enormous quantities, are separate.

Many shops sell only ready-made or second-hand men's clothes. Those for women are always made either to order or by themselves. Some sell blankets and British woollen goods of the most shameless "shoddy," others nothing but a thin, striped silk made in the neighbourhood, and largely used for *haori*. There are separate shops for fans, from three *sen* up to four or five *yen*, for *kakemonos*, or wall-pictures, and *makemonos* or rolled pictures, and floral albums, for folding screens, for the silk braid fastenings of *haori*, for *crêpe*, and for blue and white towels. The number of shops which sell nothing but smoking apparatus surprises me, though it ought not, for all men above fifteen smoke, and most women, and all men carry a pipe and pouch at their girdles. Then there are shops for pens only, for ink and inkstones, and others which sell nothing but writing-boxes.

There are large book shops which supply the country towns and the hawkers who carry books into the villages. "Pure Literature Societies" are much needed in Japan. The books for which there is the greatest demand are those which pack the greatest amount of crime into the smallest space, and corrupt the morals of all classes. A bookseller tells me that eight-tenths of his very large stock consists of novels, many of them coarsely illustrated, and the remaining two-tenths of "standard works." You will be interested to know the names of some of those which few but the most illiterate families are without, and which take the place occupied with us by the Bible and *Pilgrim's Progress*.

There are certain books for women, called collectively the *Bunko*, and respectively *Woman's Great Learn-*

ing, the moral duties of women based upon the Chinese Classics; *Woman's Small Learning*, introductory to the above; *Woman's Household Instruction*, the duties relating to dress, furniture, reception of guests, and the minutiæ of daily and ceremonial life; *The Lady's Letter-Writer;* and *Twenty-four Children*, stories of twenty-four model Chinese children. These books, which, if printed in small Roman type, would not be larger altogether than the *Cornhill Magazine*, contain, says an informant, the maxims and rules, many of them a thousand years old, on which the morals and manners of "all our women" are founded, so that their extreme similarity is easily accounted for. These books are studied and taught from early infancy. In many respects this careful training for the domestic duties of married life, and for all possible circumstances, so that a girl is never in any difficulty as to how she shall act, is far wiser then the haphazard way in which many of our girls are allowed to tumble into positions for which they have had no previous training, and to learn life's lessons by the sharp teachings of experience. There is another book which is read, and re-read, and committed to memory in every Japanese household by the women, the contents of which are, a collection of a hundred poems by a hundred poets, lives of model women, rules to secure perfect agreement between man and wife, and examples of such agreement, and other useful and ornamental knowledge, suitable for maiden, wife, and mother.

Books are remarkably cheap. Copyright is obtained by a Japanese author by the payment to Government of a sum equivalent to the selling-price of six copies of his work. They are printed from wooden blocks, on fine silky paper, doubled so that only the outsides receive the impression, but I have not seen anything in the way of binding better than stiffened paper of a heavier quality than the pages, except in the case of hand-painted picture-books, which are often bound in brocade and gold and silver stuffs.

This bookseller, who was remarkably communicative, and seems very intelligent, tells me that there is not the same demand now as formerly for native works on the history, geography, and botany of Japan. He showed me a folio work on botany, in four thick volumes, which gives root, stalk, leaf, flower, and seed of every plant delineated (and there are 400), drawn with the most painstaking botanical accuracy, and admirable fidelity to colour. This is a book of very great value and interest. He has translations of some of the works of Huxley, Darwin, and Herbert Spencer, which, he says, are bought by the young men attending the higher school. The *Origin of Species* has the largest sale. This man asked me many questions about the publishing and bookselling trade in England, and Ito acquitted himself admirably as an interpreter. He had not a single book on any subject connected with religion.

The number of shops for the sale of paper is enormous. Then there are shops where nothing is to be seen but *hibachi*, some of them of fine bronze work and very beautiful, all in sufficiently good taste to pass off as works of art; shops for brass tongs, and others where chopsticks alone are sold, from those of fine Wasaka, and inlaid lacquer, to the common wooden ones which are used once and are then thrown away.

The paper lantern shops are among the most conspicuous and interesting. You can form no conception of the extent to which lanterns are used. They are one of the idiosyncrasies of Japan. No festival, secular or religious, is complete without hundreds or thousands of them. A paper lantern burns outside most houses and shops at night, the *yadoyas*, tea-houses, and theatres keep up a perpetual illumination, and every foot-passenger and *kuruma* runner carries one with the Chinese characters forming his name upon it, in black or red, upon a white ground. They are of all sizes, from those hanging in the temples, 10 and 12 feet long, by 3 or 4 in diameter, to the small expanding ones, a foot long, by 4 or 5 inches wide, carried in the streets. Ingenuity, fancy, and taste, do their utmost to ornament them, and many of them, especially the kinds in ordinary use, are very beautiful. The usual shape is circular, but for festal occasions they are made in huge oblongs and squares — movable transparencies rather than lanterns — and in the likeness of fans and fishes. Some of the prettiest are those with merely the family crest in red on a white ground, or the name in the Chinese seal character. On inquiring the prices at one shop I found that they ranged from 8 *sen* up to 8 *yen*. I long to buy any number of them, but cannot.

Shops for *andons*, iron kettles, work-boxes (an essen tial part of every Japanese woman's outfit), kitchen utensils, tea-shops, *saké* shops, are all interesting, but yield in attractiveness to the pottery shops, which fill a whole street. Admirers of blue china would be nearly distracted with the variety, and even with the beauty of some of it, and especially with the bold handling of the designs on some of the large fish dishes. Every-where in the interior one sees horses loaded with it, and there is hardly a wayside tea-house at which I have not seen morsels, some of them very old, which I longed to buy. The *saké* cups, with the seven gods of luck within them, are very tempting, but nothing is more so than the teapots of all sizes and patterns, in every kind of ware for which Japan is famous. Every true

Japanese teapot has a hollow handle placed at right angles with a short, straight spout. At some shops they sell nothing else. Rope and hemp shops are very numerous.

One quarter, which is given up to food shops, is always thronged, but there is none of the noisy chaffering which distinguishes such quarters in our large towns. Confectioners, humble vendors of rice dumplings and barley cakes; fishmongers with stands covered with bonito slices, conger eels, soles, lobsters, starfish, and cuttle-fish; dealers in dried fish, rice, and grain; in sauces, condiments, and soy; in wine, and leaf tea, are all crowded together. Fruiterers' shops look tempting, even so early, with loquats (*Eriobotrya Japonica*) and plums (both as sour as they can be), young turnips, carrots, cucumbers, and pease and beans; and florists make a tasteful show with cut flowers, miniature shrubs, and wonderful dwarfed trees in vases. The consumption of cucumbers is something wonderful. Every man, woman, and child eats them — you can get a good-sized basket of them for four *sen* — three or four a day is not an unreasonable allowance; you would be astonished to see the number which the Fysons and I consume at every meal! Then come sellers of dried and candied fruits, egg merchants, tailors sitting in their shop fronts working sewing machines of Japanese make, cotton cleaners, rice huskers, weavers, spectacle makers, needle makers, brass founders, herb sellers, money changers, tobacco leaf cutters, picture shops in which grotesque art predominates, druggists with their stock in handsome jars of blue and white china inscribed with red Chinese characters, and dealers in "quack medicines," with conspicuous signboards three or four feet long, with Chinese characters in gold or red on a black ground.

The Japanese Government in many ways shows a

paternal regard for the well-being of its subjects, and keeps a special watch upon "quack medicines." In order to obtain leave to make and sell them, a minute description of the nature and effect of each must be sent to that all-embracing bureau, the Ministry of the Interior. Heavy penalties are attached to their unauthorised sale and manufacture, and t⁀ license to make each costs 8s. per annum. Druggists and itinerant vendors pay nominal fees for licenses to sell them. The peasants place greater faith in such compounds, and in the charms against disease sold in the temples, than in the medicines prescribed by the regular medical profession.

The neat finish of many articles is remarkable, and the beauty of some of the things turned out from dimly lighted rooms with apparently scanty appliances. Some of the finest things in iron and bronze are made by smiths squatting by a fire on the floor, one blowing the embers with a small pair of bellows, while the other hammers the iron on an anvil a foot high. But I cannot enter into the indiscriminate laudation indulged in by some travellers. Many articles, especially in lacquer, are tawdry and tasteless; some of the cottons show the vicious influence of the staring patterns of Manchester; a good deal of the china is positively ugly, the grotesque is often exaggerated, representations of the human form are nearly always out of drawing; some objects in nature are over-conventionalised, and some of the decorative articles, such as ornamental hairpins, are tawdry and vulgar.

I hope you are not tired of the shops. I have had to spend much time in searching for necessaries among them, and they certainly indicate the tastes, habits, and requirements of the people. If, as I suppose, the Niigata shops are typical, they evidence either the absence of expensive tastes, or of the means to gratify them.

ADULTERATIONS.

The Absurd in Shopping — Sadness and Jubilation — Condensed
Milk — Lemon Sugar — Essence of Coffee — Shameless Impositions
— Rose Dentifrice — Ito — Provender for the Journey.

JAPANESE shopping is an art to be acquired, apparently, and I have not patience for it. As a general rule I would rather give something approaching the price first asked by the vendor, than spend my time in haggling over it; but foreigners, who are expert, never do anything so extravagant, and, in the estimation of the shopkeeper, so absurd. If you like and wish to buy an article you don't ask its price, but that of several other things, working indifferently round to it. Perhaps the vendor says ten *yen;* you laugh as if you were very much amused, and say two *yen.* He laughs derisively, but quite good-naturedly, and you put it down, on which he says eight *yen;* you laugh again and walk about, on which he looks amused, and says seven *yen;* you say carelessly three *yen*, he looks sad and appears to calculate on his *soroban;* you move as if to go out, when most likely he claps his hands, looks jubilant, and says *yuroshi*, which means that you are to have it for three *yen*, which possibly is far more than it is worth to him. If the sellers were sour and glum, this process would be unbearable, but if you are courteous and smiling, they are as pleasant as people can be.

There are several shops which profess to sell tinned

meats, condensed milk, and such like travelling requisites, and upon these have I spent much time with little success. I bought condensed milk with the " Eagle " brand. On opening it I found a substance like pale treacle, with a dash of valerian. I bought " lemon sugar," the one cooling drink worth drinking. It turned out to be merely moistened sugar, with a phial in the middle, containing not essence of lemon, but an oily fluid with a smell of coal-tar. I saw cognac in French bottles, with French labels, selling at forty *sen* a quart, about a ninth of its cost price. I bought Smith's essence of coffee for a high price, alas ! and on opening it found a sticky and bitter paste, which Ito declares is a decoction of the leaves of *ninjin*. Lastly, I bought some semi-transparent soap on trial, and the use of it produced in half an hour a rash like scarlatina !

If truth must be told, greed leads the Japanese into the most shameless impositions. Half the goods sold as foreign eatables and drinkables are compounded of vile and unwholesome trash, manufactured in Tôkiyô and elsewhere, put up in bottles and jars with the names and labels of such highly respectable makers as Bass, Martell, Guiness, and Crosse and Blackwell, upon them. The last firm regularly appends to its advertisement in the Yokohama papers a request that its bottles and jars may be destroyed when empty, to prevent disgusting or poisonous frauds. But to secure themselves in their trade of forgery, these unconscionable villains have establishments at Tôkiyô, not only for the manufacture of the compounds, but of the labels which give them currency, and some of these are such adroit forgeries as to be completely successful, while others would effectually deceive a purchaser were it not for certain inscrutable vagaries in spelling, of which I will give you only one instance, though I have suffered grievously myself in the matter of "lemon sugar." Thus, a tooth powder in an English box with "Rose Dentifrice" at the top, takes in the buyer, but on examining the label which surrounds it, he finds "Rose Dentifruge, *a preparation unequalled for leaving the toothache*" (cleansing the teeth). This is harmless, as the forgery is probably quite as efficacious as the original.

My plans for the rest of the summer have been decided by finding that there is no steamer for Yezo for nearly a month. The land journey is about 450 miles, and I can learn nothing about the route I wish to take, but though Ito brings from his hotel rumours of impassable roads, difficulties of transit, and bad accommodation, I have no doubt that if my strength does not break down I shall get through all right, and I cannot think of any more healthful way of spending the summer than journeying through the northern mountains. Ito is invaluable both as courier and interpreter, and as I have profited by my experience, and reduced my baggage to 65 lbs., and have got a thoroughly good mosquito net, you may feel easy about me.

I am taking some sago and two tins of genuine condensed milk, this being all the portable food which my hunt through the shops has produced; but Mrs. Fyson has added a tin of biscuits, and Dr. Palm some chocolate and quinine. To-morrow I intend to plunge into the interior, and if all goes well, you will hear from me from Yezo in a few weeks. I. L. B.

FOOD.

Fish and Soy — The Use of Game and Poultry — Varieties of Vegetables — The *Raphanus sativus* — Tastelessness of Fruits — Cakes
and Sweetmeats — Cleanliness and Economy in Cooking — Cooking Utensils — Vivisection — Soups — Formal Entertainments —
Beverages — The Diet of the Poor.

I HAVE said so much and yet so little about Japanese
food, that I feel bound to supplement the notes on the
subject which occur in my letters by a few which are
rather more connected.

The range of Japanese eatables is almost unlimited,
though rice, millet, salt fish, and *Raphanus sativus*, constitute the staple food of the poorest class. Over ninety
kinds of sea and river fish are eaten, boiled, broiled, and
raw, from steaks of bonito and whale down to a minute
species which make less than a mouthful each, which
one usually sees in numbers in an inn kitchen, impaled
on bamboo skewers. Bonito, whale, highly salted and
dried salmon, sea slug, cuttle-fish, and some others, are
eaten raw. Some fish are fried in the oil of the *Sesamum Orientale*, which produces an odour which makes
one fly from its proximity. Eels and other dainties are
served with soy (*shô-yu*), the great Japanese sauce, of a
dark brown colour, made from fermented wheat and
beans with salt and vinegar, and with a dash of *saké*
occasionally added to give it a higher flavour. The
cuttle-fish always looks disgusting, and so do many of
the others. Thirteen or fourteen kinds of shell-fish are
eaten, including clams, cockles, and oysters.

Cranes and storks are luxuries of the rich, but wild duck and goose, pheasant, snipe, heron, woodcock, sky-lark, quails, and pigeons, are eaten by the middle classes, and where Shintôism prevails, or Buddhist teachings on the sacredness of life have been effaced by contact with foreigners or their indirect influence, fowls and farmyard ducks are eaten also. All these, except quails, woodcock, and pheasant, are cooked by boiling.

The variety of vegetables is infinite, but with one important exception they are remarkably tasteless. Fourteen varieties of beans are grown for food, besides pease, buckwheat, maize, potatoes, sweet potatoes (only eaten by the lowest classes), turnips, carrots, lettuce endive, cucumbers, squash, musk, and water melon spinach, leeks, onions, garlic, chilies, capsicums, eggs (*melongena*), yams, sweet basil seeds, a species of equisetum, yellow chrysanthemum blossoms, the roots and seeds of the lotus *Nelumbo nucifera*, the *Sagittaria*, *sagittata*, the *Arum esculentum* the *taro* of Hawaii, and some others. Besides cultivated vegetables they eat dock (*Lappa major*), ferns, wild ginger, water pepper, bamboo shoots (a great delicacy), and various other roots and stems. The egg-plant is enormously culti-vated. The bulbs of the tiger and white lily are also cultivated and eaten. Vegetables are usually boiled. I have left to the last the vegetable *par excellence*, the celebrated *daikon* (*Raphanus sativus*), from which every traveller and resident suffers. It is a plant of renown — it deserves the honorific! It has made many a brave man flee! It is grown and used everywhere by the lower classes to give sipidity to their otherwise tasteless food. Its leaves, something like those of a turnip, are a beautiful green, and enliven the fields in the early winter. Its root is pure white, tolerably even, and looks like an immensely magnified radish, as thick as an average arm, and from one to over two feet long. In this state it is comparatively innocuous. It is slightly dried and then pickled in brine, with rice bran. It is very porous, and absorbs a good deal of the pickle in the three months in which it lies in it, and then has a smell so awful that it is difficult to remain in a house in which it is being eaten. It is the worst smell that I know of except that of a skunk!

Mushrooms, dried, boiled, and served with sauce, are to be seen at every road-side tea-house.

Fruits, with one exception, are eaten raw, and without sugar or condiment. The finest fruit of Japan is the *kaki* or persimmon (*Diospyros kaki*), a large golden fruit on a beautiful tree. There are many varieties, but perhaps the best is a hard kind, which, after being peeled, is dried in the sun, and then tastes like a fig. The loquat is good, stewed with sugar, especially its large seeds, which taste like peach kernels. Grapes are tolerable only, and so are oranges; yellow and red raspberries grow wild, but they have less taste than an English blackberry. Among other fruits are apples, pears, quinces, plums, chestnuts, peaches, apricots, and musk and water melons, but they are sour and flavourless.

Seaweed is a common article of diet, and is dried and carried everywhere into the interior. I have scarcely seen a coolie make a meal of which it was not a part, either boiled, fried, pickled, raw, or in soup.

Pickles and relishes are enormously consumed. Cucumbers, and the *brinjal*, or egg-plant, with one or two other things pickled in brine or lees of *saké*, with or without rice-bran, are popular, and are relied on for imparting appetite; other vegetables are pickled with salt and ginger leaves, and are taken with tea the first thing in the morning, to counteract, as is supposed, the effect of the damp.

The Japanese have no puddings, tarts, creams, or custards, or anything in which milk and butter are essential; and in actual cookery sweets do not play an important part, but I have never seen elsewhere such numbers of shops for the sale of sweetmeats and confectionery, and on arriving at *yadoyas* of the better class, a tray of sweetmeats is always produced along with the tea with which a guest is welcomed, and they are offered also to "morning visitors." The finer kinds are brought from Tôkiyô, and are beautiful, flowers and leaves being simulated with botanical accuracy and truthfulness of colouring. I am ready to suspect the brilliant greens and yellows, but I believe they are quite harmless. Nearly every hamlet has its coarse confectionery, made chiefly for children, in which men, women, children, temples, drums, dogs, and many other things, are burlesqued in coarse sugar. The best are singularly insipid, and either the sugar or the rice flour mingled with it have an "old" taste. The common kinds are home-made, as may be seen in every village. Ito invested in sweetmeats everywhere. They seemed as essential to him as tobacco, and he said that all who abstain from *saké* crave for sugar. I often eked out my scanty fare with comfits made of sugar-coated beans, or with bricks of fine rice flour kneaded with sugar, and with *yokan*, which is sold in oblongs put up in dried leaves, and is made of beans and sugar rendered firm by a gelatinous substance obtained from seaweed. There is a cake called *kasuteira*, resembling sponge-cake, which is in much favour, and is quite tolerable, unless, as is frequently the case, the eggs are musty. It is said to have been introduced by the Spaniards, and that its name is a corruption of Castella. *Mochi*, a small round cake of unbaked rice dough, though insipid, is not unpalatable, and is in much favour also.

The marvel is that such a small quantity of fuel, and such a limited cooking apparatus can produce such a variety of results. Take a *yadoya*, for instance, with forty guests, from the high Government official down to *kuruma* runners and baggage coolies. It might not be difficult to provide a dinner for forty, but then it must be forty dinners, *i.e.* each person must have his separate lacquered table and from four to twelve dishes or bowls containing eatables. I abhor the viands, but I never see even a coolie taking his midday meal without fresh admiration of the neat and cleanly mode of serving, and the adaptability and elegance of the *solitaire* dinner service, with nothing " hugger-mugger," forlorn, or incomplete about it. It is very interesting to watch the cleanliness, economy, and certainty of the cooking operations, and the way in which, by frequent and dexterous manipulations of a dainty pair of brass tongs, which are worked like chopsticks with the fingers, a few ounces of charcoal can be made to cook a family meal. However dirty the clothing and even houses of the poorer classes are, I have never seen anything but extreme cleanliness in the cooking and serving of meals, and I have often preferred to spend an hour by the kitchen fire to a dignified solitude in my own room.

Each cooking utensil has its special beauty and fitness, and the people take a pride both in their cleanliness and antiquity. Many an inn kitchen contains articles in bronze and iron which are worth all the gaudy and tasteless rubbish of many a Yokohama curio shop, specially iron and bronze kettles of antique and elaborate workmanship, in design at least equal to those in the Imperial Treasury at Nara, and even exceeding in grace of form and delicacy of execution the cooking utensils in the Pompeiian room of the Naples

Museum. I have before me now two kettles of grace-ful shape in antique bronze, decorated with four or five small medallions in *niello* work, each consisting of a circle of gold, with an iris, a chrysanthemum. or a cherry blossom inlaid in gold within it. Of course the char-coal fires are smokeless, and the kettle rests on a three-legged circle of iron above the embers, so that it is not exposed to any coarse or sooty contacts.

In the large kitchens, cooking is done at a row of small fireplaces at a convenient height, which, however, are on the same economical principle as the *irori*. Fish are boiled in water and soy, and a sort of sweet *saké* called *mirinshu*, to which a little sugar is added. They are served with various relishes according to rules pre-scribed by inflexible custom. In broiling, the most common way is to sprinkle salt from above during the process, but a more piquant mode is to dash a little soy and *mirinshu* on the fish from time to time. All birds, with the exception of quail, woodcock, and pheasant, which are broiled on spits, are first cut into small pieces, and then boiled in water with a little salt. The com-mon people are also fond of "a pot-boil of birds" in which a little soy and *mirinshu* are added to the water. There are two ways of serving raw fish. In the first method the flesh is cut up into small, oblong strips, in the latter into very thin threads. The carp is frequent-ly cut up while yet alive, and survives a partial dis-memberment for some time. While one side of it is being eaten raw by the guests, the other, attached to the back bone, and the head, which is not touched, con-tinue to move about, and the movements are often quickened by sprinkling water on the poor creature. This dish, which is a delicacy, is called " A live prepara tion of Ko-i."

The chief kinds of soup used by the middle classes

are bean soup, egg soup, and clear soup. The latter is of two kinds, one water and salt, the other water and soy. Among the lower classes there are many kinds, most of which taste like dirty water with a pinch of salt, and contain cubes of bean curd, strips of dried fish, raw cuttle-fish, etc. One soup is a black liquid containing dried snails of the consistency of leather, and most are best described by the Biblical phrase, "broth of abominable things." Egg soup is usually found somewhat palatable by foreigners. In "upper circles," fish and vegetables, which have been separately boiled, are added to soups. Carp is used with bean soup only, while *serranus marginalis* is reserved for that especially ascetic soup the basis of which is salt and water.

The usual everyday meal of "well-to-do" people consists of rice, soups, boiled and broiled fish, and relishes, which occupy a far more important place than with us. Formal entertainments are divided into three classes, the *san no zen*, in which three small lacquer tables of eatables are provided for each guest; the *ni no zen*, with two, and the *honzen* with one. The following are ordinary *menus* in each style.

San no zen.

1st Table. Rice, bean soup with carp, raw fish cut into thin threads with adjuncts, boiled fish, and relishes.

2d Table. Clear soup, broiled fish, boiled vegetables.

3d Table. Clear or bean soup, boiled fish, boiled vegetables, a jar of slightly modified clear soup, and other vegetables.

Ni no zen.

1st Table. Rice, soup, boiled fish, a jar of a different soup, and relishes.

2d Table. Broiled fish, vegetables.

Honzen.

Rice, soup, broiled fish, raw fish, vegetables.

These bills of fare seem meagre, but such a number of dainties are comprised under the head relishes, that each table probably contains from eight to twelve bowls or dishes.

At all entertainments *saké*, or rice-beer, a straw-coloured fluid of a faintish taste and smell, most varieties of which contain from 11 to 17.5 per cent of alcohol, plays an important part. It is frequently heated, and is taken before what the Japanese consider as the real repast.

Before an entertainment, fish, either on a fine lacquer or porcelain dish, or on separate tables, is served with *saké* to each guest, and is known by the name of *saké no sakana* or "accompaniment to *saké*." This is independent of the one, two, or three tables of the feast. The preparation of raw fish cut into oblong strips called *sashimi* is used exclusively for this purpose, but occasionally the "*saké* accompaniment" consists of a large dish containing a preparation of fish, boiled quails, and other delicacies, cut up and piled one on the top of another. Before this preliminary, tea and sweetmeats are handed round, but are hardly touched.

A few of the combinations used in the best class of Japanese cookery are wild duck, dock root, equisetum, sea perch, lettuce, turnips; ferns, sea perch, *Aralia cordata;* crane, *Aralia cordata*, mushrooms; salt pheasant, dock root, *Aralia cordata;* cod, white fish, greens boiled in *saké*. Any three of these, in the order in which they are given, are found floating together in the soup.

With the *namasu*, or thin threads of raw fish, the adjuncts are sole, shrimps, chestnuts, ginger, *daikon;* orange, sea slug, jelly-fish, small lobsters, carrots, onions, parsley, and scraped *daikon,* four of which are usually served on the same plate.

With the *sashimi,* or oblong strips of raw fish, the combinations frequently are salmon, mushrooms, lemon juice, carp, cut up alive, large clams, strong *saké* in a jar, boiled pheasant, garlic sauce. With *Ayemono,* a vegetable "olla," *Alaria pinnatifida,* carrots, mushrooms, *beche de mer,* minced beans, mushrooms, and a kind of horsetail. These and other combinations in cookery, as with us, are partly determined by custom.[1]

The only drinks in common use are tea, hot water, *saké,* and *strochiu,* less palatable even than *saké,* a form of alcohol, which is taken cold at odd hours during the hot season. Tea, prepared with water not quite boiling and merely poured through the leaves, is the beverage usually taken with meals. Tea (*cha*) and *saké* both take the honorific before their names. *Usu-cha,* which is made of powdered tea and has the appearance and consistency of pea-soup, is in high esteem among people rich enough to afford it. It is served both before and after meals, and in that case hot water, which is the ancient national beverage, as it is to this day among the Ainos, accompanies the actual food.

It will be seen from this far from exhaustive account, that the *cuisine* of the "well-to-do" Japanese is far from despicable, yet there is something about their dishes so unpalatable to foreigners, that it is only after long experience that any Englishman, otherwise than ruefully, swallows Japanese food. The diet of the poorer classes is meagre and innutritious, revolting in appearance and taste, and the quantities of sauces and pickles with

[1] For the *menus,* combinations in cookery, and for much else, I am indebted to the kindness of Mr. Basil Hall Chamberlain, of the Imperial Naval College, Tôkiyô, who, although an accomplished scholar, does not think anything beneath him which is in any way illustrative of Japanese life and customs.

which they render it palatable are very injurious to the digestive organs. Everything which can be used for food is utilised by them. They even make a kind of curd or jelly from the water in which rice is boiled. In the cities the essential elements of the diet of an ordinary Japanese are rice, fish, and pickled *daikon;* in the interior rice, or in its place millet, beans, or pease and *daikon.* A coolie's average consumption of rice daily is two lbs. Of the luxuries of which I have written I never saw any on my northern tour — game never, and poultry and fresh fish very rarely; but any traveller wishing to acquaint himself with the delicacies of the Japanese *cuisine,* can do so at any of the better class of *yadoyas* in Yedo, Kiyôto, Ôsaka, Otsu, or even in Yokohama itself.

DISCOMFORTS.

The Canal-side at Niigata — Awful Loneliness — Courtesy — Dr. Palm's Tandem — A Noisy *Matsuri* — A Jolting Journey — The Mountain Villages — Winter Dismalness — An Out-of-the-world Hamlet — Crowded Dwellings — Riding a Cow — "Drunk and Disorderly" — An Enforced Rest — Local Discouragements — Heavy Loads — Absence of Beggary — Slow Travelling.

ICHINONO, *July* 12.

Two foreign ladies, two fair-haired foreign infants, a long-haired foreign dog, and a foreign gentleman, who, without these accompaniments, might have escaped notice, attracted a large but kindly crowd to the canal side when I left Niigata. The natives bore away the children on their shoulders, the Fysons walked to the extremity of the canal to bid me good-bye, the *sampan* shot out upon the broad, swirling flood of the Shinano, and an awful sense of loneliness fell upon me. We crossed the Shinano, poled up the narrow, enbanked Shinkawa, had a desperate struggle with the flooded Aganokawa, were much impeded by strings of nauseous manure-boats on the narrow, discoloured Kajikawa, wondered at the interminable melon and cucumber fields, and at the odd river life, and after hard poling for six hours, reached Kisaki, having accomplished exactly ten miles. Then three *kurumas* with trotting runners took us twenty miles at the low rate of 4½ *sen* per *ri*. In one place a board closed the road, but, on representing to the chief man of the village that the traveller was a foreigner, he courteously allowed me to pass, the Express Agent having accompanied me thus far to see that I "got through all right." The road was tolerably populous throughout the day's journey, and the farming villages which extended much of the way — Tsuiji, Kasayanagê, Mono, and Mari — were neat, and many of the farms had bamboo fences to screen them from the road. It was on the whole a pleasant country, and the people, though little clothed, did not look either poor or very dirty. The soil was very light and sandy. There were in fact "pine barrens," sandy ridges with nothing on them but spindly Scotch firs and fir scrub, but the sandy levels between them, being heavily manured and cultivated like gardens, bore splendid crops of cucumbers trained like peas, melons, vegetable marrow, *Arum esculentum*, sweet potatoes, maize, tea, tiger-lilies, beans, and onions; and extensive orchards with apples and pears trained laterally on trellis-work eight feet high, were a novelty in the landscape.

Though we were all day drawing nearer to mountains wooded to their summits on the east, the amount of vegetation was not burdensome, the rice swamps were few, and the air felt drier and less relaxing. As my runners were trotting merrily over one of the pine barrens, I met Dr. Palm returning from one of his medico-religious expeditions, with a tandem of two naked coolies who were going over the ground at a great pace, and I wished that some of the most staid directors of the Edinburgh Medical Missionary Society could have the shock of seeing him! I shall not see a European again for some weeks. From Tsuiji, a very neat village, where we changed *kurumas*, we were jolted along over a shingly road to Nakajo, a considerable town just within treaty limits. The Japanese doctors there, as in some other places, are Dr. Palm's cordial helpers, and five or six of them, whom he regards as possessing the rare virtues of candour, earnestness, and single-mindedness, and who have studied English medical works, have clubbed together to establish a dispensary, and under Dr. Palm's instructions are even carrying out the antiseptic treatment successfully, after some ludicrous failures!

Though Nakajo is a Shintô place, I noticed throughout the day indications of the region being "sunk in Buddhism" — sweeping roofs of temples in the greenery, wayside shrines with many *ex votos*, figures of Buddha by the road, and in some instances prayers were actually being said before the shrines by men. There were other novelties, — large tanks for the preservation of manure, sunk in the earth and covered by neatly thatched roofs, and carts with heavy, wooden wheels without tires, drawn by men and women.

We dashed through Nakajo as *kuruma* runners always dash through towns and villages, got out of it in a drizzle upon an avenue of firs, three or four deep, which extends from Nakajo to Kurokawa, and for some miles beyond, were jolted over a damp valley on which tea and rice alternated, crossed two branches of the shingly Kurokawa on precarious bridges, rattled into the town of Kurokawa, much decorated with flags and lanterns, where the people were all congregated at a shrine where there was much drumming, and a few girls, much painted and bedizened, were dancing or posturing on a raised and covered platform, in honour of the god of the place, whose *matsuri* or festival it was; and out again, to be mercilessly jolted under the firs in the twilight to a solitary house where the owner made some difficulty about receiving us, as his license did not begin till the next day, but eventually succumbed, and gave me his one up stairs room, exactly five feet high, which hardly allowed of my standing upright with my hat on. He then rendered it suffocating by closing the *amado*, for the reason often given, that if he left them open and the house was robbed, the police would not only blame him severely, but would not take any trouble to recover his property. He had no rice, so I indulged in a feast of delicious cucumbers. I never saw so many eaten as in that district. Children gnaw them all day long, and even babies on their mothers' backs suck them with avidity. Just now they are sold for a *sen* a dozen.

It is a mistake to arrive at a *yadoya* after dark. Even if the best rooms are not full it takes fully an hour to get my food and the room ready, and meanwhile I cannot employ my time usefully because of the mosquitoes. There was heavy rain all night, accompanied by the first wind that I have heard since landing, and the fitful creaking of the pines and the drumming from the shrine made me glad to get up at sunrise, or rather at daylight, for there has not been a sunrise since I came, or a sunset either. That day we travelled by Sekki to Kawaguchi in *kurumas, i.e.* we were sometimes bumped over stones, sometimes deposited on the edge of a quagmire, and asked to get out; and sometimes compelled to walk for two or three miles at a time along the infamous bridle-track above the river Arai, up which two men could hardly push and haul an empty vehicle; and as they often had to lift them bodily and carry them for some distance, I was really glad when we reached the village of Kawaguchi to find that they could go no farther, though, as we could only get one horse, I had to walk the last stage in a torrent of rain, poorly protected by my paper waterproof cloak.

We are now in the midst of the great central chain of the Japanese mountains, which extends almost without a break for 900 miles, and is from 40 to 100 miles in width, broken up into interminable ranges traversable only by steep passes from 1000 to 5000 feet in height, with innumerable rivers, ravines, and valleys, the heights and ravines heavily timbered, the rivers impetuous and liable to freshets, and the valleys invariably terraced for rice. It is in the valleys that the villages are found, and regions more isolated I have never seen, shut out by bad roads from the rest of Japan. The houses are very poor, the summer costume of the men consists of the *maro* only, and that of the women of trousers with an open shirt, and when we reached Kurosawa last night it had dwindled to trousers only. There is little traffic, and very few horses are kept, one, two, or three constituting the live stock of a large village. The shops, such as they are, contain the barest necessaries of life. Millet and buckwheat rather than rice, with the universal *daikon*, are the staples of diet. The climate is wet in summer and bitterly cold in winter. Even now it is comfortless enough for the people to come in wet, just to warm the tips of their fingers at the *irori*, stifled the while with the stinging smoke, while the damp wind flaps the torn paper of the windows about, and damp draughts sweep the ashes over the *tatami* until the house is hermetically sealed at night. These people never know anything of what we regard as comfort, and in the long winter, when the wretched bridle-tracks are blocked by snow and the freezing wind blows strong, and the families huddle round the smoky fire by the doleful glimmer of the *andon*, without work, books, or play, to shiver through the long evenings in chilly dreariness, and herd together for warmth at night like animals, their condition must be as miserable as anything short of grinding poverty can make it. The faces in this region impress me sadly as dull and apathetic. The vacant stare of the women has grown more vacant. There are no schools in these mountain villages, and medical advice, except of the old Chinese school, is hard to get. The necessaries of life are growing dearer, the Government machine at Tôkiyô wants much costly greasing, the tax-gatherer follows the harvest, and the people know the cost of progress with few of its blessings. There is another side to the picture happily. The old oppression is at an end. The Government is doing its best to mitigate the burden of taxation, and equalise its pressure, the heads of families are peasant proprietors, there are no caste distinctions, the rights of property are secure, and no "contiguous palace" mocks by its pomp and luxury the mean houses and fare of the peasantry.

I saw things at their worst that night as I tramped into the hamlet of Numa, down whose sloping street a swollen stream was running, which the people were banking out of their houses. I was wet and tired, and the woman at the one wretched *yadoya* met me, saying, "I'm sorry it's very dirty and quite unfit for so honourable a guest;" and she was right, for the one room was up a ladder, the windows were in tatters, there was no charcoal for a *hibachi*, no eggs, and the rice was so dirty and so full of a small black seed as to be unfit to eat. Worse than all, there was no Transport Office, the hamlet did not possess a horse, and it was only by sending to a farmer five miles off, and by much bargaining, that I got on the next morning. In estimating the number of people in a given number of houses in Japan, it is usual to multiply the houses by five, but I had the curiosity to walk through Numa and get Ito to translate the tallies which hang outside all Japanese houses with the names, number, and sexes of their inmates, and in twenty-four houses there were 307 people! In some there were four families, the grand-parents, the parents, the eldest son with his wife and family, and a daughter or two with their husbands and children. The eldest son, who inherits the house and land, almost invariably brings his wife to his father's house, where she often becomes little better than a slave to her mother-in-law. By rigid custom she literally forsakes her own kindred, and her "filial duty" is transferred to her husband's mother, who often takes a dislike to her, and instigates her son to divorce her if she has no children. My hostess had induced her son to divorce his wife, and she could give no better reason for it than that she was lazy.

The Numa people, she said, had never seen a foreigner, so, though the rain still fell heavily, they were astir in the early morning. They wanted to hear me speak, so I gave my orders to Ito in public. Yesterday was a most toilsome day, mainly spent in stumbling up and sliding down the great passes of Futai, Takanasu, and Yenoiki, all among forest-covered mountains, deeply cleft by forest-choked ravines, with now and then one of the snowy peaks of Aidzu breaking the monotony of the ocean of green. The horses' shoes were tied and untied every few minutes, and we made just a mile an hour! At last we were deposited in a most unpromising place in the hamlet of Tamagawa, and were told that a rice merchant, after waiting for three days, had got every horse in the country. At the end of two hours' chaffering one baggage coolie was produced, some of the things were put on the rice horses, and a steed with a pack-saddle was produced for me in the shape of a plump and pretty little cow, which carried me safely over the magnificent pass of Ori and down to the town of Okimi, among rice-fields, where, in a drowning rain, I was glad to get shelter with a number of coolies by a wood-fire till another pack-cow was produced, and we walked on through the rice-fields and up into the hills again to Kurosawa, where I had intended to remain, but there was no inn, and the farm-house where they take in travellers, besides being on the edge of a malarious pond, and being dark and full of stinging smoke, was so awfully dirty and full of living creatures, that, exhausted as I was, I was obliged to go on. But it was growing dark, there was no Transport Office, and for the first time the people were very slightly extortionate, and drove Ito nearly to his wits' end. The peasants do not like to be out after dark, for they are afraid of ghosts and all sorts of devilments, and it was difficult to induce them to start so late in the evening.

There was not a house clean enough to rest in, so I sat on a stone, and thought about the people for over an hour. Children with scald-head, *scabies*, and sore eyes swarmed. Every woman carried a baby on her back, and every child who could stagger under one carried one too. Not one woman wore anything but cotton trousers. One woman reeled about "drunk and disorderly." Ito sat on a stone hiding his face in his hands, and when I asked him if he were ill, he replied in a most lamentable voice, "I don't know what I am to do, I'm so ashamed for you to see such things!" The boy is only eighteen, and I pitied him. I asked him if women were often drunk, and he said they were in Yokohama, but they usually kept in their houses. He says that when their husbands give them money to pay bills at the end of a month, they often spend it in *saké*, and that they sometimes get *saké* in shops and have it put down as rice or tea. "The old old story!" I looked at the dirt and barbarism, and asked if this were the Japan of which I had read. Yet a woman in this unseemly costume firmly refused to take the 2 or 3 *sen* which it is usual to leave at a place where you rest,

b ause she said that I had had water and not tea, and
a er I had forced it on her, she returned it to Ito, and
is redeeming incident sent me away much comforted.

From Numa the distance here is only 1½ *ri*, but it is
over the steep pass of Honoki, which is ascended and
descended by hundreds of rude stone steps, not pleasant in the dark. On this pass I saw birches for the first
time; at its foot we entered Yamagata *ken* by a good
bridge, and shortly reached this village, in which an unpromising-looking farm-house is the only accommodation; but though all the rooms but two are taken up
with silk-worms, those two are very good and look upon
a miniature lake and rockery. The one objection to
my room is that to get either in or out of it I must pass
through the other, which is occupied by five tobacco
merchants who are waiting for transport, and who while
away the time by strumming on that instrument of dis-
may, the *samisen*. No horses or cows can be got for
me, so I am spending the day quietly here, rather glad
to rest, for I am much exhausted. When I am suffer
ing much from my spine Ito always gets into a fright
and thinks I am going to die, as he tells me when I am
better, but shows his anxiety by a short, surly manner,
which is most disagreeable. He thinks we shall never
get through the interior ! Mr. Brunton's excellent map
fails in this region, so it is only by fixing on the well-
known city of Yamagata and devising routes to it that
we get on. Half the evening is spent in consulting
Japanese maps, if we can get them, and in questioning
the house-master and Transport Agent, and any chance
travellers; but the people know nothing beyond the
distance of a few *ri*, and the agents seldom tell one
anything beyond the next stage. When I inquire
about the "unbeaten tracks" that I wish to take, the
answers are "It's an awful road through mountains,"

or " There are many bad rivers to cross," or " There are
none but farmers' houses to stop at." No encouragement is ever given, but we get on, and shall get on, I
doubt not, though the hardships are not what I would
desire in my present state of health.

Very few horses are kept here. Cows and coolies
carry much of the merchandise, and women as well as
men carry heavy loads. A baggage coolie carries
about 50 lbs., but here merchants carrying their own
goods from Yamagata actually carry from 90 to 140
lbs., and even more. It is sickening to meet these
poor fellows struggling over the mountain passes in
evident distress. Last night five of them were resting
on the summit ridge of a pass gasping violently. Their
eyes were starting out; all their muscles, rendered
painfully visible by their leanness, were quivering; rills
of blood from the bite of insects which they cannot
drive away were literally running all over their naked
bodies, washed away here and there by copious perspiration. Truly "in the sweat of their brows" they
were eating bread and earning an honest living for
their families! Suffering and hard-worked as they
were, they were quite independent. I have not seen a
beggar or beggary in this strange country. The women
were carrying 70 lbs. These burden-bearers have their
backs covered by a thick pad of plaited straw. On
this rests a ladder, curved up at the lower end like the
runners of a sleigh. On this the load is carefully
packed till it extends from below the man's waist to
a considerable height above his head. It is covered
with waterproof paper, securely roped, and thatched
with straw, and is supported by a broad padded band
just below the collar bones. Of course, as the man
walks nearly bent double, and the position is a very
painful one, he requires to stop and straighten himself

frequently, and unless he meets with a bank of convenient height, he rests the bottom of his burden on a
short, stout pole with an L-shaped top, carried for this
purpose. The carrying of enormous loads is quite a
feature of this region, and so, I am sorry to say, are red
stinging ants, and the small gad-flies which molest the
coolies.

Yesterday's journey was 18 miles in twelve hours!
Ichinono is a nice industrious hamlet, given up, like all
others, to rearing silkworms, and the pure white and
sulphur yellow cocoons are drying on mats in the sun
everywhere.   I. L. B.

A PROSPEROUS DISTRICT.

Comely Kine — Japanese Criticism on a Foreign Usage — Pleas-
ant Halt — Renewed Courtesies — The Plain of Yonezawa A
Curious Mistake — The Mother's Memorial — The Judgments of
Hades — Arrival at Komatsu — Stately Accommodation — Lati-
tude in Speech — Silk and Silk Culture — A Vicious Horse — An
Asiatic Arcadia — A Fashionable Watering-place — A Belle —
"Godowns" — The God of Wealth.

KAMINOYAMA.

A SEVERE day of mountain travelling brought us
into another region. We left Ichinono early on a fine
morning, with three pack-cows, one of which I rode
[and their calves], very comely kine, with small noses,
short horns, straight spines, and deep bodies. I thought
that I might get some fresh milk, but the idea of anything but a calf milking a cow was so new to the people that there was a universal laugh, and Ito told me
that they thought it "most disgusting," and that the
Japanese think it "most disgusting" in foreigners to
put anything "with such a strong smell and taste"
into their tea! All the cows had cotton cloths, printed
with blue dragons, suspended under their bodies to
keep them from mud and insects, and they wear straw
shoes, and cords through the cartilages of their noses.
The day being fine, a great deal of rice and *saké* was
on the move, and we met hundreds of pack-cows, all of
the same comely breed, in strings of four.

We crossed the Sakuratogé, from which the view is
beautiful, got horses at the mountain village of Shi-

rakasawa, crossed more passes, and in the afternoon
reached the village of Tenoko. There, as usual, I sat
under the verandah of the Transport Office, and waited
for the one horse which was available. It was a large
shop, but contained not a single article of European
make. In the one room a group of women and children sat round the fire, and the agent sat as usual with
a number of ledgers at a table a foot high, on which his
grandchild was lying on a cushion. Here Ito dined on
seven dishes of horrors, and they brought me *saké*, tea,
rice, and black beans. The last are very good. We
had some talk about the country, and the man asked
me to write his name in English characters, and to
write my own in a book. Meanwhile a crowd assembled, and the front row sat on the ground that the
others might see over their heads. They were dirty
and pressed very close, and when the women of the
house saw that I felt the heat they gracefully produced
fans and fanned me for a whole hour. On asking the
charge, they refused to make any, and would not receive anything. They had not seen a foreigner before,
they said, they would despise themselves for taking
anything, they had my "honourable name" in their
book. Not only that, but they put up a parcel of
sweetmeats, and the man wrote his name on a fan and
insisted on my accepting it. I was grieved to have
nothing to give them but some English pins, but they
had never seen such before, and soon circulated them
among the crowd. I told them truly that I should
remember them as long as I remember Japan, and
went on, much touched by their kindness.

The lofty pass of Utsu, which is ascended and descended by a number of stone slabs, is the last of the
passes of these choked-up ranges. From its summit in
the welcome sunlight I joyfully looked down upon the

noble plain of Yonezawa, about 30 miles long and from 10 to 18 broad, one of the gardens of Japan, wooded and watered, covered with prosperous towns and villages, surrounded by magnificent mountains not altogether timbered, and bounded at its southern extremity by ranges white with snow even in the middle of July.

In the long street of the farming village of Matsuhara a man amazed me by running in front of me and speaking to me, and on Ito coming up, he assailed him vociferously, and it turned out that he took me for an Aino, one of the subjugated aborigines of Yezo. I have before now been taken for a Chinese!

Throughout the province of Echigo I have occasionally seen a piece of cotton cloth suspended by its four corners from four bamboo poles just above a quiet stream. Behind it there is usually a long narrow tablet, notched at the top, similar to those seen in cemeteries, with characters upon it. Sometimes bouquets of flowers are placed in the hollow top of each bamboo, and usually there are characters on the cloth itself. Within it always lies a wooden dipper. In coming down from Tenoko I passed one of these close to the road, and a Buddhist priest was at the time pouring a dipper full of water into it, which strained slowly through. As he was going our way we joined him, and he explained its meaning.

According to him the tablet bears on it the *kaimiyô*, or posthumous name of a woman. The flowers have the same significance as those which loving hands place on the graves of kindred. If there are characters on the cloth, they represent the well-known invocation of the Nichiren sect, *Namu miô hô ren gé kiô*. The pouring of the water into the cloth, often accompanied by telling the beads on a rosary, is a prayer. The whole is called " The Flowing Invocation." I have seldom

seen anything more plaintively affecting, for it denotes
that a mother in the first joy of maternity has passed
away to suffer (according to popular belief) in the Lake
of Blood, one of the Buddhist hells, for a sin committed
in a former state of being, and it appeals to every
passer-by to shorten the penalties of a woman in

THE FLOWING INVOCATION.

anguish, for in that lake she must remain until the
cloth is so utterly worn out that the water falls through
it at once.

I have rarely passed the "Flowing Invocation" without seeing some wayfarer fill and empty the dipper, and
even Ito, sceptic as he is, never neglects to do the same.
In order to produce the liberation of a soul in torment,

it is essential that the cloth be bought at a temple. There the priest's information ceased, but Ito tells me that rich people can buy a cloth dexterously scraped thin in the middle, which lets the water through in a few days, while the poor man has to content himself with a closely woven cotton, which wears out with painful slowness. There are plenty of similar instances of the sordidness of priestcraft, so many that there is a common saying among the Japanese, "The judgments of Hades depend on money." Other resemblances to the Romish system of paying for masses occur in several forms *i* Buddhism, as for instance in the first and seve .ch months numbers of people visit temples in w .ich there are idols of Yemma, the Lord of Hell, for .he purpose of relieving the souls of friends who are suffering the pains of purgatory, and Yemma is expected to cancel the misdeeds which are recorded in his book in exact proportion to the sums paid to the priests.

Where the mountains come down upon the plain of Yonezawa, there are several raised banks, and you can take one step from the hill-side to a dead level. The soil is dry and gravelly at the junction, ridges of pines appeared, and the look of the houses suggested increased cleanliness and comfort. A walk of six miles took us from Tenoko to Komatsu, a beautifully situated town of 3000 people, with a large trade in cotton goods, silk, and *saké*.

As I entered Komatsu, the first man who I met turned back hastily, called into the first house the words which mean "Quick, here's a foreigner;" the three carpenters who were at work there flung down their tools, and, without waiting to put on their *kimonos*, sped down the street calling out the news, so that by the time I reached the *yadoya* a large crowd was pressing upon me. The front was mean and unpromising-looking, but on reaching the back by a stone bridge over a stream which ran through the house, I found a room 40 feet long by 15 high, entirely open along one side to a garden with a large fishpond with goldfish, a pagoda, dwarf trees, and all the usual miniature adorn ments. *Fusuma* of wrinkled blue paper splashed with gold turned this "gallery" into two rooms; but there was no privacy, for the crowds climbed upon the roofs at the back, and sat there patiently until night.

These were *daimiyô's* rooms. The posts and ceilings were ebony and gold, the mats very fine, the polished alcoves decorated with inlaid writing-tables and sword racks; spears nine feet long, with handles of lacquer inlaid with Venus's ear, hung in the verandah, the washing bowl was fine inlaid black lacquer, and the rice-bowls and their covers were gold lacquer.

In this as in many other *yadoyas* there were *kakémonos* with large Chinese characters representing the names of the Prime Minister, Provincial Governor, or distinguished General, who had honoured it by halting there, and lines of poetry were hung up, as is usual, in the same fashion. I have several times been asked to write something to be thus displayed. I spent Sunday at Komatsu, but not restfully, owing to the nocturnal croaking of the frogs in the pond. In it, as in most towns, there were shops which sell nothing but white, frothy-looking cakes, which are used for the goldfish which are so much prized, and three times daily the women and children of the household came into the garden to feed them.

The questions which the women everywhere put to me through Ito about things at home are most surprising, and show a latitude of speech very offensive to English ideas of delicacy, yet it would be quite unfair to judge of their morals either by such speech, or by many things in their habits which are at variance with our own. My impression is that the married women are virtuous and faithful, that the men are just the reverse, and that the children, who hear from their infancy the loose conversation of their parents, grow up without that purity and innocence which are among the greatest charms of children at home.

Silk is everywhere; silk occupies the best rooms of all the houses; silk is the topic of everybody's talk; the region seems to live by silk. One has to walk warily in many villages lest one should crush the cocoons which are exposed upon mats, and look so temptingly like almond comfits. The house-master took me to a silk-farm, where the farmer both raises the eggs [which are exported from Japan annually to the amount of three million dollars] and fine silk. For the eggs the cocoons are ranged in shallow basket trays for twelve or fourteen days, at the end of which time the chrysalis changes into a small white moth of mean appearance. From 100 to 130 moths are then placed on a card, which in twelve hours is covered with eggs, and is hung up by a string till the autumn. The cards are then packed in boxes, and the eggs are hatched the following spring. The best cards from this district bring 3½ *yen* each. The silk season here begins in early April by the cards being hung up. In about twenty-two days the worms appear. The women watch them most carefully, placing the cards on paper in basket trays, and brushing them each morning with a feather for three days, till all the worms are hatched. The mulberry leaves with which they are fed are minced very fine and sifted, so as to get rid of leaf fibre, and are then mixed with millet bran. The worms on being removed from the paper are placed on clean basket trays over a layer of matting. They pass through four sleeps, the first occurring ten days after hatching. The interval between the three remaining sleeps is from six to seven days. For these sleeps the most careful preparations are made by the attendants. Food is usually given five times a day, but in hot weather as many as eight times, and as the worms grow bigger their food grows coarser, till after the fourth sleep the leaves are given whole. The quantity is measured with great nicety, as the worms must neither be starved nor gorged. Great cleanliness is necessary, and an equable temperature, or disease arises; and the watching by day and night is so incessant, that, during the season, the women can do little else. After the fourth sleep the worms soon cease to feed, and when they are observed to be looking for a place to spin in, the best are picked out and placed on a straw contrivance, on which they spin their cocoons in three days. When the cocoons are intended for silk they are laid out in the sun on trays for three days, and this kills the chrysalis.

In almost every house front that I pass women are engaged in reeling silk. In this process the cocoons are kept in hot water in a copper basin, to the edge of which a ring of horsehair or a hook of very fine wire is attached. For the finest silk, the threads of five or six cocoons are lifted up and passed through the ring to the reel with the first and second fingers of the left hand, the right hand meanwhile turning the handle of the reel. Much expertness is required. The water used must be very pure, and is always filtered before it is used, or the silk loses its natural gloss.

When I left Kumatsu there were fully sixty people inside the house and 1500 outside, walls, verandahs, and even roofs being packed. From Nikkô to Kumatsu mares had been exclusively used, but there I encountered for the ı́ᵗᵗ time the terrible Japanese pack-horse. Two horridly fier ᵉ-looking creatures were at the door, with their heads tieᵘ ᵈown till their necks were completely arched. When I ḿ ᵘnted, the crowd followed, gathering as it went, frighteᵑ ᵑg the horse with the clatter of clogs and the sound of ᵃ ᵘltitude, till he broke his head rope, and the frighteneᵈ ᵐago letting him go, he proceeded down the street maı̈ᵑ ᵗ on his hind feet, squealing, and striking savagely with ᵈis fore feet, the crowd scattering to the right and left, tıı̇, as it surged past the police station, four policemen came out and arrested it, only to gather again, however, for there was a longer street down which my horse proceeded in the same fashion, and looking round, I saw Ito's horse on his hind legs and Ito on the ground. My beast jumped over all ditches, attacked all foot-passengers with his teeth, and behaved so like a wild animal that not all my previous acquaintance with the idiosyncrasies of horses enabled me to cope with him. On reaching Akayu we found a horse fair, and as all the horses had their heads tightly tied down to posts, they could only squeal and lash out with their hind feet, which so provoked our animals that the baggage horse, by a series of jerks and rearings, divested himself of Ito and most of the baggage, and as I dismounted from mine, he stood upright, and my foot catching, I fell on the ground, when he made several vicious dashes at me with his teeth and fore feet, which were happily frustrated by the dexterity of some mago. These beasts forcibly remind me of the words, "Whose mouth must be held with bit and bridle, lest they turn and fall upon thee."

It was a lovely summer day, though very hot, and the snowy peaks of Aidzu scarcely looked cool as they glittered in the sunlight. The plain of Yonezawa, with the prosperous town of Yonezawa in the south, and the frequented watering-place of Akayu in the north, i a perfect garden of Eden, "tilled with a pencil inste   of a plough," growing in rich profusion, rice, cotton maize, tobacco, hemp, indigo, beans, egg plants, walnu , melons, cucumbers, persimmons, apricots, pomegran tes; a smiling and plenteous land, an Asiatic Arcadia, prosperous and independent, all its bounteous acres be onging to those who cultivate them, who live under thei vines, figs, and pomegranates, free from oppression — a   markable spectacle under an Asiatic despotism. Y t still Daikoku is the chief deity, and material good is he one object of desire.

It is an enchanting region of beauty, indust y, and comfort, mountain girdled, and watered by the bright Matsuka. Everywhere there are prosperous ar beautiful farming villages, with large houses with carved beams and ponderous tiled roofs, each standin in its own grounds, buried among persimmons and po egranates, with flower-gardens under trellised vir s, and privacy secured by high, closely-clipped screens c pomegranate and cryptomeria. Besides the villages of Yoshida, Semoshima, Kurokawa, Takayama, and T kataki, through or near which we passed, I counted o er fifty on the plain with their brown, sweeping barn roofs looking out from the woodland. In every one there are two poles over 30 feet high for white bannerets, which are inscribed with the name of the village god, and are put up on his *matsuri* or festival day, and from the number of these visible among the trees, it seemed as if half the villages were keeping holiday. The monotonous sound of drumming filled the air, the girl children were all much painted, and large lanterns, with the characters representing the god, were hanging under all eaves, in preparation for the evening illuminations. The village of Yoshida, in which I saw the process of silk raising, is the most beautiful and prosperous of all; but even there there was not a man or woman who did not work with his or her own hands, and semi-nudity among the adults was as common as in the mountain villages, though the children, especially the girls, were elaborately dressed in silk fabrics, and wore a good deal of scarlet. I cannot see any differences in the style of cultivation. Yoshida is rich and prosperous-looking, Numa poor and wretched-looking, but the scanty acres of Numa, rescued from the mountain-sides, are as exquisitely trim and neat, as perfectly cultivated, and yield as abundantly of the crops which suit the climate, as the broad acres of the sunny plain of Yonezawa, and this is the case everywhere. "The field of the sluggard" has no existence in Japan.

We rode for four hours through these beautiful villages on a road four feet wide, and then, to my surprise, after ferrying a river, emerged at Tsukuno upon what appears on the map as a secondary road, but which is in reality a main road 25 feet wide, well kept, trenched on both sides, and with a line of telegraph poles along it. It was a new world at once. The road for many miles was thronged with well-dressed foot-passengers, *kurumas*, pack-horses, and waggons either with solid wheels, or wheels with spokes but no tires. It is a capital carriage-road, but without carriages. In such civilised circumstances it was curious to see two or four brown skinned men pulling the carts, and quite often a man and his wife — the man unclothed, and the woman unclothed to her waist — doing the same. Also it struck me as incongruous to see telegraph wires above, and below, men whose only clothing consisted of a sun-hat and fan; while children with books and slates were returning from school, conning their lessons.

At Akayu, a town of hot sulphur springs, I hoped to

sleep, but it was one of the noisiest places I have seen. In the most crowded part, where four streets meet, there are bathing sheds, which were full of people of both sexes, splashing loudly, and the *yadoya* close to it had about forty rooms, in nearly all of which several rheumatic people were lying on the mats, *samisens* were twanging, and *kotos* screeching, and the hubbub was so unbearable that I came on here, ten miles farther, by a fine new road, up an uninteresting strath of rice-fields and low hills, which opens out upon a small plain surrounded by elevated gravelly hills, on the slope of one of which Kaminoyama, a watering-place of over 3000 people, is pleasantly situated. It is keeping festival; there are lanterns and flags on every house, and crowds are thronging the temple grounds, of which there are several on the hills above. It is a clean, dry place, with beautiful *yadoyas* on the heights, and pleasant houses with gardens, and plenty of walks over the hills. The people say that it is one of the driest places in Japan. If it were within reach of foreigners, they would find it a wholesome health resort, with picturesque excursions in many directions.

This is one of the great routes of Japanese travel, and it is interesting to see watering-places with their habits, amusements, and civilisation quite complete, but borrowing nothing from Europe. The hot springs here contain iron, and are strongly impregnated with sulphuretted hydrogen. I tried the temperature of three, and found them 100°, 105°, and 107°. They are supposed to be very valuable in rheumatism, and they attract visitors from great distances. The police, who are my frequent informants, tell me that there are nearly 600 people now staying here for the benefit of the baths, of which six daily are usually taken. I think that in rheumatism, as in some other maladies, the old-fashioned

Japanese doctors pay little attention to diet and habits, and much to drugs and external applications. The benefit of these and other medicinal waters would be much increased if vigorous friction replaced the dabbing with soft towels.

THE BELLE OF KAMINOYAMA.

This is a large *yadoya*, very full of strangers, and the house-mistress, a buxom and most prepossessing widow, has a truly exquisite hotel for bathers higher up the hill. She has eleven children, two or three of whom are tall, handsome, and graceful girls. One blushed deeply at my ev lent admiration, but was not displeased, and took me up he hill to see the temples, baths, and *yadoyas* of this v ry attractive place. I am much delighted with her race and *savoir faire*. I asked the widow how long s e had kept the inn, and she proudly answered, "Three undred years," not an uncommon instance of the here lity of occupations.

My accommodatic i is unique, a *kura*, or godown, in a large conventional garden, in which is a bath-house which receives a hot pring at a temperature of 105°, in which I luxuriate. Last night the mosquitoes were awful. If the widow a id her handsome girls had not fanned me persevering] for an hour, I should not have been able to write a lin . My new mosquito net succeeds admirably, and wh I am once within it I rather enjoy the disappointment f the hundreds of drumming bloodthirsty wretches outs le.

The widow tells me th house-masters pay 2 *yen* once for all for the sign, an an annual tax of 2 *yen* on a first-class *yadoya*, 1 *yen* fo a second, and 50 cents for a third, with 5 *yen* for the lic nse to sell *saké*.

These "godowns" (from he Malay word *gadong*), or fireproof storehouses, are one of the most marked features of Japanese towns, both because they are white where all else is grey, and because they are solid where all else is perishable. Hotels, shops, and middle class (if there be a middle class) houses have their own *kuras*, but for the poorer classes and in villages there are *kuras* in which people can hire the security needed. Nobody keeps anything of value in his own inflammable dwelling. Several times I have seen a whole district burned to the ground, leaving only a few ashes, and the *kuras* standing unharmed, except by the smoke. They are all on one model, and have a handsome appearance as contrasted with the houses. The foundations are of stone, on which a tolerably solid wooden frame-work is constructed, which is covered with from twenty-five to fifty coats of mud plaster. A plaster roof of considerable thickness is placed upon these walls, and above that, leaving a space of a foot, a handsome tiled one. The doors and window shutters are

DAIKOKU.

iron or bronze, solid and handsome, much like the doors of Chubb's fireproof safes, except in a few cases, in which they are made of wood thickly coated with plaster. The outside of the building is coated with *chunam*, a pure white cement.

I am lodged in the lower part, but the iron doors are open, and in their place at night is a paper screen. A

few things are kept in my room. Two handsome
shrines from which the unemotional faces of two
Buddhas looked out all night, a fine figure of the goddess Kwan-non, and a venerable one of the god of lon-
gevity suggested curious dreams. You will remember
that I mentioned two gigantic figures, the Ni-ô, as guarding the gateways of the temples. I have noticed small
prints of these over the doors of almost all the houses,
and over the *kura* doors also. It seems that the
prints are put up as a protection against burgrurs.
Near the *yadoya* entrance there is the largest figure of
Daikoku, the god of wealth, that I have yet seen,
though I cannot recall a house in which he does not
appear in larger or smaller form. He is jolly and
roguish-looking usually, as indeed the god may be who
leads all men, and fools most. He is short and stout,
wears a cap like the cap of liberty, is seated on rice
bags, holds a mallet in his right hand, and with the left
grasps tightly a large sack which he carries over his
shoulders. The moral taught by this figure has long
since been forgotten. It teaches humility by its low
stature. Its bag represents wealth, requiring to be
firmly held when attained. The cap partly shades the
eyes, to keep them bent down on the realities of life.
The mallet represents manual labour, and the rice-bags
the riches to be acquired by following the rules which
raise the lowly! Traders, farmers, and all who have
their living to make, incessantly propitiate Daikoku,
and he is never without offerings and incense.

I. L. B

A JAPANESE DOCTOR.

Prosperity — Convict Labour — A New Bridge — Yamagata — Intoxicating Forgeries — The Government Buildings — Bad Manners
A Filature — Snow Mountains — A Wretched Town.

KANAYAMA, *July* 16.

THREE days of travelling on the same excellent road
have brought me nearly 60 miles. Yamagata *ken* impresses me as being singularly prosperous, progressive,
and go-ahead; the plain of Yamagata, which I entered
soon after leaving Kaminoyama, is populous and highly
cultivated, and the broad road, with its enormous traffic,
looks wealthy and civilised. It is being improved by
convicts in dull red *kimonos* printed with Chinese characters, who correspond with our ticket-of-leave men, as
they are working for wages in the employment of con-
tractors and farmers, and are under no other restriction
than that of always wearing the prison dress.

At the Sakamoki river I was delighted to come upon
the only thoroughly solid piece of modern Japanese
work that I have met with, a remarkably handsome
stone bridge nearly finished — the first I have seen. I
introduced myself to the engineer Okuno Chiuzo, a very
gentlemanly, agreeable Japanese, who showed me the
plans, took a great deal of trouble to explain them, and
courteously gave me tea and sweetmeats.

This remarkable bridge on a remarkable road is 192
feet long by 30 broad, with five arches of a span of 30
feet each. It has a massive stone balustrade, with

pillars at the ends and centre, surmounted by bronze finials 3 feet high. The stones are quarried 12 miles off, and each is brought down to the river-side by eight coolies and dressed on the spot. The regular size of the stones is 3 feet by 2, and, like all Japanese masonry, they are fitted together without mortar, and with such absolute nicety that the joinings are hardly visible. The estimated cost is 16,000 *yen*, or something over £3000. This bridge is most interesting, as the design and work are Japanese, and it has been erected successfully without foreign aid. I paid the engineer many compliments on his work, and doubtless they lost nothing by transmission through Ito, who has adopted a most amusing swagger of walk and speech ever since we entered this thriving *ken*. The washing away of bridges during the frequent freshets is a source of great loss and inconvenience. The rivers are innumerable, and in a poor country it cannot be expected that such structures as this should become common, even on the main roads, but iron cylinders filled with concrete would, in many places, be cheaper in the long run than wooden piers without foundations. The obvious prosperity of this region must arise partly, I think, from the fine main road which gives the cultivator a choice of markets, instead of compelling him to sell in the nearest, because of the difficulty of transit. The road is very cheerful, owing not only to the pedestrians and pack-horses, but to the immense number of man-carts and *kurumas*.

Yamagata, a thriving town of 21,000 people and the capital of the *ken*, is well situated on a slight eminence, and this and the dominant position of the *kenchô* at the top of the main street give it an emphasis unusual in Japanese towns. The outskirts of all the cities are very mean, and the appearance of the lofty white buildings of the new Government Offices above the low grey houses was much of a surprise. The streets of Yamagata are broad and clean, and it has good shops, among which are long rows selling nothing but ornamental iron kettles and ornamental brasswork. So far in the interior I was annoyed to find several shops almost exclusively for the sale of villainous forgeries of European eatables and drinkables, specially the latter. The Japanese, from the Mikado downwards, have acquired a love of foreign intoxicants, which would be hurtful enough to them if the intoxicants were genuine, but is far worse when they are compounds of vitriol, fusel oil, bad vinegar, and I know not what. I saw two shops in Yamagata which sold champagne of the best brands, Martell's cognac, Bass's ale, Medoc, St. Julian, and Scotch whisky, at about one-fifth of their cost price — all poisonous compounds, the sale of which ought to be interdicted.

The Government Buildings, though in the usual confectionery style, are improved by the addition of verandahs, and the *Kenchô, Saibanchô,* or Court House, the Normal School with advanced schools attached, and the police buildings, are all in keeping with the good road and obvious prosperity. A large two-storied hospital, with a cupola, which will accommodate 150 patients, and is to be a Medical School, is nearly finished. It is very well arranged and ventilated. I cannot say as much for the present hospital, which I went over. At the Court House I saw twenty officials doing nothing, and as many policemen, all in European dress, to which they had added an imitation of European manners, the total result being unmitigated vulgarity. They demanded my passport before they would tell me the population of the *ken,* and city. Once or twice I have found fault with Ito's manners, and he has asked me twice since if I think them like the manners of the policemen at Yamagata!

I visited a filature where the managers and engine-tenders all wore European clothes, but they were singularly courteous and communicative. It is a light, lofty, well-ventilated building, running 50 spindles (shortly to be increased to 100), worked by as many clean, well-dressed girls. Those who are learning get little besides their food, the skilled hands earn 5s. a week and food. The machinery is run by a steam-engine of twenty horse-power, made and worked by Japanese. In front of the spindles is a row of tables at which the girls are seated, on high, cushioned stools, each one with a brass pan full of water kept at a given temperature, which contains the cocoons. They lift the ends of the silk with small brushes made of twigs, and pass them through glass rings to the spindles. The working day is eleven hours. The spun silk is all sent to England. The white bears the highest price, but the yellow is the strongest. In whatever form silk is sold, it must be put up in given quantities, in wrappers, bearing impressed stamps of different values. The manager complained very much of the adulterations of silk in Europe, and specially of that mixture of silk and cotton known as Japanese silk. In the rear of the filature is a large fireproof building, with racks up to the roof, in which the cocoons are stored after they have been exposed to a high temperature in a stove-heated chamber. The manager entertained us with tea, the first of this season's crop, and remarkably delicious.

The Yamagata crowd was a suffocating and persevering one. It followed me to the filature, and after being dispersed by the police, re-accumulated, waited outside during the hour I spent there, and followed me to the tea-house, where my spoon and fork detained it for another hour.

North of Yamagata the plain widens, and fine longitudinal ranges capped with snow mountains on the one side, and broken ranges with lateral spurs on the other, enclose as cheerful and pleasant a region as one would wish to see, with many pleasant villages on the lower slopes of the hills. The mercury was only 70°, and the wind north, so it was an especially pleasant journey, though I had to go three and a half *ri* beyond Tendo, a town of 5000 people, where I had intended to halt, because the only inns at Tendo which were not *kashit-sukeya*, were so occupied with silkworms that they could not receive me.

The next day's journey was still along the same fine road, through a succession of farming villages, and towns of 1500 and 2000 people, such as Tochiida and Obanasawa, were frequent. From both these there was a glorious view of Chôkaisan, a grand, snow-covered dome, said to be 8000 feet high, which rises in an altogether unexpected manner from comparatively level country, and as the great snow-fields of Udonosan are in sight at the same time, with most picturesque curtain ranges below, it may be considered one of the grandest views of Japan. After leaving Obanasawa the road passes along a valley watered by one of the affluents of the Mogami, and after crossing it by a fine wooden bridge, ascends a pass from which the view is most magnificent. After a long ascent through a region of light, peaty soil, wooded with pine, cryptomeria, and scrub oak, a long descent and a fine avenue terminate in Shinjô, a wretched town of over 5000 people, situated in a plain of rice-fields.

The day's journey, of over twenty-three miles, was through villages of farms without *yadoyas*, and in many cases without even tea-houses. The st-- -- ----ng has quite changed. W-- --- --sappeared, and all the houses are now built with heavy beams and walls of laths and brown mud mixed with chopped straw, and very neat. Nearly all are great oblong barns, turned endwise to the road, 50, 60, and even 100 feet long, with the end nearest the road the dwelling-house. These farm-houses have no paper windows, only *amado*, with a few panes of paper at the top. These are drawn back in the daytime, and, in the better class of houses, blinds, formed of reeds or split bamboo, are let down over the opening. There are no ceilings, and in many cases an unmolested rat snake lives in the rafters, who, when he is much gorged, occasionally falls down upon a mosquito net.

Again I write that Shinjô is a wretched place. It is a *daimiyô's* town, and every *daimiyô's* town that I have seen has an air of decay, partly owing to the fact that the castle is either pulled down, or has been allowed to fall into decay. Shinjô has a large trade in rice, silk, and hemp, and ought not to be as poor as it looks. The mosquitoes were in thousands, and I had to go to bed, so as to be out of their reach, before I had finished my wretched meal of sago and condensed milk. There was a hot rain all night, my wretched room was dirty and stifling, and rats gnawed my boots and ran away with my cucumbers.

To-day the temperature is high and the sky murky. The good road has come to an end, and the old hardships have begun again. After leaving Shinjô this morning we crossed over a steep ridge into a singular basin of great beauty, with a semicircle of pyramidal hills, rendered more striking by being covered to their summits with pyramidal cryptomeria, and apparently blocking all northward progress. At their feet lies

Kanayama in a romantic situation, and though I arrived as early as noon, I am staying for a day or two, for my room at the Transport Office is cheerful and pleasant, the agent is most polite, a very rough region lies before me, and Ito has secured a chicken for the first time since leaving Nikkô!

I find it impossible in this damp climate, and in my present poor health, to travel with any comfort for more than two or three days at a time, and it is difficult to find pretty, quiet, and wholesome places for a halt of two nights. Freedom from fleas and mosquitoes one can never hope for, though the last vary in number, and I have found a way of "dodging" the first, by laying down a piece of oiled paper six feet square upon the mat, dusting along its edges a band of Persian insect powder, and setting my chair in the middle. I am then insulated, and though myriads of fleas jump on the paper, the powder stupefies them, and they are easily killed. I have been obliged to rest here at any rate, because I have been stung on my left hand both by a hornet and a gadfly, and it is badly inflamed. In some places the hornets are in hundreds, and make the horses wild. I am also suffering from inflammation produced by the bites of "horse ants," which attack one in walking. The Japanese suffer very much from these, and a neglected bite often produces an intractable ulcer. Besides these, there is a fly as harmless in appearance as our house-fly, which bites as badly as a mosquito. These are some of the drawbacks of Japanese travelling in summer, but worse than these is the lack of such food as one can eat when one finishes a hard day's journey without appetite, in an exhausting atmosphere.

July 18. — I have had so much pain and fever from stings and bites that last night I was glad to consult a Japanese doctor from Shinjô. Ito, who looks twice as

big as usual when he has to do any "grand" interpreting, and always puts on silk *hakama* in honour of it,
came in with a middle-aged man dressed entirely in silk,
who prostrated himself three times on the ground, and
then sat down on his heels. Ito in many words explained my calamities, and Dr. Nosoki then asked to see
my "honourable hand" which he examined carefully,
and then my "honourable foot." He felt my pulse and
looked at my eyes with a magnifying glass, and with
much sucking in of his breath — a sign of good breeding and politeness — informed me that I had much
fever, which I knew before; then that I must rest,
which I also knew; then he lighted his pipe and con
templated me. Then he felt my pulse and looked at
my eyes again, then felt the swelling from the hornet
bite, and said it was much inflamed, of which I was
painfully aware, and then clapped his hands three times.
At this signal a coolie appeared, carrying a handsome
black lacquer chest with the same crest in gold upon it
as Dr. Nosoki wore in white on his *haori.* This contained a medicine chest of fine gold lacquer, fitted up
with shelves, drawers, bottles, etc. He compounded a
lotion first, with which he bandaged my hand and arm
rather skilfully, telling me to pour the lotion over the
bandage at intervals till the pain abated. The whole
was covered with oiled paper, which answers the purpose of oiled silk. He then compounded a febrifuge,
which, as it is purely vegetable, I have not hesitated to
take, and told me to drink it in hot water, and to avoid
saké for a day or two!

I asked him what his fee was, and after many bows
and much spluttering and sucking in of his breath, he
asked if I should think half a *yen* too much, and when
I presented him with a *yen*, and told him with a good
deal of profound bowing on my part that I was exceed-

ingly glad to obtain his services, his gratitude quite abashed me by its immensity.

Doctors are being turned out in numbers from the Medical College in Tôkiyô, with diplomas which entitle them to practice throughout the Empire, and the medical schools connected with the provincial hospitals taught by men educated in European Medical Science give diplomas entitling their receivers to practise within the limits of the *ken* in which they are issued; but Dr. Nosoki is one of the old-fashioned practitioners, whose medical knowledge has been handed down from father to son, and who holds out, as probably most of his patients do, against European methods and drugs. A strong prejudice against surgical operations, specially amputations, exists throughout Japan. With regard to the latter, people think that as they came into the world complete, so they are bound to go out of it, and in many places a surgeon would hardly be able to buy at any price the privilege of cutting off an arm.

Except from books these older men know nothing of the mechanism of the human body, as dissection is unknown to native science. Dr. Nosoki told me that he relies mainly on the application of the *moxa* and on acupuncture in the treatment of acute diseases, and in chronic maladies on friction, medicinal baths, certain animal and vegetable medicines, and certain kinds of food. The use of leeches and blisters is unknown to him, and he regards mineral drugs with obvious suspicion. He has heard of chloroform, but has never seen it used, and considers that in maternity it must necessarily be fatal either to mother or child. He asked me (and I have twice before been asked the same question) whether it is not by its use that we endeavour to keep down our redundant population! He has great faith in *ginseng* and in rhinoceros horn, and in the powdered liver of some animal, which, from the description, I understood to be a tiger — all specifics of the Chinese school of medicines.[1] Dr. Nosoki showed me a small box of " unicorn's " horn, which he said was worth more than its weight in gold! As my arm improved coincidently with the application of his lotion, I am bound to give him the credit of the cure.

I invited him to dinner, and two tables were produced covered with different dishes, of which he ate heartily, showing most singular dexterity with his chopsticks in removing the flesh of small, bony fish. It is proper to show appreciation of a repast by noisy gulpings, and much gurgling and drawing in of the breath. Etiquette rigidly prescribes these performances, which are most distressing to a European, and my guest nearly upset my gravity by them.

The host and the *Kôchô*, or chief man of the village, paid me a formal visit in the evening, and Ito, *en grande tenue*, exerted himself immensely on the occasion. They were much surprised at my not smoking, and supposed me to be under a vow! They asked me many questions about our customs and Government,

---

[1] Afterwards in China, at a native hospital, I heard much more of the miraculous virtues of these drugs, and in Salangor, in the Malay Peninsula, I saw a most amusing scene after the death of a tiger. A number of the neighbouring Chinese flew upon the body, cut out the liver, eyes, and spleen, and carefully drained every drop of the blood, fighting with each other for the possession of things so precious, while those who were not so fortunate as to secure any of these cut out the cartilage from the joints. The centre of a tiger's eyeball is supposed to possess nearly miraculous virtues; the blood, dried at a temperature cf 110°, is the strongest of all tonics, and gives strength and courage; and the powdered liver and spleen are good for many diseases. Sultan Abdul Samat claimed the liver, but the other parts were all sold at high prices to the Chinese doctors. A little later, at Qualla Kangsa in Perak, I saw rhinoceros horns sold at a high price for the Chinese drug market, and Rajah Muda, who was anxious to claim the horns of the district, asserted that a single horn, with a particular mark on it, was worth fifty dollars for sale to the Chinese doctors.

but frequently reverted to tobacco. The use of it is absolutely universal. According to Mr. Satow it was not cultivated in Japan till 1605, and in 1612 and 1615 the Shôgun prohibited both the cultivation and use of it, but the craving for the "smoke-weed" was too strong for the edict, and in 1651 it was modified into a notification, forbidding people to smoke outside their houses. It was a long time before respectable women became smokers. Now the shops in the cities for the sale of pipes, pouches, and tobacco, are innumerable; any village which has shops at all is sure to have one for smoking apparatus; along the road-side there are stands for the same, and the *tabako-bon*, with its fire-pot and ash-pot, is a part of the furniture of even the poorest house. In some of the literature devoted to the subject it is called both "the poverty weed" and the "fool's herb," but these names are the invention of non-smokers. The pipe of a Japanese is often his sole companion. These men told me that all men "long for tobacco day and night without ceasing." A decoction of its leaves is used, as with us, for destroying insects on plants, bundles of the leaves are placed under the eaves to keep away vermin, dried leaves are laid in books to prevent the attacks of worms, and dried tobacco oil is a remedy in some forms of eye disease.[1]

[1] Mr. Satow has translated the following amusing notes on the merits and demerits of the weed, from a treatise upon it called the *Ensauki*.

1. It dispels the vapours and increases the energies.

2. It is good to produce at the beginning of a feast.

3. It is a companion in solitude.

4. It affords an excuse for resting now and then from work, as if in order to take breath.

5. It is a storehouse of reflection, and gives time for the fumes of wrath to disperse. But on the other hand — 1. There is a natural tendency to hit people over the head with one's pipe in a fit of anger. 2. The pipe comes sometimes to be used for arranging the burning charcoal in the *hibachi*. 3. An inveterate smoker has been known to walk about among the dishes at a feast with his pipe in his mouth. 4. People knock

There have been frequent and lively discussions in Japan on the use of tobacco, but the doctors have been on the whole in favour of smoking in moderation. An eminent writer, Kaibara, comparing it with tea and *saké*, condemns it altogether, saying, "Tobacco alone produces no benefit, but does more harm than anything else. It is not worth while to chide the common people for sucking it in, but for gentlemen and 'superior' men to follow after a custom imported from a barbarous country, and to take pleasure in and praise that which harms the body, are woful errors." [1]

In every agricultural place where I have had the opportunity of talking with intelligent people, I have

the ashes out of their pipes while still alight, and forget to extinguish the fire; hence clothing and mats are frequently scorched by burning tobacco ash. 6. Smokers spit indiscriminately in the *hibachi*, foot warmers, or kitchen fire, and also in the crevices between the *tatami* which cover the floor. 7. They rap the pipe violently on the edge of the fire-pot. 8. They forget to have the ash-pot emptied till it is full to overflowing.

[1] When I was in Tôkiyô I saw an amusing paper on Women's Rights translated from a native newspaper called the *Meiroku Zasshi*. The writer dreaded the increase of the power of women as one result of the introduction of European customs, and instanced the fact (less universal than formerly, alas!) that among Europeans men "are not permitted to smoke without the ladies' permission being first obtained." After giving an instance in point, in which he was the sufferer, he says, "The reason that men are thus prohibited from smoking is that the ladies do not like it. But if I smoke, I do so in virtue of my rights as a man, and if the ladies do not like it, they should leave the room. The dislike of (European) women to smoking subtracts from the pleasures of men, and there can surely be no reason in this, as it involves a limitation of the freedom of power. I find no reason for making distinctions between men and women in such a matter, and for smoking before the one and not smoking before the other. When it is not a thing prohibited by law or morals, and a distinction is made between smoking before men and women, I fail to see the reason of it. At present there is much discussion in this country as to the relations which should exist between men and women. It is well, therefore, that our learned men should take this into consideration, otherwise the power of the other sex will grow gradually, and eventually become so overwhelming that it will be impossible to control it."

tried to gain some knowledge of rural administration, and of the peasant view of the existing order of things; but no one who has not made the attempt can realise how difficult it is to get any information that will hang together, and it is impossible to get an expression of opinion which is worth anything, either from a natural incapacity for truth-telling, or from a lingering dread of espionage. These men were an exception to the general rule, and we managed to conduct a conversation which lasted till midnight with frequent relays of tea and sweetmeats.

The *Kôchô*, or responsible head-man of the village, is elected by a majority of the male inhabitants of a given district, but his appointment must be ratified by the Governor of the *ken*. The presents formerly made to him have been abolished, and he receives a fixed salary of 5 or 6 *yen* a month — little enough for the multifarious and ever-increasing duties which he has to perform. He has to put his seal to all the announcements, inquiries, and petitions which are sent to the *Kenrei* or Governor by the people of his village; to see that every one pays his Imperial taxes after the harvest; to keep the civil register of births, deaths, and marriages; to collect the provincial rates, to watch over the condition of roads, embankments, and bridges; and to give notice if the two last and ferries are in a dangerous condition.

Above him is the *Gunchô*, who is at the head of a circuit of from four to ten villages, called the *Kôri:* he receives 12 *yen* monthly, and has a handsome office, and assistants, and scribes. He superintends the *Kôchô* of his district, and settles the special expenses of each village for schools, repairs of roads, salaries, etc., and arranges monthly with the *Kôchô* the contribution of the district to the expenditure of the *ken*.

At the head of local officialdom stands the *Kenrei*, who is directly responsible to the Ministry of the Interior. In a large *ken*, such as Niigata, he has deputies who reside in the important towns, and he has a chief secretary, several advisers, and a large staff. His first duty is to maintain order by means of the police, but they are not under him but under the Police Department at Yedo. The *Kenrei* adjusts to some extent the imperial taxes, and assesses the provincial taxes, superintends roads, rivers, embankments, schools; meets, if possible, the increasing requirements of trade and commerce, by improving roads and assisting trading companies; and is magistrate in all matters relating to inheritance and adoption.

The present change in taxation from payments in rice to those in money, requires most skilful management. Land is the only subject on which the peasants are sensitive, and a very little irritation concerning it, or things naturally connected with it, is sufficient to make these usually harmless cultivators turn their " pruning hooks " into spears, and deal in vague threats of insurrection. Risings of this sort are quite common, and are as commonly put down by a few judicious words from the *Kenrei* or his deputy.

If, as is sometimes the case, the second son is to be made heir to the house and lands instead of the eldest son, or if the widow is to be made guardian of the children, or if the head of a family desires to adopt a child, the confirmation of the *Kenrei* is required. He seems to fill much the same position as the Prefect of a French Department.

I failed to extract much from the *Kôchô* as to the actual condition of the peasantry. He seemed to think that it was better formerly, but I cannot agree with him. Many hardships may and must be involved in the transition, and the peasant, accustomed to the tutelage, and, in some cases, almost the parental care of the old *régime*, is sure at first to feel keenly the drawbacks of an independent position, in which, in case of a bad harvest or other calamities, he has no feudal lord to fall back upon; but he is now, if he only knew it, in the most enviable of all positions, that of a peasant proprietor. He has the right to dispose of his land by will, to sell it, and to cultivate whatever crops he pleases, and is no longer bound to the soil as a serf, as he practically was under the old *régime;* and the innumerable prerogatives of the upper class, and the limitations of the liberty of his own, are done away with. At the present time each holding is being assessed, and title-deeds are being issued, vesting the right to the soil in the actual cultivator, but reserving all mineral rights to the Mikado, who is thus Lord of the Manor of all Japan. The chief weight of taxation does, however, fall on the peasant proprietors, even though last year the land tax was reduced to 2½ per cent on the value of the land, and the tax for local Government purposes, also chargeable on the land, was limited at its maximum to one-fifth of the land tax.

It remains to be seen whether these people are capable of retaining the singular advantages conferred upon them. Probably a more ignorant and superstitious peasantry does not exist on earth. The facilities for mortgaging land are many, and it may be that in this way small holdings will pass out of the hands of the present free-holders, and so a class of large landed proprietors, with a dependent population of labourers, may grow up, the security against this change lying in the intensely tenacious attachment to land which is a feature of the Japanese character.   I. L. B.

A FEARFUL DISEASE.

The Effect of a Chicken — Poor Fare — Slow Travelling — Stone
Ropes — Objects of Interest — *Kak'ké* — The Fatal Close — Predisposing Causes — A Great Fire — Security of the *Kuras*.

SHINGOJI, *July* 21.

VERY early in the morning, after my long talk with
the *Kôchô* of Kanayama, Ito wakened me by saying,
" You'll be able for a long day's journey to-day, as you
had a chicken yesterday," and under this chicken's
marvellous influence we got away at 6.45, only to verify
the proverb "the more haste the worse speed." Unso-
licited by me the *Kôchô* sent round the village to forbid the people from assembling, so I got away in peace
with a pack-horse and one runner. It was a terrible
road, with two severe mountain-passes to cross, and I
not only had to walk nearly the whole way, but to help
the man with the *kuruma* up some of the steepest places.
Halting at the exquisitely situated village of Nosoki, we
got one horse, and walked by a mountain road along
the head-waters of the Omono to Innai. I wish I could
convey to you any idea of the beauty and wildness of
that mountain route, of the surprises on the way, of
views, of the violent deluges of rain which turned rivu-
lets into torrents, and of the hardships and difficulties
of the day; the scanty fare of sun-dried rice dough and
sour yellow rasps, and the depth of the mire through
which we waded! We crossed the Shione and Sakatsu
passes, and in twelve hours accomplished fifteen miles!

Everywhere we were told that we should never get through the country by the way we are going.

The women still wear trousers, but with a long garment tucked into them instead of a short one, and the men wear a cotton combination of breastplate and apron, either without anything else, or over their *kimonos*. The descent to Innai under an avenue of cryptomeria, and the village itself, shut in with the rushing Omono, are very beautiful. Shrines and figures of Buddha and his disciples are very numerous in that region, and in many places there are immense upright stones without characters, with rude carvings of the sun and moon upon them. Among other ingenious devices there are an unusual number of the ropes or bolsters of stones, which have been used as embankments all the way from Nikkô. These consist of cylinders of variable length, and from 2 to 4 feet in diameter, made of split bamboo, woven in meshes small enough to prevent the escape of a 6 lb. stone. They are filled with waterworn boulders, and serviceable dams and embankments are formed by laying the cylinders one above another. Bad as the ravages of floods are, they are much mitigated by this simple arrangement.

The *yadoya* at Innai was a remarkably cheerful one, but my room was entirely *fusuma* and *shôji*, and people were peeping in the whole time. It is not only a foreigner and his strange ways which attract attention in these remote districts, but in my case, my india-rubber bath, air-pillow, and above all, my white mosquito net. Their nets are all of a heavy green canvas, and they admire mine so much, that I can give no more acceptable present on leaving than a piece of it to twist in with the hair. There were six engineers in the next room who are surveying the passes which I had crossed, in order to see if they could be tunnelled, in

which case *kurumas* might go all the way from Tôkiô
to Kubota on the Sea of Japan, and, with a small ⟶ ⟶
tional outlay, carts also.

In the two villages of Upper and Lower Innai there
has been an outbreak of malady much dreaded by
the Japanese, called *kak'ké*, which, in the last seven
months, has carried off 100 persons out of a population
of about 1500, and the local doctors have been aided
by two sent from the Medical School at Kubota. I
don't know a European name for it; the Japanese name
signifies an affection of the legs. Its first symptoms
are a loss of strength in the legs, "looseness in the
knees," cramps in the calves, swelling, and numbness.
This, Dr. Anderson, who has studied *kak'ké* in more
than 1100 cases in Tôkiyô, calls the sub-acute form.
The chronic is a slow, numbing, and wasting malady,
which, if unchecked, results in death from paralysis
and exhaustion, in from six months to three years.
The third, or acute form, Dr. Anderson describes thus.
After remarking that the grave symptoms set in quite
unexpectedly, and go on rapidly increasing, he says: —
" The patient now can lie down no longer, he sits up in
bed and tosses restlessly from one position to another,
and, with wrinkled brow, staring and anxious eyes,
dusky skin, blue, parted lips, dilated nostrils, throbbing
neck, and labouring chest, presents a picture of the most
terrible distress that the worst of diseases can inflict.
There is no intermission even for a moment, and the
physician, here almost powerless, can do little more than
note the failing pulse and falling temperature, and wait
for the moment when the brain, paralysed by the car-
bonised blood, shall become insensible, and allow the
dying man to pass his last moments in merciful uncon
sciousness.[1]

[1] *Kak'ké*, by William Anderson, F.R.C.S. Transactions of English
Asiatic Society of Japan, January 1878.

Having this paper on *kak'ké* with me, I was much interested in the account given me of the malady by one of the doctors from Kubota, with whom I rode for one stage. He said, that in the opinion of the native doctors (as well as in Dr. Anderson's), bad drainage, dampness, overcrowding, and want of ventilation, are the predisposing causes, and he added that he thought that its extreme frequency among soldiers and policemen arises from the wearing of foreign shoes, which are oftener wet than dry. Ito is so convinced of this that he never will put on his foreign boots when the roads are wet. It excites a most singular dread. It is considered to be the same disease as that which, under the name *Beri-beri*, makes such havoc at times in crowded jails and barracks in Ceylon and India. It has been unusually bad of late in Tôkiyô, and two hospitals have been opened, in one of which native treatment is to be tried, and in the other, foreign.

The next morning, after riding nine miles through a quagmire, under grand avenues of cryptomeria, and noticing with regret that the telegraph poles ceased, we reached Yusowa, a town of 7000 people, in which, had it not been for provoking delays, I should have slept instead of at Innai, and found that a fire a few hours previously had destroyed seventy houses, including the *yadoya* at which I should have lodged. We had to wait two hours for horses, as all were engaged in moving property and people. The ground where the houses had stood was absolutely bare of everything but fine black ash, among which the *kuras* stood blackened, and, in some instances, slightly cracked, but in all unharmed. Already skeletons of new houses were rising. No life had been lost except that of a tipsy man, but I should probably have lost everything but my money.

FUNERAL CEREMONIES.

Lunch in Public — A Grotesque Accident — Police Enquiries — Man or Woman? — A Melancholy Stare — A Vicious Horse — An Ill-favoured Town — A Disappointment — A *Torii*.

YUSOWA is a specially objectionable-looking place. I took my lunch, a wretched meal of a tasteless white curd made from beans, with some condensed milk added to it, in a yard, and the people crowded in hundreds to the gate, and those behind being unable to see me, got ladders and climbed on the adjacent roofs, where they remained till one of the roofs gave way with a loud crash, and precipitated about fifty men, women, and children into the room below, which fortunately was vacant. Nobody screamed — a noteworthy fact — and the casualties were only a few bruises. Four police-men then appeared and demanded my passport, as if I were responsible for the accident, and failing, like all others, to read a particular word upon it, they asked me what I was travelling for, and on being told "to learn about the country" they asked if I was making a map? Having satisfied their curiosity they disappeared, and the crowd surged up again in fuller force. The Transport Agent begged them to go away, but they said they might never see such a sight again! One old peasant said he would go away if he were told whether "the sight" were a man or a woman, and on the agent asking if that were any business of his, he said he should like to tell at home what he had seen, which awoke my sympathy at once, and I told Ito to tell them that a Japanese horse galloping night and day without ceasing, would take 5½ weeks to reach my country — a statement which he is using lavishly as I go along. These are such queer crowds, so silent and gaping, and they remain motionless for hours, the wideawake babies on the mothers' backs and in the fathers' arms never crying. I should be glad to hear a hearty aggregate laugh, even if I were its object. The great melancholy stare is depressing.

The road for ten miles was thronged with country people going in to see the fire. It was a good road and very pleasant country, with numerous roadside shrines and figures of the goddess of mercy. I had a wicked horse, thoroughly vicious. His head was doubly chained to the saddle girth, but he never met man, woman, or child, without laying back his ears and running at them to bite them. I was so tired and in so much spinal pain that I got off and walked several times, and it was most difficult to get on again, for as soon as I put my hand on the saddle he swung his hind legs round to kick me, and it required some agility to avoid being hurt. Nor was this all. The evil beast made dashes with his tethered head at flies, threatening to twist or demolish my foot at each, flung his hind legs upwards, attempted to dislodge flies on his nose with his hind hoof, executed capers which involved a total disappearance of everything in front of the saddle, squealed, stumbled, kicked his old shoes off, and resented the feeble attempts which the *mago* made to replace them, and finally walked in to Yokote and down its long and dismal street mainly on his hind legs, shaking the rope out of his timid leader's hand, and shaking me into a sort of aching jelly! I used to think that horses were made vicious either by being teased or by violence in breaking; but this does not account for the malignity of the Japanese horses, for the people are so much afraid of them that they treat them with great respect; they are not beaten or kicked, are spoken to in soothing tones, and on the whole live better than their masters. Perhaps this is the secret of their villany — " Jeshurun waxed fat and kicked."

Yokote, a town of 10,000 people, in which the best *yadoyas* are all non-respectable, is an ill-favoured, ill-smelling, forlorn, dirty, damp, miserable place, with a large trade in cottons. As I rode through on my temporary biped, the people rushed out from the baths to see me, men and women alike without a particle of clothing. The house-master was very polite, but I had a dark and dirty room, up a bamboo ladder, and it swarmed with fleas and mosquitoes to an exasperating extent. On the way I heard that a bullock was killed every Thursday in Yokote, and had decided on having a broiled steak for supper and taking another with me, but when I arrived it was all sold, there were no eggs, and I made a miserable meal of rice and bean curd, feeling somewhat starved, as the condensed milk I bought at Yamagata had to be thrown away. I was somewhat wretched from fatigue and inflamed ant bites, but in the early morning, hot and misty as all the mornings have been, I went to see a Shintô temple or *miya*, and though I went alone escaped a throng.

The entrance into the temple court was as usual by a *torii*, which consisted of two large posts 20 feet high, surmounted with cross beams, the upper one of which projects beyond the posts, and frequently curves upwards at both ends. The whole, as is often the case, was painted a dull red. This *torii* or " birds' rest " is said to be so called because the fowls, which were formerly offered but not sacrificed, were accustomed to perch upon it. A straw rope with straw tassels and strips of paper hanging from it, the special emblem of Shintô, hung across the gateway. In the paved court there were several handsome granite lanterns on fine granite pedestals, such as are the nearly universal accompaniments of both Shintô and Buddhist temples. In this part of Japan the lantern is usually pierced on one side with a crescent for the moon, and on the other with a disc for the sun, emblems which are said to refer

TORII.

to the Chinese notion of the male and female principles in nature. The temple itself was of the usual form, with a pack-saddle roof of bark thatch, and a flight of stone stairs leading to the entrance, but, unlike the Buddhist temples, there was a bar across, and the temple was as empty as the creed, for it contained nothing but a polished steel mirror, and even this, Mr. Satow says in one of his learned papers on Shintô, is kept in a box except where the temple has been at some time contaminated by Buddhism. Behind this there was a concealed shrine with a table in front of it, with two little bowls, one containing rice and the other *saké*, and a sprig of evergreen upon it. A pure Shintô temple is always built outside and inside of planed wood, and is roofed with thatch after the model of the shrines of Isé, the cradle of the creed.

As I stood at the entrance several people came up and pulled a much-frayed bell-rope which was hanging in the doorway, and clattered a most inharmonious bell. Then they clapped their hands and muttered a few words, made three genuflections, clapped their hands again, and departed, the whole performance taking about $1\frac{1}{2}$ minute. The ringing the bell and clapping the hands are to attract the attention of the god. Regular attendance on services is not enjoined, the intervention of a priest is seldom necessary, and priestcraft has hardly a place in Shintô. which, unlike Buddhism, concerns itself little with a future state of being. A number of red *torii* about a foot high, *ex votos*, were lying against the temple court wall. The village shrines and those in the groves are about five feet high and usually contain nothing.

After leaving Yakote we passed through very pretty country with mountain views and occasional glimpses of the snowy dome of Chokaizan, crossed the Omono (which has burst its banks and destroyed its bridges) by two troublesome ferries, and arrived at Rokugo, a town of 5000 people with fine temples, exceptionally mean houses, and the most aggressive crowd by which I have yet been asphyxiated.

There, through the good offices of the police, I was enabled to attend a Buddhist funeral of a merchant of some wealth. It interested me very much from its solemnity and decorum, and Ito's explanations of what went before were remarkably distinctly given. I went in a Japanese woman's dress, borrowed at the tea-house, with a blue hood over my head, and thus escaped all notice, but I found the restraint of the scanty "tied forward" *kimono* very tiresome. Ito gave me many injunctions as to what I was to do and avoid, which I carried out faithfully, being nervously anxious to avoid jarring on the sensibilities of those who had kindly permitted a foreigner to be present.

The illness was a short one, and there had been no time either for prayers or pilgrimages on the sick man's behalf. When death occurs the body is laid with its head to the north (a position that the living Japanese scrupulously avoid), near a folding screen, between which and it a new *zen* is placed, on which are a saucer of oil with a lighted rush, cakes of uncooked rice dough, and a saucer of incense sticks. The priests directly after death choose the *kaimiyô* or posthumous name, write it on a tablet of white wood, and seat themselves by the corpse; his *zen*, bowls, cups, etc., are filled with vegetable food, and are placed by his side, the chopsticks being put on the wrong, *i.e.* the left side of the *zen*. At the end of forty-eight hours the corpse is arranged for the coffin by being washed with warm water, and the priest, while saying certain prayers, shaves the head. In all cases, rich or poor, the dress is of the usual make, but of pure white linen or cotton.

At Omagori, a town near Rokugo, large earthenware jars are manufactured, which are much used for interment by the wealthy, but in this case there were two square boxes, the outer one being of finely planed wood of the *Retinospora obtusa*. The poor use what is called the "quick-tub," a covered tub of pine hooped with bamboo. Women are dressed for burial in the

silk robe worn on the marriage day, *tabi* are placed
beside them or on their feet, and their hair usually
flows loosely behind them. The wealthiest people fill
the coffin with vermilion, and the poorest use chaff, but
in this case I heard that only the mouth, nose, and ears
were filled with vermilion, and that the coffin was
filled up with coarse incense. The body is placed
within the tub or box in the usual squatting position.
It is impossible to understand how a human body,
many hours after death, can be pressed into the limited space afforded by even the outermost of the boxes.
It has been said that the rigidity of a corpse is over-
come by the use of a powder called *dosia*, which is sold
by the priests, but this idea has been exploded, and the
process remains incomprehensible.

Bannerets of small size and ornamental staves were
outside the house door. Two men in blue dresses,
with pale blue over-garments resembling wings, received each person, two more presented a lacquered
bowl of water and a white silk *crêpe* towel, and then
we passed into a large room round which were arranged a number of very handsome folding screens,
on which lotuses, storks, and peonies were realistically
painted, on a dead gold ground. Near the end of the
room the coffin, under a canopy of white silk, upon
which there was a very beautiful arrangement of artificial white lotuses [1] rested upon trestles, the face of the

---

[1] The only reason I can ascertain for the constant recurrence of the
lotus in Buddhist art and ceremonial is the idea of its being the symbol
of purity. Its scent and aspect are alike delightful, and though rooted
in mud and slime it abhors all defilement. If, therefore, men would
but take it as their model, they would escape all the contamination of
this corrupt world. Every man, it is said, has a lotus in his bosom,
which will blossom forth if he call in the assistance of Buddha. It is
on account of the generally high esteem in which the lotus is held that
it is carried before the corpse at funerals, symbolising as it does the
desire of the survivors for the new birth of their departed friend into
Paradise and the " Lotus-Seat "

corpse being turned towards the north. Six priests, very magnificently dressed, sat on each side of the coffin, and two more knelt in front of a small temporary altar.

The widow, an extremely pretty woman, squatted near the deceased, below the father and mother; and after her came the children, relatives, and friends, who sat in rows, dressed in winged garments of blue and white. The widow was painted white; her lips were reddened with vermilion; her hair was elaborately dressed and ornamented with carved shell pins; she wore a beautiful dress of sky blue silk, with a *haori* of fine white *crêpe* and a scarlet *crêpe* girdle embroidered in gold, and looked like a bride on her marriage day, rather than a widow. Indeed, owing to the beauty of the dresses, and the amount of blue and white silk, the room had a festal rather than a funereal look. When all the guests had arrived, tea and sweetmeats were passed round; incense was burned profusely; litanies were mumbled, and the bustle of moving to the grave began, during which I secured a place near the gate of the temple grounds.

The procession did not contain the father or mother of the deceased, but I understood that the mourners who composed it were all relatives. The oblong tablet with the "dead name" of the deceased was carried first by a priest, then the lotus blossom by another priest, then ten priests followed two and two, chanting litanies from books, then came the coffin on a platform borne by four men, and covered with white drapery, then the widow, and then the other relatives. The coffin was carried into the temple and laid upon trestles, while incense was burned and prayers were said, and was then carried to a shallow grave lined with cement, and prayers were said by the priests until the

earth was raised to the proper level, when all dispersed.
and the widow, in her gay attire, walked home unat-
tended. There were no hired mourners or any signs
of grief, but nothing could be more solemn, reverent,
and decorous, than the whole service. [I have since
seen many funerals, chiefly of the poor, and though
shorn of much of the ceremony, and with only one
officiating priest, the decorum was always most remarkable.] The fees to the priests are from 2 up to 40 or
50 *yen*. The graveyard which surrounds the temple
was extremely beautiful, and the cryptomeria specially
fine. It was very full of stone gravestones, and like
all Japanese cemeteries, exquisitely kept. As soon as
the grave was filled in, a life-size pink lotus plant
was placed upon it, and a lacquer tray, on which were
lacquer bowls containing tea or *saké*, beans, and sweetmeats.

The periods of mourning are very rigidly observed.
Mr. Mitford, in a note to *The Tales of Old Japan*, trans-
lates some funeral directions given in a book called the
Shorei Hikki, in which it is said, " The burial of his
parents is the most important ceremony which a man
has to go through in his whole life," [1] consequently
after it has been performed with befitting ceremony,
deep mourning for either father or mother lasts fifty
days, during which time the children must abstain
from *saké*, and visit the grave and the temple of the
burial-service daily, but no other *tera* or *miya*. For
husbands, wives, brothers, sisters, and first-born chil-

[1] The same book gives the following cautions to mourners, the two
last of which are not altogether inapplicable at home. "When invited
to a friend's or neighbour's funeral a man should avoid putting on smart
clothes or dresses of ceremony, and when he follows the coffin he
should not speak in a loud voice to the person next him, for that would
be very rude, and even should he have occasion to do so, he should
avoid entering wine-shops and tea-houses on his return from the
funeral."

dren, the deep mourning only lasts twenty days, another instance of the preponderating importance given to the filial relation. For parents the second period of mourning lasts a year, and for the relatives before mentioned ninety days, and non-observance of the period of mourning for parents or husband is vis- ited by penal servitude for one year.

Friends must visit the grave on the seventh day, and every seventh day thereafter until the fiftieth day, when the priests recite prayers, and the mourners inter- change presents. A ceremonial visit is paid to the tomb on the hundredth day, when the tombstone is erected. It is next visited on the anniversary of the death, and afterwards on the third, seventh, thirteenth, seventeenth, fiftieth, and hundredth anniversaries. A tablet with the posthumous name takes its place on the god-shelf of a house after a death, and a similar one is placed on a shelf in the temple, and offerings of food are placed before it according to the liberality of the survivors to the priests.

Laths, or long tablets, inscribed with characters in Chinese or Sanskrit, are placed upon the graves by re- lations at their periodical visits. Each family has its separate enclosure in the graveyard. I have never visited a cemetery without finding fresh flowers in bam- boo flower-holders on many of the graves, and women burning incense before the tombstones. All this rever- ence for the dead is, however, quite distinct from the ancestral worship of the Chinese. The etiquette of burial and mourning is regulated by very strict rules. The funeral ceremonies vary according to the usage of the many Buddhist sects, but are always in the hands of Buddhist priests, by a prescriptive right from which even Christian obsequies are only exempted, as they have been in some recent instances, by the courtesy of the priests.

The temple at Rokugo was very beautiful, and, except that its ornaments were superior in solidity and good taste, differed little from a Romish church. The low altar, on which were lilies and lighted candles, was draped in blue and silver, and on the high altar, draped in crimson and cloth of gold, there was nothing but a closed shrine, an incense burner, and a vase of lotuses.

POLICEMEN.

A Casual Invitation — A Ludicrous Incident — Politeness of a Policeman — A Comfortless Sunday — An Outrageous Irruption — A
Privileged Stare.

AT a wayside tea-house, soon after leaving Rokugo
in *kurumas*, I met the same courteous and agreeable
young doctor, who was stationed at Innai during the
prevalence of *kak'ke*, and he invited me to visit the
hospital at Kubota, of which he is junior physician, and
told Ito of a restaurant at which "foreign food" can be
obtained — a pleasant prospect, of which he is always
reminding me.

Travelling along a very narrow road, I as usual first,
we met a man leading a prisoner by a rope, followed by
a policeman. As soon as my runner saw the latter, he
fell down on his face so suddenly in the shafts, as nearly
to throw me out, at the same time, trying to wriggle
into a garment which he had carried on the crossbar,
while the young men who were drawing the two *kurumas* behind, crouching behind my vehicle, tried to scuttle into their clothes. I never saw such a picture of
abjectness as my man presented. He trembled from
head to foot, and illustrated that queer phrase often
heard in Scotch Presbyterian prayers, "lay our hands
on our mouths and our mouths in the dust." He literally grovelled in the dust, and with every sentence that
the policeman spoke, raised his head a little, to bow it
yet more deeply than before. It was all because he

had no clothes on. I interceded for him as the day was very hot, and the policeman said he would not arrest him, as he should otherwise have done, because of the inconvenience that it would cause to a foreigner. He was quite an elderly man, and never recovered his spirits, but as soon as a turn of the road took us out of the policeman's sight, the two younger men threw their clothes into the air, and gambolled in the shafts, shrieking with laughter!

On reaching Shingoji, being too tired to go farther, I was dismayed to find nothing but a low, dark, foul-smelling room, enclosed only by dirty *shôji*, in which to spend Sunday. One side looked into a little mildewed court, with a slimy growth of *Protococcus viridis*, and into which the people of another house constantly came to stare. The other side opened on the earthen passage into the street, where travellers wash their feet, the third into the kitchen, and the fourth into the front room. Even before dark it was alive with mosquitoes, and the fleas hopped on the mats like sand-flies. There were no eggs, nothing but rice and cucumbers. At five on Sunday morning I saw three faces pressed against the outer lattice, and before evening, the *shôji* were riddled with finger-holes, at each of which a dark eye appeared. There was a still, fine rain all day, with the mercury at 82°, and the heat, darkness, and smells, were difficult to endure. In the afternoon a small procession passed the house, consisting of a decorated palanquin, carried and followed by priests, with capes and stoles over crimson chasubles and white cassocks. This ark, they said, contained papers inscribed with the names of people and the evils they feared, and the priests were carrying the papers to throw them into the river.

I went to bed early as a refuge from mosquitoes, with

the *andon*, as usual, dimly lighting the room, and shut my eyes. About nine I heard a good deal of whispering and shuffling, which continued for some time, and on looking up, saw opposite to me, about 40 men, women, and children (Ito says 100), all staring at me, with the light upon their faces. They had silently removed three of the *shôji* next the passage! I called Ito loudly, and clapped my hands, but they did not stir till he came, and then they fled like a flock of sheep. I have patiently, and even smilingly, borne all out-of-doors crowding and curiosity, but this kind of intrusion is unbearable; and I sent Ito to the police station, much against his will, to beg the police to keep the people out of the house, as the house-master was unable to do so. This morning, as I was finishing dressing, a policeman appeared in my room, ostensibly to apologise for the behaviour of the people, but in reality to have a privileged stare at me, and above all, at my stretcher and mosquito net, from which he hardly took his eyes. Ito says he could make a *yen* a day by showing them! The policeman said that the people had never seen a foreigner.   I. L. B.

A HOSPITAL VISIT.

The Necessity of Firmness — Perplexing Misrepresentations — Gliding with the Stream — Suburban Residences — The Kubota Hospital — A Formal Reception — Bad Nursing — The Antiseptic
Treatment — A Well-arranged Dispensary — The Normal School
— Contrasts and Incongruities.

KUBOTA, *July* 23.

I ARRIVED here on Monday afternoon by the river
Omono, what would have been two long days' journey
by land having been easily accomplished in nine hours
by water. This was an instance of forming a plan
wisely, and adhering to it resolutely! Firmness in
travelling is nowhere more necessary than in Japan. I
decided some time ago, from Mr. Brunton's map, that
the Omono must be navigable from Shingoji, and a
week ago told Ito to inquire about it, but at each place
difficulties have been started. There was too much
water, there was too little; there were bad rapids, there
were shallows; it was too late in the year; all the boats
which had started lately were lying aground; but at
one of the ferries I saw in the distance a merchandise
boat going down, and told Ito I should go that way and
nc other. On arriving at Shingoji they said it was not
on the Omono at all, but on a stream with some very
bad rapids, in which boats are broken to pieces. Lastly,
they said there was no boat, but on my saying that I
would send ten miles for one, a small, flat-bottomed
scow was produced by the Transport Agent, into which
Ito, the luggage, and myself accurately fitted. Ito sen-

tentiously observed, "Not one thing has been told us on our journey which has turned out true!" This is not an exaggeration. The usual crowd did not assemble round the door, but preceded me to the river, where it covered the banks and clustered in the trees. Four policemen escorted me down. The voyage of forty-two miles was delightful. The rapids were a mere ripple, the current was strong, one boatman almost slept upon his paddle, the other only woke to bale the boat when it was half-full of water, the shores were silent and pretty, and almost without population, till we reached the large town of Araya, which straggles along a high bank for a considerable distance, and after nine peaceful hours we turned off from the main stream of the Omono just at the outskirts of Kubota, and poled up a narrow, green river, fringed by dilapidated backs of houses, boat-building yards, and rafts of timber on one side, and dwelling-houses, gardens, and damp greenery on the other. This stream is crossed by very numerous bridges.

I got a cheerful upstairs room at a most friendly *yadoya*, and my three days here have been fully occupied and very pleasant. "Foreign food" — a good beefsteak, an excellent curry, cucumbers, and foreign salt and mustard were at once obtained, and I felt my "eyes lightened" after partaking of them.

Kubota is a very attractive and purely Japanese town of 36,000 people, the capital of Akita *ken*. A fine mountain, called Taiheisan, rises above its fertile valley, and the Omono falls into the Sea of Japan close to it. It has a number of *kurumas*, but owing to heavy sand and the badness of the roads they can only go three miles in any direction. It is a town of activity and brisk trade, and manufactures a silk fabric in stripes of blue and black, and yellow and black, much used for making *hakama* and *kimonos*, a species of white silk *crêpe* with a raised woof, which brings a high price in Tôkiyô shops, *fusuma*, and clogs. Though it is a castle town, it is free from the usual "deadly lively" look, and has an air of prosperity and comfort. Though it has few streets of shops, it covers a great extent of ground with streets and lanes of pretty, isolated dwelling-houses, surrounded by trees, gardens, and well-trimmed hedges, each garden entered by a substantial gateway. The existence of something like a middle class with home privacy and home life is suggested by these miles of comfortable "suburban residences." Foreign influence is hardly at all felt, there is not a single foreigner in Government or any other employment, and even the hospital was organised from the beginning by Japanese doctors.

This fact made me greatly desire to see it, but on going there at the proper hour for visitors, I was met by the Director with courteous but vexatious denial. No foreigner could see it, he said, without sending his passport to the Governor and getting a written order, so I complied with these preliminaries, and 8 A.M. of the next day was fixed for my visit. Ito, who is lazy about interpreting for the lower orders, but exerts himself to the utmost on such an occasion as this, went with me, handsomely clothed in silk, as befitted an "Interpreter," and surpassed all his former efforts.

The Director and the staff of six physicians, all handsomely dressed in silk, met me at the top of the stairs, and conducted me to the management room, where six clerks were writing. Here there was a table solemnly covered with a white cloth, and four chairs, on which the Director, the Chief Physician, Ito, and I sat, and pipes, tea, and sweetmeats were produced. After this, accompanied by fifty medical students, whose intelligent

looks promise well for their success, we went round the
hospital, which is a large two-storied building in semi-
European style, but with deep verandahs all round.
The upper floor is used for class-rooms, and the lower
accommodates 100 patients, besides a number of resident students. Ten is the largest number treated in
any one room, and severe cases are treated in separate
rooms. Gangrene has prevailed, and the Chief Physician, who is at this time remodelling the hospital, has
closed some of the wards in consequence. There is a
Lock Hospital under the same roof. About fifty important operations are annually performed under chloroform, but the people of Akita *ken* are very conservative,
and object to part with their limbs and to foreign drugs.
This conservatism diminishes the number of patients.

Dr. Kayobashi, the new Chief Physician, is fresh
from the Medical College at Tôkiyô, and has introduced
the antiseptic treatment with great success. Beds are
not used. He approves of them, but finds it necessary
at present to yield to the strong prejudice against them.
The nursing here, as everywhere, is a weak point, to
say the least of it. There are a few male and female
nurses, but the patients usually bring friends with them,
who take charge of them, and do not carry out medical
instructions in doing so. The kitchen was not as nice
as it should be, and smelt of the *daikon* and fried fish
which the cooks were eating, and the *irori* looked very
small for much cooking; but this is accounted for by
the fact that the friends cook on the *hibachi* in the
wards. The diet is liberal, but on the whole strictly
Japanese. Meat is given in a few cases, and brandy,
port wine, and claret in many, but the wine and brandy
are always beaten up with eggs. Advice and medicine
are supplied daily to about eighty out-patients.

I was interested here, as elsewhere, to find that the

Government, in establishing hospitals on the foreign plan, is conserving the independence of the people, so that they can hardly be called charitable institutions. The out-patients pay for medicines, and the in-patients pay so much per day, and only absolutely destitute persons are received gratuitously on getting an order from the Governor.

I was better pleased with the dispensary than with the in-patient department. Its arrangements are admirable, and the lofty, light, and airy rooms leave nothing to be desired. There were sixty patients in the waiting-room, a fine room, thirty-five feet square, furnished with benches. Their names are called in alphabetical order, and on the decision of one of the junior physicians each proceeds into one of three light and conveniently fitted-up consulting rooms, devoted respectively to medical, surgical, and eye cases. Each receives a prescription which is entered in a book, and numbered with a number which corresponds with a similar one on the patient's bottle. After being prescribed for the patients pass into a large waiting-room with a counter at an opening into the dispensing room, where in due time they receive their medicines. The dispensing room is a fine room, very carefully fitted up in the most approved style, the drugs being arranged on shelves and neatly labelled with the Latin and Japanese names. A senior dispenser and four student assistants were at work there.

The odour of carbolic acid pervaded the whole hospital, and there were spray producers enough to satisfy Mr. Lister! At the request of Dr. K. I saw the dressing of some very severe wounds carefully performed with carbolised gauze, under spray of carbolic acid, the fingers of the surgeon and the instruments used being all carefully bathed in the disinfectant. Dr. K. said it was difficult to teach the students the extreme careful ness with regard to minor details which is required in the antiseptic treatment, which he regards as one of the greatest discoveries of this century. I was very much impressed with the fortitude shown by the surgical patients, who went through very severe pain without a wince or a moan. Eye cases are unfortunately very numerous. Dr. K. attributes their extreme prevalence to overcrowding, defective ventilation, poor living, and bad light.

The hospital is also a medical school with 100 students, and its diploma entitles the receiver to practise medicine in Akita *ken.* The large class-rooms are well fitted up with German and English diagrams, but the museum is scantily supplied with anatomical preparations, and the skeleton is of a low-type savage from Micronesia. It has been impossible to get a Japanese skeleton, and the only cases in which subjects for dis section can be procured are those in which the friends of patients are exceptionally grateful, and the cause of death has not been discovered during life. After our round we returned to the management room to find a meal laid out in English style, coffee in cups with handles and saucers, and plates with spoons. After this pipes were again produced, and the Director and medical staff escorted me to the entrance, where we all bowed profoundly. I was delighted to see that Dr. Kayabashi, a man under thirty, and fresh from Tôkiyô, and all the staff and students were in the national dress, with the *hakama* of rich silk. It is a beautiful dress, and assists dignity as much as the ill-fitting European costume detracts from it. This was a very interesting visit, in spite of the difficulty of communication through an interpreter.

The public buildings, with their fine gardens, and the

broad road near which they stand, with its stone-faced embankments, are very striking in such a far-off *ken*. Among the finest of the buildings is the Normal School, where I shortly afterwards presented myself, but I was not admitted till I had shown my passport and explained my objects in travelling. These preliminaries being settled, Mr. Tomatsu Aoki, the Chief Director, and Mr. Shude Kane Nigishi, the principal teacher, both looking more like monkeys than men in their European clothes, lionised me.

The first was most trying, for he persisted in attempting to speak English, of which he knows about as much as I know of Japanese, but the last, after some grotesque attempts, accepted Ito's services. The school is a commodious Europeanised building, three storeys high, and from its upper balcony the view of the city, with its grey roofs and abundant greenery, and surrounding mountains and valleys, is very fine. The equipments of the different class-rooms surprised me, especially the laboratory of the chemical class-room, and the truly magnificent illustrative apparatus in the natural science class-room. Ganot's "Physics" is the text book of that department.

There are 25 teachers, and 700 pupils between the ages of 6 and 20. They teach reading, writing, arithmetic, geography, history, political economy after John Stuart Mill, chemistry, botany, a course of natural science, geometry, and mensuration. From 6 to 14 the fees are 15 *sen* per month, after that 25, and the extra expense is defrayed by an education rate. The pupils sit on forms with backs at separate desks, the school furniture being on the American model. The two examination-rooms are fifty feet square. The whole is in admirable order. The Director said that the ambitious boys all intend to be doctors, advocates, or engineers, and that the education given in this school is an admirable preparation for the special schools connected with these professions.

I have written that foreign influence is hardly felt in Kubota, I mean the influence of direct contact with foreigners; but both the school and hospital are pervaded by foreign science and system. Before leaving, knowing what the reply would be, I asked the teacher if they taught religion, and both the gentlemen laughed with undisguised contempt. " We have no religion," the teacher said, " and all your learned men know that religion is false."

An Imperial throne founded on an exploded religious fiction, a State religion receiving an outward homage from those who ridicule it, scepticism rampant among the educated classes, and an ignorant priesthood lording it over the lower classes; an Empire with a splendid despotism for its apex, and naked coolies for its base, a bald materialism its highest creed and material good its goal, reforming, destroying, constructing, appropriating the fruits of Christian civilisation, but rejecting the tree from which they spring — such are among the contrasts and incongruities everywhere!

I. L. B.

THE POLICE FORCE.

A Silk Factory — Employment for Women — A Police Escort — The
Japanese Police Force — A Ruined Castle — The increasing Study
of Law.

KUBOTA, *July* 23.

MY next visit was to a factory of handloom silk-
weavers, where 180 hands, half of them women, are
employed. These new industrial openings for respectable employment for women and girls are very important, and tend in the direction of a much-needed social
reform. The striped silk fabrics produced are entirely
for home consumption.

Afterwards I went into the principal street, and after
a long search through the shops, bought some condensed
milk with the " Eagle " brand and the label all right,
but on opening it found it to contain small pellets of a
brownish, dried curd, with an unpleasant taste ! As I
was sitting in the shop half stifled by the crowd, the
people suddenly fell back to a respectful distance, leaving me breathing space, and a message came from the
chief of police to say that he was very sorry for the
crowding, and had ordered two policemen to attend
upon me for the remainder of my visit. The black and
yellow uniforms were most truly welcome, and since
then I have escaped all annoyance. On my return I
found the card of the chief of police, who had left a
message with the house-master apologising for the crowd
by saying that foreigners very rarely visited Kubota.

and he thought that the people had never seen a foreign woman.

I went afterwards to the central police station to inquire about an inland route to Aomori, and received much courtesy, but no information. The police everywhere are very gentle to the people, — a few quiet words or a wave of the hand are sufficient, when they do not resist them. They belong to the *samurai* class, and doubtless their naturally superior position weighs with the *heimin*. Their faces and a certain *hauteur* of manner show the indelible class distinction. The entire police force of Japan numbers 23,300 educated men in the prime of life, and if 30 per cent of them do wear spectacles, it does not detract from their usefulness. 5600 of them are stationed at Yedo, as from thence they can be easily sent wherever they are wanted, 1004 at Kiyôto, and 815 at Osaka, and the remaining 10,000 are spread over the country. The police force costs something over £400,000 annually, and certainly is very efficient in preserving good order. The pay of ordinary constables ranges from 6 to 10 *yen* a month. An enormous quantity of superfluous writing is done by all officialdom in Japan, and one usually sees policemen writing. What comes of it I don't know. They are mostly intelligent and gentlemanly-looking young men, and foreigners in the interior are really much indebted to them. If I am at any time in difficulties I apply to them, and though they are disposed to be somewhat *de haut en bas* they are sure to help one, except about routes, of which they always profess ignorance.

Kubota has a grand enclosure for the *daimiyô's* castle, three embankments, and three moats on elevated ground, and some clumps of fine timber; but all the castle that has not been removed is ruinous — ruin without picturesqueness, that ramshackle sort of ruin into which neglected wooden buildings fall. The remains are a gateway with an overhanging tiled roof, and a dilapidated group of lath and plaster houses within, only a storey high.

At Kubota, as in the other capitals of *kens*, there is a provincial court which has full jurisdiction in civil and criminal cases, but its capital sentences must be confirmed by a higher court. Judge Deputies, with full jurisdiction in civil, and partial jurisdiction in criminal cases, sit in the chief towns of districts remote from the provincial courts, and there are minor courts for petty matters in all the larger towns. With the changes in the judicial system of Japan, a crop of advocates is springing up; now that I have learned their sign, I am astonished at their numbers, and there are so many in Kubota that one would suppose it a most litigious place. Law is becoming a favourite occupation with the *samurai*, who are usually skilful in the use of the pen, and as advocates' licenses cost £2 yearly, I think the occupation must be a lucrative one. On the whole, I like Kubota better than any other Japanese town, perhaps because it is so completely Japanese and has no air of having seen better days. I no longer care to meet Europeans, indeed I should go far out of my way to avoid them. I have become quite used to Japanese life, and think that I learn more about it in travelling in this solitary way than I should otherwise. I. L. B.

ITO'S VIRTUES AND FAULTS.

"A Plague of Immoderate Rain" — A Confidential Servant — Ito's Diary — Ito's Excellences — Ito's Faults — A Prophecy of the Future of Japan — Curious Queries — Superfine English — Economical Travelling — The Japanese Pack-horse again.

KUBOTA, *July* 24.

I AM here still, not altogether because the town is fascinating, but because the rain is so ceaseless as to be truly "a plague of immoderate rain and waters." Travellers keep coming in with stories of the impassability of the roads and the carrying away of bridges. Ito amuses me very much by his remarks. He thinks that my visit to the school and hospital must have raised Japan in my estimation, and he is talking rather big. He asked me if I noticed that all the students kept their mouths shut like educated men and residents of Tôkiyô, and that all country people keep theirs open. I have said little about him for some time, but I daily feel more dependent on him, not only for all information, but actually for getting on. At night he has my watch, passport, and half my money, and I often wonder what would become of me if he absconded before morning. He is not a good boy. He has no moral sense, according to our notions; he dislikes foreigners; his manner is often very disagreeable; and yet I doubt whether I could have obtained a more valuable servant and interpreter. When we left Tôkiyô, he spoke fairly good English, but by practice and industrious study, he now speaks better than any official interpreter that I have seen, and his vocabulary is daily increasing. He never uses a word inaccurately when he has once got hold of its meaning, and his memory never fails. He keeps a diary both in English and Japanese, and it shows much painstaking observation. He reads it to me sometimes, and it is interesting to hear what a young man who has travelled as much as he has regards as novel in this northern region. He has made a hotel book and a transport book, in which all the bills and receipts are written, and he daily transliterates the names of all places into English letters, and puts down the distances and the sums paid for transport and hotels on each bill.

He inquires the number of houses in each place from the police or Transport Agent, and · the special trade of each town, and notes them down for me. He takes great pains to be accurate, and occasionally remarks about some piece of information that he is not quite certain about, "If it's not true, it's not worth having." He is never late, never dawdles, never goes out in the evening except on errands for me, never touches *saké*, is never disobedient, never requires to be told the same thing twice, is always within hearing, has a good deal of tact as to what he repeats, and all with an undisguised view to his own interest. He sends most of his wages to his mother, who is a widow — "It's the custom of the country" — and seems to spend the remainder on sweetmeats, tobacco, and the luxury of frequent shampooing.

That he would tell a lie if it served his purpose, and would "squeeze" up to the limits of extortion, if he could do it unobserved, I have not the slightest doubt. He seems to have but little heart, or any idea of any but vicious pleasures. He has no religion of any kind; he has been too much with foreigners for that. His frankness is something startling. He has no idea of reticence on any subject; but probably I learn more about things as they really are, from this very, defect. In virtue in man or woman, except in that of his former master, he has little, if any belief. He thinks that Japan is right in availing herself of the discoveries made by foreigners, that they have as much to learn from her, and that she will outstrip them in the race, because she takes all that is worth having, and rejects the incubus of Christianity. Patriotism is, I think, his strongest feeling, and I never met with such a boastful display of it, except in a Scotchman or an American. He despises the uneducated, as he can read and write both the syllabaries. For foreign rank or position he has not an atom of reverence or value, but a great deal of both for Japanese officialdom. He despises the intellects of women, but flirts in a town-bred fashion with the simple tea-house girls.

He is anxious to speak the very best English, and to say that a word is slangy or common, interdicts its use. Sometimes, when the weather is fine, and things go smoothly, he is in an excellent and communicative humour, and talks a good deal as we travel. A few days ago, I remarked, "What a beautiful day this is!" and soon after, notebook in hand, he said, "You say 'a beautiful day.' Is that better English than 'a devilish fine day,' which most foreigners say?" I replied that it was "common," and "beautiful" has been brought out frequently since. Again, "When you ask a question, you never say, 'What the d—l is it?' as other foreigners do. Is it proper for men to say it and not for women?" I told him it was proper for neither, it was a very "common" word, and I saw that he erased it from his notebook. At first he always used *fellows* for men, as, "Will you have one or two *fellows* for your

kuruma?" "*fellows* and women." At last he called
the Chief Physician of the hospital here a *fellow*, on
which I told him that it was slightly slangy, and at
least "colloquial," and for two days he has scrupulously spoken of man and men. To-day he brought a
boy with very sore eyes to see me, on which I exclaimed,
"Poor little fellow!" and this evening he said, "You
called that boy a fellow, I thought it was a bad word!"
The habits of many of the Yokohama foreigners have
helped to obliterate any distinctions between right and
wrong, if he ever made any. If he wishes to tell me
that he has seen a very tipsy man, he always says he
has seen "a fellow as drunk as an Englishman." At
Nikkô I asked him how many legal wives a man could
have in Japan, and he replied, "Only one lawful one,
but as many others (*mekaké*) as he can support, just as
Englishmen have." He never forgets a correction.
Till I told him it was slangy, he always spoke of inebri-
ated people as "tight," and when I gave him the words
"tipsy," "drunk," "intoxicated," he asked me which
one would use in writing good English, and since then
he has always spoken of people as "intoxicated."

He naturally likes large towns, and tries to deter me
from taking the "unbeaten tracks" which I prefer; but
when he finds me immovable, always concludes his
arguments with the same formula, "Well, of course you
can do as you like, it's all the same to me." I do not
think he cheats me to any extent. Board, lodging, and
travelling expenses for us both are about 6s. 6d. a day,
and about 2s. 6d. when we are stationary, and this includes all gratuities and extras. True, the board and
lodging consist of tea, rice, and eggs, a copper basin of
water, an *andon* and an empty room, for though there
are plenty of chickens in all the villages, the people
won't be bribed to sell them for killing, though they

would gladly part with them if they were to be kept to lay eggs. Ito amuses me nearly every night with stories of his unsuccessful attempts to provide me with animal food.

The travelling is the nearest approach to " a ride on a rail " that I have ever made. I have now ridden or rather sat upon seventy-six horses, all horrible. They all stumble. The loins of some are higher than their shoulders, so that one slips forwards, and the back bones of all are ridgy. Their hind feet grow into points which turn up, and their hind legs all turn outwards, like those of a cat, from carrying heavy burdens at an early age. The same thing gives them a roll in their gait, which is increased by their awkward shoes. In summer they feed chiefly on leaves, supplemented with mashes of bruised beans, and instead of straw they sleep on beds of leaves. In their stalls their heads are tied " where their tails should be," and their fodder is placed not in a manger, but in a swinging bucket. Those used in this part of Japan are worth from 15 to 30 *yen*. I have not seen any overloading or ill-treatment; they are neither kicked, nor beaten, nor threatened in rough tones, and when they die they are decently buried, and have stones placed over their graves. It might be well if the end of a worn-out horse were somewhat accelerated, but this is mainly a Buddhist region, and the aversion to taking animal life is very strong.   I. L. B.

A WEDDING CEREMONY.

The Symbolism of Seaweed — Afternoon Visitors — An Infant Prodigy — A Feat in Calligraphy — Child Worship — The Japanese Seal — A Borrowed Dress — Marriage Arrangements — A *Trousseau* — House Furniture — The Marriage Ceremony — A Wife's Position — Code of Morals for Women.

KUBOTA, *July* 25.

THE weather at last gives a hope of improvement, and I think I shall leave to-morrow. I had written this sentence when Ito came in to say that the man in the next house would like to see my stretcher and mosquito net, and had sent me a bag of cakes with the usual bit of seaweed attached, to show that it was a present. The Japanese believe themselves to be descended from a race of fishermen; they are proud of it, and Yebis, the god of fishermen, is one of the most popular of the household divinities. The piece of seaweed sent with a present to any ordinary person, and the piece of dried fish-skin which accompanies a present to the Mikado, record the origin of the race, and at the same time typify the dignity of simple industry.

Of course I consented to receive the visitor, and with the mercury at 84°, five men, two boys, and five women entered my small, low room, and after bowing to the earth three times, sat down on the floor. They had evidently come to spend the afternoon. Trays of tea and sweetmeats were handed round, and a *tabako-bon* was brought in, and they all smoked, as I had told Ito that all usual courtesies were to be punctiliously performed.

They expressed their gratification at seeing so "honourable" a traveller. I expressed mine at seeing so much of their "honourable" country. Then we all bowed profoundly. Then I laid Brunton's map on the floor and showed them my route, showed them the Asiatic Society's Transactions, and how we read from left to right, instead of from top to bottom, showed them my knitting, which amazed them, and my Berlin work, and then had nothing left. Then they began to entertain me, and I found that the real object of their visit was to exhibit an "infant prodigy," a boy of four, with a head shaven all but a tuft on the top, a face of preternatural thoughtfulness and gravity, and the self-possessed and dignified demeanour of an elderly man. He was dressed in scarlet silk *hakama*, and a dark, striped, blue silk *kimono*, and fanned himself gracefully, looking at everything as intelligently and courteously as the others. To talk child's talk to him, or show him toys, or try to amuse him, would have been an insult. The monster has taught himself to read and write, and has composed poetry. His father says that he never plays, and understands everything just like a grown person. The intention was that I should ask him to write, and I did so.

It was a solemn performance. A red blanket was laid in the middle of the floor, with a lacquer writing-box upon it. The creature rubbed the ink with water on the inkstone, unrolled four rolls of paper, five feet long, and inscribed them with Chinese characters, nine inches long, of the most complicated kind, with firm and graceful curves of his brush, and with the ease and certainty of Giotto in turning his O. He sealed them with his seal in vermilion, bowed three times, and the performance was ended. People get him to write *kakemonos* and signboards for them, and he had earned ten *yen*, or about £2, that day. His father is going to travel to Kiyôto with him, to see if any one under fourteen can write as well. I never saw such an exaggerated instance of child worship. Father, mother, friends, and servants, treated him as if he were a prince.

There are two alphabets, or rather syllabaries, in Japan — the *Hirakana*, which is a syllabary of forty-seven syllables, each being represented by several characters, which consist of abbreviated cursive forms of the more common Chinese characters, and containing some hundred signs, and the *Katagana*, which also consists of a syllabary of forty-seven syllables, but with only one sign for each. Women almost invariably use the first, but this child wrote both. In Japanese drawings you must have noticed a red seal on one side. Every one has such a seal, and the writing-boxes contain the vermilion with which the impression is made. Even young children become possessed of them. No receipt or form is valid without them. The seal is composed of the character or characters forming a person's name, engraved usually in the Chinese seal character. My visitors smoked pipes all round, and then bowed themselves out. The child was a most impressive spectacle, but not loveable. I think that sitting on seats raised above the floor, and a desire for domestic seclusion, are two initial steps of western civilisation.

The house-master, who is a most polite man, procured me an invitation to the marriage of his niece, and I have just returned from it. He has three "wives" himself. One keeps a *yadoya* in Kiyôto, another in Morioka, and the third and youngest is with him here. From her limitless stores of apparel she chose what she considered a suitable dress for me — an under-dress of sage green silk *crêpe*, a *kimono* of soft, green, striped silk of a darker shade, with a fold of white *crêpe*, spangled with gold at the neck, and a girdle of sage green corded silk, with the family badge here and there upon it in gold. I went with the house-master, Ito, to his disgust, not being invited, and his absence was like the loss of one of my senses, as I could not get any explanations till afterwards.

The ceremony did not correspond with the rules laid down for marriages in the books of etiquette that I have seen, but this is accounted for by the fact that they were for persons of the *samurai* class, while this bride and bridegroom, though the children of well-to-do merchants, belong to the *heimin*.

Marriages are arranged by the friends of both parties, and much worldly wisdom is constantly shown in the transaction. Still, youthful affections do not always run in the prescribed channels, and an attractive girl, in spite of her seclusion in her father's house, is sure to have several lovers; and the frequent suicides of lovers prove that in Japan, as elsewhere, the course of true love is not always smooth. Ito says that a lover who has formed a very decided preference fixes a sprig of the *Celastrus alatus* to the house of the lady's parents, and that if it be neglected, so is he, but if the maiden blackens her teeth he is accepted, subject to the approval of the parents. The house-master says that this is sometimes resorted to in the Kubota neighbourhood, but that marriages are usually made after the prescribed fashion.

Marriages are usually arranged when the bridegroom has passed his twentieth and the bride her sixteenth year. Marriage is the manifest destiny of Japanese female children, who are trained to its duties from their earliest infancy. The bride does not receive a dowry, but is provided with a *trousseau* according to her condi-

tion. Money considerations do not appear to weigh
much in the arrangements, but it is essential for the
lady to be discreet, amiable, and accomplished, and to
be a mistress of etiquette and domestic management.
If a father having no son gives his eldest daughter in
marriage, her husband becomes his adopted son, and
takes his name. Betrothal precedes marriage, and marriage presents are often so lavishly given as to cripple
for a time the resources of the givers. In addition to
the *trousseau* the bride's parents bestow upon her a
spinning-wheel and kitchen utensils, besides other furniture, which is not abundant, as the *tatami* answer the
purpose of beds, sofas, tables, and chairs.[1]

In this case the *trousseau* and furniture were conveyed to the bridegroom's house in the early morning,
and I was allowed to go to see them. There were several girdles of silk embroidered with gold, several
pieces of brocaded silk for *kimonos*, several pieces of
silk *crêpe*, a large number of made-up garments, a piece
of white silk, six barrels of wine or *saké*, and seven sorts
of condiments. Jewellery is not worn by women in
Japan.

The furniture consisted of two wooden pillows, finely
lacquered, one of them containing a drawer for ornamental hair-pins, some cotton *futons*, two very handsome
silk ones, a few silk cushions, a lacquer workbox, a

---

[1] Among the strong reasons for deprecating the adoption of foreign
houses, furniture, and modes of living by the Japanese, is that the expense of living would be so largely increased as to render early marriages impossible. At present the requirements of a young couple in
the poorer classes are, a bare matted room, capable or not of division,
two wooden pillows, a few cotton *futons*, and a sliding panel, behind
which to conceal them in the day-time, a wooden rice bucket and ladle,
a wooden wash-bowl, an iron kettle, a *hibachi*, a tray or two, a teapot
or two, two lacquer rice bowls, a *bentô-bako* or dinner box, a few china
cups, a few towels, a bamboo switch for sweeping, a *tabako-bon*, an iron
pot, and a few shelves let into a recess, all of which can be purchased
for something under £2.

spinning-wheel, a lacquer rice bucket and ladle, two ornamental iron kettles, various kitchen utensils, three bronze *hibachi*, two *tabako-bons*, some lacquer trays, and *zens*, china kettles, teapots, and cups, some lacquer rice bowls, two copper basins, a few towels, some bamboo switches, and an inlaid lacquer *étagère*. As the things are all very handsome the parents must be well off. The *saké* is sent in accordance with rigid etiquette.

It has often been written that marriage must be solemnised by a priest, but this is a mistake. Japanese marriage is a purely civil contract. No religious ceremony is necessary. A marriage is legalised by its registration in the office of the *Kôchô*. These people were Buddhists, but there was not even a priest present on the occasion.

The bridegroom is twenty-two, the bride seventeen, and very comely, so far as I could see through the paint with which she was profusely disfigured. Towards evening she was carried in a *norimon*, accompanied by her parents and friends to the bridegroom's house, each member of the procession carrying a Chinese lantern. When the house-master and I arrived the wedding party was assembled in a large room, the parents and friends of the bridegroom being seated on one side, and those of the bride on the other. Two young girls, very beautifully dressed, brought in the bride, a very pleasing-looking creature, dressed entirely in white silk, with a veil of white silk covering her from head to foot.

The bridegroom who was already seated in the middle of the room near its upper part, did not rise to receive her, and kept his eyes fixed on the ground, and she sat opposite to him, but never looked up. A low table was placed in front, on which there was a two-spouted kettle full of *saké*, some *saké* bottles, and some cups, and on another there were some small figures representing a fir tree, a plum tree in blossom, and a stork standing on a tortoise, the last representing length of days, and the former, the beauty of women and the strength of men. Shortly a *zen*, loaded with eatables was placed before each person, and the feast began, accompanied by the noises which signify gastronomic gratification.

After this, which was only a preliminary, the two girls who brought in the bride handed round a tray with three cups containing *saké*, which each person was expected to drain till he came to the god of luck at the bottom.

The bride and bridegroom then retired, but shortly re-appeared in other dresses of ceremony, but the bride still wore her white silk veil, which one day will be her shroud. An old gold lacquer tray was produced, with three *saké* cups, which were filled by the two bridesmaids, and placed before the parents-in-law and the bride. The father-in-law drank three cups, and handed the cup to the bride, who, after drinking two cups, received from her father-in-law a present in a box, drank the third cup, and then returned the cup to the father-in-law, who again drank three cups. Rice and fish were next brought in, after which the bridegroom's mother took the second cup, and filled and emptied it three times, after which she passed it to the bride, who drank two cups, received a present from her mother-in-law in a lacquer box, drank a third cup, and gave the cup to the elder lady, who again drank three cups. Soup was then served, and then the bride drank once from the third cup, and handed it to her husband's father, who drank three more cups, the bride took it again, and drank two, and lastly the mother-in-law drank three more cups. Now, if you possess the clear-sightedness which I laboured to preserve, you will perceive that each of the three had inbibed nine cups of some generous liquor! [1]

After this the two bridesmaids raised the two-spouted kettle, and presented it to the lips of the married pair, who drank from it alternately, till they had exhausted its contents. This concluding ceremony is said to be emblematic of the tasting together of the joys and sorrows of life. And so they became man and wife till death or divorce parted them.

This drinking of *saké* or wine, according to prescribed usage, appeared to constitute the " marriage service," to which none but relations were bidden. Immediately afterwards the wedding guests arrived, and the evening was spent in feasting and *saké* drinking, but the fare is simple, and intoxication is happily out of place at a marriage feast. Every detail is a matter of etiquette, and has been handed down for centuries. Except for the interest of the ceremony in that light it was a very dull and tedious affair, conducted in melancholy silence, and the young bride, with her whitened face and painted lips, looked and moved like an automaton.

From all that I can learn I think that Japanese wives are virtuous and faithful under circumstances which we should think most trying, as even apparent fidelity on the part of the husband is not regarded either as a virtue or a conventional requirement. On this point I think there can be no reasonable doubt.

It is obvious that the parental relation is regarded as far higher than the matrimonial, and that the tendency is to sink the wife in the mother. If the father is the servant of the child, the mother is his slave, and her lot is apt to be very hard, as her first duty is to bring chil-

---

[1] I failed to learn what the liquor was which was drunk so freely, but as no unseemly effects followed its use, I think it must either have been light Ôsaka wine, or light *saké*.

dren into the world, and then to nurse and wait upon them, while marriage places her in the position of a slave to her mother-in-law. The following translation of the Japanese "Code of Morals for Women" is deeply interesting, and throws more light upon some social customs, and upon the estimation in which women are held, than many pages of description. **I. L. B.**

JAPANESE CODE OF MORALS FOR WOMEN.[1]

" *1st Lesson.* Every girl, when of age, must marry a man of a different family, therefore her parents must be more careful of her education than that of a son, as she must be subject to her father and mother-in-law, and serve them. If she has been spoiled, she will quarrel with her husband's relatives.

2d. It is better for women to have a good mind than a beauti-- ful appearance. Women who have a bad mind, their passions are turbulent, their eyes seem dreadful, their voices loud and chattering, and when angry, will tell their family secrets, and besides, laugh at and mock other people, and envy and be spiteful towards them. These things are all improper for women to do, as they ought to be chaste, amiable, and gentle.

3d. Parents must teach their daughters to keep separate from the other sex. They must not see or hear any iniquitous thing. The old custom is, man and woman shall not sit on the same mat, nor put their clothing in the same place, shall have different bathrooms, shall not give or take anything directly from hand to hand. During the evening, when women walk out, they shall carry a lantern, and on walking out, even families, men must keep separate from their female relatives. People who neglect these rules are not polite, and bring a reproach on their families. No girl shall marry without the permission of her parents, and the management of a medium, and though she meets with such a sad fate as to be killed, she must keep as solid a mind as metal and stone, and do no unchaste thing.

4th. The house of the husband is that of the wife, and though her husband be poor she must not leave his house; if she does, and is divorced, it will be a disgrace to her all her life.

The reasons why a man may divorce his wife are seven. When she is disobedient to her father and mother-in-law; when she is unfaithful; when she is jealous; when she has leprosy; when she is childless; when she steals; when she has a chattering tongue.

[1] This translation is from a curious little book on the history and customs of Japan, by Mr. N. Macleod.

To the last reason the explanatory clause is added, "For the gabbling of a woman often destroys the peace of families." In mercy to the childless wife, the clause is added, "If she is amiable and gentle she shall not be divorced, but her husband shall adopt a child, or if his concubine have a child when his wife hath none, he shall not divorce her." At the end of all of the reasons for divorce, it is added, "When a woman is once driven out of her husband's house, it is a great reproach to her."

5th. When a girl is unmarried, she shall reverence her parents, but after marriage her father and mother-in-law more than her own parents. Morning and evening she shall inquire after the health of her father and mother-in-law, and ask if she can be of any service to them, and likewise do all they bid her; and if they scold her, she must not speak, and if she shows an amiable disposition, finally they come to a peaceful settlement of their difficulties.

6th. The wife has no lord or master but her husband, therefore she must do his bidding and not repine. The rule which women must observe is obedience. When the wife converses with her husband she must do so with a smiling face and humble word, and not be rude. This is the principal duty of women; the wife must obey the husband in all that he orders her to do, and when he is angry she must not resist, but obey. All women shall think their husbands to be heaven, so they must not resist their husbands and incur the punishment of heaven.

7th. All her husband's relatives are hers. She must not quarrel with them, or the family will be unhappy: she must be on good terms with the wife of her husband's eldest brother [he being considered the head of the family].

8th. The wife must not be jealous of her husband if he is unfaithful to her, but must admonish him in a gentle, kind manner. Of course, when she is jealous, her anger will appear in her face, and she will be disliked and abandoned by her husband; when she admonishes her husband she must always do it with a kind face and gentle words, and when he won't listen to her, she must wait till his passion is cooled and then speak to him again.

9th. Women must not chatter, or revile any one, or tell a lie. When she hears any slander she must not repeat it, and so cause disputes among families.

10th. Women shall always keep to their duty, rise early and work till late at night. She must not sleep during the day, must study economy, and must not neglect her weaving, sewing, and spinning, and must not drink too much tea or wine. She shall not hear or see any such lascivious thing as a theatre or drama; before reaching the age of forty, women shall not go to those places, or to where many people collect, such as a temple or a shrine.

11*th*. A wife must not waste her money in expensive clothing, but must dress according to her income.

12*th*. When a wife is young, she shall not speak on familiar terms with any young man, a relative of her husband's, nor yet with his servant, as the separation between the sexes must be observed. Though there is important business, she shall not write a letter to any young man.

13*th*. The ornaments and clothing must not be splendid, but neat and clean, so that she does not cause people to remark ; but she will wear clothing according to her rank.

14*th*. During such festivals as the first day or the third day of the third month and the fifth day of the fifth month, she must first visit her husband's relatives in preference to her own, and, except her husband allow her, she shall not go out or give gifts to any one.

15*th*. Women do not succeed their parents, but their father and mother-in-law, therefore she must be kinder to them than to her own parents. When a woman is married she shall seldom pay a visit to her own parents, only a messenger shall be sent; likewise to other relatives and friends. She shall not pride herself on her own descent.

16*th*. Though a woman have many servants, it is the rule of women that she do all her business herself. She shall sew the clothing and cook the food of her father and mother-in-law; she shall wash the clothing and sweep the mat of her husband, and when she nurses her child, she shall wash the linen herself. Women always shall live within the house, and also not go out without any business.

17*th*. When a woman has a female servant, she shall look after her, as her mind is ignorant, untutored, and verbose, and when she takes a spite at the relatives of her mistress's husband, she will slander them; and if her mistress is not wise, she will believe her, and will take an ill-will to her husband's family. As her husband's friends were previously strangers to her, such disputes can easily happen; therefore she must not believe her servant's words, and disturb the family peace of her husband's relatives; and such a servant she will dismiss, as such low persons must do such low things. A mistress must check her servant when she makes a mistake, and pity her stupidity, and warn her to be more careful in future.

18*th*. There are five bad qualities in women, that they slander or take a spite at some one, are jealous and ignorant; seven or eight women in ten have these maladies. This is a sign that women are comparatively inferior to men; they therefore must remedy them. The worst of these is ignorance, and it is the source of the remainder. The minds of women generally are as dark as the night, and are more stupid than men; they do not notice what is before them, and they slander innocent persons; they envy the happiness of others, and pet their children, all to the discredit of their husbands. Women are stupid, therefore they must be humble and obedient to their husbands. In all stations of life the wife must stand behind her husband; though she may have done good deeds, she must not be vain of them.

Though it be said she is bad, she shall not resist; she will continue to improve herself, and be careful not to repeat the same fault, and when she comports herself wisely, the intimacy between herself and her husband through life will be a happy one.

The foregoing lessons all girls shall be taught from their infancy, and they shall study them by reading and writing, so that they don't forget them.

A HOLIDAY.

A Holiday Scene — A *Matsuri* — Attractions of the Revel — *Matsuri* Cars — Gods and Demons — *Tableaux vivants* — A possible Harbour — A Village Forge — Prosperity of *Saké* Brewers — The Introduction of *Saké* into Japan — *Saké* and Revenue — A "great Sight."

TSUGURATA, *July* 27.

THREE miles of good road thronged with half the people of Kubota on foot and in *kurumas*, red vans drawn by horses, pairs of policemen in *kurumas*, hundreds of children being carried, hundreds more on foot, little girls, formal and precocious-looking, with hair dressed with scarlet *crêpe* and flowers, hobbling toilsomely along on high clogs, groups of men and women, never intermixing, stalls driving a "roaring trade" in cakes and sweetmeats, women making *mochi* as fast as the buyers ate it, broad rice-fields rolling like a green sea on the right, an ocean of liquid turquoise on the left, the grey roofs of Kubota looking out from their green surroundings, Taiheisan in deepest indigo blocking the view to the south, a glorious day, and a summer sun streaming over all, made up the cheeriest and most festal scene that I have seen in Japan, men, women, and children, vans and *kurumas*, policemen and horsemen, all on their way to a mean-looking town, Minato, the junk port of Kubota, which was keeping *matsuri*, or festival, in honour of the birthday of the god Shimmai. Towering above the low grey houses there were objects which at first looked like five enormous black fingers, then like trees with their branches wrapped in black, and then — comparisons ceased; they were a mys·tery.

Dismissing the *kurumas*, which could go no farther, we dived into the crowd, which was wedged along a mean street, nearly a mile long — a miserable street of poor tea-houses, and poor shop-fronts; but in fact you could hardly see the street for the people. Paper lanterns were hung close together along its whole length. There were rude scaffoldings supporting matted and covered platforms, on which people were drinking tea and *saké*, and enjoying the crowd below; monkey theatres and dog theatres, two mangy sheep and a lean pig attracting wondering crowds, for neither of these animals is known in this region of Japan; a booth in which a woman was having her head cut off every half-hour for 2 *sen* a spectator; cars with roofs like temples, on which, with forty men at the ropes, dancing children of the highest class were being borne in procession; a theatre with an open front, on the boards of which two men in antique dresses, with sleeves touching the ground, were performing with tedious slowness a classic dance of tedious posturings, which consisted mainly in dexterous movements of the aforesaid sleeves, and occasional emphatic stampings, and utterances of the word *Nô* in a hoarse howl. It is needless to say that a foreign lady was not the least of the attractions of the fair. The *cultus* of children was in full force, all sorts of masks, dolls, sugar figures, toys, and sweetmeats were exposed for sale on mats on the ground, and found their way into the hands and sleeves of the children, for no Japanese parent would ever attend a *matsuri* without making an offering to his child.

The police told me that there were 22,000 strangers in Minato, yet for 32,000 holiday-makers a force of twenty·

five policemen was sufficient. I did not see one person under the influence of *saké* up to 3 P. M., when I left, nor a solitary instance of rude or improper behaviour, nor was I in any way rudely crowded upon, for even where the crowd was densest, the people of their own accord formed a ring and left me breathing space.

We went to the place where the throng was greatest, round the two great *matsuri* cars, whose colossal erections we had seen far off. These were structures of heavy beams, thirty feet long, with eight huge, solid wheels. Upon them there were several scaffoldings with projections, like flat surfaces of cedar branches, and two special peaks of unequal height at the top, the whole being nearly fifty feet from the ground. All these projections were covered with black cotton cloth, from which branches of pines protruded. In the middle three small wheels, one above another, over which striped white cotton was rolling perpetually, represented a waterfall ; at the bottom another arrangement of white cotton represented a river, and an arrangement of blue cotton, fitfully agitated by a pair of bellows below, represented the sea. The whole is intended to represent a mountain on which the Shintô gods slew some devils, but anything more rude and barbarous could scarcely be seen. On the fronts of each car, under a canopy, were thirty performers on thirty diabolical instruments, which rent the air with a truly infernal discord, and suggested devils rather than their conquerors. High up on the flat projections there were groups of monstrous figures. On one a giant in brass armour, much like the *Niô* of temple gates, was killing a revolting-looking demon. On another a *daimiyô's* daughter, in robes of cloth of gold with satin sleeves richly flowered, was playing on the *samisen*. On another a hunter, twice the size of life, was killing a wild horse equally magnified, whose hide was represented by the hairy wrappings of the leaves of the *Chamœrops excelsa.* On others, highly coloured gods, and devils equally hideous, were grouped miscellaneously. These two cars were being drawn up and down the street at the rate of a mile in three hours by 200 men each, numbers of men with levers assisting the heavy wheels out of the mud-holes.

Two beautiful *kago*, highly gilded and decorated with lilies, each borne by four men, and each containing a child with whitened face, elaborately dressed false hair, and superb robes of flowered satin, reclining with a stately air on cushions of cloth of gold, were carried in procession. These are the children of a rich man of the place, who, at great expense, have been taught some of the antique dances to perform in public at this *matsuri.* The attraction *par excellence* was this performance. Later on they re-entered their grand car, with a temple roof and hangings of cloth of gold, and proceeded slowly down the street, the objects of the concentrated admiration of many thousand people, stopping at intervals to give their performance on the front of the car, which was a richly decorated stage, the back part being a costume-room, as well as a waiting-room for a large retinue of relatives and servants. These children performed painfully well. It was distressing to see creatures of eight and nine with such perfect dignity and self-possession. The girl managed her splendid trained dress and fan as well as the actors in the Shintomi Theatre at Yedo, danced a classical dance, with its singular posturings and jerky utterances, to perfection, and in the closing act, when she and her brother performed together, there was much spirit and vigour without the slightest exaggeration.

I went to see the woman's head cut off, and stood

with my feet in the mud for half an hour; but the trick was transparent, and the juggling very poor. I also saw a posturing and dancing dog, which so evidently went through his performance under the influence of terror that I tried to buy him, but his owner and tyrant would not take less than 50 *yen* for him. This *matsuri*, which, like an English fair, feast or revel, has lost its original religious significance, goes on for three days and nights, and this was its third and greatest day.

We left on mild-tempered horses, quite unlike the fierce fellows of Yamagata *ken*. Between Minato and Kado there is a very curious lagoon on the left, about 17 miles long by 16 broad, connected with the sea by a narrow channel, guarded by two high hills called Shinzan and Honzan. Two Dutch engineers are now engaged in reporting on its capacities, and if its outlet could be deepened without enormous cost, it would give north-western Japan the harbour it so greatly needs. Extensive rice-fields and many villages lie along the road, which is an avenue of deep sand and ancient pines much contorted and gnarled. Down the pine avenue hundreds of people on horseback and on foot were trooping into Minato from all the farming villages, glad in the glorious sunshine which succeeded four days of rain. There were hundreds of horses, wonderful-looking animals in bravery of scarlet cloth and lacquer and fringed nets of leather, and many straw wisps and ropes, with Gothic roofs for saddles, and dependent panniers on each side, carrying two grave and stately-looking children in each, and sometimes a father or a fifth child on the top of the pack-saddle.

I was so far from well that I was obliged to sleep at the wretched village of Abukawa, in a loft alive with fleas, where the rice was too dirty to be eaten, and where the house-master's wife, who sat for an hour on my floor, was sorely afflicted with skin disease. The clay houses have disappeared and the villages are now built of wood, but Abukawa is an antiquated, ramshackle place, propped up with posts and slanting beams projecting into the roadway for the entanglement of unwary passengers.

The village smith was opposite, but he was not a man of ponderous strength, nor were there those wondrous flights and scintillations of sparks which were the joy of our childhood in the Tattenhall forge. A fire of powdered charcoal on the floor, always being trimmed and replenished by a lean and grimy satellite, a man still leaner and grimier, clothed in goggles and a girdle, always sitting in front of it, heating and hammering iron bars with his hands, with a clink which went on late into the night, and blowing his bellows with his toes; bars and pieces of rusty iron pinned on the smoky walls, and a group of idle men watching his skilful manipulation, were the sights of the Abukawa smithy, and kept me thralled in the balcony, though the whole clotheless population stood for the whole evening in front of the house with a silent, open-mouthed stare.

Early in the morning the same melancholy crowd appeared in the dismal drizzle, which turned into a tremendous torrent, which has lasted for sixteen hours. Low hills, broad rice valleys in which people are puddling the rice a second time to kill the weeds, bad roads, pretty villages, much indigo, few passengers, were the features of the day's journey. At Morioka and several other villages in this region, I noticed that if you see one large, high, well-built house, standing in enclosed grounds, with a look of wealth about it, it is always that of the *saké* brewer. A bush denotes the manufacture as well as the sale of *saké*, and these are of all sorts, from the mangy bit of fir which has seen long service to the vigorous truss of pine constantly renewed. It is curious that this should formerly have been the sign of the sale of wine in England.

I really cannot do otherwise than digress upon *saké* here, for Japan without *saké* would be more unlike itself than England without beer, and the drinking of a prescribed quantity of *saké* on special occasions is a part of the traditional etiquette of the Empire. The *saké* breweries are now all quiet, as the season for making it is only from the beginning of November till the end of February, a low temperature being requisite. *Saké* is said to have been made here for 2600 years, and that in 400 A.D. two *saké* brewers came from China and introduced the improved Chinese process ; but it appears to have been made in small quantities only and in houses, and that it is only 300 years since *saké* breweries for supplying it on a large scale were established in Ōsaka, where the best is still made.[1] Seven per cent

[1] The process is a very complicated one, and I do not attempt to give its details, but will quote a generalisation of them in a paper by Mr. Korscheldt given in the Transactions of the German Asiatic Society for 1878. "In *saké* brewing we have learned an entirely new and peculiar form of fermentation industry, which differs from the European process in every respect, and which, so far as completeness is concerned, is not to be ranked below the latter. The Japanese process is as follows: —

A fungus is made to grow in a dark chamber on rice which has been steamed. This fungus alone performs the same work as is done in our breweries by the malt and yeast. Yeast is first produced from it. For this purpose the rice which is covered with fungus is mashed together with a fresh quantity of steamed rice, at a temperature of almost 0° centigrade. The substance which has been formed by the growth of the fungus changes the starch into sugar. When the change into sugar has advanced sufficiently, the mash is warmed, the mycelium of the fungus breaks up into yeast cells, and the fermentation commences. When the necessary yeast is made, the chief process is proceeded with. Steamed rice is again mashed with rice on which the fungus has grown, and yeast mash is added simultaneously. The diastase of the rice with the fungus changes the starch into sugar, which is hardly produced when it is immediately fermented by the yeast. Both processes go on with equal activity side by side. When the formation of sugar is complete, the fermentation also ceases a few days after. The mash is pressed, and

of the entire rice crop of Japan is turned into *saké.* In 1874 the annual production of it was 6,745,798 hectolitres, and its consumption 20½ litres per head of the population, and the production is annually increasing The tax on fermented liquor, which brought in £322,616 in 1875-76, brought in £474,773 in the last financial year. For revenue purposes five distinct kinds of *saké* are enumerated, and the manufacturer pays £2 a year for the license to make each, and ten per cent on the total amount of his sales. The retailer's license is £1 yearly. It is not wonderful that those who drive so extensive and lucrative a trade should have the finest houses in these northern villages.

The whole process of *saké*-making takes forty days, and European chemists say that it could not be improved upon. It is during the summer months that *saké* is subjected to what is known as Pasteur's process, though it has been practised in Japan for three centuries before Pasteur was born. *Saké* ought to have five distinct tastes — sweetness, sharpness, sourness, bitterness, and astringency, with a flavour of fusel oil in addition! It contains from 11 to 17 per cent of alcohol. I think it faint, sickly, and nauseous.[1]

the *saké* subjected to an after-fermentation, whereby the last particle capable of fermentation disappears. The *saké* then undergoes Pasteur's process, so that it may keep."

[1] *Saké* is mentioned in the earliest Japanese historical writings. Susanoô-no Mikoto, brother of the sun goddess, is said to have caused eight jars of *saké* to be brewed for him when he descended from heaven to the province of Idzumo; while in another tradition, a goddess is represented as brewing sweet *saké* with her own hands. Coming down to times perhaps less fabulous, it is related of the celebrated Empress Fingô, that, after her return from the conquest of Corea (early in the 3d century), she despatched her son (now worshipped as the god of war, under the name of Hachiman) to convey her respects to a distant divinity, and on his return, greeted him with *saké.* Possibly this story points to the same Corean origin for *saké* as belongs to most of the other arts and manufactures of the ancient Japanese. Undoubtedly, the use of *saké* dates from the earliest times, as it is perpetually mentioned in the most ancient books, both as a beverage and as an offering to the gods.

The wind and rain were something fearful all that afternoon. I could not ride, so I tramped on foot for some miles under an avenue of pines, through water a foot deep, and with my paper waterproof soaked through, reached Toyôka half drowned and very cold, to shiver over a *hibachi* in a clean loft, hung with my dripping clothes, which had to be put on wet the next day. By 5 A.M. all Toyôka assembled, and while I took my breakfast, I was not only the "cynosure" of the eyes of all the people outside, but of those of about forty more who were standing in the *doma*, looking up the ladder. When asked to depart by the house-master, they said, "It's neither fair nor neighbourly in you to keep this great sight to yourself, seeing that our lives may pass without again looking on a foreign woman;" so they were allowed to remain!   I. L. B.

A NARROW ESCAPE.

The Fatigues of Travelling — Torrents and Mud — Ito's Surliness —
   The Blind Shampooers — Guilds of the Blind — A supposed Monkey Theatre — A Suspended Ferry — A Difficult Transit — Perils
   on the Yonetsurugawa — A Boatman Drowned — Nocturnal Disturbances — A noisy *Yadoya* — Storm-bound Travellers — *Hai
   Hai!* — More Nocturnal Disturbances.

ODATÉ, *July* 29.

I HAVE been suffering so much from my spine, that I
have been unable to travel more than seven or eight
miles daily for several days, and even that with great
difficulty. I try my own saddle, then a pack-saddle,
then walk through the mud ; but I only get on because
getting on is a necessity, and as soon as I reach the
night's halting-place, I am obliged to lie down at once.
Only strong people should travel in Northern Japan.
The inevitable fatigue is much increased by the state
of the weather, and doubtless my impressions of the
country are affected by it also, as a hamlet in a quagmire in a grey mist or a soaking rain, is a far less
delectable object than the same hamlet under bright
sunshine. There has not been such a season for thirty
years. The rains have been tremendous. I have
lived in soaked clothes, in spite of my rain-cloak, and
have slept on a soaked stretcher in spite of all waterproof wrappings for several days, and still the weather
shows no signs of improvement, and the rivers are so
high on the northern road, that I am storm bound as
well as pain bound here. Ito shows his sympathy for

me by intense surliness, though he did say very sensibly, " I'm very sorry for you, but it's no use saying so over and over again ; as I can do nothing for you, you'd better send for the blind man ! "

In Japanese towns and villages, you hear every evening a man (or men) making a low peculiar whistle as he walks along, and in large towns the noise is quite a nuisance. It is made by blind men; but a blind beggar is never seen throughout Japan, and the blind are an independent, respected, and well-to-do class, carrying on the occupations of shampooing, money-lending, and music. They were anciently formed into two guilds, one by the son of an emperor who wept himself blind for the loss of his wife, and the other, by a general who plucked out his eyes that he might be delivered from the temptation of slaying the generous prince, who, after taking him captive, treated him with singular kindness. The incorporation formed by the latter contains a very large number of musicians, who are to be seen at theatres, weddings, processions, and festivals. The shampooers with their shaven pates are all blind, and many of them add money-lending at the rate of from 15 to 20 per cent a month to shampooing. It is their low whistle which one

STRAW RAIN-CLOAK.[1]

---

[1] The cloak, hat, and figure are from a sketch of myself, but the face is a likeness of a young Japanese woman.

hears at night. Next to smoking and the hot bath, shampooing is the national luxury, which no Japanese, however poor, would forego. It answers to the *lomi lomi* of Hawaii, and consists in a dexterous suppling of all the joints, and kneading of all the muscles, till aching and fatigue are done away with. The "blind man" is Ito's daily luxury, and the *kuruma* runners surrender their tired limbs to his manipulation on all occasions. The number of the blind is very great, and it is very interesting to find that, without either asylums or charity, they can make an independent living. There is an immense deal of pecuniary independence of a curious kind in the Japanese, and the further removed one is from foreigners, the more marked it is.

We have had a very severe journey from Toyôka. That day the rain was ceaseless, and in the driving mists one could see little but low hills looming on the horizon, pine barrens, scrub, and flooded rice-fields, varied by villages standing along roads which were quagmires a foot deep, and where the clothing was specially ragged and dirty. Hinokiyama, a village of *samurai*, on a beautiful slope, was an exception, with its fine detached houses, pretty gardens, deep-roofed gateways, grass and stone faced terraces, and look of refined, quiet comfort. Everywhere there was a quantity of indigo, as is necessary, for nearly all the clothing of the lower classes is blue. Near a large village we were riding on a causeway through the rice-fields, Ito on the pack-horse in front, when we met a number of children returning from school, who, on getting near us, turned, ran away, and even jumped into the ditches, screaming as they ran. The *mago* ran after them, caught the hindmost boy, and dragged him back, the boy scared and struggling, the man laughing. The boy said that they thought that Ito was a monkey-player, *i.e.* the keeper of a monkey theatre, I a big ape, and the poles of my bed the scaffolding of the stage!

Splashing through mire and water we found that the people of Tubiné wished to detain us, saying that all the ferries were stopped in consequence of the rise in the rivers, but I had been so often misled by false reports that I took fresh horses and went on by a track along a very pretty hill-side, overlooking the Yonetsu-rugawa, a large and swollen river, which nearer the sea had spread itself over the whole country. Torrents of rain were still falling, and all out-of-doors industries were suspended. Straw rain-cloaks hanging to dry dripped under all the eaves, our paper cloaks were sodden, our dripping horses steamed, and thus we slid down a steep descent into the hamlet of Kiriishi, thirty-one houses clustered under persimmon trees under a wooded hill-side, all standing in a quagmire, and so abject and filthy that one could not ask for five minutes' shelter in any one of them. Sure enough, on the bank of the river, which was fully 400 yards wide, and swirling like a mill-stream with a suppressed roar, there was an official order prohibiting the crossing of man or beast, and before I had time to think, the *mago* had deposited the baggage on an islet in the mire and was over the crest of the hill. I wished that the Government was a little less paternal.

Just in the nick of time we discerned a punt drifting down the river on the opposite side, where it brought up, and landed a man, and Ito and two others yelled, howled, and waved so lustily as to attract its notice, and to my joy an answering yell came across the roar and rush of the river. The torrent was so strong that the boatmen had to pole up on that side for half a mile, and in about three quarters of an hour they reached our side. They were returning to Kotsunagi — the very place I wished to reach, but though only 2½ miles off the distance took nearly four hours of the hardest work I ever saw done by men. Every moment I expected to see them rupture blood-vessels or tendons. All their muscles quivered. It is a mighty river, and was from eight to twelve feet deep, and whirling down in muddy eddies, and often with their utmost efforts in poling, when it seemed as if poles or backs must break, the boat hung trembling and stationary for three or four minutes at a time. After the slow and eventless tramp of the last few days this was an exciting transit. Higher up there was a flooded wood, and getting into this the men aided themselves considerably by hauling by the trees, but when we got out of this, another river joined the Yonetsurugawa, which with added strength rushed and roared more wildly.

I had long been watching a large house-boat far above us on the other side, which was being poled by desperate efforts by ten men. At that point she must have been half a mile off, when the stream overpowered the crew, and in no time she swung round and came drifting wildly down and across the river, broadside on to us. We could not stir against the current, and had large trees on our immediate left, and for a moment it was a question whether she would not smash us to atoms. Ito was livid with fear; his white, appalled face struck me as ludicrous, for I had no other thought than the imminent peril of the large boat with her freight of helpless families, when, just as she was within two feet of us, she struck a stem and glanced off. Then her crew grappled a headless trunk and got their hawser round it, and eight of them, one behind the other, hung on to it, when it suddenly snapped, seven fell backwards, and the forward one went overboard to be no more seen. Some house that night was desolate.

Reeling downwards, the big mast and spar of the un gainly craft caught in a tree, giving her such a check that they were able to make her fast. It was a saddening incident. I asked Ito what he felt when he seemed in peril, and he replied, "I thought I'd been good to my mother, and honest, and I hoped I should go to a good place."

The fashion of boats varies much on different rivers. On this one there are two sizes. Ours was a small one, flat-bottomed, 25 feet long by 2½ broad, drawing 6 inches, very low in the water, and with sides slightly curved inwards. The prow forms a gradual long curve from the body of the boat, and is very high.

The mists rolled away as dusk came on, and revealed a lovely country with much picturesqueness of form, and near Kotsunagi the river disappears into a narrow gorge with steep, sentinel hills dark with pine and cryptomeria. To cross the river we had to go fully a mile above the point aimed at, and then a few minutes of express speed brought us to a landing in a deep, tough quagmire in a dark wood, through which we groped our lamentable way to the *yadoya.* A heavy mist came on, and the rain returned in torrents; the *doma* was ankle deep in black slush. The *daidokoro* was open to the roof, roof and rafters were black with smoke, and a great fire of damp wood was smoking lustily. Round some live embers in the *irori* fifteen men, women, and children, were lying, doing nothing, by the dim light of an *andon.* It was picturesque decidedly, and I was well disposed to be content when the production of some handsome *fusuma* created *dai-miyô's* rooms out of the farthest part of the dim and wandering space, opening upon a damp garden, into which the rain splashed all night.

The solitary spoil of the day's journey was a glorious

lily, which I presented to the house-master, and in the morning it was blooming on the *kami-dana* in a small vase of priceless old Satsuma china. I was awoke out of a sound sleep by Ito coming in with a rumour, brought by some travellers, that the Prime Minister had been assassinated, and fifty policemen killed! [This was probably a distorted version of the partial mutiny of the Imperial Guard, which I learned on landing in Yezo.] Very wild political rumours are in the air in these outlandish regions, and it is not very wonderful that the peasantry lack confidence in the existing order of things after the changes of the last ten years, and the recent assassination of the Home Minister. I did not believe the rumour, for fanaticism, even in its wildest moods, usually owes some allegiance to common sense; but it was disturbing, as I have naturally come to feel a deep interest in Japanese affairs. A few hours later Ito again presented himself with a bleeding cut on his temple. In lighting his pipe — an odious nocturnal practice of the Japanese — he had fallen over the edge of the fire-pot. I always sleep in a Japanese *kimono* to be ready for emergencies, and soon bound up his head, and slept again, to be awoke early by another deluge.

I have been mistaken in thinking that the children are left without education in places in which there are no schools. In Kotsunagi, as well as in several other hamlets in which I have halted, the principal inhabitants secure a young man to teach their children, one giving him clothes, another board and lodging, the poorer people giving monthly fees, and the poorest getting their children's education gratuitously. This appears to be a very common custom. At Kotsunagi the house-master gives the teacher board and lodging, and thirty studious children are taught in a portion of the *daidokoro*.

We made an early start, but got over very little

ground, owing to bad roads and long delays. All day the rain came down in even torrents, the tracks were nearly impassable, my horse fell five times, I suffered severely from pain and exhaustion, and almost fell into despair about ever reaching the sea. In these wild regions there are no *kago* or *norimons* to be had, and a pack-horse is the only conveyance, and yesterday, having abandoned my own saddle, I had the bad luck to get a pack-saddle with specially angular and uncompromising peaks, with a soaked and extremely unwashed *futon* on the top, spars, tackle, ridges, and furrows, of the most exasperating description, and two nooses of rope to hold on by, as the animal slid down-hill on his haunches, or let me almost slide over his tail as he scrambled and plunged up-hill.

It was pretty country, even in the downpour, when white mists parted, and fir-crowned heights looked out for a moment, or we slid down into a deep glen with mossy boulders, lichen-covered stumps, ferny carpet, and damp, balsamy smell of pyramidal cryptomeria, and a tawny torrent dashing through it in gusts of passion. Then there were low hills, much scrub, immense rice-fields, and violent inundations. But it is not pleasant, even in the prettiest country, to cling on to a pack-saddle, with a saturated quilt below you, and the water slowly soaking down through your wet clothes into your boots, knowing all the time that when you halt you must sleep on a wet bed, and change into damp clothes, and put on the wet ones again the next morning. The villages were poor, and most of the houses were of boards rudely nailed together for ends, and for sides straw rudely tied on; they had no windows, and smoke came out of every crack. They were as unlike the houses which travellers see in Southern Japan as a "black hut" in Uist is like a cottage in a trim village in Kent. These peasant proprietors have much to learn of the art of living. At Tsuguriko, the next stage, where the Transport Office was so dirty that I was obliged to sit in the street in the rain, they told us that we could only get on a *ri* farther, because the bridges were all carried away, and the fords were impassable; but I engaged horses, and by dint of British dogged- ness, and the willingness of the *mago*, I got the horses singly and without their loads, in small punts across the swollen waters of the Hayakuchi, the Yuwasé, and the Mochida, and finally forded three branches of my old friend the Yonetsurugawa, with the foam of its hurry- ing waters whitening the men's shoulders and the horses' packs, and with a hundred Japanese looking on at the "folly" of the foreigner.

I like to tell you of kind people everywhere, and the two *mago* were specially so, for when they found that I was pushing on to Yezo for fear of being laid up in the interior wilds, they did all they could to help me; lifted me gently from the horse, made steps of their backs, for me to mount, and gathered for me handfuls of red ber- ries, which I ate out of politeness, though they tasted of some nauseous drug. They suggested that I should stay at the picturesquely situated old village of Kawa- guchi, but everything about it was mildewed, and green with damp, and the stench from the green and black ditches with which it abounded was so overpowering, even in passing through, that I was obliged to ride on to Odaté, a crowded, forlorn, half-tumbling-to-pieces town of 8000 people, with bark roofs held down by stones.

The *yadoyas* are crowded with storm-staid travellers, and I had a weary tramp from one to another, almost sinking from pain, pressed upon by an immense crowd, and frequently bothered by a policeman, who followed

me from one place to the other, making wholly unrighteous demands for my passport at that most inopportune
time. After a long search I could get nothing better
than this room, with *fusuma* of tissue paper, in the centre of the din of the house, close to the *doma* and *daidokoro*. Fifty travellers, nearly all men, are here, mostly
speaking at the top of their voices, and in a provincial
jargon which exasperates Ito. Cooking, bathing, eating, and, worst of all, perpetual drawing water from a
well with a creaking hoisting apparatus, are going on
from 4.30 in the morning till 11.30 at night, and on both
evenings noisy mirth, of alcoholic inspiration, and dissonant performances by *geishas*, have added to the din.

In all places lately *Hai*, "yes," has been pronounced
Hé, *Chi*, *Na*, *Né*, to Ito's great contempt. It sounds
like an expletive or interjection rather than a response,
and seems used often as a sign of respect or attention
only. Often it is loud and shrill, then guttural, at
times little more than a sigh. In these *yadoyas* every
sound is audible, and I hear low rumbling of mingled
voices, and above all the sharp *Hai*, *Hai*, of the tea-
house girls, in full chorus from every quarter of the
house. The habit of saying it is so strong that a man
roused out of sleep jumps up with *Hai*, *Hai*, and often,
when I speak to Ito in English, a stupid Hebe sitting
by answers *Hai*.

I don't want to convey a false impression of the noise
here. It would be at least three times as great were I
in equally close proximity to a large hotel kitchen in
England, with fifty Britons only separated from me by
paper partitions. I had not been long in bed on Saturday night, when I was awoke by Ito bringing in an old
hen which he said he could stew till it was tender, and
I fell asleep again with its dying squeak in my ears, to
be awoke a second time by two policemen wanting for

some occult reason to see my passport, and a third time by two men with lanterns scrambling and fumbling about the room, for the strings of a mosquito net, which they wanted for another traveller. These are among the ludicrous incidents of Japanese travelling. About five Ito woke me by saying he was quite sure that the *moxa* would be the thing to cure my spine, and as we were going to stay all day, he would go and fetch an operator; but I rejected this as emphatically as the services of the blind man! Yesterday a man came and pasted slips of paper over all the "peep-holes" in the *shôji*, and I have been very little annoyed, even though the *yadoya* is so crowded.

The number of towns of about 10,000 people is very surprising. Odaté, like many others of its size, seems to have no special reason for existence. It has, however, a trade with Noshiro, by the turbulent river Yonetsurugawa, and makes large quantities of coarse lacquer for *andons* and bowls, and the short knives which are used for reaping, as well as the hoes and mattocks which are almost the only implements used for the garden-like cultivation of Japan. It is a miserable-looking town, patched up and propped up, and the large number of iron-workers in their wretched forges, which line the streets in some places, make it look like a slum of a Staffordshire nail-making village.

The rain continues to come down in torrents, and rumours are hourly arriving of disasters to roads and bridges on the northern route.   I. L. B.

SHIRASAWA.

Good-tempered Intoxication — The Effect of Sunshine — A tedious
Altercation — "Harassed Interests" — Foreign Requirements —
Village Doings — Homogeneity of Japan — Evening Occupations
— Noisy Talk — Social Gatherings — Unfair Comparisons.

SHIRASAWA, *July* 29.

EARLY this morning the rain-clouds rolled themselves
up and disappeared, and the bright blue sky looked as
if it had been well washed. I had to wait till noon
before the rivers became fordable, and my day's journey
is only seven miles, as it is not possible to go farther
till more of the water runs off. We had very limp,
melancholy horses, and my *mago* was half-tipsy, and
sang, talked, and jumped the whole way. *Saké* is frequently taken warm, and in that state produces a very
noisy but good-tempered intoxication. I have seen a
good many intoxicated persons, but never one in the
least degree quarrelsome, and the effect very soon
passes off, leaving, however, an unpleasant nausea for
two or three days, as a warning against excess. The
abominable concoctions known under the names of
beer, wine, and brandy, produce a bad-tempered and
prolonged intoxication, and *delirium tremens*, rarely
known as a result of *saké* drinking, is being introduced
under their baleful influence.

The sun shone gloriously and brightened the hill-gir-
dled valley in which Odaté stands into positive beauty,
with the narrow river flinging its bright waters over

green and red shingle, lighting it up in glints among the conical hills, some richly wooded with *coniferæ*, and others merely covered with scrub, which were tumbled about in picturesque confusion. When Japan gets the sunshine, its forest-covered hills and garden-like valleys are turned into paradise. In a journey of 600 miles there has hardly been a patch of country which would not have been beautiful in sunlight.

We crossed five severe fords with the water half-way up the horses' bodies, in one of which the strong current carried my *mago* off his feet, and the horse towed him ashore, singing and capering, his drunken glee nothing abated by his cold bath. Everything is in a state of wreck. Several river channels have been formed in places where there was only one; there is not a trace of the road for a considerable distance, not a bridge exists for ten miles, and a great tract of country is covered with boulders, uprooted trees, and logs floated from the mountain sides. Already, however, these industrious peasants are driving piles, carrying soil for embankments in creels on horses' backs, and making ropes of stones to prevent a recurrence of the calamity. About here the female peasants wear for field-work a dress which pleases me much by its suitability — light blue trousers, with a loose sack over them, confined at the waist by a girdle.

On arriving here in much pain, and knowing that the road was not open any farther, I was annoyed by a long and angry conversation between the house-master and Ito, during which the horses were not unloaded, and the upshot of it was that the man declined to give me shelter, saying that the police had been round the week before giving notice that no foreigner was to be received without first communicating with the nearest police station, which, in this instance, is three hours off.

I said that the authorities of Akita *ken* could not by any local regulations override the Imperial edict under which passports are issued; but he said he should be liable to a fine and the withdrawal of his license if he violated the rule. No foreigner, he said, had ever lodged in Shirasawa, and I have no doubt that he added that he hoped no foreigner would ever seek lodgings again. My passport was copied and sent off by special runner, as I should have deeply regretted bringing trouble on the poor man by insisting on my rights, and in much trepidation he gave me a room open on one side to the village, and on another to a pond, over which, as if to court mosquitoes, it is partially built. I cannot think how the Japanese can regard a hole full of dirty water as an ornamental appendage to a house.

The house-masters, are, I think, somewhat harassed in their business; indeed, over government and endless and worrying changes in details, are defects of the present *régime*. Nearly every week a number of fresh notifications are issued, and the dull, puzzled brains of the peasantry have hardly taken in one batch before another appears, and the police are sharp in pulling up offenders. The house-masters are obliged to enter in a book, not only the names and destinations of all travellers, but the name of the place they last came from, and this book must be exhibited to the police on their monthly domiciliary visit. In the case of foreigners, the special harassment warrants a special charge, for there is the labour of making two copies of the passport, and a man "giving accommodation to, or lodging foreigners, without permission from the authorities," is liable to a fine, and to be flogged in default of payment. Apart from these special difficulties, I think that a house-master is entitled to make a higher charge to a foreigner, because a single foreigner occupies a whole room in which six or eight Japanese would be perfectly happy, he requires water in his room, he cooks odd food at odd times, and generally gives more trouble. So far I am quite on the house-master's side, and feel ashamed of some of my countrymen, and of many Americans, who give 15 *sen*, without a gratuity, for a good room, *futons ad libitum*, a well-replenished *hibachi*, hot water to wash in, an *andon* all night, and rice and tea without stint — fire, candle, two meals, a good room, and good attendance, for 7d.! My hotel expenses (including Ito's) are less than 3s. a-day, and in nearly every place there has been a cordial desire that I should be comfortable, and considering that I have often put up in small, rough hamlets off the great routes even of Japanese travel, the accommodation, *minus* the fleas and the odours, has been surprisingly excellent, not to be equalled, I should think, in equally remote regions in any country in the world.

I have spent the pleasant evening looking into the street of the little quiet village of 71 houses — one of thousands of similar villages, with its *Kôchô* and notification boards, its temple and graveyard, its decaying objects of worship, its *matsuri*, its social polity, its marriages and deaths, its small local interests, its police visitations, its tax paying, its land feuds, its small scandals, its superstition and ignorance — a little world, but part of great Japan. Centralisation is the principle of Japanese Government, but it is a remarkable fact that law is as strong here as in the capital itself, and the strong arm of power is none the less strong because it has reached over 600 miles of country. Though the old system of *espionage* is ended, I doubt not that the doings of Shirasawa are known at the Ministry of the Interior at Tôkiyô through numberless reports, for Japanese officialdom is nothing unless it writes.

Again the homogeneity of the country interests me greatly. I have now travelled through several regions which were until lately distinct, and not always friendly, principalities, each with its separate feudal system. Climate and vegetation have considerably changed in 5° of latitude, and in this *ken* speech itself differs widely from the speech of the central provinces. But everywhere the temples and houses are constructed on identically the same plan, and though some may be large and some small, and wooden walls and mud walls, thatched roofs and roofs of bark or shingles, may alternate, the interior of the dwelling-house has always similar recognisable features. Crops vary with the soil and climate, but there is no change in the manner of cultivation; the manuring and other agricultural processes are always the same. And far beyond all this the etiquette which governs society in all its grades is practically the same. The Akita coolie, boor as he may be, is just as courteously ceremonious in his intercourse with others as the Tôkiyô coolie; the Shirasawa maidens are as self-possessed, dignified, and courteous as those of Nikkô; the children play at the same games, with the same toys, and take the same formal steps in life at the same ages. All are bound alike by the same rigid fetters of social order, a traditional code which, if it works some evil, works also so much good that I should grieve to see it displaced by any perverted imitation of Western manners and customs.

This evening, here, as in thousands of other villages, the men came home from their work, ate their food, took their smoke, enjoyed their children, carried them about, watched their games, twisted straw ropes, made straw sandals, split bamboo, wove straw rain-coats, and spent the time universally in those little economical ingenuities and skilful adaptations which our people (the worse for them) practise perhaps less than any other. There was no assembling at the *saké* shop. Poor though the homes are, the men enjoy them; the children are an attraction at any rate, and the brawling and disobedience which often turn our working-class homes into bear-gardens are unknown here where docility and obedience are inculcated from the cradle as a matter of course. The signs of religion become fewer as I travel north, and it appears that the little faith which exists consists mainly in a belief in certain charms and superstitions, which the priests industriously foster.

A low voice is not regarded as "a most excellent thing" in man at least, among the lower classes in Japan. The people speak at the top of their voices, and though most words and syllables end in vowels, the general effect of a conversation is like the discordant gabble of a farmyard. The next room to mine is full of storm-bound travellers, and they and the house master kept up what I thought was a most important argument for four hours at the top of their voices. I supposed it must be on the new and important ordinance granting local elective assemblies, of which I heard at Odaté, but on inquiry found that it was possible to spend four mortal hours in discussing whether the day's journey from Odaté to Noshiro could be made best by road or river. I have heard from "one who knows" that the conversation even among educated Japanese is of the poorest order. Politics and public matters are tabooed, religion and kindred topics are nowhere, art has lost its interest, literature is nowhere, the elevating influence of cultivated women is absent, from old habit or present distrust every man fears to commit himself by giving an opinion on any subject which is worth speaking about, and talk degenerates into a coarse jocularity and ribaldry with which a foreigner of refinement can have no sympathy.

Japanese women have their own gatherings, where gossip and chit-chat, marked by a truly Oriental indecorum of speech, are the staple of talk. I think that in many things, specially in some which lie on the surface, the Japanese are greatly our superiors, but that in many others they are immeasurably behind us. In living altogether among this courteous, industrious, and civilised people, one comes to forget that one is doing them a gross injustice in comparing their manners and ways with those of a people moulded by many centuries of Christianity. Would to God that we were so Christianised, that the comparison might always be favourable to us, which it is not!

July 30. In the room on the other side of mine were two men with severe eye-disease, with shaven heads and long and curious rosaries, who beat small drums as they walked, and were on pilgrimage to the shrine of Fudo at Megura, near Yedo, a seated, flame-surrounded idol, with a naked sword in one hand and a coil of rope in the other, who has the reputation of giving sight to the blind. At five this morning they began their devotions, which consisted in repeating with great rapidity, and in a high monotonous key for two hours, the invocation of the Nichiren sect of Buddhists, *Namu miyô hô ren ge Kiyô*, which certainly no Japanese understands, and on the meaning of which, even the best scholars are divided; one having given me, " Glory to the salvation-bringing Scriptures; " another, " Hail, precious law and gospel of the lotus flower," and a third, " Heaven and earth! The teachings of the wonderful lotus flower sect." *Namu amidu Butsu,* occurred at intervals, and two drums were beaten the whole time!

The rain, which began again at eleven last night, fell from five till eight this morning, not in drops, but in streams, and in the middle of it, a heavy pall of blackness (said to be a total eclipse) enfolded all things in a lurid gloom. Any detention is exasperating within one day of my journey's end, and I hear without equanimity, that there are great difficulties ahead, and that our getting through in three or even four days is doubtful. I hope you will not be tired of the monotony of my letters. Such as they are, they represent the scenes which a traveller would see throughout much of Northern Japan, and whatever interest they have consists in the fact that they are a faithful representation, made upon the spot, of what a foreigner sees and hears in travelling through a large but unfrequented region.

I. L. B.

AN INUNDATION.

Torrents of Rain — An unpleasant Detention — Devastations produced by Floods — The Yadate Pass — The Force of Water — Difficulties thicken — A Primitive *Yadoya* — The Water rises.

IKARIGASEKI, AOMORI KEN, *August* 2.

THE prophecies concerning difficulties are fulfilled. For six days and five nights the rain has never ceased, except for a few hours at a time, and for the last thirteen hours, as during the eclipse at Shirasawa, it has been falling in such sheets as I have only seen for a few minutes at a time on the equator. I have been here storm-staid for two days, with damp bed, damp clothes, damp everything, and boots, bag, books, are all green with mildew. And still the rain falls, and roads, bridges, rice-fields, trees, and hill-sides are being swept in a common ruin towards the Tsugaru Strait, so tantalisingly near; and the simple people are calling on the forgotten gods of the rivers and the hills, on the sun and moon, and all the host of heaven, to save them from this " plague of immoderate rain and waters." For myself to be able to lie down all day is something, and as " the mind, when in a healthy state, reposes as quietly before an insurmountable difficulty as before an ascertained truth," so, as I cannot get on, I have ceased to chafe, and am rather inclined to magnify the advantages of the detention, a necessary process, as you would think if you saw my surroundings!

The day before yesterday, in spite of severe pain, was

one of the most interesting of my journey. As I
learned something of the force of fire in Hawaii, I am
learning not a little of the force of water in Japan.
We left Shirasawa at noon, as it looked likely to clear,
taking two horses and three men. It is beautiful scenery — a wild valley, upon which a number of lateral
ridges descend, rendered strikingly picturesque by the
dark pyramidal cryptomeria, which are truly the glory
of Japan. Five of the fords were deep and rapid, and
the entrance on them difficult, as the sloping descents
were all carried away, leaving steep banks, which had
to be levelled by the mattocks of the *mago*. Then the
fords themselves were gone ; there were shallows where
there had been depths, and depths where there had
been shallows; new channels were carved, and great
beds of shingle had been thrown up. Much wreckage
lay about. The road and its small bridges were all
gone, trees torn up by the roots or snapped short off by
being struck by heavy logs, were heaped together like
barricades, leaves and even bark being in many cases
stripped completely off ; great logs floated down the
river in such numbers and with such force that we had
to wait half an hour in one place to secure a safe crossing ; hollows were filled with liquid mud, boulders of
great size were piled into embankments causing perilous
alterations in the course of the river ; a fertile valley
had been utterly destroyed, and the men said they could
hardly find their way.

At the end of five miles it became impassable for
horses, and with two of the *mago* carrying the baggage,
we set off, wading through water and climbing along
the side of a hill, up to our knees in soft, wet soil. The
hill-side and the road were both gone, and there were
heavy landslips along the whole valley. Happily there
was not much of this exhausting work, for just as higher

and darker ranges, densely wooded with cryptomeria, began to close us in, we emerged upon a fine new road, broad enough for a carriage, which, after crossing two ravines on fine bridges, plunges into the depths of a magnificent forest, and then by a long series of fine zigzags of easy gradients, ascends the pass of Yadate, on the top of which, in a deep sandstone cutting, is a handsome obelisk, marking the boundary between Akita and Aomori *ken*. This is a marvellous road for Japan, it is so well graded and built up, and logs for travellers' rests are placed at convenient distances. Some very heavy work in grading and blasting has been done upon it, but there are only four miles of it, with wretched bridle tracks at each end. I left the others behind, and strolled on alone over the top of the pass and down the other side, where the road is blasted out of rock of a vivid pink and green colour, looking brilliant under the trickle of water. I admire this pass more than anything I have seen in Japan; I even long to see it again, but under a bright blue sky. It reminds me much of the finest part of the Brunig Pass, and something of some of the passes in the Rocky Mountains, but the trees are far finer than in either. It was lonely, stately, dark, solemn; its huge cryptomeria, straight as masts, sent their tall spires far aloft in search of light; the ferns, which love damp and shady places, were the only undergrowth; the trees flung their balsamy, aromatic scent liberally upon the air, and in the unlighted depths of many a ravine and hollow, clear, bright torrents leapt and tumbled, drowning with their thundering bass the musical treble of the lighter streams. Not a traveller disturbed the solitude with his sandalled footfall; there was neither song of bird nor hum of insect.

In the midst of this sublime scenery, and at the very top of the pass, the rain, which had been light but steady during the whole day, began to come down in streams and then in sheets. I have been so rained upon for weeks that at first I took little notice of it, but very soon changes occurred before my eyes which concentrated my attention upon it. The rush of waters was heard everywhere, trees of great size slid down, breaking others in their fall; rocks were rent and carried away trees in their descent, the waters rose before our eyes; with a boom and roar as of an earthquake a hillside burst, and half the hill, with a noble forest of cryptomeria, was projected outwards, and the trees, with the land on which they grew, went down heads foremost, diverting a river from its course, and where the forest-covered hill-side had been there was a great scar, out of which a torrent burst at high pressure, which in half an hour carved for itself a deep ravine, and carried into the valley below an avalanche of stones and sand. Another hill-side descended less abruptly, and its noble groves found themselves at the bottom in a perpendicular position, and will doubtless survive their transplantation. Actually, before my eyes, this fine new road was torn away by hastily improvised torrents, or blocked by landslips in several places, and a little lower, in one moment, a hundred yards of it disappeared, and with them a fine bridge, which was deposited aslant across the torrent lower down.

On the descent, when things began to look very bad, and the mountain-sides had become cascades bringing trees, logs, and rocks down with them, we were fortunate enough to meet with two pack-horses whose leaders were ignorant of the impassability of the road to Odaté, and they and my coolies exchanged loads. These were strong horses, and the *mago* were skilful and courageous. They said, if we hurried, we could just get to the hamlet they had left, they thought, but while they

spoke the road and the bridge below were carried away.
They insisted on lashing me to the pack-saddle. The
greât stream, whose beauty I had formerly admired,
was now a thing of dread, and had to be forded four
times without fords. It crashed and thundered, drowning the feeble sound of human voices, the torrents from
the heavens hissed through the forest, trees and logs
came crashing down the hill-sides, a thousand cascades
added to the din, and in the bewilderment produced by
such an unusual concatenation of sights and sounds we
stumbled through the river, the men up to their shoulders, the horses up to their backs. Again and again we
crossed. The banks being carried away, it was very
hard to get either into or out of the water; the horses
had to scramble or jump up places as high as their
shoulders, all slippery and crumbling, and twice the
men cut steps for them with axes. The rush of the
torrent at the last crossing taxed the strength of both
men and horses, and as I was helpless from being tied
on, I confess that I shut my eyes! After getting
through, we came upon the lands belonging to this
village — rice-fields with the dykes burst, and all the
beautiful ridge and furrow cultivation of the other
crops carried away. The waters were rising fast, the
men said we must hurry; they unbound me, so that I
might ride more comfortably, spoke to the horses, and
went on at a run. My horse, which had nearly worn
out his shoes in the fords, stumbled at every step, the
mago gave me a noose of rope to clutch, the rain fell in
such torrents that I speculated on the chance of being
washed off my saddle, when suddenly I saw a shower
of sparks; I felt unutterable things, I was choked.
bruised, stifled, and presently found myself being hauled
out of a ditch by three men, and realised that the horse
had tumbled down in going down a steepish hill, and

that I had gone over his head. To climb again on the soaked *futon* was the work of a moment, and with men running, and horses stumbling and splashing, we crossed the Hirakawa by one fine bridge, and half a mile farther re-crossed it on another, wishing as we did so that all Japanese bridges were as substantial, for they were both 100 feet long, and had central piers.

We entered Ikarigaseki from the last bridge, a village of 800 people, on a narrow ledge between an abrupt hill and the Hirakawa, a most forlorn and tumble-down place, given up to felling timber and making shingles; and timber in all its forms — logs, planks, faggots, and shingles, is heaped and stacked about. It looks more like a lumberer's encampment than a permanent village, but it is beautifully situated, and unlike any of the innumerable villages that I have ever seen.

The street is long and narrow, with streams in stone channels on either side, but these had overflowed, and men, women, and children were constructing square dams to keep the water, which had already reached the *doma*, from rising over the *tatami*. Hardly any house has paper windows, and in the few which have, they are so black with smoke as to look worse than none. The roofs are nearly flat, and are covered with shingles held on by laths, and weighted with large stones. Nearly all the houses look like temporary sheds, and most are as black inside as a Barra hut. The walls of many are nothing but rough boards tied to the uprights by straw ropes.

In the drowning torrent, sitting in puddles of water, and drenched to the skin hours before, we reached this very primitive *yadoya*, the lower part of which is occupied by the *daidokoro*, a party of storm-bound students, horses, fowls, and dogs. My room is a wretched loft, reached by a ladder, with such a quagmire at its foot that I have to descend into it in Wellington boots. It was dismally grotesque at first. The torrent on the unceiled roof prevented Ito from hearing what I said, the bed was soaked, and the water, having got into my box, had dissolved the remains of the condensed milk, and had reduced clothes, books, and paper, into a condition of universal stickiness. My *kimono* was less wet than anything else, and borrowing a sheet of oiled paper, I lay down in it, till roused up in half an hour by Ito shrieking above the din on the roof that the people thought that the bridge by which we had just entered would give way; and running to the river bank we joined a large crowd, far too intensely occupied by the coming disaster to take any notice of the first foreign lady they had ever seen.

The Hirakawa, which an hour before was merely a clear, rapid, mountain stream, about four feet deep, was then ten feet deep, they said, and tearing along, thick and muddy, and with a fearful roar,

> " And each wave was crested with tawny foam,
>   Like the mane of a chestnut steed."

Immense logs of hewn timber, trees, roots, branches, and faggots, were coming down in numbers. The abutment on this side was much undermined, but, except that the central pier trembled whenever a log struck it, the bridge itself stood firm, so firm, indeed, that two men, anxious to save some property on the other side, crossed it after I arrived. Then logs of planed timber of large size, and joints, and much wreckage, came down, fully forty fine timbers, thirty feet long, for the fine bridge above had give way. Most of the harvest of logs cut on the Yadate Pass must have been lost, for over 300 were carried down in the short time in which I watched the river. This is a very heavy

loss to this village, which lives by the timber trade.
Efforts were made at a bank higher up to catch them as
they drifted by, but they only saved about one in
twenty. It was most exciting to see the grand way
in which these timbers came down; and the moment
in which they were to strike or not to strike the pier
was one of intense suspense. After an hour of this two
superb logs, fully thirty feet long, came down close
together, and striking the central pier nearly simultaneously, it shuddered horribly, the great bridge parted
in the middle, gave an awful groan like a living thing,
plunged into the torrent, and re-appeared in the foam
below only as disjointed timbers hurrying to the sea.
Not a vestige remained. The bridge below was carried
away in the morning, so, till the river becomes fordable,
this little place is completely isolated. On thirty miles
of road, out of nineteen bridges, only two remain, and
the road itself is almost wholly carried away!

CHILDREN'S GAMES.

Scanty Resources — Japanese Children — Children's Games — A saga-
cious Example — A Kite Competition — Alphabet Cards — Contagious Merriment — Popular Proverbs — Personal Privations.

IKARIGASEKI.

I HAVE well-nigh exhausted the resources of this
place. They are to go out three times a day to see how
much the river has fallen, to talk with the house-master and *Kôchô*, to watch the children's games and the
making of shingles ; to buy toys and sweetmeats and
give them away; to apply zinc lotion to a number of
sore eyes three times daily, under which treatment, during three days, there has been a wonderful amendment ;
to watch the cooking, spinning, and other domestic processes in the *daidokoro ;* to see the horses, which are also
actually in it, making meals of green leaves of trees instead of hay ; to see the lepers who are here for some
waters which are supposed to arrest, if not to cure, their
terrible malady ; to lie on my stretcher and sew, and
read the papers of the Asiatic Society, and to go over
all possible routes to Aomori. The people have become
very friendly in consequence of the eye lotion, and
bring many diseases for my inspection, most of which
would never have arisen had cleanliness of clothing and
person been attended to. The absence of soap, the in-
frequency with which clothing is washed, and the absence of linen next the skin, cause various cutaneous
diseases, which are aggravated by the bites and stings

of insects. Scald-head affects nearly half the children here.

I am very fond of Japanese children. I have never yet heard a baby cry, and I have never seen a child troublesome or disobedient. Filial piety is the leading virtue in Japan, and unquestioning obedience is the habit of centuries. The arts and threats by which English mothers cajole or frighten children into unwilling obedience appear unknown. I admire the way in which children are taught to be independent in their amusements. Part of the home education is the learning of the rules of the different games, which are absolute, and when there is a doubt, instead of a quarrelsome suspension of the game, the fiat of a senior child decides the matter. They play by themselves, and don't bother adults at every turn. I usually carry sweeties with me, and give them to the children, but not one has ever received them without first obtaining permission from the father or mother. When that is gained, they smile and bow profoundly, and hand the sweeties to those present before eating any themselves. They are gentle creatures, but too formal and precocious.

They have no special dress. This is so queer that I cannot repeat it too often. At three they put on the *kimono* and girdle, which are as inconvenient to them as to their parents, and childish play in this garb is grotesque. I have, however, never seen what we call child's play, that general abandonment to miscellaneous impulses, which consists in struggling, slapping, rolling, jumping, kicking, shouting, laughing, and quarrelling!

Two fine boys are very clever in harnessing paper carts to the backs of beetles with gummed traces, so that eight of them draw a load of rice up an inclined plane. You can imagine what the fate of such a load and team would be at home among a number of snatch-

ing hands. Here, a number of infants watch the per
formance with motionless interest, and never need the
adjuration, "Don't touch." In most of the houses there
are bamboo cages for "the shrill-voiced Katydid," and
the children amuse themselves with feeding these vocif-
erous grasshoppers. The channels of swift water in the
street turn a number of toy water-wheels, which set in
motion most ingenious mechanical toys, of which a
model of the automatic rice-husker is the commonest,
and the boys spend much time in devising and watching these, which are really very fascinating. It is the
holidays, but "holiday tasks" are given, and in the evenings you hear the hum of lessons all along the street
for about an hour. The school examination is at the
re-opening of the school after the holidays, instead of
at the end of the session, an arrangement which shows
an honest desire to discern the permanent gain made
by the scholars.

This afternoon has been fine and windy, and the boys
have been flying kites, made of tough paper on a bamboo frame, all of a rectangular shape, some of them five
feet square, and nearly all decorated with huge faces of
historical heroes. Some of them have a humming arrangement made of whalebone. There was a very interesting contest between two great kites, and it brought
out the whole population. The string of each kite,
for 30 feet or more below the frame, was covered with
pounded glass, made to adhere very closely by means of
tenacious glue, and for two hours the kite-fighters tried
to get their kites into a proper position for sawing the
adversary's string in two. At last one was successful,
and the severed kite became his property, upon which
victor and vanquished exchanged three low bows.
Silently as the people watched and received the destruction of their bridge, so silently they watched this excit-

ing contest. The boys also flew their kites while walking on stilts, a most dexterous performance, in which few were able to take part, and then a larger number gave a stilt race. The most striking out-of-door games, are played at fixed seasons of the year, and are not to be seen now.

There are twelve children in this *yadoya*, and after dark they regularly play at a game which Ito says "is played in the winter in every house in Japan." The children sit in a circle, and the adults look on eagerly, child-worship being more common in Japan than in America, and to my thinking, the Japanese form is the best.

This game of *I-ro-ha garuta*, or Alphabet Cards, is played with small cards, each one containing a proverb. On another is a picture which illustrates it. Each proverb begins with a letter of the Japanese syllabary. The cards are shuffled and dealt, and the children appoint one of their number to be the reader. He reads a proverb on one of his cards, and the one who has the picture corresponding to the proverb read calls out. The one who first gets rid of his cards wins the game, and the one who has the last card loses it. The game was played with great animation and rapidity, but with the most amusing courtesy. All the ugly, open-mouthed, kindly lookers-on were delighted. At the end the loser, who was a little girl, had a wisp of straw put into her hair; had it been a boy, he would have had certain prescribed ink marks made upon his face. All this was gone through with stinging wood smoke aggravating the eyes, cooking going on upon the fire, carding cotton on the mats, and from the far back gloom four horses watched the dimly-lighted circle. Then tea was handed round, and I gave sweetmeats to all the children. Then Ito made a rough translation of many of the proverbs,

some of which, partly from the odd language into which
he put them, and partly from their resemblance to our
own, made me laugh uncontrollably, and my mirth, or
my unsuccessful efforts to restrain it, proving contagious,
it ended in twenty people laughing themselves into a
state of exhaustion! I feel much better for it, and
thoroughly enjoyed the evening.

Ito has since written what he says is a good transla
tion of the best sayings, or what he thinks the best,
which I send. Is it not strange to find the same ideas
gathered up into recognisably similar forms in Japan as
in England, and cast into these forms at a date when
our ancestors were clothed in paint and skins? "Speak
of a man and his shadow comes." "A tongue of three
inches can kill a man of six feet." "Curse a neighbour
and dig two graves." "Never give a *ko-bang* to a cat."
"The fly finds the diseased spot." "A small-minded
man looks at the sky through a reed." "The putting-off
man sharpens his arrows when he sees the lion." "Diseases enter by the mouth." "For a woman to rule is as
for a hen to crow in the morning." These are a few,
with clever though not always refined illustrations, but
Ito brought a book of proverbs, of which he translated
many, among the best of which are — "Good doctrine
needs not help from marvels." "Love flies with the red
petticoat " (only unmarried girls wear this piquant garment). Among those which indicate the impossible are
— "Scattering a fog with a fan." "Building bridges to
the clouds." "To dip up the ocean with a shell."
Among the most curious of the axioms are — "If you
hate a man let him live." This is another of the proofs
of the disrelish for life which is so common among
Orientals. "Many words, little sense." "Let the
preaching suit the hearer." "To be over polite is to
be rude." "The doctor can't cure himself." "Hell's

torments are measured by money." "The fortune-teller can't tell his own fortune." "There are thorns on all roses." "Inquire seven times before you believe a report." "To know the new search the old." "He is a clever man who can preach a short sermon." "Don't rub salt on a sore." "A cur is bold (or barks bravely) before his own gate." "Treat every old man as thy father." "When old men grow too old, they must obey their children." "A good son makes a happy father." "Famous swords were made of iron scrapings." "A wise man keeps to his money." "A man who lends money to a friend will never more see his friend or his money." "Trust a woman so long as thy mother's eyes are on her." "Tell not thy secrets to a servant." "Thine own heart makes the world." [1] Some of these, you will observe, contain very good teaching, and others are intensely worldly. A number more, showing a distrust and low estimate of women, were translated, but I will only give two — "A wise wife seldom crosses her husband's threshold," and "A child less wife is a curse from the gods." One beautiful proverb is, "The poet at home sees the whole world," and another is, "The throne of the gods is on the brow of a righteous man."

From proverbial philosophy to personal privation is rather a descent, but owing to the many detentions on the journey my small stock of foreign food is exhausted, and I have been living here on rice, cucumbers, and salt salmon — so salt, that, after being boiled in two waters, it produces a most distressing thirst. Even this has failed to-day, as communication with the coast has been stopped for some time, and the village is suf-

[1] Several of these proverbs, with slight verbal differences, are to be found in a copious collection of Japanese proverbs given by Mr. Griffis in *The Mikado's Empire*.

fering under the calamity of its stock of salt fish being completely exhausted. There are no eggs, and rice and cucumbers are very like the "light food" which the Israelites "loathed." I had an omelette one day, but it was much like musty leather. The Italian minister said to me in Tôkiyô, "No question in Japan is so solemn as that of food," and many others echoed what I thought at the time a most unworthy sentiment. I recognised its truth to-day when I opened my last resort, a box of Brand's meat lozenges, and found them a mass of mouldiness. One can only dry clothes here by hanging them in the wood smoke, so I prefer to let them mildew on the walls, and have bought a straw rain-coat, which is more reliable than the paper water-proofs. I hear the hum of the children at their lessons for the last time, for the waters are falling fast, and we shall leave in the morning.   I. L. B.

THE TANABATA.

Hope deferred — Effects of the Flood — Activity of the Police — A Ramble in Disguise — The *Tanabata* Festival — Mr. Satow's Reputation — The Weaving Woman.

Kuroishi, *August 5*.

After all, the waters did not fall as was expected, and I had to spend a fourth day at Ikarigaseki. We left early on Saturday, as we had to travel fifteen miles without halting. The sun shone on all the beautiful country, and on all the wreck and devastation, as it often shines on the dimpling ocean the day after a storm. We took four men, crossed two severe fords where bridges had been carried away, and where I and the baggage got very wet; saw great devastations and much loss of crops and felled timber; passed under a cliff, which for 200 feet was composed of fine columnar basalt in six-sided prisms, and quite suddenly emerged on a great plain, on which green billows of rice were rolling sunlit before a fresh north wind. This plain is liberally sprinkled with wooded villages and surrounded by hills; one low range forming a curtain across the base of Iwakisan, a great snow-streaked dome, which rises to the west of the plain to a supposed height of 5000 feet. The water had risen in most of the villages to a height of four feet, and had washed the lower part of the mud walls away. The people were busy drying their *tatami*, *futons*, and clothing, reconstructing their dykes and small bridges, and fishing for the logs which were still coming down in large quantities.

In one town two very shabby policemen rushed upon us, seized the bridle of my horse, and kept me waiting for a long time in the middle of a crowd, while they toilsomely *bored* through the passport, turning it up and down, and holding it up to the light, as though there were some nefarious mystery about it. My horse stumbled so badly that I was obliged to walk to save myself from another fall, and just as my powers were failing, we met a *kuruma*, which, by good management, such as being carried occasionally, brought me into Kuroishi, a neat town of 5500 people, famous for the making of clogs and combs, where I have obtained a very neat, airy, upstairs room, with a good view over the surrounding country, and of the doings of my neighbours in their back rooms and gardens. Instead of getting on to Aomori I am spending three days and two nights here, and as the weather has improved, and my room is remarkably cheerful, the rest has been very pleasant. As I have said before, it is difficult to get any information about anything even a few miles off, and even at the Post Office they cannot give any intelligence as to the date of the sailings of the mail steamer between Aomori, twenty miles off, and Hakodaté.

The police were not satisfied with seeing my passport, but must also see me, and four of them paid me a polite but domiciliary visit the evening of my arrival. That evening the sound of drumming was ceaseless, and soon after I was in bed Ito announced that there was something really worth seeing, so I went out in my *kimono*, and without my hat, and in this disguise altogether escaped recognition as a foreigner. Kuroishi is unlighted, and I was tumbling and stumbling along in overhaste when a strong arm cleared the way, and the house-master appeared with a very pretty lantern, hanging close to the ground from a cane held in the hand. Thus came the phrase, " Thy word is a light unto my feet."

We soon reached a point for seeing the festival procession advance towards us, and it was so beautiful and picturesque, that it kept me out for an hour. It passes through all the streets between 7 and 10 P.M. each night, during the first week in August, with an ark, or coffer, containing slips of paper, on which (as I understand), wishes are written, and each morning at seven this is carried to the river, and the slips are cast upon the stream. The procession consisted of three monster drums nearly the height of a man's body, covered with horsehide, and strapped to the drummers, end upwards, and thirty small drums, all beaten rub-a-dub-dub without ceasing. Each drum has the *tomoyé* painted on its ends. Then there were hundreds of paper lanterns carried on long poles of various lengths, round a central lantern, 20 feet high, itself an oblong 6 feet long, with a front and wings, and all kinds of mythical and mystical creatures painted in bright colours upon it, a transparency rather than a lantern in fact. Surrounding it were hundreds of beautiful lanterns and transparencies of all sorts of fanciful shapes, fans, fishes, birds, kites, drums; the hundreds of people and children who followed all carried circular lanterns, and rows of lanterns with the *tomoyé* on one side and two Chinese characters on the other, hung from the eaves all along the line of the procession. I never saw anything more completely like a fairy scene, the undulating waves of lanterns as they swayed along, the soft lights and soft tints moving aloft in the darkness, the lantern-bearers being in deep shadow. This festival is called the *tanabata* or *seiseki* festival, but I am unable to get any information about it.[1] Ito says that he knows what it means, but is un-

---

[1] Mr. F. V. Dickins, has kindly given me the following notes on this curious festival. *Tanabata* is represented by characters meaning, seventh day of seventh month. It is also known as *Seiseki*, star-even-

able to explain, and adds the phrase he always uses
when in difficulties, " Mr. Satow would be able to tell
you all about it."   I. L. B.

ing. On the above evening offerings are made and adoration paid to
Shokujo, the " weaving woman," the star *Vega*, and Kengiu, the " herd-
man," said by some to be a star in *Aquila* and by others to be parts of
Capricornus and *Sagittarius*. The following typical legend of Chinese
origin is one of the most popular concerning these stars. On the bank
of the stream of heaven, a beautiful woman lived, who occupied herself
for years unsuccessfully in the attempt to weave a web of fine silk.
The Lord of Heaven, pitying her disappointment, sent her a husband,
who lived on the lower earth, in whose love she forgot her task. Displeased with this, the Lord of Heaven sent her back to her original
home, and only allowed her to visit her husband once a year, on the
evening of the seventh day of the seventh month. The woman, the
star *Vega*, is supposed to cross the Milky Way by a miraculous bridge,
formed by birds placing their wings diagonally across the heavenly
stream.

Those who on this evening are fortunate enough to observe the mingling of the two stars, known to the Japanese as Shokujo and Kengiu,
will find their wishes realised, if not in one year, within three years.
People may wish for ability, for long life and happiness, and for children, but women and girls wish chiefly for cleverness in needlework.
Various offerings are made on this evening, and are placed on a stand,
over which are arched two bamboos connected by a rice straw rope.

POPULAR SUPERSTITIONS.

A Lady's Toilet — Hair-dressing — Paint and Cosmetics — Afternoon.
Visitors — Christian Converts — Popular Superstitions — Wraiths
and Apparitions — Spiritualism — Omens and Dreams — Love and
Revenge.

KUROISHI, *August* 5.

THIS is a pleasant place, and my room has many advantages besides light and cleanliness, as, for instance, that I overlook my neighbours, and that I have seen a lady at her toilet preparing for a wedding! A married girl knelt in front of a black lacquer toilet-box with a spray of cherry blossoms in gold sprawling over it, and lacquer uprights at the top, which supported a polished metal mirror. Several drawers in the toilet-box were open, and toilet requisites in small lacquer boxes were lying on the floor. A female barber stood behind the lady, combing, dividing, and tying her hair, which, like that of all Japanese women, was glossy black, but neither fine nor long. The *coiffure* is an erection, a complete work of art. Two divisions, three inches apart, were made along the top of the head, and the lock of hair between these was combed, stiffened with a bandoline made from the *Uvario Japonica*, raised two inches from the forehead, turned back, tied, and pinned to the back hair. The rest was combed from each side to the back, and then tied loosely with twine made of paper. Several switches of false hair were then taken out of a long lacquer box, and with the aid of a quantity of bandoline and a solid pad, the ordinary smooth chignon was produced, to which several loops and bows of hair were added, interwoven with a little dark-blue *crêpe*, spangled with gold. A single thick, square-sided, tortoise-shell pin was stuck through the whole as an ornament.

The fashions of dressing the hair are fixed. They vary with the ages of female children, and there is a slight difference between the *coiffure* of the married and unmarried. The two partings on the top of the head and the chignon never vary. The amount of stiffening used is necessary, as the head is never covered out of doors. This arrangement will last in good order for a week or more — thanks to the wooden pillow.

The barber's work was only partially done when the hair was dressed, for every vestige of recalcitrant eyebrow was removed, and every downy hair which dared to display itself on the temples and neck was pulled out with tweezers. This removal of all short hair has a tendency to make even the natural hair look like a wig. Then the lady herself took a box of white powder, and laid it on her face, ears, and neck, till her skin looked like a mask. With a camel's-hair brush she then applied some mixture to her eyelids to make the bright eyes look brighter, the teeth were blackened, or rather reblackened, with a feather brush dipped in a solution of gall-nuts and iron filings — a tiresome and disgusting process, several times repeated, and then a patch of red was placed upon the lower lip. I cannot say that the effect was pleasing, but the girl thought so, for she turned her head so as to see the general effect in the mirror, smiled, and was satisfied. The remainder of her toilet, which altogether took over three hours, was preformed in private, and when she reappeared she looked as if a very unmeaning-looking wooden doll had been dressed up with the exquisite good taste, harmony, and quietness which characterise the dress of Japanese women.

A most rigid social etiquette draws an impassable line of demarcation between the costume of the virtuous woman in every rank and that of her frail sister. The humiliating truth that many of our female fashions are originated by those whose position we the most regret,

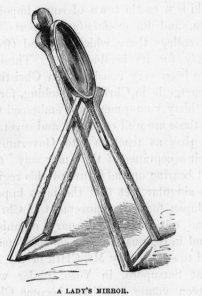

A LADY'S MIRROR.

and are then carefully copied by all classes of women in our country, does not obtain credence among Japanese women, to whom even the slightest approximation in the style of hairdressing, ornament, or fashion of garments would be a shame.

I was surprised to hear that three " Christian students" from Hirosaki wished to see me, three remarkably intelligent-looking, handsomely-dressed young men, who all spoke a little English. One of them had the brightest and most intellectual face which I have seen in Japan. They are of the *samurai* class, as I should have known from the superior type of face and manner. They said that they heard that an English lady was in the house, and asked me if I were a Christian, but apparently were not satisfied till, in answer to the question if I had a Bible, I was able to produce one.

Hirosaki is a castle town of some importance, $3\frac{1}{2}$ *ri* from here, and its ex-*daimiyô* supports a high-class school or college there, which has had two Americans successively for its head-masters. These gentlemen must have been very consistent in Christian living as well as energetic in Christian teaching, for under their auspices thirty young men have embraced Christianity. As all of these are well educated, and several are nearly ready to pass as teachers into Government employment, their acceptance of the "new way" may have an important bearing on the future of this region.

It is a singular fact that the most important work done in Japan for the advancement of Christianity has been done outside of missionary organisations altogether, and in regions in which no missionary, as such, is allowed to settle, — by Mr. Clark of the Agricultural College at Satsuporo, in Yezo, under whose teaching eighteen young men have become Christians, by Captain Jayne, a scientific teacher at a Government school in Kiushiu, under whom forty young men of the *samurai* class, now theological students in Kiyôto, received Christianity, and by Mr. Ing and Mr. Davidson at Hirosaki — all Americans, and all in Japanese employment. The latitude accorded to these teachers shows the extent to which Christianity is now tolerated.

These three students, who gave their names as Waki-yama, Akama, and Yamada, come over here to preach.

powers. Thus figures of the famous saints Nichiren and Kobodaishi carry their wearers safely to Paradise. Benten, the Japanese Venus, gives girls beauty and attractiveness; another divinity protects from snakes, of which all Japanese women have the utmost dread; another from the machinations of the fox; another gives good luck; another saves from drowning and accident; another bestows the gift of children, and makes them loveable; and so on infinitely. These amulets and figures are originally obtained from the temples, and are a source of revenue to the priests. In the rice-fields of late I have constantly seen sticks with papers inscribed with characters dangling from them. These are charms against a worm, and are obtained from the temples. Most of the horses in Akita and Aomori *ken* wear charms suspended from their necks.

The Buddhist priests sustain and foster all superstitions which they can turn to a profitable account. A rag rubbed upon the medicine god and conveyed to a sick person is, under some circumstances, supposed to have the same effect as a personal application. The amulet which saves from drowning is a certain cure for choking, if courageously swallowed. Certain superstitions govern the building of houses. Thus it is lucky to place the *kura* on the north-east side, the door to the south-east, and the cupboards on the south-west. In sleeping, the head must on no account be turned to the north, because that is the position of a corpse after death; and cold water must always be poured into the warm water in a vessel, not warm into cold, because in washing the dead the latter plan is adopted. It is very unlucky to use chopsticks of which one is bamboo and the other wood, because the tongs used to collect the ashes in the cremation grounds are made in this fash ion.

Ghosts are as much believed in in Japan as anywhere else, and they are not limited to apparitions of human beings, for the she-badger and the fox love to disport themselves after their departure from the body. Foxes play practical jokes, and steal away people's senses, and nearly always assume the shapes of beautiful women. The fox always follows his victims, who are usually men; while the badger always goes before hers, who are usually women befooled by her in the guise of loveable young men. A lover, thinking of the girl he loved as he passes her grave, is followed from the cemetery by a woman of great beauty carrying a lantern, but she is seen by a third person only as a hideous skeleton. Ghosts can be raised in various ways, some of which are like disused Hallowe'en practices. One way is to put into the *andon* a hundred rushlights, and repeat an incantation of a hundred lines. One of the rushlights is taken out at the end of each line, and the would-be ghost-seer then goes out in the dark with one light still burning, and blows it out, when the ghost ought to appear. Girls who have lost their lovers by death sometimes try this sorcery. The Japanese are terribly afraid of darkness; the poorest people keep a lamp burning all night. In these regions they will not walk along the roads after dark unless in companies. I have been compelled to make an early halt several times because the *mago* would not for double pay encounter the supernatural risks to be met with in returning at night. At Shingoji I was awoke by a great disturbance because a bald-pated monster with goggle eyes and a tongue hanging out of his mouth had looked over the folding-screens, a trick he often plays. The ghosts of suicides haunt the scene of self-destruction, specially if it be a well.

Spiritualism, as a mode of raising ghosts, has been

long practised in Japan. At Innai I saw a woman (the mediums are always women) going into a house to practise her craft. A father wished to know whether his son, who was ill of *kak'ke*, would recover. The mediums always carry a small box put up in a bundle of peculiar shape, and a light bark hat, not on the head, but in the hand. The contents of the box, if it has any, are known only to its possessor. Some say it contains the head of a dog which has been buried alive up to its neck, and has died of thirst. The medium sits down with the box in front of her, and twangs the string of a small bow ceaselessly on the lid. The inquirer sits opposite to her, and she throws water towards him out of a small cup. If it is a departed spirit which is to be summoned, a leaf from a grave-yard bouquet is used to splash the water; if the spirit of a living person, a bit of stick. The only question which the medium puts to the inquirer is whether he wishes to interview the living or the dead. In this instance of spiritualism at Innai, where Ito was present, a departed spirit was called. An incantation is said, and then the spirit speaks with the medium's voice. Ito (sceptic as he is) confessed that when at Niigata he went to a medium to ask the spirit of his dead father whether he would get safely through this journey through the interior.

Among the many ghosts in which junkmen believe, there is one malignant fellow who comes to them very politely and asks to borrow a dipper. The answer involves the exercise of much discrimination, for if a dipper with a bottom is courteously bestowed upon him, he uses it to bale water enough to swamp the junk, but if the bottom be hastily knocked out, and the dipper be thrown to him, he disappears; but in this last case, unless the act be accompanied by an incantation, the ghost turns into a sea *kappa*, a many-clawed monster, powerful enough to drag the junk to the bottom. In Minato I saw in a small temple a god hung over with offerings made by sailors in the belief that he can protect them from the ghost of the dipper.

I suppose that the common household superstitions are believed by all women and by most men of the lower classes, though "Young Japan" affects to laugh at them. Probably many of them are local, as some, for instance, which were believed at Nikkô are unknown here. One that I have met with everywhere is that those who throw clippings of nails or hair into the *kamado* or *irori* are in danger of disaster; and another, that no word containing the syllable *shi*, one meaning of which is death, must be used on New Year's Day.

Some of the superstitions are amusing. People always leave their clogs in the *doma* on entering a house, and it is believed that if you burn a *moxa* on the back of those of a tedious visitor, it will rid you of him. Purple or violet must not be worn at a marriage either by bride or bridegroom, lest divorce should come speedily, as these of all colours fade the soonest. To break the thong of a clog in front while walking is a sign of evil to the wearer's enemies, if at the back, to himself. Salt, as with us, has much mysterious significance. It must not be bought at night, and when purchased during the day, a little of it must be thrown into the fire to prevent misfortune and family quarrels. It is also sprinkled about the threshold after a funeral.

A fisherman, if he meets a priest on the road, will not catch any fish that day.

Conflagrations are frequent, and in many places the signs which portend them are carefully watched. Among these are a dog climbing on the roof of a house. a weasel crying once, and a cock crowing in the morn ing. To avert the evil a person must take a dipper in his left hand, and pour out three dippersful of water.

Many superstitions appear general among the people of the north. If a stalk of tea falls into the teacup, and stands upright for a second, a visitor is expected from the direction in which it falls. To pour tea out of the teapot in an absent fit in any way but by the spout is a sign of the approach of a priest. The shadow of a bird on the paper window is a sure sign of a visitor. These are so firmly believed in here that if any one of them happens the girls add some little adornment to their hair.

To break the chopsticks while eating is a sign of death. The north-east is a quarter in which special evil abides, and few people would build a house fronting that direction, lest destruction should come upon it. It is not possible to induce young girls to pour tea over a bowl of "red rice," as, if they did so, the marriage-day would be rainy. Few people will put on new clothes or sandals after 5 P.M. for fear of bringing bad luck. If a young man lights his pipe at the *andon* instead of the *hibachi*, he will not get a good wife. For children to eat the charred rice which sometimes remains at the bottom of the rice-pot is to ensure their marriage to persons scarred with small-pox. When small-pox is epidemic, a charm against the malady is for a person to write a notice on the front of his house that his children are absent. A young child is not allowed to look into a mirror, in the belief that if it sees its infant face and grows up to be married its first offspring will be twins.

Yesterday I saw one of the servants burying a tooth which had just been extracted, and found that it is a popular belief that a new tooth will grow in the socket, if the old one, if from the lower jaw, is thrown upon a house roof, and if from the upper, is buried as nearly as possible under the foundation. In the farming village: open wells are covered during an eclipse of the sun or moon, in the belief that poison drops from the sky at that time. I saw this done at Shirasawa a few days ago.

Of course dreams are regarded as of great importance, as the soul, in the form of a black ball, is supposed to leave the body during sleep and go off on various errands. People have a great dread of waking others suddenly, lest death should be caused by the soul not having time to return to the body from its possibly distant peregrinations. Dreams, as with us, are frequently supposed to go by contraries. Thus, it is lucky to dream of being stabbed, or of losing money; but if you dream of finding money, you are nearly sure to come to beggary. But to dream of riches with a picture of Daikoku purchased at a temple under the head, on the day of the Rat, one of the Japanese signs of the zodiac, is certain to bring an accession of fortune within a year. People also put pictures of the fabled treasure-ship under their heads on the night of the second day of the first month, in the hope of dreaming of it, which is a nearly certain sign of coming wealth.

The superstitions connected with love are endless. One is akin to those practised in England and Germany. A girl drops a long hair-pin from her head into the *tatami*, and counts the straws from it to the border — one, yes; two, no, and so on — and so divines her lover's faithfulness or its opposite.

Wherever Shintô prevails there are sacred trees, whose sacredness is denoted by a circle of rice-straw rope with straw tassels at intervals, and it is believed that the gods will visit with their vengeance those by or for whom they are desecrated. One of the darkest superstitions of Japan is intimately connected with these. I have before mentioned that disappointments in love often occasion suicide, but on some occasions they drive the disappointed maiden to seek revenge with the help of the gods. Having made a rude shape of straw, which represents the faithless lover, she repairs, "at the hour of the ox," two in the morning, to a shrine in a wood with the effigy and a hammer and nails in her hands, and nails the straw man to the sacred tree, asking the gods, as she does so, to impute the desecration to her lover, and revenge her on him. This visit is repeated at the same hour for several successive nights, till the object of vengeance fails and dies! I have seen such a tree with the straw effigy of a man nailed upon it — a token of sorrow and passion, of the family resemblance of heart to heart in all ages and lands, and of the jealousy which in Japan as elsewhere is "cruel as the grave."

These are a mere random selection from the hundreds of superstitious beliefs which I have noted down since I left Tôkiyô. Many of them have already faded from the cities, and in many parts of Southern Japan are spoken of merely in jest; but among the primitive people of the north they still hold their old sway and exercise their old terror.   I. L. B.

PRIMITIVE SIMPLICITY.

A Travelling Curiosity — Rude Dwellings — Primitive Simplicity —
The Public Bath-house — Solemn Queries — The "Few Stripes"
— A Trembling Hope.

KUROISHI.

YESTERDAY was beautiful, and dispensing for the first time with Ito's attendance, I took a *kuruma* for the day, and had a very pleasant excursion into a *cul de sac* in the mountains. The one drawback was the infamous road, which compelled me either to walk or be mercilessly jolted. The runner was a nice, kind, merry creature, quite delighted, Ito said, to have a chance of carrying so great a sight as a foreigner into a district in which no foreigner has ever been seen. In the absolute security of Japanese travelling, which I have fully realised for a long time, I look back upon my fears at Kasukabé, with a feeling of self-contempt.

The scenery, which was extremely pretty, gained everything from sunlight and colour, wonderful shades of cobalt and indigo, green blues and blue greens, and flashes of white foam in unsuspected rifts. It looked a simple, home-like region, a very pleasant land.

We passed through several villages of farmers who live in very primitive habitations, built of mud, looking as if the mud had been dabbed upon the framework with the hands. The walls sloped slightly inwards, the thatch was rude, the eaves were deep and covered all manner of lumber ; there was a smoke-hole in a few, but the majority smoked all over like brick-kilns, they had no windows, and the walls and rafters were black and shiny. Fowls and horses live on one side of the dark interior, and the people on the other. The houses were alive with unclothed children, and as I repassed in the evening unclothed men and women, nude to their waists, were sitting outside their dwellings with the

AKITA FARM-HOUSE.

small fry, clothed only in amulets, about them, several big yellow dogs forming part of each family group, and the faces of dogs, children, and people were all placidly contented! These farmers owned many good horses, and their crops were splendid. Probably on *matsuri* days all appear in fine clothes taken from ample hoards. They cannot be so poor, as far as the necessaries of life are concerned, they are only very "far back." They know nothing better, and are contented; but their houses are as bad as any that I have ever seen, and the simplicity of Eden is combined with an amount of dirt which makes me sceptical as to the performance of even weekly ablutions.

Upper Nakano is very beautiful, and in the autumn, when its myriads of star-leaved maples are scarlet and crimson, against a dark background of cryptomeria, among which a great white waterfall gleams like a snow-drift before it leaps into the black pool below, it must be well worth a long journey. I have not seen anything which has pleased me more. There is a fine flight of moss-grown stone steps down to the water, a pretty bridge, two superb stone *torii*, some handsome stone lanterns, and then a grand flight of steep stone steps up a hill-side dark with cryptomeria, leads to a small Shintô shrine. Not far off there is a sacred tree, with the token of love and revenge upon it, which I mentioned in the notes on superstitions in my last letter. The whole place is entrancing.

Lower Nakano, which I could only reach on foot, is only interesting as possessing some very hot springs, which are valuable in cases of rheumatism and sore eyes. It consists mainly of tea-houses and *yadoyas*, and seemed rather gay. It is built round the edge of an oblong depression, at the bottom of which the bath-houses stand, of which there are four, only nominally separated, and with but two entrances, which open directly upon the bathers. In the two end houses women and children were bathing in large tanks, and in the centre ones women and men were bathing together, but at opposite sides, with wooden ledges to sit upon all round. I followed the *kuruma* runner blindly to the baths, and when once in, I had to go out at the other side, being pressed upon by people from behind; but the bathers were too polite to take any notice of my most unwilling intrusion, and the *kuruma* runner took me in without the slightest sense of impropriety in so doing. I noticed that formal politeness prevailed in the bath-house as elsewhere, and that dippers and towels were handed from one to another with profound bows. The public bath-house is said to be the place in which public opinion is formed, as it is with us in clubs and public-houses, and that the presence of women prevents any dangerous or seditious consequences; but the Government is doing its best to prevent promiscuous bathing; and though the reform may travel slowly into these remote regions, it will doubtless arrive sooner or later. The public bath-house is one of the features of Japan.

Many solemn queries arise in this heathen land, which either do not occur, or occur with far less force, at home; and in my solitary ride they come up continually. Did the "one Father" make the salvation of millions of His heathen offspring depend upon the tardiness of a niggard and selfish Church, selfish and niggard both as to men and money? Did our Lord and Saviour Christ mean eternal perdition — a horror past human conception — by the mild term, "few stripes"? Was His death on Calvary an atonement or reconciliation for an elect few, or "a full, perfect, and sufficient sacrifice, oblation, and satisfaction for the sins of the whole world"? Is He the High Priest of a limited few, or is He at "the right hand of God," to make an endless intercession for the "whole world," for which He died, "that in the fulness of time He may gather together all things in one," so that "as in Adam all die, even so in Christ shall all be made alive"? Are not "the heathen His inheritance," and His redeemed "a multitude which no man can number, of all nations"?

Such and many similar questions must suggest them-

selves to any one living among these people, learning
their simple virtues and simple vices, and how kind the
heart is which beats under the straw cloak of the cultivator, realising all the time how few out of these thirty-
four millions have heard of Christ, and that of those
few the most have seen His precepts systematically
violated in the lives of His followers. Shall not the
Judge of all the earth do right?" Can we not trust
our brethren, who "are also His offspring," to the infinite compassion of Him "who spared not His own Son,
but delivered Him up for us all," and cling tremblingly,
as befits our ignorance, to the hope that when the work
of the "few stripes" is done, these shall be redeemed
from evil, and shall be gathered together, with all the
wandering children, into our "Father's house of many
mansions"? These remarks may seem a digression; but
such questions are forced upon me every hour of every
day.[1]   I. L. B.

[1] I leave these sentences as they stood in my letter; but, lest they
should be supposed to be written in disparagement of mission work, or
doubt of its necessity, I reiterate the belief expressed in the chapter on
Niigata Missions, that our Lord's parting command concerning the promulgation of His gospel is binding on all His followers until the world's
end, and that hopes and speculations as to the ultimate destiny of the
heathen have no bearing at all upon the positive duty of the Church, or
indeed any *practical* bearing of any kind.

END OF THE JOURNEY.

A hard Day's Journey — An Overturn — Nearing the Ocean — Joyful Excitement — Universal Greyness — Inopportune Policemen — A Stormy Voyage — A wild Welcome — A Windy Landing — The Journey's End.

HAKODATÉ, YEZO, *August* 12, 1878.

THE journey from Kuroishi to Aomori, though only 22½ miles, was a tremendous one, owing to the state of the roads; for more rain had fallen, and the passage of hundreds of pack-horses heavily loaded with salt-fish had turned the tracks into quagmires. At the end of the first stage the Transport Office declined to furnish a *kuruma*, owing to the state of the roads; but as I was not well enough to ride farther, I bribed two men for a very moderate sum to take me to the coast; and by accommodating each other, we got on tolerably, though I had to walk up all the hills and down many, to get out at every place where a little bridge had been carried away, that the *kurama* might be lifted over the gap, and often to walk for 200 yards at a time, because it sank up to its axles in the quagmire. In spite of all precautions, I was upset into a muddy ditch, with the *kuruma* on the top of me; but as my air-pillow fortunately fell between the wheel and me, I escaped with nothing worse than having my clothes soaked with water and mud, which, as I had to keep them on all night, might have given me cold, but did not. We met strings of pack-horses the whole way, carrying salt-fish, which is taken throughout the interior.

The mountain-ridge, which runs throughout the Main Island, becomes depressed in the province of Nambu, but rises again into grand, abrupt hills at Aomori Bay. Between Kuroishi and Aomori, however, it is broken up into low ranges, scantily wooded, mainly with pine, scrub oak, and the dwarf bamboo. The *Sesamum ignosco*, of which the incense sticks are made, covers some hills to the exclusion of all else. Rice grows in the valleys, but there is not much cultivation, and the country looks rough, cold, and hyperborean.

The farming hamlets grew worse and worse, with houses made roughly of mud, with holes scratched in the side for light to get in, or for smoke to get out, and the walls of some were only great pieces of bark and bundles of straw tied to the posts with straw ropes. The roofs were untidy, but this was often concealed by the profuse growth of the water-melons which trailed over them. The people were very dirty, but there was no appearance of special poverty, and a good deal of money must be made on the horses and *mago* required for the transit of fish from Yezo, and for rice to it.

At Namioka occurred the last of the very numerous ridges we have crossed since leaving Nikkô at a point called Tsugarusaka, and from it looked over a rugged country, upon a dark-grey sea, nearly landlocked by pine-clothed hills, of a rich purple indigo colour. The clouds were drifting, the colour was intensifying, the air was fresh and cold, the surrounding soil was peaty, the odours of pines were balsamic, it looked, felt, and smelt like home; the grey sea was Aomori Bay, beyond was the Tsugaru Strait, — my long land-journey was done. A traveller said a steamer was sailing for Yezo at night, so, in a state of joyful excitement, I engaged four men, and by dragging, pushing, and lifting, they got me into Aomori, a town of grey houses, grey roofs, and grey

stones on roofs, built on a beach of grey sand, round a
grey bay — a miserable-looking place, though the capital of the *ken*.

It has a great export trade in cattle and rice to Yezo,
besides being the outlet of an immense annual emigration from Northern Japan to the Yezo fishery, and imports from Hakodaté large quantities of fish, skins, and
foreign merchandise.   It has some trade in a pretty but
not valuable " seaweed " or variegated lacquer, called
Aomori lacquer, but not actually made there, its own
specialty being a sweetmeat made of beans and sugar.
It has a deep and well-protected harbour, but no piers
or conveniences for trade.   It has barracks and the
usual Government buildings, but there was no time to
learn anything about it, — only a short half-hour for
getting my ticket at the *Mitsu Bishi* office, where they
demanded and copied my passport; for snatching a
morsel of fish at a restaurant where " foreign food " was
represented by a very dirty table-cloth; and for running
down to the grey beach, where I was carried into a
large *sampan*, crowded with Japanese steerage passengers.

The wind was rising, a considerable surf was running,
the spray was flying over the boat, the steamer had her
steam up, and was ringing and whistling impatiently,
there was a scud of rain, and I was standing, trying to
keep my paper waterproof from being blown off, when
three inopportune policemen jumped into the boat and
demanded my passport.   For a moment I wished them
and the passport under the waves!   The steamer is a
little old paddle-boat of about 70 tons, with no accommodation but a single cabin on deck.   She was as clean
and trim as a yacht, and, like a yacht, totally unfit for
bad weather.   Her captain, engineers, and crew were
all Japanese, and not a word of English was spoken.

My clothes were very wet, and the night was colder than the day had been, but the captain kindly covered me up with several blankets on the floor, so I did not suffer. We sailed early in the evening, with a brisk northerly breeze, which chopped round to the south-east, and by eleven blew a gale; the sea ran high, the steamer laboured and shipped several heavy seas, much water entered the cabin, the captain came below every half-hour, tapped the barometer, sipped some tea, offered me a lump of sugar, and made a face and gesture indicative of bad weather, and we were buffeted about mercilessly till 4 A.M., when heavy rain came on, and the gale fell temporarily with it. The boat is not fit for a night passage, and always lies in port when bad weather is expected, and as this was said to be the severest gale which has swept the Tsugaru Strait since January, the captain was uneasy about her, but being so, showed as much calmness as if he had been a Briton!

The gale rose again after sunrise, and when, after doing sixty miles in fourteen hours, we reached the heads of Hakodaté Harbour, it was blowing and pouring like a bad day in Argyllshire, the spin-drift was driving over the bay, the Yezo mountains loomed darkly and loftily through rain and mist, and wind and thunder, and "noises of the northern sea," gave me a wild welcome to these northern shores. A rocky head like Gibraltar, a cold-blooded-looking grey town, straggling up a steep hill-side, a few *coniferæ*, a great many grey junks, a few steamers and vessels of foreign rig at anchor, a number of *sampans* riding the rough water easily, seen in flashes between gusts of rain and spin-drift, were all I saw, but somehow it all pleased me from its breezy, northern look.

The steamer was not expected in the gale, so no one met me, and I went ashore with fifty Japanese clustered on the top of a decked *sampan*, in such a storm of wind and rain that it took us 1½ hour to go half a mile; then I waited shelterless on the windy beach till the Customs' Officers were roused from their late slumbers, and then battled with the storm for a mile up a steep hill. I was expected at the hospital Consulate, but did not know it, and came here to the Church Mission House, to which Mr. and Mrs. Dening kindly invited me when I met them in Tôkiyô. I was unfit to enter a civilised dwelling; my clothes, besides being soaked, were coated and splashed with mud up to the top of my hat; my gloves and boots were finished, my mud-splashed baggage was soaked with salt water; but I feel a somewhat legitimate triumph at having conquered all obstacles, and having accomplished more than I intended to accomplish when I left Yedo.

How musical the clamour of the northern ocean is! How inspiriting the shrieking and howling of the boisterous wind! Even the fierce pelting of the rain is home-like, and the cold in which one shivers is stimulating! You cannot imagine the delight of being in a room with a door that will lock, to be in a bed instead of on a stretcher, of finding twenty-three letters containing good news, and of being able to read them in warmth and quietness under the roof of an English home! **I. L. B.**

ITINERARY OF ROUTE FROM NIIGATA TO AOMORI

	No. of Houses.	Ri.	Chô.
Kisaki	56	4	
Tsuiji	209	6	
Kurokawa	215	2	12
Hanadati	20	2	
Kawaguchi	27	3	
Numa	24	1	18
Tamagawa	40	3	
Okuni	210	2	11
Kurosawa	17	1	18
Ichinono	20	1	18
Shirokasawa	42	1	21
Tenoko	120	3	11
Komatsu	513	2	13
Akayu	350	4	
Kaminoyama	650	5	
Yamagata	21,000 souls	3	19
Tendo	1,040	3	8
Tateoka	307	3	21
Tochiida	217	1	33
Obanasawa	506	1	21
Ashizawa	70	1	21
Shinjô	1,060	4	6
Kanayama	165	3	27
Nosoki	37	3	9
Innai	257	3	12
Yusawa	1,506	3	35
Yokote	2,070	4	27
Rckugo	1,062	6	
		—	—
Carry forward		88	1

	No. of Houses.	*Ri.*	*Chô.*
Brought forward		88	1
Shingoji	209	1	28
Kubota	36,587 souls	16	
Minato	2,108	1	28
Abukawa	163	3	33
Ichi Nichi Ichi	306	1	34
Kado	151	2	9
Hinikoyama	396	2	9
Tsugurata	186	1	14
Tubiné	153	1	18
Kiriishi	31	1	14
Kotsunagi	47	1	16
Tsuguriko	136	3	5
Odaté	1,673	4	23
Shirasawa	71	2	19
Ikarigaseki	175	4	18
Kuroishi	1,176	6	19
Daishaka	43	4	
Shinjo	51	2	21
Aomori		1	24
		Ri 147	31

About 368 miles.

This is considerably under the actual distance, as on several of the mountain routes the *ri* is 56 *chô*, but in the lack of accurate information the *ri* has been taken at its ordinary standard of 36 *chô* throughout.

END OF VOL. I.

AINOS OF YEZO.

UNBEATEN TRACKS IN JAPAN

AN ACCOUNT OF

TRAVELS ON HORSEBACK IN THE INTERIOR

INCLUDING

VISITS TO THE ABORIGINES OF YEZO AND THE SHRINES
OF NIKKÔ AND ISÉ

By ISABELLA L. BIRD

AUTHOR OF 'A LADY'S LIFE IN THE ROCKY MOUNTAINS' 'SIX
MONTHS IN THE SANDWICH ISLANDS'
ETC. ETC.

IN TWO VOLUMES.—VOL. II.

WITH MAP AND ILLUSTRATIONS

———————

NEW YORK
G. P. PUTNAM'S SONS
27 AND 29 WEST 23D STREET

CONTENTS OF VOL. II.

THE ISÉ SHRINES.

ANOTHER PILGRIMAGE.

LAKE BIWA.

PROSPECTS OF CHRISTIANITY.

CREMATION.

JAPANESE PUBLIC AFFAIRS.

APPENDIX.

LIST OF ILLUSTRATIONS.

YEZO.

SEPARATED from the main island of Japan by the
Tsugaru Strait, and from Saghalien by the narrow strait
of La Perouse, in shape an irregular triangle, extending
from long. 139° 50′ E. to long. 146° E., and from lat.
41° 30′ N. to lat. 45° 30′ N., its most northern point considerably south of the Land's End, Yezo has a climate
of singular severity, a heavy snowfall, and, in its northern parts, a Siberian winter. Its area is 35,739 square
miles, or considerably larger than that of Ireland, while
its estimated population is only 123,000. The island is
a mountain mass, with plains well grassed and watered.
Impenetrable jungles and impassable swamps cover
much of its area. It has several active volcanoes, and
the quietude of some of its apparently extinct ones is
not to be relied upon. Its forests and swamps are
drained by innumerable short, rapid rivers, which are
subject to violent freshets. In riding round the coast
they are encountered every two or three miles, and often
detain the traveller for days on their margins. The
largest is the Ishkari, famous for salmon.

The coast has few safe harbours, and though exempt
from typhoons, is swept by heavy gales and a continuous
surf. The cultivated land is mainly in the neighbour-

hood of the sea, with the exception of the extensive plain around Satsuporo. The interior is forest-covered, and the supplies of valuable lumber are nearly inexhaustible, and include thirty-six kinds of useful timber trees. Openings in the forest are heavily grassed with the *Eulalia Japonica*, a grass higher than the head of a man on horseback; and the forest itself is rendered impassable, not only by a dense growth of the tough and rigid dwarf bamboo, which attains a height of eight feet, but by ropes and nooses of various vines, *lianas* in truth, which grow profusely everywhere. The soil is usually rich, and the summer being warm is favourable to the growth of most cereals and root crops. The climate is not well suited to rice, but wheat ripens everywhere. Most of the crops which grow in the northern part of the main island flourish in Yezo, and English fruit-trees succeed better than in any part of Japan. I never saw finer crops anywhere than in Mombets on Volcano Bay. Cleared land, from the richness of the soil formed by vegetable decomposition, is fitted to produce crops as in America, for twenty years without manuring, and a regular and sufficient rainfall, as in England, obviates the necessity for irrigation.

The chief mineral wealth of Yezo is in its coalfields, but the Government is jealous of the introduction of foreign capital, and till the embargo is removed, it is unlikely that this source of wealth will be utilised on a large scale, and much of the money appropriated for the developement of mines is frittered away by official "squeezes" *en route*. But this coal may eventually turn out of great importance to the world. Mr. Lyman, the able head of the Geological Survey, estimates the quantity of coal in the Yezo coalfields at *one hundred and fifty thousand million tons;* in other words, that

Yezo could yield the present annual product of Great Britain for a thousand years to come ! ! !

The official name of Yezo is the *Hokkaido* or Northern Sea Circuit, and owing to various circumstances, actual and imaginary, it is under a separate department of the Government called the Colonisation Department, known as the *Kaitakushi*, or, as we should say, the "Development Department." This department has spent enormous sums upon Yezo, some of which have been sunk in unprofitable and costly experiments, while others bear fruit in productive improvements. The appropriation of this year is over £302,000. The island differs so much in its general features and natural products from the rest of Japan, that it is exempt from the ordinary taxes, and is subject to special imposts on produce, which bring in a revenue of about £72,000 annually, a large sum to be paid by a small population.

Satsuporo, on the Ishkari River, is the creation of this Department. The chief and most hopeful of its operations there is an Agricultural College on the model of the Massachusetts Agricultural College, under native direction, but with a staff of four able American professors. Its graduation course is four years, and the number of students is limited to sixty. It gives a sound English education, with special attention to surveying and civil engineering, as required for the construction of ordinary roads, railroads, drainage and irrigation works, and such thorough instruction in agriculture and horticulture as is required by the necessities of farming in Yezo. There are model farms both at Satsuporo and Nanai, near Hakodaté, and nursery gardens for exotic trees, vegetables, and flowers. The department is introducing sheep and pigs, and by importing blood stock is endeavouring to improve the breed of horses and cattle. At Satsuporo it has extensive sawmills, a silk factory, a tannery, and a brewery, and large flour mills both there and at Nanai.

It would be uninteresting to give a list of all which the *Kaitakushi* has attempted for the development of Yezo. Many of its schemes have proved utterly abortive, and some which still exist are not carried out with the completeness and perseverance necessary for success. Its funds are undoubtedly eaten up by superfluous officials, who draw salaries and perpetrate "squeezes," and do little besides smoke and talk. Roads are much needed. The broad road from Hakodaté to Satsuporo, on which much money is always being expended, is in a permanently wretched state, and is mainly available for long strings of pack-horses, whose deep cross ruts had not disappeared even in September; and the steam-ferry of twenty-five miles on this main road is carried on by a steamer whose extreme speed is five miles an hour, and whose boilers, to use the expressive native phrase, are constantly "sick." The theories of "development" are very good; mistakes have been and are being made; some valuable practical measures are neglected in favour of Utopian experiments, and some good results are being attained.

The Government is supposed to have two objects in view in developing Yezo. One is to provide a field for emigration for the inhabitants of those parts of Japan which are supposed to be over-populated, and the other, by building up a population in Yezo, to erect a sort of bulwark against aggressive designs which are supposed to be entertained by Russia, a power which is as much distrusted in Japan as in England. Colonies have been settled in several favourable regions; grants of land have been made to a great many *samurai*, and at Satsuporo nearly 1000 soldiers are settled with their families in detached houses, each with several acres of land·

seeds and fruit-trees are sold to settlers at a very low
price, and many agricultural advantages are provided
which do not exist on the main island ; but still, either
from a natural disinclination to emigrate, or from a
dread of the taxes imposed on produce, the *Hokkaido*
fails to attract a population, and a region which could
support six millions has a scattered sprinkling, and that
mainly round the coasts, of only 123,000 souls.

The fisheries of Yezo are magnificent, and rival those
of the opposite coast of Oregon ; but they are overtaxed,
the tax levied being from 10 to 25 per cent on the yield.
Salmon is the specialty, but cuttle-fish, seaweed, and
bêche de mer are also important articles of export. There
are many fishing stations on the southern coast, but the
most important are at Ishkari in the north, near Satsuporo, the new capital. The salmon-fishing there is one
of the sights of Japan. Some of the seines are 4000
feet in length, and require seventy men to work them.
A pair of such, making three hauls a day, sometimes
catch 20,000 salmon, averaging, when cured, 10 lbs. each.
The revenue from the fisheries of the Ishkari river alone
is $50,000 annually. Yezo fish is not only sent through-
out the interior of Japan, but is shipped to China. The
Ainos, the aborigines of the island, are largely employed
in the fishing, and an immense number of emigrants
from the provinces of Nambu and Ugo resort to Yezo
for the fishing season.

Hakodaté, the northern Treaty Port, a flourishing city
of 37,000 people, is naturally the capital, with its deep
and magnificent harbour well sheltered in all winds.
Situated on a gravelly hill-slope, with a sunny exposure
and splendid natural drainage, it is fitted to recruit energies which have been exhausted by the damp heat of
Yokohama and Tôkiyô. Though it has occasionally nine
inches of snow on the ground in November, the snow-

fall is not excessive, as it is in the north of the island ,
it does not lie permanently on the ground, and there are
many sunny winter days, so many, indeed, that the
slush is worse than the snow. It has a mean annual
temperature of about 10° below that of Yedo, but the
range in the direction of cold is much greater. The
minimum is 2°, and the maximum 88°. The nights, even
in hot weather, are nearly always cool. In a period of
nine years the annual rainfall has averaged 51.9 inches,
and the average number of rain days is about 98.

Hakodaté is annually falling away as a foreign port.
In fact, its foreign trade is reduced to nothing. It has
only two foreign firms, and its foreign residents, exclusive of Chinese, only number 37. If it were not for
the number of ships of war which visit it every summer, and for the arrival of a few visitors in impaired
health, it would be nearly as dull as Niigata. But as a
Japanese port it is an increasingly thriving place. It is
unprofitable for foreign vessels to come so far to this
one point, now that Japanese steamers, which can trade
at *all* ports, are so numerous. Foreign merchandise is
now imported by Japanese merchants in Japanese ships,
and the chief articles of export — dried fish, seaweed,
and skins — are sent direct to China and the main
island in native vessels. Fine passenger steamers of the
Mitsu Bishi Company run between Hakodaté and Yokohama every ten days, and to Niigata once a month,
besides cargo boats, and junks and native vessels of
foreign rig arrive and depart in numbers with every
fair wind.

The Government buildings are extensive, and the
hospital and prisons are under admirable native management. Remote as Hakodaté is, it does not seem to me
to be behind any city of its size in enterprise, general
comfort, cleanliness, and good order. The *Kaitakushi*

has seventeen schools in the city, in which the pupils
are taught reading, writing, and arithmetic up to frac-
tions, along with universal history and geography; besides which there are numbers of private schools, which
only teach reading and writing. Some of the shopkeepers, in a most enlightened spirit, have established
an evening school for apprentices and assistants between
twelve and eighteen, who are engaged during the day,
and the fees for all these schools are moderate.

The Post Office and Custom House are efficiently
managed by Japanese officials, in conformity with foreign usages; and though the Judicial Department
gives little satisfaction, the police are so efficient that
H.B.M.'s Consul officially reports that "no thief or
criminal can escape the vigilance of the authorities!"
Japanese ship-carpenters are designing and turning out
small schooners of foreign rig, and Japanese merchants
import foreign goods, such as clothing, provisions, hard-
ware, crockery, glass, fancy goods, and alcoholic liquors,
to such an extent that the absence of a foreign store is
scarcely felt.

Such are some of the signs of progress in a city
which, when Mr. Alcock visited it in 1859 to instal the
British Consul, had a population of only 6000 people,
and was only resorted to by a few whalers!

It is the centre of missionary operations for the island;
and at present the Greeks, Romanists, Church Missionary Society, and American Methodist Episcopal Church,
have agents there, limited, of course, to the treaty distance of twenty-five miles, unless they obtain travelling
passports under the ordinary regulations.

Besides Hakodaté, there are only two towns of any
importance — Matsumae, a decayed place of about
16,000 people, formerly the residence of a very powerful *daimiyô;* and Satsuporo, the capital, a town of 3000

people, laid out on the plan of an American city, with wide, rectangular streets, lined by low Japanese houses and shops, and tasteless, detached, frame houses. The American idea is further suggested by the *Kaitakushi* offices with a capitol copied from the capitol at Washington. Besides the Government Buildings and those which have been previously mentioned, there is a hospital under the charge of an American doctor.

Near Satsuporo are several agricultural settlements, and the experiments there and elsewhere on the island prove that though the winter is long and severe, the climate and soil are specially favourable for winter wheat, maize, millet, buckwheat, potatoes, pease, beans, and other vegetables and cereals, as well as for Japanese hemp, which commands a high price, owing to the length, fineness, and silkiness of its fibre. Thousands of acres of well-watered grass-land lie utterly useless in the neighbourhood of Satsuporo on the Ishkari river.

Wild animals and game in large numbers have their home in the impenetrable forests of the interior. In the Hakodaté market, at different seasons of the year, are to be bought at moderate prices, grouse, hares, quail, snipe, teal, venison, woodcock, wild duck, and bear, and bear-furs and deer-skins are among the important articles of export.

The chief object of interest to the traveller is the remnant of the Aino race, the aborigines of Yezo, and not improbably of the whole of Japan, peaceable savages, who live on the coasts and in the interior by fishing and hunting, and stand in the same relation to their Japanese subjugators as the Red Indians to the Americans, the Jakkoons to the Malays, and the Veddas to the Sinhalese. In truth, it must be added that they receive better treatment from their masters than is accorded to any of these subject races. The Letters

which follow contain all that I could learn about them
from actual observation, but Mr. Yasuda Sadanori, First
Secretary of the *Kaitakushi* Department, has supplied
a few additional facts at the request of Sir Harry
Parkes : —

"A rough census of the Ainos made in 1873 gives
their numbers at —

Males . . .	6118
Females . . .	6163
Total . .	12,281

Since that year no separate census has been made, but
the Ainos are believed to be decreasing in number.

"As regards taxes, they pay partly in money and
partly in kind.

"The education law of the Ministry of Public Instruction does not apply to the *Hokkaido*, but a similar
system has been adopted by the *Kaitakushi* Department,
and is applied to all inhabitants of the island without
distinction of origin, the object of the Imperial Government being to teach Ainos and Japanese alike.

"Special arrangements have been made for the purpose of enabling the Ainos to live."

The "hairy Ainos," as these savages have been called,
are stupid, gentle, good-natured, and submissive. They
are a wholly distinct race from the Japanese. In complexion they resemble the peoples of Spain and Southern Italy, and the expression of the face and the manner of showing courtesy are European rather than
Asiatic. If not taller, they are of a much broader and
heavier make than the Japanese ; the hair is jet black,
very soft, and on the scalp forms thick, pendant masses,
occasionally wavy, but never showing any tendency to
curl. The beard, moustache, and eyebrows are very

thick and full, and there is frequently a heavy growth of stiff hair on the chest and limbs. The neck is short, the brow high, broad, and massive, the nose broad and inclined to flatness, the mouth wide but well formed, the line of the eyes and eyebrows perfectly straight, and the frontal sinuses well marked. Their language is a very simple one. They have no written characters, no literature, no history, very few traditions, and have left no impression on the land from which they have been driven.

In Yezo the traveller is conscious of a freer atmosphere than he has breathed on the main island, and it is not only the air which circulates more freely, but men and beasts have plenty of elbow-room. You can get a tolerable horse, and ride him where you please, without being brought up by a trespass notice or a rice-swamp; you go off the roads and gallop for miles over breezy commons by the sea-shore, covered with red roses; you can lead a half-savage life, and swim rivers, and climb mountains, and "light a fire in woods," without offending against "regulations;" in a word, you can do all that you may not do on the main island; and apart from the interest of investigation and observation, there is a charm about the thinly-peopled country, a fascination in the long moan of the Pacific between Tomakomai and Cape Erimo, in the glorious loneliness of the region round Volcano Bay, and in the breeziness and freedom of Yezo life, which makes my memories of Yezo in some respects the most delightful which I have brought away from Japan.

THE MISSION WORK.

Form and Colour — A Windy Capital — Eccentricities in House Roofs
— Social Dulness — Mission Agencies — A Disorderly Service
Daily Preaching — A Buddhist Temple — A Buddhist Sermon.

HAKODATÉ, YEZO, *August* 13, 1878.

AFTER a tremendous bluster for two days the weather
has become beautifully fine, and I find the climate here
more invigorating than that of the main island. It is
Japan, but yet there is a difference somehow. When the
mists lift they reveal not mountains smothered in greenery, but naked peaks, volcanoes only recently burnt
out, with the red ash flaming under the noonday sun,
and passing through shades of pink into violet at sun-
down. Strips of sand border the bay, ranges of hills,
with here and there a patch of pine or scrub, fade into
the far-off blue, and the great cloud shadows lie upon
their scored sides in indigo and purple. Blue as the
Adriatic are the waters of the land-locked bay, and the
snowy sails of pale junks look whiter than snow against
its intense azure. The abruptness of the double peaks
behind the town is softened by a belt of cryptomeria,
the sandy strip which connects the headland with the
mainland heightens the general resemblance of the
contour of the ground to Gibraltar, but while one
dreams of the western world a *kuruma* passes one at a
trot, temple drums are beaten in a manner which does
not recall "the roll of the British drum," a Buddhist
funeral passes down the street, or a man-cart pulled and

pushed by four yellow-skinned, little-clothed mannikins, creaks by, with the monotonous grunt of *Ha huida*.

A single look at Hakodaté itself makes one feel that it is Japan all over. The streets are very wide and clean, but the houses are mean and low. The city looks as if it had just recovered from a conflagration. The houses are nothing but tinder. The grand tile roofs of some other cities are not to be seen. There is not an element of permanence in the wide and windy streets. It is an increasing and busy place; it lies for two miles along the shore, and has climbed the hill till it can go no higher; but still houses and people look poor. It has a skeleton aspect too, which is partially due to the number of permanent "clothes-horses" on the roofs. Stones, however, are its prominent feature. Looking down upon it from above you see miles of grey boulders, and realise that every roof in the windy capital is "hodden doun" by a weight of paving stones. Nor is this all. Some of the flatter roofs are pebbled all over like a courtyard, and others, such as the roof of this house, for instance, are covered with sod and crops of grass, the two latter arrangements being precautions against risks from sparks during fires. These paving stones are certainly the cheapest possible mode of keeping the roofs on the houses in such a windy region, but they look odd.

None of the streets, except one high up the hill, with a row of fine temples and temple grounds, call for any notice. Nearly every house is a shop; most of the shops supply only the ordinary articles consumed by a large and poor population; either real or imitated foreign goods abound in Main Street, and the only novelties are the furs, skins, and horns, which abound in shops devoted to their sale. I covet the great bear furs, and the deep cream-coloured furs of Aino dogs, which are cheap as well as handsome. There are many second-hand, or, as they are called, "curio" shops, and the cheap lacquer from Aomori is also tempting to a stranger.

The foreigners, all told, number thirty-seven. There is little social intercourse, owing to antagonism in morals and manners, and when the last stranger leaves at the end of September, and the long winter sets in, it must be dreary enough for people who have not plenty of work which is worth doing. In summer, as now, it is very lively, owing to the frequent arrivals and departures of European ships of war, and the visits of health-seeking strangers, who go up to some pretty lakes which lie at the foot of the flushed volcano of Komono-taki, or adventure into the interior as far as Satsuporo, the nominal capital. The British Consul, Mr. Eusden, has been here for nine years, and the cordial and graceful hospitalities shown by Mrs. Eusden to foreigners, without distinction of nation, often leave pleasanter memories than the profuse, conventional gaieties of other naval resorts. Otherwise, to climb the peak, to go to see Nanai, one of the experimental farms of the *Kaitakushi* Department, and to shoot snipe, are the only diversions.

The four bodies of Christians which have missions here have built church edifices, of which the Romish is the largest, and the Greek the most decorated, the walls being covered with pictures. Hitherto the Greek Mission has been very successful in making converts, and though Father Nicolai is alone, he has four or five ordained native helpers. Some "sisters" have lately arrived to join the Romish Mission, and will probably give it a great impetus. The Mission of the C. M. S. is a comparatively new one, and is represented by Mr. Dening, at whose house I am staying, and Mr. Ogawa, a remarkably bright native evangelist of the *samurai* class. There have been eight baptisms at Hakodaté. Mr. Dening has out stations within treaty limits, where he preaches once a week, but Yezo is Buddhist, and in one of these places, Ono, the opposition is very strong. We made an expedition to it on pack-ponies, which went the whole way at a pace feli itously called the "Yezo Scramble." After leaving the neck of land which unites the headland with the mainland it was a charming ride in the bright sunshine, over sandy ground, covered with grass and great red roses, mingled with honeysuckle, *sedums*, the bee-haunted *Stephanandra flexuosa*, and the reddening leaves of anemones, with glimpses of the blue of the bay on the left, and of the red peaks of the volcano above dark green ravines. From the sandy village of Arakawa a bridle track, among gardens, and hamlets, and very pretty wooded country, leads to the large village of Ono, where the many exotic trees and flowers which the Government has distributed are very flourishing. On our way we met a number of men, and an Aino, with spears and muskets, *riding*, not sitting, on horses, returning from killing a bear. Near Ono there is a Government factory, where they are utilising the strong silk of the mountain silk-worm, which feeds on the tough leaves of a species of oak.

At Ono there is a schoolroom with a boarded floor, and Ogawa, the catechist, lives there; but though there has been Christian teaching for a year, there has been no result. The village was keeping *matsuri*, but when the doors of the schoolroom were opened at eight the room filled at once with a disorderly crowd of men, women, and children, who came in like a tornado, and instead of leaving their wooden clogs at the door, as is customary, clattered them on the floor with a deafening din. Three hundred people, some the worse for *saké*, clattering clogs, shouting, clustering on the window-sills, climbing on the benches, laughing, eating, lighting their pipes at the lamps, throwing off their *kimonos*, and keeping up a prolonged uproar for an hour and a quarter, were the most unpromising audience I have ever seen. Mr. Dening has a singular aptitude for languages, and has acquired not only a wonderful command of the colloquial Japanese spoken by the lower classes, but, what is even more, the tones in which they speak; and having a strong *physique*, and a very powerful voice, he perseveringly made himself heard above the uproar, which was not, as I supposed, an exceptional one stimulated by the spectacle of three foreign ladies, but is the regular accompaniment of Christian preaching in Ono. Mr. Dening gives his time, strength, and heart to his work, with a vigour, energy, and enthusiasm which could not be surpassed, and which are unchilled by opposition and disappointment, otherwise an Ono audience would have made an end of his efforts long ago, for the Buddhist priests stir up the people against the "new way." Where Shintô prevails, indifference is the rule. We left the village at 9 P.M., and, owing to the fatigue and fears of the other ladies, who were not accustomed to ride, and who were afraid of deserting the "scramble" for a gallop, we did not reach Hakodaté till 1 A.M., and then in a sorry plight, after a "scramble" of twenty-five miles. It was the first really exquisite night that I have seen in Japan; sharp tree shadows on dew-gemmed grass, broad moonlight on a silver sea, silver clouds drifting across mountain summits, and a cool, soft air, laden with the scent of sleeping flowers.

On Sunday evening a new preaching-place was opened in the main street of Hakodaté, a front room and *doma* open to the street, with kitchen extending to the back; and it is among the many instances of the toleration which Christianity enjoys, that after this place was filled, the police, who frequently passed, never interfered with the crowd which assembled outside. The people were very quiet, and tolerably stationary, quite different from the Ono "pagans." A few, who sat on the stairs leading to the upper room, called for the *tabako-bon* and smoked, and others had trays of refreshments carried to them; but they do the same in their own temples.

It appears very up-hill mission work here. The work has to be sought and made, and frequently, when the novelty has passed by, the apparent interest dies away. A medical missionary is in a very different position. His work seeks him, and grows upon him daily, with endless interesting ramifications, and he has, at least, the satisfaction of successfully ministering to the bodies of men.

Since the missionaries arrived here, the Buddhists, as at Niigata, have established daily services in one or other of the large temples which form one side of one of the streets, and I have been to see them nearly every day. The large temple is well filled every afternoon with men and women, all of the poorer classes, and as quiet and orderly as they can be. They occupy the part railed off from the holier place, in which the priests minister. Very low and sweet, though heard all over the city, is the sound of the great bronze bell which summons the hearers, and exactly at three the priests fold back the heavily-gilded doors of the chancel and light the candles and lamps which shed a "dim religious light" through the gorgeous interior, revealing the high altar, covered with an altar-cloth of green brocade, and side altars hung with white brocade embroidered with gold. On the low altar incense ascends between vases of white flowers, and a dreamy sensuousness pervades the whole building. Four priests in chasubles of black silk gauze, over pure white cassocks, with green brocade squares of a large size hanging behind them by a shoulder-strap of green silk, kneel with their backs to the people, and in front of them eight more similarly dressed, except that the brocade squares which hang behind them are alternately green and brown, and embroidered in silver. Before each is a low, lacquer desk for the service-books, and the sweet-toned bells which accompany service. Two more priests kneel at the sides of the altar. A bell sounds, fourteen shaven heads are bowed three times to the earth, more lamps are lighted; a bell sounds again, and then litanies are chanted monotonously, with bells tinkling, and the people responding at intervals, in a tongue to them unknown, *Namu Amida Butsu.* After an hour the priests glide away in procession, and one of those who have hitherto been kneeling at the altar mounts a square pulpit just within the rail which separates them from the people, sits down, not in Japanese fashion, but cross-legged, after the manner of the founder of his faith, and preaches for an hour with much energy.

Would you like to know how very diverting a sermon in Japan can be made? The following is a fragment of a translation of one of considerable length, which I have just come upon in the *Japan Mail* for June 1875. The sermon, as is proper, takes a text, which is to be found in the Chinese Classics—

"That which is evil, be it but small, do not:
That which is good, be it but small, fail not to do."

The echoes of a thousand pulpits are in the opening sentences: "These words, my good friends, are found in the section called *Kagen of the Shogaku*, which is so well known to all of you. They are indeed blessed words, and well suited to be our text this evening. These words are short, but they contain an invaluable lesson." Two or three pages of thoroughly valuable and condensed moral teaching follow. Sounder ethics on this subject could not be found, and the terse maxims are illustrated by anecdotes and comparisons level to the capacity of boor or child. I grieve that I must not copy the whole, as it would make this letter too long. The sermon concludes with an imaginary dialogue, which I can well believe would arrest the attention of the largest congregation ever gathered under one roof in Japan.

"What says the song?

> " ' Self-restraint our daily words,
> Howe'er so short, should guard
> From morn to eve.'

"A misfortune may have its origin in a word. Take, as an example, the way a husband calls to his wife. Should he summon her with a pleasant 'Here, good wife,' she will reply with a soft '*Ai, ai.*' Now take the reverse of that.

Husband. " ' What are you pottering at there? Just stir about, will you? These short days too!'

Wife. " ' I know the days are short, and that's just it. If any one comes to the door I've got to answer, and the washing to look after besides. I haven't got five or six hands to do all that, have I?'

Husband. " ' Are you going to give your husband any of your ill chat?'

Wife. " ' Well, what are you doing hugging that fire box all day, instead of lending me a hand now and then?'

Husband. "'What's that now? Look here, I'm not an ox, I'll have you know. You're not going to put a rope through my snout, and lug me all over the place. You don't do that with human beings;' and so they go on, he a fine strapping young fellow, and she a sweet-looking young girl, a rival to Benten-Sama in very beauty, by turns now red, now green, with passion.

Husband. "'It would be but a small matter though one killed a useless hussey like you outright.'

Wife. "'Oh, just please kill me now — do kill me. You didn't pick me off a dunghill though for all that. I've got a good stout father and elder brother to take care of me. See there, just you kill me now!'

Husband. "'Oh! I'll soon do that.'

"Such a hubbub!

"They are not the great things of life which call for our watchful care; they are the small affairs, the so-called trifling matters, the 'Yeas' and 'Noes,' the questions and answers in our daily home life. Peace in a household is like the joyous music in the dancing cars of the gods in the region of heaven."

So ends the sermon, and I feel that from Solomon's day downwards there is a monotonous resemblance among men, that "as in water face answereth to face so answereth the heart of man to man." I. L. B

HAKODATÉ.

Ito's Delinquency — "Missiona.y Manners" — A Predicted Failure — A Japanese Doctor — The Hakodaté Hospital — The Prison — Prison Amenities — Chrysanthemum Culture — The *Bon* Festival — A Holiday-making Crowd.

HAKODATÉ, YEZO.

I AM enjoying Hakodaté so much that, though my tour is all planned and my arrangements are made, I linger on from day to day. There has been an unpleasant *éclaircissement* about Ito. You will remember that I engaged him without a character, and that he told both Lady Parkes and me that after I had done so his former master, Mr. Maries, asked him to go back to him, to which he had replied that he had "a contract with a lady." Mr. Maries is here, and I now find that he had a contract with Ito, by which Ito bound himself to serve him as long as he required him, for $7 a month, but that hearing that I offered $12, he ran away from him and entered my service with a lie! Mr. Maries has been put to the greatest inconvenience by his defection, and has been hindered greatly in completing his botanical collection, for Ito is very clever, and he had not only trained him to dry plants successfully, but he coulc trust him to go away for two or three days and collect seeds. I am very sorry about it. He says that Ito was a bad boy when he came to him, but he thinks that he cured him of some of his faults, and that he has served me faithfully. I have seen Mr. Maries at the Consul's, and have arranged that after my Yezo tour is over Itc shall be returned to his rightful master, who will take him to China and Formosa for a year and a half, and who, I think, will look after his well-being in every way. Dr. and Mrs. Hepburn, who are here, heard a bad account of the boy after I began my travels, and were uneasy about me, but except for this original lie, I have no fault to find with him, and his Shintô creed has not taught him any better. When I paid him his wages this morning he asked me if I had any fault to find, and I told him of my objection to his manners, which he took in very good part, and promised to amend them; "but," he added, "mine are just missionary manners!"

Yesterday I dined at the Consulate, to meet Count Diesbach, of the French Legation, Mr. Von Siebold, of the Austrian Legation, and Lieutenant Kreitner, of the Austrian army, who start to-morrow on an exploring expedition in the interior, intending to cross the sources of the rivers which fall into the sea on the southern coast, and measure the heights of some of the mountains. They are "well found" in food and claret, but take such a number of pack-ponies with them that I predict that they will fail, and that I, who have reduced my luggage to 45 lbs., will succeed!

After dinner the Consul took me to the hospital, where we were received by Dr. Fucasi, who is not only at the head of the hospital and its medical and student staff, but in the lack of a European doctor has won the confidence of the whole European community. He is a very bright, keen-eyed man, and very enthusiastic in his profession. He wears a European white linen suit, but does not speak English.

The hospital consists of three well-ventilated European buildings, one of which is for sailors. It may literally be said that it has 120 "beds," for Dr. Eldridge, who organised it, and left it in a very efficient condi tion, introduced bedsteads, much to the advantage of the patients. Foreigners, mainly sailors, pay 50 *sen*, or about 1s. 8d. a day, natives 20 *sen*, and absolutely destitute persons are received gratuitously. There are six Japanese doctors on duty at this hospital, which is, besides, a school of medicine, in which instruction is given by daily lectures and clinical demonstrations. It is very clean and cheerful, and the patients looked quite as comfortable as hospital patients in England. Each bed has a shelf for the patient's use, and a tablet on which the hours for taking medicine are inscribed. Dr. Fucasi uses the antiseptic treatment, under which he considers that cures are more rapid and that pain is mitigated. There were a great number of surgical cases, and three men had actually consented to part with their legs! Dr. Fucasi showed one case with great pride, in which a man whose leg was only amputated twenty-five days ago was ready to be dismissed, and was walking about on his crutches. There were several *kak'ké* patients, and a number of severe cases of eye disease, arising from neglected ophthalmia. The number of out-patients who pay for medicines only, averages 160 daily, and is always on the increase, though there are four other hospitals in Yezo, and every village of any size has its dispensary and Japanese doctor. These evidences (and they are only a few among many) of enlightenment and progress in this remote part of the empire are not only interesting but surprising, considering that it is less than seven years since Iwakura and his mission went to Europe and America to investigate western civilisation with the view of transplanting its best results to Japanese soil.

It is quite a natural transition to the prison, which I visited afterwards with Mr. and Mrs. Eusden. It is a pleasant prison, standing in extensive gardens at some distance from the town, perhaps too pleasant! I made this remark to the chief of police, and the manager who received us, and the former replied laughingly, that some of the criminals seemed very fond of coming back.[1] There are several separate buildings, including well-ventilated dormitories, workrooms, refectories, and a cell something like a bear cage, for the detention of refractory criminals. 170 prisoners are undergoing sentence, 10 are there for murder, and 19 of the number are sentenced to penal servitude for life. Only 4 are women. The whole are under the charge of 17 warders. Considerable liberty is allowed. Hard labour consists in working on the road and dragging man-carts; light, in tilling the garden, and in employment at the workshops.

They have a tannery, and make cabinet-work, candles of vegetable wax, soap, alcohol, and scents, besides which they do engraving and block-printing. A man is usually allowed to follow his own trade, but if, being a peasant, he has not one, he is taught one in the prison. There are never more than eight employed in the same room, but to my surprise they are allowed to talk. There were only two that I should pick out as low, criminal faces among the number; most of them looked like pleasant, intelligent artisans, and only 7 per cent are unable to read and write. They wear red *kimonos*, but are free from any physical restraints, and, except the refractory cage, there is nothing of the nature of a cell. They are known by numerals only to the warders and each other. Photographs are taken and preserved of all who are sentenced for more than 100 days. They

[1] Since I visited the prison of the Naamhoi Magistrate, the great prison of Canton, where unmitigated barbarism and cruelty, the outgrowth of unmitigated rapacity, still regulate the treatment of criminals, I have felt inclined to condone what appeared to me, at the time, the exaggerated leniency of the Hakodaté system.

receive fair wages for their work as piece-work, the cost
of their keep is deducted, and the accumulated surplus
is handed to them at the expiry of the sentence, and
often amounts to a sum sufficient to set them up in
business. Great care is taken to conceal the identity
of the prisoners. Not thinking it possible that any of
them could hear me, I asked through the Consul's interpreter, for what crime a superior-looking man was
there, and the chief of police begged me to postpone
the question till we were out of hearing of the man's
comrades. There is a flower garden attached to the
prison, in which the convicts take great delight. At
present some of them are cultivating chrysanthemums.
Bad eggs or dead birds are buried at the roots, and
each plant is allowed to bear but one blossom.

It seems to me that the only telling features of punishment in this prison are the withdrawal from family
life and the withholding of liberty to move about. It
is humane to a fault, and the prisoners look really
happy. Whether this mild system produces reforma-
tory results, I cannot ascertain.

At night we went to the *Bon* festival. This is one
of the great festivals of Japan, the "feast of lanterns."
It was introduced from China in the eighth century,
and its original object undoubtedly was to procure the
release of departed spirits from the Buddhist purgatory
Offerings of food are still made at the tombs, but the
chief features of the festival are a general holiday,
abundance of *saké*, thousands of lanterns, and a general resemblance to a fair.

We went out about nine, and found the greater part
of the population of Hakodaté assembled either in the
great cemetery or on the roads leading to it, which were
turned into avenues of coloured lanterns, with pyramids, festoons, and arches of lanterns, and transparen

cies of all forms and colours, and lines of illuminated
booths bright with toys, sweetmeats, and knick-knacks.
Thousands of people, cheerful, orderly, and courteous,
thronged the roads till it was only possible to get on a
few yards at a time; children with gay dresses and fan·
tastically-arranged hair were making purchases at all
the stalls; drums, bells, gongs, stringed instruments,
kept up din and discord; the burial-ground was one
glorious illumination in undulating lines of light; the
pale junks on the silver sea hung out coloured lanterns;
it was all beautiful and wonderful. In a small Buddhist temple with a Shintô mirror, a richly-dressed priest
knelt in front of an illuminated altar, in the midst of
the soft light of countless lanterns, repeating endless
litanies to the accompaniment of a monster drum, and
a bronze bowl with a bell-like sound, which he struck
incessantly and alternately with two sticks, while an
amused crowd watched him without reverence from the
outside. At the entrance of the cemetery there were
fifteen wooden posts, each inscribed with the name of a
god. In every post there was a wheel, and each turn
of the wheel is equivalent to a prayer to the god.
Some people turned the whole fifteen carelessly as they
passed. In the same place there was a temporary
shrine, which was the chief centre of attraction. It
appeared to be full of decorated images, and was ablaze
with light, and two great pyramids of lanterns were
opposite to it. It and the flight of steps leading to it
were one swaying, struggling, mass of people, and
though some obliging officials made an attempt to make
way for us, we were forced backwards down the stairs,
and as there was more than a mere fanciful risk of being
hurt, we were obliged reluctantly to give it up, and
return home through the crowded fairy scene, and
through streets with lanterns hanging from every house

I hope to start on my long-projected tour to-morrow I have planned it for myself with the confidence of an experienced traveller, and look forward to it with great pleasure, as a visit to the aborigines is sure to be full of novel and interesting experiences. Good-bye for a long time.
I. L. B.

A CHANGE OF SCENERY.

A Lovely Sunset — An Official Letter — A "Front Horse" — Japanese Courtesy — Sedentary Amusements — The Steam Ferry — Coolies Abscond — A Team of Savages — A Drive of Horses — Floral
Beauties — An Unbeaten Track — A Ghostly Dwelling — Solitude
and Eeriness.

GINSAINOMA, YEZO, *August* 17.

I AM once again in the wilds! I am sitting outside
an upper room built out almost over a lonely lake, with
wooded points purpling, and still shadows deepening in
the sinking sun. A number of men are dragging down
the nearest hill-side the carcass of a bear which they
have just despatched with spears. There is no village,
and the busy clatter of the *cicada* and the rustle of the
forest are the only sounds which float on the still evening air. The sunset colours are pink and green; on
the tinted water lie the waxen cups of great water-
lilies, and above the wooded heights the pointed,
craggy, and altogether naked summit of the volcano
of Komono-taki flushes red in the sunset. Not the
least of the charms of the evening is that I am absolutely alone, having ridden the eighteen miles from
Hakodaté without Ito or an attendant of any kind;
have unsaddled my own horse, and by means of much
politeness and a dexterous use of Japanese substantives

[1] I venture to present this journal letter, with a few omissions, just
as it was written, trusting that the interest which attaches to aboriginal
races and little-visited regions will carry my readers through the minute-
ness and multiplicity of its details.

have secured a good room and supper of rice, eggs, and black beans for myself, and a mash of beans for my horse, which, as it belongs to the *Kaitakushi*, and has the dignity of iron shoes, is entitled to special consideration!

I am not yet off the "beaten track," but my spirits are rising with the fine weather, the drier atmosphere, and the freedom of Yezo. Yezo is to the main island of Japan what Tipperary is to an Englishman, Barra to a Scotchman, "away down in Texas" to a New Yorker — in the rough, little known and thinly-peopled; and people can locate all sorts of improbable stories here without much fear of being found out, of which the Ainos and the misdeeds of the ponies furnish the staple, and the queer doings of men and dogs, and adventures with bears, wolves, and salmon, the embroidery. Nobody comes here without meeting with something queer, and one or two tumbles either with or from his horse. Very little is known of the interior except that it is covered with forest matted together by lianas, and with an undergrowth of scrub bamboo impenetrable except to the axe, varied by swamps equally impassable, which gives rise to hundreds of rivers well stocked with fish. The glare of volcanoes is seen in different parts of the island. The forests are the hunting-grounds of the Ainos, who are complete savages in everything but their disposition, which is said to be so gentle and harmless that I may go among them with perfect safety.

Kindly interest has been excited by the first foray made by a lady into the country of the aborigines; and Mr. Eusden, the Consul, has worked upon the powers that be with such good effect that the Governor has granted me a *shomon*, a sort of official letter or certificate, giving me a right to obtain horses and coolies everywhere at the Government rate of 6 *sen* a *ri*, with a prior claim to accommodation at the houses kept up for officials on their circuits, and to help and assistance from officials generally; and the Governor has further telegraphed to the other side of Volcano Bay desiring the authorities to give me the use of the Government *kuruma* as long as I need it, and to detain the steamer to suit my convenience! With this document, which enables me to dispense with my passport, I shall find travelling very easy, and I am very grateful to the Consul for procuring it for me.

Here, where rice and tea have to be imported, there is a uniform charge at the *yadoyas* of 30 *sen* a day, which includes three meals, whether you eat them or not. Horses are abundant, but are small, and are not up to heavy weights. They are entirely unshod, and though their hoofs are very shallow and grow into turned-up points and other singular shapes, they go over rough ground with facility at a scrambling run of over four miles an hour, following a leader called a "front horse." If you don't get a "front horse" and try to ride in front, you find that your horse will not stir till he has another before him; and then you are perfectly helpless, as he follows the movements of his leader without any reference to your wishes. There are no *mago;* a man rides the "front horse," and goes at whatever pace you please, or if you get a "front horse" you may go without any one. Horses are cheap and abundant. They drive a number of them down from the hills every morning into *corrals* in the villages, and keep them there till they are wanted. Because they are so cheap they are very badly used. I have not seen one yet without a sore back, produced by the harsh pack-saddle rubbing up and down the spine, as the loaded animals are driven at a run. They are mostly very poor-looking.

As there was some difficulty about getting a horse for me, the Consul sent one of the *Kaitakushi* saddle-horses, a handsome, lazy animal, which I rarely succeeded in stimulating into a heavy gallop. Leaving Ito to follow with the baggage, I enjoyed my solitary ride and the possibility of choosing my own pace very much, though the choice was only between a slow walk and the lumbering gallop aforesaid.

I met strings of horses loaded with deer-hides, and overtook other strings loaded with *saké* and manufactured goods, and in each case had a fight with my sociably inclined animal. In two villages I was interested to see that the small shops contained lucifer matches, cotton umbrellas, boots, brushes, clocks, slates, and pencils, engravings in frames, kerosene lamps,[1] and red and green blankets, all but the last, which are unmistakable British "shoddy," being Japanese imitations of foreign manufactured goods, more or less cleverly executed. The road goes up-hill for fifteen miles, and after passing Nanai, a trim Europeanised village in the midst of fine crops, one of the places at which the Government is making acclimatisation and other agricultural experiments, it fairly enters the mountains, and from the top of a steep hill there is a glorious view of Hakodaté Head, looking like an island in the deep blue sea, and from the top of a higher hill, looking northward, a magnificent view of the volcano with its bare, pink summit rising above three lovely lakes densely wooded. These are the flushed scaurs and outbreaks of bare rock for which I sighed amidst the smothering

---

[1] The use of kerosene in matted wooden houses is a new cause of conflagrations. It is not possible to say how it originated, but just before Christmas 1879 a fire broke out in Hakodaté, which in a few hours destroyed 20 streets, 2500 houses, the British Consulate, several public buildings, the new native Christian Church, and the Church Mission House, leaving 11,000 people homeless.

greenery of the main island, and the silver gleam of the lakes takes away the blindness from the face of nature. It was delicious to descend to the water's edge in the dewy silence amidst balsamic odours, to find not a clattering grey village with its monotony, but a single, irregularly-built house, with lovely surroundings.

It is a most displeasing road for most of the way; sides with deep corrugations, and in the middle a high causeway of earth, whose height is being added to by hundreds of creels of earth brought on ponies' backs. It is supposed that carriages and waggons will use this causeway, but a shying horse or a bad driver would overturn them. As it is at present, the road is only passable for pack-horses, owing to the number of broken bridges. I passed strings of horses laden with *saké* going into the interior. The people of Yezo drink freely, and the poor Ainos outrageously. On the road I dismounted to rest myself by walking up hill, and the saddle being loosely girthed, the gear behind it dragged it round and under the body of the horse, and it was too heavy for me to lift on his back again. When I had led him for some time two Japanese with a string of pack-horses loaded with deer-hides met me, and not only put the saddle on again, but held the stirrup while I remounted, and bowed politely when I went away. Who could help liking such a courteous and kindly people?

MORI, VOLCANO BAY, *Monday.*

Even Ginsainoma was not Paradise after dark, and I was actually driven to bed early by the number of mosquitoes. Ito is in an excellent humour on this tour. Like me, he likes the freedom of the *Hokkaidô.* He is much more polite and agreeable also, and very proud of the Governor's *shomon*, with which he swag-

gers into hotels and Transport Offices. I never get on
so well as when he arranges for me. Saturday was
grey and lifeless, and the ride of seven miles here along
a sandy road through monotonous forest and swamp,
with the volcano on one side and low wooded hills on
the other, was wearisome and fatiguing. I saw five
large snakes all in a heap, and a number more twisting
through the grass. There are no villages, but several
very poor tea-houses, and on the other side of the road
long sheds with troughs hollowed like canoes out of the
trunks of trees, containing horse food. Here nobody
walks, and the men ride at a quick run, sitting on the
tops of their pack-saddles with their legs crossed above
their horses' necks, and wearing large hats like coal-
scuttle bonnets. The horses are infested with ticks,
hundreds upon one animal sometimes, and occasionally
they become so mad from the irritation that they throw
themselves suddenly on the ground, and roll over load
and rider. I saw this done twice. The ticks often
transfer themselves to the riders.

Mori is a large, ramshackle village, near the southern
point of Volcano Bay, a wild, dreary-looking place on a
sandy shore, with a number of jôrôyas and disreputable
characters. Several of the yadoyas are not respectable,
but I rather like this one, and it has a very fine view of
the volcano, which forms one point of the bay. Mori
has no anchorage, though it has an unfinished pier 345
feet long. The steam ferry across the mouth of the bay
is here, and there is a very difficult bridle-track running
for nearly 100 miles round the bay besides, and a road
into the interior. But it is a forlorn, decayed place.
Last night the inn was very noisy, as some travellers
in the next room to mine hired *geishas*, who played,
sang, and danced till two in the morning, and the
whole party imbibed *saké* freely. In this compara-

tively northern latitude the summer is already waning. The seeds of the blossoms which were in their glory when I arrived are ripe, and here and there a tinge of yellow on a hill-side, or a scarlet spray of maple, heralds the glories and the coolness of autumn.

The travellers in the next room played all day at a game which I have seen literally everywhere in Japan, wherevei men have time to kill. This great resource is called *gô*, and is played with 180 white discs cut from a species of cockle shell, and 181 black ones, made from a black pebble. The board is divided into 361 squares, and the game consists in enclosing a certain space, and preventing the opponent from doing the same. The table on which the board is set, called the *gô-ban*, has a square hollow beneath it, to which a terrible legend attaches, namely, that according to the ancient laws of the game, if a third person interfered or offered his advice to either player his head might be chopped off and placed in the hollow, which would collect the blood which dripped from it! Hence its ghastly name, which means " the blood-collector! " These men played at *gô* from seven in the morning till eleven at night. I have seen *shogi* or Japanese chess played, but not so universally _ gô.

YUBETS, YEZO.

A loud yell of " steamer," coupled with the information that " she could not wait one minute," broke in upon *gô* and everything else, and in a broiling sun we hurried down to the pier, and with a heap of Japanese, who filled two *scows*, were put on board a steamer not bigger than a large, decked steam launch, where the natives were all packed into a covered hole, and I was conducted with much ceremony to the forecastle, a place at the bow 5 feet square, full of coils of rope, shut in, and left to solitude and dignity, and the stare of eight eyes, which perseveringly glowered through the windows! The steamer had been kept waiting for me on the other side for two days, to the infinite disgust of two foreigners, who wished to return to Hakodaté, and to mine.

It was a splendid day, with foam crests on the wonderfully blue water, and the red ashes of the volcano, which forms the south point of the bay, glowed in the sunlight. This wretched steamer, whose boilers are so often "sick" that she can never be relied upon, is the only means of reaching the new capital without taking a most difficult and circuitous route. To continue the pier and put a capable, good steamer on the ferry would be a useful expenditure of money. The breeze was strong and in our favour, but even with this it took us six weary hours to steam twenty-five miles, and it was eight at night before we reached the beautiful and almost land-locked bay of Mororan, with steep, wooded sides, and deep water close to the shore, deep enough for the foreign ships of war which occasionally anchor there, much to the detriment of the town. We got off in over-crowded *sampans*, and several people fell into the water, much to their own amusement. The servants from the different *yadoyas* go down to the jetty to "tout" for guests with large paper lanterns, and the effect of these, one above another, waving and undulating, with their soft coloured light, was as bewitching as the reflection of the stars in the motionless water. Mororan is a small town very picturesquely situated on the steep shore of a most lovely bay, with another height, richly wooded, above it, with shrines approached by flights of stone stairs, and behind this hill there is the first Aino village along this coast.

The long, irregular street is slightly picturesque, but

ground by wooden stilts. When I am better acquainted
with the houses I shall describe them; at present I will
only say that they do not resemble the Japanese houses
so much as the Polynesian, as they are made of reeds
very neatly tied upon a wooden framework. They
have small windows, and roofs of a very great height,
and steep pitch, with the thatch in a series of very neat
frills, and the ridge poles covered with reeds, and ornamented. The coast Ainos are nearly all engaged in
fishing, but at this season the men hunt deer in the forests. On this coast there are several names com

AINO STORE-HOUSE AT HOROBETS.

pounded with *bets* or *pets*, the Aino for a river, such as
Horobets, Yubets, Mombets, etc.

I found that Ito had been engaged for a whole hour
in a violent altercation, which was caused by the
Transport Agent refusing to supply runners for the
kuruma, saying that no one in Horobets would draw
one, but on my producing the *shomon* I was at once
started on my journey of sixteen miles with three Japanese lads, Ito riding on to Shiraôi to get my room
ready. I think that the Transport Offices in Yezo are
in Government hands. In a few minutes three Ainos

ran out of a house, took the *kuruma*, and went the
whole stage without stopping. They took a boy and
three saddled horses along with them to bring them
back, and rode and hauled alternately, two youths
always attached to the shafts, and a man pushing
behind. They were very kind, and so courteous, after
a new fashion, that I quite forgot that I was alone
among savages. The lads were young and beardless,

AINO LODGES (*From a Japanese Sketch*).

their lips were thick, and their mouths very wide, and
I thought that they approached more nearly to the
Eskimo type than to any other. They had masses of
soft black hair falling on each side of their faces. The
adult man was not a pure Aino. His dark hair was
not very thick, and both it and his beard had an occasional auburn gleam. I think I never saw a face more
completely beautiful in features and expression, with

a lofty, sad, far-off, gentle, intellectual look, rather that of Sir Noël Paton's "Christ" than of a savage His manner was most graceful, and he spoke both Aino and Japanese in the low musical tone which I find is a characteristic of Aino speech. These Ainos never took off their clothes, but merely let them fall from one or both shoulders when it was very warm.

The road from Horobets to Shiraôi is very solitary, with not more than four or five houses the whole way. It is broad and straight, except when it ascends hills, or turns inland to cross rivers, and is carried across a broad swampy level, covered with tall wild flowers, which extends from the high beach thrown up by the sea for two miles inland, where there is a lofty wall of wooded rock, and beyond this the forest-covered mountains of the interior. On the top of the raised beach there were Aino hamlets, and occasionally a nearly overpowering stench came across the level from the sheds and apparatus used for extracting fish-oil. I enjoyed the afternoon thoroughly. It is so good to have got beyond the confines of stereotyped civilisation, and the trammels of Japanese travelling, to the solitude of nature, and an atmosphere of freedom. It was grey, with a hard, dark line of ocean horizon, and over the weedy level the grey road, with grey telegraph poles along it, stretched wearisomely like a grey thread. The breeze came up from the sea, rustled the reeds, and waved the tall plumes of the *Eulalia Japonica*, and the thunder of the Pacific surges boomed through the air with its grand, deep bass. Poetry and music pervaded the solitude, and my spirit was rested.

Going up and then down a steep, wooded hill, the road appeared to return to its original state of brushwood, and the men stopped at the broken edge of a declivity which led down to a shingle bank and a foam-

crested river of clear, blue-green water, strongly impregnated with sulphur from some medicinal springs
above, with a steep bank of tangle on the opposite
side. This beautiful stream was crossed by two round
poles, a foot apart, on which I attempted to walk, with
the help of an Aino hand; but the poles were very
unsteady, and I doubt whether any one, even with a
strong head, could walk on them in boots. Then the
beautiful Aino signed to me to come back and mount
on his shoulders; but when he had got a few feet out
the poles swayed and trembled so much, that he was
obliged to retrace his way cautiously, during which
process I endured miseries from dizziness and fear;
after which he carried me through the rushing water,
which was up to his shoulders, and through a bit of
swampy jungle, and up a steep bank, to the great
fatigue both of body and mind, hardly mitigated by
the enjoyment of the ludicrous in riding a savage
through these Yezo waters. They dexterously carried
the *kuruma* through, on the shoulders of four, and
showed extreme anxiety that neither it nor I should
get wet. After this we crossed two deep, still rivers,
in scows, and far above the grey level and the grey sea,
the sun was setting in gold and vermilion-streaked
green behind a glorified mountain of great height, at
whose feet the forest-covered hills lay in purple gloom.
At dark we reached Shiraôi, a village of eleven Japanese houses, with a village of fifty-one Aino houses,
near the sea. There is a large *yadoya* of the old style
there; but I found that Ito had chosen a very pretty
new one, with four stalls open to the road, in the centre
one of which I found him, with the welcome news that
a steak of fresh salmon was broiling on the coals; and
as the room was clean and sweet, and I was very hungry, I enjoyed my meal by the light of a rush in a
saucer of fish-oil as much as any part of the day.

The night was too cold for sleep, and at daybreak hearing a great din, I looked out, and saw a drove o fully a hundred horses all galloping down the road, with two Ainos on horseback, and a number of big dogs after them. Hundreds of horses run nearly wild on the hills, and the Ainos, getting a large drove together, skilfully head them for the entrance into the *corral*, in which a selection of them is made for the day's needs, and the remainder — that is, those with the deepest sores on their backs — are turned loose. This dull rattle of shoeless feet is the first sound in the morning in these Yezo villages. I sent Ito on early, and followed at nine with three Ainos. The road is perfectly level for thirteen miles, through gravel flats and swamps, very monotonous, but with a wild charm of its own. There were swampy lakes, with wild ducks and small white water-lilies, and the surrounding levels were covered with reedy grass, flowers, and weeds. The early autumn has withered a great many of the flowers; but enough remains to show how beautiful the now russet plains must have been in the early summer. A dwarf rose, of a deep crimson colour, with orange, medlar-shaped hips, as large as crabs, and corollas three inches across, is one of the features of Yezo; and besides, there is a large rose-red convolvulus, a blue campanula, with tiers of bells, a blue monkshood the *Aconitum Japonicum*, the flaunting *Calystegia soldanella*, purple asters, grass of Parnassus, yellow lilies, and a remarkable trailer, whose delicate leafage looked quite out of place among its coarse surroundings, with a purplish-brown campanulate blossom, only remarkable for a peculiar arrangement of the pistil, green stamens, and a most offensive carrion-like odour, which is probably to attract to it a very objectionable-looking fly, for purposes of fertilisation.

We overtook four Aino women, young and comely, with bare feet, striding firmly along ; and after a good deal of laughing with the men, they took hold of the *kuruma*, and the whole seven raced with it at full speed for half a mile, shrieking with laughter. Soon after we came upon a little tea-house, and the Ainos showed me a straw package, and pointed to their open mouths, by which I understood that they wished to stop and eat. Later we overtook four Japanese on horseback, and the Ainos raced with them for a considerable distance — the result of these spurts being that I reached Tomakomai at noon, a wide, dreary place, with houses roofed with sod, bearing luxuriant crops of weeds. Near this place is the volcano of Tarumai, a calm-looking grey cone, whose skirts are draped by tens of thousands of dead trees. So calm and grey had it looked for many a year, that people supposed it had passed into endless rest, when quite lately, on a sultry day, it blew off its cap, and covered the whole country for many a mile with cinders and ashes, burning up the forest on its sides, adding a new covering to the Tomakomai roofs, and depositing fine ash as far as Cape Erimo, fifty miles off.

At this place the road and telegraph wires turn inland to Satsuporo, and a track for horses only turns to the north-east, and straggles round the island for about seven hundred miles. From Mororan to Sarufuto there are everywhere traces of new and old volcanic action, pumice, tufas, conglomerates, and occasional beds of hard basalt, all covered with recent pumice, which, from Shiraôi eastward, conceals everything. At Tomakomai we took horses, and, as I brought my own saddle, I have had the nearest approach to real riding that

I have enjoyed in Japan. The wife of a Satsuporo doctor was there, who was travelling for two hundred miles
astride on a pack-saddle, with rope-loops for stirrups.
She rode well, and vaulted into my saddle with circus-
like dexterity, and performed many equestrian feats
upon it, telling me that she should be quite happy if
she were possessed of it.

I was happy when I left the "beaten track" to
Satsuporo, and saw before me, stretching for I know
not how far, rolling, sandy *machirs* like those of the
Outer Hebrides, desert-like and lonely, covered almost
altogether with dwarf roses and campanulas, a prairie
land on which you can make any tracks you please.
Sending the others on, I followed them at the Yezo
scramble, and soon ventured on a long gallop, and revelled in the music of the thud of shoeless feet over the
elastic soil, but I had not realised the peculiarities of
Yezo steeds, and had forgotten to ask whether mine
was a "front horse," and just as we were going at full
speed we came nearly up with the others, and my horse
coming abruptly to a full stop, I went six feet over his
head among the rose-bushes. Ito looking back saw me
tightening the saddle-girths, and I never divulged this
escapade.

After riding eight miles along this breezy belt, with
the sea on one side and forests on the other, we came
upon Yubets, a place which has fascinated me so much
that I intend to return to it, but I must confess that its
fascinations depend rather upon what it has not than
upon what it has, and Ito says that it would kill him to
spend even two days there. It looks like the end of
all things, as if loneliness and desolation could go no
farther. A sandy stretch on three sides, a river arrested
in its progress to the sea, and compelled to wander tedi-
ously in search of an outlet by the height and mass of

the beach thrown up by the Pacific, a distant forest-belt rising into featureless, wooded ranges in shades of indigo and grey, and a never-absent consciousness of a vast ocean just out of sight, are the environments of two high look-outs, some sheds for fish-oil purposes, four or five Japanese houses, four Aino huts on the top of the beach across the river, and a grey barrack, consisting of a polished passage eighty feet long, with small rooms on either side, at one end a gravelled yard, with two quiet rooms opening upon it, and at the other an immense *daidokoro*, with dark recesses and blackened rafters, a haunted-looking abode. One would suppose that there had been a special object in setting the houses down at weary distances from each other. Few as they are, they are not all inhabited at this season, and all that can be seen is grey sand, sparse grass, and a few savages creeping about.

Nothing that I have seen has made such an impression upon me as that ghostly, ghastly fishing-station. In the long grey wall of the long grey barrack there were many dismal windows, and when we hooted for admission a stupid face appeared at one of them and disappeared. Then a grey gateway opened, and we rode into a yard of grey gravel, with some silent rooms opening upon it. The solitude of the thirty or forty rooms which lie between it and the kitchen, and which are now filled with nets and fishing-tackle, was something awful, and as the wind swept along the polished passage, rattling the *fusuma*, and lifting the shingles on the roof, and the rats careered from end to end, I went to the great black *daidokoro* in search of social life, and found a few embers and an *andon*, and nothing else but the stupid-faced man deploring his fate, and two orphan boys whose lot he makes more wretched than his own. In the fishing season this barrack accommodates from 200 to 300 men.

I started to the sea-shore, crossing the dreary river, and found open sheds much blackened, deserted huts of reeds, long sheds with a nearly insufferable odour from caldrons in which oil had been extracted from last year's fish, two or three Aino huts, and two or three grand-looking Ainos, clothed in skins, striding like ghosts over the sandbanks, a number of wolfish dogs, some log canoes or "dug-outs," the bones of a wrecked junk, a quantity of bleached drift-wood, a beach of dark-grey sand, and a tossing expanse of dark-grey ocean under a dull and windy sky. On this part of the coast the Pacific spends its fury, and has raised up at a short distance above high-water mark a sandy sweep of such a height that when you descend its seaward slope you see nothing but the sea and the sky, and a grey, curving shore, covered thick for many a lonely mile with fantastic forms of whitened drift-wood, the shattered wrecks of forest-trees, which are carried down by the innumerable rivers, till, after tossing for weeks and months along with

> " —— wrecks of ships, and drifting
> spars uplifting
> On the desolate, rainy seas :
> Ever drifting, drifting, drifting,
> On the shifting
> Currents of the restless main ; "

the "toiling surges" cast them on Yubets beach, and

> " All have found repose again."

A grim repose !

The deep boom of the surf was music, and the strange cries of sea-birds, and the hoarse notes of the audacious black crows, were all harmonious, for nature, when left to herself, never produces discords either in sound or colour.

A MEETING.

The Harmonies of Nature — A Good Horse — A Single Discord — A
Forest — Aino Ferrymen —" *Les Puces ! Les Puces !* "— Baffled
Explorers — Ito's Contempt for Ainos — An Aino Introduction.

SARUFUTO.

No! Nature has no discords. This morning, to the
far horizon, diamond-flashing blue water shimmered in
perfect peace, outlined by a line of surf which broke
lazily on a beach scarcely less snowy than itself. The
deep, perfect blue of the sky was only broken by a few
radiant white clouds, whose shadows trailed slowly over
the plain on whose broad bosom a thousand corollas, in
the glory of their brief but passionate life, were drinking in the sunshine, wavy ranges slept in depths of
indigo, and higher hills beyond were painted in faint
blue on the dreamy sky. Even the few grey houses of
Yubets were spiritualised into harmony by a faint blue
veil which was not a mist, and the loud croak of the
loquacious and impertinent crows had a cheeriness
about it, a hearty mockery, which I liked.

Above all, I had a horse so good that he was always
trying to run away, and galloped so lightly over the
flowery grass that I rode the seventeen miles here with
great enjoyment. Truly a good horse, good ground to
gallop on, and sunshine, make up the sum of enjoyable
travelling. The discord in the general harmony was
produced by the sight of the Ainos, a harmless people
without the instinct of progress, descending to that vast

tomb of conquered and unknown races which has
opened to receive so many before them. A mounted
policeman started with us from Yubets, and rode the
whole way here, keeping exactly to my pace, but never
speaking a word. We forded one broad, deep river,
and crossed another, partly by fording and partly in a
scow, after which the track left the level, and after
passing through reedy grass as high as the horse's ears,
went for some miles up and down hill, through woods
composed entirely of the *Ailanthus glandulosus*, with
leaves much riddled by the mountain silk-worm, and a
ferny undergrowth of the familiar *Pteris aquilina*. The
deep shade and glancing lights of this open copsewood
were very pleasant; and as the horse tripped gaily up
and down the little hills, and the sea murmur mingled
with the rustle of the breeze, and a glint of white surf
sometimes flashed through the greenery, and dragon-flies
and butterflies in suits of crimson and black velvet
crossed the path continually like "living flashes" of
light, I was reminded somewhat, though faintly, of
windward Hawaii. We emerged upon an Aino hut
and a beautiful placid river, and two Ainos ferried the
four people and horses across in a scow, the third wading to guide the boat. They wore no clothing, but only
one was hairy. They were superb-looking men, gentle,
and extremely courteous, handing me in and out of the
boat, and holding the stirrup while I mounted, with
much natural grace. On leaving they extended their
arms and waved their hands inwards twice, stroking
their grand beards afterwards, which is their usual salutation. A short distance over shingle brought us to
this Japanese village of sixty-three houses, a colonisation
settlement, mainly of *samurai* from the province of
Sendai, who are raising very fine crops on the sandy
soil. The mountains, twelve miles in the interior, have

a large Aino population, [1] and a few Ainos live near this village and are held in great contempt by its inhabitants My room is on the village street, and as it is too warm to close the *shôji*, the aborigines stand looking in at the lattice hour after hour.

A short time ago Mr. Von Siebold and Count Diesbach galloped up on their return from Biratori, the Aino village to which I am going; and Count D., throwing himself from his horse, rushed up to me with the exclamation, *Les Puces! Les Puces!* They have brought down with them the chief, Benri, a superb but dissipated-looking savage. Mr Von Siebold called on me this evening, and I envied him his fresh, clean clothing as much as he envied me my stretcher and mosquito-net. They have suffered terribly from fleas, mosquitoes, and general discomfort, and are much exhausted; but Mr. Von S. thinks that in spite of all, a visit to the mountain Ainos is worth a long journey. As I expected, they have completely failed in their explorations, and have been deserted by Lieutenant Kreitner. I asked Mr. Von S. to speak to Ito in Japanese about the importance of being kind and courteous to the Ainos whose hospitality I shall receive; and Ito is very indignant at this. "Treat Ainos politely!" he says; "They're just dogs, not men;" and since he has regaled

[1] It is impossible to state with any exactness the Aino population of Yezo. Mr. Enslie, who was H.B.M.'s acting consul at Hakodaté from 1861 to 1863, gives it as 200,000! Foreigners in Yezo during my visit estimated it at 25,000. The Statistical Department of the Japanese Government gave it to me as 12,000, but with a qualification, as stated in the "Notes on Yezo." I am much inclined to think that this may be under the mark by some thousands, as smallpox, which caused a considerable decline in their numbers, has ceased. They are a healthy people, the children are not carried off by infantile diseases; and though there are rarely more than five in a family, they usually live to grow up. I hazard this conjecture as to their larger numbers from the population which I ascertained to exist in eight of their villages.

me with all the scandal concerning them which he has been able to rake together in the village.

We have to take not only food for both Ito and myself, but cooking utensils. I have been introduced to Benri, the chief; and though he does not return for a day or two, he will send a message along with us which will ensure me hospitality. I. L. B.

LIVING WITH THE AINOS.

Savage Life — A Forest Track — Cleanly Villages — A Hospitable
Reception — The Chief's Mother — The Evening Meal — A Sav-
age *Séance* — Libations to the Gods — Nocturnal Silence — Aino
Courtesy — The Chief's Wife.

AINO HUT, BIRATORI, *August* 23.

I AM in the lonely Aino land, and I think that the
most interesting of my travelling experiences has been
the living for three days and two nights in an Aino hut,

AINO HOUSES.

and seeing and sharing the daily life of complete savages, who go on with their ordinary occupations just as
if I were not among them. I found yesterday a most

fatiguing and over-exciting day, as everything was new
and interesting, even the extracting from men who
have few if any ideas in common with me, all I could
extract concerning their religion and customs, and that
through an interpreter. I got up at six this morning
to write out my notes, and have been writing for five

AINOS AT HOME (*From a Japanese Sketch*).

hours, and there is shortly the prospect of another savage *séance*. The distractions, as you can imagine, are
many. At this moment a savage is taking a cup of
saké by the fire in the centre of the floor. He salutes
me by extending his hands and waving them towards
his face, and then dips a rod in the *saké*, and makes six
libations to the god — an upright piece of wood with a

fringe of shavings planted in the floor of the room.
Then he waves the cup several times towards himself,
makes other libations to the fire, and drinks. Ten
other men and women are sitting along each side of the
fire-hole, the chief's wife is cooking, the men are apathetically contemplating the preparation of their food;
and the other women, who are never idle, are splitting
the bark of which they make their clothes. I occupy the
guest seat — a raised platform at one end of the fire,
with the skin of a black bear thrown over it.

I have reserved all I have to say about the Ainos till
I had been actually among them, and I hope you will
have patience to read to the end. Ito is very greedy
and self-indulgent, and whimpered very much about
coming to Biratori at all, — one would have thought he
was going to the stake. He actually borrowed for himself a sleeping-mat and *futons*, and has brought a
chicken, onions, potatoes, French beans, Japanese sauce,
tea, rice, a kettle, a stew-pan, and a rice-pan, while I
contented myself with a cold fowl and potatoes.

We took three horses and a mounted Aino guide, and
found a beaten track the whole way. It turns into the
forest at once on leaving Sarufuto, and goes through
forest the entire distance, with an abundance of reedy
grass higher than my hat on horseback along it, and as
it is only twelve inches broad and much overgrown, the
horses were constantly pushing through leafage soaking
from a night's rain, and I was soon wet up to my shoulders. The forest trees are almost solely the *Ailanthus
glandulosus* and the *Zelkowa keaki*, often matted
together with a white-flowered trailer of the Hydrangea
genus. The undergrowth is simply hideous, consisting
mainly of coarse reedy grass, monstrous docks, the large-
leaved *Polygonum cuspidatum*, several umbelliferous
plants, and a "ragweed," which, like most of its gawky

fellows, grows from five to six feet high. The forest is dark and very silent, threaded by this narrow path, and by others as narrow, made by the hunters in search of game. The "main road" sometimes plunges into deep bogs, at others is roughly corduroyed by the roots of trees, and frequently hangs over the edge of abrupt and much-worn declivities, in going up one of which the baggage-horse rolled down a bank fully thirty feet high, and nearly all the tea was lost. At another the guide's pack-saddle lost its balance, and man, horse, and saddle went over the slope, pots, pans, and packages flying after them. At another time my horse sank up to his chest in a very bad bog, and as he was totally unable to extricate himself, I was obliged to scramble upon his neck and jump to *terra firma* over his ears.

There is something very gloomy in the solitude of this silent land, with its beast-haunted forests, its great patches of pasture, the resort of wild animals which haunt the lower regions in search of food when the snow drives them down from the mountains, and its narrow track, indicating the single file in which the savages of the interior walk with their bare, noiseless feet. Reaching the Sarufutogawa, a river with a treacherous bottom, in which Mr. Von Siebold and his horse came to grief, I hailed an Aino boy, who took me up the stream in a "dug-out," and after that we passed through Biroka, Saruba, and Mina, all purely Aino villages, situated among small patches of millet, tobacco, and pumpkins, so choked with weeds that it was doubtful whether they were crops. I was much surprised with the extreme neatness and cleanliness outside the houses; "model villages" they are in these respects, with no litter lying in sight anywhere, nothing indeed but dog troughs, hollowed out of logs, like "dug-outs," for the numerous yellow dogs, which are a feature of

Aino life. There are neither puddles nor heaps, but the houses, all trim and in good repair, rise clean out of the sandy soil.

Biratori, the largest of the Aino settlements in this region, is very prettily situated among forests and mountains, on rising ground, with a very sinuous river winding at its feet and a wooded height above. A lonelier place could scarcely be found. As we passed among the houses the yellow dogs barked, the women looked shy and smiled, and the men made their graceful salutation. We stopped at the chief's house, where, of course, we were unexpected guests; but Shinondi, his nephew, and two other men came out, saluted us, and with most hospitable intent helped Ito to unload the horses. Indeed their eager hospitality created quite a commotion, one running hither and the other thither in their anxiety to welcome a stranger. It is a large house, the room being 35 by 25, and the roof 20 feet high; but you enter by an ante-chamber, in which are kept the millet-mill and other articles. There is a doorway in this, but the inside is pretty dark, and Shinondi, taking my hand, raised the reed curtain bound with hide, which concealed the entrance into the actual house, and leading me into it, retired a footstep, extended his arms, waved his hands inwards three times, and then stroked his beard several times, after which he indicated by a sweep of his hand and a beautiful smile that the house and all it contained were mine. An aged woman, the chief's mother, who was splitting bark by the fire, waved her hands also. She is the queen-regnant of the house.

Again taking my hand, Shinondi led me to the place of honour at the head of the fire, a rude, movable platform six feet long, by four broad, and a foot high, on which he laid an ornamental mat, apologising for not having at that moment a bearskin wherewith to cover it. The baggage was speedily brought in by several willing pairs of hands; some reed mats fifteen feet long were laid down upon the very coarse ones which covered the whole floor, and when they saw Ito putting up my stretcher they hung a fine mat along the rough wall to conceal it, and suspended another on the beams of the roof for a canopy. The alacrity and instinctive hospitality with which these men rushed about to make

AINO MILLET-MILL AND PESTLE.

things comfortable were very fascinating, though comfort is a word misapplied in an Aino hut. The women only did what the men told them.

They offered food at once, but I told them that I had brought my own, and would only ask leave to cook it on their fire. I need not have brought any cups, for they have many lacquer bowls, and Shinondi brought me on a lacquer tray a bowl full of water from one of their four wells. They said that Benri, the chief, would wish me to make his house my own for as long as I cared to stay, and I must excuse them in all things in which their ways were different from my own. Shi·nondi and four others in the village speak tolerable Japanese, and this of course is the medium of communication. Ito has exerted himself nobly as an interpre·ter, and has entered into my wishes with a cordiality and intelligence which have been perfectly invaluable; and though he did growl at Mr. Von Siebold's injunctions regarding politeness, he has carried them out to my satisfaction, and even admits that the mountain Ainos are better than he expected; "but," he added, "they have learned their politeness from the Japanese!" They have never seen a foreign woman, and only three foreign men, but there is neither crowding nor staring as among the Japanese, possibly in part from apathy and want of intelligence. For three days they have kept up their graceful and kindly hospitality, going on with their ordinary life and occupations, and though I have lived among them in this room by day and night, there has been nothing which in any way could offend the most fastidious sense of delicacy.

They said they would leave me to eat and rest, and all retired but the chief's mother, a weird, witch-like woman of eighty, with shocks of yellow-white hair, and a stern suspiciousness in her wrinkled face. I have come to feel as if she had the evil eye, as she sits there watching, watching always, and for ever knotting the bark thread like one of the Fates, keeping a jealous watch on her son's two wives, and on other young women who come in to weave—-neither the dulness nor the repose of old age about her; and her eyes gleam with a greedy light when she sees saké, of which she drains a bowl without taking breath. She alone is suspicious of strangers, and she thinks that my visit bodes no good to her tribe. I see her eyes fixed upon me now, and they make me shudder.

I had a good meal seated in my chair on the top of the guest-seat to avoid the fleas, which are truly legion. At dusk Shinondi returned, and soon people began to drop in, till eighteen were assembled, including the sub-chief, and several very grand-looking old men, with full, grey, wavy beards. Age is held in much reverence, and it is etiquette for these old men to do honour to a guest in the chief's absence. As each entered he saluted me several times, and after sitting down turned towards me and saluted again, going through the same ceremony with every other person. They said they had come "to bid me welcome." They took their places in rigid order at each side of the fireplace, which is six feet long, Benri's mother in the place of honour at the right, then Shinondi, then the sub-chief, and on the other side the old men. Besides these, seven women sat in a row in the background splitting bark. A large iron pan hung over the fire from a blackened arrangement above, and Benri's principal wife cut wild roots, green beans, and seaweed, and shred dried fish and venison among them, adding millet, water, and some strong-smelling fish-oil, and set the whole on to stew for three hours, stirring the "mess" now and then with a wooden spoon.

Several of the older people smoke, and I handed round some mild tobacco, which they received with waving hands. I told them that I came from a land in the sea, very far away, where they saw the sun go down, so very far away that a horse would have to gallop day and night for five weeks to reach it, and that I had come a long journey to see them, and that I wanted to ask them many questions, so that when I went home I might tell my own people something about them. Shinondi and another man, who understood Japanese, bowed, and (as on every occasion) translated what I said into Aino for the venerable group opposite.

Shinondi then said "that he and Shinrichi, the other
Japanese speaker, would tell me all they knew, but
they were but young men, and only knew what was
told to them. They would speak what they believed
to be true, but the chief knew more than they, and
when he came back he might tell me differently, and
then I should think that they had spoken lies." I said
that no one who looked into their faces could think that
they ever told lies. They were very much pleased, and

SHINONDI AND SHINRICHI.

waved their hands and stroked their beards repeatedly.
Before they told me anything, they begged and prayed
that I would not inform the Japanese Government that
they had told me of their customs, or harm might come
to them!

For the next two hours, and for two more after supper, I asked them questions concerning their religion
and customs, and again yesterday for a considerable
time, and this morning, after Benri's return, I went over
the same subjects with him, and have also employed a

considerable time in getting about 300 words from them, which I have spelt phonetically of course, and intend to go over again when I visit the coast Ainos.[1]

The process was slow, as both question and answer had to pass through three languages. There was a very manifest desire to tell the truth, and I think that their statements concerning their few and simple customs may be relied upon. I shall give what they told me separately when I have time to write out my notes in an orderly manner. I can only say that I have seldom spent a more interesting evening.

About nine the stew was ready, and the women ladled it into lacquer bowls with wooden spoons. The men were served first, but all ate together. Afterwards *saké*, their curse, was poured into lacquer bowls, and across each bowl a finely-carved "*saké-stick*" was laid. These sticks are very highly prized. The bowls were waved several times with an inward motion, then each man took his stick and, dipping it into the *saké*, made six libations to the fire, and several to the "god," a wooden post, with a quantity of spiral white shavings falling from near the top. The Ainos are not affected by *saké* nearly so easily as the Japanese. They took it cold, it is true, but each drank about three times as much as would have made a Japanese foolish, and it had no effect upon them. After two hours more talk one after another got up and went out, making profuse

[1] These words are given in the Appendix. I went over them with the Ainos of a remote village on Volcano Bay, and found the differences in pronunciation very slight, except that the definiteness of the sound which I have represented by *Tsch* was more strongly marked. I afterwards went over them with Mr. Dening, and with Mr. Von Siebold at Tôkiyô, who have made a larger collection of words than I have, and it is satisfactory to find that we have represented the words in the main by the same letters, with the single exception that usually the sound represented by them by the letters *ch*, I have given as *Tsch*, and I venture to think that this is the most correct rendering

salututions to me and to the others. My candles had been forgotten, and our *séance* was held by the fitful light of the big logs on the fire, aided by a succession of chips of birch bark, with which a woman replenished a cleft stick that was stuck into the fire-hole. I never saw such a strangely picturesque sight as that group of magnificent savages with the fitful firelight on their faces, and for adjuncts the flare of the torch, the strong lights, the blackness of the recesses of the room and of the roof, at one end of which the stars looked in, and the row of savage women in the background — eastern savagery and western civilisation met in this hut, savagery giving, and civilisation receiving, the yellow-skinned Ito the connecting-link between the two, and the representative of a civilisation to which our own is but an "infant of days."

I found it very exciting, and when all had left crept out into the starlight. The lodges were all dark and silent, and the dogs, mild like their masters, took no notice of me. The only sound was the rustle of a light breeze through the surrounding forest. The verse came into my mind, "It is not the will of your Father which is in Heaven that one of these little ones should perish." Surely these simple savages are children, as children to be judged; may we not hope as children to be saved through Him who came "not to judge the world, but to save the world"

I crept back again and into my mosquito net, and suffered not from fleas or mosquitoes, but from severe cold. Shinondi conversed with Ito for some time in a low musical voice, having previously asked if it would keep me from sleeping. No Japanese ever intermitted his ceaseless chatter at any hour of the night for a similar reason. Later, the chief's principal wife, Noma, stuck a triply-cleft stick in the fire-hole, put a potsherd with a wick and some fish-oil upon it, and by the dim light of this rude lamp sewed until midnight at a garment of bark cloth which she was ornamenting for her lord with strips of blue cloth, and when I opened my eyes the next morning she was at the window sewing by the earliest daylight. She is the most intelligent-looking of all the women, but looks sad and almost stern, and speaks seldom. Although she is the principal wife of the chief, she is not happy, for she is childless, and I thought that her sad look darkened into something evil as the other wife caressed a fine baby boy. Benri seems to me something of a brute, and the mother-in-law obviously holds the reins of government pretty tight. After sewing till midnight she swept the mats with a bunch of twigs, and then crept into her bed behind a hanging mat. For a moment in the stillness I felt a feeling of panic, as if I were incurring a risk by being alone among savages, but I conquered it, and after watching the fire till it went out, fell asleep till I was awoke by the severe cold of the next day's dawn.

AINO HOSPITALITY.

WHEN I crept from under my net, much benumbed with cold, there were about eleven people in the room, who all made their graceful salutation. It did not seem as if they had ever heard of washing, for when water was asked for, Shinondi brought a little in a lacquer bowl, and held it while I bathed my face and hands, supposing the performance to be an act of worship! I was about to throw some cold tea out of the window by my bed, when he arrested me with an anxious face, and I saw what I had not observed before, that there was a god at that window, a stick with festoons of shavings hanging from it, and beside it a dead bird. The Ainos have two meals a day, and their breakfast was a repetition of the previous night's supper. We all ate together, and I gave the children the remains of my rice, and it was most amusing to see little creatures of three, four, and five years old, with no other clothing than a piece of pewter hanging round their necks, first formally asking leave of the parents before taking the rice, and then waving their hands. The obedience of the children is instantaneous. Their parents are more demonstrative in their affection than the Japanese are, caressing them a good deal, and two of the men are devoted to children who are not their own. These little ones are as grave and dignified as Japanese children, and are very gentle.

I went out soon after five, when the dew was glittering in the sunshine, and the mountain hollow in which Biratori stands was looking its very best, and the silence of the place, even though the people were all astir, was as impressive as that of the night before. What a strange life! knowing nothing, hoping nothing, fearing a little, the need for clothes and food the one motive principle, *saké* in abundance the one good! How very few points of contact it is possible to have! I was just thinking so when Shinondi met me, and took me to his home to see if I could do anything for a child sorely afflicted with skin disease, and his extreme tenderness for this very loathsome object made me feel that human affections were the same among them as with us. He had carried it on his back from a village, five miles distant, that morning, in the hope that it might be cured. As soon as I entered, he laid a fine mat on the floor, and covered the guest-seat with a bearskin. After breakfast he took me to the lodge of the sub-chief, the largest in the village, 45 feet square, and into about twenty others all constructed in the same way, but some of them were not more than 20 feet square. In all, I was received with the same courtesy, but a few of the people asked Shinondi not to take me into their houses, as they did not want me to see how poor they are. In every house there was the low shelf with more or fewer curios upon it, but besides these, none but the barest necessaries of life, though the skins which they sell or barter every year would enable them to surround themselves with comforts, were it not that their gains represent to them *saké* and nothing else. They are not nomads. On the contrary, they cling tenaciously to the sites on which their fathers have lived and died. But anything more deplorable than the attempts at cultivation which surround their lodges could not be seen. The soil is little better than white sand, on which without manure they attempt to grow millet, which is to them in the place of rice, pumpkins, onions, and tobacco, but the look of their plots is as if they had been cultivated ten years ago, and some chance-sown grain and vegetables had come up among the weeds. When nothing more will grow, they partially clear another bit of forest, and exhaust that in its turn.

In every house the same honour was paid to a guest. This seems a savage virtue which is not strong enough to survive much contact with civilisation. Before I entered one lodge, the woman brought several of the finer mats, and arranged them as a pathway for me to walk to the fire upon. They will not accept anything for lodging, or for anything that they give, so I was anxious to help them by buying some of their handiwork, but found even this a difficult matter. They were very anxious to give, but when I desired to buy they said they did not wish to part with their things. I wanted what they had in actual use, such as a tobacco-box and pipe-sheath, and knives with carved handles and scabbards, and for three of these I offered 2½ dollars. They said they did not care to sell them, but in the evening they came saying they were not worth more than 1 dollar 10 cents, and they would sell them for that; and I could not get them to take more. They said it was "not their custom." I bought a bow and three poisoned arrows, two reed-mats, with a diamond pattern on them in reeds stained red, some knives with sheaths, and a bark cloth dress. I tried to buy the *saké*-sticks with which they make libations to their gods, but they said it was "not their custom " to part with the *saké*-stick of any living man — however, this morning Shinondi has brought me, as a very valuable present, the stick of a dead man! This morning the man who sold the arrows brought two new ones, to replace two which were imperfect. I found them, as Mr. Von Siebold had done, punctiliously honest in all their transactions. They wear very large earrings with hoops an inch and a half in diameter, a pair constituting the dowry of an Aino bride, but they would not part with these.

A house was burned down two nights ago, and "custom" in such a case requires that all the men should work at rebuilding it, so in their absence I got two boys to take me in a "dug-out" as far as we could go up the Sarufutogawa, a lovely river, which winds tortuously through the forests and mountains in unspeakable loveliness. I had much of the feeling of the ancient mariner —

> " We were the first
> Who ever burst
> Into that silent sea."

For certainly no European had ever previously floated on the dark and forest-shrouded waters. I enjoyed those hours thoroughly, for the silence was profound, and the faint blue of the autumn sky, and the soft blue veil which "spiritualised " the distances, were so exquisitely like the Indian summer.

The evening was spent like the previous one, but the hearts of the savages were sad, for there was no more *saké* in Biratori, so they could not "drink to the god," and the fire and the post with the shavings had to go without libations. There was no more oil, so after the strangers retired the hut was in complete darkness.

Yesterday morning we all breakfasted soon after daylight, and the able-bodied men went away to hunt. Hunting and fishing are their occupations, and for "indoor recreation" they carve tobacco-boxes, knife-sheaths, *saké*-sticks, and shuttles.   It is quite unneces-

AINO STORE-HOUSE.

sary for them to do anything; they are quite contented to sit by the fire, and smoke occasionally, and eat and sleep, this apathy being varied by spasms of activity when there is no more dried flesh in the *kuras*, and when skins must be taken to Sarufuto to pay for *saké*. The women seem never to have an idle moment.   They rise early to sew, weave, and split bark, for they not only clothe themselves and their husbands in this nearly indestructible cloth, but weave it for barter, and the lower class of Japanese are constantly to be seen wearing the product of Aino industry. They do all the hard work, such as drawing water, chopping wood, grinding millet, and cultivating the soil, after their fashion; but to do the men justice, I often see them trudging along, carrying one and even two children. The women take the exclusive charge of the *kuras*, which are never entered by men.

I was left for some hours alone with the women, of whom there were seven in the hut, with a few children. On the one side of the fire the chief's mother sat like a Fate, for ever splitting and knotting bark, and petrifying me by her cold, hateful eyes. Her thick, grey hair hangs in shocks, the tattooing round her mouth has nearly faded, and no longer disguises her really handsome features. She is dressed in a much ornamented bark-cloth dress, and wears two silver beads tied round her neck by a piece of blue cotton, in addition to very large earrings. She has much sway in the house, sitting on the men's side of the fire, drinking plenty of *saké*, and occasionally chiding her grandson Shinondi for telling me too much, saying that it will bring harm to her people. Though her expression is so severe and forbidding, she is certainly very handsome, and it is a European, not an Asiatic, beauty.

The younger women were all at work; two were seated on the floor weaving without a loom, and the others were making and mending the bark coats which are worn by both sexes. Noma, the chief's principal wife, sat apart, seldom speaking. Two of the youngest women are very pretty — as fair as ourselves, and their comeliness is of the rosy, peasant kind. It turns out

that two of them, though they would not divulge it
before men, speak Japanese, and they prattled to Ito
with great vivacity and merriment; the ancient Fate
scowling at them the while from under her shaggy eyebrows. I got a number of words from them, and they
laughed heartily at my erroneous pronunciation. They
even asked me a number of questions regarding their
own sex among ourselves, but few of these would bear
repetition, and they answered a number of mine. As
the merriment increased the old woman looked increasingly angry and restless, and at last rated them sharply,
as I have heard since, telling them that, if they spoke
another word, she should tell their husbands that they
had been talking to strangers. After this not another
word was spoken, and Noma, who is an industrious
housewife, boiled some millet into a mash for a mid-day
lunch. During the afternoon a very handsome young
Aino, with a washed, richly-coloured skin and fine clear
eyes, came up from the coast, where he had been working at the fishing. He saluted the old woman and
Benri's wife on entering, and presented the former with
a gourd of *saké*, bringing a greedy light into her eyes
as she took a long draught, after which, saluting me, he
threw himself down in the place of honour by the fire,
with the easy grace of a staghound, a savage all over.
His name is Pipichari, and he is the chief's adopted son.
He had cut his foot badly with a root, and asked me to
cure it, and I stipulated that it should be bathed for some
time in warm water before anything more was done,
after which I bandaged it with lint. He said " he did
not like me to touch his foot, it was not clean enough,
my hands were too white," etc.; but when I had dressed
it, and the pain was much relieved, he bowed very low
and then kissed my hand! He was the only one among
them all who showed the slightest curiosity regarding

though I have made a bowl of beef-tea with the remains of my stock, it can only last one day.

I was so tired with these nocturnal expeditions and anxieties, that on lying down I fell asleep, and on waking found more than the usual assemblage in the room, and the men were obviously agog about something. They have a singular, and I hope an unreasonable, fear of the Japanese Government. Mr. Von Siebold thinks that the officials threaten and knock them about; and this is possible; but I really think that the *Kaitaikushi* Department means well by them, and, besides removing the oppressive restrictions by which, as a conquered race, they were fettered, treats them far more humanely and equitably than the U. S. Government, for instance, treats the North American Indians. However, they are ignorant; and one of the men who had been most grateful because I said I would get Dr. Hepburn to send some medicine for his child, came this morning and begged me not to do so, as, he said, "the Japanese Government would be angry." After this they again prayed me not to tell the Japanese Government that they had told me their customs; and then they began to talk earnestly together.

The sub-chief then spoke, and said that I had been kind to their sick people, and they would like to show me their temple, which had never been seen by any foreigner; but they were very much afraid of doing so, and they asked me many times "not to tell the Japanese Government that they showed it to me, lest some great harm should happen to them." The sub-chief put on a sleeveless Japanese war-cloak to go up, and he, Shinondi, Pipichari, and two others accompanied me. It was a beautiful but very steep walk, or rather climb, to the top of an abrupt acclivity beyond the

village, on which the temple or shrine stands. It
would be impossible to get up, were it not for the
remains of a wooden staircase, not of Aino construction. Forest and mountain surround Biratori, and the
only breaks in the dense greenery are glints of the
shining waters of the Sarufutogawa, and the tawny roofs
of the Aino lodges. It is a lonely and a silent land, fitter
for the *hiding* place than the *dwelling* place of men.

When the splendid young savage, Pipichari, saw
that I found it difficult to get up, he took my hand
and helped me up, as gently as an English gentleman
would have done; and when he saw that I had greater
difficulty in getting down, he all but insisted on my
riding down on his back, and certainly would have
carried me, had not Benri, the chief, who arriv d while
we were at the shrine, made an end of it by taking my
hand and helping me down himself. Their instinct f
helpfulness to a foreign woman strikes me as so odd,
because they never show any courtesy to their own
women, whom they treat (though to a less extent than
is usual among savages) as inferior beings.

On the very edge of the cliff, at the top of the zigzag,
stands a wooden temple or shrine, such as one sees in
any grove, or on any high place on the main island,
obviously of Japanese construction, but concerning
which Aino tradition is silent. No European had ever
stood where I stood, and there was a solemnity in the
knowledge. The sub-chief drew back the sliding doors,
and all bowed with much reverence. It was a simple
shrine of unlacquered wood, with a broad shelf at the
back, on which there was a small shrine containing a
figure of the historical hero Yoshitsuné, in a suit of inlaid brass armour, some metal *gohei*, a pair of tarnished
brass candlesticks, and a coloured Chinese picture representing a junk. Here, then, I was introduced to the

is never to be met with. The features, expression, and aspect, are European rather than Asiatic.

The "ferocious savagery" of the appearance of the men is produced by a profusion of thick, soft, black

AN AINO PATRIARCH.

hair, divided in the middle, and falling in heavy masses nearly to the shoulders. Out of doors it is kept from falling over the face by a fillet round the brow. The beards are equally profuse, quite magnificent, and generally wavy, and in the case of the old men they give a truly patriarchal and venerable aspect, in spite of the yellow tinge produced by smoke and want of cleanliness. The savage look produced by the masses of hair and beard, and the thick eyebrows, is mitigated by the softness in the dreamy brown eyes, and is altogether obliterated by the exceeding sweetness of the smile, which belongs in greater or less degree to all the rougher sex.

I have measured the height of thirty of the adult men of this village, and it ranges from 5 feet 4 inches to five feet 6½ inches. The circumference of the heads averages 22.1 inches, and the arc, from ear to ear, 13 inches. According to Mr. Davies, the average weight of the Aino adult masculine brain, ascertained by measurement of Aino skulls, is 45.90 ounces avoirdupois, a brain weight said to exceed that of all the races, Hindoo and Mussulman, on the Indian plains, and that of the aboriginal races of India and Ceylon, and is only paralleled by that of the races of the Himalayas, the Siamese, and the Chinese Burmese. Mr. Davies says, further, that it exceeds the mean brain weight of Asiatic races in general. Yet with all this the Ainos are a stupid people.

Passing travellers who have seen a few of the Aino women on the road to Satsuporo speak of them as very ugly, but as making amends for their ugliness by their industry and conjugal fidelity. Of the latter there is no doubt, but I am not disposed to admit the former. The ugliness is certainly due to art and dirt. The Aino women seldom exceed five feet and half an inch in height, but they are beautifully formed, straight, lithe, and well-developed, with small feet and hands, well-arched insteps, rounded limbs, well-developed busts, and a firm, elastic gait. Their heads and faces are small; but the hair, which falls in masses on each side of the face like that of the men, is equally redundant

They have superb teeth, and display them liberally in smiling. Their mouths are somewhat wide, but well formed, and they have a ruddy comeliness about them which is pleasing, in spite of the disfigurement of the band which is tattooed both above and below the mouth, and which, by being united at the corners, enlarges its apparent size and width. A girl at Shirôai, who, for some reason, has not been subjected to this process, is the most beautiful creature in features, colouring, and natural grace of form, that I have seen for a long time. Their complexions are lighter than those of the men. There are not many here even as dark as our European brunettes. A few unite the eyebrows by a streak of tattooing, so as to produce a straight line. Like the men, they cut their hair short for two or three inches above the nape of the neck, but instead of using a fillet they take two locks from the front and tie them at the back.

They are universally tattooed, not only with the broad band above and below the mouth, but with a band across the knuckles, succeeded by an elaborate pattern on the back of

TATTOOED FEMALE HAND.

the hand, and a series of bracelets extending to the elbow. The process of disfigurement begins at the age of five, when some of the sufferers are yet unweaned. I saw the operation performed on a dear little bright girl this morning. A woman took a large knife with a sharp edge, and rapidly cut several horizontal lines on the upper lip, following closely the curve of the very pretty mouth, and before the slight bleeding had ceased carefully rubbed in some of the shiny soot which collects on the mat above the fire. In two or three days the scarred lip will be washed with the decoction of the bark of a tree to fix the pattern, and give it that blue look which makes many people mistake it for a daub of paint. A child who had this second process performed yesterday has her lip fearfully swollen and inflamed. The latest victim held her hands clasped tightly together while the cuts were inflicted, but never cried. The pattern on the lips is deepened and widened every year up to the time of marriage, and the circles on the arm are extended in a similar way. The men cannot give any reason for the universality of this custom. It is an old custom, they sa   and part of their religion, and no woman could mai y without it. Benri ancies that the Japanese custom f blackening the eth is equivalent to it; but he is mis ken, as that ce emony usually succeeds marriage. Th v begin to t too the arms when a girl is five or six, and vork fror the elbow downwards. They expressed thems lves as very much grieved and tormented by the recent pro vition of tattooing. They ay the gods will be ang y and that the women can't m   ry unless they are tat oed ; and they implored both Mr.   n Siebold and m to intercede with the Japanese Governn nt on their vehali in this respect. They are less apathet o on th s than on any subject, and repeat frequently, "It's a part of our religion."

The children are very pretty and attractive, and their faces give promise of an intelligence which is lacking in those of the adults. They are much loved, and are caressing as well as caressed. The infants of the mountain Ainos have seeds of millet put into their mouths as soon as they are born, and those of the coast

Ainos a morsel of salt fish; and whatever be the hour
of birth, " custom" requires that they shall not be fed
until a night has passed. They are not weaned until
they are at least three years old. Boys are preferred to
girls, but both are highly valued, and a childless wife
may be divorced. Children do not receive names till
they are four or five years old, and then the father
chooses a name by which his child is afterwards known.
Young children when they travel are either carried on
their mothers' backs in a net, or in the back of the
loose garment; but in both cases the weight is mainly
supported by a broad band which passes round the
woman's forehead. When men carry them they hold
them in their arms. The hair of very young children
is shaven, and from about five to fifteen the boys wear
either a large tonsure or tufts above the ears, while the
girls are allowed to grow hair all over their heads.

Implicit and prompt obedience is required from infancy; and from a very early age the children are utilised by being made to fetch and carry and go on messages. I have seen children apparently not more than
two years old sent for wood; and even at this age they
are so thoroughly trained in the observances of etiquette, that babies just able to walk never toddle into
or out of this house without formal salutations to each
person within it, the mother alone excepted. They
don't wear any clothing till they are seven or eight
years old, and are then dressed like their elders. Their
manners to their parents are very affectionate. Even
to-day, in the chief's awe-inspiring presence, one dear
little nude creature, who had been sitting quietly for
two hours staring into the fire with her big brown eyes,
rushed to meet her mother when she entered, and threw
her arms round her, to which the woman responded by
a look of true maternal tenderness and a kiss. These

little creatures, in the absolute unconsciousness of innocence, with their beautiful faces, olive-tinted bodies, —
all the darker, sad to say, from dirt — their perfect
docility, and absence of prying curiosity, are very bewitching. They all wear silver or pewter ornaments
tied round their necks by a wisp of blue cotton.

Apparently the ordinary infantile maladies, such as
whooping-cough and measles, do not afflict the Ainos
fatally; but the children suffer from a cutaneous affection, which wears off as they reach the age of ten or
eleven years, as well as from severe toothache with
their first teeth.

COSTUME AND CUSTOMS.

Aino Clothing — Holiday Dress — Domestic Architecture — House-hold Gods — Japanese Curios — The Necessaries of Life — Clay Soup — Arrow Poison — Arrow Traps — Female Occupations — Bark Cloth — The Art of Weaving.

AINO clothing, for savages, is exceptionally good. In the winter it consists of one, two, or more coats of skins, with hoods of the same, to which the men add rude moccasins when they go out hunting. In summer they wear *kimonos*, or loose coats, made of cloth woven from the split bark of a forest tree. This is a durable and beautiful fabric in various shades of natural buff, and somewhat resembles what is known to fancy work-ers as "Panama canvas." Under this a skin or bark-cloth vest may or may not be worn. The men wear these coats reaching a little below the knees, folded over from right to left, and confined at the waist by a narrow girdle of the same cloth, to which is attached a rude, dagger-shaped knife, with a carved and engraved wooden handle and sheath. Smoking is by no means a general practice, consequently the pipe and tobacco-box are not, as with the Japanese, a part of ordinary male attire. Tightly-fitting leggings, either of bark-cloth or skin, are worn by both sexes, but neither shoes nor san-dals. The coat worn by the women reaches half-way between the knees and ankles, and is quite loose and without a girdle. It is fastened the whole way up to the collar-bone; and not only is the Aino woman com-

pletely covered, but she will not change one garment
for another except alone or in the dark. Lately a
Japanese woman at Sarufuto took an Aino woman into
her house, and insisted on her taking a bath, which she
absolutely refused to do till the bath-house had been
made quite private by means of screens. On the
Japanese woman going back a little later to see what
had become of her, she found her sitting in the water
in her clothes; and on being remonstrated with, she
said that the gods would be angry if they saw her without clothes!

Many of the garments for holiday occasions are exceedingly handsome, being decorated with "geometri-
cal" patterns, in which the "Greek fret" takes part, in
coarse blue cotton, braided most dexterously with scarlet
and white thread. Some of the handsomest take half a
year to make. The masculine dress is completed by an
apron of oblong shape decorated in the same elaborate
manner. These handsome savages, with their powerful
physique, look remarkably well in their best clothes. I
have not seen a boy or girl above nine who is not
thoroughly clothed. The "jewels" of the women are
large, hoop earrings of silver or pewter, with attach-
ments of a classical pattern, and silver neck ornaments,
and a few have brass bracelets soldered upon their arms.
The women have a perfect passion for every hue of red,
and I have made friends with them by dividing among
them a large turkey-red silk handkerchief, strips of
which are already being utilised for the ornamenting
of coats.

The houses in the five villages up here are very good.
So they are at Horobets, but at Shiraôi, where the aborigines suffer from the close proximity of several grog
shops, they are inferior. They differ in many ways from
any that I have before seen, approaching most nearly to

the grass houses of the natives of Hawaii. Custom does not appear to permit either of variety or innovations; in all the style is the same, and the difference consists in the size and plenishings. The dwellings seemed ill-fitted for a rigorous climate, but the same thing may be said of those of the Japanese. In their houses, as in their faces, the Ainos are more European than their conquerors, as they possess doorways, windows, central fireplaces, like those of the Highlanders of Scotland, and raised sleeping-places.

The usual appearance is that of a small house built on at the end of a larger one. The small house is the vestibule or ante-room, and is entered by a low doorway screened by a heavy mat of reeds. It contains the large wooden mortar and pestle with two ends, used for pounding millet, a wooden receptacle for millet, nets or hunting gear, and some bundles of reeds for repairing roof or walls. This room never contains a window. From it the large room is entered by a doorway, over which a heavy reed-mat, bound with hide, invariably hangs. This room in Benri's case is 35 feet long by 25 feet broad, another is 45 feet square, the smallest measures 20 feet by 15. On entering, one is much impressed by the great height and steepness of the roof, altogether out of proportion to the height of the walls.

The frame of the house is of posts, 4 feet 10 inches high, placed 4 feet apart, and sloping slightly inwards. The height of the walls is apparently regulated by that of the reeds, of which only one length is used, and which never exceed 4 feet 10 inches. The posts are scooped at the top, and heavy poles, resting on the scoops, are laid along them to form the top of the wall. The posts are again connected twice by slighter poles tied on horizontally. The wall is double; the outer part being formed of reeds tied very neatly to the framework in small, regular bundles, the inner layer or wall being made of reeds attached singly. From the top of the pole, which is secured to the top of the posts, the frame-work of the roof rises to a height of twenty-two feet, made, like the rest, of poles tied to a heavy and roughly-hewn ridge-beam. At one end under the ridge-beam there is a large triangular aperture for the exit of smoke. Two very stout, roughly-hewn beams cross the width of the house, resting on the posts of the wall, and on props let into the floor, and a number of poles are laid at the same height, by means of which a secondary roof formed of mats can be at once extemporised, but this is only used for guests. These poles answer the same purpose as shelves. Very great care is bestowed upon the out-side of the roof, which is a marvel of neatness and pretti-ness, and has the appearance of a series of frills, being thatched in ridges. The ridge-pole is very thickly cov-ered, and the thatch both there and at the corners is elaborately laced with a pattern in strong peeled twigs. The poles, which, for much of the room, run from wall to wall, compel one to stoop, to avoid fracturing one's skull, and bringing down spears, bows and arrows, arrow-traps, and other primitive property. The roof and rafters are black and shiny from wood smoke. Immediately under them, at one end and one side, are small, square windows, which are closed at night by wooden shutters, which during the day-time hang by ropes. Nothing is a greater insult to an Aino than to look in at his window.

On the left of the doorway is invariably a fixed wooden platform, eighteen inches high, and covered with a single mat, which is the sleeping-place. The pil-lows are small stiff bolsters, covered with ornamental matting. If the family be large there are several of these sleeping platforms. A pole runs horizontally at a fitting distance above the outside edge of each, over which mats are thrown to conceal the sleepers from the rest of the room. The inside half of these mats is plain, but the outside, which is seen from the room, has a diamond pattern woven into it in dull reds and browns. The whole floor is covered with a very coarse reed-mat, with interstices half an inch wide. The fireplace, which is six feet long, is oblong. Above it, on a very black

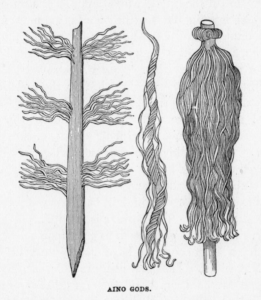

AINO GODS.

and elaborate framework, hangs a very black and shiny mat, whose superfluous soot forms the basis of the stain used in tattooing, and whose apparent purpose is to prevent the smoke ascending, and to diffuse it equally throughout the room. From this framework depends the great cooking-pot, which plays a most important part in Aino economy.

Household gods form an essential part of the furnishing of every house. In this one, at the left of the entrance, there are ten white wands, with shavings depending from the upper end, stuck in the wall; another projects from the window which faces the sunrise, and the great god, a white post, two feet high, with spirals of shavings depending from the top, is always planted in the floor, near the wall, on the left side, opposite the fire, between the platform bed of the householder and the low, broad shelf placed invariably on the same side, and which is a singular feature of all Aino houses, coast and mountain, down to the poorest, containing, as it does, Japanese curios, many of them very valuable objects of antique art, though much destroyed by damp and dust. They are true curiosities in the dwellings of these northern aborigines, and look almost solemn ranged against the wall. In this house there are twenty-four lacquered urns, or tea-chests, or seats, each standing two feet high on four small legs, shod with engraved or filigree brass. Behind these are eight lacquered tubs, and a number of bowls and lacquer trays, and above are spears with inlaid handles, and fine Kaga and Awata bowls. The lacquer is good, and several of the urns have *daimiyô's* crests in gold upon them. One urn and a large covered bowl are beautifully inlaid with Venus' ear. The great urns are to be seen in every house, and in addition there are suits of inlaid armour, and swords with inlaid hilts, engraved blades, and *répoussé* scabbards, for which a collector would give almost anything. No offers, however liberal, can tempt them to sell any of these antique possessions. "They were presents," they say in their low, musical voices; "they were presents from those who were kind to our fathers; no, we cannot sell them; they were presents." And so gold lacquer, and pearl inlaying, and gold niellowork, and *daimiyô's* crests in gold, continue to gleam in the smoky darkness of their huts. Some of these things were doubtless gifts to their fathers when they went to pay tribute to the representative of the Shôgun and the prince of Matsumæ, soon after the conquest of Yezo. Others were probably gifts from *samurai*, who took refuge here during the rebellion, and some must have been obtained by barter. They are the one possession which they will not barter for *saké*, and are only parted with in payment of fines at the command of a chief, or as the dower of a girl.

Except in the poorest houses, where the people can only afford to lay down a mat for a guest, they cover the coarse mat with fine ones on each side of the fire. These mats and the bark-cloth are really their only manufactures. They are made of fine reeds, with a pattern in dull reds or browns, and are 14 feet long by 3 feet 6 inches wide. It takes a woman eight days to make one of them. In every house there are one or two movable platforms 6 feet by 4 and 14 inches high, which are placed at the head of the fireplace, and on which guests sit and sleep on a bearskin or a fine mat. In many houses there are broad seats a few inches high, on which the elder men sit cross-legged, as their custom is, not squatting Japanese fashion on the heels. A water-tub always rests on a stand by the door, and the dried fish and venison or bear for daily use hang from the rafters, as well as a few skins. Besides these things there are a few absolute necessaries, — lacquer or wooden bowls for food and *saké*, a chopping-board and rude chopping knife, a cleft stick for burning strips of birch-bark, a triply-cleft stick for supporting the potsherd in which, on rare occasions, they burn a wick with oil, the component parts of their rude loom, the bark of which they make their clothes, the reeds of which they make their mats, — and the inventory of the essentials of their life is nearly complete. No iron enters into the construction of their houses, its place being supplied by a remarkably tenacious fibre.

I have before described the preparation of their food,

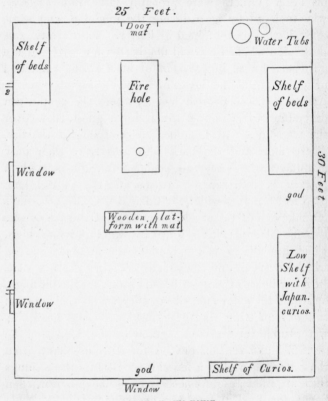

PLAN OF AN AINO HOUSE.

which usually consists of a stew " of abominable things." They eat salt and fresh fish, dried fish, seaweed, slugs, the various vegetables which grow in the wilderness of tall weeds which surrounds their villages, wild roots and berries, fresh and dried venison and bear; their carni-

more out of observation than here. The traps consist of a large bow with a poisoned arrow, fixed in such a way that when the bear walks over a cord which is attached to it he is simultaneously transfixed. I have seen as many as fifty in one house. The simple contrivance for inflicting this silent death is most ingenious.

The women are occupied all day, as I have before said. They look cheerful, and even merry when they smile, and are not like the Japanese, prematurely old, partly perhaps because their houses are well ventilated, and the use of charcoal is unknown. I do not think that they undergo the unmitigated drudgery which falls to the lot of most savage women, though they work hard. The men do not like them to speak to strangers, however, and say that their place is to work and rear children. They eat of the same food, and at the same time as the men, laugh and talk before them, and receive equal support and respect in old age. They sell mats and bark-cloth in the piece, and made up, when they can, and their husbands do not take their earnings from them. All Aino women understand the making of bark-cloth. The men bring in the bark in strips, five feet long, having removed the outer coating. This inner bark is easily separated into several thin layers, which are split into very narrow strips by the older women, very neatly knotted, and wound

WEAVER'S SHUTTLE.

into balls weighing about a pound each. No preparation of either the bark or the thread is required to fit it
for weaving, but I observe that some of the women
steep it in a decoction of a bark which produces a
brown dye to deepen the buff tint.

The loom is so simple that I almost fear to represent
it as complicated by description. It consists of a stout
hook fixed in the floor, to which the threads of the far
end of the web are secured, a cord fastening the near
end to the waist of the worker, who supplies, by dexterous rigidity, the necessary tension ; a frame like a
comb resting on the ankles, through which the threads
pass, a hollow roll for keeping the upper and under
threads separate, a spatula-shaped shuttle of engraved
wood, and a roller on which the cloth is rolled as it is
made. The length of the web is fifteen feet, and the
width of the cloth fifteen inches. It is woven with
great regularity, and the knots in the thread are carefully kept on the under side.[1] It is a very slow and
fatiguing process, and a woman cannot do much more
than a foot a day. The weaver sits on the floor with
the whole arrangement attached to her waist, and the
loom, if such it may be called, on her ankles. It takes
long practice before she can supply the necessary tension by spinal rigidity. As the work proceeds she
drags herself almost imperceptibly nearer the hook. In
this house and other large ones two or three women
bring in their webs in the morning, fix their hooks,
and weave all day, while others, who have not equal
advantages, put their hooks in the ground and weave
in the sunshine. The web and loom can be bundled up
in two minutes, and carried away quite as easily as a

[1] I have not been able to obtain from any botanist the name of the
tree from the bark of which the thread is made, but suppose it to be a
species of *Tiliaceæ*.

knitted sofa blanket. It is the simplest and perhaps the most primitive form of hand-loom, and comb, shuttle, and roll, are all easily fashioned with an ordinary knife.

RELIGION OF AINOS.

A Simple Nature Worship — Aino Gods — A Festival Song — Religious Intoxication — Bear Worship — The Annual Saturnalia — The Future State — Marriage and Divorce — Musical Instruments — Etiquette — The Chieftainship — Death and Burial — Old Age — Moral Qualities.

THERE cannot be anything more vague and destitute of cohesion than Aino religious notions. With the exception of the hill shrines of Japanese construction dedicated to Yoshitsuné, they have no temples, and they have neither priests, sacrifices, nor worship. Apparently through all traditional time their *cultus* has been the rudest and most primitive form of nature worship, the attaching of a vague sacredness to trees, rivers, rocks, and mountains, and of vague notions of power for good or evil to the sea, the forest, the fire, and the sun and moon. I cannot make out that they possess a trace of the deification of ancestors, though their rude nature worship may well have been the primitive form of Japanese Shintô. The solitary exception to their adoration of animate and inanimate nature appears to be the reverence paid to Yoshitsuné, to whom they believe they are greatly indebted, and who, it is supposed by some, will yet interfere on their behalf.[1] Their gods, that is, the outward symbols of

[1] Yoshitsuné is the most popular hero of Japanese history, and the special favourite of boys. He was the brother of Yoritomo, who was appointed by the Mikado in 1192, *Sei-i Tai Shôgun* (barbarian-subjugat-

their religion, corresponding most likely with the Shintô *gohei*, are wands and posts of peeled wood, whittled nearly to the top, from which the pendent shavings fall down in white curls. These are not only set up in their houses, sometimes to the number of twenty, but on precipices, banks of rivers and streams, and mountain passes, and such wands are thrown into the rivers as the boatmen descend rapids and dangerous places. Since my baggage horse fell over an acclivity on the trail from Sarufuto, four such wands have been placed there. It is nonsense to write of the religious ideas of a people who have none, and of beliefs among people who are merely adult children. The traveller who formulates an Aino creed must "evolve it from his inner consciousness." I have taken infinite trouble to learn from themselves what their religious notions are, and Shinondi tells me that they have told me all they know, and the whole sum is a few vague fears and hopes, and a suspicion that there are things outside themselves

ing great general) for his victories, and was the first of that series of great Shôguns whom our European notions distorted into "Temporal Emperors" of Japan. Yoshitsuné, to whom the real honour of these victories belonged, became the object of the jealousy and hatred of his brother, and was hunted from province to province, till, according to popular belief, he committed *hara-kiri*, after killing his wife and children, and his head, preserved in *saké*, was sent to his brother at Kamakura. Scholars, however, are not agreed as to the manner, period, or scene of his death. Many believe that he escaped to Yezo and lived among the Ainos for many years, dying among them at the close of the twelfth century. None believe this more firmly than the Ainos themselves, who assert that he taught their fathers the arts of civilisation, with letters and numbers, and gave them righteous laws, and he is worshipped by many of them under a name which signifies Master of the Law. I have been told by old men in Biratori, Usu, and Lebungé, that a later Japanese conqueror carried away the books in which the arts were written, and that since his time the arts themselves have been lost, and the Ainos have fallen into their present condition! On asking why the Ainos do not make vessels of iron and clay as well as knives and spears, the invariable answer is, " The Japanese took away the books."

more powerful than themselves, whose good influences may be obtained, or whose evil influences may be averted, by libations of *saké*.

The word worship is in itself misleading. When I use it of these savages it simply means libations of *saké*, waving bowls and waving hands, without any spiritual act of deprecation or supplication. In such a sense and such alone they worship the sun and moon (but not the stars), the forest, and the sea. The wolf, the black snake, the owl, and several other beasts and birds have the word *kamoi*, god, attached to them, as the wolf is the "howling god," the owl "the bird of the gods," a black snake the "raven god," but none of these things are now "worshipped," wolf-worship having quite lately died out. Thunder, "the voice of the gods," inspires some fear. The sun, they say, is their best god, and the fire their next best, obviously the divinities from whom their greatest benefits are received. Some idea of gratitude pervades their rude notions, as in the case of the "worship" paid to Yoshitsuné, and it appears in one of the rude recitations chanted at the Saturnalia which in several places conclude the hunting and fishing seasons:—

" To the sea which nourishes us, to the forest which protects us, we present our grateful thanks. You are two mothers that nourish the same child; do not be angry if we leave one to go to the other.

" The Ainos will always be the pride of the forest and of the sea."

The solitary act of sacrifice which they perform is the placing of a worthless, dead bird, something like a sparrow, near one of their peeled wands, where it is left till it reaches an advanced stage of putrefaction. " To drink for the god " is the chief act of " worship," and thus drunkenness and religion are inseparably con nected, as the more *saké* the Ainos drink the more devout they are, and the better pleased are the gods. It does not appear that anything but *saké* is of sufficient value to please the gods. The libations to the fire and the peeled post are never omitted, and are always accompanied by the inward waving of the *saké* bowls.

The peculiarity which distinguishes this rude mythology is the "worship" of the bear, the Yezo bear being one of the finest of his species, but it is impossible to understand the feelings by which it is prompted, for they worship it after their fashion, and set up its head in their villages, yet they trap it, kill it, eat it, and sell its skin. There is no doubt that this wild beast inspires more of the feeling which prompts worship than the inanimate forces of nature, and the Ainos may be distinguished as bear-worshippers, and their greatest religious festival or Saturnalia as the Festival of the Bear. Gentle and peaceable as they are, they have a great admiration for fierceness and courage; and the bear, which is the strongest, fiercest, and most courageous animal known to them, has probably in all ages inspired them with veneration. Some of their rude chants are in praise of the bear, and their highest eulogy on a man is to compare him to a bear. Thus Shinondi said of Benri the chief, "He is as strong as a bear," and the old Fate praising Pipichari called him "The young bear."

In all Aino villages, specially near the chief's house, there are several tall poles with the fleshless skull of a bear on the top of each, and in most there is also a large cage, made gridiron fashion, of stout timbers, and raised two or three feet from the ground. At the present time such cages contain young but well-grown bears, captured when quite small in the early spring. After the capture the bear cub is introduced into a dwelling-house, generally that of the chief, or sub-chief, where it is suckled by a woman, and played with by the children, till it grows too big and rough for domestic ways, and is placed in a strong cage, in which it is fed and cared for, as I understand, till the autumn of the following year, when, being strong and well-grown, the Festival of the Bear is celebrated. The customs of this festival vary considerably, and the manner of the bear's death differs among the mountain and coast Ainos, but everywhere there is a general gathering of the people, and it is the occasion of a great feast, accompanied with much *saké* and a curious dance, in which men alone take part.

Yells and shouts are used to excite the bear, and when he becomes much agitated a chief shoots him with an arrow, inflicting a slight wound which maddens him, on which the bars of the cage are raised, and he springs forth, very furious. At this stage the Ainos run upon him with various weapons, each one striving to inflict a wound, as it is good luck to draw his blood. As soon as he falls down exhausted, his head is cut off, and the weapons with which he has been wounded are offered to it, and he is asked to avenge himself upon them. Afterwards the carcass, amidst a frenzied uproar, is distributed among the people, and amidst feasting and riot the head, placed upon a pole, is worshipped, *i.e.* it receives libations of *saké*, and the festival closes with general intoxication. In some villages it is customary for the foster-mother of the bear to utter piercing wails while he is delivered to his murderers, and after he is slain to beat each one of them with a branch of a tree. [Afterwards at Usu, on Volcano Bay, the old men told me that at their festival they despatch the bear after a different manner. On letting it loose from the cage two men seize it by the ears, and others simultaneously place a long, stout pole across the nape of its neck, upon which a number of Ainos mount, and after a prolonged struggle the neck is broken. As the bear is seen to approach his end, they shout in chorus, " We kill you, O bear! come back soon into an Aino."] When a bear is trapped or wounded by an arrow, the hunters go through an apologetic or propitiatory ceremony. They appear to have certain rude ideas of metempsychosis, as is evidenced by the Usu prayer to the bear and certain rude traditions, but whether these are indigenous, or have arisen by contact with Buddhism at a later period, it is impossible to say.

They have no definite ideas concerning a future state, and the subject is evidently not a pleasing one to them. Such notions as they have are few and confused. Some think that the spirits of their friends go into wolves and snakes; others, that they wander about the forests; and they are much afraid of ghosts. A few think that they go to " a good or bad place," according to their deeds; but Shinondi said, and there was an infinite pathos in his words, " How can we know? No one ever came back to tell us ! " On asking him what were bad deeds, he said, " Being bad to parents, stealing, and telling lies." The future, however, does not occupy any place in their thoughts, and they can hardly be said to believe in the immortality of the soul, though their fear of ghosts shows that they recognise a distinction between body and spirit.

Their social customs are very simple. Girls never marry before the age of seventeen, or men before twenty-one. When a man wishes to marry, he thinks of some particular girl, and asks the chief if he may ask for her. If leave is given, either through a "go-between" or personally, he asks her father for her, and if he consents, the bridegroom gives him a present, usually a Japanese " curio." This constitutes betrothal, and the marriage, which immediately follows, is celebrated by carousals and the drinking of much *saké*. The bride receives as her dowry her earrings and a highly-ornamented *kimono*. It is an essential that the husband provides a house to which to take his wife Each couple lives separately, and even the eldest son does not take his bride to his father's house. Polygamy is only allowed in two cases. The chief may have three wives; but each must have her separate house. Benri has two wives; but it appears that he took the second because the first was childless. [The Usu Ainos told me that among the tribes of Volcano Bay polygamy is not practised, even by the chiefs.] It is also permitted in the case of a childless wife; but there is no instance of it in Biratori, and the men say that they prefer to have one wife, as two quarrel.

Widows are allowed to marry again with the chief's consent; but among these mountain Ainos a woman must remain absolutely secluded within the house of her late husband for a period varying from six to twelve months, only going to the door at intervals, to throw *saké* to the right and left. A man secludes himself similarly for thirty days. [So greatly do the customs vary, that round Volcano Bay I found that the period of seclusion for a widow is only thirty days, and for a man twenty-five; but that after a father's death the house in which he has lived is burned down after the thirty days of seclusion, and the widow and her children go to a friend's house for three years, after which the house is rebuilt on its former site.]

If a man does not like his wife, by obtaining the chief's consent he can divorce her; but he must send her back to her parents with plenty of good clothes. but divorce is impracticable where there are children and is rarely if ever practised. Conjugal fidelity is a virtue among Aino women; but "custom" provides that, in case of unfaithfulness, the injured husband may bestow his wife upon her paramour, if he be an unmarried man; in which case the chief fixes the amount of damages which the paramour must pay; and these are usually valuable Japanese curios.

The old and blind people are entirely supported by their children, and receive until their dying day filial reverence and obedience.

If one man steals from another, he must return what he has taken, and give the injured man a present besides, the value of which is fixed by the chief.

Their mode of living you already know, as I have shared it, and am still receiving their hospitality. "Custom" enjoins the exercise of hospitality on every Aino. They receive all strangers as they received me, giving them of their best, placing them in the most honourable place, bestowing gifts upon them, and, when they depart, furnishing them with cakes of boiled millet.

They have few amusements, except certain feasts. Their dance, which they have just given in my honour, is slow and mournful, and their songs are chants or recitative. They have a musical instrument, something like a guitar, with three, five, or six strings, which are made from sinews of whales cast up on the shore. They have another, which is believed to be peculiar to themselves, consisting of a thin piece of wood, about five inches long and two and a half inches broad, with a pointed wooden tongue, about two lines in breadth and sixteen in length, fixed in the middle, and grooved on three sides. The wood is held before the mouth, and the tongue is set in motion by the vibration of the breath in singing. Its sound, though less penetrating, is as discordant as that of a Jew's harp, which it somewhat resembles. One of the men used it as an accompaniment of a song; but they are unwilling to part with them, as they say that it is very seldom that they can find a piece of wood which will bear the fine splitting necessary for the tongue.

They are a most courteous people among each other. The salutations are frequent — on entering a house, on leaving it, on meeting on the road, on receiving anything from the hand of another, and on receiving a kind or complimentary speech. They do not make any acknowledgments of this kind to the women, however. The common salutation consists in extending the hands and waving them inwards, once or oftener, and stroking the beard; the formal one in raising the hands with an inward curve to the level of the head two or three times, lowering them, and rubbing them together; the ceremony concluding with stroking the beard several times. The latter and more formal mode of salutation is offered to the chief, and by the young to the old men. The women have no "manners!"

They have no "medicine men," and though they are aware of the existence of healing herbs, they do not know their special virtues or the manner of using them. Dried and pounded bear's liver is their specific, and they place much reliance on it in colic and other pains. They are a healthy race. In this village of 300 souls, there are no chronically ailing people; nothing but one case of bronchitis, and some cutaneous maladies among children. Neither is there any case of deformity in this and five other large villages which I have visited, except that of a girl, who has one leg slightly shorter than the other.

They ferment a kind of intoxicating liquor from the root of a tree, and also from their own millet and Jap anese rice, but Japanese *saké* is the one thing that they care about. They spend all their gains upon it, and drink it in enormous quantities. It represents to them all the good of which they know, or can conceive. Beastly intoxication is the highest happiness to which these poor savages aspire, and the condition is sanctified to them under the fiction of "drinking to the gods." Men and women alike indulge in this vice. A few, however, like Pipichari, abstain from it totally, taking the bowl in their hands, making the libations to the gods, and then passing it on. I asked Pipichari why he did not take *saké*, and he replied with a truthful terseness, "Because it makes men like dogs."

Except the chief, who has two horses, they have no domestic animals except very large, yellow dogs, which are used in hunting, but are never admitted within the houses.

The habits of the people, though by no means destitute of decency and propriety, are not cleanly. The women bathe their hands once a day, but any other washing is unknown. They never wash their clothes, and wear the same by day and night. I am afraid to speculate on the condition of their wealth of coal-black hair. They may be said to be very dirty, as dirty fully as masses of our people at home. Their houses swarm with fleas, but they are not worse in this respect than the Japanese *yadoyas*. The mountain villages have, however, the appearance of extreme cleanliness, being devoid of litter, heaps, puddles, and untidiness of all kinds, and there are no unpleasant odours inside or outside the houses, as they are well ventilated and smoked, and the salt fish and meat are kept in the godowns. The hair and beards of the old men, instead of being snowy as they ought to be, are yellow from smoke and dirt.

They have no mode of computing time, and do not know their own ages. To them the past is dead, yet like other conquered and despised races they cling to the idea that in some far-off age they were a great nation. They have no traditions of internecine strife, and the art of war seems to have been lost long ago. I asked Benri about this matter, and he says that formerly Ainos fought with spears and knives as well as with bows and arrows, but that Yoshitsuné, their hero god, forbade war for ever, and since then the two-edged spear, with a shaft nine feet long, has only been used in hunting bears.

The Japanese Government of course exercises the same authority over the Ainos as over its other subjects, but probably it does not care to interfere in domestic or tribal matters, and within this outside limit despotic authority is vested in the chiefs. The Ainos live in village communities, and each community has its own chief, who is its lord paramount. It appears to me that this chieftainship is but an expansion of the paternal relation, and that all the village families are ruled as a unit. Benri, in whose house I am, is the chief of Biratori, and is treated by all with very great deference of manner. The office is nominally for life; but if a chief becomes blind, or too infirm to go about, he appoints a successor. If he has a "smart" son, who he thinks will command the respect of the people, he appoints him; but if not he chooses the most suitable man in the village. The people are called upon to approve the choice, but their ratification is never refused. The office is not hereditary anywhere.

Benri appears to exercise the authority of a very strict father. His manner to all the men is like that of a master to slaves, and they bow when they speak to him. No one can marry without his approval. If any one builds a house he chooses the site. He has absolute jurisdiction in civil and criminal cases, unless (which is very rare) the latter should be of sufficient magnitude to be reported to the Imperial officials. He compels restitution of stolen property, and in all cases fixes the fines which are to be paid by delinquents. He also fixes the hunting arrangements and the festivals. The younger men were obviously much afraid of incurring his anger in his absence.

An eldest son does not appear to be, as among the Japanese, a privileged person. He does not necessarily inherit the house and curios. The latter are not divided, but go with the house to the son whom the father regards as being the "smartest." Formal adoption is practised. Pipichari is an adopted son, and is likely to succeed to Benri's property to the exclusion of his own children. I cannot get at the word which is translated "smartness," but I understand it as meaning general capacity. The chief, as I have mentioned before, is allowed three wives among the mountain Ainos, otherwise authority seems to be his only privilege.

The Ainos have a singular dread of snakes. Even their bravest fly from them. One man says that it is because they know of no cure for their bite, but there is something more than this, for they flee from snakes which they know to be harmless.

They have an equal dread of their dead. Death seems to them very specially "the shadow fear'd of man." When it comes, which it usually does from bronchitis in old age, the corpse is dressed in its best clothing, and laid upon a shelf for from one to three days. In the case of a woman her ornaments are buried with her, and in that of a man his knife and

saké-stick, and, if he were a smoker, his smoking apparatus. The corpse is sewn up with these things in a
mat, and, being slung on poles, is carried to a solitary
grave, where it is laid in a recumbent position. Nothing will induce an Aino to go near a grave. Even if a
valuable bird or animal falls near one, he will not go to
pick it up. A vague dread is for ever associated with
the departed, and no dream of Paradise ever lights for
the Aino the "Stygian shades."

Benri is, for an Aino, intelligent. Two years ago
Mr. Dening of Hakodaté came up here and told him
that there was but one God who made us all, to which
the shrewd old man replied, "If the God who made
you made us, how is it that you are so different, you so
rich, we so poor?" On asking him about the magnificent pieces of lacquer and inlaying which adorn his
curio shelf, he said that they were his father's, grandfather's, and great-grandfather's at least, and he thinks
they were gifts from the daimiyô of Matsumae soon
after the conquest of Yezo. He is a grand-looking
man, in spite of the havoc wrought by his intemperate
habits. There is plenty of room in the house, and this
morning, when I asked him to show me the use of the
spear, he looked a truly magnificent savage, stepping
well back with the spear in rest, and then springing
forward for the attack, his arms and legs turning into
iron, the big muscles standing out in knots, his frame
quivering with excitement, the thick hair falling back
in masses from his brow, and the fire of the chase in his
eye. I trembled for my boy, who was the object of the
imaginary onslaught, the passion of sport was so admirably acted.

As I write, seven of the older men are sitting by the
fire. Their grey beards fall to their waists in rippled
masses, and the slight baldness of age not only gives

them a singularly venerable appearance, but enhances the beauty of their lofty brows. I took a rough sketch of one of the handsomest, and showing it to him, asked if he would have it, but instead of being amused or pleased he showed symptoms of fear, and asked me to burn it, saying it would bring him bad luck, and he should die. However, Ito pacified him, and he accepted it, after a Chinese character, which is understood to mean good luck, had been written upon it, but all the others begged me not to "make pictures" of them, except Pipichari, who lies at my feet like a staghound.

The profusion of black hair, and a curious intensity about their eyes, coupled with the hairy limbs and singularly vigorous *physique*, give them a formidably savage appearance, but the smile, full of "sweetness and light," in which both eyes and mouth bear part, and the low, musical voice, softer and sweeter than anything I have previously heard, make me at times forget that they are savages at all. The venerable look of these old men harmonises with the singular dignity and courtesy of their manners, but as I look at the grand heads, and reflect that the Ainos have never shown any capacity, and are merely adult children, they seem to suggest water on the brain rather than intellect. I am more and more convinced that the expression of their faces is European. It is truthful, straightforward, manly, but both it and the tone of voice are strongly tinged with pathos.

Before these elders Benri asked me, in a severe tone, if I had been annoyed in any way during his absence. He feared, he said, that the young men and the women would crowd about me rudely. I made a complimentary speech in return, and all the ancient hands were waved, and the venerable beards were stroked in acknowledgment.

These Ainos, doubtless, stand high among uncivilised peoples. They are, however, as completely irreclaimable as the wildest of nomad tribes, and contact with civilisation, where it exists, only debases them. Several young Ainos were sent to Tôkiyô, and educated and trained in various ways, but as soon as they returned to Yezo they relapsed into savagery, retaining nothing but a knowledge of Japanese. They are charming in many ways, but make one sad, too, by their stupidity, apathy, and hopelessness, and all the sadder that their numbers appear to be again increasing, and as their *physique* is very fine, there does not appear to be a prospect of the race dying out at present.

They are certainly superior to many aborigines, as they have an approach to domestic life. They have one word for *house*, and another for *home*, and one word for husband approaches very nearly to house-band. Truth is of value in their eyes, and this in itself raises them above some peoples. Infanticide is unknown, and aged parents receive filial reverence, kindness, and support, while in their social and domestic relations there is much that is praiseworthy.

I must conclude this letter abruptly, as the horses are waiting, and I must cross the rivers, if possible, before the bursting of an impending storm.

I. L. B.

A TIPSY SCENE.

A Parting Gift — A Delicacy — Generosity — A Seaside Village —
Pipichari's Advice — A Drunken Revel — Ito's Prophecies — The
Kôchô's Illness — Patent Medicines.

SARUFUTO, YEZO, *August 27.*

I LEFT the Ainos yesterday with real regret, though
I must confess that sleeping in one's clothes, and the
lack of ablutions, are very fatiguing. Benri's two
wives spent the early morning in the laborious operation of grinding millet into coarse flour, and before I
departed, as their custom is, they made a paste of it,
rolled it with their unclean fingers into well-shaped
cakes, boiled them in the unwashed pot in which they
make their stew of "abominable things," and presented
them to me on a lacquer tray. They were distressed
that I did not eat their food, and a woman went to a
village at some distance and brought me some venison
fat as a delicacy. All those of whom I had seen much
came to wish me good-bye, and they brought so many
presents (including a fine bearskin) that I should have
needed an additional horse to carry them had I accepted but one half.

I rode twelve miles through the forest to Mombets,
where I intended to spend Sunday, but I had the worst
horse I ever rode, and we took five hours. The day was
dull and sad, threatening a storm, and when we got out
of the forest, upon a sand-hill covered with oak scrub,
we encountered a most furious wind. Among the many

views which I have seen, that is one to be remembered. Below lay a bleached and bare sand-hill, with a few grey houses huddled in its miserable shelter, and a heaped-up shore of grey sand, on which a brown-grey sea was breaking with clash and boom in long, white, ragged lines, with all beyond a confusion of surf, surge, and mist, with driving brown clouds mingling sea and sky, and all between showing only in glimpses amidst scuds of sand.

At a house in the scrub a number of men were drinking *saké* with much uproar, and a superb-looking Aino came out, staggered a few yards, and then fell backwards among the weeds, a picture of debasement. I forgot to tell you that before I left Biratori, I inveighed to the assembled Ainos against the practice and consequences of *saké*-drinking, and was met with the reply, "We must drink to the gods, or we shall die," but Pipichari said, "You say that which is good; let us give *saké* to the gods, but not drink it," for which bold speech he was severely rebuked by Benri.

Mombets is a stormily-situated and most wretched cluster of twenty-seven decayed houses, some of them Aino, and some Japanese. The fish-oil and seaweed fishing trades are in brisk operation there now for a short time, and a number of Aino and Japanese strangers are employed. The boats could not get out because of the surf, and there was a drunken debauch. The whole place smelt of *saké*. Tipsy men were staggering about and falling flat on their backs, to lie there like dogs till they were sober, — Aino women were vainly endeavouring to drag their drunken lords home, and men of both races were reduced to a beastly equality. I went to the *yadoya* where I intended to spend Sunday, but besides being very dirty and forlorn, it was the very centre of the *saké* traffic, and in its open space there were men in all stages of riotous and stupid intoxication. It was a sad scene, yet one to be matched in a hundred places in Scotland every Saturday afternoon. I am told by the *Kôchô* here that an Aino can drink four or five times as much as a Japanese without being tipsy, so for each tipsy Aino there had been an outlay of 6s. or 7s., for *saké* is 8d. a cup here!

I had some tea and eggs in the *daidokoro*, and altered my plans altogether, on finding that if I proceeded farther round the east coast as I intended, I should run the risk of several days' detention on the banks of numerous "bad rivers," if rain came on, by which I should run the risk of breaking my promise to deliver Ito to Mr. Maries by a given day. I do not surrender this project, however, without an equivalent, for I intend to add 100 miles to my journey, by taking an almost disused track round Volcano Bay, and visiting the coast Ainos of a very primitive region. Ito is very much opposed to this, thinking that he has made a sufficient sacrifice of personal comfort at Biratori, and plies me with stories, such as that there are "many bad rivers to cross," that the track is so worn as to be impassable, that there are no *yadoyas*, and that at the Government offices we shall neither get rice nor eggs! An old man who has turned back unable to get horses is made responsible for these stories. The machinations are very amusing. Ito was much smitten with the daughter of the house-master at Mororan, and left some things in her keeping, and the desire to see her again is at the bottom of his opposition to the other route.

Monday.— The horse could not or would not carry me farther than Mombets, so, sending the baggage on, I walked through the oak wood, and enjoyed its silent solitude, in spite of the sad reflections upon the enslavement of the Ainos to *saké*. I spent yesterday quietly in my old quarters, with a fearful storm of wind and rain outside. Pipichari appeared at noon, nominally to bring news of the sick woman, who is recovering, and to have his nearly healed foot bandaged again, but really to bring me a knife sheath which he has carved for me. He lay on the mat in the corner of my room most of the afternoon, and I got a great many more words from him. The house-master, who is the *Kôchô* of Sarufuto, paid me a courteous visit, and in the evening sent to say that he would be very glad of some medicine, for he was "very ill and going to have fever." He had caught a bad cold and sore throat, had bad pains in his limbs, and was bemoaning himself ruefully. To pacify his wife, who was very sorry for him, I gave him some "Cockle's Pills," and the trapper's remedy of "a pint of hot water with a pinch of cayenne pepper," and left him moaning, and bundled up under a pile of *futons*, in a nearly hermetically sealed room, with a *hibachi* of charcoal vitiating the air. This morning, when I went and inquired after him in a properly concerned tone, his wife told me very gleefully that he was quite well and had gone out, and had left 25 *sen* for some more of the medicines that I had given him, so with great gravity I put up some of Duncan and Flockhart's most pungent cayenne pepper, and showed her how much to use. She was not content, however, without some of the "Cockles," a single box of which has performed six of those "miraculous cures" which rejoice the hearts and fill the pockets of patent medicine makers' I. L. B.

VISIT TO A VOLCANO.

A Welcome Gift — Recent Changes — Volcanic Phenomena — Interesting Tufa Cones — An Aggressive Trailer — Semi-strangulation — A Fall into a Bear-trap — The Shiraôi Ainos — Horsebreaking and Cruelty.

OLD MORORAN, VOLCANO BAY, YEZO, *September 2.*

After the storm of Sunday, Monday was a grey, still, tender day, and the ranges of wooded hills were bathed in the richest indigo colouring. A canter of seventeen miles among the damask roses on a very rough horse only took me to Yubets, whose indescribable loneliness fascinated me into spending a night there again, and encountering a wild clatter of wind and rain; and another canter of seven miles the next morning took me to Tomakomai, where I rejoined my *kuruma,* and after a long delay, three trotting Ainos took me to Shiraôi, where the "clear shining after rain," and the mountains against a lemon-coloured sky, were extremely beautiful; but the Pacific was as unrestful as a guilty thing, and its crash and clamour and the severe cold fatigued me so much that I did not pursue my journey the next day, and had the pleasure of a flying visit from Mr. Von Siebold and Count Diesbach, who bestowed a chicken upon me.

I like Shiraôi very much, and if I were stronger would certainly make it a basis for exploring a part of the interior, in which there is much to reward the explorer. Obviously the changes in this part of Yezo have been comparatively recent, and the energy of the force which has produced them is not yet extinct. The land has gained from the sea along the whole of this part of the coast to the extent of two or three miles, the old beach with its bays and headlands being a marked feature of the landscape. This new formation appears to be a vast bed of pumice, covered by a thin layer of vegetable mould, which cannot be more than fifty years old. This pumice fell during the eruption of the volcano of Tarumai, which is very near Shiraôi, and is also brought down in large quantities from the interior hills and valleys by the numerous rivers, besides being washed up by the sea. At the last eruption pumice fell over this region of Yezo to a medium depth of 3 feet 6 inches. In nearly all the rivers good sections of the formation may be seen in their deeply-cleft banks, broad, light-coloured bands of pumice, with a few inches of rich, black, vegetable soil above, and several feet of black sea-sand below. During a freshet which occurred the first night I was at Shiraôi, a single stream covered a piece of land with pumice to the depth of nine inches, being the wash from the hills of the interior, in a course of less than fifteen miles.

Looking inland, the volcano of Tarumai, with a bare grey top and a blasted forest on its sides, occupies the right of the picture. To the left and inland are mountains within mountains, tumbled together in most picturesque confusion, densely covered with forest and cleft by magnificent ravines, here and there opening out into narrow valleys. The whole of the interior is jungle, penetrable for a few miles by shallow and rapid rivers, and by nearly smothered trails made by the Ainos in search of game. The general lie of the country made me very anxious to find out whether a much-broken ridge lying among the mountains is or is not a series of tufa cones of ancient date ; and apply·

ing for a good horse and Aino guide on horseback, I left Ito to amuse himself, and spent much of a most splendid day in investigations and in attempting to get round the back of the volcano and up its inland side. There is a great deal to see and learn there. Oh that I had strength! After hours of most tedious and exhausting work I reached a point where there were several great fissures emitting smoke and steam, with occasional subterranean detonations. These were on the side of a small, flank crack which was smoking heavily. There was light pumice everywhere, but nothing like recent lava or scoriæ. One fissure was completely lined with exquisite, acicular crystals of sulphur, which perished with a touch. Lower down there were two hot springs with a deposit of sulphur round their margins, and bubbles of gas, which, from its strong, garlicky smell, I suppose to be sulphuretted hydrogen. Farther progress in that direction was impossible without a force of pioneers. I put my arm down several deep crevices which were at an altitude of only about 500 feet, and had to withdraw it at once, owing to the great heat, in which some beautiful specimens of tropical ferns were growing. At the same height I came to a hot spring — hot enough to burst one of my thermometers, which was graduated above the boiling point of Fahrenheit; and tying up an egg in a pocket-handkerchief and holding it by a stick in the water, it was hard boiled in 8½ minutes. The water evaporated without leaving a trace of deposit on the handkerchief, and there was no crust round its margin. It boiled and bubbled with great force.

Three hours more of exhausting toil, which almost knocked up the horses, brought us to the apparent ridge, and I was delighted to find that it consisted of a lateral range of tufa cones, which I estimate as being from 200 to 350, or even 400 feet high. They are densely covered with trees of considerable age, and a rich deposit of mould; but their conical form is still admirably defined. An hour of very severe work, and energetic use of the knife on the part of the Aino, took me to the top of one of these through a mass of entangled and gigantic vegetation, and I was amply repaid by finding a deep, well-defined crateriform cavity of great depth, with its sides richly clothed with vegetation, closely resembling some of the old cones in the island of Kauai. This cone is partially girdled by a stream, which in one place has cut through a bank of both red and black volcanic ash. All the usual phenomena of volcanic regions are probably to be met with north of Shiraôi, and I hope they will at some future time be made the object of careful investigation.

In spite of the desperate and almost overwhelming fatigue, I have enjoyed few things more than that "exploring expedition." If the Japanese have no one to talk to they croon hideous discords to themselves, and it was a relief to leave Ito behind and get away with an Aino, who was at once silent, trustworthy, and faithful. Two bright rivers bubbling over beds of red pebbles run down to Shiraôi out of the back country, and my directions, which were translated to the Aino, were to follow up one of these and go into the mountains in the direction of one I pointed out till I said "Shiraôi." It was one of those exquisite mornings which are seen sometimes in the Scotch Highlands before rain, with intense clearness and visibility, a blue atmosphere, a cloudless sky, blue summits, heavy dew, and glorious sunshine, and under these circumstances scenery beautiful in itself became entrancing.

The forest is a true forest, extending northwards for over 100 miles, with unknown eastern and western

limits. The principal trees are two species of oak,
three varieties of maple, beeches of enormous size, ash
and elm, all entangled by a wild vine with enormous
cordate leaves and a redundant vigour which is almost
irritating. A most aggressive trailer it is. It goes up
to the tops of the tallest trees, and, not content with
overrunning them, leaps from one tree top to another,
clothes dead trees with more than their living beauty,
twists, loops, and knots itself as if it did not know
what to do with its strength, crushes feeble trees in its
embrace, hangs loops and nooses down everywhere,
makes arbours, disports itself, runs altogether riot, and
is at once the pride and the peril of the forest. Some of
its stems are as thick as a man's leg, and will bear a
heavier strain, they say, than a frigate's best hawser.
Then there is a trailer of the hydrangea genus, with
clusters of white blossoms, which is not riotous, and
contents itself with climbing to the top of the tallest
trees, and clinging to them with the tenacity of ivy,
besides the wild hop, and the mistletoe growing on
oaks, and many others less striking. The undergrowth
is composed mainly of ugly weeds six feet high, and in
some places solely of the dwarf, dark-leaved bamboo.
In the openings the ground is covered densely with a
plumed, reed-like grass, the *Eulalia Japonica*, which in
that rich soil attains a height of eight feet : and bamboo
and grass would be equally impossible to penetrate
without the use of the bill-hook, were it not for the
remains of the trails made by Aino hunters.

The trailers are so formidable that we had to stoop
over our horses' necks at all times, and with pushing
back branches and guarding my face from slaps and
scratches, my thick dogskin gloves were literally frayed
off, and some of the skin of my hands and face in addition, so that I returned with both bleeding and swelled.

It was on the return ride fortunately that, in stooping to escape one great liana the loop of another grazed my nose, and, being unable to check my unbroken horse instantaneously, the loop caught me by the throat, nearly strangled me, and in less time than it takes to tell it I was drawn over the back of the saddle, and found myself lying on the ground, jammed between a tree and the hind leg of the horse, which was quietly feeding. The Aino, whose face was very badly scratched, missing me, came back, said never a word, helped me up, brought me some water in a leaf, brought my hat, and we rode on again. I was little the worse for the fall, but on borrowing a looking-glass I see not only scratches and abrasions all over my face, but a livid mark round my throat as if I had been hung! The Aino left portions of his bushy locks on many of the branches. You would have been amused to see me in this forest, preceded by this hairy and formidable-looking savage, who was dressed in a coat of skins with the fur outside, seated on the top of a pack-saddle covered with a deer hide, and with his hairy legs crossed over the horse's neck, a fashion in which the Ainos ride any horses over any ground with the utmost serenity.

It was a wonderful region for beauty. I have not seen so beautiful a view in Japan as from the river-bed from which I had the first near view of the grand assemblage of tufa cones, covered with an ancient vegetation, backed by high mountains of volcanic origin, on whose ragged crests the red ash was blazing vermilion against the blue sky, with a foreground of bright waters flashing through a primeval forest. The banks of these streams were deeply excavated by the heavy rains, and sometimes we had to jump three and even four feet out of the forest into the river, and as much up again, fording the Shiraôi river only more than twenty times, and often

naked children, all as dirty as they could be, with unkempt, elf-like locks, were huddled round the fires.
Still, bad as it looked and smelt, the fire was the hearth,
and the hearth was inviolate, and each smoked and dirt-
stained group was a family, and it was an advance upon
the social life of, for instance, Salt Lake City. The
roofs are much flatter than those of the mountain
Ainos, and as there are few store-houses, quantities of
fish, " green " skins, and venison, hang from the rafters,
and the smell of these and the stinging of the smoke
were most trying. Few of the houses had any guest-
seats, but in the very poorest, when I asked shelter
from the rain, they put their best mat upon the ground,
and insisted, much to my distress, on my walking ove
it in muddy boots, saying, " It is Aino custom." Even
in those squalid homes the broad shelf, with its rows
of Japanese curios, always has a place. I mentioned
that it is customary for a chief to appoint a successor
when he becomes infirm, and I came upon a case in
point, through a mistaken direction, which took us to
the house of the former chief, with a great empty bear
cage at its door. On addressing him as the chief, he
said, " I am old and blind, I cannot go out, I am of no
more good," and directed us to the house of his successor. Altogether it is obvious, from many evidences
in this village, that Japanese contiguity is hurtful, and
that the Ainos have reaped abundantly of the disad-
vantages without the advantages of contact with Japanese civilisation.

That night I saw a specimen of Japanese horse-break-
ing as practised in Yezo. A Japanese brought into
the village street a handsome, spirited young horse,
equipped with a Japanese *demi-pique* saddle, and a
most cruel gag bit. The man wore very cruel spurs,
and was armed with a bit of stout board two feet long

by six inches broad. The horse had not been mounted before, and was frightened, but not the least vicious. He was spurred into a gallop, and ridden at full speed up and down the street, turned by main force, thrown on his haunches, goaded with the spurs, and cowed by being mercilessly thrashed over the ears and eyes with the piece of board, till he was blinded with blood. Whenever he tried to stop from exhaustion, he was spurred, jerked, and flogged, till at last, covered with sweat, foam, and blood, and with blood running from his mouth and splashing the road, he reeled, staggered, and fell, the rider dexterously disengaging himself. As soon as he was able to stand, he was allowed to crawl into a shed, where he was kept without food till morning, when a child could do anything with him. He was "broken," effectually spirit-broken, useless for the rest of his life. It was a brutal and brutalising exhibition, as triumphs of brute force always are.

A WET TRIP.

The Universal Language — The Yezo *Corrals* — A "Typhoon Rain" — Difficult Tracks — An Unenviable Ride — Drying Clothes — A Woman's Remorse.

THIS morning I left early in the *kuruma* with two kind and delightful savages. The road being much broken by the rains, I had to get out frequently, and every time I got in again they put my air-pillow behind me, and covered me up in a blanket; and when we got to a rough river, one made a step of his back by which I mounted their horse, and gave me nooses of rope to hold on by, and the other held my arm to keep me steady, and they would not let me walk up or down any of the hills. What a blessing it is that, amidst the confusion of tongues, the language of kindness and courtesy is universally understood, and that a kindly smile on a savage face is as intelligible as on that of one's own countryman! They had never drawn a *kuruma*, and were as pleased as children when I showed them how to balance the shafts. They were not without the capacity to originate ideas, for when they were tired of the frolic of pulling, they attached the *kuruma* by ropes to the horse, which one of them rode at a "scramble," while the other merely ran in the shafts to keep them level. This is an excellent plan.

Horobets is a fishing station of antique and decayed aspect, with eighteen Japanese and forty-seven Aino houses. The latter are much larger than at Shiraôi, and their very steep roofs are beautifully constructed. It was a miserable day, with fog concealing the mountains and lying heavily on the sea, but as no one expected rain, I sent the *kuruma* back to Mororan and secured horses. On principle I always go to the *corral* myself to choose animals, if possible, without sore backs, but the choice is often between one with a mere *raw*, and others which have holes in their backs into which I could put my hand, or altogether uncovered spines. The practice does no immediate good, but by showing the Japanese that foreign opinion condemns these cruelties an amendment may eventually be brought about. At Horobets, among twenty horses, there was not one that I would take, — I should like to have had them all shot. They are cheap and abundant, and are of no account. They drove a number more down from the hills, and I chose the largest and finest horse I have seen in Japan, with some spirit and action, but I soon found that he had tender feet. We shortly left the high-road, and in torrents of rain turned off on " unbeaten tracks," which led us through a very bad swamp and some much swollen and very rough rivers into the mountains, where we followed a worn-out track for eight miles. It was literally "*foul* weather," dark and still, with a brown mist, and rain falling in sheets. I threw my paper waterproof away as useless, my clothes were of course soaked, and it was with much difficulty that I kept my *shomon* and paper money from being reduced to pulp. Typhoons are not known so far north as Yezo, but it was what they call a "typhoon rain " without the typhoon, and in no time it turned the streams into torrents barely fordable, and tore up such of a road as there is, which at its best is a mere water-channel. Torrents, bringing tolerable-sized stones, tore down the track, and when the horses had been struck two or three times by these, it was with difficulty that they could be induced to face the rushing water. Constantly in a pass, the water had gradually cut a track several feet deep between steep banks, and the only possible walking place was a stony gash not wide enough for the two feet of a horse alongside of each other, down which water and stones were rushing from behind, with all manner of trailers matted overhead, and between avoiding being strangled and attempting to keep a tender-footed horse on his legs, the ride was a very severe one. The poor animal fell five times from stepping on stones, and in one of his falls twisted my left wrist badly. I thought of the many people who envied me my tour in Japan, and wondered whether they would envy me that ride !

After this had gone on for four hours, the track, with a sudden dip over a hill-side, came down on Old Mororan, a village of thirty Aino and nine Japanese houses, very unpromising-looking, although exquisitely situated on the rim of a lovely cove. The Aino huts were small and poor, with an unusual number of bear skulls on poles, and the village consisted mainly of two long dilapidated buildings, in which a number of men were mending nets. It looked a decaying place, of low, mean lives. But at a "merchant's" there was one delightful room with two translucent sides — one opening on the village, the other looking to the sea down a short, steep slope, on which is a quaint little garden, with dwarfed fir-trees in pots, a few balsams, and a red cabbage grown with much pride as a "foliage plant."

It is nearly midnight, but my bed and bedding are so wet that I am still sitting up and drying them, patch by patch, with tedious slowness, on a wooden frame placed over a charcoal brazier, which has given my room the dryness and warmth which are needed when a person has been for many hours in soaked clothing, and has nothing really dry to put on. Ito bought a chicken for my supper, but when he was going to kill it an hour later, its owner in much grief returned the money, saying she had brought it up, and could not bear to see it killed. This is a wild, outlandish place, but an intuition tells me that it is beautiful. The ocean at present is thundering up the beach with the sullen force of a heavy ground swell, and the rain is still falling in torrents.

I. L. B.

A SURPRISE.

LEBUNGÉ, VOLCANO BAY, YEZO, *September* 6.

"Weary wave and dying blast
Sob and moan along the shore,
All is peace at last."

AND more than peace. It was a heavenly morning. The deep blue sky was perfectly unclouded, a blue sea with diamond flash and a "many-twinkling smile" rippled gently on the golden sands of the lovely little bay, and opposite, forty miles away, the pink summit of the volcano of Komono-taki, forming the south-western point of Volcano Bay, rose into a softening veil of tender blue haze. There was a balmy breeziness in the air, and tawny tints upon the hill, patches of gold in the woods, and a scarlet spray here and there heralded the glories of the advancing autumn. As the day began, so it closed. I should like to have detained each hour as it passed. It was thorough enjoyment. I visited a good many of the Mororan Ainos, saw their well-grown bear in its cage, and tearing myself away with difficulty at noon, crossed a steep hill and a wood of scrub oak, and then followed a trail which runs on the amber sands close to the sea, crosses several small streams, and passes the lonely Aino village of Maripu, the ocean always on the left and wooded ranges on the right, and in front an apparent bar to farther progress in the volcano of Usu-taki, an imposing mountain, rising abruptly to a height of nearly 3000 feet, I should think.

In Yezo, as on the main island, one can learn very little about any prospective route. Usually when one makes an inquiry, a Japanese puts on a stupid look, giggles, tucks his thumbs into his girdle, hitches up his garments, and either professes perfect ignorance, or gives one some vague second-hand information, though it is quite possible that he may have been over every foot of the ground himself more than once. Whether suspicion of your motives in asking, or a fear of compromising himself by answering, is at the bottom of this, I don't know, but it is most exasperating to a traveller. In Hakodaté I failed to see Captain Blakiston, who has walked round the whole Yezo sea-board, and all I was able to learn regarding this route was that the coast was thinly-peopled by Ainos, that there were Government horses which could be got, and that one could sleep where one got them; that rice and salt fish were the only food; that there were many "bad rivers," and that the road went over "bad mountains;" that the only people who went that way were Government officials twice a year, that one could not get on more than four miles a day, that the roads over the passes were "all big stones," etc. etc. So this Usu-taki took me altogether by surprise, and for a time confounded all my carefully-constructed notions of locality. I had been told that the one volcano in the bay was Komono-taki, near Mori, and this I believed to be eighty miles off, and there, confronting me, within a distance of two miles, was this grand, splintered, vermilion-crested thing, with a far nobler aspect than that of "*the*" volcano, with a curtain range in front, deeply scored, and slashed with ravines and abysses whose purple gloom was unlighted even by the noonday sun. One of the peaks was emitting black smoke from a deep crater, another, steam and white smoke from various rents and fissures in its side, vermilion peaks, smoke, and steam, all rising into a sky of brilliant blue, and the atmosphere was so clear that I saw everything that was going on there quite distinctly, especially when I attained an altitude exceeding that of the curtain range. It was not for two days that I got a correct idea of its geographical situation, but I was not long in finding out that it was not Komonotaki! There is much volcanic activity about it. I saw a glare from it last night thirty miles away. The Ainos said that it was "a god," but did not know its name, nor did the Japanese who were living under its shadow. At some distance from it in the interior rises a great dome-like mountain, Shiribetsan, and the whole view is grand.

After passing through miles of scrub and sand we came quite suddenly upon the agricultural settlement of Mombets, where the Government has placed a colony of 600 Japanese, and the verses apply, "The valleys are so thick with corn that they laugh and sing — the wilderness and the solitary place shall be glad for them, and the desert shall rejoice and blossom as the rose." For two miles, careful manuring and assiduous hand labour have turned a sandy waste into a garden, a sea of crops without a weed, hundreds of acres of maize, wheat, millet, beans, tobacco, hemp, egg plants, peaches, apricots, pumpkins, and all the good things of Northern Japan, beautiful and luxuriant, with a good bridle road, fenced from the crops by a closely-cropped willow hedge, and numbers of small, neat Japanese houses, with gardens bright with portulaccas, red balsams, and small yellow chrysanthemums, all glowing in the sunshine, a perfect oasis, showing the resources which

Yezo possesses for the sustenance of a large population.

I have not seen above three or four Japanese together
since I left Hakodaté, and I was much impressed with
their ugliness, the lack of force in their faces, and the
feeble *physique* of both men and women, as compared
with that of the aborigines. The Yezo Japanese don't
look altogether like the Japanese of the main island.
They are as the colonists of Canada or Australia as
compared with the small farmers of England, rougher,
freer, more careless in their dress and deportment, and
they are certainly affected, as people always are, by the
cheapness and abundance of horses, which they ride
cross-legged, in imitation of the Ainos. Till I reached
Mombets, all the Japanese I have seen have led a life
of irregular and precarious industry, very different from
that of the peasant proprietors of the main island; and
in the dull time they loaf and hang about "grog shops"
not a little, and are by no means improved by the habit
of lording it over an inferior race.

A little beyond Mombets flows the river Osharu,
one of the largest of the Yezo streams. It was much
swollen by the previous day's rain; and as the ferry-
boat was carried away, we had to swim it, and the
swim seemed very long. Of course, we and the baggage got very wet. The coolness with which the Aino
guide took to the water without giving us any notice
that its broad, eddying flood was a swim, and not a
ford, was very amusing.

From the top of a steepish ascent beyond the Osha-
rugawa, there is a view into what looks like a very
lovely lake, with wooded promontories, and little bays,
and rocky capes in miniature, and little heights, on
which Aino houses, with tawny roofs, are clustered;
and then the track dips suddenly, and deposits one, not

by a lake at all, but on Usu Bay, an inlet of the Pacific, much broken up into coves, and with a very narrow entrance, only obvious from a few points. Just as the track touches the bay, there is a road-post, with a prayer-wheel in it, and by the shore an upright stone of very large size, inscribed with Sanskrit characters, near to a stone staircase and a gateway in a massive stone-faced embankment, which looked much out of keeping with the general wildness of the place. On a rocky promontory in a wooded cove, there is a large, rambling house, greatly out of repair, inhabited by a Japanese man and his son, who are placed there to look after Government interests, exiles among 500 Ainos. From among the number of rat-haunted, rambling rooms which had once been handsome, I chose one opening on a yard or garden with some distorted yews in it, but found that the great gateway and the *amado* had no bolts, and that anything might be appropriated by any one with dishonest intentions; but the house-master and his son, who have lived for ten years among the Ainos, and speak their language, say that nothing is ever taken, and that the Ainos are thoroughly honest and harmless. Without this assurance I should have been distrustful of the number of wide-mouthed youths who hung about, in the listlessness and vacuity of savagery, if not of the bearded men who sat or stood about the gateway with children in their arms.

Usu is a dream of beauty and peace. There is not much difference between the height of high and low water on this coast, and the lake-like illusion would have been perfect had it not been that the rocks were tinged with gold for a foot or so above the sea by a delicate species of *fucus*. In the exquisite inlet where I spent the night, trees and trailers drooped into the water and were mirrored in it, their green, heavy shad ows lying sharp against the sunset gold and pink of the rest of the bay; log canoes, with planks laced upon their gunwales to heighten them, were drawn upon a tiny beach of golden sand, and in the shadiest cove, moored to a tree, an antique and much-carved junk was "floating double." Wooded, rocky knolls, with Aino huts, the vermilion peaks of the volcano of Usu-taki redder than ever in the sinking sun, a few Ainos mending their nets, a few more spreading edible seaweed out to dry, a single canoe breaking the golden mirror of the cove by its noiseless motion, a few Aino loungers, with their "mild-eyed, melancholy" faces and quiet ways suiting the quiet evening scene, the unearthly sweetness of a temple bell — this was all, and yet it was the loveliest picture I have seen in Japan.

In spite of Ito's remonstrances and his protestations that an exceptionally good supper would be spoiled, I left my rat-haunted room, with its tarnished gilding and precarious *fusuma*, to get the last of the pink and lemon-coloured glory, going up the staircase in the stone-faced embankment, and up a broad, well-paved avenue, to a large temple, within whose open door I sat for some time absolutely alone, and in a wonderful stillness; for the sweet-toned bell which vainly chimes for vespers amidst this bear-worshipping population had ceased. This temple was the first symptom of Japanese religion that I remember to have seen since leaving Hakodaté, and worshippers have long since ebbed away from its shady and moss-grown courts. Yet it stands there to protest for the teaching of the great Hindu; and generations of Aino heathen pass away one after another; and still its bronze bell tolls, and its altar lamps are lit, and incense burns for ever before Buddha. The characters on the great bell of this temple are said to be the same lines which are often graven on temple bells, and to possess the dignity of twenty-four centuries;

> ' All things are transient;
> They being born must die,
> And being born are dead;
> And being dead are glad
> To be at rest."

The temple is very handsome, the baldachino is superb, and the bronzes and brasses on the altar are specially fine. A broad ray of sunlight streamed in, crossed the matted floor, and fell full upon the figure of Sakya-muni in his golden shrine; and just at that moment a shaven priest, in silk-brocaded vestments of faded green, silently passed down the stream of light, and lit the candles on the altar, and fresh incense filled the temple with a drowsy fragrance. It was a most impressive picture. His curiosity evidently shortened his devotions, and he came and asked me where I had been and where I was going, to which, of course, I replied in excellent Japanese, and then stuck fast.

Along the paved avenue, besides the usual stone trough for holy water, there are on one side the thousand-armed Kwan-non, a very fine relief, and on the other a Buddha, throned on the eternal lotus blossom, with an iron staff, much resembling a crozier, in his hand, and that eternal apathy on his face which is the highest hope of those who hope at all. I went through a wood, where there are some mournful groups of graves on the hill-side, and from the temple came the sweet sound of the great bronze bell and the beat of the big drum, and then, more faintly, the sound of the little bell and drum, with which the priest accompanies his ceaseless repetition of a phrase in the dead tongue of a distant land. There is an infinite pathos about the lonely temple in its splendour, the absence of even possible worshippers, and the large population of Ainos, sunk in yet deeper superstitions than those which go to make up popular Buddhism. I sat on a rock by the bay till the last pink glow faded from Usu-taki and the last lemon stain from the still water; and a beautiful crescent, which hung over the wooded hill, had set, and the heavens blazed with stars:

> "Ten thousand stars were in the sky,
> Ten thousand in the sea,
> And every wave with dimpled face,
> That leapt upon the air,
> Had caught a star in its embrace,
> And held it trembling there."

The loneliness of Usu Bay is something wonderful — a house full of empty rooms falling to decay, with only two men in it — one Japanese house among 500 savages, yet it was the only one in which I have slept in which they bolted neither the *amado* nor the gate. During the night the *amado* fell out of the worn-out grooves with a crash, knocking down the *shôji*, which fell on me, and rousing Ito, who rushed into my room half-asleep, with a vague vision of blood-thirsty Ainos in his mind. I then learned what I have been very stupid not to have learned before, that in these sliding wooden shutters there is a small door through which one person can creep at a time called the *jishindo*, or "earthquake door," because it provides an exit during the alarm of an earthquake, in case of the *amado* sticking in their grooves, or their bolts going wrong. I believe that such a door exists in all Japanese houses.

The next morning was as beautiful as the previous evening, rose and gold instead of gold and pink. Before the sun was well up I visited a number of the Aino lodges, saw the bear, and the chief, who, like all the rest, is a monogamist, and, after breakfast, at my request, some of the old men came to give me such information as they had. These venerable elders sat cross-legged in the verandah, the house-master's son, who kindly acted as interpreter, squatting, Japanese fashion, at the side, and about thirty Ainos, mostly women, with infants, sitting behind. I spent about two hours in going over the same ground as at Biratori, and also went over the words,[1] and got some more, including some synonyms. The *click* of the *ts* before the *ch* at the beginning of a word is strongly marked among these Ainos. Some of their customs differ slightly from those of their brethren of the interior, specially as to the period of seclusion after a death, the non-allowance of polygamy to the chief, and the manner of killing the bear at the annual festival. Their ideas of metempsychosis are more definite, but this, I think, is to be accounted for by the influence and proximity of Buddhism. They spoke of the bear as their chief god, and next the sun and fire. They said that they no longer worship the wolf, and that though they call the volcano and many other things *kamoi*, or god, they do not worship them. I ascertained beyond doubt that worship with them means simply making libations of *saké*, and "drinking to the god," and that it is unaccompanied by petitions, or any vocal or mental act.

These Ainos are as dark as the people of southern Spain, and very hairy. Their expression is earnest and pathetic, and when they smiled, as they did when I could not pronounce their words, their faces had a touching sweetness which was quite beautiful, and European, not Asiatic. Their own impression is that they are now increasing in numbers after diminishing for many years. I left Usu sleeping in the loveliness of an autumn noon with great regret. No place that I have seen has fascinated me so much.

[1] See Appendix A.

SOLITUDE.

The Sea-shore — A "Hairy Aino" — A Horse Fight — The Horses of
Yezo — "Bad Mountains" — A Slight Accident — Magnificent
Scenery — A Bleached Halting-Place — A Musty Room — Aino
"Good-breeding."

A CHARGE of 3 *sen* per *ri* more for the horses for the
next stage, because there were such "bad mountains to
cross," prepared me for what followed — many miles of
the worst road for horses I ever saw. I should not
have complained if they had charged double the price.
As an almost certain consequence, it was one of the
most picturesque routes I have ever travelled. For
some distance, however, it runs placidly along by the
sea-shore, on which big, blue, foam-crested rollers were
disporting themselves noisily, and passes through several Aino hamlets, and the Aino village of Abuta, with
sixty houses, rather a prosperous-looking place, where
the cultivation was considerably more careful, and the
people possessed a number of horses. Several of the
houses were surrounded by bears' skulls grinning from
between the forked tops of high poles, and there was a
well-grown bear ready for his doom and apotheosis. In
nearly all the houses a woman was weaving bark-cloth,
with the hook which holds the web fixed into the
ground several feet outside the house. At a deep river
called the Nopkobets, which emerges from the mountains close to the sea, we were ferried by an Aino completely covered with hair, which on his shoulders was

wavy like that of a retriever, and rendered clothing quite needless either for covering or warmth. A wavy, black beard rippled nearly to his waist over his furry chest, and, with his black locks hanging in masses over his shoulders, he would have looked a thorough savage had it not been for the exceeding sweetness of his smile and eyes. The Volcano Bay Ainos are far more hairy than the mountain Ainos, but even among them it is quite common to see men not more so than vigorous Europeans, and I think that the hairiness of the race as a distinctive feature has been much exaggerated, partly by the smooth-skinned Japanese.

The ferry scow was nearly upset by our four horses beginning to fight. At first one bit the shoulders of another; then the one attacked uttered short, sharp squeals, and returned the attack by striking with his fore feet, and then there was a general *mêlée* of striking and biting, till some ugly wounds were inflicted. I have watched fights of this kind on a large scale every day in the *corral.* The miseries of the Yezo horses are the great drawback of Yezo travelling. They are brutally used, and are covered with awful wounds from being driven at a fast "scramble" with the rude, un-girthed pack-saddle and its heavy load rolling about on their backs, and they are beaten unmercifully over their eyes and ears with heavy sticks. Ito has been barbarous to these gentle, little-prized animals ever since we came to Yezo; he has vexed me more by this than by anything else, especially as he never dared even to carry a switch on the main island, either from fear of the horses or their owners. To-day he was beating the baggage-horse unmercifully, when I rode back and interfered with some very strong language, saying, " You are a bully, and, like all bullies, a coward." Imagine my aggravation when, at our first halt, he brought out his note-book as usual, and quietly asked me the meaning of the words "bully" and "coward." It was perfectly impossible to explain them, so I said a bully was the worst name I could call him, and that a coward was the meanest thing a man could be. Then the provoking boy said, "Is bully a worse name than devil?" "Yes, far worse," I said, on which he seemed rather crestfallen, and he has not beaten his horse since, in my sight at least.

The breaking-in process is simply breaking the spirit by an hour or two of such atrocious cruelty as I saw at Shiraôi, at the end of which the horse, covered with foam and blood, and bleeding from mouth and nose, falls down exhausted. Being so ill used, they have all kinds of tricks, such as lying down in fords, throwing themselves down head foremost and rolling over pack and rider, bucking, and resisting attempts to make them go otherwise than in single file. Instead of bits they have bars of wood on each side of the mouth, secured by a rope round the nose and chin. When horses which have been broken with bits gallop they put up their heads till the nose is level with the ears, and it is useless to try either to guide or check them. They are always wanting to join the great herds on the hill-side or sea-shore, from which they are only driven down as they are needed. In every Yezo village the first sound that one hears at break of day is the gallop of forty or fifty horses, pursued by an Aino, who has hunted them from the hills. A horse is worth from twenty-eight shillings upwards. They are very sure-footed when their feet are not sore, and cross a stream or chasm on a single rickety plank, or walk on a narrow ledge above a river or gulch without fear. They are barefooted, their hoofs are very hard, and I am glad to be rid of the perpetual tying and untying and replacing of the straw shoes of the well-cared-for horses of the main island. A man rides with them, and for a man and three horses the charge is only sixpence for each 2½ miles. I am now making Ito ride in front of me, to make sure that he does not beat or otherwise misuse his beast.

After crossing the Nopkobets, from which the fighting horses have led me to make so long a digression, we went right up into the "bad mountains," and crossed the three tremendous passes of Lebungétogé. Except by saying that this disused bridle-track is impassable, people have scarcely exaggerated its difficulties. One horse broke down on the first pass, and we were long delayed by sending the Aino back for another. Possibly these extraordinary passes do not exceed 1500 feet in height, but the track ascends them through a dense forest with most extraordinary abruptness, to descend as abruptly, to rise again sometimes by a series of nearly washed-away zigzags, at others by a straight, ladder-like ascent deeply channelled, the bottom of the trough being filled with rough stones, large and small, or with ledges of rock with an entangled mass of branches and trailers overhead, which render it necessary to stoop over the horse's head while he is either fumbling, stumbling, or tumbling among the stones in a gash a foot wide, or else is awkwardly leaping up broken rock steps nearly the height of his chest, the whole performance consisting of a series of scrambling jerks at the rate of a mile an hour.

In one of the worst places the Aino's horse, which was just in front of mine, in trying to scramble up a nearly breast-high and much-worn ledge, fell backwards, nearly overturning my horse, the stretcher poles, which formed part of his pack, striking me so hard above my ankle that for some minutes afterwards I thought the bone was broken. The ankle was severely cut and bruised, and bled a good deal, and I was knocked out of the saddle. Ito's horse fell three times, and eventually the four were roped together. Such are some of the *divertissements* of Yezo travel.

Ah, but it was glorious! The views are most magnificent. This is really Paradise. Everything is here, — huge headlands magnificently timbered, small, deep, bays into which the great green waves roll majestically, great, grey cliffs, too perpendicular for even the most adventurous trailer to find root-hold, bold bluffs and outlying stacks cedar-crested, glimpses of bright, blue ocean dimpling in the sunshine or tossing up wreaths of foam among ferns and trailers, and inland ranges of mountains forest-covered, with tremendous gorges between, forest filled, where wolf, bear, and deer make their nearly inaccessible lairs, and outlying battlements, and ridges of grey rock with hardly six feet of level on their sinuous tops, and cedars in masses giving deep shadow, and sprays of scarlet maple or festoons of a crimson vine lighting the gloom. The inland view suggested infinity. There seemed no limit to the forest-covered mountains and the unlighted ravines. The wealth of vegetation was equal in luxuriance and entanglement to that of the tropics, primeval vegetation, on which the lumberer's axe has never rung. Trees of immense height and girth, specially the beautiful *Salisburia adiantifolia* with its small fan-shaped leaves, all matted together by riotous lianas, rise out of an impenetrable undergrowth of the dwarf, dark-leaved bamboo, which, dwarf as it is, attains a height of seven feet, and all is dark, solemn, soundless, the haunt of wild beasts, and of butterflies and dragonflies of the most brilliant colours. There was light without heat, leaves and streams sparkled, and there was nothing of the half-smothered sensation which is often produced by the choking greenery of the main island, for frequently, far below, the Pacific flashed in all its sunlit beauty, and occasionally we came down unexpectedly on a little cove with abrupt cedar-crested headlands and stacks, and a heavy surf rolling in with the deep thunder music which alone breaks the stillness of this silent land.

There was one tremendous declivity where I got off to walk, but found it too steep to descend on foot with comfort. You can imagine how steep it was, when I tell you that the deep groove being too narrow for me to get to the side of my horse, I dropped down upon him from behind, between his tail and the saddle, and so scrambled on!

The sun had set and the dew was falling heavily when the track dipped over the brow of a headland, becoming a waterway so steep and rough that I could not get down it on foot without the assistance of my hands, and terminating on a lonely little bay of great beauty, walled in by impracticable-looking headlands, and being itself the entrance to an equally impracticable-looking, densely-wooded valley running up among densely-wooded mountains. There was a margin of grey sand above the sea, and on this the skeleton of an enormous whale was bleaching. Two or three large "dug-outs," with planks laced with stout fibre on their gunwales, and some bleached drift-wood, lay on the beach, the foreground of a solitary, rambling, dilapidated grey house, bleached like all else, where three Japanese men with an old Aino servant live to look after "Government interests," whatever these may be, and keep rooms and horses for Government officials — a great boon to travellers who, like me, are belated here.

Only one person has passed Lebungé this year, except two officials and a policeman.

There was still a red glow on the water, and one horn of a young moon appeared above the wooded headland; but the loneliness and isolation are over-powering, and it is enough to produce madness to be shut in for ever with the thunder of the everlasting surf, which compels one to raise one's voice in order to be heard.   In the wood, half a mile from the sea, there is an Aino village of thirty houses, and the appearance of a few of the savages gliding noiselessly over the beach in the twilight added to the ghastliness and loneliness of the scene.   The horses were unloaded by the time I arrived, and several courteous Ainos showed me to my room, opening on a small courtyard with a heavy gate.   The room was musty, and, being rarely used, swarmed with spiders.   A saucer of fish-oil and a wick rendered darkness visible, and showed faintly the dark, pathetic faces of a row of Ainos in the verandah, who retired noiselessly with their grace-ful salutation when I bade them good-night.   Food was hardly to be expected, yet they gave me rice, pota-toes, and black beans boiled in equal parts of brine and syrup, which are very palatable.   The cuts and bruises of yesterday became so very painful with the cold of the early morning that I have been obliged to remain **here**.   **I. L. B.**

THE MISSING LINK.

HAKODATÉ, *September* 12.

LEBUNGÉ is a most fascinating place in its awful isolation. The house-master was a friendly man, and much attached to the Ainos. If other officials entrusted with Aino concerns treat the Ainos as fraternally as those of Usu and Lebungé, there is not much to lament. This man also gave them a high character for honesty and harmlessness, and asked if they might come and see me before I left; so twenty men, mostly carrying very pretty children, came into the yard with the horses. They had never seen a foreigner, but either from apathy or politeness, they neither stare nor press upon one as the Japanese do, and always make a courteous recognition. The bear-skin housing of my saddle pleased them very much, and my boots of unblacked leather, which they compare to the deer-hide moccasins which they wear for winter hunting. Their voices were the lowest and most musical that I have heard, incongruous sounds to proceed from such hairy, powerful-looking men. Their love for their children was most marked. They caressed them tenderly, and held them aloft for notice, and when the house-master told them how much I admired the brown, dark-eyed, winsome creatures, their faces lighted with pleasure, and they saluted me over and over again. These, like other Ainos, utter a short, screeching sound when they are not pleased, and then one recognises the savage.

These Lebungé Ainos differ considerably from those of the eastern villages, and I have again to notice the decided sound or *click* of the *ts* at the beginning of many words. Their skins are as swarthy as those of Bedaween, their foreheads comparatively low, their eyes far more deeply set, their stature lower, their hair yet more abundant, the look of wistful melancholy more marked, and two who were unclothed for hard work in fashioning a canoe, were almost entirely covered with short, black hair, specially thick on the shoulders and back, and so completely concealing the skin as to reconcile one to the lack of clothing. I noticed an enormous breadth of chest, and a great development of the muscles of the arms and legs. All these Ainos shave their hair off for two inches above their brows, only allowing it there to attain the length of an inch. Among the well-clothed Ainos in the yard there was one smooth-faced, smooth-skinned, concave-chested, spindle-limbed, yellow Japanese, with no other clothing than the decorated bark-cloth apron which the Ainos wear in addition to their coats and leggings. Escorted by these gentle, friendly savages, I visited their lodges, which are very small and poor, and in every way inferior to those of the mountain Ainos. The women are short and thick-set, and most uncomely.

From their village I started for the longest, and by reputation, the worst stage of my journey, seventeen miles, the first ten of which are over mountains. So solitary and disused is this track, that on a four days' journey we have not met a human being. In the Le-

bungé valley, which is densely forested, and abounds
with fordable streams and treacherous ground, I came
upon a grand specimen of the *Salisburia adiantifolia*,
which, at a height of three feet from the ground,
divides into eight lofty stems, none of them less than 2
feet 5 inches in diameter. This tree, which grows
rapidly, is so well adapted to our climate, that I wonder it has not been introduced on a large scale, as it
may be seen by every body in Kew Gardens. There
is another tree with orbicular leaves in pairs, which
grows to an immense size.

From this valley a worn-out, stony bridle-track ascends
the western side of Lebungétogé, climbing through a
dense forest of trees and trailers to a height of about
2000 feet, where, contented with its efforts, it reposes,
and, with only slight ups and downs, continues along
the top of a narrow ridge within the seaward mountains, between high walls of dense bamboo, which, for
much of that day's journey, is the undergrowth alike
of mountain and valley, ragged peak, and rugged ravine. The scenery was as magnificent as on the previous day. A guide was absolutely needed, as the track
ceased altogether in one place, and for some time the
horses had to blunder their way along a bright, rushing
river, swirling rapidly downwards, heavily bordered
with bamboo, full of deep holes, and made difficult by
trees which have fallen across it. There Ito, whose
horse could not keep up with the others, was lost, or
rather lost himself, which led to a delay of two hours.
I have never seen grander forest than on that two day's
ride.

At last the track, barely passable after its recovery,
dips over a precipitous bluff, and descends close to the
sea, which has evidently receded considerably. Thence
it runs for six miles on a level, sandy strip, covered

near the sea with a dwarf bamboo about five inches high, and farther inland with red roses and blue campanula.

At the foot of the bluff there is a ruinous Japanese house, where an Aino family has been placed to give shelter and rest to any who may be crossing the pass. I opened my *bentô bako* of red lacquer, and found that it contained some cold, waxy potatoes, on which I dined, with the addition of some tea, and then waited wearily for Ito, for whom the guide went in search. The house and its inmates were a study. The ceiling was gone, and all kinds of things, for which I could not imagine any possible use, hung from the blackened rafters. Everything was broken and decayed, and the dirt was appalling. A very ugly Aino woman, hardly human in her ugliness, was splitting bark fibre. There were several *irori*, Japanese fashion, and at one of them a grand-looking old man was seated apathetically contemplating the boiling of a pot. Old, and sitting among ruins, he represented the fate of a race which, living, has no history, and perishing, leaves no monument. By the other *irori* sat, or rather crouched, the "MISSING LINK." I was startled when I first saw it. It was, shall I say? a man, and the *mate*, I cannot write the husband, of the ugly woman. It was about fifty. The lofty Aino brow had been made still loftier by shaving the head for three inches above it. The hair hung, not in shocks, but in snaky wisps, mingling with a beard which was grey and matted. The eyes were dark but vacant, and the face had no other expression than that look of apathetic melancholy which one sometimes sees on the faces of captive beasts. The arms and legs were unnaturally long and thin, and the creature sat with the knees tucked into the armpits. The limbs and body, with the exception of a patch on each side, were thinly covered with fine black hair, more than an inch long, which was slightly curly on the shoulders. It showed no other sign of intelligence than that evidenced by boiling water for my tea. When Ito arrived he looked at it with disgust, exclaiming, "The Ainos are just dogs; they had a dog for their father," in allusion to their own legend of their origin.

The level was pleasant after the mountains, and a canter took us pleasantly to Oshamambé, where we struck the old road from Mori to Satsuporo, and where I halted for a day to rest my spine, from which I was suffering much. Oshamambé looks dismal even in the sunshine, decayed and dissipated, with many people lounging about in it doing nothing, with the dazed look which over-indulgence in *saké* gives to the eyes. The sun was scorching hot, and I was glad to find refuge from it in a crowded and dilapidated *yadoya*, where there were no black beans, and the use of eggs did not appear to be recognised. My room was only enclosed by *shôji*, and there were scarcely five minutes of the day in which eyes were not applied to the finger-holes with which they were liberally riddled; and during the night one of them fell down, revealing six Japanese sleeping in a row, each head on a wooden pillow.

The grandeur of the route ceased with the mountain passes, but in the brilliant sunshine the ride from Oshamambé to Mori, which took me two days, was as pretty and pleasant as it could be. At first we got on very slowly, as besides my four horses there were four led ones going home, which got up fights and entangled their ropes, and occasionally lay down and rolled; and besides these there were three foals following their mothers, and if they stayed behind, the mares hung back neighing, and if they frolicked ahead, the mares

wanted to look after them, and the whole string showed
a combined inclination to dispense with their riders
and join the many herds of horses which we passed. It
was so tedious that, after enduring it for some time, I
got Ito's horse and mine into a scow at a river of some
size, and left the disorderly drove to follow at leisure.

At Yurapu, where there is an Aino village of thirty
houses, we saw the last of the aborigines, and the interest of the journey ended. Strips of hard sand below
high-water mark, strips of red roses, ranges of wooded
mountains, rivers deep and shallow, a few villages of
old grey houses amidst grey sand and bleaching drift-
wood, and then came the river Yurapu, a broad, deep
stream, navigable in a canoe for fourteen miles. The
scenery there was truly beautiful in the late and
splendid afternoon. The long blue waves rolled on
shore, each one crested with light as it curled before it
broke, and hurled its snowy drift for miles along the
coast with a deep booming music. The glorious inland
view was composed of six ranges of forest-covered
mountains, broken, chasmed, caverned, and dark with
timber, and above them bald, grey peaks rose against a
green sky of singular purity. I longed to take a boat
up the Yurapu, which penetrates by many a gorge into
their solemn recesses, but had not strength to carry out
my wish.

After this I exchanged the silence or low musical
speech of Aino guides for the harsh and ceaseless
clatter of Japanese. At Yamakushinoi, a small hamlet
on the seashore, where I slept, there was a sweet, quiet
yadoya, delightfully situated, with a wooded cliff at the
back, over which a crescent hung out of a pure sky;
and besides, there were the more solid pleasures of fish,
eggs, and black beans. Thus, instead of being starved
and finding wretched accommodation, the week I spent

on Volcano Bay has been the best fed, as it was certainly the most comfortable, week of my travels in Northern Japan.

Another glorious day favoured my ride to Mori, but I was unfortunate in my horse at each stage, and the Japanese guide was grumpy and ill-natured, a most unusual thing. Otoshibé and a few other small villages of grey houses, with "an ancient and fish-like smell," lie along the coast, busy enough doubtless in the season, but now looking deserted and decayed, and houses are rather plentifully sprinkled along many parts of the shore, with a wonderful profusion of vegetables and flowers about them, raised from seeds liberally supplied by the *Kaitakushi* Department from its Nanai experimental farm and nurseries. For a considerable part of the way to Mori there is no track at all, though there is a good deal of travel. One makes one's way fatiguingly along soft sea sand or coarse shingle close to the sea, or absolutely in it, under cliffs of hardened clay or yellow conglomerate, fording many small streams, several of which have cut their way deeply through a stratum of black volcanic sand. I have crossed about 100 rivers and streams on the Yezo coast, and all the larger ones are marked by a most noticeable peculiarity, *i.e.* that on nearing the sea, they turn south, and run for some distance parallel with it, before they succeed in finding an exit through the bank of sand and shingle which forms the beach and blocks their progress.

I have not said anything about the crows, which are a feature of Yezo, and one which the colonists would willingly dispense with. There are millions of them, and in many places they break the silence of the silent land with a Babel of noisy discords. They are everywhere, and have attained a degree of most unpardonable impertinence, mingled with a cunning and sagacity which almost put them on a level with man in some circumstances. Five of them were so impudent as to alight on two of my horses, and so be ferried across the Yurapugawa. In the inn-garden at Mori I saw a dog eating a piece of carrion in the presence of several of these covetous birds. They evidently said a great deal to each other on the subject, and now and then one or two of them tried to pull the meat away from him, which he resented. At last a big, strong crow succeeded in tearing off a piece, with which he returned to the pine where the others were congregated, and after much earnest speech they all surrounded the dog, and the leading bird dexterously dropped the small piece of meat within reach of his mouth, when he immediately snapped at it, letting go the big piece unwisely for a second, on which two of the crows flew away with it to the pine, and with much fluttering and hilarity they all ate or rather gorged it, the deceived dog looking vacant and bewildered for a moment, after which he sat under the tree and barked at them inanely. A gentleman told me that he saw a dog holding a piece of meat in like manner in the presence of three crows, which also vainly tried to tear it from him, and after a consultation they separated, two going as near as they dared to the meat, while the third gave the tail a bite sharp enough to make the dog turn round with a squeak, on which the other villains seized the meat, and the three fed triumphantly upon it on the top of a wall. In many places they are so aggressive as to destroy the crops unless they are protected by netting. They assemble on the sore backs of horses and pick them into holes, and are mischievous in many ways. They are very late in going to roost and are early astir in the morning, and are so bold that they often came " with many a stately flirt and flutter" into the verandah where I was sitting. I never watched an assemblage of them for any length of time without being convinced that there was a Nestor among them to lead their movements. Along the sea-shore they are very amusing, for they "take the air" in the evening seated on sand-banks facing the wind, with their mouths open. They are threatening to devour the settlers, and a crusade is just now being waged against them, but they are Legion.

On the way I saw two Ainos land through the surf in a canoe, in which they had paddled for nearly 100 miles. A river canoe is dug out of a single log, and two men can fashion one in five days, but on examining this one, which was twenty-five feet long, I found that it consisted of two halves, laced together with very strong bark fibre for their whole length, and with high sides also laced on. They consider that they are stronger for rough sea and surf work when made in two parts. Their bark-fibre rope is beautifully made, and they twist it of all sizes, from twine up to a nine-inch hawser.

Beautiful as the blue ocean was, I had too much of it, for the horses were either walking in a lather of sea foam or were crowded between the cliff and the sea, every larger wave breaking over my foot and irreverently splashing my face, and the surges were so loud tongued and incessant, throwing themselves on the beach with a tremendous boom, and drawing the shingle back with them with an equally tremendous rattle, so impolite and noisy, bent only on showing their strength, reckless, rude, self-willed, and inconsiderate! This purposeless display of force, and this incessant waste of power, and the noisy self-assertion in both, approached vulgarity!

Towards evening we crossed the last of the bridgeless rivers, and put up at Mori, which I left three weeks before, and I was very thankful to have accomplished my object without disappointment, disaster, or any considerable discomfort. Had I not promised to return Ito to his master by a given day, I should like to spend the next six weeks in the Yezo wilds, for the climate is good, the scenery beautiful, and the objects of interest are many.

The peaks of the volcano of Komono-taki were blazing in the setting sun, and with a glass I was able then, and from a point above the lakes, to trace its configuration pretty easily. It may still prove mischievous, and in its last recent eruption it covered the ground in its neighbourhood with pumice to a depth of three feet. The lava ejected by it and the other volcanoes of this coast appears to differ considerably from that of the flows from the flank and summit craters of Mauna Loa on Hawaii, as it is light and porous, consisting almost entirely of pumice, which on Hawaii appears rarely, and then only as the *froth* on streams, which solidify into dense basalt, either jagged or smooth. The highest peak is estimated at a height of 3300 feet, but the great crater, which is about three-quarters of a mile in diameter, lies 500 feet lower, and contains six smaller craters, one of which was active in 1872. One of these is about 100 feet deep. Steam escapes from many apertures in their sides. The slopes of the volcano have a scathed and dreary look, from the remains of a forest charred in the last great eruption, and the immediate neighbourhood cannot be profitably tilled till a greater depth of soil has accumulated over the last layer of pumice. In the meantime nature is doing her best to provide it by covering the ground with young woods.

Another splendid day favoured my ride from Mori to

Togénoshita, where I remained for the night, and I had
exceptionally good horses for both days, though the one
which Ito rode, while going at a rapid "scramble,"
threw himself down three times and rolled over to rid
himself from flies. I had not admired the wood between
Mori and Ginsainoma (the lakes) on the sullen, grey
day on which I saw it before, but this time there was
an abundance of light and shadow and solar glitter, and
many a scarlet spray and crimson trailer, and many a
maple flaming in the valleys, gladdened me with the
music of colour. From the top of the pass beyond the
lakes there is a grand view of the volcano in all its
nakedness, with its lava beds and fields of pumice, with
the lakes of Onuma, Konuma, and Ginsainoma, lying in
the forests at its feet, and from the top of another hill
there is a remarkable view of windy Hakodaté, with its
headland looking like Gibraltar. The slopes of this
hill are covered with the *Aconitum Japonicum*, of which
the Ainos make their arrow poison.

The *yadoya* at Togénoshita was a very pleasant and
friendly one, and when Ito woke me yesterday morning,
saying, "Are you sorry that it's the last morning? I
am," I felt we had one subject in common, for I was
very sorry to end my pleasant Yezo tour, and very sorry
to part with the boy who had made himself more useful and invaluable even than before. It was most
wearisome to have Hakodaté in sight for twelve miles,
so near across the bay, so far across the long, flat, stony
strip which connects the headland upon which it is
built with the mainland. For about three miles the
road is rudely macadamised, and as soon as the barefooted horses get upon it they seem lame of all their
legs; they hang back, stumbling, dragging, edging to
the side, and trying to run down every opening, so that
when we got into the interminable main street I sent

Ito on to the Consulate for my letters, and dismounted, hoping that as it was raining I should not see any foreigners; but I was not so lucky, for first I met Mr Dening, and then, seeing the Consul and Dr. Hepburn coming down the road, evidently dressed for dining in the flag-ship, and looking spruce and clean, I dodged up an alley to avoid them; but they saw me, and did not wonder that I wished to escape notice, for my old *betto's* hat, my torn green paper waterproof, and my riding skirt and boots, were not only splashed but *caked* with mud, and I had the general look of a person "fresh from the wilds." **I. L. B.**

ITINERARY OF TOUR IN YEZO.

Hakodaté to

	No. of houses. Jap. Aino.		*Ri.*	*Chô.*
Ginsainoma . .	4		7	18
Mori	105		4	
Mororan . . .	57		11	
Horobets . .	18	47	5	1
Shiraoi . . .	11	51	6	32
Tomakomai . .	38		5	21
Yubets . . .	7	3	3	5
Sarufuto . . .	63		7	5
Biratori . . .		53	5	
Mombets . .	27		5	1

From Horobets to

	Jap. Aino.		*Ri.*	*Chô.*
Old Mororan .	9	30	4	28
Usu	3	99	6	2
Lebungé . . .	1	27	5	22
Oshamambé .	56	38	6	34
Yamakushinai .	40		4	18
Otoshibé . . .	40		2	3
Mori	105		3	29
Togénoshita . .	55		6	7
Hakodaté .	37,000 souls		3	29

About 358 English miles.

JAPANESE PROGRESS.

A Dubious Climate — Missionary Ardour — A Political Move — An Opinion on the Government — "Squeezes" — Lack of Persever- ance — A Japanese Ironclad —Realities of Progress.

HAKODATÉ, Yezo.

THE weather has been abominable since I returned, with the mercury hanging about 80°, the mosquitoes rampant, the air so damp that mildew has to be removed from leather every few hours, and a hot, depressing wind with a hot, drizzling rain. If I complain of the lifelessness of the climate of Japan, and its lack of morn- ing and evening freshness, people always say, "Wait till October," and I am beginning to think that October and November are the only pleasant months, for the cold of winter is spoken of as "raw and penetrating."

The steamy atmosphere does not affect Mr. Dening's missionary zeal, which is perfectly indefatigable. Be- sides the two Sunday preachings and two weekly preachings at Ono and Arikawa, and two weekly preach- ings and three Bible classes in Hakodaté in addition, he is going to open a new station at Nanai, where there are many *samurai*, and it is from among these, and not from among the common people — in whom the religious instinct and the spirit of religious inquiry seem quite dead, — that converts have been made. The foundation- stone of an English Episcopal Church has been laid since I returned, by Mr. Eusden, H.B.M.'s Consul, in the presence of the eight Japanese converts, whose names were placed in a cavity in the stone, and a few others, with a considerable crowd of native onlookers. It shows the toleration granted to Christianity that this small body of Christians should have been able to purchase a site on the main street on which to erect a conspicuous religious edifice.

Some important public events have occurred lately. A portion of the Imperial Guard has mutinied in Tôkiyô (not from political motives, however), much blood has been shed, and the Prime Minister has issued a proclamation warning people "not to be excited." Almost coincidently with this event Japan has taken the first step in the direction of constitutional Government by the issuing of a proclamation by the Mikado empowering the election of Provincial Assemblies in March of next year, which are to have control of the local taxation. The qualification for electors is fixed so very low that suffrage will be almost universal, and voting is to be by ballot! Although it is a small and somewhat hampered concession to the principle of popular government, it is an important step for an Asiatic despotism to take under present circumstances. It is placing a degree of power in the hands of millions of ignorant peasants, who, until lately, were practically serfs, and it seems to me not only a sign of the fidelity of the Government to its promises, but of its confidence in the general approval of the existing order of things. I think none the worse of the Government for delaying this step, and for taking it now with extreme caution.

There is a great deal of indiscriminate and unwise laudation of everything Japanese, and much harm has been done by it; but, on the other hand, the carping and sneering with which every fresh Japanese movement is received in other quarters is very unbecoming, and very lacerating to the feelings of a people unduly sensitive to foreign criticism. I scarcely venture to give an opinion, but it is impossible to avoid forming one gradually, and I am more and more inclined to think that Iwakura, Sanéyoshi, Terashima, and others who have guided affairs since the Restoration, are both able and patriotic; that they have shown, and are showing, most extraordinary capacity in the conduct of affairs, hampered as they are by the not always harmonious demands of foreign Governments; that though they are ambitious they are also honest men, and that their actions and policy prove them to be actuated by an intense desire to promote the national well-being and greatness, and not their individual aggrandisement.

Of course among so many changes, many of them of a fundamental nature, we must expect some bungling to occur, and it has occurred, and some expensive experiments have turned out abortive. Some of the innovations, too, are little better than patchwork, and some strike one as totally incongruous. Supposing the heads of the Government to be honest men, we must not overlook the fact that they have to work through a large army of officials, and that Asiatic officialdom, though it has never touched such depths of corruption in Japan as in China and some other countries, is essentially untrustworthy where money is concerned, and that the idea of being content with a salary is a new one to the official mind. Here, in Yezo, enormous sums have been undoubtedly squandered, and only a limited part of the liberal appropriations for the *Kaitakushi* Department has reached the objects for which it was intended, in consequence of the repeated "squeezes," and the same thing may be stated in greater or less degree concerning most grants for public works.

But taking Yezo as an example of what has been done by the present Government, we find complete security for life and property — the chief *desideratum* of any government, aborigines enjoying nearly equal rights with their conquerors, rapid detection of crime, prisons and hospitals on the most enlightened systems, liberal provision made for education and medical aid in remote districts, complete religious toleration, taxation on equitable principles, an agricultural college, and model farms, a Custom-House and Post-Office admirably managed, trade unhampered by vexatious restrictions, and improvements in active operation in many parts of the island.

On the other hand, some of the weak points of Japanese administration are epitomised here. Public money is eaten up by an army of underpaid officials, who are to be seen idling and " kicking their heels" in all the public offices, four or five of them doing the work which would be accomplished by a single Englishman. This arises partly from the number of over-educated young men, trained in Japan or elsewhere at Government expense, for whom Government employment must be found, and partly from the fact that when a Japanese receives anything but a most subordinate position, he creates as many " situations" as possible for his friends. Though crime is readily detected, the administration of justice is very unsatisfactory, specially in civil cases. Much money has been literally sunk in expensive experiments, and vast resources, such as the coal-fields, remain undeveloped, from a jealousy of the introduction of foreign capital. A necessity for Yezo is good roads, yet the main road from Hakodaté to Satsuporo, on which thousands of *yen* are constantly spent, is in such a condition from the use of bad materials, and from broken bridges and choked, ill-constructed drains, that a wheeled conveyance can scarcely pass over its whole length. Schemes are started on a grand scale, and, after much public money has been spent upon them, they are either abandoned, after some progress has been made, without any apparent reason, or because it is found that some insuperable obstacle to their success has been overlooked, or the attention of the officials lapses and grows languid, and deterioration sets in.

I observed many instances of this last failing at the experimental farm at Nanai. The managers imported at a cost of 1000 *yen* a fine Arabian horse, a really beautiful creature, of which they were very proud so long as he was a novelty, but he is now suffering from most discreditable neglect. His fetlock is badly cut from careless hobbling, and from lack of grooming his beautiful skin is covered with hundreds of ticks. Several other things are suffering similarly from lack of persevering supervision, and that on an establishment overloaded with officials. Piers which would be of great value are carried out as at Mori, 350 feet into the sea, where they are perfectly useless, and are then allowed to decay, and small enterprises, which would cost little, but would confer immense benefit on the island, are ignored in favour of costly projects which make a show, but are comparatively useless.

One of the expensive projects of the Empire is before me now in the form of a very fine ironclad, with a crew in European uniform, and drilled in European fashion, and a band playing European music on European instruments. The Hakodaté Japanese are wild with pride about this costly production, and disparage the British war-vessel *Audacious*, and the Russian corvette,[1]

[1] The captain of this corvette, after criticising the Japanese naval drill as compared with the British, of which it is an imitation, remarked abruptly to me, "Your Prime Minister is a great man. Berlin has shown him a great diplomatist. He has given England more than the *prestige* of twenty victories."

ered," not sewn together, but laced vertically, leaving a decorative lacing six inches wide between each two widths. Instead of reefing in a strong wind, a width is unlaced, so as to reduce the canvas vertically, not horizontally. Two blue spheres commonly adorn the sail. The mast is placed well abaft, and to tack or veer it is only necessary to reverse the sheet. When on a wind the long bow and nose serve as a head-sail The high, square, piled-up stern, with its antique carving, and the sides with their lattice-work, are wonderful, together with the extraordinary size and projection of the rudder, and the length of the tiller. The anchors are of grapnel shape, and the larger junks have from six to eight arranged on the fore-end, giving one an idea of bad holding-ground along the coast. They really are much like the shape of a Chinese "small-footed" woman's shoe, and look very unmanageable. They are of unpainted wood, and have a wintry, ghastly look about them.[1]

I have parted with Ito finally to-day, with great regret. He has served me faithfully, and on most common topics I can get much more information through him than from any foreigner. I miss him already, though he insisted on packing for me as usual, and put all my things in order. His cleverness is something surprising. He goes to a good, manly master, who will help him to be good, and set him a virtuous example, and that is a satisfaction. Before he left he wrote a letter for me to the Governor of Mororan, thanking him on my behalf for the use of the *kuruma* and other courtesies.

A Japanese letter always begins with a compliment,

---

[1] The duty paid by junks is 4s. for each twenty-five tons, by sailing ships of foreign shape and rig £2 for each 100 tons, and by steamers £5 for each 100 tons.

usually to the health of the person addressed, and in the case of an inferior at least concludes with an expression of humiliation, followed by the names of the sender and the person addressed, the latter with a honorific title. I was made to regret that I had not been able "to worship the Governor's most exalted visage," and to thank him "with veneration for the use of his august *kuruma*, and for the other exalted kindnesses which it had pleased him to show." The letter concluded with, "My august mistress lifts this up for your august information. I knock my head against the floor. Tremblingly said."

I cannot get a complete literal translation of this remarkable document, but Mr. Chamberlain kindly gave me some samples of Japanese letters which will interest you from the extreme orientalism of their expressions, though possibly they do not go very far beyond "your obedient humble servant."

Invitation to an Official Dinner.

"As [I] am desirous of making an august feast on the approaching 15th day at the summer palace at Shiba, [I] am desirous of [your] august approach to that place on that day at three o'clock in the afternoon. [I] lift this up for [your] august information. Tremblingly said.

"10th year of Meiji, 12th moon, 13th day."
[Name of sender and person addressed with an honorific title.]

Letter from a High Official to thank for the Present of a Book.

"The exalted letter has been worshipfully perused, and [I] joyfully congratulate [you] on [your] ever-increasing august robustness,[1] notwithstanding the perpetual chilly winds. My communication regards the volume entitled *Corean Primer* in [your] august possession, which was mentioned the other evening when [I] worshipped your eyebrow [*i.e.* met you], and which [you] have augustly condescended to send [to me]. The above being a valuable and wonderful book, shall be garnered for ever in [my] library, and taken out and perused.

"Respectful veneration.

"10th moon, 13th day."

[Names.]

Letter from a Servant to his Master, who was Travelling in the Interior.

"That through the fierce heat the exalted master should have augustly arrived unhurt in the mountains is a subject for joyful congratulation and great felicity, which is felt with veneration. Meanwhile, in the exalted house there is no change, and all within the august gate are augustly without hurt, therefore pray condescend to feel augustly at ease. [Your] august despatch reached [my] hands last night, and [I] therefore have this morning without delay augustly forwarded up [to you] eight newspapers and five letters, and pray [you] may condescend to receive them. Pray condescend to take august care [of your health] during the great heat.

"7th moon, 22d day."

[Names.]

The style of letters is completely different to that of conversation, and to that used in books, and almost

---

[1] This is a usual form, and is used quite irrespectively of any knowledge the writer may have of the state of the health of the person he addresses.

forms a language apart. It is almost entirely Chinese, and the grandest and most unusual expressions are sought after to give it elegance, and to bring out markedly the abasement of the sender and the illustriousness of the person addressed. The honorifics and all this paraphernalia of a peculiar style are used even by parents in addressing their children. The Japanese are great letter-writers, and a good epistolary style and good handwriting are greatly esteemed.

Ito writes to his mother at great length once a week, to a number of young friends, and even to acquaintances such as Kanaya, only made since we left Tôkiyô Everywhere I have observed that the young men and women spend much of their leisure time in writing, and one important branch of industry is the designing of decorated paper and envelopes, of which the variety is infinite. Dexterity in the use of the camel's hair brush, which serves for a pen, is regarded as an essential result of education.   I. L. B.

A CYCLONE.

Pleasant Prospects — A Miserable Disappointment — Caught in a
Typhoon — A Dense Fog — Alarmist Rumours — A Welcome at
Tôkiyô — The Last of the Mutineers.

H.B.M.'s Legation, Yedo, *Sept.* 21.

A PLACID sea, which after much disturbance had
sighed itself to rest, and a high, steady barometer promised a fifty hours' passage to Yokohama, and when Dr.
and Mrs. Hepburn and I left Hakodaté, by moonlight,
on the night of the 14th, as the only passengers in the
Hiogo Maru, Captain Moore, her genial, pleasant master, congratulated us on the rapid and delightful passage before us, and we separated at midnight with many
projects for pleasant intercourse and occupation.

But a more miserable voyage I never made, and it
was not until the afternoon of the 17th that we crawled
forth from our cabins to speak to each other. On the
second day out, great heat came on with suffocating
closeness, the mercury rose to 85°, and in lat. 38° 0' N.
and long. 141° 30' E. we encountered a "typhoon,"
otherwise a "cyclone," otherwise a "revolving hurri-
cane," which lasted for twenty-five hours, and "jetti-
soned " the cargo. Captain Moore has given me a very
interesting diagram of it, showing the attempts which
he made to avoid its vortex through which our course
would have taken us, and to keep as much outside it as
possible. The typhoon was succeeded by a dense fog,
so that our fifty-hour passage became seventy-two hours,

and we landed at Yokohama near upon midnight of the 17th, to find traces of much disaster, the whole low-lying country flooded, the railway between Yokohama and the capital impassable, great anxiety about the rice crop, the air full of alarmist rumours, and paper money, which was about par when I arrived in May, at a discount of 13 per cent! In the early part of this year (1880) it has touched 42 per cent.

Late in the afternoon the railroad was re-opened, and I came here with Mr. Wilkinson, glad to settle down to a period of rest and ease under this hospitable roof. The afternoon was bright and sunny, and Tôkiyô was looking its best. The long lines of *yashikis* looked handsome, the castle moat was so full of the gigantic leaves of the lotus, that the water was hardly visible, the grass embankments of the upper moat were a brilliant green, the pines on their summits stood out boldly against the clear sky, the hill on which the Legation stands looked dry and cheerful, and, better than all, I had a most kindly welcome from those who have made this house my home in a strange land.

Tôkiyô is tranquil, that is, it is disturbed only by fears for the rice-crop, and by the fall in *satsu*. The military mutineers have been tried, popular rumour says tortured, and fifty-two have been shot. The summer has been the worst for some years, and now dark heat, moist heat, and nearly ceaseless rain prevail. People have been "rained up" in their summer quarters. "Surely it will change soon," people say, and they have said the same thing for three months.   I. L. B.

NOTES ON TOKIYO.[1]

A Metamorphosis — "Magnificent Distances" — Climate — The Castle — The Official Quarter — The "Feudal Mansions of Yedo" — Commercial Activity — The Canals — Streets and Shop Signs — Street Names.

WITH Yedo,[2] the mysterious city of the Shôgun, I have nothing to do, and gladly leave it to the researches of the learned members of the Asiatic Society of Japan. Yedo is in fact no more. The moats, walls, and embankments, the long lines of decaying *yashikis*, and the shrines of Shiba and Uyeno, with the glories of their gilded and coloured twilight, alone recall its splendid past. The palace within the castle no longer exists, the last Shôgun lives in retirement at Shidzuoka; the *daimiyô* are scattered through the suburbs; not a "two-sworded" man is to be seen; Mutsuhito, the "Spiritual Emperor," the son of the gods, dressed in European clothes, drives through streets of unconcerned spectators in a European carriage; twelve years have metamorphosed ancient Yedo into modern Tôkiyô, and if the old city, with its buildings and customs, be not altogether forgotten, it is due to the careful and loving labours of foreign scholars.

[1] These Notes merely refer to a few of the features of Tôkiyô, at the present time. A third volume would scarcely exhaust its interests and peculiarities.

[2] The British Legation, with pathetic Conservatism, still uses this name officially, and all scholars who cling to the past of the Empire, and ignore the "vulgarity" of Western innovation, do the same.

The first thing a stranger tries to do, is to get a gen-eral idea of the town, but the ascent of Atagayama and other elevated places proves a failure ; there is no one point from which it can be seen, and the only way of grasping it satisfactorily would be from a balloon! From every altitude, however, dark patches of forest, the low elevation crowned by the walls of the Castle topped by dark groves of pine and cryptomeria, broken hills and hollows with groups of temples, hills with streets straggling over their crests, shady places where the dead lie, parks, temple grounds, and garden-bor-dered streets, sweeping, tiled roofs of temples, small oblong buildings glaring with white cement, long lines of low, grey roofs, green slopes, gleams of moats and canals, and Europeanised buildings, conspicuous by their windows and their ugliness, are sure to be seen, and the eye soon learns to distinguish as landmarks the groves of Shiba, Uyeno, and the Castle. On fine days Fujisan looms grandly in the distance, and the white sails of junks, on the blue waters of the Gulf of Yedo, give life to a somewhat motionless scene.

No view of Tôkiyô, leaving out the impression pro-duced by size, is striking, indeed there is a monotony of meanness about it. The hills are not heights, and there are no salient objects to detain the eye for an in-stant. As a city it lacks concentration. Masses of greenery, lined or patched with grey, and an absence of beginning or end, look suburban rather than metropoli-tan. Far away in the distance are other grey patches ; you are told that those are still Tôkiyô, and you ask no more. It is a city of "magnificent distances" without magnificence. You can drive in a crooked line fifteen miles from north to south, and eleven miles from east to west at least, and are still in Tôkiyô. The blue waters of the gulf are its only recognisable boundary. It is an aggregate of 125 villages, which grew together round the great fortress of the Mikado's chief vassal, and which, while retaining their parks, country houses, gardens, lakes, streams, and fields, their rustic lanes and sylvan beauty, have agreed to call themselves Tôkiyô, and in certain quarters, such as the neighbourhood of the Nippon-Bashi, Asakusa, and the Shimmei-mai, have packed themselves pretty closely together. The bright Sumida, which once enclosed a part of the city, has now a transpontine Tôkiyô, the populous district of Hondjo on its other side, and on the east and west miniature hills and valleys with rice-fields, pines, camellias, and bamboo, come up into the suburbs. There is no smoke, and no hum or clatter ascends.

I do not intend to describe Tôkiyô. This has been done often, and in some cases well, in so far as it is possible to do it at all. The Notes which follow were taken for my own information, and, in connection with the more pictorial accounts given by other travellers, may help my readers to some additional knowledge of the city which has been raised to the dignity of the capital of Japan.

Tôkiyô is situated in lat. 35° 39′ N. and in long. 139° 45′ E., at the head of the Gulf of Yedo, where the Sumida, the Kanda, and several small streams fall into the sea. Thus it is slightly south of Gibraltar, but its isotherm is that of Bologna and Marseilles. Its annual rainfall is about 60 inches. That of 1878, however, was 69.460 inches, of which 18 inches fell in September. The average number of rain-days is 98. The months of least rain are December, January, and February, and those of the greatest are usually June and July. The snow-fall is very light, and snow rarely lies long on the ground. Days on which the mercury never rises above the freezing-point are very rare, and only occur with a

persistent north-west wind; but it often falls below 32°
at night, for weeks together, and the average number
of such nights is 75 per season. It is quite a mistake
to suppose that Japan has no winter. The cold is penetrating and merciless, owing to the humidity of the
climate. People suffer more at Tôkiyô with the mer
cury at 36°, than in Colorado, when it is below zero.
As the cold increases, so does the amplitude of the Tô-
kiyans, for they put on one wadded garment above
another, and withdrawing their hands into the wide and
sticking out sleeves, looked like trussed poultry. Bare
heads are not seen in winter, and at the top of this
mass of padding, two eyes peer from among folds of
cotton.

Heat sets in in June, and often continues without a
break until the middle or end of September. In August the mercury occasionally rises to 96°; foreigners
fly from the capital, and the enforced clothing of the
natives is minimised. In January and February the
mercury falls as low as 25°. "Typhoons," or revolving
hurricanes, occur in July, August, and September, and
earthquakes so frequently, that it requires a pretty
smart shock to disturb the equanimity of the residents;
but there has not been a really severe one since 1854,
when a considerable portion of the city was destroyed.
Tôkiyô has a long summer-time, beginning really early
in May, and extending into October, and its winter is
bright and sunny until February, when the weather
breaks, with snow, rain, and gales. The soil is alluvial,
with a large proportion of clay; but the streets dry
immediately after rain, and there are neither holes nor
ruts for the retention of stagnant water. Such, in
brief, are its general climatic conditions.

Its population, like that of most eastern cities, has
been much exaggerated, and the withdrawal of the re-

tainers of the *daimiyô* has reduced it to the manageable
size of New York and Paris. It has 236,961 houses,
inhabited by 1,036,771 persons, of whom 536,621 are
males and 500,150 are females, a disparity more easily
accounted for in Tôkiyô than elsewhere.

The Castle, with its surroundings, the first object
which impresses a stranger on arriving from Yokohama
by railroad, formerly known as the "Official Quarter,"
and still retaining a strong flavour of officialism, is the
nucleus round which the city has crystallised; and
though the Castle Palace within the inner enclosure
has disappeared, the Castle itself is much as it was
when completed by Iyémitsu, two centuries and a half
ago.

Its broad moats of deep, green waters, covered thickly with magnificent lotus blossoms in the late summer,
and with wild-fowl in the early winter, are very imposing, from their depth and width, the height of their
ramparts, and the greenness of the lawn-like turf with
which they are covered, and the size of the trees by
which they are crowned. These ramparts, in some
places, are 100 feet high, and there are eleven miles of
moats. Equally imposing are the stupendous walls,
formed of polygonal blocks of stone, laid without mortar, rising almost perpendicularly from the water, with
kiosk-shaped towers on their angles, and a three-storeyed tower overhanging the Hasu-ike gate. The gates,
twenty-seven in number, are composed of massive timbers on handsome stone foundations, and, in the lower
castle, are approached by bridges and causeways.
Their height varies from ten to eighteen feet, and the
inner ones have two-storeyed buildings above them,
with high, ornamental roofs, and long, upturned eaves.
On the lower ground, fronting the sea, the nearly perpendicular, stone-faced embankments are 60 feet high

The Palace was burned down in 1873; and within the inner moat there is little but the beautiful Fukiagé Gardens mentioned on page 36, the Treasury godowns, a three-storeyed tower, and a drill-ground for troops. Altogether, the Castle is by far the most impressive feature of Tôkiyô, from its vastness, and from the size of the stones used in the walls, some of which are 16 feet in length. It is, moreover, very puzzling, and though I spent some weeks within its moats, I always found a little difficulty in retracing my way to Kôjimachi.

The old " Official Quarter " is remarkable for the long, dreary lines of the external buildings of a number of the *yashikis*, which were formerly the residences of *daimiyô*, and are now either falling into decay or are utilised as public offices, whilst not a few have altogether disappeared, and the spaces on which they stood are enclosed with palisades, and are used for exercising troops, dressed in European fashion, and drilled by French officers. Modern officialism has taken possession of this quarter, which contains, among much else, the buildings occupied by the Supreme Council, the Imperial Treasury, which includes the Finance Department, and several bureaus; the Departments of the Interior, Justice, Education, Religion, War, and Marine; the headquarters of the French Military Mission; the Engineering, Military, and Foreign Language Colleges; the Military Hospital, the Exhibition Building, the Government Printing-Office, the Barracks of the Imperial Guard, and of a few infantry and artillery regiments, the Municipal Offices, the Shôkonsha, a new Shintô shrine, erected to the memory of those who fell in the civil war, and the racecourse and beacon. It is significant of the change which has turned Yedo into Tôkiyô, that the flags of four " barbarian " nations —

England, Russia, Italy, and Germany — are displayed
from four conspicuous buildings which have been
erected in this formerly sacred region. Many of the
Government Departments are accommodated in the
yashikis of the former Princes of the Empire, and
the French Military Mission has its quarters in the Ii
Kamon *yashiki*, situated on a hill close to the British
Legation, its great, dull red portal being the most conspicuous object in the neighbourhood.

Next to the Castle, the most characteristic features
of the city are these "Feudal Mansions of Yedo,"
the *yashikis* of the former *daimiyô*, which lie within
the Castle moat in great numbers, and are scattered
over the northern and southern quarters of the town.
Whether they are occupied as Departments or not, the
street fronts of the outer buildings always present
the same dreary, silent, monotonous, rat-haunted look,
grimness without grandeur.

All are on the same pattern, with insignificant variations regulated by etiquette. All are surrounded by
uncovered ditches with stone-faced sides, crossed at
the gateways by stone platforms, and varying in width
from eighteen inches to trenches which may almost be
called moats. Inside the ditch are foundations, from
one to six feet in height, of blocks of stone of irregular shape, carefully fitted without mortar, on which
stand the *nagoya*, the quarters formerly occupied by
the two-sworded retainers of the princes as the exterior
defences of the mansion. They are long, continuous
lines of building, mile after mile of them, their dismal
frontage only broken by gateways of heavy timbers
clamped with bronze or iron. Heavily-tiled roofs, with
the crest of the *daimiyô* on the terminal tiles, the upper
storeys, where they have them, covered with white
plaster, the lower painted black, or faced with dark

coloured tiles placed diagonally, with their joints covered with white plaster and forming a diamond pattern,
the windows broader than high, massively barred, and
often projecting from the walls, form a style of street
architecture as peculiar as it is unimposing.

The gateways, which at intervals break the dreary
lines. are striking and picturesque, subject, like the
roofs, to variations which, to the initiated, indicate the
former owner's rank. The chief entrances consist of
two large, weighty, folding doors, studded outside with
heavy knobs of metal, the great posts on which they
swing, and the ponderous beam overhead often being
sheathed with the same. They are equipped with por-
ters' lodges and postern gates for use in case of fire or
earthquake. Among the grandest are those of the
yashiki, now occupied by the War Department, and of
that lately occupied by the Education Department;
but there are others of singular stateliness, including
the dull red portal previously mentioned.

The *nagoya* run round a large area, which may be
regarded as having been the camp of the former owner,
the mansion itself, the kernel of the whole, standing in
the middle in a courtyard, sometimes altogether
flagged, and at others pebbled, with flagged pathways,
privacy being secured by a plastered wall or wooden
screen. These mansions differ from ordinary Japanese
houses mainly in the number and size of the rooms [as
may be seen in the *yashiki* occupied by the Offices of
the Government of Tôkiyô], among which are a hall of
audience, waiting rooms, private apartments, and separate suites of rooms, often of great extent, for the
ladies of the household, with small guard-rooms for the
retainers on duty. The posts and beams are of finely
grained, unvarnished wood, ornamented at the joints
with pieces of metal, pierced or engraved, and bearing

the owner's crest. The paper screens and sliding
doors are either plain or heavily covered with gold-leaf
adorned with paintings, and the floors are finely matted
Of furniture there is and was none. These mansions,
however, belong to Yedo rather than to Tôkiyô, and to
the province of the antiquary.[1]

The fire look-out stations, or wooden towers, erected
on the top of the main hall, are still conspicuous
objects. The gardens were often of immense extent
and great beauty, and the groves of those of the Mito
and Owari *yashikis* are prominent landmarks.

Though the long lines of the *nagoya* of these feudal
mansions are still characteristic of the region within
the inner moat, the *yashikis* are fast disappearing. The
Yamato and Kaga *yashikis* have been removed, and
their sites are covered with the bungalows of foreigners
in Japanese service. Some have been burned, and the
nagoya of others have been turned into shops, but it is
to be hoped that the Government will defer to the
desire expressed by foreigners for the conservation of
relics of the recent past, and that those occupied officially will be kept in repair.

These great wooden camps, for they were nothing
else, go far to account for the immense area occupied
by this singular city, for each *yashiki* of importance
covers many acres of ground, and there were 268
daimiyô, most of whom possessed three *yashikis* apiece,
and were attended to the capital by 1000, 2000, and
even 3000 armed retainers. The process of decay has
been a rapid one, for it was only in 1871 that these

[1] The *yashikis*, with their exterior and interior arrangements, and the
rigid etiquette which governed even their smallest details, have been
carefully and brilliantly described by Mr. M'Clatchie, of H.B.M.'s
Consular service, in a paper called "The Feudal Mansions of Yedo,"
published in the Transactions of the English Asiatic Society of Japan
for 1879.

princes were called upon to retire into private life, when their town dwellings, as well as their castles scattered throughout Japan, became the property of the Government.

Outside the Official Quarter are the city, and the districts of north, east, and south Tôkiyô, containing Shiba and Uyeno, with their temples, groves, shrines, avenues, and gardens, and the gorgeous tombs of eleven of the Shôguns of the Tokugawa dynasty; Tsukiji, the "Foreign Concession," and centre of foreign Missions; Asakusa, with the great popular temple of Kwan-non and its surrounding exhibitions; Oji with its temples and tea-houses; Mukojima with its tea-houses, cherry avenues, and shrines; Meguro with its rural beauty,. its temples, and cremation-ground, and the tombs of Gompachi and Kamurasaki; Takanawa, famous for attacks on the British Legation, and for the tombs of the "Forty-seven ronins," and Shinagawa, of evil fame, the suburb which lies nearest to Yokohama, are all names which have become familiar from the reports of travellers and Mr. Mitford's *Tales of Old Japan*.

Of all Tôkiyô, the city proper is the most densely populated district, and not the least interesting, as it is thoroughly Japanese, and few traces of foreign influence are to be seen. The Nipponbashi, or Bridge of Japan, is there, the geographical centre of the Empire, from which all distances are measured; the main street and numerous canals run through it, and every part of it is occupied with shops, storehouses, fireproof warehouses, and places of wholesale business, and their deep, heavily-tiled roofs almost redeem it from insignificance. The canals are jammed with neatly-roofed boats piled with produce, and on the roadways, loaded pack-horses, coolies, and man-carts with their shouting and struggling teams, leave barely room for the sight-seer. No streets of Liverpool or New York present more commercial activity. No time is lost, — "*Presto*" is the motto, — and loading, unloading, packing, unpacking, and warehousing, are carried on during daylight with much rapidity and noise. One would think that all the rice of Japan had accumulated in the storehouses which line the canals, as well as the energy, bustle, and business of the Empire.

The canals, which form, as at Niigata, a convenient network of communication, are water-streets as well as waterways, and are always thronged with loaded boats, and at certain times with pleasure-boats, and nocturnal boat processions illuminated with paper lanterns. The tide runs through them and keeps them sweet, but at low-water they look dirty and dismal, with their ragged fringe of sheds, and boats lying on the slime in which hundreds of children wallow with amphibious satisfaction. So many moats and canals involve a large number of bridges, but few of these are of stone. Yaetai-bashi, one of the longest, has twenty-four spans of thirty feet each. Tôkiyô, in few things "behind the age," possesses waterworks, and the supply is brought from a distance of nine miles in curious, square, wooden pipes, the mains from one to two feet square, and the distribution pipes four inches square; but there are no filtering beds, and the water is more abundant than absolutely pure.

The Japanese are the most irreligious people that I have ever seen — their pilgrimages are picnics, and their religious festivals fairs; but a pious spirit must have existed once at Tôkiyô, for an immense quantity of ground is taken up not only with temples, colleges for priests, pagodas and shrines, but with the grounds belonging to them, as at Shiba, Asakusa, and Uyeno. It is said that, including the shrines to Inari Sama, the patron of agriculture, there are over 3000 buildings in the capital dedicated to Shintô and Buddhist divinities, and the Buddhists are still erecting temples on a grand scale. Asakusa has already been described, and the shrines of the Shôguns in Shiba vary so little in their main features from those of Nikkô that it is needless to write of them, specially as nothing but the most detailed and technical description could give the reader any idea of their peculiar beauty, which is ever suggesting the regret that the work of the artist should be in a material so perishable as wood. The immense groves of the temples of Shiba and Uyeno have been turned into public parks, whose broad carriage-roads and shady avenues vie with those of any parks in Europe. Besides groups and streets of temples, there are temples stowed away in unlikely, crowded, or obscure localities, and some of these are great resorts of the populace, such as a small shrine in the narrow business street called Shimmei-mai, the walls and court of which are nearly concealed by *ex votos* offered by sufferers from toothache, who believe themselves to have been healed by the god to whom it is dedicated. Other small temples are resorted to by childless wives, and the altars of one divinity, who is supposed to secure the faithfulness of husbands, are always thronged with suppliants, of whose earnestness there can be no doubt.

The streets of the capital number 1400, very few retaining the same name along their entire length. They are of unpainted wood, and no description can give an idea of their monotonous meanness. Except that they are the scenes of a bustle which exists nowhere else in Japan but in Ôsaka, the lines of the Tôkiyô shops differ in few respects from those of Niigata, described in Letter XXI.; it is emphatically a city of shopkeepers,

ENTRANCE TO SHRINE OF SEVENTH SHŌGUN, SHIBA, TŌKIYŌ.

and great numbers of its streets have the short, shop curtains hanging along their entire length. Most of them, as elsewhere, are of small dimensions, resembling dolls' houses as much by their size as by the smallness and exquisite neatness of their wares. Unless accompanied by a Japanese or an intelligent foreign resident, it is impossible even to guess at the uses of half the things which are exposed for sale, and pilgrimages among the shops are by no means an insignificant aid to learning something of the requirements and mode of living of the people, though it is at Tôkiyô more than anywhere else that one feels how much there is to learn, and how comparatively little could be learned, even by the assiduous application of many years. A great number of the articles sold are actually made at Tôkiyô, and, as befits a capital, it is a grand emporium for the productions of the whole Empire.

The street signs do little to relieve the monotony of the low, grey houses, nor do the shops (except the toy-shops which are gorgeous) make much show, with their low fronts half-concealed by curtains. Confectioners usually display a spiked white ball a foot and a half in diameter; *saké*-dealers a cluster of cypress trimmed into a sphere; the sellers of the crimson pigment with which women varnish their lips a red flag; goldbeaters a great pair of square spectacles, with gold instead of glass; druggists and herbalists a big bag resembling in shape the small ones used in making their infusions; kite-makers a cuttle-fish; sellers of cut flowers a small willow tree; dealers in dried and salt fish, etc., two fish, coloured red, and tied together by the gills with straw, indicating that they can supply the gifts which it is usual to make to betrothed persons; but the Brobdignagian signs in black, red, and gold, which light up the streets of Canton, are too "loud" and explicit for

Japanese taste, which prefers the simple and symbolical.

Many of the streets remain exclusively Japanese, and their shops sell nothing but Japanese goods; but others have been westernised, and are simply repulsive-looking, as, to my thinking, are most of the other European innovations. It may be said, once for all, that there is not a fine street in Tôkiyô, though some in which the roofs are deep and heavily tiled are slightly picturesque. On the whole they are flimsy, unpicturesque, and perishable, and singularly unimpressive except from the crowds which frequent them. There are no side-walks, but the roadways are so beautifully clean that they are not missed. External cleanliness is a characteristic of the city. The sewage is carried out for the fertilisation of the neighbouring country by men and horses in neat, covered pails, and, as a whole, the city is remarkably sweet, though it must be confessed that sundry black ditches give off, in hot weather, odours which suggest "drain fever." Public bath-houses abound.

The theatres are mainly confined to Saruwaka Street, and most dissipations and amusements have their respective localities.

The street names are a study in themselves,[1] and are very numerous, as a single street sometimes receives as many as twenty for twenty parts of its length. Japan has no Aboukirs, Agincourts, or Almas to commemorate. Owing to her insular position, her wars, such as they have been, have been mainly internecine, and it has not been the custom to perpetuate by street names either the heroes or victories of civil strife. A few, in-

---

[1] Mr. Griffis, author of the *Mikado's Empire*, contributed a very interesting paper upon this subject to the Transactions of the English Asiatic Society of Japan.

deed, are called after the soldier-emperor Hachiman;
some are named after famous wrestlers, priests, or nuns;
the great theatre street after Saruwaka, the founder of
the modern Japanese theatre; and one after Kinda
Miyamoto, an ancient fencing-master who murdered his
father, and is the hero of many fictitious tales of revenge. The popular deities, and the dragon, the favourite mythical monster, play a very insignificant part in
street nomenclature.

Of the 1400 streets of Tôkiyô, about two-thirds de-
rive their names from natural objects, another proof of
the love of nature which is so strong among the Japanese. There is a *Matsu* or Pine Street in nearly every
one of the ninety-six subdivisions of the city. Scores
of streets are named after the willow and bamboo,
and a number after the cedar, peony, rush, rice-plant,
wormwood, holly, and chrysanthemum. Among the
more fanciful names are Plum Orchard, Pure Water,
Sun Shade, Morning Sun, Flowing River, Mountain
Breeze, and New Blossom; and beasts and birds are
not forgotten, for there are Badger, Tortoise, Monkey,
Stork, Bear, and Pheasant Streets re-duplicated, and
twenty streets are called after that unworthy brute the
Japanese horse, Pack Horse Relay Street being the oldest in Tôkiyô. Invention languishes there as with us.
There are more than twenty timber streets; and the
names of trades are frequently repeated, such as Car-
penter, Blacksmith, Dyer, Sawyer, Farmer, Coolie,
and Cooper. A farther descent is to File, Kettle, Pot,
and Table. Many are named from Salt, Wheat, Indigo,
Charcoal, Hair, Leather, Pen, Mat, and Fan, and there
are Net, and Fresh, Roasted, and Salt Fish Streets. A
few are called after such obsolete military weapons as
are only to be found in the Museum, others are named
Abounding Gladness, Same Friend, Conjugal Love
Congratulation, and Peace.

The Restoration, which has changed so much, has not been without its effect on street nomenclature, for since Yedo became Tôkiyô, and the Shôgunate fell, about a sixth of the street names, which were associated with the power of the usurping vassal, were altered, but many of the former survive in popular usage.

The puzzling repetition of the same names arises from the fact, to which allusion has previously been made, that the capital is an aggregation of 125 villages more or less distant from each other. A letter has to be addressed not only with the name of the person to whom it is sent, and his street and number, but with that of the ward of the city, and of the ancient village, to which latter name the people are tenaciously attached. No city is better supplied with materials for a census, for over each doorway there is a slip of wood inscribed with the name of the householder, and the number and sexes of his household, besides the designation of the street and the number of the house, which compensates for the absence of conspicuous boards with street names upon them.

MODERN INSTITUTIONS.

The Cemeteries — Cremation — Sharp Criticism — Stereotyped Ideas — Modern Constructive Art — The College of Engineering — Principal Dyer — The Telegraph Department — The Foreign Residents — Forms of Flattery — The Flower *Festa* — A Memory of Fuji — Costly Entertainments — The Brain of New Japan.

Two estimable features in the Japanese character are the respect in which they hold their dead, and the attention which they pay to everything which can render their cemeteries beautiful and attractive. Though Tôkiyô cannot boast of burial-grounds of equal beauty with those of Kiyôto, its many cemeteries are all carefully kept; and from the gorgeous shrines of Shiba and Uyeno, where the Shôguns " lie in glory," down to the modest tomb in which the ashes of a coolie rest, there are no grim contrasts between death and life, and "the house appointed for all living" is neat, ornamental, and befitting the position which its occupant filled in life. The solid granite monuments, often elaborate, are always tasteful. They vary from the simple upright obelisk or stone pillar on a square pedestal, merely inscribed with the name of the deceased, to the massive granite base and carved column surmounted by a bronze Buddha seated on a lotus blossom, the figure being occasionally as much as eight feet high. The square family mausoleums, carefully swept, with their rows of solid pillars on stone pedestals, the fresh flowers in bamboo flower-holders by many tombs, the exquisite neatness of the narrow streets of the dead, and the number of visitors always engaged in reverently tending the graves, lighting fresh incense sticks, and replacing the faded bouquets with newly gathered ones, are among the most interesting sights, not only of Tô-kiyô, but of Japan, and the solidity of the abodes of the dead contrasts curiously with the perishableness of the houses of the living.

Cremation, which was interdicted by the Government some years ago, is now again permitted, on the grounds that the Government declines to interfere with personal wishes, that in so vast a city burial by interment alone would, after a time, produce results injurious to the public health, and that after some years room would scarcely be found for the dead among the living. These reasons were given me in writing by Mr. Masakata Kusamoto, the enlightened Governor of Tôkiyô *Fu*, and are worthy of careful consideration. Five cremation grounds exist in the capital, and within the last four years the number of bodies disposed of by burning has annually increased. Corpses can be burned for sums varying from 3s. 8d. to 20s., and though the arrangements are very simple, no disagreeable results are to be observed in the neighbourhoods.

Tôkiyô, not Yedo, being my text, its Europeanised buildings deserve notice, for they are an increasingly marked and very repulsive feature of the capital, and in some districts are taking the place of houses of Japanese construction. They present little variety, and with a few exceptions, of which the Engineering College is the chief, are models of ugliness and bad taste. They look "run up" not built. They are garish, staring, glaring, angular, white, many-windowed, temporary-looking, unsuited to the climate, offensive to the eye, suggestive of the outskirts of new cities in America, and at their best and cleanest look more like confectionery than ought else.

Stereotyped ideas in architecture have marked the past of Japan. The architect who constructed a massive, sweeping roof, with deep eaves, supported it on circular pillars on a raised platform, and called it a temple, created a style of ecclesiastical architecture from which no builder has dared to swerve for 800 years. So it may be feared that the innovator, be he British or American, who designed the first of these tasteless, Europeanised structures, has ploughed a groove so deep that no future projector will get out of it, that even Mr. Chastel de Boinville, the architect to the Government, and of the one appropriate and handsome building which Tôkiyô possesses, will find himself fettered by newly-created prejudices in favour of erections half-barrack, half-warehouse, and that the harmonious greys, velvety-browns, and dull reds are discarded for ever by modern Japan.

My first impression was that most of the Europeanised or rather Americanised buildings in the Official Quarter, in so far as they are of wood, were military or police barracks or cavalry stables ; and the houses built of brick, which are the residences of some of the ministers, are like some of the tasteless villas of Holloway or New Barnet, while others are so like the staring taverns which deform the approaches to London, that one involuntarily looks for the great board with " Hanbury's Entire," or " Guinness' Stout " upon it. They look " got up " cheaply of soft brick, and, between porous bricks and bad mortar, some of them already show signs of disintegration.

The wooden houses are worse, being mainly vicious and exaggerated copies of some of the worst of the constructions in the European settlements, or illustrations of ideas imported from Denver or Virginia City.   Cracking, warping, and shrinking, ill-concealed by a coating of white paint or plaster, are obvious on many new buildings, and most, from the fragile materials used, and the hasty mode of erection, are already in want of repair.   Much money has been spent on the public buildings, most have some pretension to architecture, and are supposed to be improvements on Japanese construction, and it is really a pity that the Government, which means well, has not been better advised.   In truth, the Anglo-American architecture, which is daily gaining ground in Tôkiyô, and is being copied by the provincial capitals, means the union of the cold and discomfort of Japanese houses with the ugliness and discomfort of third-rate suburban villas in America.   In public buildings it means the abandonment of the simple grandeur of the massive, curved roof, with its deep, picturesque eaves, and carefully moulded corner and terminal tiles, the shady verandahs, the carved scrolls of the grand entry, the imposing arrangement of rafters, the solid and decorated panels, and the general combination of strength and airiness, light and shade, dignity and simplicity, which are seen in perfection in the Goshô at Kiyôto and in some of the *yashikis* at Tôkiyô, in favour of buildings which possess size without majesty, with layers of white plaster or paint hiding a badly put-together framework of wood, suggestive of the pastry-cook's art, with shallow roofs, unshaded windows in scores, tawdry porches, an absence of verandahs, and a general flatness of inexpressive physiognomy terrible to behold, nothing in the style of the tawdry and ephemeral-looking erections affording the slightest clue to the purpose for which they were originally built and are at present used.   As examples of this modern constructive art, it is only necessary to mention as among the best the Imperial University, and as ordinary speci mens, the buildings which conceal the present residence of the Mikado, and the police stations all over Tôkiyô.

It is singular that the Japanese, who rarely commit a solecism in taste in their national costume, architecture, or decorative art, seem to be perfectly destitute of perception when they borrow ours. Their tasteless, Americanised structures, and the "loud," gaudy, "tapestry" carpets which they lay down on the floors of their public buildings when they relinquish their own beautiful mats, are instances in point.

Among the most noteworthy of the new and old buildings which distingnish Tôkiyô, and show the advance which Japan is making in civilisation, education, and philanthropy, are the Imperial University, the Medical, Naval, and Military Schools, the Imperial College of Engineering, which is really a technical university, the Paper Money "Mint," the Normal School for girls, endowed by the Empress, the Military, Naval, and *Kak'ké* Hospitals, the Post Office, Telegraph Office, and Railway Terminus, besides Government Offices and Departments too numerous to mention.

The glory and pride of Japanese educational institutions is the Imperial College of Engineering, and the Japanese may justly be proud of it, for it is not only the finest modern building in Japan, worthy to take a humble place beside the Cam or Isis — academical in its aspects, noble in its proportions, suited for its purpose, and placed in an elevated and commanding position — but, in the opinion of many competent judges, is the most complete and best equipped engineering college in the world, and destined shortly to make Japan, as she ought to be, entirely independent of foreigners for the carrying out of the great projects of improvement on which her future progress depends. To a Japanese mind this stately building is the embodiment and apotheosis of material progress, the god of every educated Japanese. This shrine of progress consists of an imposing arrangement of stone-faced brick buildings in a mixed Tudor style, forming three sides of a handsome and spacious quadrangle.

The college buildings contain a library and common hall of ecclesiastical as well as academical appearance, a general lecture hall, class-rooms, chemical demonstration rooms, secretary's office, Principal's and Professors' rooms, class anterooms, general drawing-office, engineering drawing-office, surveying drawing-office, boiler-house, mining lecture and demonstration rooms, architectural drawing-office, printing-office, natural philosophy instrument room, natural philosophy laboratories and demonstration rooms, museum, dormitories, kitchens, chemical laboratory, engineering laboratory, metallurgical laboratory, Professors' houses, telegraph and mineralogical museums, and two or three other minor departments.

No expense has been or is spared upon the equipments of this magnificent college. Whatever other institutions are starved, it gets whatever Principal Dyer chooses to ask. Its museum, illustrative of civil and mechanical engineering, is a superb one, and it is said that no similar school in the world possesses a collection of models at once so accurate in their construction, or so valuable for teaching purposes. The Telegraph and Mineralogical Museums are equally carefully arranged, and not only do concise and admirable catalogues accompany each museum, but descriptions are given with each model and instrument, which convey the leading idea of its construction and utility in the smallest possible space. To the non-scientific visitor the museum of Japanese products, manufacturers, and models of

Japanese machinery, though by no means as complete as it ought to be and will be, is the most interesting of all, and year by year, as the old style of things disappears, will gain in value, and in time may come to be the only place in which the Japanese of the future can study the former industries of his country, and the simple methods by which great results were obtained.

This college is under the ministry of Public Works. Principal Dyer, who has made it what it is, is intensely a Scotchman, and not only very able in his own profession, but a man of singular force, energy, and power of concentration, with a resolute and indomitable will. He is felt in the details of every department of the College, and combines practical sagacity with a large amount of well-directed enthusiasm. It is said that of the foreign teachers in Japanese employment he is the one whose resolute independence and determination to carry out his own plans in his own way have been respected by the Government, and I venture to predict that he will be the last one whose services will be dispensed with. His highly-efficient teaching staff consists of nine English professors, with several qualified Japanese assistants, all working energetically; and among the former have been and are several men who have thrown themselves heartily into different departments of Japanese study. The discipline and tone of the College leave little to be desired. A fine spirit pervades the students, and it seems that the only complaint made by their teachers is that it is difficult to make them understand the necessity for recreation.

Classes are held in English language and literature, technical drawing, mathematics, natural philosophy, chemistry, engineering, telegraphic engineering, mechanical engineering, architecture, mineralogy, geology, mining, and metallurgy, with branches under several of these heads. The course lasts six years, and a considerable part of it is occupied with practical instruction at the well-equipped works at Akabané, the largest mechanical engineering establishment in Japan, where all sorts of engines and mechanical appliances are turned out. The enlightened system of education which is pursued is supplemented by a very valuable and always increasing library, containing over 13,000 volumes, mostly on technical subjects, and by a reading-room liberally supplied with periodicals.

The question arises, What is to be done with the fifty "masters in engineering" who hereafter will be turned out annually by what is usually termed by foreigners "Mr. Dyer's college," and how is work to be provided for them in a country which has overspent itself, and is obliged to economise? Japan cherishes visions of costly engineering undertakings of all kinds, but these are expensive, and in her present temper she intends not only not to contract any new debts, but to pay off the old. Mr. Dyer would reply that his business is to turn out competent engineers, and not to forecast their future, and I pass from the subject in the hope of an era of remunerative improvements.

Museums are worthily occupying the attention of the Government. The *Kaitakushi* Department has a collection of objects imperfectly illustrating the industries and mode of living of the Ainos in its museum in Shiba, and the National Museum contains objects of variety and beauty the like of which are not to be found anywhere else, and which, had they not been purchased by the nation, would have passed into the hands of foreign *connoisseurs*. Many of the creations of ancient art which are arranged in Uyeno are unique and priceless, and the authorities deserve great credit for the extent, value, and arrangement of this museum.

The last building which I notice is the Telegraph Building, opened in March 1878, under the auspices of Mr. Gilbert, the chief superintendent. The whole telegraph system of Japan is now worked by native officials, foreigners having been dispensed with in the summer of last year. This building, though in the vicious Europeanised style, is well arranged for its objects, its lower floor being occupied by reception-rooms, offices, and a broad counter for messages, and nearly the whole of the upper by an operating-room, to which the messages are conveyed in a lift. The Morse instruments, including "sounders," are used for ordinary messages, and on short local lines Wheatstone's alphabetical instruments, specially arranged for recording the Roman alphabet and Japanese syllabary. Part of this room is taken up by a test-box and a test-board, which accommodates eighty circuits, into which the wires from all Japan are led, and another part by a time-transmitter and regulator clock, whereby the telegraphic time all over Japan is adjusted daily. In another room batteries with a thousand cells are kept upon tables. A telephone connected with the Engineering College for experimental purposes is the latest instance of the eagerness with which the Japanese are appropriating foreign inventions. The Morse instruments, test-box, time-transmitter, and everything for out and indoor use, except wire, are made by Japanese in the workshops of the Telegraph Department, and the instruments, for delicacy of finish and accuracy, are said to bear comparison with any which are manufactured in Europe. The manipulators there and elsewhere are Japanese, and they have proved such apt scholars that they manage their telegraph system with a carefulness and accuracy which allow of no hostile criticism.

In truth, Tôkiyô is a wonderful city of enterprise

and bustle, the focus of the new order of things, not only the seat of a Government of singular capacity and activity, but the headquarters of an education which is revolutionising Japan. Doctors, schoolmasters, and engineers are being dispersed from it over the Empire, who not only carry with them a new education, medicine, and science, but new ideas of government, philosophy, and the position of women, as well as the pushing, progressive, Tôkiyô spirit of unmitigated materialism. It must be observed that the education and stimulation of the brain are carried on with little reference to man's moral nature, and that distortion of one part of his being and dwarfing of another must be the sure result. In addition, the indirect, and in some cases the direct, influence of some of the foreign teachers has been against Christianity, and in favour of materialism. The new education lays "the axe to the root of the tree" of the old *cultus* and beliefs, substituting nothing. Probably there is scarcely an atheism so blank, or a materialism so complete, on earth as that of the educated modern Japanese.

Of the foreigners in Japanese Government employment the greater number are in Tôkiyô. They are allowed to live anywhere outside the dreary limits of Tsukiji, and they form a society among themselves, mixing but little with the colony of missionaries in the Concession. Their number decreases, for the Government parts with them as soon as it thinks that Japanese can fill their places, and the constant changes among them are unfavourable to the pleasantest kind of social intercourse. The most recent clearance has been at the Naval College, where only two of the English staff, and those not in the College proper, have been retained. Many of them apply themselves with praiseworthy assiduity to the study of the Japanese language, and of

special subjects connected with Japan, and their dili-
gence bears good fruit in papers of great and permanent interest contributed by them to the English and
German Asiatic Societies, both of which hold regular
meetings in Tôkiyô. Those who merely teach, and hold
a..oof from Japanese interests, must have rather a "dull
time," and the ladies, very few of whom interest themselves in anything Japanese except curios, must be
duller still.

The capital, as one of the three imperial cities or *Fu*,
has a local jurisdiction, and a governor, assisted by a
large staff. The present Governor, Masakata Kusumoto, is the one who cleansed and renovated Niigata,
and under his vigorous administration order and cleanliness reign in Tôkiyô, though the number of robberies
on winter nights retains formidable proportions in spite
of nearly 6000 policemen. There are no beggars, and
there is no quarter given up to poverty and squalor, or
poverty and squalor in combination with crime, and fes-
tering centres of misery of any kind are not to be
found. Vice, though legalised, is prohibited from displaying its seductions in the ordinary streets, the resorts
of the dissolute being confined to special quarters of
the city.

Over 10,000 cavalry, infantry, and artillery are quartered in Tôkiyô, but these are more likely to prove a
source of difficulty than of strength. Large numbers
are recruited from the *heimin* or lowest class, and the
uncouthness of their bucolic faces contrasts with the
intelligence of those of the policemen, who are mostly
samurai. On days when large numbers of them get
leave, they are to be seen staggering about the streets
in a state of intoxication, creating a disorder which is
as rare in Tôkiyô as in any other Japanese city.

The paucity of horse vehicles, where horses are

abundant and roads are excellent, is a curious fact. In
the Official Quarter a few carriages are to be seen, and
on one street clumsy vans, drawn by contemptible
ponies, run as omnibuses, but elsewhere one may walk
about week after week without seeing anything but
kurumas or man-carts and coolies, and coolies and pack-
horses are used for the transport of all goods which
cannot be conveyed by canal. It is not unusual to see
100 men carrying a log of felled and squared timber, or
a stone of enormous size. There are over 23,000 *kurumas;* their number is rapidly increasing, and they are
used by everybody as the handiest means of abbreviat-
ing the "magnificent distances" of the city.

Tôkiyô is the centre of the publishing trade, and
nearly every trade and manufacture in Japan is more
or less represented there. I will notice but one. In
several passages in the previous letters melancholy
allusions have been made to certain imitations, which,
though they may be "the sincerest form of flattery,"
are also the most impertinent form of swindling. Of
the manufacture of forged labels and imitative compounds of the most nauseous or unwholesome description Tôkiyô is the centre, and it has reduced systematic
forgery to a trade. Nor is this iniquity confined to
back slums and holes and corners, but it is carried on
in the face of day at unscreened windows, where presses
may be seen at work imitating the English Government
Inland Revenue stamp, Dr. Collis Browne's signature,
or the attractive label of "Preston's Sugar of Lemons,"
or the tempting cover of the "Ramornie" meat tins, the
"Eagle Brand," Bass's "Red Diamond" label, etc., fortunately not always with that strict attention to English orthography which would render the deception
complete. It is complete enough, however, for the
unfortunate Japanese victims, and from Nagasaki to

Hakodaté spurious eatables, drinkables, and medicines are sold, dealing sickness with a liberal hand, introducing *delirium tremens* and other woes where they were previously unknown, and turning innocent into "deadly things." I write feelingly, as a sufferer from an evil compound, supposed to consist of soap, vitriol, oil of lemons, and sugar, sold for that best of all refreshing drinks, "Preston's Sugar of Lemons." Elsewhere, a perfumer, who aspires to be the Rimmel of Japan, bottles aggressively nauseous odours in Rimmel's and Farina's bottles, adroitly imitating even the seal or capsule, and "Pears' Soap" appears as a scarifying compound, admirable *possibly* as "a counter-irritant." Again, men may be seen industriously filling Bass's bottles from casks of native beer, and Guinness's with the same beer coloured with liquorice and refuse treacle. Are we to class these forgeries as among the signs of manufacturing progress in Japan?

Tôkiyô is a stronghold of amusement and pleasure, as well as of politics, education, and business, but its theatres, *geishas*, wrestlers, jugglers, and other diversions have been so minutely described by other writers, that I gladly let them alone in favour of the Flower *festa* of the different seasons, which are among the most attractive sights of the capital. The well-tended gardens of the suburbs, with their stiffly-clipped hedges, the back plots a few feet square, with their gardens in miniature, even in the most crowded streets, or perhaps pots alone, with flowering plants, as regularly changed in their succession as those in the balconies of houses in Belgravia, attest that love of the beauties of nature, which is one of the most pleasing features of the Japanese character, and which finds its more systematic gratification in resorting to special places where special flowers are to be seen in their glory. In February, when the Japanese plum tree, with its crowded blossoms, chiefly varying from those of our apricot in size and variety of shape and colour, is in perfection, crowds go out to Kamédo and Omurai on the river, and to Tabata — places distinguished for the number and beauty of these trees. This is only a foretaste of the festival in April, when Japan is at its best, and the winter, especially dreaded by the Japanese, is forgotten, and the different varieties of the cherry, the pride of the flowering trees, are in their beauty. Then all Tôkiyô, in holiday costume, flocks to the hill plateau of Aska-yama, to Ódsi, and especially to Uyeno, which has the aspect of a fair for two or three weeks. Numbers of temporary tea-houses are constructed of bamboo, and are decorated with flags and lanterns, and dainties, toys, and confectionery are everywhere sold, girls and children sing and dance; but the beauty of the cherry blossoms is the soul of the festival, and all day long crowds of all ages throng the park, luxuriating with genuine enjoyment in the delight of the "cherry viewing," and sipping tea and cherry-blossom water.

In June the wistaria festival is held, and thousands of people visit Kamédo, where bowers of this trailer, with pendent clusters of blossoms, surround a piece of water, and amidst feasting, singing, and music, verses in praise of its beauty are written on slips of paper and are hung upon the boughs. The "iris viewing" shortly follows, when the ponds and flower-beds of Hari Kiri are glorious with irises of the loveliest colours, and again pleasure-loving Tôkiyô creates a vast picnic, and crowds the garden suburb of Mukôjima by the river; and boats, gay with flags in the daytime, and with lanterns at night, throng the broad stream, and the riverside roads are cheery with groups bound to the bowers and tea-houses of the iris gardens. The "Festival of the Chrysanthemums" in October, one of the five great national festivals of Japan, has several centres, and the imperial flower is nowhere seen in greater perfection than in Tôkiyô.

Perpetual floral attractions of a very curious kind are offered by the "art gardeners" of Sugamo and Somei, pleasant suburbs, and in Dango Saka, where the tea-house grounds and gardens are always crowded with holiday-making guests. Except in the gardens of the Buddhist monastery of Hang-tse in China, I have never seen anything approaching in singularity to these productions, but the gardeners of Tôkiyô are far more daring than the monks. Bushes and shrubs cut into the life-size resemblances of men and women, are equipped with faces of painted wood or paper, the clothes, fans, or weapons being formed of carefully trained leaves and flowers, which fall in artistic draperies of delightfully harmonised colours. In one scene a tree represents a monster fan, two others a bridge with a ship passing underneath it, then a landscape with a picnic and a setting sun of gold-coloured chrysanthemums is wonderfully executed. Chinese women walking, and animals, specially hares and rabbits, are also represented by this singular art. Scenes from well-known plays are the most enduringly popular of all these scenes, and one of the mythic heroes of Japan, shown in combat with an eight-headed monster, while the lady for whom he is fighting sits apart, clothed in red, yellow, and white chrysanthemums, the whole forming a landscape over thirty feet long, is always the centre of joyous crowds in late October, when the sun is warm and the air is still.

It would be treachery to many delicious memories were I to omit to say that Fuji, either as a cone of dazzling snow, or rosy in the autumn sunrise, or as a lofty spiritual presence far off in a veil of mist, or purple against the sunset gold, is one of the great sights of Tôkiyô. Even of Shiba, that dream of beauty, among whose groves the city hum is unheard, one might weary, but of Fuji never, and as time goes on, he becomes an infatuating personality, which raises one above the monotonous clatter and the sordid din of mere material progress. One vision of Fuji I shall never forget. After spending an afternoon alone among the crowds which throng the great temple of Kwan-non at Asakusa, as I turned a corner at dusk to go down a hill, my *kuruma*-runner looked round and said, "Fuji!" and I saw a glory such as I had not seen before in Japan. The heavens behind and overhead were dark and covered with clouds, but in front there was a clear sky of pure, pale green, into which the huge cone of Fuji rose as a mass of ruddy purple, sublime, colossal, while above the green, which was streaked with some lines of pure vermilion, the clouds were a sea of rippling rose-colour, and in the darkness below, at the foot of a solemn, tree-covered embankment, lay the castle moat, a river of molten gold, giving light in the gloom. Actual darkness came on, and still Fuji rose in purple into the fading sky, lingering in his glory, and never, while the earth and heavens last, will just the same sight be seen again.

One of the most recent phases of Tôkiyô has been the sort of craze it has taken for giving extravagant entertainments to guests. The Government and the people have gone wild on the subject, and poor, and burdened with debt and taxation as the nation is, it is a matter for regret that a course of such decidedly "unremunerative" expenditure should have been entered upon. Mr. E. J. Reed, M.P., was the first guest of the series, and he has been followed by General Grant, a grandson

of Queen Victoria, Prince Henry of Prussia, and the
Duke of Genoa. In addition to the sums expended by
Government, Tôkiyô spent $50,000 in entertaining
General Grant, and the entertainment given to him in
the hall and grounds of the Engineering College was
one of the most successful *fêtes* ever seen in the capital,
owing to the number and beauty of the lanterns used
for illumination. All this is very modern and "progressive."

Whatever else may or may not be seen or enjoyed, the
street life of Tôkiyô is an inexhaustible source of pleasure. The middle and lower classes have an outdoorish-
ness and visibility about them which offer a thousand
points of interest. The shop life, the canal life, the
child life, Tôkiyô on wheels, on foot, and under umbrellas, the crowds and their unvarying good temper and
good behaviour, the flower festivals, the *fêtes*, the *matsuri* with their processions, the cheerful funerals, the
throngs in the popular temples, the picnics, the water
processions by day and night, the perpetual illumination with coloured lanterns, the quaint incongruities,
the changing and shifting, the abundance of movement,
the ceaseless industry, the personal independence and
liberty enjoyed by all classes shown by a demeanour
neither servile nor self-assertive, the tiny houses and
doll-like women, the old and the new mingling in a city
no part of which is more than three centuries old, form
a series of separate and combined pictures, which at
once bewilder and fascinate.

Banks, a Chamber of Commerce, dispensaries, exhibition buildings, newspaper and telegraph offices, a railway station, steamboat offices, photographic galleries,
and powder magazines, are all essential features of the
new capital.

Truly Yedo, the City of the Shôguns, is no more. A

city of camps, "the necessity of feudalism," it perished with the *old régime*, to be born again as a city of business, politics, amusement, bustle, energy, and progress. Tôkiyô, the city of the future, is the *brain* of New Japan, but Kiyôto, the historic capital, the home of art and poetry, must remain its *heart*.

A JAPANESE CONCERT.

A "Dirty Sky" — "Rags" — Mr. Mori — A Ministerial Entertainment — The "Shiba Pavilion" — An Amateur Orchestra — The Japanese Wagner — An Aristocratic *Belle* — A Juvenile *Danseuse* — An Agonising Mystery — The "Dead March" in *Saul* — Japanese Music — Musical Instruments — Lady Parkes.

H.B.M.'s LEGATION, YEDO, *October* 11.

THE weather produces a lassitude which makes letter-writing difficult. Every now and then a bright, hot day occurs, but usually it rains as it has been raining for weeks past, and the sailor's phrase, "a dirty sky," is the only one which describes the dull brown clouds and stagnant brown mists. The mercury hovers about 80°, the air is quite still, and stillness and heat together make one expect a thunderstorm, which never comes; but instead we have had a smart shock of earthquake, which seemed equally suitable to the weather. Everything is moist or sticky, boots mildew four hours after they have been blacked, writing-paper has to be dried near a charcoal brazier before it is used, soap jellifies, ink turns mouldy, appetite for solid food entirely fails, every one is more or less ailing. Sir Harry, much worn out, has gone to Hakone, Lady Parkes, who has been suffering from intermittent fever, has gone to Yokohama, and Mr. Chamberlain, the two children, "Rags," and I, are all feeble. "Rags" takes very little notice of me when his own people are here, but now he is most attentive to me, lies by my chair, sleeps on my hearthrug at night, assumes a very cordial manner, and expects me to feed him and attend to his comfort. Mr. Chamberlain has been here for a fortnight, which has been a great pleasure to me, not only because he is an excellent *cicerone*, but because he is such a thorough lover of Japan, as well as a Japanese student, and is never bored by being asked any number of questions, even though many of them are trivial and unintelligent. I have been utilising the bad weather by studying several volumes of the Japan *Weekly Mail*, and files of the *Tôkiyô Times*, and the "Transactions" of the Asiatic Society for several years, the three combined being better than all the books of travels put together for steeping one in a Japanese atmosphere.

The few bright days have been very bright, and like our English midsummer (when we have summer at all). On one of the brightest we, with Miss Gordon Cumming, who arrived in the middle of September, went to an afternoon entertainment given to the diplomatic body in the Shiba Pavilion, one of the Mikado's smaller palaces, by Mr. Arenori Mori, Vice-minister for foreign affairs.[1] Mr. Mori is one of the most progressive of Japanese politicians, and, under an Oriental despotism, is "an advanced Liberal." He would tolerate everything. He is in favour of "Women's Rights;" he was married much in English civil fashion; his wife dresses tastefully in English style, and receives his guests along with himself; he regards Shintô only as a useful political engine, and has even formally proposed the adoption of the English language in Japan, if we would agree to a phonetic system of spelling. He was in America for some years, speaks English tolerably well, and, unlike most of his countrymen, knows how to wear the European dress.

[1] Recently appointed Minister to England.

He received us at the door of the Pavilion, ar 1 conducted us to a room where nearly the whole diplomatic
corps was assembled; the Chinese ministers being conspicuous in blue silk robes with squares of gold embroidery on the back and front, long amber necklaces,
and white hats covered with crimson fringe. The only
costumes besides these were worn by two young Japanese ladies, daughters of nobles, who looked awkward
and timid sitting on chairs in dark silk *kimonos* and
very thick and heavy girdles. The room consisted of a
suite of rooms in Japanese style, thrown open to the
verandah, and looking upon a large garden very beautifully laid out, bounded on the sea side by a massive
stone embankment, which is concealed from the house
by grass mounds and trees. This very attractive
pleasure-ground is a dexterous artificial composition
of closely shaven lawns, lakes with small islands and
stone bridges, stone lanterns, shrubberies, distorted
pines, and flagged and gravelled walks. Not a stray
twig or leaf was visible, and the walks were so exquisitely smooth that it seemed as if a lady's train
might rudely ruffle them. From the mounds there is
a fine view of the Gulf of Yedo, and junks and fishing-
boats sail within a few yards of the garden wall. The
house, a very simple and pretty Japanese building, is
Europeanised by a tawdry Brussels carpet, black and
gold lacquer chairs, and black and gold tables with
books of Japanese pictures upon them.

Tea in cups with handles and saucers was handed
round by servants in black dress suits, with white ties.
The diversion provided was a juggling performance
upon mats laid on the lawn, and consisted mainly of
clever but tedious feats of balancing balls, cups, sticks,
and vases, with a drumming accompaniment, a great
waste of time and skill. There was an interlude of a

very abundant "collation," with all sorts of food, ice cream, abundance of claret cup, champagne, and "mint julep," serve̴ on a long table, with about twenty waiters rustling about in European clothes. The china was all English, and not pretty. Mr. Mori complimented me with much *bonhommie* on my "unprecedented tour," and remarked that people rarely travelled in Northern Japan. After more juggling, the party broke up, and I regretted the loss of an afternoon, as lost it was, for this entertainment was a mere imitation of an English reception, and had nothing distinctively Japanese about it.

A very interesting one was given a few days afterwards by Mr. Satow, in his beautiful Japanese house, the furnishing of which is the perfection of Japanese and European good taste and simplicity. The drawing-room is purely Japanese, with ceiling and posts of planed wood, walls of carefully roughened greenish grey plaster, a polished alcove and fine *tatami*, with here and there a Persian carpet over them; a rich, quiet-coloured couch, a few chairs, a solitary table with a lamp, a stand with some rare books, a very few bronze ornaments and some fine engravings, and flowers in vases hanging on the walls, completed its furnishing. There were only the two English Secretaries, the wife of one of them, and myself. The little dinner was worthy of one of Disraeli's descriptions, and was served by noiseless attendants in Japanese dress. Shortly after we went to the drawing-room, thirteen gentlemen and ladies of remarkably dignified and refined appearance entered with musical instruments, carried by servants, who then retired. These musicians were an amateur orchestra under the leadership of a Japanese composer, who aspires to be the Wagner of Japan, and who composed the music with which the evening was occupied.

The orchestra consisted of six ladies, two of whom were elderly widows, and six men. On the floor were five *kotos*, each one six feet long. A young girl, daughter of a noble who has filled several high official positions, played on a most exquisitely made antique instrument, called the *shô*, formed of several reeds beautifully lacquered in gold, banded with silver, and set in a circular box of fine gold lacquer. This needed to be constantly warmed at a stand of rich lacquer, containing a charcoal brazier. The girl was very pretty for a Japanese, and perfectly bewitching by the dignified grace of her manner; but her face and throat were much whitened with powder, and her lower lip was patched with vermilion. Her " evening dress " consisted of a *kimono* of soft, bronze green silk, with sleeves hanging nearly to her ankles, an under vest, showing at the neck, of scarlet *crêpe* splashed with gold, a girdle of 3½ yards of rich silver brocade made into a large lump at the back, and white cloth socks. She wore a large *chignon*, into which some scarlet *crêpe* was twisted, a loop of hair on the top of her head, and a heavy tortoise-shell pin with a branch of pink coral at one end, stuck through the *chignon*. The other young ladies were dressed in *kimono* of dark blue silk, with blue girdles brocaded with silver; and the two elderly widows wore dark silk *kimono* and *haori* of the same. The men all wore silk *hakama* and *haori*.

These people were all thoroughly well-bred Japanese. I cannot describe the grace, dignity, and courtesy of their manners, and the simple kindliness with which they exerted themselves on our behalf. Their demeanour was altogether natural, and it was most interesting to see an etiquette, manner, and tone, perfect in their way, yet not in the slightest particular formed upon our models.

Besides this very interesting orchestra, there was a very conspicuous performer in the shape of a child of nine, daughter of one of the Mikado's chief attend-ants, a being of unutterable dignity and abstraction.

> "It was neither man nor woman,
> It was neither brute nor human ; "

but most certainly, it was not "a ghoul," but a female presence trained from its infancy to perfect self-posses-sion, and to a complete knowledge of the etiquette per-taining to its sex and age — a little princess, the out-come of one of the most highly artificial systems of civilisation.

Imagine some lamps upon the floor, with the orches-tra behind them, the *kotos* on the floor, the music on lacquer desks, such as are used in temples ; and at the other end of the room, ourselves lounging in easy chairs. Into the open space between us this being glided, made a profound bow, which, like the bow of royalty, included the whole company, and remained standing like a statue till the music recommenced. On her entrance she was dressed in a *kimono* of rich striped silk, with a girdle of scarlet brocade. Her hair was divided circularly, and the centre drawn up in loops, mixed with scarlet *crêpe*, and secured by a gay pin. The rest hung quite straight and smooth behind and down each cheek, while the front was cut straight and short and combed down to her eyebrows, much in the style of a digger Indian. Her face was so whitened with powder, that no trace of "complex-ion" could be seen, and her lower lip was reddened. After a short time she returned to her attendants, who stood in the lobby, and re-appeared in a *kimono* of white silk *crêpe* and *hakama* of scarlet satin, such as the Empress wears, and with a fan of large size and extreme beauty in her hand.

Again the instruments wailed and screeched forth their fearful discords, and the miniature court lady entertained us with two prolonged dances illustrative of the music, which represented the four seasons. Really, the performance was not a dance at all, but a series of dramatic posturings executed with faultless accuracy. Much use was made of the fan, the little figure swayed rhythmically, and the feet, though they moved but little, were occasionally used to *stamp* an emphasis, as in the ancient lyric drama. The expression of the face never changed; it might have been a mask. We were completely ignored, the upturned eyes heeded us not, the training was perfect, the dramatic abstraction complete. The perfect self-possession with which this little "princess" went through the dance was most remarkable, and the bow at the end, which once more included the whole audience, was a work of art. The dignity was painful, not ludicrous. I often wished that the small maiden would falter a little, or be embarrassed, or show some consciousness of our presence. Nor when it was over and she had received our thanks, was there the slightest relapse into childhood. Mr. de Saumarez, who is passionately fond of Japanese children, vainly tried to win her into friendliness, but she scarcely spoke; she was absolutely indifferent; the face remained motionless; the dignity was real, not a veneering.

Of the musical performance, as is fitting, I write with great diffidence. If I was excruciated, and experienced twinges of acute neuralgia, it may have been my own fault. The performers were happy, and Mr. Satow's calm, thoughtful face showed no trace of anguish. Oriental music is an agonising mystery to me. I wondered at the time, and still wonder, whether the orchestral music of the Temple on Mount Zion would not

have been equally discordant to western ears. A gulf
not to be spanned divides the harmonies of the East
from those of the West. The performers were anxious
to hear some of our music, and Mrs. Mounsey played
some of our most beautiful and plaintive airs, the musicians standing round her with a look of critical intelligence on their faces, which was not hopeful. They
thanked her gracefully, but even their Oriental politeness was unable to fabricate a compliment. Then she
played the "Dead March" in *Saul* with more than
funereal slowness, but an almost scornful criticism sat
upon their faces, the instrument and the "March" alike
were obviously vapid, trivial, and destitute of feeling.
These faces were all well-bred and keenly intelligent.

There were five *kotos*, two *shô*, a Corean *fuyé* or flute,
and eventually a Japanese *fuyé*. There were two or
three vocal performances. These *may* have obeyed
some rules, but the vocalists certainly did not take
parts, and each seemed at liberty to execute excursions
of his own devising. The music was absolutely monotonous, and inflicted a series of disappointments, for
every time that it seemed to tremble upon the verge of
a harmony it relapsed into utter dissonance. There was
no *piano*, it was all *forte*, *crescendo*, and *fortissimo*. Dr.
Mueller says, however — and he has studied the Japanese and their music intelligently — "If I am asked
what impression our music makes upon the Japanese, I
am sure I shall not be far wrong in saying that they
find it far more detestable than we do theirs. A prominent Japanese said, not to me, indeed, for their politeness would forbid it, 'Children, coolies, and women
may find pleasure in European music; but an educated
Japanese can never tolerate it!'"

Japanese music, like most of their arts and sciences,
is mainly Chinese and Corean, and its theory has the

usual spirit of mystical Chinese speculation, which, basing the forces and phenomena of nature upon the number *five*, declares that as sounds belong to such phenomena, there must be *five* tones, but in stringed instruments the Japanese make use of chromatic divisions, though the five tones alone are recognised officially. The key-notes themselves stand in a definite relation to the months, so that in each month of the twelve a separate and perfectly defined key rules, so that in each the murmuring of the wind in wind instruments is confined to a special key! I will not lead you farther into the fog in which I speedily found myself in spite of Mr. Satow's possibly lucid explanations, as even the initiated say that Japanese music is incomprehensible, partly because the text of much of the older music has been lost, and the players no longer know the meaning formerly attached to it.

Our complicated instruments, such as those with valves, key-boards, and hammers, are unknown. The Japanese use only stringed instruments, which are played either with a bow or with various kinds of sharpened appliances, wind instruments of wood or shell with metal tongues, and instruments of percussion, made of wood or metal, in which stretched skins are used.

The *koto* has several varieties, one of which has been known for 1500 years. The special one played at Mr. Satow's has 13 strings of waxed silk stretched from two immovable bridges, placed on a sounding-board of very hard wood 6 feet long, standing on four very low feet, with two openings on the under side. It is played with ivory finger caps, and always, before beginning, the performers rubbed their hands vigorously together.

The *shô* is a beautiful-looking instrument, richly decorated in gold, and exquisitely finished. It has seventeen pipes of very different lengths, let into a wind chest, each pipe being provided with a metal tongue. Its sounds, taken singly, are powerful and highly melodious. It is used as the fundamental instrument in tuning in the Japanese orchestras, it leads the melody, and the voice is always in unison with it. The *kangura fuyé*, or Japanese flute, claims an antiquity of twelve centuries, and the *koma fuyé*, or Corean flute, is also very ancient.

In all Japanese wind instruments the measure of the skill of the player is the length of time for which he can hold on a note. The power and penetrating qualities of the *shô* and flutes are tremendous; they leave not a single nerve untortured! The vocal performance was most excruciating. It seemed to me to consist of a hyena-like howl, long and high (a high voice being equivalent to a good voice), varied by frequent guttural, half-suppressed sounds, a bleat, or more respectfully "an impure shake," very delicious to a musically-educated Japanese audience which is both scientific and highly critical, but eminently distressing to European ears. Another source of pain to me is that the tuning of the *koto* harmonises with our *minor scale*, the fourth and seventh being omitted in deference to the number *five*.

Altogether it was a most interesting evening, and I was most favourably impressed with the grave courtesy, musical enthusiasm, and strictly Japanese demeanour of the amateurs, and sincerely hope that whatever be the fate of the " *Music* of the Future," the *manners* of the future will be the same as the manners of the present.

I have been purposing to go to Kiyôto, by the Naka-sendo, or inland mountain route, a journey of fourteen days, and have engaged a servant interpreter for the impossible task of replacing Ito! The rain, however has never ceased for four days, and at the last moment I have been obliged to give up this land journey, the less regretfully, as my new servant, though a most respectable-looking man, knows hardly any English, and I shrink from the solitude of detentions in rain and snow in lonely and elevated *yadoyas.*

Lady Parkes and the children are shortly going to England, and this pleasant home, in which I have received unbounded kindness and hospitality, will be broken up ere I return. Lady Parkes carries with her the good-will and regret of the whole foreign community, for, besides the official and semi-official courtesies and hospitalities which she has shown as a necessity of Sir Harry's position, she has given liberally of those sympathies in sorrow and of those acts of thoughtful and unostentatious kindness, which are specially appreciated by those who are "strangers in a strange land." People only need to be afflicted in "mind, body, or estate," to be sure of soft, kind words genuinely spoken, and generous attempts at alleviation. Gossip and unkind speech have been met by quiet coldness, and she has laboured long and earnestly to promote good feeling among all classes. She will be much missed by the higher classes of Japanese women, for she has used all the opportunities within her power to win their confidence and friendship, striving quietly to bring them forward, and to encourage them to take a more active part in the influential sphere of social duty. Tôkiyô and Yokohama are about to show their regret for her departure by giving her magnificent farewell entertainments.

My last day has come, and the rain still falls in torrents from a dingy sky !　　　　　　　　　I. L. B.

A MISSIONARY CENTRE.

The *Hiroshima Maru* — A Picturesque Fishing Fleet — A Kind Reception — A Mission Centre — A Model Settlement — The Native Town — Foreign Trade — The Girls' Home — Bible Classes — The First Christian Newspaper — Defects in Mission Schools — Manners and Etiquette — "Missionary Manners" — The Truth Foreshadowed — Separation in Foreign Society — A Vow.

KÔBE, *October* 20.

THE day before I left Tôkiyô, the rain fell in such torrents that I could not even send my servant into Yokohama with my baggage; the next day I dispensed with him, giving him a suitable compensation, and have not yet been suffered to miss him.

On a cool and brilliant afternoon, dashing through the blue water, amidst crowds of *sampans*, in the *Juno's* steam-launch, and afterwards on the broad white deck of the Shanghai mail steamer, *Hiroshima Maru*, with Fuji standing out in his magnificent loneliness against a golden sky — a violet dome crested with snow, I was a little in love with Yokohama — at a distance! That *Hiroshima*, a large American sidewheel, deck-over-deck, unrigged steamer, is a historic boat, for she was the *Golden Age* on the old Panama route, and, in the palmy days of California, used to carry 1000 passengers at a time to the golden land. One of her large cabins is still called the El Dorado, and the other L'Esperance, and the last being allotted to me, proved a good omen, for I never made a more charming voyage, Captain

Furber's genial kindness, excellent accommodation, a refined *cuisine*, brilliant sunshine, grand coast views, and a waveless sea, all combining to make it pleasant. After such dingy, drowning weather, one appreciates the sunshine heartily.

On the evening of the second day, ahead, astern, around, near and far, wherever we could see, great flaring lights were bobbing and curtseying just above the water, and as they drifted by, and the eye became accustomed to them, they appeared as a confused multitude of fitful fires hanging over the bows of hundreds of fishing-boats, plying their trade at the mouth of the Kii Channel, by which we were entering the inland sea, and groups of figures always struggling at the boats' heads, now in the glare, and now in the darkness, the fiery light in its redness and fitfulness, and the phosphorescent light in its whiteness and steadiness, formed one of the most picturesque illuminations I ever beheld. These lights are much used in fishing, specially for squid. By long wooden handles the fishermen hold over the side of their boats iron cages, in which they burn, like the Ainos, birch bark strips, which give a clear and vivid light, very speedily extinct. It is supposed that the fish, confused by the glare, are more readily taken. I wished the followers of Yebis a good haul that night, for the sake of the pleasure they had given me.

We anchored here in the early morning in torrents of rain, accompanied by a high wind, and neither had ceased when Mr. Gulick came off for me, and in a very short time took me to his New England home. He is a son of one of the early missionaries to the Sandwich Islands, who has six missionary children, four of whom are in Japan, three living here under the same roof with their venerable mother. Mrs. Gulick is also a born

Sandwich Islander, a sister of my friends Mrs. Sever ance and Mrs. Austin of Hawaii; the house is built like a Hilo house, and has many Polynesian "effects" about it, and you can imagine how we revel in Hawaiian talk, and how the fires of Kilauea, the glorious forests of Hilo, the waving palms, the dimpling seas, the coral caves, the purple nights, and all the never-to-beforgotten beauties of those enchanted islands, mingle in our speech with some personal recollections and some gossip, and I dream my tropical dream once more.

This is the headquarters of mission-work under the auspices of the "American Board." Somehow when one thinks of Kôbe it is less as a Treaty Port than as a Mission centre. It was partly to see the process of missionary work that I came. Everything is at high pressure, and a hearty, hopeful spirit prevails among all who have got over the initial difficulties of the language, which press heavily on new-comers. The missionaries are all intensely American in speech, manner, and tone, and set about their work with a curious practicality and a confident apportionment of means to ends which I have not seen before in this connection. They are quite a community, mixing little, if at all, with the other foreign residents, but forming a very affectionate and intimate family among themselves. Kôbe being a place of energetic effort, and of reputed success, is the spot in Japan in which to gauge in some degree the prospects of Christianity; but I shall defer saying much on the subject till I have been to Kiyôto and Ôsaka.

Kôbe is a bright, pleasant-looking settlement, by far the most prepossessing of the "Treaty Ports" that I have seen, situated on an inland sea, on the other side of which the mountainous island of Kiushiu rises. Westwards, wooded points and promontories, melting into a blue haze, or fiery purple in the sunset, appear to close the channel, while eastwards a stretch of land-locked water, crowded with white sails, leads to the city of Ôsaka, the commercial capital of Japan. A range of steep, somewhat bare, and very picturesquely-shaped hills, with pines in their hollows, and temples, *torii*, and tea-houses on their heights, rises immediately behind Kôbe, which, with Hiogo, the old Japanese town, of which it is a continuation, is packed along the shore for a distance of three miles, the Kiyôto and Hiogo Railway, opened in great state by the Mikado in February 1877, running through the town, down to a pier which enables ships of large tonnage to receive cargo direct from the railway trucks. The Foreign Concession, beautifully and regularly laid out on a grand scale for the population which it has never attracted, is at the east end. It is a "model settlement," well lighted with gas, and supplied with water, kept methodically clean, and efficiently cared for by the police. The Bund has a fine stone embankment, a grass parade, and a magnificent carriage-road, with the British, American, and German Consulates, and some "imposing" foreign residences on the other side. Several short streets run back from this, crossing a long one parallel with the Bund. The side-walks are very broad, and well paved with stones laid edgewise, with curb-stones and handsome paved water-ways, and the carriage-roads are broad and beautifully kept. The foreign houses are spacious and solid, and the railroad, and the station and its environments, are of the most approved English construction.

But where are the people? Roads without houses, carriage-ways without carriages, side-walks without foot-passengers, and a solitude so dreary that three men stopping in the street to talk is a sight which might

collect the rest of the community to stare at it, are fea
tures of what was intended to be an important place.
It is mainly English, but there are only about 170

A HIOGO BUDDHA.

British residents, and this includes all the British firms
from Ôsaka, who migrated here when the railroad was
opened. There is an English "omnibus" Church behind the Bund, in which service is conducted once on
Sunday by an American Congregational clergyman,

and once by Mr. Foss, the missionáry of the English "S.P.G." A number of foreign, wooden houses straggle up the foot-hills at the back, some of them unmistakable English bungalows, while those which look like Massachusetts homesteads are occupied by American missionaries. In spite of the solitude and stagnation of the streets of the settlement, Kôbe is a pertinaciously cheerful-looking place. In sunshine it is all ablaze with light, and even in wind and rain its warm colouring saves it from dismalness. A large native town has grown up at Kôbe, as a continuation of Hiogo, and the two are active, thriving, and bustling; their narrow streets being thronged with people, *kurumas*, and oxcarts, while sweeping roofs of temples on heights and flats, *torii*, great bronze Buddhas, colossal stone lanterns, and other tokens of prevailing Buddhism, give the native town a variety and picturesqueness very pleasing to the eye. The crowded junk harbour, the number of large steamers, both Japanese and British, lying off the Bund, and the blue mountains across the water, make it as pretty to look from as to look at.

As at Hakodaté, foreign trade is decreasing, and Japanese trade is rapidly increasing. It is quite interesting to find how widely the exports differ in different parts of Japan. In Yezo it was fish, seaweed, and skins, here it is mainly tea, silk, copper, vegetable wax, tobacco, camphor, mushrooms, and fans, of which *four millions* were exported last year, mainly to America. The rapid increase in the native town is quite wonderful; it is said that Hiogo and Kôbe between them have a population of 50,000 people.

The Secretary of the American Board of Missions most kindly wrote, commending me to the missionaries here, and I am made very welcome consequently. Yesterday evening we went to tea at the "Girls' Home," a boarding-school for twenty-seven Japanese girls, the prettiest house in Kôbe, in very attractive grounds. This is conducted by three ladies, with Japanese assistance. The girls live in Japanese fashion, but learn our music, in which they are very anxious to excel. The ladies who keep it speak Japanese fluently, and do a great deal of outside mission-work, not only in Kôbe, but in villages at a distance, where they hold meetings for women.

This morning I went to the Bible classes, which are attended by forty-six men and twelve women, some of them quite elderly. The plan is for each woman to read a few verses aloud from the New Testament, and give her ideas upon them, and such ideas they are as would never occur to a European, or to any one who had had the *sough* of Christianity about his ears from infancy. They ask many questions, and show an interest and vivacity which, at least, must keep the teacher alert, and there was so much laughter that one would hardly have imagined the Bible to be the subject. No traditional reverence has gathered round it, they possess but a few fragments, and it is to them simply a story of facts with a moral code attached. Several of their questions were startling, but natural. "What is the name of God's wife?" one woman asked, on hearing of the Divine Son. We visited more classes where there were 100 pupils, and then went to church, where the sermon was cold and hard, as if Christianity had grown sapless and wizened with age.

This Mission has at Kôbe nine men missionaries, all but one with wives, and five single ladies; in Ôsaka four men and three single ladies, and in Kiyôto, three men and one single lady. Two are Medical Missionaries, and through their popular work several villages within treaty limits have been opened to Christianity,

two of which now possess churches and pastors of theii
own. In Kôbe there are three preaching places, and
two "out-stations;" in Ôsaka three, and one "out-
station;" in Kiyôto three, and two "out-stations," besides numerous women's meetings and classes. Nearly
all the missionaries itinerate regularly within treaty
limits, and irregularly with passports beyond them
They have girls' boarding-schools in the three towns,
and, as another agency, a newspaper with a Japanese
editor, but under Mr. Gulick's supervision, the *Shichi
Ichi Zappo*, or Weekly Messenger, established in January 1876. It has a circulation of about 1100 among
native Christians, and this is always slowly increasing
It gives general news, but as it abstains from unfavourable criticism on the actions of the Government, and
praises it dexterously every now and then, it has escaped a "press warning." It treats of the progress of
Christianity, and of other subjects interesting to the
professors of the new faith. It may become a really
valuable organ if its expression of native Christian
opinion is not unduly hampered. As, for instance just
now, the editor wrote a kindly but serious criticism on
the way in which girls' Christian schools are conducted,
setting forth that there is a failure in domestic training,
and that, consequently, young men would not, indeed
could not, seek for wives among the girls educated by
the missionaries. This seems to me the weak point of
the different female schools that I have heard of. Of
course, the first object is to give a Christian training,
and raise the standard of morality, which must be lcw
enough if it is represented truthfully by a superior sort
of girl, who told the teacher that to form connections
with foreigners is the great ambition of girls in her
position. Besides instruction in Christianity, the usual
branches of a polite education, including music, are

taught, and further time is taken up by teaching the Chinese character, which girls are very anxious to learn. In Japanese training great stress is laid upon the housewifely education, and to be accomplished in all housewifely arts is a just object of desire with every right-minded Japanese girl. This very essential part of education is almost of necessity crowded out in the foreign schools, and I have not hesitated to express my opinion to my missionary friends as to the injurious consequences. Here they sit on the floor and eat Japanese food in Japanese fashion, but in some other foreign schools they sit on chairs at dining tables, and eat meat, European fashion, with knives and forks, table napkins, if I mistake not, being used also. Very few Japanese can afford to give these luxuries to their wives. To foreigners, a girl in some degree accustomed to our usages, and speaking a little English, is, in many cases, more attractive than one solely Japanese in her language and habits, and with misguided female ambition on the one side, and the habits which prevail in the East on the other, there is much reason to fear that results may occur which would be to none so painful as to the missionaries themselves.

Another difficulty which presents itself very definitely to me, is regarding manners and etiquette. You remember Ito telling me, when I found fault with his manners, that they were "just missionary manners." It is in some cases true that the missionaries, disliking the hollowness and insincerity which underlie a good deal of Japanese politeness, discourage its courtesies as a waste of time, and that young men, who have been for some time under missionary training, are apt to shock one by a brusquerie and regardlessness of manner and attitude, which would be displeasing even in Europeans; but I don't refer to this, but to the una voidable ignorance of foreign ladies of the thousand and one details of Japanese female etiquette. Thus, I have heard a native critic say that the girls trained by the foreign ladies use their chop-sticks "disgracefully;" that they don't know at what height to carry a tray of tea; that their girdles are badly tied; that their bows are short and ungraceful; that they enter a room awkwardly, etc. This critic is a Christian, and most anxious for the success of the foreign schools.

Ah, well! If we are not a stiff-necked, we are a stiffbacked generation, and the American back is even stiffer than ours, and with the best intentions, we can never emulate the invertebrate obeisances of Orientals. Still it is very distasteful to me to see a low and graceful bow acknowledged by a hasty "bob," and all the graceful national courtesies ignored, nor does this "laying the axe to the root of the tree" of hoary national custom commend Christianity. I abhor the denationalisation of nations, and should like to see Japanese courtesies studied and met at least half-way, and the etiquette of Japanese politeness informed and infused throughout by the truth and sincerity of the religion of Jesus Christ, which enjoins courtesy and "honour" to "all men," as it enjoins truth and charity. It is noteworthy that a medical missionary here, by an almost Oriental courtesy and suavity of deportment, has commended himself so much to the upper classes and to men in influential positions, that he has obtained from Government various important openings for mission work, which his more brusque and stiff-backed brethren would have sought for years in vain. I am just writing to you what I have said to my friends with some earnestness, for the Christian religion is unpopular enough in Japan, without weighting it with the millstone of an implied and practised antagonism to the

ancient laws of good breeding, which, like the costumes, fit the people, and from which we might advan-
tageously learn not a little.

Except in a few cases the missionaries of the different denominations know nearly nothing of the two
great national faiths. Frequently, on asking the meaning of various significant heathen ceremonies, I receive
the reply, " Oh, I take no interest in their rubbish," or
" Oh, it's not worth knowing," or " Oh, it's just one of
their absurdities," or " I really have no time to get information on these matters," the last being a sufficient
reason, and certainly applicable to the Kôbe missionaries, who devote their time to their work with most
praiseworthy energy. With regard to Shintô, except
to the antiquary or student, its superstitions are simply
rubbish, but it constantly occurs to me that even the
corrupt form of Buddhism which prevails in Japan, as
it possesses an ethical code and definite teachings concerning immortality, might be used as a valuable auxil-
iary in the preaching of Christianity by a teacher who
had studied it; for all its lotus imagery, its doctrine of
purity, and its penalties for unrighteousness, are but
testimonies to the Truth that " without holiness no man
can see the Lord," and shadows of the loftier teaching
of Him to whom all that is TRUE in every creed and
age bears reverent witness.

In Kôbe, as elsewhere, there is a complete separation
between the foreign and the missionary community. It
is possible that missionaries lump the laity together as
taking no interest in their work, and shun them as being
uncongenial and antagonistic, and certainly most foreigners speak of them as of a pariah caste, and many
as if their presence in Japan were an outrage, while
scarcely any take the slightest trouble to learn what, if
any, are the results from the work of such a large num-

ber of agents. It is a pity, and many hard things are said on both sides which were better unsaid, as they are not always true.

The few days since I have arrived have gone very fast. One of my objects in coming here is to visit the Shrines of Isé, the "holy places" of Shintôism, and as yet I have not been able to see any one who has been there, or who can suggest the most interesting way of going. The servant difficulty is a great one, but Mr. Flowers, H.B.M.'s Consul, kindly says, that, if I cannot do better, an English-speaking Japanese from the Consulate shall go with me. As usual, kind people are taking much trouble to aid me. There is not much to see in these towns, except the busy street life and the large number of temples, but the walks on the hills, and the variety of views from them, are beautiful. Some of the Shintô shrines are on picturesque heights, and are approached through avenues of red *torii*. In one of these avenues, consisting of about 120 of these erections, there were miniature flag poles, seven inches long, planted at the base of every *torii*, each one with a red paper flag inscribed with Chinese characters. The translation is "The man is forty years old who makes this request. He was born in the year of the Dog. If it be granted, he will give 500 of these flags." The request was not given.　　　　　　　　　I. L. B.

THE KIYÔTO COLLEGE.

Mountain-girdled Kiyôto — Third-class Travelling — The Home of Art — The Kiyôto College — Captain Jayne — Mr. Davis — The Curriculum — Philosophical Ardour — Discussions and Difficulties — Total Abstinence — The First Christian Pastor — Japanese Impressions of Scotland — Increased Demand for the Christian Scriptures.

NIJÔSAN YASHIKI, KIYÔTO, *October* 30.

THIS is truly delightful. As the Hebrew poets loved to sing of mountain-girdled Jerusalem, so Japanese poetry extols Kiyôto, which is encompassed, not with forest-smothered ranges like those of Northern Japan, but with hills more or less rugged, wooded here, broken into grey peaks there, crimson with maples, or dark with pines, great outbreaks of yellowish rock giving warmth and variety, and the noble summit of Hiyeizan crowning the mountain wall which bounds the city on the north. On fine days, when the sun rises in pink and gold, and sets in violet and ruddy orange, these mountains pass through colours which have no names, the higher ranges beyond the Gulf of Ôsaka look faintly through a veil of delicious blue, and I grudge the radiant hours passing, because rain and mist persistently return to dim the picture. There is a pleasure in being able to agree cordially with every one, and every one loves Kiyôto.

I came here a fortnight ago with Mrs. Gulick, intending to spend two or three days alone in a *yadoya*, but on arriving found that it had been arranged that I should be received here, where I have spent a fortnight delight fully, seeing a great many of the sights with my hostess, and others with Mr. Noguchi, an English-speaking Japanese, deputed by the Governor to act as my *cicerone*.

We travelled third class, as I was most anxious to see how the "common people" behaved. The carriage was not divided higher than the shoulders, and was at once completely filled with Japanese of the poorest class. The journey lasted three hours, and I unweariedly admired the courtesy of the people to each other and to us, and their whole behaviour. It was beautiful — so well bred and kindly, such a contrast to what one would probably have seen near great seaport cities at home; and the Japanese, like the Americans, respect themselves and their neighbours by travelling in decent and cleanly clothing. Respect to age and blindness came out very prettily on the journey. Our best manners fall short of theirs in grace and kindliness. It is quite a mistake always to travel first class, for then one only hears the talk of foreigners, which is apt to be vapid and stale.

An hour's journey took us to Ôsaka; more third class cars, filled with passengers, were attached; we steamed off again, the hills drew nearer to each other; we crossed several rivers down which boats with mat sails were dropping with the current, saw the rapid Yodo, thought of Francis Xavier, and as pagodas and temple roofs appeared among the trees the train pulled up in a trim, prosaic station, where hundreds of *kuruma*-runners clamoured for our custom; and, chafing at the incongruity and profanation of a railway station in this historic capital, I realised in half an hour that Kiyôto is unlike the other cities of Japan. It is the home of art, given up to beauty, dress, and amusement; its women are pretty, their *coiffures* and girdles are bewitching, surprises of bright colour lurk about their attire; the children are pictures, there is music everywhere; beautiful tea-houses and pleasure-grounds abound, and besides all this, the city is completely girdled by a number of the grandest temples in Japan, with palaces and palace gardens of singular loveliness on the slopes of its purple hills.

This place is the American Mission School for girls,

THE ROKKUKADO.

a very large semi-Japanese house, with glass slides instead of *shôji*, and without *amado*, which makes it very cold. It is built on the site of the *yashiki* of a *kugé* or noble of the Mikado's court, and is in a spacious enclosure, with temple grounds behind it, and the sweet-toned bells of many temples make the hours musical by night and day. There is room for fifty girls, but the number is limited to eighteen at present, because Miss Starkwether, the lady principal, is alone, and seems likely to remain without American assistance. This school gives an industrial training, and Miss Stark-wether is most conscientiously anxious that the girls should attend strictly to the rules of Japanese etiquette and good breeding.

This mission, in this rigidly secluded city, is a most interesting one, for it has been brought about mainly by Japanese. If you have read my letters carefully, you will long have known that no foreigners, unless in Japanese employment, can live outside of treaty limits. In this case a Japanese Company, consisting of one Christian Japanese, and two who are not Christians, holds the college and school property, and employs as teachers, under a civil contract, Mr. Davis, Mr. Learned, and Miss Starkwether, who, as its servants, have obtained permits to live here for five years. The governor of the city is opposed strongly to Christian-ity, and permits of residence have been refused to the two ladies who were to assist in the girls' school.

Close by is the Kiyôto College, the most interesting feature of mission work in Japan. The college came about in this way. In Higo province, in the island of Kiushiu, there is a Government school, in which an American, Captain Jayne, who was really a teacher of military tactics, taught science in English for five years, his pupils being young men of the *samurai* class, many of whom intended to enter the army. Under his influence about forty of these became Christians, and anxious to spread Christianity in Japan. Some of them were much opposed, and even turned adrift by their parents, but, remaining stead fast, desired theological instruction, and this Japanese company, assisted by Americans, bought this ground and established the college. There are over 100 youths in it now, 60 of whom are Christians, and between 40 and 50 are studying for the Christian ministry. Though the object of the college is a Christian one, attendance at the morning prayers is not compulsory, neither is the receiving of religious instruction. Practically, however, few of the students reject either.

Mr. Davis, the head, is genial, enthusiastic, vehement, and, what is so rare in this day, a firm believer in the truth of what he teaches. He is sanguine regarding the spread of Christianity in Japan, and his students imbibe something of his hopeful spirit. He distinguished himself in the American war, and a soldierly frankness and spirit are so blended with a very earnest Christianity, that his military rank clings to him, and he is often called "Colonel Davis." Mr. Learned, a very silent but scholarly man, is his coadjutor, and Mr. Neesima, a Japanese, at present the only ordained Japanese pastor, and some younger men, assist. The course is very extensive, extending over five years, and the theological students are anxious to increase it to six! The ordinary course includes Japanese, reading, spelling, language lessons, international and common school geography, international arithmetic, written arithmetic, algebra, general and Japanese history, geometry, natural philosophy, chemistry, physiology, rhetoric, with Japanese and English composition and declamation, and a course of Biblical study. The theological course includes mental and moral philosophy, sacred geography, theology, homiletics, pastoral theology, and church history, with classes on prophecy and the Epistles. The weakness in the teaching staff is obvious, but permits have been applied for for two more foreign teachers, and in the meantime, by energy and enthusiasm, Mr. Davis gets the work carried on.

For several mornings I have gone to the college to hear some of the classes taught. The first day I arrived at the end of morning prayers, and was surprised to see how very few decline either the prayers or the religious instruction. All my acquaintances among the Tôkiyô teachers speak of the good conduct, courtesy, docility, and appetite for severe and continued study which characterise their students, and it is just the same here. I pity the instructors who have to deal off-hand with the difficulties of these earnest youths, many of whose questions show them to be deep thinkers, and indisposed to accept anything on trust, or to pass over the most trivial matter without understanding it. Their absorption in study is so complete that they never even look at me. I find the mental and moral philosophy classes peculiarly interesting, these being subjects on which the young men are keenly alive, and thought in these directions is greatly stimulated by the extensive circulation of the works of Mill, Herbert Spencer, and Comte; while the researches and speculations of Darwin and Huxley tend to intensify the interest in a special direction. The students, as a whole, are remarkably ugly, and it is curious to see their earnest, thoughtful faces, several of them with spectacles, drinking in thoughtfully and critically the philosophy of Sir W. Hamilton, an alien philosophy in an alien tongue.

Mr. Davis lectures for half an hour, and in the remaining half the students question him and state their difficulties in English. One of their questions, or rather difficulties, as to the possibility of conceiving of colour without form has taken up a great part of two mornings. Obviously they decline to accept anything either from teacher or class-book without understanding it. Many of their questions are carefully prepared, and are very tough. There is less enthusiasm, as is natural, in the Church History class. It must discourage these neophytes to find that Christianity was scarcely brighter or purer as it neared its source, and that its history is full of wrangling and bitterness. It was odd to hear the differences between the Jesuits and the Jansenists discussed in Japan, and to notice the intense interest which the students showed in anything which bore, even remotely, on the special tenets of Calvin. This morning one of the classes was a debating-club rather than a class, the subject started being, "Whether the eye furnishes us with facts, or only with data from which we elaborate facts," and the students were prepared with quotations from Reid, Stewart, Brown, and Hamilton. In the next class a student was called upon to give the distinctive features of the Baconian teaching, and this he did so admirably and with such conciseness, that his definition might have been printed. I was very much interested, also, with a class on "the Messianic Psalms," the seventy-second being the subject. The hour was spent almost entirely in the suggestion of difficulties by the students, who failed to see that it has any Messianic reference, and regarded it as applicable to Solomon. They had fortified themselves by a very careful study of the Old Testament in English, and their honest difficulties on this and other subjects are far removed from the flippancy of doubt. Some of them are quite new, and show very forcibly the questions which arise when the Bible is presented for the first time to an educated people; others might occur to any one among ourselves, such as, "You say Christ and His Father are one. Then, when Christ was on earth, there was no God in heaven; to whom, then, did men pray?" and, "If in the old days a pious Jew did not understand the references in a prophecy or its meaning, would the prophet be able to explain it?"

These young men bear their own expenses and wear the Japanese dress, but their Japanese politeness has much deteriorated, which is a pity, and the peculiar style of manner and attitude which we recognise as American does not sit well upon them. They are an earnest body of students, their moral tone is very high, they all abstain from *saké*, they are all heartily convinced of the truth of Christianity, they are anxious to be furnished with every weapon of attack against the old heathenism and the new philosophies, and they mean to spend their lives in preaching Christianity. Several of them already preach in the vacation, and just now, one, named Hongma, is meeting with singular success at Hikone on Lake Biwa, the changed lives of some of the converts being matter of notoriety. It is to such men as these that the conversion of Japan will be owing if their sanguine views are realised; but who can say what the Japanese church of the future will be, or whether its teachings will be in accordance with those of any of our creeds?

The practical sagacity with which the Americans manage their missions is worthy of notice. So far from seeking for a quantity of converts, they are mainly solicitous for quality. They might indeed baptize hundreds where they are content with tens. [The same remark applies to Dr. Palm and the missionaries of the C.M.S. at Hakodaté and Niigata.] There are hundreds of men and women scattered throughout this neighbourhood who are practically Christians, who even meet together to read the Bible, and who subscribe for Christian objects, but have never received baptism. Two matters test the sincerity of would-be converts. The first is that they are expected to build their own churches, support their own pastors, and sustain their own poor, and the next, that abstinence from *saké*, though not an article of membership, is tacitly required, the missionaries of the American Board being, without an exception, rigid " teetotallers." *Saké* enters so largely into all social customs and ceremonials that the abandonment of it on the part of the converts involves a nearly complete social separation from their heathen friends. You will remember the important part which *saké* played in the marriage ceremony at Kubota, of which, indeed, the formal drinking of twenty-seven cups of it constituted the obvious part. The Kôbe Christians have so altogether broken with the old usage that recently their marriages have been celebrated by a religious service at church, the legal registration being in the office of the *Kôchô*, and *saké* has been altogether banished from the marriage-feast. The Kôbe church, just opened, cost its 350 members 915 dollars. They pay their pastor, provide dispensary medicines for those of their number who are too poor to pay for them, and compensate such of their members as are too poor to abstain from Sunday work for their loss of a day's wages. The making the congregations self-supporting, and training the Japanese Christians to independence, is part of the work of all the American missionaries. Probably, after a time, when the number of converts is largely increased, they may evolve both a theology and a church order which will surprise their teachers. I have had several interesting conversations with some of the students who speak English well, and I gather from them that they earnestly desire to establish a national church, not altogether on the lines of the pattern supplied to them; and it is not impossible that in religion, as in other matters, the foreigners may first be used, and then be dispensed with. In the meantime, the progress, slow as it is, which Christianity is making among the upper classes, is very interesting, and the interest is focussed among these young men.

Yesterday evening, after a delightful interview with Akamatz, the most influential priest of the Monto sect of Buddhists, I went to tea with Mr. and Mrs. Neesima in their pleasant Japanese house. The tea was on a table, we sat on chairs, and there was no difference between the meal and one at a foreign house except for the exquisitely beautiful porcelain on the table, some of it old Satsuma. Such treasures at home would be locked up in cabinets. Mr. Neesima is a *samurai*. He is a Christian pastor, ordained in America, and teaches natural philosophy, etc., in the Kiyôto College. He wears a European dress, and having been abroad for many years, knows how to wear it. His wife teaches needlework in the girls' home, and dresses as a Japanese. Mr. N.'s study is just like a literary man's room at home, with its walls well covered with English and American editions of our standard works in several departments. He has relations in very influential positions, and has himself served the Government abroad. He was brought up a Shintôist, and as he grew up became an atheist. Having received the best education which could be got, he went to Tôkiyô to learn Dutch, in order that he might visit America, and study navigation and foreign shipbuilding, with the view of introducing the latter trade into Japan, whose prosperity, even then, was very dear to him. In Tôkiyô he saw some Christian tracts in Chinese, and learned from them the notion of a Creator with claims on all His creatures. With the strong sense of filial duty in which the Japanese are brought up, the decided opposition of his parents had hindered him from leaving home, but he became convinced that if the Christian God had indeed created him, He had a prior claim to his obedience, and that duty compelled him to go and strive to advance the prosperity of his country, which he felt must be very dear to the Creator.

At that time Japanese were prohibited from leaving Japan, and a penalty of death [practically only imprisonment] awaited the disobedient on their return, though it was not likely to be inflicted on any one who should bring back a valuable art. With the object of learning Christianity and visiting America, Mr. N. went to Yezo, but after managing to get on board a ship bound for China, found, to his disappointment, that the American captain knew nothing about religion. On landing in China he sold his two swords, bought a New Testament, obtained a considerable intellectual acquaintance with Christianity, and on the long voyage to Boston, acquired English, which he speaks with considerable freedom and vigour. In Boston he fell among people with whom Christianity was a life as well as a creed, passed through the mysterious change known as " conversion," and, under the power of the new impulse, abandoned shipbuilding, believing that he was bound to spread a religion which would bring a better and truer prosperity to his country than trade, spent five years in studying theology at Andover, and three years in a scientific course at Amherst, with a break in which he accompanied Mr. Tanaka, the acting Minister of Education, to England, France, Sweden, Denmark, Russia, and Germany, eventually remaining for some time in Berlin. On returning home after being ordained in America, he organised the company by which the teachers in this college are engaged, and devotes himself to the Christianising and elevating of his countrymen, in the full belief that it is through the first that the last must come. These are merely the bald outlines of a most interesting history. There was much that was singular in his adventures, as I have heard from others, his own modesty making him withhold some of the most interesting events in his history, but I am afraid of repeating them incorrectly, so I leave them out. Mr. N. is a gentleman to begin with, and has quiet, easy, courteous manners. He is a genial, enlightened Christian, and an intensely patriotic Japanese. He gives a sad account of the lack of truth, and the general corruption of morals, among his countrymen. He takes a less hopeful view of the prospects of Christianity than his American colleagues, thinks that there is a great unlikelihood of its spreading much in the cities, but hopes for successful results from the preaching of the students in the country districts. I asked him what, in his opinion, are the leading faults of his countrymen, and he replied without a moment's hesitation, " Lying and licentiousness." It is curious that two Japanese, holding high official positions, and both heathen, should have given me exactly the same answer.

I asked him what made the greatest impression upon him in England, and he said, " The drunkenness, and the innocent faces of the children." The former, specially in Scotland, horrified him. He supposed, from his New England experience, that " Christians " did not put wine on their tables, and told Mr. Tanaka so ; consequently, when Mr. T. was entertained at a dinner where wine played a prominent part, " he supposed that the Scotch were not Christians." Mr. Neesima was in Edinburgh at the time of the General Assemblies, and was astonished to find that " a good deal of wine was drunk by ministers at dinners." " Some of them got very stupid and sleepy with it," he said ; " I wish they could know how sad and sore my heart felt for them." This seemed to impress him more than the Commissioner's procession, or the Free Assembly in a crowded and hot debate. He spoke at some length as to the spread of the "English Philosophy" among the educated youth of Japan.

You know that only parts of the Bible have, as yet, been translated. The Old Testament, though the translators are hard at work upon it, is not printed, and the New consists of the four Gospels, the Acts, Romans, Galatians, Hebrews, and St. John's Epistles. I wonder what the effect of the Mosaic record, and of the importance attached to the Jewish nation, will be on people who believe Japan the sum and centre of all things? The demand for the books of the New Testament is increasing rapidly. Very many thousand copies have been sold during the last year, and there must be altogether a prodigious number in circulation.

I. L. B.

THE MONTO SECT.

The Protestants of Buddhism — The "English-Speaking" Priest —
The Nishi-Honguwanji Temple — A Monto Altar — Nirvana —
Hidéyoshi's Summer Palace — Metempsychosis — Buddha as a
Democrat — The Prospects of Christianity — The Priest's Estimate
of Belief in England — The Conflict of Opinion in Japan — A
Question.

NIJÔSAN YASHIKI, KIYÔTO, *November* 1.

OF the many sects and sub-sects into which Buddhism
is divided, none interests me so much as the Shinshiu,
sometimes called the Monto Sect, founded by Shinran
in 1262. Protesting against celibacy, penance, fasting,
pilgrimages, nunneries, monasteries, cloistered and her-
mit isolation from society, charms, amulets, and the
reading of the Scriptures in an unknown tongue, claiming freedom of thought and action, and emancipation
from Shintô, traditional, and State influence, and holding that the family is the source and example of
purity, Shinran married a noble lady of Kiyôto, and
founded a married priesthood. If the Monto is not
the largest sect, it stands first in intelligence, influence,
and wealth, it is putting forth immense energies, and
has organised theological schools on a foreign system,
in which its acolytes are being trained in Buddhist and
Western learning for the purpose of enabling them not
only to resist or assail both Shintô and Christianity,
but the corruptions of the Buddhist faith. At this
hour new college buildings are arising in Kiyôto to be
splendidly equipped for teaching purposes, and the

plan is to send certain of the young priests to England
to learn Sanskrit, and to fortify themselves with arguments against Christianity; and it is not in Kiyôto
alone that this vigorous sect is training a priesthood to
meet the needs of the day.

Foremost in this movement, which has for its object
a new reformation, and the re-establishment of Buddhism as a moral power in Japan, is Akamatz, a priest of
great intellect, high culture, indomitable energy, wide
popularity, and far-reaching ambitions for the future of
his faith. He spent some years in England, studying
Sanskrit and Christianity, and is known to the Japanese in Kiyôto as "the English-speaking priest." Mr.
de Saumarez gave me a letter to him, and he wrote me
a note in English, asking me to go and see him at the
Nishi-Honguwanji temple.

The Monto sect builds large temples in the centres
of great cities, and often in pairs, connected by a
covered corridor. These are the temples whose huge
sweeping roofs and vast enclosures near the railway
station impressed me on the day of my arrival, and not
less impressive were they to-day as I approached them
in my favourite *kuruma* through streets of shrine and
idol makers, in whose shops the gorgeous paraphernalia
of a gorgeous worship make a resplendent display.
The comely walls with heavily tiled roofs, the broad,
granite-lined water-channels outside, along which the
water ripples brightly, the massive gateways which
give access to the temple-courts, the gardens with their
bridges, artificial lakes and islands, the luxurious pleasure-grounds of the summer palace of an ancient Shôgun,
and the imposing group formed by the twin temples,
with their background of enormous trees, are among
the vastest sights of Kiyôto.

The sky was murky and threatening, a drift of brown

cloud lay across Hiyeizan, occasional gusts of wind lifted the sand in the temple-courts, and the gloom seemed to suit these grand structures of an ancient faith. In the stately courts there were neither priests nor worshippers, and I shivered as I crossed them, guided by my *kuruma*-runner, to whom the utterance of the simple word Akamatz conveyed my wishes. He deposited me at the side of the great temple, where a flight of steps led up to a small room where two priests were writing, and there, taking off my boots, I waited for the "English-speaking priest." I was disappointed with his appearance. He is barely five feet high, and decidedly ill-favoured, with hair about an inch long, very bristly, a bristly black mustache, and bristly scanty beard. His brow, however, is fine, and his eyes are bright and keen. He wore a cassock of figured blue brocade, a deep chasuble of figured brown silk grenadine, and a stole of crimson cloth of gold, and carried a brown rosary in his left hand. In describing Buddhist vestments, it is impossible to avoid drifting into the use of terms by which the vestments in the Roman Church are known. Akamatz is very gentlemanly and courteous, speaks English remarkably well, with great vigour of expression, and talked, as it seemed to me, with surprising frankness. He took me over the temples, and showed me all that was to be seen. My visit lasted for three hours, and I would gladly have made it longer, I was so deeply interested with his mind and conversation.

This great temple of Nishi-Honguwanji may be regarded as the cathedral of the Monto sect,[1] and the

[1] The statements concerning the Monto sect and its tenets, which are given in this Letter, rest on the authority of Mr. Akamatz. I have not met a European whose information on the subject is sufficient to enable me to judge of their accuracy ; but the character of this priest stands very high, and there is no reason to suppose that he misinformed me.

Abbot or High Priest and its other dignitaries represent Bishop, Dean, and Chapter. They are at the
head of 10,000 Monto temples, whose financial and
ecclesiastical concerns they manage, and whose patronage they dispense. There are 100 priests here, besides
acolytes, but much of their business is secular. They
look very unlike ordinary "*bonzes*," because of their
hair and beards, and there is little of the stupid or
sanctimonious expression which is usual on the faces
of Buddhist priests. Their creed does not require anything like asceticism or separation from the duties and
delights of other men, and in so much is healthier and
more human.

We walked round the outside of the public rooms,
which are numerous, large, and lofty, by a deep corridor,
from which we saw the interior, through the open *shôji*,
and the dull gleam of rich dead gold hinted of the
artistic treasures within. For in these dimly-lighted
rooms, most of which have been set apart for guests for
centuries, there are paintings nearly 300 years old, and
the walls are either panelled in gold, or are formed of
fusuma, heavily overlaid with gold-leaf, on which, in the
highest style of Japanese art, are depicted various sacred
emblems — the lotus, the stork, the peony, and the
Cleyera Japonica — executed very richly and beautifully with slightly conventionalised fidelity to nature.
From thence we passed into the great temple, the simple splendour of which exceeds anything I have yet
seen. The vast oblong space has a flat roof, supported
on many circular pillars of finely-planed wood; a third
part is railed off for the sanctuary; the panels of the
folding-doors and the panels at the back are painted
with flowers on a gold ground; behind a black lacquer
altar stands a shrine of extreme splendour, gleaming in
the coloured twilight; but on the high altar itself there

were only two candlesticks, two vases of pure white chrysanthemums, and a glorious bronze incense burner. An incense burner was the only object on the low altar. Besides these there were six black lacquer desks, on each desk a roll of litanies, and above the altar six lamps burned low. It was imposingly magnificent. "As handsome as a Monto altar," is a proverbial saying. This sect rejects images and all sensuous paraphernalia addressed to the popular taste, and, according to Mr. Akamatz, teaches "the higher life" by the rule of the Scriptures, which, written in characters of the unlearned, and in the tongue of the common people, "are able to make them wise" unto a salvation which can only be obtained by purity and righteousness. Furthermore, it teaches that the maxims and doctrines promulgated by the other sects are corruptions of the truth; that celibate vows, fasting, and abstinence from the moderate use of the good things of life, are inventions of the vanity or superstition of men; that a married priesthood is the best conservator of the purity of society; and that priestcraft, in the ordinary sense, is a delusion and a snare. Their sons, if not by birth, at all events by adoption from the family of another priest, succeed them, and formerly, in time of war, they have laid aside their robes, put on armour, and formed themselves into battalions.

We passed by a covered bridge into the other temple, in which the principal object is a gorgeous shrine, in which Sakya-muni stands with his hands folded, looking calmly down upon flowers, candles, and an incense burner, as calmly as he looks upon thousands of worshippers on festal days, the spiritual children of those who, for 2000 years, have called him blessed. In front of the altar there was a stand with four MS. rolls upon it, "the original words of Buddha." Besides this there was nothing, and in the vast, dim temple, only a man and woman knelt at the sanctuary rails, telling their beads with a look of extreme devotion, and the low murmur, " *Namu amida Butsu,*" thrilled plaintively through the stillness; and it was as thrilling to hear the priest, in presence of the symbols of his faith, discoursing on its mysteries.

He either could not or did not care to answer many of my questions regarding the symbolisms of ritual. He said he was not acquainted with the details of the other sects. I asked the meaning of the universal recurrence of the lotus. " The lotus," he said, " is purity; with its fair blossom it grows out of slime and mud, so righteousness grows out of the filth of the human heart." As to the differences among the Buddhist sects, he said, " Their doctrines differ as widely from each other as do those of Christians; but as you all believe in one God and Christ, so all Buddhists agree in reverence for Amida, and in belief in immortality and in the transmigration of souls." He said, " You are limited by your ' Creator;' we do not believe in any creator, but that spirit (eternal) produced atoms, which, by what in English you would call ' fortuitous combination,' produce all we see. Buddha is not, as your God, supreme, but *above all*. When you die you do not become gods, but we become Buddhas." I said that I saw bronze and stone Buddhas everywhere, with faces on which stagnation is depicted, and from which all human emotion is banished; Buddha is not sleeping or waking or thinking, he exists only. " Even so," he answered; " *the end of righteousness is rest*. Nirvana cannot be easily explained. You ask, Is it absorption? I answer Yes and No. It may be termed absorption, yet not altogether so; individuality may cease, but individual consciousness may remain latent — the eternal ages are long. You have not in your language the words by which I could speak more clearly of Nirvana. Misery is the very essence of all life. To attain Nirvana is to be delivered from the merciless necessity of being born again, to reach a state 'in which there are neither ideas, nor a consciousness of the absence of ideas.' This is life in death, or death in life; English has no words for it." I asked him what the objects of the Buddhist faith are, and he answered unhesitatingly, "To make men pure, and to keep alive belief in the immortality of the soul, which is the basis of all righteousness. Buddha is incarnate in all good deeds. If I am indolent and stay in my room, I am myself; if I rise and preach righteousness, I am Buddha."

Speaking on such themes in the temples and galleries, I hardly noticed where we were tending, till, crossing a bridge and passing through some buildings, I found that we were in the most exquisite garden that I have seen in Japan, a fairy-like creation, small, but seeming large, and well worthy to be the retreat of one of the greatest of the Shôguns. There were fountains and a small lake, over whose clear waters, through which large gold-fish were glancing, hung the fantastic balconies of Hidéyoshi's summer palace, an irregular three-storeyed building of most picturesque appearance. Small stone bridges cross the water, winding paths in deep shade lead to unexpected summer-houses, enormous trees give stateliness, the huge roofs of the temples rise above the shady foreground, scarlet maples are reflected scarlet in the motionless water, the quaint trunks and dark green fronds of the cycas rise out of rocky islets; and the whole was solemnised by a dark November sky. We passed the end of the lake on a stone terrace and entered the Shôgun's retreat, which is fantastically arranged with steep, narrow staircases,

nefarious-looking *roomlets*, irregular balconies, large
rooms with deep recesses, and a small, singular-looking
chamber, used for the mysterious rites of *cha-no-yu*, or
tea-meetings. Two attendants, silent like all else, were
waiting to draw aside the *shôji*, that I might see the
different beautiful views on the different storeys, the
most beautiful, to my thinking, being the enchanted-
looking garden, with the grand curved roofs of the temples above the stately trees, and the blotches of scarlet
in the lake below.

Tea and *bonbons* were served on a gold lacquer tray
in antique Kaga cups, by these noiseless attendants, in
the large room of the summer palace, with its dark
posts and ceiling and dull gleams of dead gold, the
little light there was falling on the figure of the priest
in his vestments, as he still discoursed on his faith.
The solemnity was nearly oppressive, and the deserted
palace, the representative of a dead faith (for dead it
surely is), the deepening gloom, the sighing of a doleful
wind among the upper branches, the rattling of the
shôji, the low boom of the temple drum in the distance,
and the occasional sound of litanies wafted on the wailing breeze, wrought on me so like a spell, that I felt as
if I were far from the haunts of living men. It was
not this alone, but I was entangled in a web of metaphysics, or lost in chaos where nothing had form, and
birth and death succeeded each other through endless
eternities, life with misery for its essence, death only
the portal to re-birth into new misery, and so on in
interminable cycles of unsatisfying change, till at last
righteousness triumphs, and the soul being born into
misery no more, reaches its final goal in practical annihilation.

Mr. Akamatz said a great deal about transmigration,
in which he avowed his implicit belief as an essential

article of faith. I asked him if the pure, on dying pass into Nirvana, which appears to me but a synonym for *negation*, a conception impossible to the western mind. "Where are the pure?" he replied. Then I asked him if those who die unrighteous pass into the divers torments figured on the *kakemonos* of the Chi-onin temple for a period of purification? "No," he said, "their spirits undergo metempsychosis, they are re-born into the bodies of animals." I suggested that this shut out all hope of purification, as they were then out of reach of all teaching and good influences. "Not so, for Buddha becomes incarnate in other animals, and conveys to them such teaching as they can receive. If the torments of the Chionin hells are the end of all to some, who knows? the eternal ages are long." You cannot imagine the profound melancholy of this refrain, which occurred at least six times in the priest's conver-sation, "long" in the dreary past, and "long" in the dreary future, man walking " in a vain show " through cycles of misery to a goal of annihilation. So have Sakya-muni and his followers taught for more than 2000 years, and so teaches this most enlightened priest of this most enlightened sect, who having studied Chris-tianity and the philosophies of East and West, has no better hope than "not to be."

I asked him his opinion of the present religious state of Japan, and after very much interesting conversation, he summed up thus: — "Shintôism is truly the rudest form of nature worship, slightly embellished by Confu-cian and Buddhist contact. As a religion it is dead, as a political engine it is failing, it never had life. Buddh-ism was once strong, it is now weak, it may or may not revive. Its vital truths — purity, metempsychosis, and immortality, cannot die." I told him that, in spite of certain superstitious observances, I could not but regard the Japanese as a most irreligious people. "It is so now," he said. "The Confucian philosophy spread rapidly long ago among the higher classes, and educated and thinking men denied immortality, and became what you would call materialists. Gradually their unbelief sank downwards through the *heimin*, and there is little real belief in Japan, though much superstition still exists." I asked him if his sect addressed itself specially to the upper classes. "Pure Buddhism knows no classes," he said; "Buddha was what you call a democrat. All souls are equal, all men by righteousness can become Buddhas. Your Christ was a democrat, and desired to make of men a brotherhood, but you have one doctrine for rich and one for poor, and one church for rich, into which poor cannot enter, and one for poor, where you teach men to obey the rich; this is not our way." I asked him what he thought of the prospects of Christianity in Japan, and among much else he said, "There have been missionaries called Protestants in Japan for fifteen years, there are now over 100, and they count 1600 baptized persons. The college here is sending out young *samurai* to preach, very ardent, and well equipped for teaching; Christianity may make great progress in some of the country parts of Japan, for many are *weary, weary, weary, and it is easy*, and they will be disposed to receive it but not in the large towns." This corresponds closely with Mr. Neesima's opinion on the same subject. I asked him what he considered the most prevalent "unrighteousnesses" among his countrymen, and he gave the reply which I have mentioned as having been given me three times before, "truthlessness and licentiousness."

After speaking a great deal of the demerits of Christianity, he said that he considered that a far more pow-

erful influence than it is now working in Japan in "the
English philosophy," as taught by Mill, Herbert Spencer, and others, while the scientific writings of Huxley,
and Darwin's *Origin of Species*, are stimulating inquiries "which Christianity cannot answer." These books
are translated, and the higher education, rapidly extending, is enabling the young men to acquaint themselves
with a wide range of similar works in English. Besides
this, he said, there are English, Scotch, and German
teachers who assail Christianity openly in their lectures, and teach an undisguised materialism. "The
Confucian philosophy is being rapidly replaced here by
your English philosophy," he said. "This philosophy is
threatening your beliefs at home, your priests are adapt-
ing their teaching, perhaps their creeds, to it. *God and
immortality are quickly disappearing in England*, so men
grow more wicked, and despise your doctrines of purity,
which are not consistent. Jesus Christ is first abandoned, yet men say they believe in God, yet not as
Creator but Father, then they no longer believe in God.
It may be well just now, but it will not be well soon,
for without immortality there will be no righteousness.
In Japan this philosophy threatens both Buddhism and
Christianity; it is your own philosophy which Christianity will have to fight here among the educated, and
not Shintô or Buddhism. Buddhism may yet revive;
it teaches men purity, it shows that the end of righteousness is rest; purity is the plain road to rest; the
moral teachings of Buddha are higher than those of
Christ. Christ's precepts are powerless. Do men keep
them in England?" Mr. Akamatz said a great deal
that was very interesting regarding the tendencies of
religious thought in England. He has deeply studied
one or two branches of our literature, and is evidently
a deep, though a metaphysical, thinker, as well as a stu-

dent of Christianity. Can this priest, who is regarded as the ablest and most enlightened man in the Buddhist hierarchy, truly believe in his own metaphysics and in the doctrine of prolonged metempsychosis?

It was twilight when we left the palace of Hidéyoshi and returned to the vast, dim temple, where four lamps, burning low, feebly lit the gorgeousness of the sanctuary and the figure of Buddha, serene for ever within his golden shrine. Is it the Hindu teacher in his passionless repose, who, from the dimness of the dead ages, offers men an immortality of unconsciousness, or is it the eternal Son of God, the living Brother of our humanity, who in the living present offers to "the weary" rest and service in an endless life, and fellowship in His final triumph over evil, who shall mould the religious future of Japan? I. L. B.

ARTISTIC TASTES.

Kiyôto Shopping — Artistic Patterns — Solitude in Decoration — A
Japanese *Étagère* — Honest Work — Vitiation of Japanese Art —
Kiyôto Brocades — The Board of Industries — The New Hospital.

NIJÔSAN YASHIKI, KIYÔTO.

THE "elegant repose" of Kiyôto degenerates into
wearisome dawdling in the shops. They are slower
than anywhere else. One can hardly buy the merest
trifle in less than an hour. Three or four men and
sharp, business-like boys squat on the floor round a
hibachi, with two or three wooden basins for money,
several ledgers and ink boxes, and a *soroban* or two
among them. They offer you the *tabako-bon* and produce tea after every little purchase ; and if I go with a
Japanese, they waste more time in asking my age, income, where my husband is, if I am "learned," and
where I have been.

But the beauty of the things in many of the small,
dingy shops is wonderful. Kiyôto is truly the home of
art. There are wide *mousseline de laines,* with patterns
on them of the most wildly irregular kind, but so artistic in grace of form and harmony of colour that I should
like to hang them all up merely to please my eyes.
From the blaze of gold and silver stuffs, stiff with bul-
lion, used chiefly for ecclesiastical purposes, which one
sees in some shops, one turns for rest to silk brocades
in the most artistic shades of brown, green, and grey,
with here and there a spray or figure only just suggested

in colour or silver, and to silk *crêpes* so exquisitely fine
that four widths at a time can be drawn through a finger ring, and with soft sprays of flowers or bamboo
thrown on their soft, tinted grounds with an apparent
carelessness which produces ravishing effects.

If I have not written much about Japanese art, it is
not that I do not enjoy it, but because the subject is
almost stale. I see numbers of objects everywhere,
and especially here, which give me great pleasure, and
often more than pleasure. It is not alone the costly
things which *connoisseurs* buy, but household furnishings
made for peasant use, which are often faultless in form,
colour, and general effect. As on the altars and on the
walls of Japanese houses you see a single lotus, iris,
peony, or spray of wistaria ; so on cups, vases, or lacquer
made for Japanese use the effect of solitary decoration
is understood, and repetition is avoided. Thus, a spray
of bamboo, a single stork among reeds, a faint and
almost shadowy suggestion of a bamboo in faint green
on grey or cream, or a butterfly or grasshopper on a
spray of cherry blossom, is constantly the sole decoration of a tray, vase, or teapot, thrown on with apparent
carelessness in some unexpectedly graceful position.
Instead of the big birds and trees and great blotchy
clouds in gold paint, which disfigure lacquer made for
the English market, true Kiyôto lacquer, made for those
who love it, is adorned mainly with suggested sprays of
the most feathery species of bamboo, or an indication
of the foliage of a pine, or a moon and light clouds, all
on a ground of golden mist. There are few shops
which have not on their floors just now some thoroughly
enjoyed spray of bamboo, or reddening maple, or two or
three chrysanthemums in some exquisite creation of
bronze or china.

The highest art and some unspeakably low things go

together, but every Japanese seems born with a singular perception of, and love of beauty or prettiness. The hundreds of shops in Kiyôto, in which numbers of beautiful objects are carefully arranged, are bewildering. I long to buy things for all my friends at home, but either they would despise them, or huddle them together with other things in or on some vile piece of upholstery! You should see a real Japanese *étagère* of plain black lacquer of flawless polish, with irregular shelves curiously arranged, and a very few real treasures displayed upon it, in order to learn Japanese tastefulness.

Inlaid bronze, or bronze with flowers in silver or gold relief, is one of the most beautiful manufactures of Kiyôto. I saw a pair of vases a foot high to-day at one of the workshops fostered by the Government, which were simply perfect, copied from one in the imperial treasury at Nara. An English workman who "scamps" his work, and turns out a piece of original vulgarity, or a badly executed imitation of a real work of art, should see what honest, careful, loving labour does here in perfection of finish for one shilling a day. It is true that work at which a Japanese would hardly look passes muster with foreigners. I went with Mr. Noguchi to-day to the Awata pottery, where 200 men are employed in making a cream-coloured, crackled ware for exportation, and there wasted two and a half hours in buying a tea-service, not only because tea and the *tabako-bon* were introduced so often, but because, being made for the English market, nearly all the cups were crowded with gaudy butterflies, and there was scarcely a cup or saucer that was perfectly circular.

I cannot join in the uncritical admiration of modern Japanese art which is fashionable in some quarters. The human figure is always badly drawn, and the representations of it are grotesque and exaggerated. Japanese sculpture is nearly always caricature, and even as such is deficient in accuracy and delicacy of finish. Generally, in their best modern productions, they do but imitate themselves, and an attempt to please the western buyer results in lacquer overburdened with expensive ornament, gorgeous screens heavy with coarse gilding, and glaringly incongruous painting, or costly embroideries in silks of harsh, crude colours, china overloaded with colour, pattern, and gilding, and bronzes crowded with incongruous collections of men and beasts, all the work of the craftsman, and not of the artist.

In order to correct the tendencies to imperfect copying, and degradation of true Japanese art, the Government of Kiyôto has established a "Board for the Promotion of Industries," which is doing most praiseworthy work in raising the standard of excellence in silk weaving, and in the making of bronze, porcelain, and embroidery. It has also established schools in which apprentices are taught different trades under teachers paid by Government, and in every way is trying to elevate the productions of the native manufacturers. I spent a very interesting day with Mr. Noguchi among the Nishigin silk weavers, and the bronze and porcelain makers. There are silks and brocades just now on the looms in Nishigin which would make a Frenchman die of despair, and these exquisite productions are made in imperfectly lighted and very small rooms, where four or five weavers at most are throwing heart and soul into their work. There was one brocade for a girdle thirty-two inches wide, of rich silk of a soft grey tint. On it were thrown with artistic grace very slight sprays of bamboo in silver, with their shadows in a darker shade of grey than the ground. It was a picture in itself, and only one of several almost equally beautiful. The bronze workshops, which turn out such beautiful and finished works of art as were sent to the Paris Exhibition, are no better than ordinary blacksmith's shops, and the appliances are of the rudest description.

This same "Board of Industries" has established female industrial schools, to one of which I went with Mr. Noguchi, and saw some very beautiful Japanese rugs being made to order. These schools are of two grades, one under Imperial patronage for the daughters of the nobility and gentry, the other, which has 500 pupils, mostly day boarders, for *jôrô*-girls, *geishas*, and tea-house servants, the attendance of the two former classes being compulsory during certain hours, the fees for instruction being deducted from their wages. The teaching includes music, dancing, needlework of all kinds, reading, writing, and the use of the *soroban*, together with silk-reeling, the weaving of Japanese rugs, and the preparation of wadding as the lining for clothes. In the school for the higher classes the greatest attention is paid to deportment and to all the punctilious observances of Japanese etiquette for ladies, and the result is a grace and winning courtesy on the part of the pupils, which are most truly fascinating.

Many of the white, semi-foreign buildings which jar upon the intense nationality of Kiyôto, are elementary schools, of which there are 445 in the *Fu*. Every city district is obliged to establish and maintain one of these, except in the case of very poor districts, where two are allowed to unite. In these the pupils are taught foreign history, "philosophy," geography, and mathematics, besides passing through the Chinese classics, and the usual course of Japanese study.

One of the finest novelties here is the scarcely-finished hospital, which has a very fine situation, and large grounds surrounded by a wall, outside of which is a stream of swiftly-running clear water. The hospital is composed of several two-storeyed buildings, with deep verandahs round each, and has the most approved arrangements for ventilation and general wholesomeness. It has cost a great deal, but the money is most worthily spent, as the building will not only receive 600 patients, but will be equipped as efficiently as possible as a medical school.

With its schools, hospitals, lunatic asylum, prisons, dispensaries, alms-houses, fountains, public parks and gardens, exquisitely beautiful cemeteries, and streets of almost painful cleanliness, Kiyôto is the best-arranged and best-managed city in Japan.   I. L. B.

UJI.

Hugging a *Hibachi* — A Japanese "Institution" — Industrious Pov-
erty — Uji Tea-houses — Tea-making — Our First Evening — Nara
— A Treasury of Antiquities — A Row of Petitioners — Inappro-
priate Travelling Gear — A Shrine of Pilgrimage — An Ancient
Monastery — A Trudge through Mud — Higenashi — Mushroom
Culture — Roughing it — The High Road — A Rubbing Stone.

YAMADA, PROVINCE OF ISÉ, *November* 10.

A JOURNEY of five days has brought us here to the
celebrated Isé shrines. The weather began by being
bad, but has improved, and though the impassable state
of the roads prevented us from visiting the monastery
of Koyeisan and the castle of Takatori, we have passed
through lovely scenery, much of which is altogether
Arcadian, and Mrs. Gulick is an excellent travelling
companion, uniformly cheerful, unselfish, kind, and interested, and we have been fortunate in *kuruma*-run-
ners, accommodation, and, indeed, in everything but the
weather of the three first days. As compared with the
rough, unkempt regions of Northern Japan, this is a
highly luxurious country, and as fleas and mosquitoes
are either dead or in winter quarters, there is really
little to complain of. The splendour of the colouring
is very great at this season, and as the aforesaid pests
are absent, this would really be the best time for travelling in Japan if it were not for the intolerable cold.
Time which should be usefully occupied, is completely
taken up in hugging a *hibachi*, by which means the

hands and chest are kept tolerably warm, while the rest of the body is shivering, or in tenderly piling one live ember upon another with toy tongs, the size of large scissors. The last resource is the *kotatsu*, and, casting dignity aside, I often avail myself of it. This, which is a Japanese "institution," consists of a square, wooden frame, standing over a basin of lighted charcoal, and supporting a large wadded quilt or *futon*, under which you creep, and, drawing it up to your chin, and holding it there, you spend a warm, lazy, and undignified evening. Five or six, or even more, people can creep under one, and I doubt not that at this very hour half the families of Japan are huddled under *kotatsu*.

I must reiterate the difference between a *house*, as we understand it, and a house in Japan. All buildings consist of a raised flooring, vertical beams, and a wooden roof, but their outer walls are mainly light wooden frames, with paper panes, sliding in grooves, enclosed at night by wooden shutters, the whole being merely a porous screen from the inclemency of the weather. Under these circumstances the invitation to creep under the *kotatsu* is as welcome as the "sit in" of the Scotch Highlands or the "put your feet in the stove" of Colorado.

Mr. and Mrs. Gulick and I left Kiyôto at eight on the 5th in a grey-brown drizzle, and reached Nara the same night, following the well-beaten track of nearly all foreigners who visit the old capital, halting at the celebrated Inari Temple of Fushimi, formerly a distinct town, and the residence of Xavier, and celebrated also for the final defeat of the Shôgun's army in 1869. We travelled through seven miles of continuous streets before we got into the country, much of the distance being among the dwellings of the poorest classes; but it is industrious poverty, without vice or squalor, and

nearly every mean, contracted, dingy abode is display·
ing at least one great, bulging chrysanthemum, such as
would drive the Temple gardener wild with envy.

We crossed the broad Ujikawa, which runs out of
Lake Biwa, by a long and handsome bridge, and went
as far as the pretty little town of Uji, which has some
of the loveliest tea-houses in Japan, hanging over the
broad swift river, with gardens and balconies, fountains,
stone lanterns, and all the quaint conventionalities
which are so harmonious here. These tea-houses are
ceaselessly represented by Japanese art, and if you see
a photograph of an ideal tea-house, you may be sure it
is at Uji. We got an exquisite upper room in one of
them for lunch, looking up the romantic gorge through
which the river cuts its way from Lake Biwa, and over
a miniature garden lighted by flaming maples. It was
altogether ideal, and I felt that we were coarsely real
and out of place! I had not before seen a European
man in one of these fairy-like rooms, and Mr. Gulick
being exceptionally tall, seemed to fill the whole room,
and to have any number of arms and legs! I knew
that the tea-house people looked at us with disgust.

The tea-plant, which is a camellia, and is now covered
with cream-white blossoms crowded with stamens and
faintly fragrant, is very pretty, for it is allowed to grow
into broad bushes from three to four feet high, and its
rich dark-green masses in rows contrast well with the
reddish soil. Uji is one of the most famous of the
Japan tea-districts, and its people told us that two
crops a year have been taken from the same shrubs for
300 years. The Japanese say that tea was drunk in
the Empire in the ninth century, when a Buddhist
priest brought the tea-seed from China; but it seems
that its culture died out, and that it was naturalised a
second time in the twelfth century, when a Buddhist

priest again brought seed from China, shortly after
which tea was planted at Uji. It now grows all over
Japan, except in Yezo, and, besides being the great
beverage of all classes, is exported annually to America to the amount of about 16,000,000 pounds from
Yokohama only. I have never seen any tea worth less
than sixteenpence a pound, and that is only drunk by
the poorer classes. The Japanese are great tea epi-
cures, and the best tea drunk by those who can afford
it costs thirteen shillings per pound! The water used
for tea-making must not boil, and it must rest barely a
minute on the leaves, or the result will be bitter and as-
tringent. The infusion is a pale straw colour, delicate
and delicious. No Japanese would touch the dark,
rank infusion made from black tea which we like so
well. To drink it thus, in big cups, and above all with
milk, they regard as among our many coarse habits!

The drizzle turned into heavy rain, and after two
hours of thorough soaking we were hurried into Nara
in the darkness, and shot out of our *kurumas* at the
first *yadoya* we came to, the men evidently not being
minded to run farther. It was a bad inn, with old mats,
low ceilings, a throng of travellers, and no end of
bad smells. There I missed Ito, for every bit of baggage came wet into my room with muddy wrappers and
straps. Then we had to cook our "foreign food" –
simple stirabout— over a miserable *hibachi*, and we ate
like pigs with all our wet and muddy things lying
about us, the open *shôji* letting in the view of all our
coolies bathing, the servant crouching on the floor, and
our light, a candle stuck into a bottle. Since that
night we have been in comfortable *yadoyas*, and our
kuruma-runners have attended to our baggage, but I
always miss Ito when we are cooking the stirabout over
the *hibachi*. Moreover, that evening I forgot how to

make it, and put the flour into boiling milk, and the result was tough lumps. We could not sleep for the closeness of the air and the general restlessness of our fellow-travellers; but it was almost worth lying awake to realize the fact that fleas and mosquitoes are at an end for the season.

The next day was a murky drizzle, with a temperature at 70°, but in spite of that I enjoyed the sights of the old imperial city, in which seven Mikados reigned in the eighth century. People differ about Nara. Some of my friends rave about it, others run it down. I thought it lovely even in the mist, with great natural beauty heightened by religious art, and a grey melancholy of arrested decay, which is very solemn. Among the many interesting things are a number of sacred deer, which wander about the majestic groves and avenues, and follow one about greedily, begging for cakes, which their pertinacity compels one to buy. The town, which contains over 21,000 people, runs along the slope of a range of picturesque hills, and from the forest, which in part resembles a collection of our finest English parks, there are magnificent views over the ancient province of Yamato. Every one buys images of the sacred deer, hair-pins made from their horns, charms and combs, and the pilgrims, who come in great numbers to the famous Shintô temple of Kasuga, sling these upon their girdles. We went out early, and spent much of the day, I cannot say in sight-seeing, but in enjoying the sights, nearly all of which lie in the magnificent park or forest on the hill, and are mostly connected with religion.

Among the most curious is a monstrous wooden magazine, made of heavy timbers, laid horizontally, supported on pillars consisting of solid trunks of trees eight feet high, the most drearily uncouth building that can be imagined. It has a most singular interest, for it was built for the safe deposit of the Mikado's furniture and property, just before the Court quitted Nara for Kiyôto at the end of the eighth century, and is said to have been examined every sixty-first year since, and repaired when necessary. More curious still is the fact that, not only has a wooden building escaped the destructive agencies of a thousand years, but that the actual articles mentioned in the inventory of the eighth century are there, and can easily be distinguished from later accumulations. There was an exhibition at Nara not long ago, and a few wonderful things from the Imperial Treasury are still to be seen at the rear of the great temple, but among the objects replaced in the monster "godown" were screens, pictures, masks, books, sculptures, soap in round cakes the size of quoits, copper bowls and dishes, beads and ornaments, tortoise-shell "back-scratchers," pottery and glass, dresses, bells, hats, weapons, and utensils of various kinds, bronzes, writing paper, clay statuettes, wooden statues, etc. etc. What would we not give for such a collection made by Charlemagne or Alfred?

Mr. Gulick bargained with some *kuruma*-runners to take us to Miwa, and on leaving him to return to Kôbe I was amused to find that I have gained more confidence in Japanese travelling in six months than Mrs. Gulick has in several years, and she felt a good deal of trepidation in starting upon the "unbeaten track;" but everything has gone very smoothly, and she is enjoying the tour as much as I am. We reached Miwa, a town of about 1200 people, after dark, and got delightful accommodation with very kindly people in the upper room of a *kura*, with a fine view of an avenue of pine trees, which leads to a famous shrine of Shintô pilgrimage. The entertainment of pilgrims seems indeed the great business of Miwa. As Mrs. Gulick speaks Japanese, we are always on very sociable terms with our hosts, and our room was soon filled with the hostess and her daughters and servants, besides infants of various ages. These women were astonished that we wore our dresses up to our throats, and when Mrs. Gulick remarked that, according to our ideas, it did not look womanly or "correct" to wear them as they do, open to their girdles, they were yet more surprised,

MY KURUMA-RUNNER.

and as each new-comer entered, the hostess repeated to her this singular foreign notion.

Then our three *kuruma*-runners glided in, and after prostrating themselves, knelt in a row on the floor. The eldest,[1] a tall and very ugly man, having nothing but a *maro* and a short, loose jacket, had wrapped a red blanket round his lower limbs; the second, a youth,

[1] This is a sketch from a crayon portrait in the Engineering College at Tôkiyô, representing a low class coolie, but minus his pleasant smile and look of goodness, it is a faithful likeness of my invaluable runner.

disdained this concession to our prejudices; and the third, a man of feeble *physique*, who had delayed us on the way, considered his panoply of tattooing sufficient clothing. Bowing over and over again, the older man preferred a petition that we would engage the three for the ten days' journey round to Kiyôto; they would be our servants, he said, and do whatever we desired. Mrs. Gulick represented to them that they had no recommendations, that they might desert us on the way, that they might become useless from drinking too much *saké*, etc. etc. To this they replied, that they would be faithful unto death, that they would not touch *saké*, that they would serve us well, etc., and pleaded most earnestly, but we were obdurate, till the elder man said, "We *too* wish to worship at Isé!" This was quite irresistible, so we told them that we would engage the two strong ones at six *sen* a *ri* for as long as they pleased us, but could not take the weakly one over the mountains. Then they pleaded for him, saying that he had a large family, and was very poor, and they would help him, and having obtained "leave to toil," they got up quite happy, whipped off the covers of our baggage, put up my stretcher in no time, and arranged the room quite neatly. These faithful fellows are the comfort of our tour with their unweariable good nature, strict honesty, and kindly, pleasant ways. They are never tired, never ask for help on the steepest and miriest ways, seek our comfort before their own, attend on us like servants, help us to pack, take us to respectable, clean *yadoyas*, and are faultless. At night, after they have had their bath, they come to our room to wish us good night and arrange the next day's journey, and every morning at daylight the *fusuma* glide apart, and the shining skulls are to be seen bobbing their good morning on the mats, to show that they are "on hand,"

the elder one always in the "full dress" of his red
blanket. While we get our breakfast they do our packing with a quietness and celerity which leave nothing
to be desired, and the goodness of the expression of the
elder man and his thoughtful kindness, preach many a
sermon and suggest many a thought and query. He is
a peasant proprietor, but when times are not busy, leaves
his land in his wife's care, and draws a *kuruma*. He buys
toys for his children everywhere, so that the well in the
kuruma is full of them; and having "worshipped at
Isé," and purchased many charms for friends and neighbours, he will go home with a glad heart. These runners tell us that their expenses are 20 *sen* a day, and
they earn from 40 to 60, according to the distance we
travel.

The morning at Miwa opened with heavy rain, which
never ceased during the whole day. In the deep mud
our weakly coolie broke down, and we had to dismiss
him with a present. The mountain roads were deep in
mire and water, the *kurumas* often sank up to their axles,
and though we walked nearly all day, *i.e.* floundered
through the mud, the men had great difficulty in getting
along, and sometimes the services of three or four
peasants were required to get the baggage *kuruma* up
the steep, slippery hills. I got on comparatively easily
in my mountain dress and high boots, though both were
soaked within half an hour of starting; but Mrs. Gulick,
who wore long skirts and a long waterproof cloak over
them, between the weight of the skirts and of the water
with which they were saturated, foot gear which always
seemed sticking in the mud, and the attempt to hold up
an umbrella, had a hard time; but her cheerfulness
never failed, and the worse it was and the more unlikely
it seemed that we should reach a *yadoya* for the night,
the more heartily we and the runners laughed. It was.

in truth, excellent fun, very unlike the dismalness of some equally rainy days in Northern Japan.

After leaving Miwa, and passing for a mile or two through farming villages, a great *torii* spanned the road, the mists rolled aside, the valley contracted, a wall of finely outlined hills blocked it up, and we suddenly found ourselves in a most picturesque mountain town of about 2000 people, with a torrent rushing down a stone channel in the middle, waterfalls reverberating all around, warm-tinted, deep-eaved, steep-roofed houses forming streets whose charming quaintness delights the eye, or perched on rocks or terraces on the steep hillsides — Swiss all over, even to the sale of rosaries, pictures, and wood-carvings in the dainty shops. But not Swiss are the grey temples on the heights, the priests' houses on grand, stone-faced embankments hanging over dizzy ledges, and the red *torii* at the feet of superb flights of stairs which lead up mountain sides to ancient shrines of nature worship, hidden among groves of gigantic cryptomeria, rising from among maples flaunting in scarlet and gold. It was all so unexpected, so off the beaten track of foreign travel, and we had tumbled unawares into one of the most famous places in Japan, celebrated in poetry and painting, and one of the most popular of the many places of pilgrimage. Beautiful Hasé-dera! I shall never forget its exquisite loveliness in the November rain. We splashed through mire and water, climbed heights, saw temples, forgot hunger and soaked clothes, and lingered long, for Nature, in this glorious valley, has done her best to simulate the beauties of a far-off island; and as we looked down into the cleft through which the loud-booming Yamagawa was flinging itself in broad drifts of foam, and at the steep mountain on the other side aflame with maples, we exclaimed simultaneously, "A Hawaiian gulch!"

It is hard to write plain prose about Hasé-dera. Its steep-roofed houses are piled in a *cul-de-sac*, deeply cleft by the Yamagawa ; it is blocked in by a densely-wooded mountain side, dark with cryptomeria and evergreen oaks lighted up by maples ; thickly-wooded heights rise on every side, rocky precipices descend to the river ; and heights and precipices are covered with temples, monasteries, and priests' houses — the great temple to Kwan non being built half upon the rock and half upon a platform built out of the rock. This is reached by a grand flagged ascent in three zigzags, under a corridor, with beds of tree peonies on stone-faced embankments, step above step on each side, bringing crowds of strangers to the "peony viewing" in the flowery month of April. Flights of stone stairs, grand stone embankments, religious buildings, abbots' and monks' houses with grey walls and sweeping roofs, terraces, shrines, stone and bronze lanterns, chapels, libraries, gateways, idols, one above another, and jutting out on every piece of vantage ground which hangs over the cleft of the Yamagawa, attest the former grandeur of this " Monastery of the Long Valley," which, founded in the seventh or eighth century, was destroyed by fire at least twelve times before the fifteenth !

The great temple of the Goddess of Mercy, like several other popular temples, is dark and dingy ; and a hall outside, sixty feet long, devoted to the display of tawdry *ex voto* pictures, is as mangy and worm-eaten as a celebrated image of Binzuru, the great medicine god, who occupies a chair at one end of it, and is being rubbed out of all semblance of humanity. The outer wall of the back of the chapel is hung with tresses of the hair both of women and men, offered along with vows. The view from the temple platform, of height above height crowned with monastic buildings, of the steep-roofed houses of Hasé below, piled irregularly above the rushing Yama, and of mountain, forest, and hill-sides aflame with maples, was one which we were loth to leave; and when, after climbing a steep zigzag which leads up the face of a singular ridge, called, Ata-gosan, we looked our last upon the "Monastery of the long valley," it was with a regret that I have hardly felt elsewhere in Japan.

This knife-like ridge, the summit rock of which is gashed to allow the track to pass through, has a red Shintô shrine at its extremity, a glorious view of Hasé on the one side, and on the other a steep valley terraced for rice. The rain, which had moderated a little, took a mean advantage of us there, and lasted all day, turn-ing every rivulet into a torrent, and every gash on the hill-sides into a waterfall. The scenery, however, looked lovely, for the flaming colours on the hill-sides simulated the effect of sunshine, and the tawny rice harvest against the dark evergreens gave warmth and contrast. All day we trudged through mire up and down steep hills, passing beautiful brown-roofed villages on heights, spurs, and slopes, temples on stone-faced embankments, groves of superb cryptomeria, hills with coloured woods, ravines terraced for rice with stone embankments like steep stairs only six feet wide — a lovely region of beauty, industry, and peace. We met never a horse or foot passenger the whole day, and sometimes made less than a mile an hour, owing to the steepness and deep mud of the road. When evening came on, we lost each other, and I reached the village of Sambon-matsu, or Higenashi, alone, to find total darkness, not a chink in the *amado* of any house giving evidence of light within. By dint of much shouting we succeeded in getting the door of a *yadoya* opened, and there I sat for some time in the *doma*, looking into what appeared like immensity

— a lofty blackened space dimly visible by the light of an *andon*, in which some misty, magnified figures were gliding about in the smoke. After a time I succeeded in conveying my apprehensions about Mrs. Gulick to the house-master, and six of us turned out into the rain with paper umbrellas and lanterns to search for her, and soon met her stumbling bravely along in the pitch darkness, dragging her soaked clothes with difficulty. and laughing at my fears.

In spite of the dampness and cold we were soon asleep, to be awoke at daylight by a sound as if of pitiless rain; but on opening the *amado* there was a delightful surprise, for the clouds were rolling up in rosy masses, the sky was intensely blue, the sun, which we had not seen for a week, was rising above the mountains, and colour was every moment deepening in his light. The Nushitoyama inn is on an abrupt height above the beautiful Kitsugawa, and its balcony looks down upon a sharp curve of the river, which was flashing in the sunlight below lofty grey cliffs, over which scarlet trailers hung. A little mill with an overshot wheel, hill above hill glowing with autumn colouring, in light and shadow, a great camellia tree loaded with pink blossoms, palms (*Chœmerops excelsa*), oranges, bamboo groves, steep-roofed houses rising one above the other, and everything flashing with sunlit rain-drops, made a picture of autumn beauty. But odes of a thousand years ago represent the dread with which the Japanese peasant contemplates the coming winter,[1] and our hostess

[1] Such as the following, among many others, translated by Mr. F. V Dickins:—

> "The hamlet bosomed mid the hills,
> Aye lonely is. In winter time,
> The solitude with misery fills
> My mind. For now the rigorous clime,
> Hath banished every herb and tree,
> And every human face from me."

shivered when we admired, and said that another six weeks would shut out her beautiful village from the world.

We had a delightful day's journey through lovely scenery in brilliant sunshine, but the people were so busy with their harvest work that we could not get a third *kuruma*, and had to do a good deal of walking. The road follows the course of the Kitsugawa, which it crosses at the considerable town of Nobara, on a bridge of planks, supported, as many others are in that region, on bamboo creels eight feet in diameter, filled with stones. On the way, in damp woods, there were rocks with rows of pieces of decaying wood placed aslant against them, and on inquiry I learned that these represent the mushroom culture for which the provinces of Yamato and Isé are famous. Mushrooms are an article of diet everywhere. They are among the brown horrors in a brown liquid, which are among the "temptations" of every tea-house; and there is an immense demand for them, specially for a kind tasteless when fresh, but highly flavoured when dry. Much skill is brought to bear on their production, but being quite ignorant of the mode of culture elsewhere, I cannot make any comparisons. These ingenious people select logs of two kinds of oak, make longitudinal incisions in them, and expose them in groves to damp and heat till they are partly rotten, when, the worst parts being removed, they are placed aslant against rocks as I saw them, and mushrooms appear upon them in abundance the next spring. After the first crop has been gathered they are placed in water in the morning, and in the afternoon are taken out and beaten with a mallet, which beating is so successful, that after being placed aslant again for two or three days fresh mushrooms appear. The people say that if the logs are beaten heavily the mushrooms are very large, but if lightly a good number of small ones spring up in succession. The ingenuity of the Japanese in providing themselves with food is q uite marvellous.

There was the usual beautiful terrace cultivation, villages jutted out from hill-sides on stone-faced embankments, or nestled among flaming woods, and temples and *torii* everywhere testified to the devotion of a past age. At Nobara, where the mud in the streets was ten inches deep, the police bothered us for twenty minutes, fancying that there was an informality in our passports; but the sun was still high when we climbed a sandy ridge of great height, with an extensive view of hundreds of hills, mostly sandy, covered with pine and azalea, their waving ranges glorified in the sunshine. Reaching Aido in the late afternoon, a disagreeable innkeeper wanted us to remain, saying the *yadoya* at Tsiji was "piggy;" but we went on, and after much delay, owing to lack of transport, luckily met an unloaded horse, put our baggage on him, and pushed up into the mountains at sunset, along a track shut up with a torrent in a ravine whose sides were scarlet and crimson, with summits rising sharply into a lemon-coloured sky. It was too cold for anything but walking, and though the road was all up-hill, we had not walked ourselves warm when we reached the wild little mountain hamlet of Awoyama by moonlight, only to find that neither horses nor coolies could be got for the next day. It was a pretty rough place, with oxen under the same roof, but we got a good room, and our faithful runners made it as comfortable as they could.

The first chill of the winter was severe. The room was very damp, and the *amado* were partially nailed up, so it had not a chance of sunshine. We gropingly cooked our stirabout by the dim light of an *andon,*

could not see to write; kept our candles for Yamada;
shivered, hugged *hibachis* and kettles; got heaps of
futons and slept under them, regardless of their weight;
woke in the night from the cold, buried our heads and
faces in shawls, and got up before daylight, still shivering, to find a bleak, windy, and dubious morning, on
which rice and eggs were comfortless and unsustaining
food.

We were much detained again by difficulties of transport, but the day turned out very fine, and Mrs. Gulick
did not think walking any hardship in the lovely country, so that by the afternoon we had got through the
mountains, passed Kaido, Onoki, and Kaminoro, and no
end of villages and temples, and reached Rokken, on
the broad " carriage-road " which connects the great
highway of the Tôkaidô with the Isé shrines. Here
there were waggons in numbers carrying passengers,
and hundreds of *kurumas*, and pack-cows with velvet
frontlets embroidered in gold, and men making the old-
fashioned waggon-wheels which have no tires, and all
the industries of a large and prosperous population.

In order to spend Sunday here we engaged additional
runners, and came from Rokken, twelve and a half
miles, at a great pace, our men swinging paper-lanterns
and hooting merrily as they ran. The whole distance
nearly is lined with villages, towns, and good houses,
with tiled walls, enclosing large areas, a populous and
prosperous region, much advanced in all material things.
Passing through Ichida and the large town of Matsu-
saka, which abounds with curio shops, under a clear
sky, and with a sharp north wind benumbing our limbs,
we reached Kushida, where we ferried the Kushida-
gawa in a scow — a handsome new bridge on twelve
piers not being quite finished — and then under a glorious moon reached a broad, shallow river called the

Miyégawa, where we were detained, not reluctantly, for a length of time waiting ferriage. It was a very picturesque scene with the dark, wooded banks, the numerous fishing-punts with lights, and the number of patient fishers standing up to their waists in the cold water with lanterns hanging from their necks. Buddhist and Shintô temples, *torii*, and images succeeded each other along the road; there were huge trees and sacred groves girdled by the straw rope with its dependent tassels; nearly every house had Shintô emblems over the door, and rattling over the remaining *ri* we reached Yamada, the cradle of the ancient faith. It looked solid and handsome in the moonlight, and looks more solid and handsome still in the daylight, for its houses are two storeyed, and mostly in the solid *kura* style, and turn their gable-ends to the street. The roofs are heavily tiled, the stone embankments are in fine order, and altogether, apart from the grandeur of the camphor and cryptomeria groves, and the stately entrances and stone-bordered avenues of the Gekû shrine, Yamada is the handsomest town I have seen in Japan.

Vice and religion are apt to be in seeming alliance in this country; the great shrines of pilgrimage are nearly always surrounded by the resorts of the dissolute, and nowhere are these so painfully numerous as on the stately road which connects the Gekû with the Naikû shrine, three miles off. It was some time before our runners succeeded in lodging us in a *yadoya* which was not *kashitsukeya*, but we are in good quarters at the ancient house kept by Matsushima Zenzaburo, from among whose thirty rooms we chose one upstairs, which is full of sunshine and pleasantness. But, oh, for a good fire! It is very cold at night and after sunset.

Nov. 10. — Sunday was a day of sunshine and glitter,

quite perfect. We read the English service in the morning, and in the afternoon, with our faithful runners, visited the Gekû shrines in their glorious groves. There our men "worshipped," that is, they threw some *rin* on the white cloth in front of the gateway of the shrines, prostrated themselves, rubbed their hands, and went away rejoicing. My runner has rheumatism in his neck, and not having been cured by his application to the medicine god of Hasé-dera, he rubbed a celebrated rubbing-stone at the corner of the sacred enclosure with great vigour, and then rubbed himself, and to-day he is free from pain! The camphor groves alone are well worth a visit, for they are gloriously beautiful, but no beauty of nature or sunshine can light the awful melancholy of the unutterable emptiness of the holiest places of Shintô.

In the evening our host came up for a friendly talk, and made many inquiries concerning Christianity, and Mrs. Gulick made a praiseworthy attempt to explain its essentials to our runners, with how much success may be judged from the question which they asked to-day, "If we were to worship your God, should we have to go to your country?" being quite willing, apparently, to add another deity to their already crowded Pantheon.

I. L. B.

THE ISÉ SHRINES.[1]

"The Divine Palaces of the most holy gods of Isé" — Sanctity of the
Isé Shrines — The *Kami-dana* — The Isé Charms — The Gekû
Camphor Groves — The Temple Grounds — The Sacred Enclosure
— The Shrines — The "Holy of Holies" — The Japanese Regalia
— The Shintô Mirror.

THESE temples of Isé, the Gekû and the Naikû, called
by the Japanese by a name which literally means "The
two great divine palaces," rank first among Shintô
shrines in point of sanctity, and are to Shintôists, even
in the irreligious present, something of what Mecca is
to Mussulmans, and the Holy Places of Jerusalem to
Greeks and Latins. Tens of thousands of pilgrims still
resort to them annually, and though the pilgrimage season is chiefly in the spring months, there is no time of
the year in which there is an absolute cessation of visitors. The artisans of Tôkiyô now think it possible to
gain a livelihood without beseeching the protection of
the Isé divinities, and the shop-boys of the trading
cities no longer beg their way to and from Yamada in
search of the Isé charms; but it will be long before
the Japanese householder, specially the credulous peasant, learns to feel safe without the paper ticket inscribed
with the name Tenshôkô-daijin, the principal deity of
Isé, which is only to be obtained at the Isé shrines.

[1] The account of the Isé shrines in my letter is so incomplete and
fragmentary, that I prefer to give these Notes taker on the spot, and
corrected subsequently by the help of a paper by Mr. Satow.

In the foregoing Letters I have alluded to the fact that in every Japanese house there is a *kami-dana*, or "shelf for gods," on which is a wooden miniature of a Shintô shrine containing paper tickets, on which the names of various gods are written, one of which is always the deity aforesaid. This ticket is believed to contain between two thin slips some shavings of the wan'ls used by the priests of Isé at the two annual festivals, which are supposed to effect the purification of the nation from the "sin" of the preceding six months, and is supposed to protect its possessor from misfortune for half a year, at the end of which time the *o-harai*, as it is called, ought to be changed for a new one ; but from what I learned at the Gekû, it appears that modern negligence is content to renew the charm once in one, two, and three years, or even longer. It is to be supposed that these *o-harai* bear as much relation to the wands of purification as the relics profusely scattered throughout the world bear to the Holy Cross, of which they are said to be fragments. The old *o-harai* ought to be burned or cast into a river or the sea, but are usually employed to heat the bath used by the virgin priestesses after their posturings at the annual festival of the patron-god of any locality. They were hawked about Japan up to 1868, but this practice was prohibited by Government a few years ago, and they can only be obtained at the Isé temples themselves, or at certain accredited agencies. This fact of the universal distribution of the *o-harai* connects every family in Japan with the Isé shrines and Shintô superstition, and gives the shrines a central position as regards the national faith.

The two groups of shrines are distant about three and a half miles from each other. The majority of the pilgrims lodge in Furuichi, a town which occupies the crest of the ridge between the two temples, and is almost made up of *yadoyas*, tea-houses, and *jôrôyas*, mostly of large size, with solid gables turned towards the street. Yamada, which is conterminous with Furuichi, is also full of houses of entertainment. These towns contain about 40,000 people, and for Japan are marvels of solid and picturesque building. A Japanese pilgrimage is not a solemn or holy thing, and the great shrines of Shintô pilgrimage possess more than the usual number of vicious attractions.

It is sufficient to describe the Gekû shrine, which is exactly copied from the Naikû. Both stand in the midst of ancient cryptomeria, each stately tree in Shintô fancy worthy to be a god, but it is the camphor groves, the finest in Japan, covering the extensive and broken grounds with their dark magnificence, which so impress a stranger with their unique grandeur as to make him forget the bareness and meanness of the shrines which they overshadow.

The grand entrance is reached from Yamada by crossing a handsome bridge, which leads to a wide space enclosed by banks faced with stone. On the right is a building occupied by the temple-attendants, where fragments of the wood used in building the shrines, packets of the rice offered to the gods, and sundry other charms, are offered for sale. Close to this there is a massive *torii*, the entrance to the temple-grounds, which are of great extent, and contain hills, ravines, groves, and streams. Very broad and finely-gravelled roads, with granite margins and standard lamps at intervals, intersect them, and their *torii*, stone bridges, stone staircases, and stone-faced embankments, are all on a grand scale and in perfect repair. On the left hand, within the entrance, there are some plain buildings, one of which is occupied by several temple-attendants in white silk vest-

ments, whose business it is to sell the *o-harai* to all com-
ers. Heavy curtains, with the Mikado's crest upon
them, are draped over the entrances to this and the
building at the gate, and may be taken as indicating
that Shintô is under "State" patronage.

Passing through stately groves by a stately road, and
under a second massive *torii*, the visitor reaches the
famous Gekû shrine, and, even in spite of Mr. Satow's
realistic description, is stricken with a feeling of disappointment, for he is suddenly brought up by a great
oblong enclosure of neatly planed wood, the upright
posts, which are just over nine feet high, being planted
at distances of six feet, the intervals being completely
filled up with closely-fitting and very heavy planking
laid horizontally. The only ornaments are bamboo receptacles on each post, containing sprigs of *Cleyera
Japonica*, changed occasionally. This monotonous looking enclosure rests on a raised platform of broken stone,
supported on a rough stone-faced embankment about
three feet high. One corner of this is formed by a
large, irregularly shaped, dark stone, worn perfectly
smooth from being constantly rubbed by the hands of
persons who believe that by rubbing the stone first, and
then any painful part of the body, the pain will be
cured. The front of this extraordinary enclosure is
247 feet long, the rear 235 feet, one side 339 feet, and
the other 335 feet. It has five entrances, the principal
one, 18 feet wide, facing the road, being formed by a
torii. At a distance of 24 feet from three of these entrances are high wooden screens, and a similar screen,
at a distance of 76 feet, hides the main entrance, much
in the same way that the great brick screens in Canton
conceal the gateways of the private dwellings of the
mandarins. Within the entrance *torii* there is a wooden
gateway with a thatched roof, but a curtain with the

Mikado's crest conceals all view of the interior court. In front of this gateway the pilgrims make their obeisances and throw down their *rin* upon a white cloth. The other entrances are closed with solid gates. There is no admission except for the specially privileged, but a good view into the enclosure is gained by climbing a bank upon its west side.

Within the thatched gateway there is a pebbled court, on the right of which is a long narrow shed, one of three buildings set apart for the entertainment of the envoys sent by the Mikado after the annual harvest festival. In a straight line from the second gateway a flagged pavement, passing under a *torii* at a distance of 99 feet, reaches another thatched gateway, through which there is a third court, formed by palisades the height of a man, placed close together. Another thatched gateway gives entrance to the last enclosure, an area nearly square, being 134 feet by 131, surrounded by a very stout palisade. Within this stands the *shôden* or shrine of the gods, and on the right and left two treasuries. The impression produced by the whole resembles that made upon the minds of those who have made the deepest researches into Shintô — there is nothing, and all things, even the stately avenues of the Gekû, lead to NOTHING. Japanese antiquaries say that the architecture of Shintô temples resembles that of the primeval Japanese hut, and these, which have been rebuilt since 1868, represent this architecture in its purest form. The *shôden* is 34 feet long by 18 wide, and stands on a platform raised on posts 6 feet high, which is approached by nine steps 15 feet wide, with a balustrade on each side. A balcony 3 feet wide, with a low rail, runs all round the building, and is covered by the eaves of the roof, which is finely thatched with bark to the depth of a foot. The ridge pole and a number of cigar-shaped beams and rafters at each end, crossing each other above the roof, are supposed to be merely the development of the roof of the primeval hut. The building has sides of closely-fitting planks, and the whole, like all else, is of planed wood, destitute of any other ornament than occasional plates of pierced and engraved brass. The treasuries are mere "go-downs," without balconies. They contain silken stuffs, silk fibre, and saddlery for the sacred horses.

In the north-west corner of the area is a plain building, containing the *gohei*, wands with dependent pieces of paper, frequently mentioned before, usually worshipped as gods, but at Isé only believed to have the power of attracting the spirits of the gods to the spot, which was their original meaning. In the north-east corner, within a special enclosure, there is another plain building, in which the water and food offered to the gods of the Gekû are set out. The daily offerings to the principal deity consist of sixteen saucers of rice, four saucers of salt, four cups of water, and such fish, birds, and vegetables as may be contributed by the surrounding villages, and the three secondary deities receive one-half each. The chief deity of the Gekû is "The Goddess of Food," and of the Naikû, the great "Sun Goddess."

Having followed Shintô to its centre at Isé, the bare wooden building, which is the kernel of the Gekû enclosure, and the Shintô "Holy of Holies," assumes a very special interest, but here, again, there is nothing but disappointment, for the *shôden* only contains four boxes of unpainted wood, furnished with light handles, resting on low stands, and covered with what is said to be white silk. In each box is a mirror wrapped in a brocade bag, which is never renewed, only re-covered. Over one mirror is placed a cage of unpainted wood, which is covered with a curtain of coarse silk, which conceals both cage and box. The three other boxes stand outside this cage, but are also covered, and the coverings are all that can be seen when the shrines are opened on festival days. It is in these mirrors that the spirits of the gods are supposed to dwell. Much ingenious rubbish has been devised to account for the presence of a looking-glass in every Shintô temple; but the fact is, that the original Isé mirror, of which all the rest are copies, merely represents the great Sun Goddess, the supposed ancestress of the Mikado, and, together with the sword, which constitute the Japanese regalia, found a resting-place at Isé, after many wanderings, in the year 4 B.C. The polished surface is neither a mirror of truth nor of the human soul, but is simply a very intelligible symbol of a rude compound of nature and myth worship, nature as the Sun, deified as the myth Amaterasu or the " Sun Goddess."

The Gekû was founded in the year 478 A.D., and it has been customary from time immemorial to rebuild a temple alternately on either site once in twenty years. The Naikû has the same fourfold enclosure as the Gekû. There are several smaller shrines within the groves, but they are unimportant. The river Izuzu flows through the camphor woods, and in it the pilgrims wash their hands before worshipping at the temple.

The Isé shrines were unknown to Europeans till 1872, when the Government very liberally gave Mr. Satow and a small party of foreigners the opportunity of visiting them. They are now open to passport holders under certain restrictions, and are singularly interesting to those who have made either an original or second-hand study of Shintô, for relics of Isé are in every house, the deities of Isé are at the head of the

national Pantheon, a pilgrimage to Isé forms an episode
in the life of every Shintôist, and throughout Japan
thousands of heads are daily bowed in the direction of
" the Divine Palaces of the most holy gods of Isé."

ANOTHER PILGRIMAGE.

A Dreary Shrine — The Legend of Futami-sama — A Double Temple —A Street of Shops — The Naikû Shrine — Evening Shadows — The Melancholy of Shintô — Unsanctified Pilgrim Resorts.

YAMADA, ISÉ, *November* 11, 1878.

IN order to complete the round of Shintô pilgrimage, we left Yamada early this morning, ferried the Shiwoaigawa, rested at Futamiya, a neat village entirely composed of tasteful tea-houses, went on to Futami-sama in our *kurumas*, and then walked over the sand and rocks of a very pretty coast to a resort of pilgrims, which, even at this dead season, attracts large numbers, many of whom were bands of young girls.[1] Shells, coralline, and curiosities, were offered for sale at booths under the grey cliffs, together with rude, coloured woodcuts of Fuji by sunrise, as seen from the shore; but it was all dull and grey, and Fuji had to be taken altogether for granted. Farther on there were booths where melancholy-looking women sold small *torii*, earthenware frogs, straw circles, and other *ex votos*, and then we came rather suddenly on the queerest and dreariest shrine of pilgrimage that I have ever seen.

A small promontory of grey sea gravel, with a low wall built round it, extended into the still, grey sea,

[1] I have not been able to meet with any European who has visited this remarkable spot; it has hitherto escaped even Mr. Satow's diligent researches among the holy places of Shintô.

terminating in a large *torii* of unpainted wood, and a wooden altar table, on which were laid four big, green stones, a piece of worm-eaten wood, two *zen* or small tables with offerings of rice, a number of bits of green pottery an inch long, with a distant resemblance to frogs [said to be the servants of the gods], three wands with *gohei*, and a number of *rin*. On and about it were heaps of circles of twisted straw, with *gohei* attached, some new and fresh, others old and musty; a more grotesque collection of rubbish I have never seen, and it was being added to constantly by relays of pilgrims. This promontory points to three isolated rocks, one behind the other, on which the dull waves broke in drifts of foam. The centre rock is of imposing size. It has a small *torii* on its summit, and a heavy straw cable, wound round it, connects it with the rock between it and the shore, heavy straw tassels dangling between the two.[1]

We then travelled for some miles among lovely, wooded hills, with hamlets and rice valleys, to the village of Assama, left our *kurumas*, ascended the noble hill Assamayama, where flaming maples lighted up forests of pine and cryptomeria, rejoiced in the abundance of its *Microlepia tenuifolia*, and *Gleichenia*, spent an hour at a very large tea-house with a magnificent view near the summit, and enjoyed what we saw, or thought we saw, of a grand panorama of wooded hills, deep valleys, indented coasts, and beauti-

[1] Mr. Satow has since told me that, in a Japanese guide to Isé, the following legend is given of the origin of the sacredness of this queer place: — When the younger brother of the Sun goddess was on his way to the lower world, he was overtaken by night at this spot, and sought shelter with an old couple. To protect them from a pestilence, which he foresaw would attack the village, he fastened a straw rope round their house, and the plague, when it came, left it untouched. This is the origin of the straw bands offered at this shrine.

ful islands, revelled in splotches of scarlet and crimson here and there among the dark coniferæ, marvelled at a rude double temple, one half Shintô, with the chief object of adoration a rude block of rock shaped like a junk, the other half filled with idols of Kwan-non, shivered for half an hour over *hibachi*, hurried down the mountain, regained our *kurumas*, and, after a short, picturesque jolt, rattled down a steep wooded hill to the entrance to the Naikû shrine. Near it is a most peculiar street, composed entirely of most peculiar shops, which consist solely of covered *doma* or "earth-spaces," with hundreds of whistles, wooden flutes, rice ladles, and small, rude images of Daikoku, ranged on racks up the walls.

The entrance to the shrines is very grand; a straight avenue for a short distance, from which one road turns to the right under a *torii*, and then goes forward to a solid stone bridge, while the main road, which is very broad and handsome, turns up-hill towards the temples. On the left, there is a building for the sale of *o-harai* (see p. 279), a house for officials, a covered platform for sacred dances, and a treasury on stilts ; above these, a terrace of large stones with an extensive pebbled area, enclosed by a straw rope, and a flight of steps leading to the shrines, the arrangement of which is exactly that of the Gekû, except that the principal entrance is closed by doors instead of a curtain. There our runners "worshipped," and threw down their *rin* on a white cloth. Do they think, I wonder, that we have added the gods of Isé to our objects of worship?

The sombre evening fell fast, and in its shadows the darkness of the superb groves of camphor and crypto-meria, some of which are of colossal size, became absolutely funereal. We were the only visitors ; a dismal wind sighed through the trees, dim lamps, one by one, began to glimmer through the gloom, our footsteps sounded harshly on the gravel, and in the profound melancholy which surrounds the shrines of a faith which was always dead, and has never lifted men towards a higher life,[1] I involuntarily quickened my pace, for I felt as if the ghosts of the dead ages were after me! It was good to see houses and living men again, and to be able to hire lanterns for our *kurumas*.

A fine road runs from the Gekû to the Naikû shrines, a distance of about 3½ miles, terminating at the Naikû in a fine stone bridge, with uprights with bronze finials, and a lofty *torii*. The towns Uji, Ushidani, and Furui-chi, occupy much of the distance. They flourish by the entertainment of pilgrims, and the sale of trumpery relics, and in the dim light looked solid and handsome with their long lines of *yadoyas*, tea-houses, *jôrôyas*, and various places of entertainment, suggestive of everything but sanctity. Along the road, at suitable distances on both sides, are grand stone lanterns, roofed with bronze, standing on stone pedestals of five steps each, and their dim, melancholy light, altogether unworthy of their superb appearance, made the descent into the absolute darkness of Yamada almost appalling.

Our host has come in to ask us to write lines of poetry to hang upon his walls, so I must conclude.

I. L. B.

[1] See Appendix B.

LAKE BIWA.

My *Kuruma*-runner — Stupid Curiosity — The City of Tsu — A Buddhist Temple — Road Mending — The Pass of Tsuzaka — The Tô
kaidô — Lake Biwa — The "Temperance Pledge" — A *Matsuri*.

OTSU, LAKE BIWA, *November* 15.

THREE more days of travelling have brought us here,
and in three hours we shall be in Kiyôto. I wish we
were beginning our tour instead of ending it, or rather
that we were starting on another. Everything has been
so smooth and pleasant, and so unexpectedly interesting,
and the people have been so kind and courteous, as they
always are, away from the beaten track. Mrs. Gulick's
cheerfulness and kindness have never varied, and, if I
had ever felt inclined to grumble, the unwearied good
nature, brightness, and kindness of my runner would
have rebuked me. I cannot tell you how sorry I am to
part with this faithful creature, or how I shall miss his
willing services, hideous face, and blanket-swathed form.
But no, he is not hideous! No face, beaming with honesty and kindness, can ever be so, and I like to look at
his, and to hope that one day it may be said of him, as
of a child, "of such is the kingdom of heaven."

We left Yamada early on the 12th, retraced our route
as far as Rokken, and reached the important town of
Tsu, late in the afternoon, by a fine road leading through
a very prosperous and populous country of rice-swamps
of large size, between wooded hills and the sea. The
evening was cold and clear, and the town looked its best.

The crowded *yadoya* was very unpromising-looking, but we got a quiet back room, and, by dint of hugging *hibachi*, and loading ourselves with *futons*, managed to keep ourselves from freezing, and not to be more than a little stiff with cold when we got up the next morning to find a brilliant frosty day with a keen north wind. The servants watched our ways with stupid curiosity, asked us if we slept in our shoes, and remarked that it was very long since we had blacked our teeth! Policemen with courteous manners paid us a visit; in the evening Mrs. Gulick went to a lonely quarter of the town to call upon the parents of a girl who had been in the American School in Kiyôto, and the next morning, the father returned the visit, dressed very richly in silk, and bringing a present of fine sweetmeats, with a symbolical piece of seaweed attached.

Few people in England have heard of Tsu, and when I proposed to visit it, I found few among the foreigners at Kôbe who knew of it, and it lies so off the track of foreign travel, that Europeans are a rare spectacle, and, consequently, we trailed a prodigious crowd after us, with policemen hovering upon its skirts to keep us from undue pressure. This obscure Tsu is a city of 83,000 people, divided into three parts by rivers which are crossed by fine bridges, with long, parallel streets crossed by shorter ones at right angles, fine public buildings, a normal school, a new hospital on a height, two streets of temples, an open room inscribed in English with "News for every man's reading," and chairs and tables covered with newspapers inside, a great trade in coarse blue pottery, silks, and green mosquito gauze, curio shops in numbers, with the finest antique bronzes I have seen, and small pieces of old gold lacquer on which *connoisseurs* might spend a fortune, pottery and sweetmeat shops, the remains of a *daimiyô'*s castle, with a fine moat.

stone-faced embankments, with towers at their corners, a large telegraph office, and, in the outskirts, rows of wheelwrights' sheds, where men were making cart-wheels without tires. The main street terminates in a fine double-roofed gateway and a pavement lined with booths, leading into temple grounds, as at Asakusa. There is a popular temple, crowded and shabby, but the lanterns in its portico, the candles and lamps by the shrine, the cat-like tread of priests, the bell-accompanied litanies, and the mumbled petitions of worshippers, heathen though they are, were, in some sense, refreshing after the intolerable emptiness of Shintô.

Tsu, though so near the shrines of Isé, is a Buddhist city, and its two streets of temples, with their grand gateways, paved courts, and priests' houses, are quite imposing. Some of these gateways are pierced by "Saxon" arches, the only architectural arches I have seen in Japan. Somehow I left Tsu with regret; it looked a very prosperous and thoroughly Japanese city, and the people were remarkably kind also. We left at eleven, when the sun was high and bright, lighting up the shining evergreens and glowing autumnal tints of a pretty, hilly region, where villages with their deep brown roofs peeped from among pines and maples. Soon after leaving Tsu we diverged to the village of Isshinden, visited two of the grandest temples in Japan, which appear to be unknown to foreigners, had a delightful day's journey through very pretty country, and, in the afternoon, passing under a fine *torii*, struck the beaten track at Séki on the Tôkaidô, the historic highway of Japan, the great road from Tôkiyô to Kiyôto. From Séki to Otsu it is a narrow carriage-road, in some places full of ruts and holes, the latter having been "mended" for the recent journey of the Mikado, by being filled up with twigs covered with mats. After leaving Séki it plunges

at once into lovely country, pursues the course of a
mountain stream, with which it is shut in by steep,
picturesque hills, and then further progress is apparently
barred by a ridge with a beautiful village with houses on
stone terraces clustering on its wooded acclivity. This
mountain wall, the pass of Tsuzuka, is crossed by sixteen or seventeen zigzags, from 50 to 100 feet in length,

TEMPLE GATEWAY AT ISSHINDEN.

built out from the hill-side on fine terraces, very steep,
with sharp turns, and stout railings to prevent the unwary from tumbling over. We climbed it in the lemon-
coloured twilight, revelling in the beautiful view, and
enjoying the balsamic odours of pines which came up
on the frosty air, got lanterns on the summit, and, after
a rattling run of an hour in the darkness, reached the

town of Tsuchiyama, whose pine-covered hills stood out boldly against a starlit sky; slept in a large *yadoya*, where the servants showed unusual agility; hugged *hibachi*, were half-frozen during the night in a detached suite of rooms in a garden; yesterday crossed the Matsuno-gawa, and followed its course for some time, and then, after some miles of wrinkled white sandhills, arrived at Lake Biwa, crossed the Sétagawa, paid a second visit to the beauties of Ishiyama, and reached the interminable street of Otsu after dark.

The Tôkaidô is the most beaten track of travel in Japan, but in this cold weather travellers are scarce, and we and our runners were the only guests in the great rambling tea-house last night. From Séki here there are long towns and long villages nearly the whole way, with numbers of great tea-houses and *yadoyas* with from twenty to forty rooms, together and in detached suites, with running streams, stone bridges, and all the quaintnesses possible to the conceit of the owners. The house masters and mistresses are active and polite, the servants agile and well dressed, the accommodation admirable, the equipments beautiful — in short, the Tôkaidô is the Japan of tourists, and needs no description of mine. The industries of its villages are manifold, some produce and sell nothing but *saké* gourds of all sizes (a *saké* gourd being an essential part of the equipment of most Japanese travellers), others make shrines, and ornamental baskets and basket hats are the specialties of Mina-Kochi, a large town with fine stone-faced embankments, the remains of a *daimiyô's* castle.

Lake Biwa is a noble sheet of water forty-five miles long,[1] its west shore and head dark with masses of

---

[1] I have omitted my letters from Lake Biwa and its neighbourhood, as well as most of those from Kiyôto, because these regions are on the "beaten track;" but no popular resorts in Japan are lovelier than

piled-up, forest-covered mountains, and its east a smiling region of garden cultivation. It is said that besides Otsu, Hikone, and some other towns, 1800 thriving villages fringe its coasts, its waters are whitened with sails, and a brisk traffic is also carried on by small

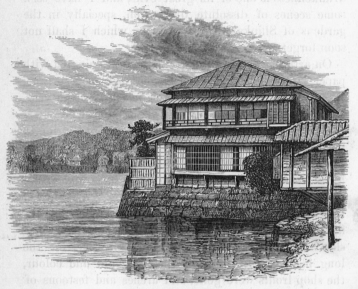

A LAKE BIWA TEA-HOUSE.

steamers. It is a great resort of pleasure-seekers, and its tea-houses are famous.

Near Kusatsu I noticed some men's top-knots hung up on a shrine, and found, on inquiry, that it is not uncommon for people who have suffered very deeply from the evils of intemperance, to take a vow of "total abstinence" and offer it to the god Kompira, who is sup-

Hiyeizan, the "priests' mountain," Sakamoto the "priests' village," and the hill groves and temples of Miidera and of Ishiyama-no-dera — scenes which Japanese art and literature are perpetually reproducing in painting and poetry.

posed to take special cognisance of vows, and to punish those who break them with great severity. Such persons cut off their top-knots and hang them up on the shrines of this idol in token of their resolves. Japan is not a quarter as intemperate as Britain, but still drunkenness is one of its great evils, and I have seen some scenes of dissolute dissipation, specially in the gardens of Shinkakuji, near Kiyôto, which I shall not soon forget.

On arriving here we found the town illuminated with paper lanterns, and that, by exceptional good fortune, we had lighted upon the grandest *matsuri* of the year, that of the god Shinnomiya. Thousands of strangers had already arrived, and thousands more are pouring in from Kiyôto and the countless villages of Lake Biwa; but full as Otsu is, our worthy host only asks 8d. each for our room — a very good one — a *hibachi, andon,* and unlimited rice and tea for two meals. We hurried through a supper of bonito steak with a carrion-like flavour, and spent the evening among the crowds outside, seeing a veritable transformation scene, for the long, mean streets were glorified by light and colour, the shop fronts were gone, and arches and festoons of coloured lanterns turned the whole into fairyland.

To begin with, every house had a lantern three feet long hanging outside it, with the characters forming the god's name on one side and a black or red *tomoyé* on the other.

The removal of *fusuma* had transformed shops into large spaces, with backs and sides of splendid folding screens with peonies, lotuses, and irises painted on a dead gold ground. The mats were covered with Kiyôto rugs; a *hibachi,* and two or three fanciful lamps were in the centre of each; a man crouched over every *hibachi,* and in most cases two or three friends were smoking or sipping tea with him. Apparently the people vied with each other in the beauty of the decorations which they displayed to the streets. Some of the houses really looked like fairy scenes, especially two, in which the trappings of the idol cars were displayed, mythological scenes in very ancient needlework, so exquisitely fine, that for some time I supposed them to be paintings, lacquer and gold filagree stands supporting valuable rock crystal balls, and black and gold lacquer railings —all the bequest of centuries of heathenism. On every floor there was a vase of magnificent chrysanthemums, and an orderly crowd of many thousands quietly promenaded the narrow streets, admiring and comparing, the *tableaux vivants* in the house fronts nowise moved by all. At the intersections of all the streets there were strings of lanterns one above another in harmoniously blended colours to a height of twenty-five feet, and *matsuri* cars for to-day's

TOMOYE.[1]

procession twenty feet high, with canopied platforms on their tops, reached by gangways from the house roofs, with festoons of lanterns, and on each car ten boys beating drums and gongs, and two men playing flutes, kept up a din truly diabolical.

We dived down a dark, lonely street, and passing through a slit in the wall of the court of the great Shintô temple, came upon a blaze of light, and a din of

---

[1] The *tomoye* is found throughout Japan. All terminal tiles of roofs or walls which do not bear the badge of the owner's family, are impressed with it. It is seen on one side of all lanterns used in *matsuri* illuminations, on all drums at the *tanabata* festival, among the wood-carving and arabesques of temples, and is the most common ornament in the Empire, besides being the second badge of the once powerful house of Arima. It is supposed (in Buddhism) to be a sign of the heaping up of myriads of good influences, good luck, long life, etc.; but it seems impossible to explain its origin.

revelry partly inspired by *saké*. Along the pavements
there were brilliantly-lighted booths for the sale of
oranges and persimmons, and heathenish toys of all
kinds, among which toy *torii*, *mikoshi* or arks containing
"divine" property or emblems, shrines, and festival
cars were selling in hundreds, to decorated doll children. The temple platforms were illuminated, and
mikoshi of black lacquer, gorgeous with gold, were displayed under their canopies; priestesses in white *kimono* and crimson silk *hakama*, with attendants beating
small drums, and vases of chrysanthemum and *Cleyera
Japonica* around them, sat on other platforms, painted
and motionless; a temple attendant thumped a big
drum, and piles of plain deal *zen*, with offerings of *Cleyera Japonica*, rice, and *saké*, were heaped up before the
principal idol's shrine. The shrine of the fox god was
also a great centre of attraction, and round shrines and
platforms in the soft, coloured light surged a crowd of
men, women, and children, dressed in their best, buying, selling, laughing, singing, clattering bells, and
blowing flutes — light, mirth, and music being at their
height about ten, when a few small drops of rain fell,
the crowd melted away, and in a few minutes the
streets were dark and silent.

But this morning is fine, and Otsu is gay and
crowded. At an early hour, with much discord supposed to be music, the *mikoshi* were brought in state
from the sacred platforms, and were placed on the cars,
which are being dragged through the streets at the rate
of a mile in an hour and a half, the priestesses performed a sacred dance, the offerings were multiplied,
and the festival is at its height. Otsu is famous for the
number and magnificence of its *matsuri* cars, of which
there are thirteen, but we only saw three. The Shintô
"godowns" must be treasures of priceless antique art,
bare as the temples are.

Each car consists of a massive, oblong, black lacquer body on a lacquer platform, on two solid, tireless wheels of brown lacquer, with a smaller wheel in front. On the top there is a platform with a heavy railing of black and gold lacquer, a solid back, and a lofty canopy of black lacquer lined with red lacquer, heavily gilded, and with a big gilded eagle at its summit. In front there were male and female figures, one standing, the other seated, in cloth of gold dresses of great beauty. Behind these, ten boys, as last night, were ceaselessly beating drums and gongs, and two men were playing flutes, all at the level of the house roofs. Below the platform there were valances of very rich needlework, and at the back a *kakemono* of glorious needlework, almost or quite priceless, the ground being worked in a fine gold thread no longer made. An antiquity of eight centuries is claimed for these decorations. The cars were dragged along by a curious team, marshalled by two men in glazed peaked hats and winged garments of calico, carrying ancient staffs with rings at the top of much-corroded iron, such as are often placed in the hands of statues of Buddhas, the team consisting of thirty men in blue and white striped trousers and dark-blue *haori* with the characters representing the god upon them. These tugged the unwieldy erections by stout ropes, and as many more, similarly attired, assisted the ponderous wheels with levers. The master of the ceremonies was a manikin in a European dress suit of black broadcloth, with a broad expanse of shirt front, and a white necktie with long ends!!!

Kiôto, November 16.— We arrived here yesterday morning, and it is a tribute to the security which foreigners enjoy in this orderly and peaceable land, that two foreign ladies, without even a servant, have travelled for nearly 200 miles, and mainly through a region in which Europeans are rarely seen, not only without a solitary instance of extortion, incivility, or annoyance, but receiving courtesy and kindness everywhere.

I. L. B.

ITINERARY OF ROUTE FROM KIYÔTO TO YAMADA
(Shrines of Isé), AND BY TSU TO KIYÔTO.

	Ri.	Chô
Kiyôto to Nara	11	20
Nara to Tambaichi	2	18
Miwa	2	5
Hasé-dera or Hatsusé	1	23
Haibara	1	8
Higenashi	2	23
Nobari-shita	2	12
Awoyama	4	3
Rokken	4	13
Matsuzaka	1	18
Kushida	1	26
Yamada	1	
Rokken	5	8
Tsu	3	
Kubota	1	
Kusuhara	3	
Séki	1	
By Tôkaidô to Kiyôto	24	
	73	23

About 185¼ miles.

PROSPECTS OF CHRISTIANITY.

Water-Ways in Ôsaka — Glimpses of Domestic Life — Ladies' Pets — The Position of Women — Imperial Example — The Medical Mission — A Japanese Benevolent Institution — A Comfortless Arrival — A Christian Gathering — The Prison at Otsu — Prospects of Christianity — Blankness of Heathenism.

KÔBE, *December* 3, 1878.

ON my way from Kiyôto I spent three days at Ôsaka with Miss M——, who, having the charge of two Japanese children, and being in Japanese employment, is allowed to live in a little house in the most densely peopled part of the great commercial capital with its 600,000 souls. Aided by her kindness and her small amount of Japanese, I saw many of the Ôsaka sights and most of the huge, busy city, but was impressed by nothing so much as by the numerous waterways and their innumerable bridges, a few of which are stone or iron ; the canals quayed with stone ; the massive flights of stone stairs down to the water ; the houses with overhanging balconies draped with trailers ; the broad, quayed roadways along the rivers, with weeping willows on one side and ancient *yashikis* and rice godowns on the other ; the hundreds of junks and small boats moving up or down with every tide ; the signs of an enormous commerce everywhere, the floating tea-houses, and house-boats with matted roofs, and the islands with tea-houses and pleasure-grounds. But the sights of Ôsaka, like those of Kiyôto, are on the best beaten

tourist track, and you can read more or less about them
in every book on Japan.

I made the acquaintance of Mr. and Mrs. Warren of
the C. M. S., and of Dr. Taylor and others connected
with the American mission. Mr. Warren has great
facility in colloquial Japanese, and a hearty, hopeful
spirit, preaches and itinerates extensively, has a daily
evening service attended by from forty to fifty people,
and has large expectations of success. The American
ladies conduct girls' schools, but very specially endeavour to make acquaintance with Japanese women
in their own homes with the assistance of a Japanese
Bible-woman, and I had some curious glimpses into the
domestic life of the richer people, one being a visit to a
lady whose husband holds high official rank, and whose
house is purely Japanese. Miss —— had become acquainted with her through her desire to know the way
in which European mothers care for their own and their
children's health, which led the way to intelligent inquiries into Christianity. On our visit we were conducted through various large rooms into a low one
about ten feet square, with lattice fret-work, only ad-
mitting a dim light. The lady, who is haggard and by
no means pretty, but who, fortunately for herself, is a
mother, received us with much dignity, and immediately
opened the conversation by inquiries about the position
of European women. She looked intelligent, restless,
and unhappy, and, I thought, chafed under the restraints of custom, as she said that no Japanese woman
could start for foreign countries alone, and she envied
foreigners their greater liberty. She produced a map
and traced my route upon it, but seemed more interested in other countries than in her own. A very
pretty girl, with singular grace and charm of manner,
came in and sat down beside her, equally well dressed

in silk, but not a legal wife. The senior wife obtains great credit for her kind and sisterly treatment of her, which, according to Japanese notions, is the path of true wisdom. There was an attendant in the shape of a detestable "Chin," something like a King Charles's spaniel with a broken nose: an artificially dwarfed creature, with glassy, prominent eyes, very cross and delicate, and dressed in a warm coat. These objection able lap-dogs are "ladies' pets" all over Japan.

My impression is, that, according to our notions, the Japanese wife is happier in the poorer than in the richer classes. She works hard, but it is rather as the partner than the drudge of her husband. Nor, in the same class, are the unmarried girls secluded, but, within certain limits, they possess complete freedom. Women undoubtedly enjoy a more favourable position than in most other heathen countries, and wives are presumably virtuous. Infanticide is very rare. The birth of a daughter is far from being an occasion of mourning, and girls receive the same affection and attention as boys, and for their sphere are equally carefully educated.

The women of the upper classes are much secluded, and always go out with attendants. In the middle ranks it is not proper for a wife to be seen abroad in her husband's absence, and, to be above suspicion, many, under these circumstances, take an old woman to keep them company. There are many painful and evil customs to which I cannot refer, and which are not likely to be overthrown except by the reception of a true Christianity, some of them arising out of morbidly exaggerated notions of filial piety; but even in past times women have not been "downtrodden," but have occupied a high place in history. To say nothing of the fact that the greatest of the national divinities is a goddess, nine empresses have ruled Japan by "divine right," and in literature, especially in poetry, women divide the foremost places with men.

At present the reform in the marriage-laws which legalises the marriage of members of different classes, the establishment of high-class schools for young women, the training in the mission-schools, the widening of the area of female industrial occupation, the slow but sure influence of European female example, the weakening of the influence of Buddhism, which, in its rigid dogma, exalts the conventual above the domestic life, and above all, the slow permeation of at least a portion of the community with Christian ideas on the true dignity and position of maid, matron, and mother, and the example of the gentle Empress Haruku, who timidly takes the lead in all that specially concerns the elevation of her sex, are all tending to bring about a better future for Japanese women, who, even at the worst, enjoy an amount of liberty, considerate care, and respect, which I am altogether surprised to find in a heathen country. It is even to be hoped that things may not go too far, and that the fear of the *Meiroku Zasshi*, that "the power of women will grow gradually, and eventually become so overwhelming that it will be impossible to control it," may not be realised![1]

The Medical Mission, both at Hiogo and Ôsaka, is under the charge of Dr. Taylor, a blunt and unaffected, as well as zealous and honest, missionary, by no means enthusiastic, or inclined to magnify what is emphatically "a day of small things." I visited both his dispensaries,

---

[1] Within the last few months, since the establishment of representative Local Assemblies with control over local taxation, women have been awaking to an idea of their "rights," and in some cases have actually written to the papers, stating that, where they pay taxes and bear part of the national burdens, it is only just that they should exercise the elective franchise!

or rather consulting-rooms, and it is interesting to observe that both he and Dr. Berry (who has been very successful, and has won the goodwill of the Government by his courtesy and suavity) employ a different manner of working from that pursued by Dr. Palm at Niigata, being less independent, and less *apparently* missionary. Dr. Taylor works almost exclusively through the native doctors, and receives no money either for advice or medicine. He acts much as a consulting-physician. The doctors bring the patients to him, he writes prescriptions, which are made up at any drug store, and afterwards lectures on the more important cases. There are 500 Japanese doctors in Ôsaka, and a number of these have organised a private hospital, of which they have asked Dr. T. to be consulting-physician. The six whom I saw were remarkably shrewd, superior-looking men. Dr. Taylor has many requests to go to outlying towns at stated intervals, and in these cases the doctors pay his expenses.

The dispensary in Hiogo is strictly a *Japanese Benevolent Institution*, to which eight Japanese doctors give monthly subscriptions, besides gratuitous advice to the very poor. Dr. Taylor goes there, and sees about forty patients every Monday, his travelling expenses being paid. Where people cannot pay for medicines, etc., a group of benevolent persons subscribes to procure them, and the Kôbe native Christians provide medicines and other requisites for all indigent persons belonging to their body. In surgical cases from a distance a room is taken at a neighbouring *yadoya*, and the patient pays a nurse; but in the case of the destitute, all the expenses are borne by the subscriptions to the dispensary. Dr. Taylor prays when the patients have assembled, but does not give an address.

At Ikinagi, forty miles from Kôbe, the Japanese doctors conduct a similar dispensary, organised by Dr. Berry, and dispensaries now exist in many other places, as the indirect result of medical missionary work, and the now "flourishing" mission-stations of Sanda, Hikone, and Akashi, were all opened by direct medical missionary effort.

On November 26, Mrs. Gulick and I went a day's journey into the mountains, through exquisite scenery, glorious with autumnal colouring, to Arima, a picturesque village, much resorted to by foreigners during the heat of summer, and famous for bamboo-baskets and straw-boxes, which can now be bought in any quantity in London; and from thence rattled down, through a woodland region, to Sanda, a town of 2000 people (formerly a *daimiyô's* town), in a rice valley. We reached it in the dusk of a chilly November afternoon, but I will not dwell upon the cold and discomfort, or tell how we got the key of an unoccupied house, all damp and decayed-looking, with the floor littered with the rubbish left by the last occupant; how a man came in and sawed up some damp wood; how we made a fire in a stove, which, having been heavily oiled, gave off a black, abominable smoke, which compelled us to dispense with it; how we found some food among the remains of some old stores, and spent nearly four hours in preparing it for supper and breakfast; how hopelessly cold the night was, and how dark and drizzling the morning, for our discomfort arose out of what constituted the interest of our visit — that we were unexpected.

The upper part of Sanda is on a steepish hill, and is almost entirely composed of large old houses, with grounds enclosed by high walls, the dwellings of *samurai*, who clustered round the castle, which is the nucleus of the whole. It is among this class that the Christian converts are found, and they have built a neat little church, which is self-supporting. We went forth with a lantern to pay some visits among these people, but were left in the dark to stumble up the hill, and to feel our way to the first house, a large rambling mansion, with an old lady at its head, who was sitting under the *kotatsu* (p. 261) with her two sons and their wives, and invited us to "creep in," which we did for a time, and then one of her daughters-in-law guided us to several other large houses, where our reception was courteous, and, lastly, to a handsome dwelling occupied by the leading physician in Sanda. We were taken into a well-lighted room, with fine *kakemono* on the walls, an antique bronze in a recess, a grand *hibachi* in the centre, and a fine lamp hanging over a group of an elderly lady in the place of honour, the physician, his wife, twin daughters, and seven visitors, including a fine bright-looking young man, second master in the Government school. Each person was sitting on his heels on a wadded silk cushion, and each saluted us with three profound bows. Tea, cakes, and sugared slices of sweet potato were passed round, of which we partook, and were much laughed at for our awkwardness with the chopsticks. There were light, warmth, comfort, and friendliness, giving me a new idea of what home life may be among the middle classes, and a frank geniality of manner, slightly European, in pleasant combination with Oriental courtesy. Of this group all are Christians except the head of the house, and he is an intelligent inquirer, and the object of the gathering was to read and discuss the Christian Scriptures for mutual instruction, the Government teacher presiding. This reunion takes place once a week. It was really very interesting to drop in upon it, and to know that this and similar gatherings and groups of Christians in this and other places have come about as results of medical missionary work, and that in Sanda and elsewhere the "new way" is aided by the influence of its reception by people of education and position. In Sanda, as in many other places, a number of persons have become Christians, and use their influence and money in favour of Christianity, who, for various reasons, have not sought baptism, and are not numbered among the converts.

I do not share the sanguine expectations of those about me as to a rapid spread of Christianity, but that it is destined to be a power in moulding the future of Japan, I do not doubt. Among favourable signs are that it is received as a life rather than as a doctrine, and that various forms of immorality are recognised as incompatible with it. It is tending to bind men together, irrespectively of class, in a true democracy, in a very surprising way. The small Christian congregations are pecuniarily independent, and are vigorous in their efforts. The Kôbe congregation, numbering 350 members, besides contributing nearly 1000 dollars to erect a church, sustaining its own poor, providing medicine and advice for its indigent sick, and paying its own pastor, engages in various forms of benevolent effort, and compensates Christians who are too poor to abstain from work on Sunday for the loss of the day's wages. At Ôsaka the native Christians have established a Christian school for their girls. The Christian students in Kiyôto are intensely zealous, preach through the country in their vacations, and aim at nothing less than the Christianising of Japan. Christian women go among the villages as voluntary missionaries to their own sex. Missionaries and students who itinerate in the interior find, as a result of medical or other missionary effort, that companies of persons meet to read such

of the Scriptures as are translated, and every true con
vert appears anxious to bring others within the pale of
the Christian society.

Doubtless there is an indirect influence against Christianity, but overtly, quiet toleration is the maxim of
the Government, and the profession of Christianity does
not involve the loss of official position. Thus, the
Director of the junior department of the Naval College
is an energetic Christian, the second teacher in the
Sanda School is the same, and I have heard of others
whose renunciation of the national faith has not involved temporal loss. The Government requested Dr.
Berry to take charge of the hospital here, and also to
inspect and report upon prisons, at the very time that
he was engaged in earnest medical missionary work — a
fact which must have had some significance among its
own subjects. In this region the Buddhist priests have
ceased to claim the right to interfere with the wishes of
a Christian or his relatives regarding his interment, or
to perform heathen rites over his grave. The edicts
against Christianity have been removed from public
places, and quite lately the Department of Religion,
formerly the first in the State, was abolished, and its
business transferred to a bureau of the Home Department. This, however, is only an indication of progress
in a western direction, and of increasing indifference to
religion. Even in prisons the *laissez faire* principle is
adopted. Several copies of such of the New Testament
books as have been translated, and some other Christian books were given some time ago by Mr. Neesima
to the officer of the prison at Otsu, who, not caring to
keep them, gave them to a man imprisoned for man-
slaughter, but a scholar. A few months ago a fire
broke out, and 100 incarcerated persons, instead of trying to escape, helped to put out the flames, and to a

man remained to undergo the rest of their sentences. This curious circumstance led to an inquiry as to its cause, and it turned out that the scholar had been so impressed with the truth of Christianity that he had taught it to his fellow-captives, and Christian principle, combined with his personal influence, restrained them from defrauding justice. The scholar was afterwards pardoned, but remained in Otsu to teach more of the "new way" to the prisoners.

There cannot, however, be a greater mistake than that Japan is "ripe for the reception of Christianity." Though the labours of many men and women in many years have resulted in making 1617 converts to the Protestant faith,[1] while the Romanists claim 20,000, the Greeks 3000, and a knowledge of the essentials of Christianity is widely diffused through many districts, *the fact remains that 34,000,000 of Japanese are sceptics or materialists, or are absolutely sunk in childish and degrading superstitions, out of which the religious significance, such as it was, has been lost.*

The chief obstacles in the way of Christianity are, if I judge correctly, the general deadness of the religious instinct and of religious cravings, the connection of the national faiths with the Japanese reverence for ancestors, a blank atheism among the most influential classes, a universal immorality which shrinks from a gospel of self-denial, and the spread of an agnostic philosophy imported from England, while the acts of "Christian" nations and the lives of "Christian" men are regarded as a more faithful commentary on the Law of Sinai and the Sermon on the Mount than that which is put upon them by the missionaries.[2]

[1] A number which the ten months which have elapsed since this letter was written have increased by fifteen hundred.

[2] The ruling spirit of Japan is represented in the following extracts from a paper called, "Of what good is Christianity to Japan?" which

The days when a missionary was "dished up for dinner"[1] at foreign tables are perhaps past, but the anti-

appeared in one of the most influential of the Japanese papers on October 19, 1878: —

"The Christian religion seems to be extending by degrees throughout our country. . . . We have no wish to obey it, nor have we any fear of being troubled by it. As we can enjoy sufficient happiness without any religion whatever, the question as to the merits or demerits of the different forms never enters our head. Indeed, we are of those who, not knowing the existence of religions in the universe, are enjoying perfect happiness. We have no intention of either supporting or attacking the Christian religion. In fact, religion is nothing to us. . . . We do not consider believers in Christianity to be odd or foolish persons, but we take them to be those who are guided in their morals by their religion, and therefore we may say that believers in the Christian religion are those who, spending time and labour, import their morals from a foreign country." The writer, after asking the question, "In associating with foreigners, in what way can we benefit our country ?" urges that though the morality of Japan is not blameless, it is rather superior than inferior to that of some western people, while in "intellect," *i. e.* the arts and sciences, Japan is immeasurably behind them. He argues that "Christian believers," therefore, are "wasting their time" upon morals, and concludes thus: — "How careless the Christian believers are in judging the importance of matters! If the time and trouble wasted on improving our morality, which is not deficient in us, were directed towards gaining intellectual knowledge, which *is* deficient in us, the benefit accruing to our country would be not a little. The present Japan is an active country, busy in gaining intellectual acquirements, and therefore no time ought to be allowed to be wasted on any useless affairs." — *Hochi Shimbun.*

[1] In his *Voyages of a Naturalist*, Mr. Darwin, in his severely truthful style, defends missionaries from malignant and vulgar attacks. His manly pages on the subject are well worth reading, but I only quote two or three sentences. "There are many who attack, even more acrimoniously than Kotzebue, the missionaries, their system, and the effects produced by it. Such reasoners never compare the present state with only twenty years ago, nor even with that of Europe at this day, but they compare it with the high standard of gospel perfection. They expect the missionaries to do that which the Apostles themselves failed to do. Inasmuch as the condition of the people falls short of this high standard, blame is attached to the missionary, instead of credit for that which he has effected." Mr. Darwin, after mentioning many sinful habits of the past, says, "They forget, or will not remember, that all these have been abolished, and that dishonesty, intemperance, and licentiousness, have been greatly reduced by the introduction of Christianity. But it is useless to argue against such reasoners. I believe that, disappointed in not finding the field for licentiousness

missionary spirit is strong, and the missionaries give a great deal of positive and negative offence, some of which might, perhaps, be avoided. They would doubt-less readily confess faults, defects, and mistakes, but with all these, I believe them to be a thoroughly sincere, conscientious, upright, and zealous body of men and women, all working, as they best know how, for the spread of Christianity, and far more anxious to build up a pure Church than to multiply nominal converts. The agents of the different sects abstain from even the appearance of rivalry, and meet for friendly counsel, and instead of perpetuating such separating names as Episcopalians, Baptists, Congregationalists, etc., "the disciples are called CHRISTIANS FIRST."

Without indulging in any unreasonable expectations, it cannot be doubted that the teaching of this large body of persons, and the example of the unquestionable purity of their lives, is paving the way for the reception of the Christianity preached by Japanese evangelists with the eloquence of conviction, and that every true convert is not only a convert but a propagandist, and a centre of the higher morality in which lies the great hope for the future of Japan.

I ardently long to see this people Christianised, not with the nominal Christianity of Christendom, but with the pure, manly, self-sacrificing Christianity of Christ and His apostles. Japanese religious art has done much to please the eye, yet the impression, on the whole, is one of profound melancholy. The religious zeal which covered the land with temples and monasteries, terraced mountain sides in stone, and ascended them by colossal flights of stone stairs, has perished.

quite so open as formerly, they will not give credit to a morality which they do not wish to practise, or to a religion which they undervalue, if not despise." — P. 414.

Myth and Nature worship are reduced to rubbing and clapping the hands, and throwing *rin* upon temple floors. Buddhism, degenerate and idolatrous, is losing its hold over men's fears, and prostrate Buddhas and decaying shrines are seen all over the land. The chill of an atheistic materialism rests upon the upper classes; an advancing education bids religion and morality stand aside, the clang of the new material progress drowns the still, small voice of Christ, the old faiths are dying, the religious instincts are failing, and religious cravings scarcely exist. Even at its best and highest there is an intense mournfulness about Japanese Buddhism, pointing, as it does, to an unattainable perfection, and holding up the terrors of hell to those who fall short of it, but recognising no availing "sacrifice for sin," no "merciful and faithful High Priest," no Father in heaven yearning over mankind with an infinite love, no higher destiny than practical annihilation, being "without hope, and without God in the world."

I. L. B.

CREMATION.

Fine Weather — Cremation in Japan — The Governor of Tôkiyô —
An Awkward Question — An Insignificant Building — Economy
in Funeral Expenses — Simplicity of the Cremation Process —
The Last of Japan.

H.B.M.'s LEGATION, YEDO, *December* 18.

I HAVE spent the last ten days here, in settled fine
weather, such as should have begun two months ago,
if the climate had behaved as it ought. A cloudless
sky, a brilliant sun, and a temperature rarely falling
to the freezing-point, are very delightful. I miss Lady
Parkes and the children sorely, and she is mourned by
every one, not only because she took, as no one else
can, the social lead in the English-speaking community,
but because of her thoughtful kindness and genuine
sympathy with sorrow, no less than for her high sense
of truth and justice, and for her judicious reticence of
speech, nowhere more important than in such a mixed
society as this. The time has flown by, however, in
excursions, shopping, select little dinner parties, farewell calls, and visits made with Mr. Chamberlain to
the famous groves and temples of Ikegami, where the
Buddhist bishop and priests entertained us in one of
the guest-rooms, and to Enoshima and Kamakura,
"vulgar" resorts which nothing can vulgarise so long
as Fujisan towers above them.

I will mention but one "sight" which is so far out
of the beaten track that it was only after prolonged

inquiry that its whereabouts was ascertained. Among
Buddhists, specially of the Monto sect, cremation was
largely practised till it was forbidden five years ago, as
some suppose in deference to European prejudices.
Three years ago, however, the prohibition was with-
drawn, and in this short space of time the number of
bodies burned has reached nearly nine thousand annu-

FUJISAN, FROM A VILLAGE ON THE TÔKAIDÔ.

ally. Sir H. Parkes applied for permission for me to
visit the Kirigaya ground, one of five, and after a few
delays it was granted by the Governor of Tôkiyô at
Mr. Mori's request, so yesterday, attended by the Legation linguist, I presented myself at the fine *yashiki* of
the Tôkiyô *Fu*, and quite unexpectedly was admitted
to an audience of the Governor. Mr. Kusamoto is a

well-bred gentleman, and his face expresses the energy and ability which he has given proof of possessing. He wears his European clothes becomingly, and in attitude, as well as manner, is easy and dignified. After asking me a great deal about my northern tour and the Ainos, he expressed a wish for candid criticism, but as this in the East must not be taken literally, I merely ventured to say that the roads lag behind the progress made in other directions, upon which he entered upon explanations which doubtless apply to the past road-history of the country. He spoke of cremation and its "necessity" in large cities, and terminated the interview by requesting me to dismiss my interpreter and *kuruma*, as he was going to send me to Meguro in his own carriage with one of the Government interpreters, adding very courteously that it gave him pleasure to show this attention to a guest of the British Minister, "for whose character and important services to Japan he has a high value."

An hour's drive, with an extra amount of yelling from the *bettos*, took us to a suburb of little hills and valleys, where red camellias and feathery bamboo against back-grounds of cryptomeria contrast with the grey monotone of British winters, and, alighting at a farm road too rough for a carriage, we passed through fields and hedgerows to an erection which looks too insignificant for such solemn use. Don't expect any ghastly details. A longish building of "wattle and dab," much like the northern farmhouses, a high roof, and chimneys resembling those of the "oast houses" in Kent, combine with the rural surroundings to sug gest "farm buildings" rather than the "funeral pyre," and all that is horrible is left to the imagination.

The end nearest the road is a little temple, much crowded with images, and small, red, earthenware urns and tongs for sale to the relatives of deceased persons, and beyond this are four rooms with earthen floors and mud walls; nothing noticeable about them except the height of the peaked roof and the dark colour of the plaster. In the middle of the largest are several pairs of granite supports at equal distances from each other, and in the smallest there is a solitary pair. This was literally all that was to be seen. In the large room several bodies are burned at one time, and the charge is only one *yen*, about 3s. 8d., solitary cremation costing five *yen*. Faggots are used, and 1s. worth ordinarily suffices to reduce a human form to ashes. After the funeral service in the house, the body is brought to the cremation ground, and is left in charge of the attendant, a melancholy, smoked-looking man, as well he may be. The richer people sometimes pay priests to be present during the burning, but this is not usual. There were five "quick-tubs" of pine hooped with bamboo in the larger room, containing the remains of coolies, and a few oblong pine chests in the small rooms containing those of middle-class people. At 8 P.M., each "coffin" is placed on the stone trestles, the faggots are lighted underneath, the fires are replenished during the night, and by 6 A.M. that which was a human being is a small heap of ashes, which is placed in an urn by the relatives and is honourably interred. In some cases the priests accompany the relations on this last mournful errand. Thirteen bodies were burned the night before my visit, but there was not the slightest odour in or about the building, and the interpreter told me that, owing to the height of the chimneys, the people of the neighbourhood never experience the least annoyance, even while the process is going on. The simplicity of the arrangement is very remarkable, and there can be no reasonable doubt that it serves the purpose of the innocuous and complete destruction of the corpse as well as any complicated apparatus (if not better), while its cheapness places it within the reach of the class which is most heavily burdened by ordinary funeral expenses.[1] This morning the Governor sent his secretary to present me with a translation of an interesting account of the practice of cremation and its introduction into Japan.

S.S. " Volga," Christmas Eve, 1878. — The snowy dome of Fujisan reddening in the sunrise rose above the violet woodlands of Mississippi Bay as we steamed out of Yokahama Harbour on the 19th, and three days later I saw the last of Japan — a rugged coast, lashed by a wintry sea.   I. L. B.

[1] The following very inaccurate but entertaining account of this expedition was given by the *Yomi-uri-Shimbun,* a daily newspaper with the largest, though not the most aristocratic circulation in Tôkiyô, being taken in by the servants and tradespeople. It is a literal translation made by Mr. Chamberlain. "The person mentioned in our yesterday's issue as ' an English subject of the name of Bird ' is a lady from Scotland, a part of England. This lady spends her time in travelling, leaving this year the two American continents for a passing visit to the Sandwich Islands, and landing in Japan early in the month of May. She has toured all over the country, and even made a five months' stay in the Hokkaido, investigating the local customs and productions. Her inspection yesterday of the cremation ground at Kirigaya is believed to have been prompted by a knowledge of the advantages of this method of disposing of the dead, and a desire to introduce the same into England (!) On account of this lady's being so learned as to have published a quantity of books, His Excellency the Governor was pleased to see her yesterday, and to show her great civility, sending her to Kirigaya in his own carriage, a mark of attention which is said to have pleased the lady much (!) "

JAPANESE PUBLIC AFFAIRS.[1]

THE new era dates from 1868. Up to the twelfth century Japan was ruled by the Mikado, who was believed
to be directly descended from the gods who created the
country. This ruler by "divine right," exercised his
absolute power through the *Kugé* or court nobles,
mostly connections of his own, who monopolised the
chief offices, constituted the membership of the two
great councils which arranged religious and secular
affairs, and filled the principal posts in the eight execu
tive departments of the empire.

After the twelfth century, when the feudal system
rose, the governing power gradually passed out of the
hands of the Mikado and his nobles into those of the
great feudal families, and in 1603 became concentrated
in Iyéyasu, the head of the Tokugawa dynasty, successive members of which exercised it for two centuries
and a half. All this time a shadowy Mikado nominally
reigned in the old palace in Kiyôto, but power and
splendour had passed to his chief vassal, who, under the
title of Shôgun, actually ruled from the Castle of Yedo,

[1] The authorities for the statements in this sketch are — Mr. Mounsey's *Satsuma Rebellion;* figures and facts supplied by the courtesy of
the Statistical Department of the Japanese Government; two lectures
on "The National Debt of Japan," by Mr. Mayét, Counsellor to the
Japanese Finance Department; the Finance Estimates for the year
ending June 30, 1880; and the Reports presented by the heads of the
Mint, Post Office, Telegraph, and Education Departments, to Sanjo
Sanéyoshi, the Prime Minister.

and was usually strong enough to impose his will on his sovereign. It was this system of dual government which gave rise to the fiction of "spiritual" and "tem poral" emperors.

The *daimiyô* were feudal princes, who, having originally conquered their domains by the sword, exercised independent jurisdiction within their limits, but were bound to render certain acts of homage to the Shôgun, whose government was composed of those among them on whose loyalty he could rely. The *samurai*, their "two-sworded" retainers, who had won their provinces for them, and had been rewarded by grants of land, were not only the fighting men of the Empire, but its most public-spirited and best-educated class.

Of these political orders the *kugé*, who were poor, but still retained their old *prestige*, numbered about 150 families; the *daimiyô*, with their quasi-independent position, 268; and the *samurai*, the "backbone of the nation," about 400,000 households. Below these there was the *heimin*, a vast, unrecognised mass of men without position, farmers, artisans, merchants, and peasants, separated by laws forbidding intermarriage from the pariah castes of the *eta*, who handled raw hides and other contaminating things; and the *hinin*, "not humans," paupers, allowed to squat on waste lands, who lived by beggary, carried bodies from the execution grounds, and performed other degraded offices, this mass, without political privileges, numbering 32,000,-000. The Shôgun was the actual depository of power, but, above all was the secluded Mikado, theoretically the source of all authority, and "a name to conjure with."

The reasons for the Revolution must be sought for elsewhere, but it must not be overlooked that contact with western power and civilisation, and the diffusion

of western ideas through the medium of translated literature, were among its predisposing causes; that it
was a few leading men in a few of the clans, together
with a very few *daimiyô* who had not succumbed to the
luxury and effeminacy of their class, who organised and
successfully carried out the dethronement of the *Shôgun*, and the restoration of the Mikado; and that it is
the leading men of the clans, and not men of the old
aristocracy, who have held the reins of power ever
since.

In 1868 Keiki, the last Shôgun, retired into private
life, and in 1869 nearly the whole of the *daimiyô* peti-
tioned to be allowed to yield up their fiefs and quasi-
sovereign rights to the Mikado, praying him to take
absolute power, and to establish the internal relations
of the country upon such a footing "that the Empire
will be able to take its place side by side with the other
countries of the world." This proposal was accepted,
a tenth of their former revenues was allotted to them;
a provision was made for their retainers, and by 1871
when the clans were finally abolished, the feudal system
of Japan, with its splendour and oppressiveness, had
ceased to exist. There has been no very important
movement against the new Government except the Satsuma Rebellion in 1877, which cost Japan 13,000 killed,
and 21,000 wounded men, and £8,400,000 in money,
besides enormous losses arising from the destruction of
property and the depression of trade.

Since 1868 Japan, casting away her traditions of seclusion, and detaching herself from the fellowship of
Oriental nations, has astonished the world by the rapidity of her progress, the skill with which she has selected
and appropriated many of the most valuable results of
western civilisation, the energy with which she has re-
constructed herself, and the governing capacity which

has been shown by men untrained in statecraft. In
the glitter and *éclat* of this unique movement we must
not forget that the Japanese throne is still founded on
a religious fiction, that the Government is still "despotic and idolatrous," that the peasantry are ignorant
and enslaved by superstition; that taxation presses
heavily on the cultivator; that money raised with difficulty is spent ofttimes on objects non-essential to the
progress, and alien to the genius, of the nation; that
the official class still suffers from the taint which pervades Asiatic officialdom; that the educational system
is not only incomplete, but suffers from radical defects;
that the reform of the legal system is only in its infancy; that the means of internal communication are
infamous; that the tone of morality is universally low;
that the nation is a heathen nation, steeped in heathen
ideas and practices; and that the work of making
Japan a really great empire is only in its beginning.
For what she has already done she claims from western
nations hearty sympathy and cordial co-operation, freedom to consolidate and originate internal reforms unem-
barrassed by pressure applied by stronger powers for
selfish purposes, and to be aided by friendly criticism
rather than retarded by indiscriminate praise.

The pages which follow bring together very briefly
some of the most outstanding facts connected with the
present position of Japan, and refer the thoughtful
reader to the carefully prepared pages from which they
are taken.

In 1869 the present Mikado, in the presence of the
grandees of the Empire, swore solemnly "that a delib-
erative assembly should be formed; that all measures
should be decided by public opinion; that the uncivilised customs of former times should be broken through;
that the impartiality and justice displayed in the work-

ings of nature should be adopted as the basis of action; and that intellect and learning should be sought for throughout the world in order to establish the foundations of the Empire." Though this oath of progress was but the word of a boy brought up in the seclusion of Kiyôto, it represented the conviction and settled purpose of the men who led the Revolution, and have piloted the Empire through the perils of the last eleven years. It is now 1880, and the first instalment of representative institutions, though in their most elementary form, was granted last year.

The composition of the Government is subject to change, but in its main features is as follows: — The Mikado is an absolute sovereign. He administers affairs through a Supreme Council, which consists of the Prime Minister, the Vice-Prime Minister, and the heads of the great Departments of State, and meets on fixed days in the Mikado's presence. This is the actual Government. Below this is a Legislative Council, composed of eminent men, and presided over by an Imperial prince. It elaborates such new laws, and reforms in old ones, as are determined on by the Supreme Council, but cannot initiate any legislative measures without its consent. There is also an "assembly of local officials," consisting of one superior officer from each of the three *Fu* (the cities of Tôkiyô, Kiyôto, and Ôsaka) and the thirty-five *Ken* (administrative departments); but it meets but rarely, and is a strictly consultative body, its functions being to advise on matters concerning taxation.

The chief Departments of State are Foreign Affairs, Finance (which embraces the Mint, Tax, Paper Money, Statistical, Audit, Loan, Record, and Paymaster's Departments, and the State Printing-office), War, Marine, Education, Public Works, Justice, Colonisation, the Imperial household, and the Interior, the most important of all (into which the Department of Religion was merged not long ago), which embraces everything not covered by the other Departments, and which has a capacity for centralisation which could scarcely be exceeded.

A Government so constituted is strictly a despotism ruling through a bureaucracy, but a step towards constitutionalism has been taken lately by the calling together of provincial parliaments. All males above 20, who pay land-tax amounting to £1 annually, are entitled to vote, persons who have been sentenced to penal servitude for one year for offences not commutable by fine, and bankrupts who have not paid their liabilities in full, alone excepted. Voting is by ballot. The property qualification for members consists in the annual payment of £2 of land-tax; but persons holding Government or religious appointments are ineligible. The functions of these "primary assemblies" are at present limited to the discussion and arrangement of the expenditure to be met out of the local taxes, and the method of levying such taxes; but a possible enlargement is provided for in the edict by which they were instituted. These novel elections passed off quietly, and the newly constituted bodies, which met in March 1879, confined themselves to the business before them, and to settling their forms of procedure. The importance of this initial step in a constitutional direction on the part of an Asiatic despotism has not been sufficiently recognised by foreigners.

For administrative purposes Japan is divided into three *Fu* and thirty-five *Ken*, each with a Governor or Prefect, and a staff of officials responsible to the Ministry of the Interior, the Island of Yezo, for some occult reason, being under the Colonisation Department.

Official salaries, judged by western notions, are not

high. The "Premier," Sanjo, receives only £1920 annually, and the chief and vice-ministers of the different departments £1440 and £960 respectively.

Protected by her insular position, Japan ought not to have any enemies, and a large armed force, besides being an expense and a source of internal danger, is a standing temptation to her to make aggressions upon her weaker neighbors. On the abolition of the *samurai* or military class, she created a standing army, raised by conscription, and equipped, drilled, and disciplined on European models, by a commission of French officers. It consists of 35,560 men in time of peace, and 50,230 when on a war footing, besides a reserve of 20,000, not yet completely organised. The war estimates for 1880 are £1,438,020.

The navy consists of thirteen ships on active service, ironclad, ironbelted, composite, and wooden, all steamers, carrying 2250 men and 87 guns, besides 10 training-ships and 4 yachts, which, with the addition of 897 unattached men and officers, brings up its total strength to 27 vessels, 4242 men, and 149 guns. The naval drill and discipline are English. The principal navy yard is at Yokosuka, near Yokohama. The naval estimates for 1880 are £527,994.

The police force, a very important body, with very multifarious and responsible duties, is composed of 23,334 men, 5672 of whom are quartered in Tôkiyô. The pay of the chief commissioner is £60 per month, inspectors receive from £12 to £3, and constables from £2 : 10s. to 16s. according to their grade. The police estimates for 1880 are £497,000. Taken altogether, this force, which is composed mainly of men of the *samurai* class, is well-educated and efficient, performs its duties with far less of harassment to the people than might be expected from Asiatic officials, and may turn out to be more reliable than the army.

One of the earliest undertakings of the new Government was the establishment of a mail route between
Tôkiyô and Ôsaka in 1871, the signal for the disappearance of the unclothed runner with the letters in the
cleft of a stick, who figures so frequently in accounts of
Japan. So rapid was postal progress that by the date
of the last report 34,545 miles of mail routes had been
opened, the mileage is annually increasing, and the service both by sea and land is so admirably conducted as
to rival in some degree our own, on which it is modelled.
The foreign mail service is carefully managed, and the
Japanese post office, after a thorough trial, has proved
itself so efficient that the foreign postal agencies are
being abolished one after the other, the last remaining
being the French, which will shortly close.

With stamps of all denominations, post-cards, stamped
envelopes and newspaper wrappers, facilities for regis-
tering letters, money order offices, post-office savings
banks, a G. P. O. and branches, receiving agencies,
street and wayside letter-boxes, postal deliveries, and a
" dead letter " office, the foreigner need be at no loss
with regard to his correspondence, and if he can read
the Chinese character, he may instruct himself by maps
of mail routes, a postal guide giving details of post-office
business, a postal history of Japan, and a general post-
office directory of the Empire, not yet completed!

The last Report given to the public by Mr. Maye-
shima, the Postmaster-General, is an ably prepared and
comprehensive document, and gives a most satisfactory
account of increasing business and diminishing expenses, and in the estimates for 1880 it is assumed (and
not unreasonably) that the revenue will cover the expenditure. In the year ending with June 1878, the number
of letters, newspapers, etc., sent through the post was
47,192,286, an increase over the preceding year of 23

per cent, and over 1876 of 56 per cent, and of this large number only 62 were stolen, and only 91 were "missing"! Of the aggregate number nearly 25 millions were letters, 763,000 were registered letters, 10 millions were post-cards, *and 9½ millions were newspapers.* The number of money orders issued was 204,367, representing £558,072, a decrease of 21 per cent on the previous year, but the post-office savings banks, which number 292, show an increase of 131, an increase in the number of deposits of 83 per cent, in the amount deposited of 270 per cent, and in depositors of 5000, the average amount deposited by each depositor being about £3 : 10s. The Post-Office employs 7000 persons, of which number thirteen are foreigners.

The telegraphic system of Japan merits high encomiums for its trustworthiness and general efficiency. The first short line was erected in 1869 : telegraph progress has been going on since at the rate of about 600 miles a year; a thousand miles were in course of construction when the new buildings in Tôkiyô were opened in 1878, and eight thousand miles are now in operation. Bell's Telephones have been imported, and are used successfully in connection with the Public Works' Department. The number of persons employed in the Telegraph service is 1410. The tariff for European messages is considerably higher than for Japanese. During the year ending with June 1878, 1,045,442 messages were transmitted, only 23,000 of which were foreign, an increase of 364,503 messages in one year. The native newspapers are growing into the habit of presenting their readers with telegraphic news items, and the Japanese have taken as readily to the telegraph as to other innovations.

Railroad development has been very slow. Only 76½ miles are open, and though 500 are projected, it is not likely that much progress will be made for some years to come. The cost of construction cannot be ascertained, as Japanese officials arrange all contracts and payments without furnishing information to the foreign engineers. The lines are substantially built, with earthworks for a double way, and neat stations on the English model. One source of difficulty and expense, which helps to retard railroad progress, is that the beds of the rivers, by repeated embankments, have mostly been raised higher than the land through or over which they pass, and whether bridging or tunnelling be the least costly process, is a problem. I have already pointed out very frequently that Japan is miserably furnished with the means of internal communication, and that good roads are among her most urgent needs.

The Japanese mercantile marine is constantly increasing in importance, and the *Mitsu Bishi* steamers, as to management, *cuisine*, and general comfort, bear comparison with some of our own leading lines. This company has now nearly all the steam coasting traffic of Japan in its hands, and an efficient mail service to Shanghai and Hong Kong. The total Japanese steam tonnage is 36,543 tons, but, in addition, there are a number of lake and river steamers, of which no statistics exist. The number of steamers above 100 tons is 57.

The number of vessels of foreign rig and build is increasing. There are now 76 of the latter class above 100 tons, and the total tonnage is 27,319 tons. The picturesque but comparatively unseaworthy junk is likely to be slowly displaced by the handier schooner of foreign construction. In 1872 the number of junks above 6 tons was 17,258, but, though junk statistics have not been taken since, the number is now estimated at 15,000 only. Some of these are as much as 190 tons, but, taking the average at 31, the total junk navy is

468,750 tons. The fishing fleet is enormous, and a large portion of the very large coast population is engaged in this industry. The boats under 6 ton and over 18 feet long number 33,047, and the boats under 18 feet 399,399.

The mercantile marine regulations are tolerably stringent. Marine Schools have been formed for giving theoretical and practical instruction in navigation and engineering, and all masters, officers, and engineers of native owned vessels, must pass examinations and possess certificates, in order to obtain or retain nautical positions. That the examinations are not a matter of form may be inferred from the fact that at the last, out of 219 candidates, 69, including 9 foreigners, failed to "pass!" The coasts are now fairly well lighted, and most of the channels, shoals, and sunken rocks, have been surveyed and buoyed.

Japan has two Mints, a paper money mint at Têkiyô, and a metallic mint at Ôsaka; the latter, one of the largest and most complete in the world. It, like the other public works of the new era, was organised by foreigners, but, of the foreign staff, only two remain, the chemist and assayer, and the engineer, with a Japanese staff of 602 persons, including a doctor. The total value of the coinage struck from 1870 to the date of the last report exceeds £17,000,000.

The gold coinage is mainly confined to 5 *yen* pieces, which are nearly equal to a sovereign. The silver coins are the *yen*, the trade dollar, and 50, 20, 10, and 5 *sen* pieces. In the year ending 30th June 1879, 92,073 gold coins were struck; of silver *yen*, 1,879,354; of the trade dollar, 32,717; of 10 *sen*, 201,509; and of the 5 *sen*, 2,894,201. The copper coins are 2 *sen*, 1 *sen*, ½ *sen*, and 1 *rin*, and of these 83 millions were struck. There was, however, a deficiency in "small change," be-

cause of the quantities of small silver coin sent by
Government to China and the Straits Settlements, where
it was sold at a considerable discount. The value of the
coinage for the year was £686,911, and the total value
struck at the Ôsaka mint since its commencement
exceeds £17,000,000 sterling. The Government paper
money in circulation, which consists of notes from 10 *sen*
upwards, amounts to £22,675,598; but in addition,
£7,000,000 of notes have been issued by the Japanese
banks, not on the security of a certain quantity of coin,
but on that of Government paper. The depreciation of
this Government paper is a very disquieting symptom —
the discount occasionally reaching 52 per cent. People
naturally infer that Government credit is bad, the paper
issues being based on insufficient metallic reserves.
During my journeys in Japan I never saw a gold coin in
circulation; small silver coins were difficult to obtain
even in Yokohama, and from Nikkô northwards, except
at Niigata, I never saw any silver, or a single copper
coin of the new coinage, the circulating *media* being
paper, under a *yen* in value ; the large, oval *tempo*, and
the old *rin* with a hole in the middle, my own specimens
of the new silver and copper coinage being regarded as
curiosities, marked preference being shown, as in Scot
land, for "notes," no matter how old or soiled.

The newspaper press, which consists mainly of
"dailies" and "weeklies" is one of the singular features
of the new era. The first newspaper was started in 1871,
they numbered 211 in the middle of 1879, their number
is always on the increase, and they have an aggregate
circulation of nearly 29 million copies. Eleven millions
and a quarter passed through the Post Office in the year
ending 30th June 1879, an increase of over 100 per
cent on the number carried in 1876. They circulate
among all classes, and I have reason to think that

a desire to read them is a strong stimulant to the desire for education in the country districts. The staple of many of them is sensational news items, current rumours, and novelettes, which are said to minister to depraved tastes, and to corrupt the morals of the young. The better class discuss finance, commerce, morals, Christianity, the position of women, the Western movement, innovations, education, law reform, and all subjects which affect Japan, but politics are handled with extreme caution, for the press is shackled by rigid press laws, enforced by heavy penalties, and these were rendered more stringent in 1878. Their tone can be judged of by their leading articles, of which translations appear weekly in the *Japan Mail*. Ignorance of the first principles of political economy, as we understand them, is usually shown, but many subjects are treated with breadth and ability, and the articles are pervaded by remarkable earnestness and an intense though narrow patriotism.

The administration of law is undergoing extensive reform and alteration, and as its present condition can only be regarded as tentative, the remarks which follow are confined to the criminal code.

Under the old *régime* Japanese law was based upon the Chinese codes known as those of the Ming and Tsing dynasties, and the criminal code promulgated in 1871 and altered and supplemented in 1873, was mainly an adaptation of these to the needs of modern Japan. These codes, with some additions notified in 1877, at present constitute the whole penal law of the country, only press offences and some minor infringements of administrative and police regulations being excluded from its operation, but military and naval offenders are not amenable to the jurisdiction of the ordinary courts. The excessive penalties of the Chinese codes have been

modified in deference to modern humanitarian teachings, and Japanese law in practice rarely errs on the
side of undue severity.

There are twenty degrees of punishment, ten of
which involve from ten to one hundred days' imprisonment, and the other ten, penal servitude from one year
up to captivity for life. In some cases imprisonment,
where it is unaccompanied with "hard labour," may be
undergone in the offender's own house, his relations
being responsible for his safe custody, and punishment
undergoes a few other modifications varying with the
rank of the criminal. Persons who, before discovery,
make a full confession of other crimes than those
against the person are exempted from penalties.

The system of criminal procedure consists of a series
of private examinations of the accused person and witnesses. The accused is not assisted by experts or
friends, he cannot interrogate the witnesses, nor can he
compel those to appear who could give evidence in his
favour. The prosecutor, who is always an official, sits
on the bench with the judges, and trial is merely an investigation. Torture, though not formally abolished,
is, it is believed, rarely practised, and the use of an " Investigation Whip" is left to the discretion of the judges,
who, if they resort to it at all, do so only when they
are satisfied of the guilt of an accused person who pro-
tests his innocence.

The law, severe to female criminals in some respects,
is tender in others, and allows them to expiate grave
offences, except that of "violation of filial duty," by
fines, and shows a peculiar lenity to the very young and
very old, persons between the ages of 10 and 15, and
between 70 and 80, being allowed to commute any punishment, except that of death, by the payment of a
fine, while those between 7 and 10 and between 80 and

90 can only be punished for theft and wounding, and those under 7 and over 90 are ineligible for punishment at all!

Wilful murder, under which head infanticide is classed, is punished with death, and assaults are severely dealt with, a mere blow with the hand being visited with 20 days' penal servitude. Assaults on Government officials are punished according to the rank of the official assaulted, and the penalties are exceptionally severe, extending even unto death. Offences against property are treated severely, robbery by armed men, if it succeeds, being punishable by beheading, and if it fails, by hanging. Common robbery is visited with penal servitude for life, and accidental homicide, during the commission of a robbery, by hanging.

The domestic laws, as we may term them, are strongly in favour of husbands and parents. Thus, a husband may assault his wife as much as he pleases if he avoids making a cutting wound, and even then the public prosecutor cannot take cognisance of the offence except at the wife's request, but if a wife commits a common assault on her husband, she is liable to 100 days' penal servitude, and for a husband to slay an offending wife and her paramour is no crime at all, unless a certain time has elapsed since the discovery of the offence. A parent who beats a child to death only incurs 2½ years of penal servitude, and a parent bringing a false and malicious accusation against a child is not punished at all; but a child who disobeys the lawful commands of his parent is liable to penal servitude for 100 days. Non-observance of the prescribed period of mourning for parents is visited with penal servitude for one year. A senior relative is not punished for an assault on a junior, unless an incised wound be inflicted, and even then the penalty is mitigated according to the nearness of the relationship. A recent statute prohibits parents and husbands from selling their wives or daughters to the *jôrôyas* without their consent, under severe penalties. Discarding the son of a wife in favour of that of a concubine is visited with 90 days' penal servitude, and a father who turns his son-in-law out of doors, and gives his wife to a second husband, incurs the same penalty. Breaches of the seventh commandment are punished by penal servitude for one year, without distinction of sex.

Lovers arrested in the act of committing suicide, are punished by ten years of penal servitude. Trafficking in opium is forbidden under pain of beheading, and inciting to the use of it, under pain of hanging. Gambling is punished by penal servitude for 80 days, unless the stakes have been limited to something which can be eaten or drunk. Misconduct not specially provided against in the codes is termed " impropriety," and may be visited with from 30 to 100 days of penal servitude. Among "improprieties" are breaking idols, disseminating false, malicious, or alarming reports, and publishing written matter which may cause difficulties in the administration of the Government, the latter being a heading under which all free expression of opinion is liable to be classed.

The Government is thoroughly in earnest in the reform of its judicial system, and has been engaged for some time past in the compilation of a new penal code, which, it is understood, will be modelled on the French criminal law. Whether the French or any other European system is suited to the present condition of the Japanese people is a question of great importance and difficulty, and the Government will probably not be in a hurry to decide it. A new code on a European model will compel the careful training of the Judges who are to apply it, the reorganisation of the Courts, and the establishment of a system of procedure which will admit of evidence being taken according to fixed rules. It will also demand that accused persons in criminal cases shall be openly tried and defended, and that there shall be a free examination of witnesses, both by the prosecution and defence. A system of procedure so novel and alien to custom and precedent, could only be carried out effectively by judges of independent position, aided by an educated bar, but the officials who at present occupy the bench are removable at the will of the Minister of Justice, and barristers are not yet recognised in Japanese courts.[1] Legal reform is one of the most important questions which the Government has to face, and the promulgation of a code, however admirable, is only the initial step. It not only involves the reconstruction of the Courts, the abolition of the present system of procedure, and the creation of a new judicature, but a revolution in Japanese traditional notions of justice, and in the customs which are interwoven with centuries of national life. In the present preliminary stage of reform, the administration of justice fails to command the confidence of foreigners, and foreign governments are naturally unwilling to surrender the extra-territorial rights acquired by treaty, which place their subjects in Japan, as in other Oriental countries, under the jurisdiction of their own laws.

Nothing is more surprising than the efforts which the Government is making to educate the people, and it is addressing itself to this task annually with increasing thoroughness. The new educational system was planned on a noble scale in 1873, by an ordinance which divided the Empire into seven school districts, and gave one

---

[1] The "advocates" mentioned on p. 317, vol. i., are what in England would be called "attorneys."

school to every 600 inhabitants. It is based upon elementary schools, and ascends through Middle and Normal Schools to Foreign Language Schools, and Colleges for Special Sciences. The Education Report for 1877, published in 1879, gives the number of elementary schools at 25,459, with a total of 59,825 teachers, 58.267 of whom were males and 1558 females. The total number of scholars was 2,162,962, or 1,594,792 boys and 568,220 girls, school age being from six to fourteen. The increase on the previous year was 12.27 per cent, but the percentage of daily attendance, which was 70.77, was a decrease of 4.13 per cent.

In these schools the older pupils learn both the *kata-kana* and the Chinese characters ; they read geography and history, are exercised in arithmetic with western numerals and signs, and are trained to give " object lessons " to the younger scholars, a form of instruction which finds increasing favour. Something is done for health by means of light and heavy gymnastics, and among recent innovations is the orderly marching to and from seats. In some schools the boys are trained to give precedence to girls. Examinations take place at the re-opening after the holidays, and officers appointed by the Education Department inspect the schools and report upon their efficiency. Different text books to the number of 174 are used, mostly of foreign origin, and often misleading from the imperfections of the translation.

The course of study and the regulations for the primary schools were modelled on those of the Government Normal Schools, uniformity being the object aimed at ; but it has been found that the neglect of local custom, aptitude, and requirements, and the ignoring of the differences between a rural and urban population produced very unsatisfactory results, and the system is

undergoing modifications which will increase its efficiency. Simpler text-books are being prepared, as, for
instance, one on geography, in which the physical conditions, productions, etc., of the special locality for
which it is required are treated of. The standard of
instruction has been raised too high for a peasant population, and has increased the difficulty of obtaining
competent teachers; and hard and fast rules as to
school terms, in regions where children pursue industrial occupations, have prevented many from attending
schools at all.

It was intended that the elementary school system
should be administered by the people, but it has been
found that it has largely fallen into the hands of local
Government officials. In the report issued in 1877 Mr.
Tanaka, then acting Minister of Education, remarks
that although at first "educational matters required
direct interference on the part of public officers, it
would be a misfortune for the interests of schools to be
left continually so," and fears "lest, owing to a want of
interest on the part of the people, a retrograde movement may set in." He foreshadows Japanese school
boards by saying that "school matters should be committed as far as possible to the self-management of the
people, by making them understand that it is their duty
to assume the matters of schools to themselves," and
advises the local governments to give them all the
encouragement and help which can assist them in the
performance of this duty.

It must not be overlooked that the initial difficulty
in Japanese education arises from the complexity of the
language and of the ideographic symbols, and that the
teaching of 3000 of the latter is undertaken in the
primary schools! The supply of properly qualified
teachers for the lower grades of schools, though increas

ing, is still deficient, and imperfect training is still answerable for defects, many men taking their places as
pedagogues after only 100 days in the normal schools.

The total revenue for the year was £1,340,000, of
which sum £537,000 was made up by local votes,
£161,000 by voluntary contributions, £78,000 by fees,
and £109,000 by Government aid, the expenditure
being £1,072,000, and the total value of school property
£2,593,000; teachers' salaries averaged something under
£9 a year, and school fees about 8d. for each child. It
is to be noted that besides £161,000 in money voluntarily contributed for the primary schools, they received
large donations of land, 310 buildings, 16,576 sets of
school apparatus, 26,507 complete sets of books, and
miscellaneous contributions to the amount of £1200.
Within the last five years the voluntary contributions
in money only *have exceeded one million seven hundred
thousand pounds!*

The middle schools have increased rapidly in numbers
during the last four years, in consequence mainly of an
increased desire for the acquisition of the higher common branches of learning. The course of instruction
extends over 2½, 3, 4, or 5 years, and the studies, slightly
modified by local considerations are as follows: — writing, grammar, composition, drawing, language, foreign
languages (English being taught in 15 schools), geography, history, arithmetic, algebra, geometry, physics,
chemistry, astronomy, geology, natural history, physiology, agriculture, mechanics, commerce, book-keeping,
statistics, mental and moral philosophy, political economy, law, and gymnastics. This is a very ambitious
course, for which the instruction in the primary schools
can scarcely be regarded as preparatory. There were
389 middle schools, with 910 teachers, only 23 of whom
were females. In these schools there is the first ap-

pearance of the foreign element in education, 15 foreign men and 1 foreign woman being employed. The number of students was 20,522, an increase of nearly 9000 over the previous year, but the female students only number 1112.

The educational system includes schools for special sciences, of which there were 52 in different localities, with 161 teachers and 3361 students. These colleges teach law, medicine, agriculture, commerce, navigation, chemistry, mathematics, etc. Mathematics was the specialty of the larger number of them, and medical and commercial schools come next in order, the medical being by far the most important.

The edifice is crowned by the University of Tôkiyô, which includes departments of law, literature, and science, the Tôkiyô Medical College, a preparatory department formerly known as an English language school, and a botanic garden. The number of students in the three first departments was 710, and the instructors numbered 56, 32 being Japanese, and 24 foreign. The preparatory course includes English, mathematics, geography, physics, chemistry, history, political economy, philosophy, natural history, drawing, etc., and covers three years. The special course of *Law* embraces International and the various branches of English Law; *Science* includes Chemistry, Physics, and Engineering; and *Literature*, which is a new department, includes the different branches usually taught under that head. The complete graduation course is five years. During 1875–1876 nineteen students of special ability were sent to foreign countries, of which number more than half have completed their education, and have obtained the master's or bachelor's degree of the universities or colleges to which they were sent. They receive loans of £200 a year, a heavy debt with which to start upon poorly-salaried life at home.

The Medical Department, which is mainly under German influence, divides its students into two classes, medical and pharmaceutical, and provides two courses, preparatory and special. The supply of instructed practitioners is so limited that a short and simple course of medicine for day students was organised in 1876, and in 1877, 293 students availed themselves of it. The preparatory course includes geology, botany, natural history, mineralogy, geography, physics, mathematics, chemistry, German, Latin, etc.; and the special course comprises medicine, surgery, obstetrics, zoölogy, botany, materia medica, anatomy, histology, physics, physiology, and chemistry. A hospital, library, anatomical rooms, botanical and zoölogical collections, and an extensive supply of surgical and medical apparatus, are attached to the department, and in 1877, 117 corpses were subjected to dissection. The hospital treated 836 in-patients and 4290 out-patients in the same period. At least seven-tenths of the medical practitioners of the Empire still pursue the method of the Chinese schools, and the Medical College promises a most important advance in curative and surgical science. The total number of day and resident medical students, including those in the preparatory department, was 1040, with 24 Japanese and 11 foreign instructors. The annual cost of the four departments of the University of Tôkiyô is estimated at £55,000.

There were two Normal Colleges (*i.e.* Normal schools for training teachers for the middle schools), with 25 instructors and 177 students; and 96 Normal schools (for training teachers for the elementary schools), 5 of which were for females. The latter contained 7222 males and 727 females, and were instructed by 766 male and 24 female teachers. The scarcity of competent teachers for the elementary schools is still severely felt, and the Government is most anxious to extend the supply and increase the acquirements of teachers by rendering the course of study and training in these schools more complete and efficient. The Normal School course covers two years, and usually comprehends history, geography, mathematics, physics, chemistry, natural history, moral philosophy, political economy, physiology, book-keeping, composition, pedagogics, practice of teaching, hygiene, singing, and gymnastics, to which logic and the elements of English are occasionally added.

The foreign language schools were at one time regarded as of great importance, and certain progressive persons, notably Mr. Mori, the present Minister to England, cherished hopes of the introduction of English under certain modifications into Japan as the written and eventually as the spoken language, and many people here seem to suppose that this project has made much headway. It is a remarkable fact that in the single year dealt with by the last report (that for 1877) the number of foreign language schools decreased from 92 to 28, and that the chief reason assigned for the decrease is that "the people have learned that foreign languages are not very useful or serviceable outside of the large cities opened for commerce, and that they cannot be profitably studied by the mass of the population." In the same year the number of native teachers decreased by 298, and that of foreign teachers by 35; that of male studerts by 4223, and that of females by 347. In the schools which remain English is taught in 25, German in 1, Chinese in 1, and French, German, Russian, and Chinese in 1, the total number being 28, with 109 teachers, 27 of whom are foreign, and 1522 students, 120 of whom were females.

The total number of foreign teachers in Government

employment was 97, 65 of whom were English and American.

Increased attention is being paid to female education, the various mission schools are producing considerable rivalry, and the Empress Haruku has come prominently forward as a patroness of "the higher education of women." In the elementary schools, the number of female teachers was 1558, an increase of over 100 per cent on the number in 1875, and with the advantages offered by 5 Normal schools, the number of women who are qualifying themselves for the profession of teaching is increasing considerably. The number being trained in the Normal schools was 727, an increase of 264 on the previous year; but in the middle schools there was a decrease in the already small number of female students. In the primary schools the number of girls had increased 8.34 per cent, while the number of boys had only increased 3.93, but still of the total number of children in these schools, the girls are only one-third. The pupils in the schools for female handicraft number nearly 3000. Mr. Tanaka is strongly in favour of the multiplication of female teachers. He writes, "The education of children should be so conducted as to develop grace and gentleness of manners and deportment. If they are brought up under the influence of the gentler qualities of female teachers, a much better result may be expected to be attained than where they are trained entirely by men."

Instruction is everywhere conveyed on Western principles, and the pupils in the upper schools are required to sit on benches and work at desks. In the Government colleges, innovation is carried so far that the students eat food prepared in European fashion, and use knives and forks.

Intellectual ardour, eager receptiveness, admirable

behaviour, earnest self-control, docility, and an appetite for hard and continuous work, characterise Japanese students; and their average intellectual power and general ability are regarded by their foreign teachers as equal to those of Western students. Further comparisons must be left to the future. The earnest work done by both teachers and students has already resulted in the turning out of a number of young men, well equipped both in the intellectual and technical training needed for practical work; and it is not too much to expect that in a few years the empire will be able to dispense with the services of foreigners in most of the Government departments, and that the resources of Japan will be developed by the Japanese.

It remains to be pointed out that in the absence of a compulsory law, only 39.9 per cent of the population of school age is at school, *i.e.* that 3,158,000 children are not receiving any instruction, that a large proportion of the peasantry is in the lowest stage of mental development, that throughout extensive districts the children are surrounded by influences tending towards intellectual and moral debasement, and that a vast and not altogether inert mass of ignorance and superstition still exists to impede progress, embarrass the Government, and break out in trivial local disturbances.

The primary school system, besides its need (as pointed out in Mr. Tanaka's able reports) of being placed on a sound and efficient basis, is marked, I think, by two radical defects, — the general omission of moral training (the moral teaching of the Chinese classics being suffered to fall into disuse under the new system, the classics being used chiefly as a vehicle for teaching the Chinese character), and the revolutionary attempt to force European methods, culture, and modes of thought upon an unprepared people. Till the ele-

mentary education is rendered more thorough and efficient, various perils attend upon the higher education,
and in the present lack of careers for men of culture
solely, there is some risk that one or two of the higher
colleges which aim at imparting culture, but do not profess to give a thorough training in those branches of
knowledge which are of practical utility in work-a-day
life may increase the number of glib and superficial
smatterers who despise manual labour, affect expensive
foreign habits, and render the task of government increasingly difficult by rushing into the newspapers with
wild philosophical speculations, Utopian social schemes,
and crude political theories.

These remarks are not made in any spirit of invidi-
ous criticism. Japan deserves the very highest credit
for spending twice as much upon her elementary schools
as upon her Navy, for her desire to construct her educational system upon the best models, for her readiness
to correct defects and learn by failures, and for her noble efforts to bring education within the reach of all
classes; but we must bear in mind that the primary
school system is still in its infancy, that three millions
of children are without education, that very much has
yet to be done, and that the future of the empire is undoubtedly imperilled by a vast mass of ignorance and
superstition on the one hand, and by a superficial exotic
culture on the other.

The problem of "how to make ends meet" has
vexed the brains and tested the resources of Japanese
statesmen ever since 1871, when the Mikado assumed
the responsibility of the debts which the *daimiyô* had
contracted to Japanese subjects before the Restoration,
and of the paper money of all sorts and values which
they had issued, substituting for it a uniform paper currency. The reduction to order of the chaotic confu-

sion of the financial system under the feudal *régime* was carried out with so much vigour and ability, that by 1873 the Government was able to publish estimates of the national revenue for that year, which, as might be expected, were faulty in form, and not altogether accurate in detail. Each subsequent year has brought an improvement, and the estimates for the twelve months ending with June 1880 are as correct in form, and on the whole as explicit in detail, as those of some European states, and are accompanied by a Finance Report which reflects great credit upon Mr. Okuma, the Finance Minister.

It must be borne in mind, however, that official accounts of expenditure have only been issued down to 1875, that there is no public body which has power to look into and audit accounts, and that confidence in Japanese financial statements must rest partly on the character of the Finance Minister, and partly on the fact that the Government has been able to pay its way without having recourse to oppressive or risky expedients. This confidence is increased by the manly tone of Mr. Okuma's last report, in which, after regretting that the financial system still falls short of completeness, he "begs respectfully to observe that the essence of finance is to be as exact and minute as possible, and that records are only of utility when they are complete and methodical;" and expresses his earnest desire that from this year onwards, "additional accuracy may be attained, and both estimates and accounts of the national finances become more and more methodical." This is much to be desired in the interests of Japan, but that which has already been accomplished in the short period of nine years reflects great credit upon a country which had special difficulties to encounter in the unification of its financial system.

Japan has not been behind other civilised nations in the rapid contraction of a National Debt, which at the present time amounts to £72,000,000, but a comparatively small portion of this has been incurred voluntarily, or has been spent upon the material progress which has astonished the world. The legacy of debt inherited from the old *régime* amounted to £14,215,000, and to this sum we must add £40,312,000, which was required to redeem the hereditary pensions of the higher nobles and the military caste, as well as those granted to Shintô priests. In other words, it cost Japan £54,527,-000 in round numbers to close accounts with her historic past. The Government was also forced to resort to loans to meet war expenses, mainly incurred through risings against its authority; the Satsuma Rebellion in 1877 added £8,400,000 to its indebtedness, and the Formosa Expedition demanded loans amounting nearly to £2,000,000 more. What may be termed the *voluntary* debt of the new *régime* may be estimated at £9,855,000, and £3,600,000 may be termed Industrial Loans, including the London Railway Loan. Only one-thirtieth of the whole National Debt is due to foreigners, and the average rate of interest on both *foreign* and *domestic* debt is 4¼ per cent, the rate of interest on private debts being 12.20 per cent. The interest on the debt demands £3,183,000 annually, out of a revenue of £11,130,000. Paper money issued by the Government to the amount of £24,000,000, but diminished by the withdrawal of £1,477,000, constitutes 32.2 per cent of the debt, and has been spent, as it appears, mainly on the politically necessary, but unproductive expenses of the redemption of the paper money, and the assumption of the debts of the *daimiyô*, in order to make the unification of the empire possible, on extraordinary war expenses, mainly in order to preserve its in tegrity, and the formation of a Reserve Fund, consisting partly of ready money, for the purpose of meeting un· foreseen contingencies and perils. It does not appear that the Government issue of paper has largely increased the circulating medium, because it has been required to replace former paper issued by the *daimiyô*, and coin which has left the country in consequence of the imports being largely in excess of the exports. The National Debt stands at the present time thus—

Domestic debt bearing interest . . .	£45,726,226	0 0
Domestic debt bearing no interest, including Government paper money . . .	24,735,544	0 0
Total of domestic debt . .	£70,461,770	0 0
Foreign debt	2,365,824	0 0
Total of domestic and foreign debt in round numbers (about) . . .	£72,827,590	0 0

The chief source of revenue is the Imperial Land Tax, which has been reduced to 2½ per cent on the selling value of the land, and it is estimated that this tax will produce £8,200,000 during the current year. Then follow the tax on alcoholic liquors, which it is estimated will yield £901,000; the export and import duties, £428,000; the profits on Government industrial undertakings, £238,000; postage stamps, £210,000; the tax on legal documents, £107,000; the tax on companies, £100,000; the tax on tobacco, £69,000; the tax on the produce of the Hokkaidô (Yezo), £72,000; and the tax on vehicles, £54,000.

For the year ending June 30, 1880, the revenue is estimated at £11,130,000, being an increase of £475,000 over the preceding year, this increase being accounted for mainly by increased receipts from import and export duties, from land, mining, liquor, ship, boat, and vehicle taxes; from increased post-office receipts and copyright fees, and from the increasing number of persons taking out attorney's horse, cattle-dealers', and druggists' licenses.

The expenditure, for the reason that all surplus is to be applied to the reduction of debt, is estimated at exactly the same sum as the revenue. Among its chief items are the interest on the National Debt, £3,130,000; the army, which costs £1,438,000; the administration of *fu* and *ken*, £757,000; the navy, £527,000; the police, £497,000; and colonisation, £302,000. This year's appropriation for embankments is £289,000; for education, £227,000; for industrial undertakings, £201,000; and for the Civil List and appanages of Imperial Princes, £175,000. It is noteworthy that the charge for the Ministry of Public Worship appears for the last time in 1876–1877, and that the appropriation for the "Temples of the Gods," which was £44,000 in 1875–1876 and 1877, has decreased to £27,000 for 1879–1880.[1]

The magnitude of the national debt is the outstanding feature of Japanese finance, but it may be a surprise to some readers to learn that the cost of the projects entered upon by the new *régime* and of the reconstruction of the Empire is under £10,000,000; that 53.7 per cent of the whole debt is regarded by Mr. Mayét, the Councillor to the Finance Department, as "directly profitable;" that a reserve fund of £5,000,000 has been created out of surplus revenue; and that the following *extraordinary* expenses have been met out of *ordinary* revenue: — The creation and equipment of an army, with large military workshops, barracks, etc.; the purchase and construction of a navy of 27 ships of all

[1] For general tables of revenue and expenditure for 1879–1880 the reader is referred to Mr. Okuma's estimates given in Appendix C.

classes, including ironclads, and the establishment of
arsenals, building-yards, and docks; the equipment of
the coast with an efficient system of lighthouses; the
construction of 8000 miles of telegraph, with telegraph
offices; the establishing an efficient post-office system,
with Postal Savings Banks; reform in the civil administration, and in the civil and penal codes; the re-ar-
rangement of the Land Tax, and the establishment of
a uniform system of taxation for the whole Empire; the
establishment of custom-houses, the mint, and a Government printing-office; the issue of new paper money,
and a new coinage; the establishment of a University,
Medical College, and Technical University (College of
Engineering); the establishment of and provision for
primary, middle, and higher schools up to 1876; the
colonisation and survey of Yezo; the introduction of
the breeding of sheep, and improvements in the breeds
of horses and cattle, and the establishment of model
farms, tree-nurseries, acclimatisation gardens, agricultural colleges, industrial colleges, and museums; extraordinary embassies to Europe and America; participation
in the Exhibitions of Vienna, Philadelphia, and Paris,
and the education of several hundred youths in Europe
and America, etc. etc.

The Finance Minister, far from accepting the dictum
of Lorenzo von Stein (*Lehrbuch der Finanz-wissenschaft*),
quoted by the able Councillor to the Finance Department, has recently devised and made public an elaborate scheme for the liquidation of the whole debt of
Japan by 1905, without either increasing taxation or
trenching on the reserve fund. The success of the arrangement involves a complete absence of financially
or politically disturbing events; but though Japanese
paper is subject to very severe depreciation as compared with gold, and the rise in the price of the neces-

saries of life is a disquieting symptom, I think that we are not in a position to say that Mr. Okuma's project is an altogether chimerical one, although it is impossible to agree with the strongly optimist view of it taken by Mr. Mayét, or with von Stein's view that " a state with out a national debt is either not doing enough for the future, or is demanding too much from the present."

The foreign commerce [1] of Japan is a subject of great practical interest, to foreigners because it forms nearly their sole object for intercourse, and to the Japanese, because they depend upon it for the development of their material resources. It dates from the abolition of the exclusive system, which was pursued down to 1858. Before that year the Japanese, having no foreign market, in which to dispose of their surplus productions, were without one of the principal incentives to indus- try. They grew food, or manufactured commodities in quantities sufficient to meet their own wants; the har- vest of the year constituted the material wealth of the country, and the store of national capital admitted of little or no augmentation. But when foreigners came to their doors and offered them money or foreign wares in exchange for their productions, a potent stimulus to increased exertion was afforded them, and its effect testifies to their intelligence and industry.

The products which Japan furnishes to other coun- tries consist of raw silk, silkworms' eggs, tea, rice, cop- per, tobacco, camphor, vegetable wax, dried and salted fish, and various art manufactures in silk, metals, and chinaware. The first four items constitute the staple

[1] In Appendix D will be found three returns compiled at the British Legation, Tôkiyô, which furnish in a condensed form particulars of the import and export trade of Japan for a period of thirteen years; also a return showing the large amount of foreign tonnage which that trade employs, and a table of foreign residents, the majority of whom are engaged in mercantile occupations.

articles of export. The highest value which these items reached in any one year was, in the case of raw silk, nearly fifteen millions of dollars [£3,000,000 sterling], in that of silkworms' eggs more than four millions, in that of tea nearly eight millions, and in that of rice upwards of four and a half millions; while the collective value of the other exports in a single year has amounted to seven millions. The extent of the transactions in these commodities varies considerably in different years, but the average value of the total export trade of Japan for the three years 1876–1878 was twenty-five millions and a half of dollars [£5,100,000].

Japan has rendered a most material service to the silk-growers of France and Italy by providing them with fresh silk ova, when their own supplies were nearly destroyed by the disease which attained its height in 1864. A more striking instance of international commercial benefit has rarely been witnessed, for it is doubtful whether a sufficient supply of the requisite kind of silkworms' eggs could have been procured from any other quarter, and the emergency arose very shortly after the opening of the country.

In return for her products Japan takes from Europe and America, cotton yarn, cotton and woollen manufactures of all kinds, iron, machinery, kerosene oil, and many minor articles, such as cutlery, leather, and ornamental wares; while from China she receives sugar, and occasional supplies of raw cotton, which is an uncertain crop in Japan. The average value of the imported goods for the three years, 1876-1878, was twenty-eight millions of dollars [£5,600,000]. Of these goods, cotton and woollen manufactures form the principal items; cottons were imported in 1878 to the amount of nearly thirteen millions of dollars, but woollens have fallen off since 1872, when the highest importation of seven millions and a half of dollars was reached. The demand for cotton manufactures appears to be nearly stationary, while that for cotton yarn [as distinguished from cotton cloth] is steadily increasing.

The latter circumstance may be regarded as a solid and favourable feature of the trade. Every cottage possesses its own loom, which is worked by the women of the family, who can produce fabrics which, besides being genuine, are stronger and better suited to their wants and tastes than those of Manchester make, and by using a large proportion of foreign yarn, which can be supplied to them cheaper than they can spin it themselves, the people are furnished with abundant materials for the extension of their own manufactures, and are guarded against the bad consequences of a failure of their home cotton crop. Thus the native industry, instead of being supplanted by that of the foreigner, works in unison with it, and the result is a large increase in the national production.

Of the general effect of the opening of Japan to foreign trade it is difficult to judge, as we must weigh against an apparent improvement in the dwellings, clothing, and feeding of the people in the neighbourhood of its principal centres, the enhanced price of the necessaries of life throughout the country. It has created a new order of native traders and merchants, whose activity may be noticed in many of the large towns: while the foreign demand for Japanese metal-work and ceramic wares, fans, fine bamboo work, enamels, and the numerous articles known by the name of "curios," has largely benefited the skilled artisans of the country, and has opened to them new and extensive fields of employment. Thus foreign traffic is bringing forward a middle class, which may be looked to as a means of promoting not only the commercial prosperity of the country, but also its political wellbeing.

The future of the foreign commerce of Japan depends upon the increase of production. Silk growing, next to ordinary agriculture, forms her principal industry, and the Government has wisely paid great attention to the improvement of the quality of the silk which is produced. It has also shown a laudable desire to foster other industries, without always perceiving, however, that it is only those which are to some extent natural to the country which can profit by such encouragement; and, like other young and paternal governments, it has not yet realised that free competition is essential to the growth of healthy enterprise, and that privileges and monopolies only serve to impede the expansion of trade. The population of Japan is essentially an agricultural one, and it is certainly a mistake to attempt prematurely to convert an agricultural people into a manufacturing one.

Undoubtedly, it is to the development of her very large mineral and agricultural resources that Japan must look for her advancement in wealth. But though capital is the one thing needed for the working of her mineral treasures, and the nation has very little of its own, the Government has rigidly excluded the introduction of foreign capital, and the result of this and other restrictive measures is shown in the limited increase in the exports, in the costly character of internal transport, owing to the primitive condition of the roads, and the high freights of the Japanese Steam-ship Company, which monopolises the coast carrying trade, and in the slow development of the enormous coal-fields, the mines, and other productive enterprises, which cannot be undertaken without considerable outlay.

"Dense population" and "garden cultivation" are phrases which travellers constantly apply to Japan, but the highest estimate only gives 230 inhabitants to the

square mile, and though the tillage of the area ac
tually occupied deserves the highest praise, it is estimated by the Japanese Government that only *two-tenths*
of the soil is actually under cultivation, and that the
forests alone greatly exceed the area under culture of
all kinds. A new trade in wheat is springing up, and
there is little doubt that many of the vast upland tracts
which are now lying waste, as being unsuited for the
growth of rice, might be profitably utilised for wheat
and other cereals. The island of Yezo, with a rich soil,
and an area larger than Ireland, has hardly yet been
touched by the plough, and between her adaptability to
the growth of wheat, and her immense coal-fields, is a
mine of future wealth. On the whole, there is no doubt
that it is mainly to her undeveloped agricultural resources that Japan must look for increased exports and
greater commercial prosperity, but there is nothing to
lead us to suppose that she will soon become a wealthy
nation.

This brief review of some of the most important
elements of the progress of the Japanese Empire necessarily omits much which, as stated in the reports of the
heads of departments of the Japanese Government, is
fitted to excite both surprise and admiration. I have
endeavoured to avoid indiscriminate laudation on the
one side, and unreasonable blame on the other. Japan
has done much; but though she has done many things
well and wisely, much is still undone. Some reforms
of importance have been left untouched, and others
have been undertaken so superficially, that, while certain places present a fair outside, little improvement, on
the whole, in those special directions, has been effected.
Reform, not only in the laws, but in the administration
of them, is urgently required. The army needs better
discipline and better officers, if it is to be a source of

strength, and not of weakness, to the State. The Press
laws need a thorough reform, and the obnoxious restrictions on political meetings and societies which came into
force on April 6, 1880, need to be rescinded as arbitrary
and unworthy of the age. According to the Japanese
newspapers, " the whole population of the country is
actuated by one burning desire for representative institutions, and the longing for constitutional liberty has
pervaded all classes," and this demand must be wisely
met in fulfilment of the pledges given by the Government of the Restoration ; while, at the same time, the
heimin, or commonalty, numbering *thirty millions*, must
be trained to the exercise of political responsibilities.
An improved system of roads needs to be created if
the resources of the country are to be developed into
bearing the strain of taxation without undue pressure
on the cultivator. Three millions of children of school
age require to be brought under instruction, and the
standard of teaching to be raised throughout all the elementary schools. *Thoroughness* has to be studied in all
departments, and perseverance to be steadily required
from all subordinate officials.

The carrying out of the reforms which have been
already begun, the placing them upon a solid basis, the
judicious inauguration of new ones, the wise selection
of such further fruits of western civilisation as may bear
transplantation to Japanese soil, the courageous abandonment of experiments which have failed from their
inherent unsuitability to Japan, the resolute pursuit of
a pacific foreign policy, the exercise of a wise discrimination between true and false progress, and the persevering conservation of all that the Empire has actually
gained during the last ten years, are sufficient to tax the
energy and sagacity of the best and ablest men in
Japan for many years to come. The extraordinary

progress which the Empire has made justly claims our admiration, and, judging from the character of the men who take the lead in public affairs, and from the wisdom and sobriety which they have gained by ten years of experience, we may reasonably hope for the consolidation of reforms already inaugurated, and that those which are to come will be faithfully carried out with due regard for the interests of all classes, and with the honesty and solidity which alone can ensure permanent success.

Of the shadows which hang upon the horizon of Japan, the darkest, to my thinking, arises from the fact that she is making the attempt, for the first time in history, to secure the fruits of Christianity without transplanting the tree from which they spring. The nation is sunk in immorality, the millstone of Orientalism hangs round her neck in the race on which she has started, and her progress is political and intellectual rather than moral; in other words, as regards the highest destiny of man, individually or collectively, it is at present a failure. The great hope for her is that she may grasp the truth and purity of primitive Christianity, as taught by the lips and life of our Lord Jesus Christ, as resolutely as she has grasped our arts and sciences; and that, in the reception of Christianity, with its true principles of manliness and national greatness, she may become, in the highest sense, "The Land of the Rising Sun" and the light of Eastern Asia.

APPENDIX A.

AINO WORDS TAKEN DOWN AT BIRATORI AND USU, YEZO.

ABOVE, *kaschke, rekita.*

Afternoon, *to-keishi, tokes.*

Again, *ishu kanna.*

All, *obitta.*

Already, *tane.*

And, *ka.*

Angry, *yarushika.*

Arm, *amonine.*

Arrow, *eye.*

BAD, *ipocasch.*

Bark, *yara.*

Bear, *hokuyak, peri.*

Beard, *ticksa, reki.*

Before, *noschki.*

Below, *ranta.*

Beyond, *aya.*

Bird, *tskap.*

Blue, *matek.*

Boat, *chip.*

Bone, *poné.*

Bow, *ku.*

Boy [small], *cuspo.*

Bright, *bekeri.*

Brother[elder],*kiani-guru.kuimbo.*

" [younger], *kiaki-ni-guru.*

Brown, *una.*

Broad, *bira.*

Business, *ukosarange.*

CHILD [male], *sikatch.*

" [female], *makatch.*

Child [my], *kuboho.*

" [your], *iboho.*

Cloud, *nitchkuru, nischi, kuroro.*

Coat, *amip.*

Cold, *mi-une.*

" [it is], *meiragi.*

" [very], *meiupki.*

Coming down, *shan.*

Corpse, *rai guru.*

Crippled, *takushuto.*

DANCE, *ontori.*

Day, *tō.*

" [after to-morrow], *oya-tschiun.*

" [before yesterday], *hoschenu-mani.*

" [this], *tanto.*

Dawn, *ankes.*

Dead, *rai.*

Deep, *oho.*

Dew, *kuruppi, kuru-uppi.*

Dishonourable, *nanu, ischamu* (*lit.* without sight).

Dog, *set-ta.*

EAR, *kisara.*

Earth, *tschiri, tui.*

Eclipse,*tschǔpp-rai*(the sun dies).

Elbow, *hitoki.*

End, *itoki.*

Evening, *schiri-kunné* (the earth is black).

Every, *keshi.*
Eye, *shki.*
Eyebrow, *ranuma.*

FACE, *namihu.*
Far off, *torima.*
Father, *atspo. hambi. mitch.*
Female, *matni.*
Fierce, *ninren.*
Finger, *askibits. embi.*
Fire, *abé.*
Fish, *isep. chi-ep.*
  " [smoked], *fumbé.*
Flea, *taiki.*
Flower, *ebni.*
Formerly, *fusiko.*
Fox, *turepp.*
From, *kara.*

GHOST, *kamoi-yashi.*
God, *kamoi.*
Go-down, *pū.*
Good, *pirika.*
Good-bye, *saramba.*
Grandfather, *ikasi.*
Grass, *kina.*
Green, *shin-nin.*
Guest, *marubuto.*

HAIR, *noma. atōpp.*
Hairy, *noma-us.*
Hand, *teké, take.*
Hateful, *kopandé.*
Haughty, *uku-aino-buri-kuru* (to take the form of an Aino.)
Hat, *tshesek. sesik.*
Head, *saba. chapu.*
Heart, *tschambi.*
Heavy, *pashi.*
High, *kuweri.*
Hill, *ken.*

House, *tschesai. rikōp.*
  " [my], *ku-tschesai.*
Husband, *hoku. tschesaikoru. kuru.*
  " [your], *ihoku.*
  " [my], *kuhoku.*
  " [without], *hoku-tschaku.*

I, *tshoki.*
Ice, *konru.*
Infant, *bō.*
Insect, *kikiri.*

KIND, *yié-yié-kiri.*

LAKE, *tān.*
Large, *poro.*
Lie, *shungé.*
Little, *obari.*
Living, *shitnu.*
Long, *tanné.*

MALE, *binné.*
Man, *okkai. hoku. guru. aino.*
  " [old], *onné.*
  " [that], *tanguru.*
  " [this], *tō-anguru.*
  " [single], *okkai-po.*
Master [of a hut], *kayatono.*
Mat, *tsarubi.*
Men, *okkai-po-po.*
Midday, *tō-gap. tō-noschké.*
Middle, *noschké.*
Midnight, *an-noschké.*
Millet, *ié-sa-mam.*
Moon, *antsikara. tschŭpp-kunné* (night sun).
Mother, *habo.*
Mountain, *nobori.*
  " [top], *tschiri-kitai.*
Mouth, *parof.*

OAR, *kadji.*
Old, *hekai.*
Owl, *kamoi-tsikapp* (bird of the gods).

PEOPLE, *kuru.*
Poison, *tschuruku.*
Promontory, *itu.*

RAIN, *apto. weni.*
Red, *kuré.*
River, *bets.*
Road, *ru.*
Robber, *roku-guru* (a robbing man).
Roof, *cada. tschisai-katai.*
Root, *shinrichi.*

SALT, *tschipo.*
Sea, *atui, adōi.*
Shoulder, *tapsau.*
Short, *takné.*
Singing praises or chants, *yairapp.*
Sister [elder], *k'sabo.*
    " [younger], *mataké, ma-chi-ribi, turesch.*
Skin of beast, *no-ma.*
Sky, *cando.*
Small, *poné.*
Smell, *fura.*
Smoke, *shupuya.*
Snake, *takoni.*
    " [black], *paskuro-kamoi.* (raven god).
Snow, *ubashi.*
Spring, *paikaru. paika.*
Song, *ma.*
    " [for several voices], *o-ma.*
Stars, *notchiu.*
Storm, *poro-reira* (*lit.* a great wind).

Straw, *wattesu.*
Suddenly, *nischopp.*
Summer, *tschaku.*
    " [end of], *tschaku-kes.*
Sun, *tschūpp.*
Sunset, *hiri-kunné.*
Sustenance, *aino-ikiri.*
Sweet, *pan.*

TEETH, *memoki.*
Temple, *kamoi-tschisai.*
That, *tān.*
This, *tambi, tanni.*
Thing, *ambi.*
    " [living], *shitnu-ambi.*
    " [dead], *rai-no-ambi.*
    " [spread on floor], *ishoka rambi.*
Throat, *letchi.*
Thunder, *kamoi-fumi.*
Time [a long], *ohono.*
    " [short], *ponno.*
To-day, *tando.*
Together, *tora.*
To-morrow, *ururu. nischatta.*
Tongue, *parumbé.*
Torn, *periké.*

UGLY, *kai-guru-korats* (like a corpse).
Under, *shiragata.*

VALLEY, *nai. metu.*
Very, *shiri.*
Village, *kotan.*

WALL, *tomamu.*
War, *sara-kamai.*
Water, *waka.*
    " [hot], *oshai. usai.*
    " [salt], *ruru-waka.*

Weather, *shukus.*
Which, *niwa.*
White, *ritara. tsaru.*
Wife, *matchi.*
Wind, *tera.*
Window, *puyara.*
Winter, *mata.*
With difficulty, *rai-korats* (like dying).
Within, *oshipé.*
Without, *tschamu.*
Wolf, *holaiku. ushi-kamoi* (the howling god).

Woman, *menoko.*
　"　[old], *pakko.*
Wood, *nitchkuni.*
Wrist, *dekutasch.*

YEAR, *ba.*
　"　[next], *oya ba.*
　"　[this], *tan ba.*
Yesterday, *numani. numanchi*
You, *yani.*
Young, *pe ure. hekatsu.*

VERBS.

To ascend, *rikin.*
　" bathe, *shushi.*
　" be angry, *ruschké.*
　" be in pain, *yunin.*
　" blow, *rui.*
　" bury, *iwakté.*
　" catch, *koyeki.*
　" die, *ri-orkai.*
　" drink, *iku.*
　" eat, *ebé.*
　" fight, *uraiki.*
　" forget, *oira.*
　" get angry, *aino-sesek* (glow like an Aino).
　" get cold, *meandi.*
　" get better, *toōsa.*
　" get up, *aschkai.*
　" give, *koré.*
　" go up a river, *petorasch.*
　" go up a mountain, *hinnaisho.*

To hear, *nu.*
　" kill, *raigi.*
　" like, *yeramasch.*
　" live, *hitoku.*
　" make, *karu.*
　" pound, *uta.*
　" return, *oshipi.*
　" root up, *rishipi.*
　" rub, *shirishiru.*
　" run, *hoyupp.*
　" run away, *kira.*
　" scratch, *hiki.*
　" see, *nukara.*
　" seize, *kora.*
　" sing, *sakehan.*
　" sing praises, *i-uko-yairapp*
　" speak, *itaku.*
　" spring, *teriké.*
　" tell lies, *iko-shiunnke.*
　" touch, *moi-moi.*

NUMERALS.

1. *schnape.*
2. *tupaisch.*
3. *lepaisch.*

4. *mepe.*
5. *aschkei.*
6. *u-an.*

7. *aruan.*	30. *ito hots.*
8. *topaishi.*	31. *schnape icashima ito hots,* etc.
9. *schnapaishi.*	40. *tu hots.*
10. *wambi.*	41. *schnape icashima tu hots,* etc.
11. *schnape icashima wambi.*	50. *elê hots,* etc.
12. *tupaisch icashima wambi.*	60. *lê hots,* etc.
And so on up to twenty.	70. *wambi icashima iné hots,* etc.
20. *hots.*	80. *iné hots,* etc.
21. *schnape icashima hots.*	90. *wambi aschkine hots,* etc.
And so on up to thirty.	100. *aschkiné hots* or *sneyik.*

The foregoing words are spelt phonetically. In pronouncing them the vowels must be sounded as in English. The sound represented by the letters *tsch* is a very peculiar click.

APPENDIX B.

NOTES ON SHINTÔ.

SCHOLARS hesitate to decide whether Shintô is or is not "a genuine product of Japanese soil." The Japanese call their ancient religion *kami no michi* (the way of the gods); foreigners adopt the Chinese form of the same, and call it Shintô. By Shintô is meant the primitive religion which was found spread over Japan when the Buddhist propagandists arrived in the sixth century, and which, at the restoration of the Mikado to full temporal power, in 1868, became once more the " State religion." By *" Pure Shintô "* is meant the ancient faith as distinguished from that mixture of it with Buddhism and Confucianism which is known as *Riyôbu Shintô,* and it is of pure Shintô that I present my readers with a few notes, in order, if possible, to make the religious allusions in the foregoing letters interesting and intelligible.[1]

Japanese cosmogony and mythology are one, and in both Japan is the Universe. There are three confused mythical periods, dur-

[1] For a sketch of the History of Shintô and its Revival, the reader is referred to several papers of profound research in the Transactions of the English Asiatic Society of Japan for 1874, called " The Revival of Pure Shintô," by Mr. Ernest Satow, Japanese Secretary to H. B. M.'s Legation at Yedo; to an article on " The Mythology and Religious Worship of the Ancient Japanese," by the same learned writer, in the *Westminster Review* for June 1878; and to a paper called " Shintôism," by Mr. Kemperman, in the Transactions of the German Asiatic Society of Japan for 1878.

ing which the islands of Japan and many gods were called into being. The third of these begins with the supremacy of Amate-rasu, the Sun-Goddess, the great divinity of the Shintô religion. This "heaven-lighting" divinity, finding that Japan was disturbed by the unending feuds of the earthly gods, among whom Okuni-nushi, their ruler, could not keep order, despatched Ninigi-no-Mikoto, a heavenly god, to Higa in Kiushiu, and compelled Okun-inushi to resign his disorderly rule into his hands. Since then Okuninushi has ruled over the invisible, and Ninigi and his successors, the Mikados, over the visible. The gods and their offspring did not, however, always submit quietly to the new authority, and there were evident struggles for supremacy between the earthly and heavenly powers, which were finally brought to an end in 660 B.C. by Jimmu Tennô, the fifth in descent from the Sun-Goddess, who overthrew the Kiushiu rebels, and passing over into the main island, subjugated a large portion of it, and settled there with his warriors.

Whatever the actual facts may be, this event is the dawn of Japanese history, and the starting-point of Japanese chronology. The 7th of April is fixed as the anniversary of Jimmu Tennô's ascension to the throne; he is deified and worshipped in a thousand shrines, and from him the present Mikado claims direct descent. The dogma of "the divine right of kings" in his case means nothing less than that he is descended from the great Sun-Goddess through seven generations of celestial, five of terrestrial gods, and 122 divine Mikados, who have preceded him; and the three divine insignia of power — the mirror, the sword, and the stone — have descended to him directly from his ancestress, whose gifts they were.

According to Hirata, a Shintô revivalist who wrote early in this century, and from whose writings Mr. Satow has made many translations, "to compel obedience from human beings, and to love them, was all the sovereign had to do, and there was no necessity for teaching them vain doctrines, such as are preached in other countries. Hence the art of government is called *Matsurigoto*, which literally means 'worshipping.' Accordingly, the early sovereigns worshipped the gods in person, and prayed that their people might enjoy a sufficiency of food, clothing, and shelter from the elements, and twice a year, in the sixth and twelfth months, they celebrated the festival of the 'General Purification'" [observed to the present day] "by which the whole nation was purged of calamities, offences, and pollutions." In the beginning of the thirteenth century the reigning Mikado interpreted the directions of his divine ancestors by ordering that "even in the slightest matters" [certain most holy things] "are not to be placed *after* the Emperor." "As it is the duty of subjects to imitate the practice of the incarnate god who is their sovereign, the necessity of worshipping his ancestors and the gods from whom they spring is to be enjoined upon every man." As to these gods, it was declared, on their own authority, that "The gods who do harm are to be appeased, so that they may not punish those who have offended them; and all the gods are to be worshipped, so that they may be induced to increase their favours."

Thus the Shintô religion is closely interwoven with the theory of government. The Mikado's throne is founded on a religious fiction. He is the lineal descendant of the gods, nay, he is himself a god, and in virtue of his godhead, his palace is a temple His heavenly origin has been, through all historic days, the foun dation of Japanese government, and it and the duty of obeying his commands without questioning, whether they are right or wrong, are the highest of Shintô dogmas.

From the death of Jimmu Tennô, the first Mikado, to the introduction of Buddhism, is a period (according to the unreliable Japanese chronology) of 1236 years. Between 97 and 30 B.C., Sujin, the reigning Mikado, and of course a demi-god, appeared as a reformer, called on the people to turn their minds to the worship of the gods, performed a symbolic purification, built special shrines for the worship of several of the *kami* or gods, removed the mirror, sword, and stone from the palace where they had hitherto been kept to a shrine built for their custody, and appointed his daughter their priestess. This mirror rested, at least till 1871, in the shrines of Isé, of which a description is given near the end of this volume.

In the middle of the sixth century, as is supposed, Buddhist missionaries arrived from Korea, and proselytised so successfully in high quarters that a decree was issued about the middle of the eighth century, ordering the erection of two Buddhist temples and a seven-storied pagoda in every province. The long and complete supremacy of Buddhism is due, however, to a master-stroke of religious policy achieved by a priest, best known under his posthumous name of Kôbô-daishi, in the ninth century, who, in order to gain and retain a hold for his creed over the mass of the people, taught that the Shintô gods were but Japanese manifestations of Buddha, a dogma which reconciled the foreign with the native religion, and gave Buddhism several centuries of ascendency over both Shintô and Confucianism, till it was supplanted, about two hundred years ago, in the intellects of the educated, by the Chinese philosophical system of Choo He, which in its turn is being dis, placed by what is known in Japan as the "English Philosophy," represented by Mill, Herbert Spencer, and others. At the Restoration of the Mikado to temporal power, in 1868, Shintô was reinstated as the State religion, owing to its value as a political engine, but it was impossible to re-introduce its long abandoned usages alongside of Western civilisation, and the number of those who honour the old faith in its purity is believed to be very small.

The Buddhaising the old gods, and incorporating the ancient traditions of the divine ancestors and early heroes of the Japanese with the ethical code and doctrinal dogmas of Buddhism, produced a harmony or jumble upon which the reigning Mikado, pleased with the fusion, bestowed the name of *Riyôbu Shintô*, or "twofold religious doctrine." From that time Shintô and Buddhist priests frequently celebrated their ceremonies in the same temples, the distinctive feature of Shintô, the absence of idols, effigies, and other visible objects of worship, disappeared, and the temples were crowded with wooden images of the old Shintô divinities, alongside of those of Buddha and his disciples, only a very few temples in a very few districts retaining the simplicity of the ancient faith. Since 1868 the images, and all the gaudy and sensuous paraphernalia of Buddhism, have been swept out of a large number of the temples, but the splendour of the buildings still remains, as at Shiba in Yedo, and the plain wooden structure, with the thatched tent-roof and the perfectly bare interior, is only seen in its primitive simplicity in the "Shrines of Isé" and a few other places. In the eighteenth century an attempt was made by certain scholarly and able men to revive "pure Shintô," and adapt it to those cravings of humanity which Buddhism had partially met; but the attempt failed, and has resulted mainly in affording materials for the researches of Mr. Satow and other foreign scholars.

The characteristics of "Pure Shintô" are the absence of an ethical and doctrinal code, of idol-worship, of priestcraft, and of any teachings concerning a future state, and the deification of heroes, emperors, and great men, together with the worship of certain forces and objects in nature. It is said that the *kami* or gods number 14,000, of whom 3700 are known to have shrines ; but, practically, the number is infinite, or "eight millions." Each hamlet has its special god, as well as each *miya* or shrine; and each child is taken to the shrine of the district in which it is born, a month after birth, and the god of that shrine becomes his patron. Each god has his annual festival, while many have particular days in each month on which people visit their shrines.

The temples are of unpainted wood, and the tent-like roofs are thickly thatched. They are destitute of idols, effigies, images, ornaments, and ecclesiastical paraphernalia of any kind. In the bare shrines of this truly barren creed the only objects are a circular steel mirror, *the gohei*, small offerings of *saké*, rice, and other vegetable food, on unlacquered wooden trays, and some sprigs of the evergreen *Cleyera japonica*. The mirror is a copy of the one given by the Sun-Goddess, as an emblem of herself, to Ninigi, when she sent him down to govern the world; but even this is only exposed to view in temples in which Shintô has been at some time jumbled up with Buddhism. A plain *gohei* is a slim wand of unpainted wood, with two long pieces of paper, notched alternately on opposite sides, hanging from it. In some shrines which were long in Buddhist hands, such as that of Iyéyasu at Nikkô, gilded metal takes the place of paper. The *gohei* represent offerings of rough and white cloth, which were supposed to have the effect of attracting the god to the spot where they were offered, but gradually came to be considered as the gods themselves. In idea they resemble the white wands, with dependent shavings, which are worshipped by the Ainos of Yezo. In the pure Shintô temples, which do not even display the mirror, there is a kind of receptacle concealed behind the closed doors of the actual shrine, which contains a case only exposed to view on the day of the annual festival, and which is said to contain the spirit of the deity to whom the temple is dedicated, the "august spirit substitute," or " God's seed."

The prominent Shintô emblem of purely Japanese origin, the *torii*, stands at the entrance of temple grounds, in front of shrines and sacred trees, and in every place specially associated with the native *kami*. In some places, as at the great Inari or Fox temple at Fushima, near Kiyôto, there are avenues composed of several hundred of these, and, whether large or small, the *torii* is a favourite subject for an *ex voto*. In the latter case it is frequently of stone. The *torii* proper consists of two tree-trunks, planted in the ground, on the top of which rests another tree with projecting ends, and a horizontal beam below. The name means "bird's rest," for on it the fouls *offered* but not *sacrificed* to the gods were accustomed to perch. It is of unpainted wood, properly, but large numbers are painted bright red. The Buddhists have curved the upper timber and have added other ornaments. In the persecution waged against the Romish Christians of Nagasaki a few years ago, the token of recantation required was that they should pass under this Shintô emblem.

The remaining Shintô emblem is a rope of rice straw, varying in thickness from the heavy cable which often hangs across a *torii* or temple entrance, to the rope no thicker than a finger which hangs across house doors, or surrounds sacred trees, and which has straw tassels or strips of white paper dangling from it.

There are about 98,000 Shintô temples in Japan, but this number includes all the wayside shrines and the shrines in the groves, which are about five feet high. There are about 20,000 Shintô officials, including the whole of the *kannushi* or "shrine keepers," and these may all be described as officials of the Government. Their duties are few. They are allowed to marry, and do not shave their heads. There is an appropriation of about £44,000 annually for Shintô shrines, and of £14,000 for Public Worship. In the old order the Department which dealt with the affairs of the earthly and heavenly gods held the highest place in the order of official precedence; but so out of harmony was it with the new *régime*, that within four years of its re-establishment it descended from a dignity superior to that of the Council of State into a department subordinate thereto. Within a year the department for administering the affairs of the celestial and terrestrial gods sank into being a Board of Religious Instruction, and early in 1877 underwent the further humiliation of being quietly transferred to a sub-department of the Ministry of the Interior. Thus, in less than ten years, the oldest and most solemn institution in the State has passed out of existence, and it is difficult to understand how the dogma of the divine origin and relationships of the Mikado, and the identification of politics with religion, survive the change.

The claims of Shintô to be regarded as a religion are very few. It has no worship, properly so called, and no sacrifices, no hell or purgatory for bad men, and the immortality of the soul is only assumed from the immortality of the gods. It inculcates reverence for ancestors, and imitation of their worthy deeds; but its chief feature is its recognition of certain ceremonial defilements and forms of purification.

On certain occasions the priests assemble in the larger temples and chant certain words to an excruciating musical accompaniment; but this is in no sense what we understand by public worship, and the worshippers are seldom admitted within Shintô temples. The gods are supposed to be present in the temples dedicated to them, and a worshipper attracts their attention by pulling the cord of a metal globe, half bell, half rattle, which hangs at the open entrance. There are specified forms of prayer, but worship usually consists merely in clapping the hands twice, and making one or more genuflexions; and persons undertake pilgrimages of several hundred miles to do no more than this, with the addition of casting a few copper coins on the temple floor, and buying a charm or relic.

The festival days of the gods of the larger temples are celebrated by music, dancing, and processions, in which highly decorated cars take part, on and in which are borne certain sacred emblems, usually kept in the storehouses of the temples. On these occasions ancient classical dances or posturings are given on covered platforms within the temple grounds, and in these a maiden appears, dressed in white and bearing a *gohei* in her hand, who is popularly called a priestess. The history and meaning of nearly all the ceremonies are unknown to the modern Japanese.

Certain ceremonies are usually attended to even by the most careless. In nearly all Japanese houses there is a *kami-dana* or god-shelf, on which is a miniature temple in wood, which contains tablets covered with paper, on which are written the names of the gods in which the household place their trust, and monumental tablets with the posthumous names of the ancestors and deceased members of the family. Fresh flowers, and specially the leafy twigs of the *Cleyera japonica*, are offered there, together with *saké*, water, and the first portion of the rice boiled for the food of the household. At night a lamp is lit in front of the shrine, as on the god-shelf of the Buddhists, and the glow-worm glimmer of these lamps is one of the evening features of the cities of Japan.

Shintô is the easiest and least exacting of religions. The intervention of a priest is not ordinarily needed, for there are no angry deities to propitiate, or any terrors of hell to avert, and both sexes are capable of offering prayers. Of such there are many.

and so lately as 1873 a new edition of certain forms was published; but among the peasantry it seems sufficient to frame a wish
without uttering it, and most Shintôists, in Northern Japan, at
least, content themselves with turning to the sun in the early
morning, rubbing the hands slowly together, and bowing. There
are gods of all things; of wisdom, happiness, protection of human
abodes, of harvest, of learning, of the gate and front court, of the
well, the kitchen fireplace, and everything else to which superstiti-
tions of unknown origin are attached by the ignorant. The directions for prayer are, "Rising early in the morning, wash your face
and hands, rinse out the mouth, and cleanse the body. Then
turn to the province of Yamato, strike the palms of the hands together, and worship," *i.e.* bow to the ground. The following is a
specimen of one of the most enlightened of the old Shintô prayers,
translated by Mr. Satow, from a book called *Kimpi Mishô*, put forward by the Mikado Juntoku in the first half of the thirteenth
century : —

"From a distance I reverently worship with awe before Ame no
Mi-hashira, and Kuni no Mi-hashira (the god and goddess of
wind), to whom is consecrated the palace built with stout pillars
at Tatsuta no Tachinu, in the department of Heguri, in the province of Yamato. I say with awe, Deign to bless me by correcting
the unwitting faults which, seen and heard by you, I have committed, by blowing off and clearing away the calamities which evil
gods might inflict, by causing me to live long like the hard and
lasting rock, and by repeating to the gods of heavenly origin, and
the gods of earthly origin, the petitions which I present every day
along with your breath, that they may hear with the sharp-
earedness of the forth-galloping colt." Another addressed to the
kami-dana is as follows, "Reverently adoring the great god of the
two palaces of Isé in the first place, the eight hundred myriads of
celestial gods, the eight hundred myriads of terrestrial gods, all
the fifteen hundred myriads" (these numbers are figurative expressions) "of gods to whom are consecrated the great and small
temples in all provinces, all islands, and all places of the great
Land of Eight Islands, the fifteen hundreds of myriads of gods
which they cause to serve them, and the gods of branch palaces
and branch temples, and Sohodo no Kami" [the scare-crow],
"whom I have invited to the shrine set up on this divine shelf,
and to whom I offer praises day by day — I pray with awe that
they will deign to correct the unwitting faults which, heard and

seen by them, I have committed, and blessing and favouring me according to the powers which they severally wield, will cause me to follow the divine example, and to perform good works in the Way."

As a religion Shintô is nearly extinct, and, as an engine of government, its power is undoubtedly on the wane. Western science is upsetting its cosmogony, Western philosophy its mythology, and its lack of an ethical code makes it powerless even among a people of such easy morals as the Japanese. Motoori, its modern exponent and revivalist, emphatically states that the Chinese invented morals because they were an immoral people, but that in Japan there was no such necessity. " To have acquired the knowledge that there is no *michi* [ethics] to be practised and learned is really to have learned to practice the way of the gods." Mr. Mori, the present minister to England, gives it as his opinion that " the leading idea of Shintô is a reverential feeling towards the dead. As to the political use of it, the State is quite right in turning it to account in support of the absolute Government which exists in Japan." Sir H. S. Parkes says of it, "Japanese, in general, are at a loss to describe what Shintô is. . . . Infallibility on the part of the head of the State, which was naturally attributed to rulers claiming divine descent, was a convenient doctrine for political purposes in China and Japan." Mr. Von Brandt, a student of Japanese archæology, lately German Minister to Japan, writes of it, "Little is known of Shintô that might give it the character of a religion as understood by western nations." Kaempfer, one of the most painstaking and accurate observers, writes thus: — " The whole Shintô religion is so mean and simple that, besides a heap of fabulous and romantic stories of their gods, demi-gods, and heroes, inconsistent with reason and common sense, their divines have nothing either in their sacred books, or by tradition, wherewithal to satisfy the inquiries of curious persons about the nature and essences of their gods, about their power and government, about the future state of the soul, and such other essential points whereof other heathen systems are not altogether silent." Its lack of a moral code, of general definiteness, and of teachings concerning a future state, sufficiently explain the easy conquest which Buddhism made of nearly the whole nation, and the ascendency which it still retains over the uneducated. Shintô, with its absence of a ritual, of doctrinal teaching, of sensuousness, of definite objects of worship, is rather a system than a religion. It is hollow and empty; it has literally nothing in it which can influence men's lives; it appeals to no instincts of good or evil, and promises no definite destiny; and all attempts to resuscitate it, either as a bulwark against Christianity, or as a substitute for Buddhism (which contains many of the elements of a religion, and much to gratify, if not to satisfy, many of the cravings of human nature), must necessarily fail.

These notes are the merest outline of Shintô, but the most elaborate treatise can do no more than successfully demonstrate its utter emptiness of all that to our ideas constitutes religion, and excite surprise that it should still retain any place among a people so intelligent as the Japanese. The explanation probably lies in the fact that it is interwoven with that reverence for ancestors which is so marked a feature of Chinese and Japanese character, and in that general indifference to any religion which pervades Japan, making its people content with this most shadowy and barren of creeds, which neither enjoins duties nor demands sacrifices, nor holds out terrors of "judgment to come."

APPENDIX C.

TABLES OF THE ESTIMATED REVENUE AND EXPENDI-
TURE FOR THE FINANCIAL YEAR 1879–80. [NOTE.—
5 *YEN* ARE ABOUT EQUAL TO £1 STERLING.]

REVENUE.

I. — First Species of Tax:—

		Yen.
Customs — Export Duties	. .	895,113.000
" Import "	.	1,247,215.000
" Miscellaneous Receipts,		38,982.000

	Yen.
Total	2,181,310.000

II. — Second Species of Tax:—

		Yen.
Land Tax	. . .	41,000,950.000
Mining Tax	. . . .	11,537.000
Tax on Salaries	. . .	81,992.000
Tax on Produce of the Hokkaidô	.	363,971.000

	Yen.
Total	41,458,450.000

III. — Third Species of Tax :—

		Yen.
Tax on Alcoholic Liquors	. .	4,507,272.000
Tax on Tobacco	. . . .	348,674.000
Stamps on Legal Documents	. .	539,168.000
Postage Stamps	. . . .	1,050,000.000
Tax on Ruled Paper for Petitions	.	82,485.000
Licenses to Attorneys	. .	9,500.000
Ship and Boat Tax	. .	138,357.000
Vehicle Tax	. . . .	270,348.000
Tax on Companies	. . .	500,000.000
Shooting Licenses	. . . .	45,652.000
Horse and Cattle Dealers' Licenses		63,578.000

Carry forward . .	7,555,034.000

Brought forward . .	7,555,034.000
Tax on Weights and Measures .	2,925.000
Copyright Fees	3,409 000
Passport and other License Fees .	2,570.000
Druggists' Licenses . . .	79,131.000

Yen.

Total 7,643,069.000

IV. — Profits of Industrial Works : —

Yen.

Sado and Four other Mines under the control of the Ministry of Public Works	218,960.000
Railways under the control of the Ministry of Public Works . .	391,100.271
Akabane and Three other Workshops under the control of the Ministry of Public Works . .	32,265.603
Shimmachi Cotton Mill and Two other Places under the control of the Ministry of the Interior .	12,585.000
Mint under the control of Ministry of Finance	506,000.000
Printing Office under the control of the Ministry of Finance .	30,000.000
Yokosuka Shipbuilding Yard and Two others under the control of the Ministry of Marine . .	4,028.840

Yen.

Total 1,194,939.714

V. — Receipts from Government Property and other Miscellaneous Receipts : —

Yen.

Sale of Government Property .	497,586.970
Rent of Government Property .	142,156.051
Rent of Government Land at Open Cities and Ports	72,817.150
Miscellaneous Receipts . . .	1,647,745.709

Yen.

Total 2,360,305.880

Revenue — *continued.*

VI. — Refunds : —

	Yen.
Refund of Advances . . .	532,360.577
Refund of Loans made by Imperial Princes and the former *Han*	200,350.285
Refund of Estate-rated Loan .	80,593.578

	Yen.
Total	813,304.440

Grand Total of Revenue . .	55,651,379.034
	£11,130,000

EXPENDITURE.

I. — Redemption of National Debt : —

	Yen.
Domestic Debt —	
Principal . .	2,764,111.368
Interest . .	14,753,058.200
Redemption of Paper Money . .	2,000,000.000

	Yen.
Total . .	19,518,169.568

Foreign Debt —	
Principal . .	816,424.000
Interest . .	857,318.400
Commission .	8,368.712

	Yen.
Total . .	1,682,111.112

	Yen.
Total of both Items . .	21,200,280.680

II. — Civil List and Appanages of the Imperial
Princes 877,000.000

EXPENDITURE — *continued.*

III. — Pensions for Meritorious Services, to Shintô and Buddhist Priests, etc. —

	Yen
Retiring Pensions to Soldiers of the Old Imperial Guards and Line .	15,640.977
Pensions of Shintô and Buddhist Priests	125,281.000
Annuities attached to the order of Merit	152,280.000
Gratuities to the Military and Cost of Treatment of the Wounded .	266,202.000
Grant to those who took part in the Campaign in Kiushiu . .	500,000.000

Total. . . . . .   *Yen.* 1,059,403.977

IV. — Council of State, Ministries, Senate, Colonisation, Commission, and Special Bureaus : —

	Yen.
Council of State	300,860.000
Ministry for Foreign Affairs . .	170,960.000
" of the Interior .	1,275,500.000
" of Finance . .	1,505,300.000
" of War . . .	7,190,100.000
" of Marine . .	2,636,300.000
" of Public Instruction	1,139,970.000
" of Public Works .	591,300.000
" of Justice . .	1,314,800.000
" of the Imperial Household . . .	308,700.000
Senate	142,480.000
Colonisation Commission .	1,513,174.178
Land-tax Reform Bureau .	97,000.000
General Post Office . . .	1,050,000.000

Total . . . . .   *Yen.* 19,236,444.178

V. — Cost of Establishing Industrial Undertakings : —

	Yen.
Mines at Sado and Five other places under control of the Ministry of Public Works . .	232,798.000
Kiyôto and Kôbe Railway, do. .	33,300.000
Telegraph, do.	140,000.000
Workshops at Akabane and Four other places, do	165,502.000
Shimosa Sheep Farm and Three other places under control of the Ministry of the Interior .	72,793.000
Mint under the control of the Ministry of Finance . . .	50,000.000
Yokosuka Shipbuilding Yard under control of the Ministry of Marine	70,200.000

	Yen.
Total	764.593.000

VI. — Supplementary Grants of Capital for carrying on Undertakings : —

	Yen.
Kamaishi Mine under the control of the Ministry of Public Works	29,355.792
Telegraphs under do. . . .	101,335.000
Shinagawa and Fukagawa Workshops under do. . . .	28,842.000
Shimosa Sheep Farm and One other place under control of the Ministry of the Interior . . .	80,958.000

	Yen.
Total	240,490.792

VII. — Administrations of Cities and Prefectures 3,786,700.000

EXPENDITURE — *continued.*

		Yen.
VIII. — Police : —		
Central Police Bureau (Tôkiyô) .	1,316,820.400	
Police in 2 Cities and 35 Prefectures	1,169,632.000	

		Yen.
Total		2,486,452.400
XI. — Temples of the Gods . . .		135,000.000

X. — Building, Repairs, and Embankments in Cities and Prefectures : —

	Yen.	
Building and Repairs . . .	540,700.000	
Embankments	1,446,500.000	

		Yen.
Total		1,987,200 000
XI. — Diplomatic and Consular Services		500,000.000

XII. — Miscellaneous Expenditure

	Yen.
Fund for Relief of Agricultural Distress and Encouragement of Saving .	1,200,000.000
Erection of Museum in the Public Garden at Uyeno, under control of the Ministry of the Interior .	29,585.000
Charges for repairs of the Prisons and Lockups under control of the Central Police Bureau . .	90,561.901
Appropriation for the Sydney Exhibition	29,817.300
Erection of Barracks at Kanazawa	36,253.960
Erection of the Imperial Palace .	270,000.000
Relief to the (Hokkaidô) Militia .	26,407.146
Domestic Industrial Exhibition .	43.890.000
Miscellaneous	151,298.700

		Yen.
Total		1,877,814.007
XIII. — Contingent Fund		1,500,000.000

Grand Total of Expenditure	Yen. 55,651,379.034
	£11,130,000

Revenue and Expenditure are equally balanced.

NATIONAL DEBT.

Domestic Debt — Interest Bearing Debt — *Yen.*

New Debt, 4 per cent interest .	11,327.675
Bonds in exchange for *kinsatsu*, 6 per cent interest	1,923.700
Voluntarily Capitalised Pension Bonds, 8 per cent . . .	14,168.900

Capitalised Pension Bonds — *Yen.*

At 5 per cent do.	31,412.555	
At 6 per cent do.	25,001.590	
At 7 per cent do.	107,997.015	
At 10 per cent do.	8,876.370	
Total .		173,287.530

Bonds for Pensions distributed to ex-Shintô Priests, at 8 per cent . .	423.325
Public Works Loan at 6 per cent .	12,500.000
Loan for Suppression of Rebellion at 5 per cent	15,000.000
	Yen.
Total	228,631.130
Debt bearing no Interest	9,439.732
Amount of Paper Money in circulation . .	113,427.992
Total	351,498.854

APPENDIX D. — FOREIGN TRADE.

(I.) — Synoptic Table of the Import Trade of Japan

DESCRIPTION OF GOODS.	* 1865.	1867.	1868.	1869.	1870.
Yarn	$875,307	$1,350,688	$1,763,191	$2,612,240	$3,700,277
Shirtings	2,028,361	2,684,078	1,724,854	1,760,440	1,730,532
Other cotton manufactures .	2,280,100	1,713,539	1,234,538	878,343	1,843,644
Mousseline de laine (included in other woollens up to the year 1874)	-	-	-	-	-
Other woollen and woollen and cotton goods . .	6,701,067	3,184,471	2,610,838	2,010,553	1,995,364
Metals	526,864	209,171	693,780	632,255	330,681
Arms and ammunition . .	1,066,822	1,618,840	2,730,651	1,857,625	206,908
Raw cotton . . .	1,159	757,104	783,084	858,940	771,144
Sugar	208,174	1,660,554	345,267	1,597,944	2,482,293
Rice	-	787,602	1,315,705	2,769,182	12,755,331
Kerosene	-	-	-	-	-
Government goods. (No returns until the year 1873.) .	-	-	-	-	-
Other miscellaneous. — Foreign	347,963	1,619,169	1,491,043	1,776,690	3,231,007
Other miscellaneous. — Eastern	41,121	367,172	307,420	602,419	2,083,460
Total . . .	$14,076,938	$15,952,388	$15,000,371	$17,356,631	$31,120,641

Total,

Incomplete Returns —
* *Note.* — The absence of Returns for 1866 is due to the destruction of the *Mousseline de laine.* — These Returns are based upon the custom-house statistics; *Metals.* — The quantities of Metals imported in 1873 and following years on account *Government Goods.* — These figures are exclusive of foreign merchant-vessels

(II.) — Synoptic Table of the Export Trade of Japan

DESCRIPTION OF GOODS.	* 1865.	1867.	1868.	1869.	1870.
Silk, all kinds, and cocoons .	$14,842,879	$5,598,510	$10,761,081	$5,042,795	$5,309,583
Silkworms' eggs . .	727,445	2,302,572	4,199,138	2,728,500	3,473,150
Tea	1,934,971	2,006,023	3,084,580	2,019,130	3,848,231
Copper	-	61,510	-	124,735	461,093
Tobacco	12,334	33,140	18,475	21,906	54,112
Wax (vegetable) . .	50,865	123,443	254,224	98,420	64,190
Camphor	32,706	97,293	114,489	168,202	228,869
Coal	12,983	262,629	73,584	101,680	159,117
Dried fish . . .	95,485	300,375	193,689	183,941	328,391
Rice	-	-	-	-	-
Miscellaneous . . .	781,762	1,338,179	1,735,873	986,336	1,176,490
Total . . .	$18,491,430	$12,123,674	$20,435,133	$11,475,645	$15,143,246

Total,

* *Note.* — The absence of Returns for 1866 is due to the destruction

APPENDIX D. — FOREIGN TRADE.

FOR THIRTEEN YEARS, ENDING DECEMBER 31, 1878.

1871.	1872.	1873.	1874.	1875.	1876.	1877.	1878.
$3,609,444	$5,933,342	$3,357,046	$3,575,554	$4,057,850	$4,151,514	$4,088,890	$7,560,963
3,489,450	2,256,926	3,365,898	3,706,628	2,616,723	2,997,595	2,312,929	2,548,621
912,584	1,874,887	3,070,544	1,826,568	2,276,311	1,893,053	1,951,856	2,629,635
-	-	-	1,074,931	2,393,157	2,263,273	2,373,621	2,779,983
2,056,789	7,572,180	7,304,307	2,244,490	2,383,610	2,011,843	3,004,457	3,013,675
536,291	416,642	451,202	1,131,185	1,043,382	898,531	1,592,052	1,888,006
293,120	83,617	577,645	20,885	44,576	51,954	461,729	296,878
60,340	67,376	146,569	1,152,066	363,669	724,911	424,439	289,207
3,308,549	2,266,880	2,108,855	2,579,406	3,482,588	2,743,820	2,872,143	3,073,282
768,190	-	34,192	14,873	5,579	-	-	
-	89,694	323,374	292,646	590,032	455,792	602,725	1,856,881
-	-	797,395	1,809,115	3,475,277	806,801	670,537	494,110
2,398,433	4,600,233	5,332,115	3,642,626	4,441,537	4,021,959	4,698,436	6,144,012
312,415	1,026,664	574,226	1,155,656	999,903	947,953	846,722	759,049
$17,745,605	$26,188,441	$27,443,368	$24,226,629	$28,174,194	$23,969,004	$25,900,541	$33,334,392

300,489,143 dollars.

custom-house records at Kanagawa by fire in that year.
the actual importation in the year 1874 and succeeding years was much larger.
of the Japanese Government, have been included under the head of " Government Goods,"
purchased by the Japanese Government.

FOR THIRTEEN YEARS, ENDING DECEMBER 31, 1878.

1871.	1872.	1873.	1874.	1875.	1876.	1877.	1878.
$8,457,839	$8,189,143	$7,750,015	$5,894,567	$5,992,913	$14,306,450	$10,320,308	$9,223,875
2,184,688	1,963,159	3,032,460	731,275	474,921	1,902,271	346,998	682,606
4,651,292	5,445,438	4,398,711	7,792,244	6,915,692	5,427,218	4,409,320	4,412,457
416,630	1,353,545	765,815	559,397	425,160	289,708	828,111	866,384
269,359	669,340	274,529	259,687	201,148	83,496	229,288	107,547
161,834	347,542	377,670	215,642	186,244	177,398	164,977	106,367
138,575	152,879	71,026	119,812	136,073	182,477	240,065	309,972
483,130	573,527	489,278	551,360	858,883	765,726	717,819	857,322
410,034	324,000	716,399	901,583	663,639	922,580	835,660	1,031,355
-	3,122,931	521,709	839,619	17,091	810,760	2,260,936	4,641,653
2,011,424	2,153,028	2,253,382	2,299,399	2,046,081	2,710,767	2,513,226	4,019,881
$19,184,805	$24,294,532	$20,660,994	$20,164,585	$17,917,845	$27,578,851	$22,866,708	$26,259,419

$256,595,667

of the custom-house records at Kanagawa by fire in that year.

(III.) — SUMMARY OF IMPORTS AND EXPORTS FOR THIRTEEN YEARS ENDING DECEMBER 31, 1878.

YEAR.	Imports.	Exports.	Total.
1865	$14,076,938	$18,490,230	$32,567,168
1867*	15,952,388	12,123,674	28,076,062
1868	15,000,371	20,435,133	35,435,504
1869	17,356,631	11,475,645	28,832,276
1870	31,120,641	15,143,246	46,263,887
1871	17,745,605	19,184,805	36,930,410
1872	26,188,441	24,294,532	50,482,973
1873	27,443,368	20,660,994	48,104,362
1874	24,226,629	20,164,585	44,391,214
1875	28,174,194	17,917,845	46,092,039
1876	23,969,004	27,578,851	51,547,855
1877	25,900,541	22,866,708	48,767,249
1878	33,334,392	26,259,419	59,593,811
Total	**$300,489,143**	**$256,595,667**	**$557,084,810**
Average annual trade	**$23,117,549**	**$19,738,128**	**$42,852,677**

* No Returns for 1866, owing to destruction of Kanagawa records.

(IV.) — RETURN OF BRITISH AND FOREIGN SHIPPING ENTERED AT ALL PORTS OF JAPAN FOR NINETEEN YEARS.

YEAR.	BRITISH.		OTHER FOREIGN COUNTRIES.		TOTAL.	
	Ships.	Tons.	Ships.	Tons.	Ships.	Tons.
1860	122	45,279	119	43,103	241	88,382
1861	126	52,347	128	47,776	254	100,123
1862	181	57,362	230	71,678	411	129,040
1863	262	87,000	215	71,356	477	158,356
1864	313	118,907	130	44,235	443	163,142
1865	264	99,649	151	67,223	415	166,872
1866	254	100,195	188	81,943	442	182,138
1867	348	139,006	251	159,154	599	298,160
1868	496	192,185	461	389,581	957	581,766
1869	897	410,105	713	659,293	1,610	1,069,398
1870	661	319,471	902	841,704	1,563	1,161,175
1871	349	166,929	560	734,241	909	901,170
1872	382	204,077	520	756,427	902	960,434
1873	405	234,459	599	804,948	1,004	1,039,407
1874	367	237,432	532	732,510	899	969,942
1875	350	252,146	481	699,377	831	951,523
1876	356	302,039	345	378,518	701	680,557
1877	403	315,518	343	308,459	746	623,977
1878	487	417,691	351	331,181	838	749,529

(V.) — RETURN OF FOREIGN RESIDENTS AND FIRMS AT THE
OPEN PORTS OF JAPAN, FOR FIVE YEARS, FROM 1874–78.

YEAR.	BRITISH.		OTHER FOREIGN COUNTRIES.		CHINESE.		TOTAL.	
	Residents.	Firms.	Residents.	Firms.	Residents.	Firms.	Residents.	Firms.
1874	1,170	155	1,238	215	2,723	95	5,131	465
1875	1,282	109	1,301	148	-	-	-	-
1876	1,242	80	1,472	141	-	-	-	-
1877	1,156	83	1,336	149	2,107	53	4,599	285
1878	1,087	92	1,410	151	3,028	40	5,505	287

INDEX.

385